The Chef's Art

*T*he Chef's Art
Secrets of Four-Star Cooking at Home

Wayne Gisslen

John Wiley & Sons, Inc.
New York · Chichester · Brisbane · Toronto · Singapore

Senior Editor: Claire Thompson
Production Coordination: Claire Huismann and Lori Martinsek of Publication Services
Photography: J. Gerard Smith

Library of Congress Cataloging-in-Publication Data
Gisslen, Wayne, 1946–
    The chef's art: Secrets of four-star cooking at home / Wayne Gisslen.
      p.   cm.
    Includes index.
    ISBN 0-471-83684-2
    1. Cookery.   I. Title.
  TX714.G58 1992
  641.5—dc20   92-13393

Printed in the United States of America
10 9 8 7 6 5 4 3 2 1

Acknowledgments

Many people have provided guidance, advice, and ideas for the development of this book. First of all, I wish to express my gratitude to those who reviewed the entire manuscript and were most generous with their assistance: Philip Panzarino, Lynn Huffman, Fred Faria, Michael Piccinino, Jeff Graves, and Mike Jung.

I am particularly indebted to Jim Smith, whose photography is such an essential part of this project; Jim is a consummate professional and a joy to work with. My heartfelt thanks to my editor, Claire Thompson, and to the rest of the staff at John Wiley & Sons who worked so hard on this book. In addition, I am grateful to Joan Garvin of De Bragga and Spitler, Inc., New York and to John Baird of the Milltown (New Jersey) Meat Center for coming to my aid when I needed special assistance or information. Most of all, I wish to thank my wife, Mary Ellen Griffin, who assisted me with research, recipe testing, editing, and the formulation and development of much of this book.

Preface

As the title of this book suggests, *The Chef's Art: Secrets of Four-Star Cooking at Home* is not an ordinary cookbook. It was, in fact, originally designed as an advanced textbook for student chefs and as a reference book for professional cooks.

Why should an amateur cook be interested in the professional approach to cooking? Many reasons could be listed, but perhaps the most important are these:

- You will understand how cooking works. Consequently, you will know how to get exactly the results you want. In other words, you will become a better cook.
- You will know how to organize your steps so that you can work quickly and with less effort.

The professional approach to cooking is concerned with developing this kind of understanding. It is not, as is sometimes thought, primarily about cooking large volumes of food. A home cook, who rarely has to worry about preparing meals for hundreds or even dozens of people at one time, may not think of professional techniques as being particularly applicable to the home. But remember that much of the food served in fine restaurants is not cooked in large batches but is prepared to order, one serving at a time. Even elaborate dishes are often finished and served in only a few minutes. This book takes you into the kitchens of such restaurants, where you can observe the techniques that professional chefs use to prepare high-quality dishes with skill and efficiency.

This book's title is meant to draw your attention to the book's approach to its subject matter, not to suggest that the techniques discussed are proprietary secrets revealed only to professionals. The only real "secret" of professional cooking is that there are no secrets. The techniques are based on easily understandable concepts that are as relevant to the home cook as to the professional.

The theme of this book is contemporary North American cuisine. Its intention is to bring classical culinary theory up to date with discussion of cooking as it is practiced today in top American restaurants.

A professional's training is grounded in classical theory and technique, passed down by generations of chefs. This background provides a systematic basis upon which to build further knowledge and experience. At the same time, modern cuisine is changing rapidly and is being strongly affected by a vast array of influences. Today's cooks are learning new ideas from regional American cooks, from skilled cooks versed in the cuisines of foreign lands, and from imaginative chefs experimenting with new techniques.

In other words, modern cooking theory retains its classical core, but it has also changed a great deal in the last few decades. Cooks today want to know not only what constitutes classical theory, but also how it has changed, what the influences have been, what is happening today, and what can be expected in the future.

For the benefit of readers who have had little or no exposure to basic cooking terminology and to primary food preparation techniques, Chapter 2 provides a summary of the essential information. It is suggested that you review this chapter before proceeding to later chapters. Readers whose curiosity is stimulated and who would like more detailed information about basic techniques may consult my book *Professional Cooking,* which is a widely used text for student chefs and the single most comprehensive guide to the art and science of food preparation.

Picking up where *Professional Cooking* leaves off, *The Chef's Art* introduces a more extensive range of techniques, ingredients, and recipes, including a number that are relatively elaborate. This does not mean, however, that all the procedures explained here or all the recipes included are complicated or difficult. Many of the preparations are simple and straightforward but are included because they introduce techniques or ingredients that may not be treated in more basic cookbooks. The purpose is to give the reader a broader exposure to the practices of the modern kitchen.

Some of the procedures, on the other hand, require lengthy explanations. The emphasis in these explanations is on understanding how and why the techniques work, how to perform them, and when to use them. Greater understanding enables the cook to view basic theory not as a set of rules that must be followed but as tools to use to get the best results.

Special manual techniques are illustrated by approximately 200 step-by-step photographs. Additional photographs illustrate finished, plated dishes in order to demonstrate various styles of food presentation. More than 600 recipes for all types of menu items serve as practical examples of the food types and cooking methods discussed.

This book can be used in many ways—as a reference book, a source for recipes and menu ideas, or a problem-solving guide. No matter how you use it, however, you are encouraged to read Chapter 1 before turning to any of the later chapters or trying one of the recipes. This chapter serves as an introduction to the book's approach to modern cooking theory and as a guide to using the recipes.

Contents

Recipe Table of Contents

The Chef's Art

CHAPTER

1

The Professional Approach to Cooking

*D*edicated home cooks, who know that preparing a dinner party for a dozen friends and family members requires a great deal of time and effort, sometimes wonder how a restaurant can serve so many meals, most of them cooked to order, in such a short time. Of course, the restaurant stoves are bigger, and the cooks have more pots and pans and other equipment available, but surely there must be more to it than that.

In this book, you will discover many of the techniques used by professional chefs, and you will find a great variety of recipes that allow you to try these techniques. Originally designed as a textbook for the student chef and as a reference book for the professional, this book explains in step-by-step detail many procedures that will enhance your cooking skills and make your time in the kitchen easier and more creative.

In this first chapter, we examine the professional approach to cooking and discuss how this approach can be applied to home cooking.

COOKING BY METHOD

For most people, home cooking is primarily a matter of habit or, when trying out new dishes, of following recipes. Professional cooking, on the other hand, emphasizes theory, technique, and general procedures. This distinction between home cooking and professional cooking has existed for at least 200 years—that is, as long as restaurants have existed.

Modern restaurants originated around the time of the French Revolution at the end of the eighteenth century. The chefs of these early restaurants included many who had formerly worked as private cooks for the old nobility and had suddenly found themselves out of work as a result of the Revolution. These chefs found that they had to develop a new approach to cooking in order to cope with the demands of the restaurant. Home cooking was and is based on recipes, whether these recipes are written or committed to memory. The cuisine of the restaurants, as developed by these chefs, was based on techniques and procedures. Old-fashioned recipe-based cooking was not flexible enough to allow restaurant chefs to prepare efficiently a large variety of dishes at once, many of them cooked to order.

Theories and Procedures

Thus began the distinction between professional cooking and home cooking that still exists in its basic form. Home cooking is, at its roots, regional cooking. A *regional cuisine,* in turn, is a set of traditional recipes from a limited area, based on local ingredients and the practices of the local people. Ultimately, regional cooking has its roots in peasant cooking. *Professional cuisine,* on the other hand, is a system of methods and procedures rather than a set of recipes.

To put it another way, the one is based on heritage and the other relies on basic theories and procedures. A regional dish is prepared a certain way mainly because of tradition. It is done this way because this is how it has always been done. A professional cook in the classic tradition, however, prepares a dish by applying basic principles. A dish is done a certain way because the principles of roasting, braising, and so on explain how and why the desired results can be achieved.

These principles are not magic tricks or dark secrets (this book's subtitle notwithstanding) that are revealed only to professional chefs, to be used only in professionaly equipped kitchens. They are easily understandable concepts that apply to the home kitchen as well as to the restaurant.

Learning to cook with the skill and efficiency of a professional does not mean memorizing hundreds of recipes. It means learning how cooking works and how to apply this basic knowledge to any kitchen task. With this understanding, home cooks can organize their work so that both simple family meals and complex dinner parties can be prepared with less work and with tastier results. With this understanding, home cooks are not tied to the exact ingredients and instructions of written recipes but are able to change and adjust recipes and to create new dishes and new combinations. They know that a recipe is not an immutable law but simply a way of applying basic techniques to specific ingredients.

Simplicity and Complexity

One misconception about restaurant cooking or professional cuisine is that it is complex—too complex to be useful for the home cook. In fact, the difference between regional or home cooking and professional cuisine has nothing to do with complexity. Many regional or peasant dishes require dozens of ingredients and complex procedures that take hours to complete. On the other hand, classic dishes from the grand cuisine include simple roasts and grilled items.

If there is complexity in professional cuisine, it is in the theory rather than in the recipes. But this theory, once learned, simplifies cooking immensely because it makes it systematic. Learning a basic theory that can then be applied to any preparation is easier than learning hundreds or thousands of recipes by rote without understanding why they work.

Throughout the history of cooking, two opposite trends can be seen. One is the urge to simplify and to emphasize the plain, natural tastes of basic, fresh ingredients. The other is the urge to invent—that is, to highlight the creativity of the chef, with an accent on fancier, more complicated presentations. Both these forces are valid and healthy; they continually refresh and renew the art of cooking. The urge to simplify is a natural reaction after a period of creativity and invention. At the same time, it is inevitable that talented chefs will want to display their skills with their use of sauces, garnishes, spices, and artistic arrangements.

The danger of simplicity is boredom. A simple dish, if not prepared well, can be completely uninteresting. It's understandable that a cook may try to "fix" it by adding seasonings, sauces, and other ingredients. But one of the most important lessons cooks can learn is that a simple dish, perfectly prepared from good quality ingredients, is superior to a complex, elaborate dish indifferently prepared. They must also learn that the simplest dishes often require the most care in preparation.

THE RECIPE

A recipe is a set of instructions for producing a certain dish. A professional cook, however, is trained to read a recipe in terms of basic principles. In other words, a professional sees a recipe not solely as instructions for making a specific item but as a way of applying basic principles and techniques to specific ingredients.

The main purpose of learning basic cooking principles is to understand the recipes you use. No matter how detailed a recipe may be, it assumes that you already have certain knowledge—for example, that you understand the terminology it uses and that you know how to measure ingredients. A written recipe can't tell you everything, and some judgment by the cook is always required. There are at least three reasons for this:

1. **Food products are not uniform.** Because they are natural products, vegetables, fruits, meats, and fish can never have the uniformity of manufactured products, such as paper clips or drinking glasses. One carrot may be more tender than another, one steak more marbled than another, one apple riper than another. These variations affect how foods are handled, cooked, and seasoned.

2. **Kitchens do not have the same equipment.** Different stoves have different heat outputs. Different pans distribute heat at different rates. Liquid evaporates from wide pots faster than from tall, narrow ones, even if they have the same volume capacity.

3. **It is impossible to give exact instructions for many processes.** How do you set the burner if the instructions call for "medium heat"? What is the proper consistency for a sauce when the instructions say to "cook until thick"?

An experienced cook has developed the ability to make judgments about these variables.

Measurement

Careful measurement is one of the most important parts of cooking. It is essential for consistent quality each time a dish is prepared.

Weighing is the most accurate method of measuring ingredients. In the professional kitchen, it is the method used for most solid ingredients. Volume measures are used for liquids but are usually not accurate enough for solids. For example, the weight of chopped onions needed to fill one cup will vary considerably, depending on such factors as how large or small they are cut. Six ounces of chopped onion, on the other hand, is always six ounces, regardless of these other factors.

Recipes for consumers usually specify quantities by volume, and home cooks are used to measuring in this way, even though using volume measures for solid ingredients is not only inaccurate but often awkward and usually more time-consuming than simply placing the ingredients on a scale. For example, cooks often have difficulty trying to figure out just how large a "medium" onion is or how to measure ½ cup of sliced ham, 1 cup of lettuce, or, even more absurd, 1 cup of uncooked spaghetti.

Except for very small quantities such as a teaspoon or a tablespoon, the recipes in this book call for weighing solid ingredients, so you are strongly urged to buy a simple kitchen scale. Although it may seem uncomfortable to use at first, you will soon see how much quicker and easier it is than having to measure everything by cupfuls.

To be able to weigh ingredients, you must observe the difference between AP (as purchased) weight and EP (edible portion) weight. AP weight is the weight of the item as purchased, before any trimming is done. EP weight is the weight after all nonedible and nonservable parts, such as stems or peels, have been trimmed off. If a recipe doesn't specify which weight it is referring to, you must judge from the instructions.

- If a recipe calls for "2 lb potatoes" and the first instruction is "scrub and peel the potatoes and remove the eyes," you know that AP weight is specified.
- If the recipe calls for "2 lb peeled, diced potatoes," you know that the EP weight is specified and you need more than 2 lb AP.

For more information on measuring and on units of measure, please refer to Appendix 2, pages 619–621.

Recipe Format

The original version of this book was designed as a textbook for professional cooks. Therefore, the recipes included in it are not just directions for producing various dishes. They are also instructional. That is, they are intended to illustrate and reinforce the techniques and principles discussed in the text and to provide practice in applying these principles in various ways in order to enhance your skills and versatility in the kitchen.

For this reason, you will note some variations from recipe to recipe. Some are written in great detail, while others have somewhat less detail, requiring more judgment to be supplied by the cook. In many cases, they allow room for interpretation and variation.

The recipe format used in this book breaks the procedure down into stages of production. The basic outline of this format is as follows:

RECIPE TITLE

		U.S.		Metric	
	PORTIONS:	4	16	*4*	*16*
Ingredients					
Ingredient A		*X* oz	*4X* oz	*Y g*	*4Y g*
Ingredient B					

Mise en place:

1.

2.

Cooking:

1.

2.

Presentation:

1.

2.

Variations

Although this is the basic pattern, there are variations in format. For example, if no cooking is required, as for some salads and other cold dishes, there is no section labeled "Cooking." The remaining sections of this chapter provide further explanation of each element of the recipe format and variations.

Ingredient List and Yields. In most cases, quantities are listed for 4 portions and for 16 portions. With two sets of measurements to work with, it should be easy to multiply or divide the quantities to get any yield desired.

In some types of recipes, yields are given as total quantities rather than as number of portions. For example, yields for a sauce may be given as 1 pint, 2 quarts, 5 deciliters, and 2 liters. Yield for a pâté may be listed as 2 pounds, 8 pounds, and so on.

Both U.S. and metric measurements are given. Please note that the metric quantities are *not equivalent* to the U.S. quantities. For people working with metric units, the quantities are given in practical, round numbers. This means that the portion sizes for the metric quantities are slightly different, usually larger, than the portion sizes for the U.S. quantities. This difference, however, rarely amounts to more than about ½ ounce, or 15 grams, per portion.

The lists of ingredients are generally subdivided into groups to make them easier to read. These groups correspond to different stages in the production procedure. For example, in a recipe for a complex salad that is composed of assorted greens, a dressing, a vegetable mixture, and a meat or seafood preparation, the ingredients for each of these components are listed in a separate grouping.

Mise en Place. All professional cooks are well versed in the concept of *mise en place* (pronounced "meez on plahss"). Even if they are not familiar with the French term (which means "put in place"), they are familiar with kitchen setup or preprearation. They know well that much planning, organization, and preliminary kitchen work must take place before the first customer walks in the door if the service period is to go smoothly.

The concept of mise en place and how it is put into practice is discussed in more detail later in this chapter, beginning on page 9.

The primary mise en place or preparation for any recipe includes gathering and processing the ingredients as listed. For example, if a recipe calls for 4 ounces of diced onion, you must peel, dice, and weigh some onion. These steps are assumed and are not spelled out in the procedure.

After the ingredients are assembled and prepared, additional parts of the recipe may often be done in advance. This will vary depending on many factors, including time available, storage capacity and equipment available, and the nature of the rest of the menu. Therefore, the steps listed as mise en place in the recipes in this book should be taken only as suggestions. Depending on your own needs, you may want to do more parts of a recipe in advance or reserve more of the procedure for the last minute before serving.

In some recipes in this book, no separate mise en place is indicated. Some of these are recipes that are prepared in one continuous procedure. In other cases, you should analyze the recipe and determine the mise en place according to your own needs and schedule.

Cooking. This heading is used for the major part of the recipe procedure. If much of the procedure is done in advance (as mise en place) and the final cooking is brief, this section may be labeled "Finishing" instead of cooking.

If no cooking is required or if the whole recipe procedure is done in advance or is one continuous process, the heading "Procedure" may be used. (For example, see the terrine recipes in Chapter 11.)

Presentation. Some recipes include instructions for arranging the item on the plate. Once again, these are suggestions, and the cook is invited to devise other styles of plating.

Three basic principles of plating should be kept in mind:

1. *Cook foods properly.* No matter how carefully the foods are arranged on the plate, they won't be attractive unless they are handled and cooked with care and to the correct doneness. Dried-out meat or fish and overcooked, mushy or broken vegetables won't look appetizing no matter how they are plated.

2. *Be neat.* Cut foods properly and with sharp knives. Plate the foods carefully. Use clean plates. Be careful not to dribble sauce all over the rim; wipe it clean if you do.

3. *Serve foods at the proper temperature.* Serve hot foods hot, on hot plates. Serve cold foods cold, on cold plates. Observe all guidelines for safe and sanitary food handling. Although many popular modern dishes are properly served at room temperature or slightly warm, they should not be held at these temperatures. Dishes served warm should be cooked, allowed to cool for a few minutes, and served at once. Refrigerated dishes to be served cool or at room temperature should be removed from refrigeration shortly before serving to temper them and should not be allowed to stand on the counter for long periods.

The traditional style of arranging food on the plate calls for the main-course item to be placed in front on the plate, closest to the diner, with a vegetable and a starch item behind it. Modern cooks, however, have devised a great variety of imaginative and artistic plate arrangements. The following suggestions are examples of plating styles. The color photographs in this book illustrate many of these ways of arranging food.

- Place the main item in the center of the plate, and arrange the vegetables and other garnish around it. This is a commonly used method. It allows the main item to dominate the plate even when the portion size is small.

- Slice the main item, and overlap the slices on the plate. The slices may be fanned out across the plate, placed in a row down the center, arranged in a crescent at the front of the plate, or arranged in a circle with the garnish in the center. Slicing a meat can add eye appeal by showing an attractive cut surface, and it allows the main item to cover more of the plate.

- Place the main item on a bed of vegetables. The vegetables add flavor and height to the main item, while the main item releases juices that soak into and flavor the vegetable.

- Instead of using a flat bed of vegetables, mound them. Lean slices of the main item against this mound.

- Stacking or layering meat and vegetables gives height to the presentation and creates a sense of abundance. For example, place the main item on a bed of vegetables, top with another vegetable or meat garnish, then top the whole mound with an avalanche of a light, delicate garnish such as fried julienne of leeks or other fried herbs or shredded vegetables (see page 499).

- Arrangement of items on the plate may be in a careful, artistic arrangement. Pieces of garnish, for example, can be evenly spaced in a neat circle, arc, or other pattern. Avoid too elaborate a pattern, however. If the arrangement is too artistic, it can create the impression that the cook spent too long playing with the food in the kitchen. Also, don't spend so much time arranging the food that it is cold by the time it reaches the table.

- The opposite approach is to use a random-looking pattern that creates the impression that the food was quickly plated and rushed to the dining room without thought to the design, perhaps with garnish scattered casually about. Of course, to be effective, the arrangement is not actually careless or haphazard but is planned in advance.

- Sauces are used to enhance the presentation in many ways. The following are three commonly used techniques:

  1. Pour the sauce onto the plate first, to make a pool. Arrange the main item and garnish on top of this pool. This is especially effective when the color of the sauce makes a pleasing contrast with the foods.

  2. Pool the sauce as in step 1, then drop a small amount of a sauce of contrasting color on it. This can be done by splashing it on, dropping it on with a spoon in a random pattern, or piping lines or circles with a squeeze bottle. The sauces can then be marbleized by dragging a knife blade through them, either in random swirls or a careful pattern. For best results, the two (or more) sauces should be of about the same consistency.

  3. Drizzle a small amount of sauce randomly about the plate. This technique is often used with flavored oils (see page 36) or other intensely flavored liquids, when only a small quantity is desired. Two or more sauces may be used on one plate.

Variations. Many recipes are followed by variations. Some of these variations contain detailed instructions and ingredient quantities to produce a different dish, but one that is related to the main recipe. In other cases, the variations are brief or general suggestions for changing or modifying the main recipe. Presenting new recipes in the form of variations shows how different dishes are related by method and how common basic techniques can be applied to different ingredients.

Users of these recipes are encouraged to devise their own variations, using their understanding of fundamental cooking principles.

PLANNING YOUR WORK

Even on the simplest level, some preliminary preparation is necessary. Even if you prepare only one short recipe, you must first assemble your tools and ingredients, wash, trim, cut, and measure the ingredients, and prepare your equipment (e.g., preheat the oven, line or grease baking sheets, and so on). Only then can you begin the actual cooking. When many items are to be prepared in a commercial kitchen, the situation is much more complex. Dealing with this complexity is the basis of kitchen organization.

While the prepreparation in a home kitchen is usually unplanned and more or less haphazard, the mise en place in a restaurant kitchen is thoroughly and systematically planned and carried out. In any restaurant kitchen, there is far too much work to leave until the last minute, so some work must be done in advance. At the same time, most foods are at their best quality as soon as they have finished cooking, and they deteriorate as they are held. Careful planning is necessary to resolve this conflict. The goal is to do as much work as possible in advance without loss of quality.

The amateur cook can benefit greatly by following the professional's example. If you take a few minutes to analyze your recipes in advance and plan your tasks accordingly, your kitchen work can flow more smoothly and quickly. Family meals become less of a chore. Even elaborate dinner parties can be planned so that you can spend more time with your guests and less time in the kitchen with too much last-minute work.

The method for planning mise en place can be used by the home cook as well as the professional. Planning generally follows these steps:

1. *Break each recipe or menu item into individual steps.*

If you turn to any recipe in this book, you will note that the procedures are divided into a sequence of steps. Usually this sequence must be followed to make a finished product.

2. *Determine which steps may be done in advance.*

The first step of any recipe, whether written or not, is always part of advance preparation: *assembling and preparing the ingredients.* This includes cleaning and cutting the produce and cutting and trimming meats.

Succeeding steps of a recipe may be done in advance if the foods can then be held or stored without loss of quality. Frequently, separate components of a recipe, such as a sauce or a stuffing, can be completely prepared in advance, and the dish can be assembled at the last minute. Similarly, many casseroles can be assembled in advance, refrigerated, and then baked when needed.

In general, items cooked by dry-heat methods, such as broiled steaks, sautéed fish, and french-fried potatoes, do not hold well and should be cooked as close as possible to serving time. (Large roasts are an exception to this rule.) Foods cooked by moist heat, such as soups, stews, braised meats, and boiled vegetables, are better suited to reheating and can be cooked in advance. Delicate items, such as most fish, should always be freshly cooked.

3. *Save work by consolidating tasks when possible.*

For example, if you need chopped onions for more than one recipe, do them all at once. This may seem obvious, but many cooks overlook it and prepare one recipe at a time without referring to the others, thus spending more time in the kitchen than necessary. A few minutes of planning time can save much more work time.

4. *Determine how long it takes to prepare each stage of each recipe. Plan a production schedule beginning with the preparations that take the longest.*

Many operations can be carried on at once, because they don't all require your complete attention the full time. It may take several hours to cook a stew or make bread, but you don't have to stand and watch them the whole time.

5. *Determine the best way to hold the item at its final stage of prepreparation.*

Refrigerator temperatures are best for preserving the quality of most foods, whether they are raw, partially cooked, or fully cooked and awaiting final cooking or reheating. Some components, such as sauces, can be kept warm or hot for short periods, but most ingredients become overcooked if they are kept hot too long.

In a restaurant, the mise en place may be extensive, involving the preparation of large quantities of stocks, sauces, breadings, batters, as well as the trimming and cutting of vegetables, meats, and fish. Naturally, the preparation for a dinner at home is much simpler. Nevertheless, for the home cook the advantages of careful planning are similar.

As we discussed earlier, some of the recipes in this book indicate a suggested mise en place. For the remaining recipes, as well as for most recipes from other sources, you will need to plan the advance preparation yourself. Most cooks organize their work in some fashion, whether they realize it or not, but a more systematic approach, as described in the preceding discussion, brings a more professional efficiency to kitchen tasks.

2

Basic Cooking Methods

*B*ecause this book was originally designed as an advanced-level textbook for students of professional cooking, it begins with the assumption that the reader already has an understanding of basic cooking techniques, procedures, and theories and has had some experience in applying them. The amateur cook picking up this book for the first time will find a great deal of information that is immediately useful, but a brief summary of these basic principles, normally studied during the first year of a formal culinary education, will give the reader a better background for using this book. Such a summary is the subject of this chapter.

Readers who would like a more detailed understanding of these basic principles and techniques should consult any of a number of texts and references currently available, among them my book, *Professional Cooking,* which is a widely used textbook for chefs in training. Consult the Bibliography (page 623) for further information.

By understanding the basic theory, as summarized in this chapter, cooks build a solid foundation for further development, and they learn to control the cooking process with greater accuracy. This book goes beyond the basics, beginning with Chapter 3, and introduces some of the complexities that make these basics more practical and adaptable to all situations.

BASIC PREPARATIONS

Many of the techniques discussed in this section are categorized by professional cooks as mise en place (see Chapter 1). That is, they are procedures such as cutting vegetables and making thickening agents that are necessary for preparing the ingredients before cooking or assembling the finished dish.

Cutting

Cutting foods into uniform shapes and sizes is important for two reasons: it ensures even cooking, and it enhances the appearance of the product.

Cutting neat slices, strips, and dice is a cumulative process. This means that to cut a potato into ¼-inch dice, for example, you must first cut it into slices ¼ inch thick. Stack these slices, a few at a time, and cut them into ¼-inch sticks. Cut these strips, a few a time, crosswise into ¼-inch dice. Using this method, a cook can dice a potato neatly and accurately in less than a minute. For accuracy, speed, and safety, a professional cook almost always cuts foods on a cutting board, in contrast to the practice of many home cooks of holding the food in the hands and cutting against the thumb.

The most commonly used cut for most vegetables is, of course, a simple slice. Other commonly used cuts and shapes are described in the following list:

1. *Brunoise* (pronounced "broon wahz"): tiny dice measuring about ⅛ inch (3 mm) on a side.
2. *Small dice:* cubes measuring about ¼ inch (6 mm) on a side.
3. *Medium dice:* cubes measuring about ½ inch (12 mm) on a side.
4. *Large dice:* cubes measuring about ¾ inch (2 cm) on a side.
5. *Julienne:* thin strips measuring about ⅛ inch by ⅛ inch by 2 to 3 inches (3 mm × 3 mm × 6 cm).

6. *Batonnet:* thicker strips or sticks measuring about ¼ inch by ¼ inch by 2 to 3 inches (6 mm × 6 mm × 6 cm).

In addition, the following terms describe other cutting techniques:

1. *Chop:* to cut into irregularly shaped pieces.

2. *Concassé* (pronounced "con cass say"): chopped coarsely.

3. *Mince:* to chop into very fine pieces.

4. *Shred:* to cut into thin strips, either with a knife or with the coarse blade of a grater.

Flavoring Elements

Some of the most important flavoring elements are combinations of aromatic vegetables, herbs, and spices. These are widely used to flavor roasts, pot roasts, gravies, stocks, soups, and other preparations.

Mirepoix

Mirepoix (pronounced "meer pwah") is, in its most basic form, a combination of onions, carrots, and celery. It is a preparation that is used in all areas of cooking, including for flavoring stocks, soups, meats, poultry, fish, and vegetables. The standard proportions are as follows: to make 1 pound of mirepoix, use ½ pound of onions, ¼ pound of carrots, and ¼ pound of celery.

To make a white mirepoix, omit the carrots. White mirepoix is used when it is important to keep a stock or other preparation as white as possible.

Chop the vegetables coarsely into relatively uniform-sized pieces. Since mirepoix is rarely served but used only as a flavoring and removed or strained out before the food that it has flavored is served, it is not necessary to cut it neatly. The size depends on how long it will cook. Cut into large pieces when it will cook for a long time, as for brown stock (see page 606). Cut it into smaller pieces for releasing flavors in a short time, as when making fish stock (see page 607).

Bouquet Garni

A *bouquet garni* (pronounced "boo kay gar nee") is a bundle of fresh herbs and aromatic vegetables used to flavor stocks and other liquid preparations. The flavorings are tied in a bundle with string so that they can be removed easily. A bouquet garni normally includes sprigs of thyme and parsley, a bay leaf, a stalk of celery, and sometimes a small leek.

Sachet

Because dried herbs are more readily available and more widely used than fresh herbs, and because dried herbs cannot be tied into a bundle, they are instead tied into a small piece of cheesecloth. This bundle is called a *sachet* (pronounced "sa shay"), which means "bag." A spice bag can be made with any combination of herbs and spices, dried or fresh. Tying the spices in a bag makes it easy to remove them from a stock or sauce at any time during or after cooking.

A sachet used to flavor stock usually contains thyme, bay leaf, peppercorns, parsley sprigs or stems, whole cloves, and sometimes garlic.

Thickening Agents

The classic thickening agents for sauces, soups, and other liquids include three based on starches and one based on egg yolks.

If a starch is used for thickening, it must first be mixed with a fat or a cold liquid in order to separate the starch granules. This is the basic principle of the first three thickeners described in this section. If a dry flour or other starch is added to a hot liquid without first mixing it with a fat or cold liquid, it is likely to form lumps.

Roux

A roux (pronounced "roo") is a cooked mixture of equal parts by weight of fat and flour. Clarified butter (see below) is the preferred fat because of its flavor, but animal fats (e.g., chicken fat or beef drippings) are used for special items, such as pan gravies. Vegetable oil can also be used, but it contributes no flavor.

The ingredients, quantities, and exact procedure for making roux are detailed in the recipe on page 608.

Beurre Manié

Beurre manié (pronounced "burr mahnyay") is a mixture of equal parts soft, raw butter and flour worked together to form a smooth paste. It is used for quick thickening at the end of cooking. To use, drop small pieces into a simmering sauce or other liquid and stir with a wire whip until smooth.

Slurry

A *slurry* is a mixture made by stirring a starch, usually cornstarch, with cold water or other cold liquid to make a very thin, smooth paste. To use, slowly stir the slurry into the hot liquid to be thickened and stir, while simmering, until thickened. Other starches used this way include arrowroot and potato starch.

Liaison

A *liaison* is a mixture of raw egg yolks and heavy cream, used to give richness to sauces and soups. The liaison also has a slight thickening power due to the coagulation of the egg yolks. Caution must be used when thickening with egg yolks because of the danger of curdling if the yolks are overcooked. Follow these steps when employing a liaison to enrich and thicken a hot liquid:

1. Beat together the egg yolks and cream in a bowl. Normal proportions are 2 to 3 parts cream to 1 part egg yolks.
2. Very slowly add a little of the hot liquid to the liaison, beating constantly. This is known as *tempering*.
3. Off the heat, add the tempered liaison to the rest of the hot liquid, stirring well as you pour it in.
4. Return the liquid to low heat to warm it gently, but to avoid curdling do not heat it higher than 180°F (82°C), which is below the simmering point.

Miscellaneous Preparations

Three other preparations need brief attention.

Clarified Butter

Butter consists of butterfat, water, and milk solids. *Clarified butter* is purified butterfat, with the water and milk solids removed. It is used for many cooking operations, such as sautéing (because the milk solids of unclarified butter burn at high temperatures) and making hollandaise sauce (because the water of whole butter would change the consistency of the sauce).

To clarify butter, melt it in a heavy saucepan over moderate heat. Skim the froth from the surface. Carefully pour off the clear, melted butter into another container, leaving the milky water at the bottom of the saucepan.

Breading

To bread a food item means to coat it with bread crumbs or other crumbs or meal before deep-frying, panfrying, or sautéing. The usual method for applying these coatings is called the *standard breading procedure*. The food is first dredged in flour and then dipped in egg wash (a mixture of beaten eggs and liquid, usually water or milk) in order to make a firmer coating that adheres well to the food. The standard breading procedure consists of the following steps:

1. Dry the food product to be breaded in order to get a thin, even coating of flour.
2. Season the product.
3. Dip it in flour to coat evenly. Shake off excess.
4. Dip in egg wash to coat completely. Remove and let the excess drip off.
5. Dip in bread crumbs. Cover with crumbs and press on gently. Remove and carefully shake off excess.
6. Fry immediately or hold for a short time in a single layer on a rack or a pan of dry crumbs.

Gelatin

To dissolve unflavored gelatin, stir it slowly into cold liquid to avoid lumping. Let it stand for 5 minutes to absorb water. Then heat it until dissolved, or add a hot liquid and stir until dissolved.

To speed setting, dissolve the gelatin in up to half of the liquid and add the remainder of the liquid cold to lower the temperature.

Do not add raw pineapple or papaya to the gelatin. They contain enzymes that break down the gelatin and prevent it from congealing properly. If cooked or canned, however, these fruits can be used.

Add solid ingredients when the gelatin is partially set or thick and syrupy. This will keep them evenly mixed rather than floating or settling.

To unmold gelatin, follow these steps:

1. Run a thin knife blade around the top edges of the mold to loosen.
2. Dip the mold in hot water for 1 or 2 seconds.
3. Quickly wipe the bottom of the mold. Invert a plate over the mold and flip the plate and mold over together. If the gelatin doesn't slip out of the mold, give it a gentle shake. If it still doesn't come out, repeat steps 2 and 3.

EFFECTS OF HEAT ON FOODS

A cook uses heat in order to make certain changes in foods. Skillful cooks know exactly how to apply heat to create just the changes they want to make in foods. To develop these skills, you should know something about how the components of foods react to heat.

Foods are composed of proteins, carbohydrates, fats, and water, plus small amounts of minerals, vitamins, pigments, and flavor elements. It is important to understand how these components react when heated or mixed with other foods.

Proteins

Proteins are major components of meats, poultry, fish, eggs, milk, and milk products, and they are present in smaller amounts in nuts, beans, and grains. As proteins are heated, they become firm, or *coagulate*. As the temperature increases, they shrink, become firmer, and lose more moisture. Exposure of proteins to excessive heat toughens them and makes them dry. Most proteins complete coagulation—that is, they are fully cooked—at 160° to 185°F (71° to 85°C), well below the boiling point of water.

Connective tissues are special proteins that help to hold muscle tissue together. Without connective tissue, meats would fall apart, but too much connective tissue makes meats tough. Fortunately, certain kinds of connective tissue, called *collagen,* break down into gelatin and water when cooked slowly with moisture.

Acids, such as lemon juice and vinegar, speed coagulation and help dissolve connective tissue.

Carbohydrates

Carbohydrates include all the various forms of starch and sugar. Aside from nutritional considerations, cooks are concerned with two kinds of changes that heat causes in carbohydrates.

1. *Gelatinization* occurs when starches absorb water and swell to a larger size. This is the reaction that causes sauces or gravies to thicken when a starch is added to them and heated. Acids interfere with gelatinization, so sauces thickened with a starch are thinner if they contain an acid.

2. *Caramelization* is the browning of sugars caused by heat. Because some starches are broken down into sugars during this process, there are additional sugars available for caramelization. The golden brown color of baked bread and pastries and the browning of potatoes in a sauté pan are two examples of this phenomenon.

Fiber

Fiber is the name for a group of complex substances that help give structure and firmness to plants, including fruits, vegetables, and grains. The reason fruits and vegetables become softer when cooked is in part because of the breaking down of fiber by heat.

Acids make fiber firmer. Thus, if lemon juice is added to a vegetable before cooking, the cooking time will be longer. Sugars also make vegetables and fruits firmer, so fruit cooked with sugar will hold its shape better than fruit cooked without sugar.

Alkalis, such as baking soda, soften fiber. Thus if baking soda is added to green vegetables to keep them greener, they will be softer and mushier. (Baking soda also destroys some vitamins.)

Fats

Fats are present in many foods and are also important as cooking mediums. Fats can be either solid or liquid at room temperature.

High heat breaks down fats; when hot enough, fats break down rapidly and start to smoke. The temperature at which this happens is called the *smoke point,* and it varies for different fats. Fats that have been broken down by excessive heat, whether they are cooking fats or fats present in the food, can give an unpleasant flavor to foods. Stable fats—that is, those with a high smoke point—should be used for deep-frying.

Minerals, Vitamins, Pigments, and Flavor Components

All of these components may be leached out of, or dissolved away from, foods during cooking. Vitamins, pigments, and flavors may also be destroyed by heat, by long cooking, and by other compounds present in the foods. Note that many of the same factors that result in the loss of flavor and color also result in the loss of vitamins and minerals. Thus, the tastiest and most appetizing vegetables, for example, are often the ones that are the most nutritious as well.

Acids, such as lemon juice, enhance certain vegetable pigments. They make white vegetables, such as cauliflower, whiter, and they make red vegetables, such as beets and red cabbage, a brighter red. On the other hand, alkalis, such as baking soda, turn the white pigments yellowish and red pigments an unappetizing greenish-blue. By contrast, acids turn green vegetables brownish, while alkalis turn them an unnatural shade of bright green.

COOKING METHODS

Cooking methods are classified as moist-heat methods and dry-heat methods. *Moist-heat cooking methods* are those in which the heat is conducted to the food by water (including stocks, sauces, and so on) or by steam. *Dry-heat cooking methods* are those in which the heat is conducted without moisture—that is, by hot air, hot metal, infrared radiation (from a broiler), or hot fat.

Different cooking methods are suited to different kinds of foods. For example, some meats are high in connective tissue and will be tough unless this tissue is broken down slowly by moist heat. Other meats are low in connective tissue and are naturally tender. They are at their best and juiciest when cooked with dry heat to a rare or medium-done stage.

Moist-heat Methods

To *boil* means to cook in a liquid that is bubbling rapidly. Water boils at 212°F (100°C) at sea level. Boiling is generally reserved for certain vegetables and starches. The high temperature would toughen the proteins of meats, fish, and eggs, and the rapid bubbling breaks up delicate foods.

To *simmer* means to cook in a liquid that is bubbling gently; the temperature ranges from about 185° to 205°F (85° to 96°C). Foods cooked in liquid are usually simmered rather than boiled, because the high temperature and intense agitation of boiling are harmful to most foods.

To *poach* means to cook in a liquid, usually a small amount, that is hot but not actually bubbling. Poaching temperatures range from about 160° to 180°F (71° to 82°C). Poaching is used to cook delicate foods, such as fish and eggs out of the shell.

To *steam* means to cook foods by exposing them directly to steam. Restaurants often have special equipment for steaming; however, in the home kitchen, foods are usually steamed on a rack above boiling water. Steaming may also refer to cooking an item tightly wrapped or in a covered pan so that it cooks in the steam formed by its own moisture.

Steaming is widely used for vegetables because it cooks them rapidly without agitation and it minimizes the dissolving away of nutrients that occurs when vegetables are boiled.

To *braise* means to cook in a small amount of liquid, usually in a covered pan and usually after first browning the food by panfrying or other dry-heat method. For a more detailed discussion of braising as it is applied to meats, see pages 341–344.

Dry-heat Methods Without Fat

To *roast* means to cook foods by surrounding them with hot, dry air, usually in an oven. Cooking uncovered is essential to roasting. Covering a pan holds in steam, changing the process from a dry-heat method to a moist-heat method. For the same reason, water should not be added to a roasting pan during cooking.

Meats and poultry are usually roasted on a rack. The rack prevents the meat from simmering in its own juices and fat, and it also allows hot air to circulate all around the product.

The terms "broiling" and "grilling" are often used interchangeably, but in this book they are used for two distinct procedures. To *broil* means to cook with radiant heat from above. Thus, one cooks a food *under* a broiler. To *grill* means to cook on an open grid over a heat source, such as burning charcoal or an electric element. One cooks *on* a grill.

Both broiling and grilling are rapid, high-heat cooking methods that are used most often for tender meats, poultry, and fish, and for a few vegetable items. Because the heat is so high, broiling and grilling should be done with careful attention, because the foods can quickly become overcooked.

Pan-broiling is done in a sauté pan or skillet without added fat. Fat that is rendered from the food must be poured off as it accumulates or the process would become pan-frying. No liquid is added, and the pan is not covered.

Dry-heat Methods With Fat

To *sauté* means to cook quickly in a small amount of fat. Because it is a rapid cooking method requiring high heat, it is used primarily for tender, quick-cooking meats, poultry, fish, and vegetables, usually cut into small or thin pieces so that they will cook in a short time.

A sauté pan should be preheated thoroughly so that it is hot when the food is added. If this is not done, the food will not sauté but will more likely begin to simmer in its own juices. Similarly, do not add too much food to the pan at once or the temperature of the pan will be lowered too much and the food will simmer in its juices.

To *panfry* means to cook in a moderate amount of fat over moderate heat. There is no exact dividing line between sautéing and panfrying, except that the term "panfrying" is usually used when slightly larger pieces of foods, such as chops, are being cooked, when slightly more fat is used, and when the cooking time is longer.

To *deep-fry* means to cook a food submerged in hot fat. Most foods are fried at 350° to 375°F (175° to 190°C). If you don't have a fryer controlled by a thermostat, be sure to use a fat thermometer to monitor the temperature of the fat. If the temperature is too low, the food will take too long to cook and will consequently absorb more fat. Don't fry too much food at once, because adding too much food to the fry kettle greatly lowers the temperature. Deep-fried foods do not hold well, so fry as close as possible to serving time.

CHAPTER

3

Sauces

*I*n the classical kitchen brigade, the saucier ranks above all other station chefs and just below the sous chef. It is true that the saucier's responsibilities include more than just preparing sauces; they extend to producing such items as stews and sautés. Even more significant, however, the ranking of the saucier is an indication both of the importance of sauces in fine cuisine and of the difficulty and complexity of preparing them well and the training that this requires.

Sauces are widely misunderstood in this country and, as a result, are often dismissed as needless complication or, even worse, as tools for disguising poor quality food or for destroying the purity of simple cooking.

Nevertheless, sauces are as important in the best kitchens today as they were in Escoffier's day. The reason is that they are some of the glories of modern cooking. From the chef's point of view, they provide some of the most exacting outlets for cooks to exercise their skill and creativity. From the diner's point of view, they provide some of the most exciting and memorable dining experiences, even if the diner isn't aware of the quality of the sauce and remembers only the meat or fish it accompanied. A well-made sauce is not so much a food as a complex seasoning that enhances a food and lifts it to a higher level of excellence.

This chapter details a range of sauce-making techniques used today, building upon your basic knowledge of sauces.

BASIC TECHNIQUES

Because of the importance of sauces in classical European and American cooking, the fundamentals of sauce making are an important part of the training of every chef. Therefore, even relatively inexperienced cooks are, or should be, familiar with the basic techniques of sauce production. For this reason, this chapter does not go into detail on material that is covered in basic cookbooks, such as the making of stocks, roux, mother sauces, and the most familiar small sauces. Instead, we begin with a brief review of these basics and then proceed to cover in greater detail a number of advanced techniques, with attention to some of the finer points of modern sauces.

While the basic techniques of sauce making today are essentially the same as those of Escoffier, the applications have changed somewhat. Modern cooks often use no starch to thicken many of their sauces, and they place greater emphasis on some specialized techniques that have almost become hallmarks of modern haute cuisine. Those techniques are covered in detail in this chapter.

Review: Stocks

In Escoffier's kitchen, and in most of the great kitchens since Escoffier's time, most sauces were based on stocks. Of the hot sauces, only the butter sauces—hollandaise and béarnaise, plus a few minor specialized sauces—were entirely stock-free. Today, on the other hand, a greater number of non–stock-based sauces are popular and widely used. Nevertheless, good stock is still the foundation of many of the most important sauces. In the finest restaurants, careful attention to stock-making can make the difference between sauces that are merely good and those that are memorable.

Two factors are necessary for good stocks: good ingredients and proper production procedures. Care in selection of ingredients and in preparation of the stock can ensure a quality product. A good stock is one that is distinguished by the following characteristics:

Flavor

Body

Clarity

The flavor of a stock is derived, of course, from its ingredients: bones, vegetables, and seasonings. It should be strong and well balanced but neutral enough so that the stock can be used for a variety of purposes (except in the case of specialized stocks such as ham or game stock).

The body of the stock depends on its gelatin content, which is derived from bones, especially bones high in cartilage.

Clarity depends on careful preparation: skimming the cooking stock whenever necessary and simmering the stock slowly without ever letting it boil.

Regarding ingredients, Escoffier's words should be heeded: "In the matter of stock it is, above all, necessary to have a sufficient quantity of the finest materials at one's disposal." A stock pot should not be a garbage disposal, into which all sorts of scraps are carelessly thrown. Never use spoiled or stale ingredients in a stock; you will ruin it.

Bones are, of course, the most important ingredients. Bones with a lot of cartilage, such as knuckle bones, release the most gelatin into the stock. Bones from young animals have more cartilage than bones from older animals. Special ingredients with a very large quantity of gelatin, such as calf's feet, pig's feet, and pork rind (skin), may be simmered with the stock to increase its gelatin content. This technique is especially useful in the preparation of aspics and jellied consommés.

Many chefs feel that veal bones are superior to beef bones for making brown stocks. This is not only because veal bones release more gelatin, but also because they give the stock a more neutral flavor. Thus, the stock can be used in more ways. Stocks made from all beef bones have a more pronounced beefy flavor that is not appropriate for all dishes.

Meat was once commonly used in stocks, but because of its cost, it is rarely used today. If meat trimmings are available, they can certainly be added to the stock pot.

In addition to the basic mirepoix vegetables—onions, celery, carrots—other vegetables may be used for flavor, such as leek and mushroom trimmings. Carrots are often omitted if it is necessary to keep the stock very white. Tomato products should be used only in brown stocks because of their color.

Starch Thickeners

In classical cooking, the majority of sauces are made of three kinds of ingredients:

1. A liquid, the body of the sauce
2. A thickening agent
3. Additional seasoning and flavoring ingredients

The second of these components, thickening agents, is the subject of this section.

In order to accomplish its primary purpose, namely enhancing the flavor of a food, a sauce must have enough body or thickness to cling lightly to the food. Otherwise, it will just run off the food like water and lie in a puddle on the plate. This doesn't mean, however, that the sauce has to be thick and pasty.

For most traditional sauces, thickening agents have generally been starches. *Flour* is the most widely used starch for thickening, but there are several others as well, including *cornstarch, arrowroot, tapioca, waxy maize* or other modified starch, *potato starch,* and *pregelatinized* or *instant starches.*

The usual methods for incorporating a starch in a liquid involve first mixing the starch with a fat or a cold liquid. The purpose of this procedure is to separate the starch granules so that they do not form lumps. The following are the basic starch preparations:

1. *Roux* is a cooked mixture of equal parts (by weight) of starch and fat.
2. *Beurre manié* is an uncooked mixture of equal parts flour and raw butter. Sometimes a larger proportion of butter is used to give added richness to the sauce.
3. A *slurry* is a thin mixture of starch and cold water or other liquid. Slurries are often used with cornstarch and other highly purified starches. A flour slurry, called whitewash, makes an inferior sauce and is not recommended.

Cooking Starches. Once the starch, in the form of a roux, beurre manié, or slurry, is combined with a liquid, it must be cooked until the starch gelatinizes and thickens the sauce, and until there is no longer any taste of raw starch.

You should be aware, however, that there is more to cooking a starch-bound sauce than just simmering it until it is thickened. The best-quality sauces have a light, silky-smooth texture and a brilliant, glossy appearance. Since starches affect these qualities of a sauce, we must learn how to avoid the faults that result from careless or improper cooking of starches.

It is helpful to read Escoffier in order to get some insight into this problem. In speaking of a basic brown sauce or Espagnole thickened with a flour roux, Escoffier insisted that the sauce must be simmered for at least 6 hours, or preferably for six or eight hours the first day, then for additional time a second or even a third day. The reason for this long cooking is that flour consists not only of starch but also of proteins and other components. The starch is the only component that actually thickens the sauce, while the other elements only cloud the sauce and detract from its texture. Through long simmering, these impurities are gradually thrown off in the form of scum, which is skimmed from the surface by the cook.

If this is the case, then why not use a purer form of starch, such as arrowroot, cornstarch, or potato starch, instead of flour? In fact, Escoffier asked this question himself more than half a century ago. He felt that only habit made cooks continue to use flour, and that with better understanding, practices would change; chefs would use purer forms of starch.

It is interesting that in spite of this advice, Escoffier continued to use flour, as have cooks since his time. Note also that he felt that, even with a pure starch, *an Espagnole still has to simmer for an hour.*

No matter what starch is being used, the sauce must be cooked long enough to cook the starch completely and to incorporate the starch so well into the sauce that it becomes completely smooth. You must taste the sauce to make sure it is completely cooked. Even a sauce that looks smooth may feel slightly gritty on the tongue because of incompletely cooked starch granules.

You may want to experiment with different starches to learn how they thicken and how their textures differ. Try adding them in the form of roux, beurre manié and slurry and cook them for various lengths of time to see how the cooking times affect the texture. When working with various starch thickeners, keep the following guidelines in mind:

1. Purer forms of starch, such as cornstarch, potato starch, arrowroot, and so on, have roughly twice the thickening power of bread flour, so you will need only about half as much.

2. To make roux, use equal weights of starch product and fat, whether you are using flour or a purer starch. In other words, use only enough fat to coat all the starch granules, but no more than is needed.

3. Simmer the sauce long enough to completely cook the starch and to create a smooth texture. Adding a starch slurry at the end of cooking time to rescue a sauce that is too thin may result in a poor sauce.

4. Remember that long simmering concentrates the flavor of a sauce by evaporating part of the water. If you reduce the cooking time of a sauce because you are using a different starch, you must use a stronger stock to get the same flavor.

5. Skim the sauce as necessary while the sauce is cooking.

6. To get the smoothest texture, strain the sauce through a fine sieve or cheesecloth after cooking.

Starchless Sauces

As we have said, a sauce must have enough body or thickness to cling lightly to the food it is served with. This does not mean that a sauce must be thick and pasty, only that it should not be too thin and watery.

It is possible for a sauce to have a good consistency without having any starch in it at all. Other ingredients or components, other than starch, may provide a slight thickness. The most familiar example is a simple tomato sauce that is nothing more than a seasoned tomato purée. In this example, the sauce gets its consistency from the thickness of the main ingredient, a vegetable purée. Tomato purée and other vegetable purées can be used as either major or minor ingredients to give body to a sauce.

Other components are also used to thicken sauces. These include butter, cream, and the natural gelatin in a stock that has been concentrated by reduction. Incorporating these components in sauces requires special techniques, which are the subjects of the sections that follow. It is important to remember that these same techniques can be used with starch-thickened sauces, too. In fact, these aren't really new techniques, but old techniques used in new ways.

Modern chefs have tended more and more to make sauces without starch thickeners. This has led many people, including many cooks, to mistakenly believe that the classical techniques of Escoffier are no longer of any use. The fact is that the old techniques are still the basis of fine cooking. A typical modern white wine sauce for fish is essentially the same as the classical Sauce Vin Blanc or White Wine Sauce (page 41), the only difference being that the modern sauce often has no flour thickener and may contain extra butter or cream instead. To look at it another way, a white wine sauce may be made either with fish velouté (fish stock plus roux) or with unthickened fish stock (preferably a stock that is strong and concentrated).

This last example gives us a clue to how we might think about modern sauces. Classical chefs, as part of their *mise en place,* prepared quantities of the mother sauces— espagnole and demiglaze, veloutés of chicken and veal, béchamel, and so on—and then used these for making the variety of small sauces needed for the day's menu. Modern chefs, instead of preparing these mother sauces or leading sauces, might instead simply prepare some concentrated stocks and then use these during the service period to prepare the necessary small sauces.

Cooking modern, starch-free sauces requires a knowledge of all the classical sauce-making techniques, except that the roux is used less frequently.

Deglazing

To *deglaze* means to swirl or stir a liquid in a sauté pan, or other pan, over heat, in order to dissolve cooked particles of food and caramelized juices remaining on the bottom. As you will recall, this technique is used in making brown stock; the pan in which the bones were browned is deglazed, and this liquid is added to the stock to give it flavor and color.

Deglazing is important in classical cooking, especially when sautéing items to order. A liquid such as wine or stock is used to deglaze a sauté pan, and the liquid is then reduced over high heat. This reduction, with the added flavor of the pan drippings, is added to the sauce that is served with the item.

In modern kitchens, deglazing is especially important. In classical kitchens, the cooks began the service period with a bain marie full of sauces ready to be served. Today, cooks might start a service period with only a few sauces prepared or even with no sauces at all and only a supply of good stocks on hand. More sauces are prepared to order as part of the cooking procedure or recipe for each item.

The simplest sauce of all is made by merely adding stock or even water to the cooking pan. After simmering, straining, and seasoning, the liquid is served with the meat. The meat is served *au jus,* meaning "with natural juices."

Procedure for Deglazing a Pan

1. Remove the cooked item from the pan and keep it warm.
2. Remove excess grease from the pan, if necessary, and discard it.
3. If any flavoring ingredients, such as chopped shallots, are to be sautéed, add these to the pan and cook as directed in the recipe.
4. Add the deglazing liquid to the pan. The most commonly used liquids are the following:
   Stock
   Wine
   Water
   Vinegar
   Spirits, such as brandy
5. Set the pan over heat and stir or swirl the liquid in the pan to dissolve particles of food on the bottom of the pan. If necessary, scrape the bottom of the pan lightly with a wooden spoon.
6. Finish the sauce as directed in the recipe, either by adding additional ingredients and cooking further or by adding the reduction to a prepared sauce.
7. For the best appearance, either the deglazing liquid or the finished sauce should be strained to remove brown food particles.

Procedure Variations

The same procedure is used when making starch-thickened sauces. Use one of the following techniques:

1. Make a roux by adding flour to the pan after step 3 (if necessary, add more fat to the pan to make the roux). Cook the roux to the proper stage (that is, white, blond, or brown roux), depending on the recipe. Then add the deglazing liquid.
2. Instead of stock, use a starch-thickened sauce, such as demiglace or velouté, as the basic liquid.
3. Or thicken the finished sauce with beurre manié.

Reduction

To *reduce* a liquid is to simmer or boil it, evaporating part of the water in order to make it more concentrated. This process is called *reduction*. The term *reduction* is also used to mean a concentrated liquid that is made by this process.

Reduction is a basic technique in the production of sauces. To review briefly, *glace de viande*, or meat glaze, is made by reducing brown stock until it becomes thick and syrupy. Glace de viande not only has a strong, concentrated flavor, but when cooled it is solid and rubbery, because of a high concentration of gelatin. In the same way, *glace de volaille* (chicken glaze) and *glace de poisson* (fish glaze) are made by reducing the appropriate stocks.

One of the reasons for simmering both mother sauces and small sauces for long periods is to concentrate them by reduction. For example, *demiglaze* (also called *demi-glace*) is made by combining equal parts brown sauce (espagnole) and brown stock, and reducing by half.

To sum up, there are two main reasons for reducing liquids:

1. To concentrate the flavors of the liquid.
2. To thicken or adjust the texture of the liquid.

Reduction thickens a liquid because only the water evaporates, not the solid ingredients such as starch, fats, gelatin, vegetable particles, and so on. Of course, the more solids a liquid contains, the more it will thicken when reduced. For example, a good quality stock high in gelatin will become syrupy when reduced, but a poorly made stock with little gelatin content will not thicken as much.

The technique of reduction may be used at any stage of sauce making. A liquid may be reduced before being combined with other sauce ingredients. For example, when we make Bordelaise Sauce (page 44), we simmer red wine with spices, herbs, and shallots until it is one-fourth its original volume. This reduction is then used as a highly concentrated flavoring agent for the sauce.

A finished or nearly finished sauce may also be reduced until it is thickened to the desired consistency. This technique is used not only to concentrate the flavor but also to give the sauce just the right texture.

Deglazing and Reduction Combined. Deglazing and reducing are often used in combination. In fact, this is almost unavoidable. When you add a few ounces of wine or stock to a hot sauté pan, the liquid almost immediately begins to boil. Within seconds, much of the moisture has evaporated, leaving a flavorful reduction in the pan. By continuing to reduce this deglazing liquid as necessary, you produce a powerful flavoring ingredient that is an important part of many modern sauces.

Red and white table wines are often used as deglazing liquids, and it is particularly important to reduce them sufficiently. First of all, the alcohol must be cooked off so that it does not give an unpleasant flavor to the sauce. Second, table wine that is not reduced is not a good flavoring agent; it tends to water down the sauce unless it is reduced well. (It may be reduced either before or after it is combined with other ingredients, such as stock.)

By contrast, fortified wines such as sherry and madeira should not be heavily reduced, because they are added in small quantities and their delicate flavors are destroyed by excessive cooking. They are usually added shortly before the end of cooking.

Butter, Cream, and Egg Yolks

Butter, cream, and egg yolks have long been used in classical cuisine to enrich sauces. These ingredients have standard uses in culinary practice that beginning cooks learn early in their studies. To review briefly, these uses are as follows:

1. *Heavy cream* is added to sauces to make them richer and to give them a creamier flavor. Simple examples are the addition of cream to béchamel sauce to make cream sauce, and the addition of cream to chicken velouté to make suprême sauce.

2. *Butter* is added to sauces at the end of their production by using a technique called finishing with butter, or *monter au beurre* (pronounced "mohn tay oh burr"). To finish a sauce with butter, simply add a few pieces of soft butter to a hot sauce and swirl it until it melts and blends in. This procedure gives richness, shine, smoothness, and flavor to a sauce.

3. *Egg yolks* are added to sauces as part of a *liaison,* which is a mixture of raw egg yolks and heavy cream. A liaison must be tempered by stirring in a little of the hot sauce, before it is added to the bulk of the sauce. A liaison not only adds richness to the sauce, but it also has a slight binding or thickening power.

The use of these ingredients in sauces is part of the reason that classical French cooking developed a reputation for richness and heaviness. Ironically, nouvelle cuisine, although it is usually perceived to be "lighter," has produced sauces that are much richer than those prepared in Escoffier's kitchen. While the classical cream sauce is made by adding some heavy cream to a basic white sauce or béchamel, today some cream sauces are made almost entirely of heavy cream reduced over heat, with some flavoring ingredients added.

This discussion does not mean to pass judgment on either classical or modern sauces or to be critical of them. In fact, both the older and newer styles are excellent if properly made.

Emulsions. An *emulsion* is a uniform mixture of two unmixable substances, such as fat and water. Familiar examples of emulsions include such products as salad dressings, mayonnaise, and hollandaise sauce. It is important to understand emulsions in sauce making, because when we mix heavy cream (about 35 percent fat) and butter (about 80 percent fat) with sauces that are largely water, we want to keep the fat in suspension in the sauce. In other words, we want to maintain an emulsion.

A liquid fat, such as oil or melted butter, can be made into a *temporary emulsion* with water simply by vigorous mixing. Thus, if an oil and vinegar dressing is mixed or shaken hard, the oil and vinegar will stay mixed for a short time. The oil is broken up into tiny droplets that stay suspended in the vinegar. However, the droplets soon start gathering together and rising to the top. The harder the mixture is whipped, the tinier the droplets of oil will be, and the longer it will stay in suspension. This is how milk is homogenized. The milk is forced through very small holes so that the fat is broken up into such tiny droplets that the cream does not rise to the top.

When we make mayonnaise or hollandaise sauce, we create a *permanent emulsion* by using egg yolks, which serve as an *emulsifying agent.* An emulsifying agent works by combining with the tiny fat particles in a way that keeps them from joining together and separating out.

Therefore, when we use egg yolks in a sauce, either in a liaison with cream or as the basic thickening agent for hollandaise or béarnaise, we create a relatively stable emulsion.

On the other hand, when we add fat to a sauce without using an emulsifying agent, we must consider whether we need to use other techniques to keep the sauce from separating. These factors are considered in the following sections.

Butter. Because butter is, of course, mostly fat, we must pay special attention to sauces rich in butter, in order to keep the butter from separating. Keeping the following principles in mind will help you be succesful when making such sauces.

1. If a mixture of approximately *equal quantities of butter and water* are boiled rapidly in a thin layer for several minutes, they will combine to form an emulsion that will stay mixed reasonably well (that is, long enough to be served and eaten by the customer). For example, a mixture of equal parts butter and a rich chicken stock could be boiled together hard until bound and then served as a sauce.

   Caution: This technique works only with small quantities of butter and liquid in a thin layer on the bottom of a pan. Do not attempt to boil larger quantities of fat and water together. This can be very dangerous. The layer of fat floats on top and holds in the steam, until the water literally explodes, spraying hot liquid all over the kitchen.

2. If you boil an unequal mixture of fat and water (either a little butter in a large quantity of liquid, or a lot of butter with a little liquid in it), the fat will tend to separate.

3. Remember that boiling causes water to evaporate. Therefore, if you continue to boil the emulsified mixture described in the preceding point number one (equal parts fat and water), the water will gradually evaporate. When you reach the point where you have much less liquid than fat, the sauce will separate. This sauce can often be rebound by adding back some water and boiling again.

4. Fresh, raw butter is already a sort of emulsion. It might be described as a sauce waiting to be made. Remember that butter is about 15 percent water, which is bound up uniformly with the fat. Therefore, *when finishing a sauce with butter, use raw butter rather than melted or clarified butter.* The emulsified state of the raw butter will help it blend readily with the sauce. By contrast, melted butter is much harder to mix into a sauce.

The most important butter sauces in classical cooking are, of course, hollandaise sauce and its cousin béarnaise sauce. These sauces consist of melted butter, egg yolk, and a small amount of vinegar reduction or lemon juice. For your convenience, recipes for these sauces are included in Appendix 1.

You should also be familiar with the subject of hot butter sauces. The most common of these is simply melted butter, or *beurre fondu,* used as a dressing for vegetables and for such dishes as boiled lobster. Others that are well known include the following:

- Beurre noisette, or brown butter: raw butter heated until lightly browned.
- Beurre noir, or black butter: raw butter heated until dark brown and flavored with a few drops of vinegar or lemon juice (and sometimes with capers).
- Beurre meunière: brown butter flavored with lemon juice and chopped parsley.

The major techniques considered in this section are those relating to finishing sauces with butter and to a sauce called *beurre blanc.*

Finishing with Butter. As we have already said, *monter au beurre* means to finish a sauce by swirling in some raw butter. The actual amount of butter used may vary from about one-half ounce to as much as three or four ounces or more per pint of sauce. This should be done at the very end, shortly before the sauce is to be served. If the sauce is allowed to stand, the butter may separate out.

The raw butter has a slight binding or thickening effect on the sauce, depending on how much is used. This is for two reasons. The first is that the butter naturally gives a richer texture to the sauce, because fat itself has a richer texture. The second is that, as we said earlier, raw butter is a kind of emulsion, since it contains about 15 percent water. Therefore, swirling raw butter into a sauce creates a sort of temporary emulsion, giving the sauce a slightly thicker texture. However, this binding effect is lost if the sauce is overheated or allowed to stand too long and the butter separates out.

In recipes written by modern chefs, you may sometimes see the instruction, "Thicken the sauce by stirring in the butter." This may be a little misleading unless you understand that they are talking about *monter au beurre,* and that the thickening effect is only slight.

The technique of finishing a sauce with butter is an important one in classical cooking. It is called for regularly by Escoffier in his discussions of sauce making, and it is very important in modern cooking, as well. Although beginning discussions of this technique are often limited to the basic procedure of stirring raw butter into a sauce, the technique also can be used for adding many different flavors to sauces.

You may be familiar with the subject of *compound butters,* also known as flavored butters, which are simply mixtures of softened raw butter and various herbs, seasonings, condiments, and other flavoring ingredients. (Compound butters are given further consideration later in this chapter, page 71.)

Using a flavorful compound butter for the technique of *monter au beurre* is an excellent and versatile way of adding both flavor and richness to sauces. For an example of this procedure, see the recipe variation on page 59.

A Word About Beurre Manié. Beurre manié (see page 25) is always introduced to students as a starch thickener, which is what it is. That is, it can be thought of as a sort of uncooked roux that is stirred into sauces and soups.

However, adding beurre manié is also a form of *monter au beurre.* The only difference is that the raw butter that you are stirring into the sauce contains some flour, and thus has greater thickening power. Because of the raw butter it contains, beurre manié is more than just a starch thickener. It also helps to enrich the sauce like *monter au beurre.*

Therefore, you can use this technique instead of or in addition to *monter au beurre,* when your sauce requires greater thickening.

Beurre Blanc. The sauce called *beurre blanc* (French term meaning "white butter") is an extremely popular sauce today, especially for all kinds of seafood dishes. It is a very rich sauce because it consists mostly of butter, but its taste and texture are usually rather light.

Recipes for variations of beurre blanc are on page 68. You may want to refer to them while reading this section. Note that the sauce is made by beating a large quantity of raw butter into a very small quantity of flavorful liquid, usually a reduction.

To help us understand this sauce or family of sauces better, we can look at it from two points of view:

- Beurre blanc is something like hollandaise sauce made without egg yolks. Because egg yolks serve as an emulsifying agent, beurre blanc is not as stable as hollandaise. Careful control of the heat is needed to form the emulsion; if it becomes too hot (more than about 140°F (60°C)), it will separate. It does not hold or reheat well, so it is usually made as close to service time as possible.

- Beurre blanc production can be thought of as *monter au beurre* carried to its extreme. To finish a sauce with butter, you stir some raw butter into a hot sauce. Beurre blanc is made the same way, except that the amount of butter is much larger than the amount of liquid.

As we discussed, raw butter is already a kind of emulsion, because moisture is bound up in it. This fact enables us to make this sauce. The object is to melt the butter into the base liquid in such a way as to keep the emulsion from separating.

You will find the procedures for making beurre blanc and variations in the recipe section, page 68.

Cream. Reduced cream sauces are widely used in today's kitchens. In general, these sauces are made by adding heavy cream to a base liquid (such as reduced cooking liquids or deglazing liquids, stock, or wine) and boiling the sauce until reduced and thickened to the desired degree.

In the case of starch-thickened sauces, the addition of cream thins out the sauces. Therefore, if the same consistency is to be kept, the sauce must be reduced either before or after the cream is added.

In the case of modern, starchless sauces, cream is added not only to enrich, but also to thicken a sauce.

The difference between these modern sauces and classical, starch-bound sauces is that in the modern sauces the amount of cream added is often (but not always) much greater. In fact, one of the recipes in this chapter is for a sauce made of only cream, herbs, and a little lemon juice.

When heavy cream is added to an unthickened liquid and then reduced, the effect is to thicken the sauce lightly. There are at least two reasons why this happens. First, heavy cream is at least 35 percent butterfat, so the result is a little like finishing a sauce with diluted butter. (Cream consists of butterfat, water, and milk solids, just like butter. The difference is that cream has more water and milk solids.) Also, when the sauce is then reduced, some of this water content is driven off, increasing the concentration of butterfat. Remember, too, that the fat content of the cream is in *emulsion,* so you are making a sauce that gets its texture in part from emulsification, as we discussed earlier.

A second factor is related to the milk protein content of the cream. Like all proteins, they coagulate or become firmer when heated. This coagulation may even be increased when the sauce contains some acid, as it often does, especially if wine has been added. Heavy reduction of cream thus results in thickening.

Note on Curdling. A process by which milk proteins solidify or coagulate and separate from the whey is called *curdling*. As you know, one of the problems of cooking with cream is its tendency to curdle. Acids (such as lemon juice, vinegar, and wine) and heat are common causes of curdling.

Starches stabilize milk and cream. This is why you can safely add small amounts of lemon juice to béchamel sauce or suprême sauce. (How stable the sauce is depends on how much starch it contains.)

You might think, then, that if cream is added to an unthickened sauce, you cannot add any acids. Yet the opposite is true. Many reduced cream sauces contain acids such as wine and lemon juice. Why don't these sauces curdle?

The answer is that they do. Or, more accurately, the proteins coagulate, just as in curdling, but they don't actually form large curds and separate. The trick is to control the curdling so that you get the results you want. The cream is added to an acidic base, or an acid is added to cream, often over high heat, so that the mixture is boiling very quickly. The proteins coagulate rapidly and uniformly so that the mixture stays smooth.

If this doesn't quite make sense to you, remember that commercial sour cream is lightly acidic and "curdled," but it is also smooth rather than lumpy and separated.

Crème Fraîche. The French term *crème fraîche* (pronounced "krem fresh"), although it literally means "fresh cream," refers to a thick, slightly aged or cultured heavy cream. It is widely used for cooking in France and throughout Europe, and many recipes call for it. It is ideal for cooking because it is more flavorful than our heavy cream, and it blends easily into sauces.

While crème fraîche is sometimes available in the United States, it is usually very expensive. A close approximation can be made by culturing heavy cream with buttermilk (see the recipe on page 61). Or simply substitute heavy cream in recipes that call for crème fraîche.

General Procedure for Making Reduced Cream Sauces

The following is a very general procedure that can be applied to a variety of cream sauces. More specific procedures are given in the recipe section of this chapter.

1. Bring to a boil the liquid that forms the base of the sauce, if any. (If not, start with step 2.) This liquid may consist of one or more of the following:
   a. Deglazing liquid
   b. Cooking liquid
   c. Stock
   d. Wine
   e. Vinegar

   The liquid may also contain solid ingredients such as spices or chopped shallots (either raw shallots or sweat in butter). Reduce the liquid as necessary.
2. Add heavy cream. Bring to a boil. Reduce until thickened to desired consistency.
3. Add any additional ingredients to finish, such as herbs, lemon juice, or raw butter.

Whipped Cream. An interesting variation on the technique of adding a little cream to finish a sauce just before serving is to whip the cream and fold or stir it into the sauce. The sauce must then be plated and served at once. The result is a sauce with a slightly foamy or bubbly appearance. The flavor is the same as when unwhipped cream is used, but the foamy look can increase eye appeal.

Egg Yolks. The most common uses for egg yolks in sauce making are as part of an egg-yolk-and-cream liaison (page 29) and as a binding agent or emulsifier for hollandaise and béarnaise. We need not review these techniques again here.

There is another minor use of egg yolks in a type of sauce that some chefs call a *mousseline* and that others call *sabayon*. This should not be confused with the classical mousseline, made by folding whipped cream into hollandaise sauce (see page 42).

This sauce is made like the warm, whipped dessert also called sabayon. In this technique, raw egg yolks are whipped with other liquids (sometimes including cream) over gentle heat, until the mixture is light and frothy. The egg yolks are cooked gently and provide the binding power for the sauce.

The detailed procedure is included with the recipe on page 70.

Vegetable Purées

As we mentioned at the beginning of our discussion of starchless sauces (see page 26), vegetable purées can be used to thicken sauces. In fact, some sauces like tomato sauce consist primarily of a vegetable purée. (A fresh vegetable purée is sometimes called a *coulis* [pronounced "koo lee"]. This French term was originally used primarily for purée soups made from game or poultry, but today it is used most often to refer to fresh vegetable purées, and to fresh tomato sauce in particular.)

The degree of thickening depends on the amount of purée added and the nature of the vegetable. Starchy vegetables provide more thickening, for example, than leafy ones. A puréed garlic clove will add little thickness, but a large proportion of tomato purée will thicken more.

Thickening with vegetable purées can be done in two ways:

1. *Add a previously prepared purée to the sauce.* For example, you might add some tomato purée to an unthickened brown sauce.

2. *Purée the sauce and vegetable(s) together.* For example, you might take a braising liquid containing a garlic clove and diced carrots, reduce it, and force it through a sieve with the vegetables, then use this as your sauce.

Many other vegetables can be puréed and used in sauces, including sweet red peppers, fresh peas, onions, mushrooms, and so on. (See pages 50–54 for sauces consisting primarily of vegetable purées.)

Vegetable Juices

Fresh vegetable juices, heated, seasoned, and finished with a little butter or oil, make light, nutritious sauces for many modern dishes, from ravioli to seafood and meat entrées.

A vegetable juicer is necessary to make these sauces. This device extracts juice by pulverizing the vegetable and spinning the pulp in a fine sieve to separate the juice by centrifugal force.

Recipes for typical sauces are on page 56.

Procedure for Making Vegetable Juice Sauces

1. Scrub and trim the vegetables as necessary. In most cases, peeling is not necessary.
2. Pass the vegetables through the juicer to get the required amount of juice.
3. Put the juice in a saucepan and add the desired seasonings.
4. Bring to a boil. In most cases, it is necessary only to heat the juice, but in the case of some watery vegetables, the juice should be reduced somewhat to concentrate the flavor.
5. Whip in raw butter (monter au beurre). Quantities are variable, but a general rule of thumb is to use 2 oz of butter per pint of juice (60 g butter per 5 dl juice).

Tips and Variations

1. It is usually best to make these sauces just before serving and then serve them at once. If allowed to stand, the butter may separate. The sauce can also be served this way, with separate beads or swirls of butter and colored juice making a pattern on the plate.
2. Olive oil or other oil is sometimes used instead of butter. Oil will not easily blend into the juice, but the sauce can be served in this separated state as described above.

3. Use a little lemon or lime juice if the acidity will enhance the flavor and color of the juice (red beets, for example), but avoid using acids with most green vegetables, because the acidity will destroy the green color of the juice.

4. Flavored oils (page 36) can be used in place of the butter. Some examples of good flavor combinations are red beet juice and horseradish oil, and carrot juice and ginger oil.

Modern Sauces: A General Procedure

We will summarize the techniques we have discussed so far by presenting the general outline of a procedure that can be applied to a wide variety of today's popular sauces.

This general procedure is meant to give a framework that will help you understand and remember the many different recipes for sauces that you will encounter. Nevertheless, it might not be completely meaningful until you have worked with a number of different recipes. After you have studied further, come back and read this procedure again. Each time you make a sauce, compare it with this general procedure to see which steps are used. Then you should be able to apply it on a practical level, not just a theoretical one.

To use the procedure, remember the following points:

- All the steps are, in themselves, optional. Thus, you can start with almost any step, and skip steps as necessary. (Of course, you must use enough steps to make a complete sauce.) Note that by selecting the right steps, you can use the procedure to prepare everything from a simple sauce of reduced cooking juices with a little butter, to a reduced cream sauce, to beurre blanc.

- The procedure begins with the sauté pan or other pan in which a meat, poultry, or fish item was cooked. If you are not deglazing a pan and are making a sauce separately from any such cooked item, skip the first step.

- The basic procedure is for sauces that are *not* thickened with starch. To use the procedure for *starch-thickened sauces,* include one of the four steps or substeps that are enclosed in brackets ([ ]).

General Sauce-Making Procedure

1. Discard excess cooking fat from the sauté pan or roasting pan.
2. Add to the pan any flavoring ingredients to be sautéed or sweat, such as chopped shallots, onion, or garlic. (If you are starting with this step, you must also add butter or other fat.) Cook to the desired degree. For sweating, cook very slowly.
[3. Add flour to make a roux. Stir in and cook.]
4. Add liquids to the pan. These may include wine, stock, vinegar, water, cooking liquids or juices, and so on. If you are deglazing a pan, stir to dissolve browned bits of food and caramelized juices on the bottom of the pan.
[4a. Thickened sauces such as demiglaze or velouté may be included among the liquids added.]
5. Add to the liquid any solid flavoring ingredients that are not to be sautéed but are to be cooked in the sauce.
[5a. Whip in a prepared roux.]
6. Reduce the liquid in the pan as necessary over moderate or high heat.

7. If desired, repeat steps 4 through 6 with additional liquids.
8. Add heavy cream and reduce.
9. Strain the sauce (or strain it instead after step 11).
10. Add final flavoring and seasoning ingredients, including lemon juice, herbs, salt, and pepper.
11. Stir in raw butter (either as monter au beurre or as the main ingredient of beurre blanc).

[**11a.** Or whip in beurre manié.]

Flavored Oils

Flavored oils make a light, interesting alternative to vinaigrettes and other sauces when used to dress a wide variety of dishes. They are especially suitable for simple steamed or sautéed items, but they can be used with various cold foods as well. When used as a sauce, the oil is usually drizzled around or over the item on the plate. A tablespoon or so (15 ml) per portion is often sufficient.

The simplest way to flavor an oil is simply to put some of the flavoring ingredient in the oil and let it stand until the oil has taken on enough of the flavor. For most flavorings, however, this is not the best way to extract maximum flavor. For the best release of flavors, the flavoring ingredient may require some kind of preparation before adding it to the oil. For example, dry ground spices should be mixed with a little water.

The following procedures list three basic methods for making flavored oils, depending on the type of ingredients. Recipes are included in the second half of this chapter. In addition, a number of ingredients require special treatment and do not fit into these three basic categories. Recipes for two of these, lobster and shrimp, are included as well.

Unless otherwise indicated, use a mild or flavorless oil, such as safflower, canola, corn, or grapeseed. In some cases, as with garlic, the flavoring goes well with olive oil, but usually the objective is to have the pure taste of the flavoring ingredient unmasked by the taste of the oil.

Procedures for Making Flavored Oils

Method 1: For fresh roots (such as horseradish, garlic, shallots, ginger), for citrus zests, and for strong herbs (fresh rosemary, sage, thyme, oregano)

1. Chop the roots or the herbs into fine pieces by hand or in a food processor, or grate the citrus zests.
2. Use olive oil, if desired, with garlic; for the other flavorings, use a flavorless oil. In a jar or other closeable container, combine with the oil in the following poportions: For each pint (5 dl) of oil, add approximately:

   2 to 3 tbsp (about 30 g) chopped root, or
   3 to 4 tbsp (about 30 g) grated citrus zest, or
   ¾ to 1 cup (about 100 g) chopped herbs.

3. Shake the container well. Let stand for ½ hour at room temperature, then refrigerate.
4. The oil is ready to use as soon as it has taken on the desired flavor, which may be as soon as 1 hour, depending on the ingredient. After 2 days, strain the oil through a paper coffee filter. Store in the refrigerator.

Method 2: For tender fresh herbs (parsley, basil, tarragon, chervil, cilantro)

1. Drop the fresh herbs in boiling water and blanch for 10 seconds. Drain immediately and refresh under cold water. Dry well.
2. Purée the herbs in a blender with just enough oil to make a paste.
3. Measure the volume of the paste and add about 3 to 4 times its volume of oil. For these herbs, use either flavorless oil or olive oil.
4. Place in a container, shake well, and let stand for about 30 minutes. Then place in a refrigerator.
5. The next day, after the herbs have settled to the bottom, filter the oil through a paper coffee filter or cheesecloth. Store the oil in the refrigerator.

Method 2 Variation: For chives

Do not blanch the chives. Simply chop them, then begin with step 2 of the procedure. Filtering is optional.

Method 3: For dried, ground spices and other powders (cinnamon, cumin, curry powder, ginger, mustard, wasabi or Japanese green horseradish, paprika)

1. For each pint (5 dl) of oil, measure 3 to 4 tablespoons (20 to 25 g) of powder. Mix just enough water into the powder to make a paste.
2. Transfer the mixture to a jar and add the oil. Shake well.
3. Let stand at room temperature for one day. Shake the jar several times.
4. When the oil has taken on enough flavor, filter through a paper coffee filter. Store the oil in the refrigerator.

RECIPES

This section, giving detailed procedures and recipes for various sauces, begins with a discussion of classical sauces, predominantly roux-thickened sauces, followed by recipes and techniques that are generally thought of as "modern."

As was stressed in the first half of this chapter, the techniques for making the classical sauces are still the basis of the sauce chef's art. It is extremely important for the aspiring chef to master these classical sauces, for the same techniques are used for most of the sauces made in the best modern kitchens.

There is a common misconception today that the culinary revolutions that started with nouvelle cuisine discarded all the old practices and started afresh. Nothing could be further from the truth. The major change is that a chef's training today is often more haphazard than it was in the past. Many of the sauces that chefs often consider so new and different are really derived from the classic repertory, with perhaps some subtle changes to bring them up to date.

However, it is true that there have been changes in the way sauces are made. The remaining recipe sections in this chapter deal with techniques that are generally considered modern. These techniques are discussed more theoretically in the first part of this chapter. We now give specific recipes that illustrate them.

Modern haute cuisine is often more spontaneous than the older classical cuisine. Chefs frequently make sauces to order at the last minute, as a part of the main dish, rather than prepare an elaborate *mise en place* of sauces ahead of time. But good cooks know that doing a sauce at the last minute is no excuse for doing it poorly. They must have their sauce-making techniques perfectly mastered.

This spontaneous cooking style explains in part why there are relatively few recipes in this chapter. Many sauces are not made independently but are part of the recipe for the meat or fish item. This chapter gives you a sampling of the kinds of sauces popular today and gives you the understanding to deal with the sauces that are parts of other recipes. Also, by learning the techniques used here, and by experimenting with the recipe variations to see how a few changes let you create a new sauce, you will learn to develop your own recipes.

Incidentally, today's spontaneous cooking style has also had an effect on the names of sauces. The classical sauces discussed in the next section all have standard names that have been applied to these sauces since the last century. This codification of names, which is usual in classical cuisine, has a definite advantage. At one time, you could walk into almost any fine restaurant in the world, see the classical names on the menu, and know exactly what was offered. Today, however, many sauces and many dishes have no standardized names because the names were invented by the chef. So the price of creativity is a certain amount of confusion among customers.

Starch-thickened Sauces and Other Classical Sauces

The following recipes are for most of the commonly used small sauces, as well as a few that are not so common. They are all based on the five leading sauces (see recipes in Appendix 1, pages 608–614). The recipes for these small sauces are given in abbreviated format rather than in detail, since you should be familiar with the basic techniques for making small sauces from the leading sauces. All of these small sauces, including the less familiar ones, are valuable for adding variety and flexibility to your skills.

This set of recipes does not pretend to be a complete account of all the classical sauces. For more information on all the classical sauces, refer to Escoffier and to such standard handbooks as *Le Répertoire de la Cuisine* (see the Bibliography, page 623). Time devoted to studying these numerous sauces is well spent, for they are an inexhaustible source of ideas for the cook.

Remember that you can use the small sauce ingredients to make sauces without starch thickeners. As explained in the first half of this chapter, this is done by making the sauces with stock rather than starch-thickened leading sauces. If you take this approach, you must then rely on the other techniques explained in this chapter (such as reduction, monter au beurre, and so on) in order to bring the sauces to the proper consistency.

Regarding terms used for reduction, remember that *to reduce by (x fraction)* means to reduce until x fraction of the liquid has evaporated. In other words, if instructions say "reduce by three-fourths," you are to reduce until three-fourths of the liquid has evaporated or until one-fourth is left. *To reduce au sec* means to reduce until the liquid is dry or nearly dry.

Variations on Béchamel

For each variation, add the listed ingredients to the basic quantity of béchamel sauce as indicated and season to taste with salt and white pepper. See pages 608–609 for béchamel recipe. To ensure smoothness, the sauces should be strained after they are completed but before solid garnish is added.

		U.S.		*Metric*	
	BASE SAUCE:	**1 pt**	**2 qt**	*5 dl*	*2 l*
Cream Sauce					
Heavy cream, heated or tempered		2–4 oz	8–16 oz	*6–12 cl*	*25–50 cl*
Béchamel		1 pt	2 qt	*5 dl*	*2 l*

Mornay Sauce					
Gruyère cheese, grated		2 oz	8 oz	*60 g*	*250 g*
Parmesan cheese, grated		1 oz	4 oz	*30 g*	*125 g*
Butter		1 oz	4 oz	*30 g*	*125 g*
Liaison (optional):					
Egg yolks		1	4	*1*	*4*
Heavy cream		1 oz	4 oz	*3 cl*	*12 cl*
Béchamel		1 pt	2 qt	*5 dl*	*2 l*

Stir the cheese into the béchamel until smooth and melted. Finish with raw butter. The liaison is valuable if the sauce is to be used for glazing or gratinéing, because it helps the sauce brown more quickly.

Mustard Sauce					
Dijon mustard		2 oz	8 oz	*6 cl*	*25 cl*
Béchamel		1 pt	2 qt	*5 dl*	*2 l*

Soubise Sauce					
Onions, fine dice		8 oz	2 lb	*250 g*	*1 kg*
Butter		1 oz	4 oz	*30 g*	*125 g*
Béchamel		1 pt	2 qt	*5 dl*	*2 l*

Cook the onions slowly in the butter without browning. Simmer with the sauce 5 minutes. Force through a fine sieve.

Nantua Sauce					
Crayfish butter or shrimp butter		2–3 oz	8–12 oz	*60–90 g*	*250–375 g*
Heavy cream		2 oz	8 oz	*6 cl*	*25 cl*
Béchamel		1 pt	2 qt	*5 dl*	*2 l*

	U.S.		Metric	
BASE SAUCE:	**1 pt**	**2 qt**	*5 dl*	*2 l*
Cardinale Sauce				
Fish stock	8 oz	1 qt	*25 cl*	*1 l*
Béchamel	1 pt	2 qt	*5 dl*	*2 l*
Lobster butter	2–3 oz	8–12 oz	*60–90 g*	*250–375 g*
Heavy cream	2 oz	8 oz	*6 cl*	*25 cl*

Add the stock to the béchamel and reduce by one-third. Finish with the lobster butter and cream.

Variations on Velouté

For each variation, add the listed ingredients to a basic velouté or to one of the secondary leading sauces (the first three recipes that follow), as indicated. Season to taste with salt and white pepper. Velouté recipe is on page 609.

	U.S.		Metric	
BASE SAUCE:	**1 pt**	**2 qt**	*5 dl*	*2 l*
Allemande Sauce				
Liaison:				
Egg yolks	1	4	*1*	*4*
Heavy cream	2 oz	8 oz	*6 cl*	*25 cl*
Lemon juice	¾ tsp	1 tbsp	*4 ml*	*15 ml*
Veal velouté	1 pt	2 qt	*5 dl*	*2 l*

Reduce the velouté slightly, then add the tempered liaison and the lemon juice.

	U.S.		Metric	
Suprême Sauce				
Heavy cream	4 oz	1 pt	*12 cl*	*5 dl*
Butter (optional)	½ oz	2 oz	*15 g*	*60 g*
Lemon juice, to taste				
Chicken velouté	1 pt	2 qt	*5 dl*	*2 l*

Reduce the velouté by one-fourth before adding the cream. Season with a few drops of lemon juice. Finish the sauce with a little butter, if desired.

	BASE SAUCE:	U.S.		Metric	
		1 pt	**2 qt**	*5 dl*	*2 l*

White Wine Sauce

Dry white wine		2 oz	8 oz	*6 cl*	*25 cl*
Fish velouté		1 pt	2 qt	*5 dl*	*2 l*
Heavy cream		2 oz	8 oz	*6 cl*	*25 cl*
Butter		½ oz	2 oz	*15 g*	*60 g*
Lemon juice, to taste					

Reduce the wine by one-half. Add the velouté and reduce slightly. Add the remaining ingredients.

Aurora Sauce

Tomato purée		3 oz	12 oz	*1 dl*	*4 dl*
Veal or chicken velouté or allemande or suprême sauce		1 pt	2 qt	*5 dl*	*2 l*

Bercy Sauce

Shallots, chopped		1 oz	4 oz	*30 g*	*125 g*
White wine		2 oz	8 oz	*6 cl*	*25 cl*
Fish velouté		1 pt	2 qt	*5 dl*	*2 l*
Butter		1 oz	4 oz	*30 g*	*125 g*
Parsley, chopped		1 tbsp	4 tbsp	*4 g*	*14 g*
Lemon juice					

Combine shallots and wine; reduce by two-thirds. Add velouté and reduce slightly. Finish with raw butter, parsley, and lemon juice. Do not strain.

Curry Sauce

Mirepoix, cut brunoise		2 oz	8 oz	*60 g*	*250 g*
Butter		½ oz	2 oz	*15 g*	*60 g*
Curry powder		1 ½ tsp	2 tbsp	*3 g*	*12 g*
Garlic clove, crushed		½	2	*½*	*2*
Thyme		small pinch	¼ tsp	*small pinch*	*¼ g*
Bay leaf		small piece	1	*small piece*	*1*
Parsley stems		1–2	4–8	*1–2*	*4–8*
Velouté (veal, chicken, or fish)		1 pt	2 qt	*5 dl*	*2 l*
Heavy cream		1 oz	4 oz	*3 cl*	*12 cl*
Lemon juice					

Sweat the mirepoix in the butter. Add the curry powder, garlic, and herbs; cook another minute. Add velouté; simmer 20 minutes. Strain. Add the cream and lemon juice to taste

		U.S.		Metric	
BASE SAUCE:		**1 pt**	**2 qt**	**5 dl**	**2 l**
Herb Sauce					
Chopped parsley, chives, and tarragon, to taste					
White wine sauce		1 pt	2 qt	5 dl	2 l
Horseradish Sauce					
Grated horseradish		1 oz	4 oz	30 g	125 g
Allemande sauce		1 pt	2 qt	5 dl	2 l
Hungarian or Hongroise Sauce					
Onion, minced		1 oz	4 oz	30 g	125 g
Paprika		1 ½ tsp	2 tbsp	4 g	15 g
Butter		½ oz	2 oz	15 g	60 g
White wine		2 oz	8 oz	6 cl	25 cl
Veal or chicken velouté		1 pt	2 qt	5 dl	2 l

Sweat the onion and paprika in butter. Add wine and reduce by half. Add velouté and simmer 10 minutes. Strain.

		U.S.		Metric	
Ivory or Albufera Sauce					
Glace de viande		1 oz	4 oz	30 g	125 g
Suprême sauce		1 pt	2 qt	5 dl	2 l
Mushroom Sauce					
Mushrooms, sliced		2 oz	8 oz	60 g	250 g
Butter		½ oz	2 oz	15 g	60 g
Lemon juice		1 ½ tsp	1 oz	8 ml	3 cl
Suprême, allemande, white wine sauce, or any velouté		1 pt	2 qt	5 dl	2 l

Sauté mushrooms in butter with lemon juice to keep them white. Add appropriate sauce.

		U.S.		*Metric*	
	BASE SAUCE:	**1 pt**	**2 qt**	*5 dl*	*2 l*
Normandy Sauce					
Mushroom cooking liquid or mushroom trimmings		2 oz	8 oz	*60 g*	*250 g*
Oyster liquid		2 oz	8 oz	*6 cl*	*25 cl*
Fish velouté		1 pt	2 qt	*5 dl*	*2 l*
Liaison:					
Egg yolks		2	8	*2*	*8*
Heavy cream		4 oz	1 pt	*12 cl*	*5 dl*
Butter		1 ½ oz	6 oz	*45 g*	*180 g*

Combine the mushroom liquid or trimmings, oyster liquid, and velouté. Reduce by one-third. Strain. Finish with liaison and raw butter.

Diplomate Sauce					
Lobster butter (p. 77)		2 oz	8 oz	*60 g*	*250 g*
Diced lobster		1 oz	4 oz	*30 g*	*125 g*
Diced truffle		½ oz	2 oz	*15 g*	*60 g*
Normandy sauce		1 pt	2 qt	*5 dl*	*2 l*

Poulette Sauce					
White mushroom trimmings		4 oz	1 lb	*125 g*	*500 g*
Allemande sauce		1 pt	2 qt	*5 dl*	*2 l*
Chopped parsley		1 tbsp	4 tbsp	*4 g*	*15 g*
Lemon juice, to taste					

Simmer the mushroom trimmings with the velouté when making the allemande sauce. Strain and add remaining ingredients.

Venetian Sauce					
Shallots, chopped		1 tbsp	1 oz	*7 g*	*30 g*
Chervil		1 tsp	4 tsp	*1 g*	*4 g*
White wine		2 oz	8 oz	*6 cl*	*25 cl*
Tarragon vinegar		2 oz	8 oz	*6 cl*	*25 cl*
White wine sauce		1 pt	2 qt	*5 dl*	*2 l*
Tarragon, to taste					

Combine the shallots, chervil, wine, and vinegar. Reduce by two-thirds. Add sauce and simmer 2 to 3 minutes. Strain. Add tarragon.

Variations on Demiglaze

For each variation, add the listed ingredients to the basic quantity of demiglaze as indicated. The demiglaze recipe is on page 610. Season to taste. For smoothness, strain the finished sauce before adding solid garnish.

		U.S.		Metric	
BASE SAUCE:		**1 pt**	**2 qt**	*5 dl*	*2 l*
Bercy Sauce					
White wine		4 oz	1 pt	*12 cl*	*5 dl*
Shallots, chopped		2 oz	8 oz	*60 g*	*250 g*
Demiglaze		1 pt	2 qt	*5 dl*	*2 l*

Reduce wine and shallots by three-fourths. Add demiglaze and simmer 10 minutes.

Bordelaise Sauce					
Dry red wine		4 oz	1 pt	*12 cl*	*5 dl*
Shallots, chopped		1 oz	4 oz	*30 g*	*125 g*
Crushed peppercorns		⅛ tsp	½ tsp	*0.25 g*	*1 g*
Thyme		small pinch	¼ tsp	*small pinch*	*0.25 g*
Bay leaf		small piece	1	*small piece*	*1*
Demiglaze		1 pt	2 qt	*5 dl*	*2 l*
Butter		1 oz	4 oz	*30 g*	*125 g*
Poached beef marrow, sliced or diced		2 oz	8 oz	*60 g*	*250 g*

Reduce the red wine, shallots, peppercorns, and herbs by three-fourths. Add the demiglaze. Simmer 15 minutes. Strain. Finish with raw butter and garnish with the marrow.

Charcutière Sauce					
Onions, chopped		2 oz	8 oz	*60 g*	*250 g*
Butter		½ oz	2 oz	*15 g*	*60 g*
White wine		4 oz	1 pt	*12 cl*	*5 dl*
Demiglaze		1 pt	2 qt	*5 dl*	*2 l*
Dry mustard		1 tsp	4 tsp	*2 g*	*8 g*
Lemon juice		2 tsp	1 ½ oz	*1 cl*	*4 cl*
Sugar		¼ tsp	1 tsp	*1 g*	*5 g*
Garnish:					
Cornichons (small sour pickles), cut julienne					

Sweat the onions in the butter without browning. Add the wine and reduce by two-thirds. Add the demiglaze and simmer. Add the mustard dissolved in the lemon juice and the sugar. Strain. Add garnish.

	U.S.		Metric	
BASE SAUCE:	1 pt	2 qt	5 dl	2 l

Chasseur Sauce

Mushrooms, sliced	3 oz	12 oz	90 g	375 g
Shallots, minced	1 oz	4 oz	30 g	125 g
Butter	1 oz	4 oz	30 g	125 g
White wine	4 oz	1 pt	12 cl	5 dl
Demiglaze	1 pt	2 qt	5 dl	2 l
Diced tomato	4 oz	1 lb	125 g	500 g
Chopped parsley	1 tbsp	4 tbsp	4 g	15 g

Sauté the mushrooms and shallots in butter. Add the wine and reduce by three-fourths. Add demiglaze and tomato. Simmer 5 minutes. Add parsley. Do not strain.

Diable Sauce

White wine	4 oz	1 pt	12 cl	5 dl
Shallots, chopped	2 oz	8 oz	60 g	250 g
Crushed peppercorns	¼ tsp	1 tsp	0.5 g	2 g
Demiglaze	1 pt	2 qt	5 dl	2 l
Cayenne				

Reduce the wine, shallots, and peppercorns by two-thirds. Add demiglaze and simmer 20 minutes. Season well with cayenne. Strain.

Lyonnaise Sauce

Onions, minced	2 oz	8 oz	60 g	250 g
Butter	1 oz	4 oz	30 g	125 g
White wine vinegar	2 oz	8 oz	6 cl	25 cl
Demiglaze	1 pt	2 qt	5 dl	2 l

Lightly brown the onions in the butter. Add the vinegar and reduce by one-half. Add demiglaze and reduce slightly. Straining is optional.

Madeira Sauce

Madeira wine	2 oz	8 oz	6 cl	25 cl
Demiglaze	1 pt	2 qt	5 dl	2 l

Reduce demiglaze slightly and dilute with madeira to original volume.

		U.S.		Metric	
	BASE SAUCE:	**1 pt**	**2 qt**	*5 dl*	*2 l*
Mushroom Sauce					
Mushrooms, sliced		4 oz	1 lb	*125 g*	*500 g*
Shallots, minced		½ oz	2 oz	*15 g*	*60 g*
Butter		1 oz	4 oz	*30 g*	*125 g*
Demiglaze		1 pt	2 qt	*5 dl*	*2 l*
Sherry		1 oz	4 oz	*3 cl*	*12 cl*
Lemon juice					

Brown the mushrooms and shallots in butter. Add demiglaze and simmer 10 minutes. Finish with the sherry and a few drops of lemon juice. Do not strain.

Perigueux Sauce

Garnish Madeira sauce with finely diced truffle.

Piquante Sauce

		1 pt	**2 qt**	*5 dl*	*2 l*
Shallots, minced		2 oz	8 oz	*60 g*	*250 g*
Wine vinegar		2 oz	8 oz	*6 cl*	*25 cl*
White wine		2 oz	8 oz	*6 cl*	*25 cl*
Demiglaze		1 pt	2 qt	*5 dl*	*2 l*
Capers		1 oz	4 oz	*30 g*	*125 g*
Cornichons (small sour pickles) cut brunoise		1 oz	4 oz	*30 g*	*125 g*
Chopped parsley		1½ tsp	2 tbsp	*2 g*	*7 g*
Tarragon		¼ tsp	1 tsp	*0.25 g*	*1 g*

Reduce the shallots, vinegar, and wine by two-thirds. Add demiglaze and simmer 10 minutes. Garnish with remaining ingredients.

Poivrade Sauce

		1 pt	**2 qt**	*5 dl*	*2 l*
Mirepoix:					
Onion		4 oz	1 lb	*125 g*	*500 g*
Carrot		2 oz	8 oz	*60 g*	*250 g*
Celery		2 oz	8 oz	*60 g*	*250 g*
Butter		1 oz	4 oz	*30 g*	*125 g*
Red wine vinegar		2 oz	8 oz	*6 cl*	*25 cl*
Game marinade (p. 460)		12 oz	3 pt	*4 dl*	*15 dl*
Demiglaze		1 pt	2 qt	*5 dl*	*2 l*
Crushed peppercorns		¼ tsp	1 tsp	*0.5 g*	*2 g*

Brown the mirepoix in the butter. Add the vinegar and marinade. Reduce by one-half. Add the demiglaze. Simmer slowly until reduced by one-third. Add the peppercorns. Simmer 10 minutes. Strain. *Note:* Since this sauce is for game, game stock may be used to make the demiglaze.

	BASE SAUCE:	U.S.		Metric	
		1 pt	2 qt	5 dl	2 l

Red Wine Sauce

	1 pt	2 qt	5 dl	2 l
Mirepoix:				
Onion, diced	8 oz	2 lb	250 g	1 kg
Carrot, diced	4 oz	1 lb	125 g	500 g
Celery, diced	4 oz	1 lb	125 g	500 g
Garlic, chopped	1 clove	4 cloves	1 clove	4 cloves
Red wine	1 qt	1 gal	1 l	4 l
Demiglaze	1 pt	2 qt	5 dl	2 l
Butter	2 oz	8 oz	60 g	250 g

Combine the mirepoix, garlic, and wine. Reduce by one-half. Add the demiglaze and reduce again by one-half. Strain. Finish with raw butter.

Robert Sauce

This is the same as Charcutière Sauce but without the garnish of the pickles.

Rouennaise Sauce

	1 pt	2 qt	5 dl	2 l
Raw duck livers	4	16	4	16
Bordelaise sauce, without marrow	1 pt	2 qt	5 dl	2 l
Foie gras butter (p. 78), optional	2 oz	8 oz	60 g	250 g

Pass the duck liver through a fine sieve. Add this to warm bordelaise sauce. Heat the sauce gently, while stirring, to cook the liver; do not let it boil or the sauce will separate. Strain if necessary. Add the optional butter if desired.

Venison Sauce

	1 oz	4 oz	30 g	125 g
Red currant jelly	1 oz	4 oz	30 g	125 g
Heavy cream	3 oz	12 oz	1 dl	4 dl
Poivrade sauce	1 pt	2 qt	5 dl	2 l

Variations on Tomato Sauce

For each variation, add the listed ingredients to the basic quantity of tomato sauce as indicated. The recipes for tomato sauce begin on page 611.

		U.S.		Metric	
BASE SAUCE:		**1 pt**	**2 qt**	*5 dl*	*2 l*
Creole Sauce					
Onion, small dice		2 oz	8 oz	*60 g*	*250 g*
Celery, small dice		2 oz	8 oz	*60 g*	*250 g*
Green pepper, small dice		1 oz	4 oz	*30 g*	*125 g*
Garlic, chopped		½ clove	2 cloves	*½ clove*	*2 cloves*
Oil, as needed					
Tomato sauce (without roux)		1 pt	2 qt	*5 dl*	*2 l*
Bay leaf		½	2	*½*	*2*
Thyme		pinch	½ tsp	*pinch*	*0.5 g*
Grated lemon rind		¼ tsp	1 tsp	*0.5 g*	*2 g*
Cayenne, to taste					

Sauté the vegetables lightly in oil. Add sauce, herbs, lemon rind, and cayenne. Simmer 15 minutes. Remove bay leaf.

Portugaise Sauce					
Onions, brunoise		2 oz	8 oz	*60 g*	*250 g*
Olive oil		½ oz	2 oz	*15 ml*	*6 cl*
Tomatoes, peeled, seeded, and chopped		8 oz	2 lb	*250 g*	*1 kg*
Garlic, crushed		½ tsp	2 tsp	*1 g*	*4 g*
Tomato sauce		1 pt	2 qt	*5 dl*	*2 l*
Chopped parsley		1–2 tbsp	4–8 tbsp	*4–7 g*	*15–30 g*

Brown the onion lightly in the oil. Add the tomato and garlic. Reduce by one-third. Add the sauce and parsley.

Variations on Hollandaise and Béarnaise

For each variation, add the listed ingredients to the basic quantity of hollandaise or béarnaise as indicated. Recipes for the mother sauces begin on page 613.

	BASE SAUCE:	U.S.		Metric	
		1 pt	**2 qt**	**5 dl**	**2 l**
Choron Sauce					
Tomato paste		1 oz	4 oz	30 g	125 g
Béarnaise sauce		1 pt	2 qt	5 dl	2 l
Foyot Sauce					
Glace de viande		1 oz	4 oz	30 g	125 g
Béarnaise sauce		1 pt	2 qt	5 dl	2 l
Maltaise Sauce					
Orange juice		1–2 oz	4–8 oz	3–6 cl	12–25 cl
Grated orange rind		1 tsp	4 tsp	2 g	10 g
Hollandaise sauce		1 pt	2 qt	5 dl	2 l

If possible, use blood oranges, which have sweet red juice.

Mousseline Sauce					
Heavy cream		4 oz	1 pt	12 cl	5 dl
Hollandaise sauce		1 pt	2 qt	5 dl	2 l

Immediately before serving, whip the cream and fold it into the sauce.

Noisette Sauce					
Beurre noisette		1 oz	4 oz	30 g	125 g
Hollandaise sauce		1 pt	2 qt	5 dl	2 l

Purée Sauces

As we discussed in the first half of this chapter, one way of thickening a sauce or changing its consistency is to combine it with a purée. And, as you know, one of the most common sauces, tomato sauce, gets its consistency entirely or almost entirely from a vegetable purée.

Most of the recipes in this section are simply seasoned vegetable purées, thinned out to sauce consistency with a liquid such as stock or cream. The majority of these are, in fact, variations of tomato sauce, but there are also sauces based on other vegetables. The purpose of these is mainly to teach you the techniques and to stimulate your thinking. You might want to experiment with other ingredients and see what sauces you can invent. In addition, please refer to Chapter 10 for a further discussion of vegetable purées, including recipes.

One of the recipes in this section is more like a standard brown sauce. In fact, it is made like espagnole sauce, except that no roux is used. Instead, the mirepoix is puréed with the sauce to thicken it. If you make this sauce, note how the texture is different from a regular espagnole sauce. The sauce is not as smooth as a roux-thickened sauce. Also, the thickening isn't as effective as a roux, and the vegetable purée tends to settle out.

Making Purées. Three main techniques are used to purée vegetables and other ingredients:

1. Puréeing the product in a food processor or blender
2. Passing the product through a food mill
3. Forcing the product through a fine sieve

Of these three methods, the third one, forcing through a fine sieve, usually makes the smoothest purée, but it is also the most time-consuming. If you want a smooth purée but the product is difficult to force through the sieve, you can use one of the other methods first, then pass the purée through the sieve to make it smoother. For a discussion of the use of the drum sieve for puréeing vegetables, see page 496 in Chapter 10.

FRESH TOMATO SAUCE

		U.S.		Metric	
	YIELD:	**1 pt**	**2 qt**	*5 dl*	*2 l*
Ingredients					
Ripe tomatoes (see note)		2 lb 8 oz	10 lb	*1250 g*	*5 kg*
Onion		4 oz	1 lb	*125 g*	*500 g*
Garlic (optional)		1 clove	4 cloves	*1 clove*	*4 cloves*
Olive oil		1 oz	4 oz	*3 cl*	*12 cl*
Salt					
White pepper					
Butter (optional)		½ oz	2 oz	*15 g*	*60 g*

Note: If good ripe tomatoes are not available, use whole canned Italian tomatoes. If the tomatoes are not of the best quality, the sauce can be improved by the addition of a little tomato paste.

Mise en Place:

1. Peel and seed the tomatoes. Chop coarsely. If using canned tomatoes, crush lightly and drain briefly in a sieve.

2. Peel the onion. Cut into small dice.

3. Peel and mince the garlic.

Cooking:

1. Heat the olive oil in a saucepan over moderate heat. Add the onion and garlic. Cook slowly for 2 or 3 minutes, but do not let it brown.

2. Add the tomato. Simmer for about 15 minutes, until the tomato is soft and the juices are slightly reduced.

3. Purée the mixture by forcing it through a sieve or food mill.

4. If the sauce is too thin, return it to the saucepan and reduce it over moderate heat until it reaches the desired consistency.

5. Season with salt and pepper.

6. Stir in the raw butter, if desired.

Variations

Tomato Butter Sauce

Butter	4 oz	1 lb	*125 g*	*500 g*

Increase the raw butter to the quantity indicated. Add it as close to service time as possible.

Tomato Cream Sauce

Crème fraîche or heavy cream, hot	8 oz	1 qt	*25 cl*	*1 l*

Reduce the tomato sauce by one-half, until it is quite thick. Just before service, set the pan of sauce over heat and stir in the cream.

Tomato Sauce with Herbs

Flavor the basic tomato sauce or tomato butter sauce with fresh herbs, such as chives, parsley, or chervil.

Tomato Sauce for Fish

Dilute the basic tomato sauce with one-half its quantity (or less) of fish stock. Reduce again to proper consistency.

Tomato Olive Sauce

Olivada (black olive paste)	1 ½ oz	6 oz	*45 g*	*175 g*

Omit the onion and use four times the quantity of garlic. Add the olive paste to the finished sauce.

Hot Tomato Jalapeño Salsa

Jalapeño peppers	8	32	*8*	*32*

Mince the peppers, discarding seeds and stem end. Omit the onion from the basic recipe. Add the minced peppers to the garlic just before adding the tomato.

Provençale Sauce

Include the optional garlic in the basic recipe and add chopped parsley before service.

COULIS OF TOMATO AND RED BELL PEPPER

		U.S.		Metric	
	YIELD:	**1 pt**	**2 qt**	*5 dl*	*2 l*
Ingredients					
Red bell peppers		2	8	*2*	*8*
Onion, chopped		4 oz	1 lb	*125 g*	*500 g*
Garlic cloves, chopped		3	12	*3*	*12*
Olive oil		2 oz	8 oz	*60 ml*	*25 cl*
Tomatoes (fresh or canned), chopped		1 lb	4 lb	*500 g*	*2 kg*
Salt					

Procedure:

1. Char and peel the peppers, following the directions on page 521. Dice the peppers.
2. Sweat the onion and the garlic in the olive oil.
3. Add the peppers and sweat another few minutes.
4. Add the tomatoes. Bring to a simmer. If using canned tomatoes, remove from the heat at once. If using fresh, raw tomatoes, simmer 5 minutes.
5. Purée the mixture in a blender, then force through a sieve.
6. Simmer the purée a few minutes to reduce to desired consistency. Season to taste.

RED PEPPER SAUCE

		U.S.		Metric	
YIELD:		1 pt	2 qt	5 dl	2 l
Ingredients					
Sweet red peppers		2 lb	8 lb	1 kg	4 kg
Olive oil or vegetable oil		½ oz	2 oz	15 ml	6 cl
Basil		pinch	½ tsp	pinch	0.5 g
Salt		¼ tsp	1 tsp	1 g	5 g
White pepper		pinch	½ tsp	pinch	1 g
Chicken stock		4 oz	1 pt	12 cl	5 dl
Butter or olive oil		½ oz	2 oz	15 g	60 g
Salt					
White pepper					
Lemon juice					

Procedure:

1. Wash the peppers, cut them in half and remove the cores, seeds, and membranes. Cut them into small dice.

2. Heat the oil in a saucepan over low heat. Add the peppers, basil, salt, and white pepper.

3. Cover and cook over very low heat until the peppers are soft, stirring occasionally. This will take about 30 minutes.

4. Transfer the peppers to a strainer to drain off excess liquid.

5. Purée the peppers. Check the purée to make sure all the bits of skin have been removed. If not, pass through a fine sieve.

6. Stir the stock into the purée. Bring to a boil and reduce to a sauce consistency.

7. Stir in the butter or olive oil.

8. Taste and adjust the seasonings with lemon juice, salt, and pepper.

Variation

Substitute heavy cream for the chicken stock.

SPINACH SAUCE

		U.S.		Metric	
	YIELD:	**1 pt**	**2 qt**	*5 dl*	*2 l*
Ingredients					
Spinach (untrimmed weight)		1 lb	4 lb	*500 g*	*2 kg*
Butter		½ oz	2 oz	*15 g*	*60 g*
Shallots, minced		1 oz	4 oz	*30 g*	*125 g*
White veal stock, chicken stock, or fish stock		8 oz	1 qt	*25 cl*	*1 l*
Heavy cream		2 oz	8 oz	*6 cl*	*25 cl*
Butter		1 oz	4 oz	*30 g*	*125 g*
Salt					
Pepper					
Cayenne					

Procedure:

1. Trim and wash the spinach. Drop the leaves into boiling water and cook until tender.

2. Drain and cool quickly under cold water. Drain and squeeze out excess moisture.

3. Chop the spinach as finely as possible.

4. Heat the first quantity of butter in a saucepan and cook the shallots slowly without browning for a minute.

5. Add the stock and spinach. Bring to a boil.

6. Purée the mixture.

7. Heat the spinach purée in a saucepan. Stir in the cream. Cook quickly over moderately high heat until the sauce thickens slightly.

8. Stir in the butter and season to taste.

Variation

Watercress Sauce

Use watercress instead of spinach. Remove large, coarse stems. Do not boil the watercress. Blanch it for a few seconds, then cool and drain.

BROWN SAUCE THICKENED WITH VEGETABLE PURÉE

		U.S.		Metric	
	YIELD:	1 pt	2 qt	5 dl	2 l
Ingredients					
Carrot		2 oz	8 oz	60 g	250 g
Leek		2 oz	8 oz	60 g	250 g
Onion		4 oz	1 lb	125 g	500 g
Shallots		1 oz	4 oz	30 g	125 g
Garlic cloves		3	12	3	12
Butter		2 oz	8 oz	60 g	250 g
Tomato (fresh or canned), chopped		4 oz	1 lb	125 g	500 g
Sachet:					
Bay leaf		½	2	½	2
Thyme		⅛ tsp	½ tsp	0.1 g	0.5 g
Parsley stems		6	25	6	25
Peppercorns, crushed		¼ tsp	1 tsp	0.5 g	2 g
Rich brown stock		1 ½ pt	3 qt	75 cl	3 l
Salt					
Butter (optional)		2 oz	8 oz	60 g	250 g

Procedure:

1. Pare and cut the carrot into small dice. Using the white part and some of the green of the leek, wash it carefully and slice it thin. Peel and chop the onions, shallots, and garlic.

2. Cook the vegetables in butter over low heat until they just start to brown.

3. Add the tomato, sachet, and stock. Bring to a boil. Simmer over low heat until the liquid is reduced by two-thirds and the vegetables are soft.

4. Remove the sachet and force the sauce, including the vegetables, through a fine sieve. Or purée in a blender or food processor, then pass through a sieve.

5. Return the sauce to a simmer. If necessary, simmer to reduce the sauce a little more, to arrive at a light sauce consistency.

6. Season to taste.

7. If desired, monter au beurre.

Vegetable Juice Sauces

The following basic recipe for Asparagus Sauce illustrates the procedure for making light sauces from vegetable juices, as discussed in the first part of this chapter. Other vegetable juice sauces can be made the same way, as indicated by the variations following the main recipe.

ASPARAGUS SAUCE

		U.S.		Metric	
	YIELD:	**1 pt**	**2 qt**	***5 dl***	***2 l***
Ingredients					
Asparagus juice (see Mise en Place)		1 pt	2 qt	*5 dl*	*2 l*
Salt					
Butter		2 oz	8 oz	*60 g*	*250 g*

Mise en Place:

Run enough raw asparagus through a vegetable juicer to get the required amount of juice.

Cooking:

1. Place the juice in a saucepan. Season to taste. Bring to a boil.
2. Stir in the butter.

Variations

For broccoli, carrot, fennel, kohlrabi, radish, and zucchini juices, make the sauce as in the basic recipe. Add additional seasonings as desired. In the case of zucchini, olive oil can be used as an alternative to butter.

For celery juice and red beet juice, begin with twice as much juice and reduce it by one-half. Finish as in the basic recipe. For red beet juice, add a little lemon or lime juice to season and to intensify the color.

Reduction Sauces

The sauces in this section are made primarily by reducing liquids, such as stock and wine, with other ingredients to intensify their flavor and to thicken them slightly.

If you compare these recipes to such classical sauces as bordelaise sauce, bercy sauce, and poivrade sauce, you will see that they are very similar. As we have said several times, these "modern" sauces are made by the same techniques that are used for the classical sauces. However, since they may contain no roux, they are often reduced more heavily to give them more body. In all of the recipes, you may increase the amount of stock and reduce the sauce more, in order to increase the flavor intensity and the amount of thickening. Of course, your results depend on how good a stock you are using.

The classical sauces are standardized, so you cannot change the basic flavors and proportions and still use the classical name. These modern-style sauces, however, have no such restrictions. You may experiment with the ingredients, change the proportions, and add new flavoring ingredients. This kind of experience will increase your sauce-making skills and your sensitivity to how different techniques and ingredients work.

In nearly all cases, these sauces can be made to order to serve with a sautéed meat item. Simply use the first liquid in the recipe, such as wine or vinegar, to deglaze the sauté pan. Then proceed as usual with the sauce recipe.

PEPPER SAUCE

		U.S.		Metric	
	YIELD:	1 pt	2 qt	5 dl	2 l
Ingredients					
Butter		2 oz	8 oz	60 g	250 g
Carrots, chopped		6 oz	1 ½ lb	180 g	750 g
Onions, chopped		8 oz	2 lb	250 g	1 kg
Leeks, chopped		8 oz	2 lb	250 g	1 kg
Garlic, chopped		2 oz	8 oz	60 g	250 g
Crushed peppercorns		2 tsp	8 tsp	4 g	15 g
Bay leaf		1	4	1	4
Parsley stems		4	16	4	16
Thyme		¼ tsp	1 tsp	0.25 g	1 g
Brandy		4 oz	1 pt	12 cl	5 dl
Red wine vinegar		3 oz	12 oz	18 cl	75 cl
Strong brown stock or game stock, or part stock and part demiglaze		3 pt	6 qt	1.5 l	6 l
Butter (optional; see note)		4 oz	1 lb	125 g	500 g
Salt					

Note: Or use a smaller quantity of beurre manié.

Procedure:

1. Heat the butter in a sauce pot. Add the vegetables, pepper, and herbs. Sauté over low heat until the vegetables just start to brown.

2. Add the brandy. Boil to evaporate the alcohol (or flame it carefully) and reduce au sec.

3. Add the vinegar and reduce slightly.

4. Add the stock. Simmer until reduced by two-thirds. This should take at least an hour.

5. Strain the sauce. Press down on the vegetables in the strainer to extract all liquid.

6. Just before service, reheat the sauce and monter au beurre.

Variation

Use the unbuttered sauce (that is, after step 5) to deglaze the pans in which meat or game is cooked. Finish with the butter.

RED WINE SAUCE

		U.S.		Metric	
	YIELD:	1 pt	2 qt	5 dl	2 l
Ingredients					
Dry red wine		1 pt	2 qt	5 dl	2 l
Shallots, minced		2 oz	8 oz	60 g	250 g
Strong brown stock or demiglaze		1½ pt	3 qt	75 cl	3 l
Butter (optional)		2–4 oz	8–16 oz	60–125 g	250–500 g
Salt					
Pepper					

Procedure:

1. Combine the wine and shallots and reduce au sec (until thick and syrupy).

2. Add the stock. Reduce by one-third.

3. Strain the sauce.

4. Just before service, reheat the sauce and, if desired, monter au beurre.

5. Adjust the seasonings.

Variations

For a slightly different flavor, sweat the shallots in butter before adding the wine.

Red Wine Garlic Sauce

	2 oz	8 oz	60 g	250 g
Garlic	2 oz	8 oz	60 g	250 g
Butter	1 oz	4 oz	30 g	125 g

Sweat the garlic with the shallots in the butter. Add the red wine and continue with the basic recipe. *Optional:* When straining the sauce, force the vegetables through the sieve and add the purée to the sauce.

White Wine Sauce

Use dry white wine instead of red wine. Use white stock, chicken stock, or velouté instead of the brown stock or demiglaze. If necessary, bind the sauce with beurre manié before straining.

White Wine Garlic Sauce

Prepare the white wine sauce, but add the garlic as indicated in the instructions for red wine garlic sauce.

White Wine Sauce with Compound Butter

Substitute an appropriate compound butter, such as escargot butter, shellfish butter, watercress butter, etc. (see page 76), for the plain raw butter in the monter au beurre step.

PORT WINE SAUCE

		U.S.		*Metric*	
YIELD:		**1 pt**	**2 qt**	*5 dl*	*2 l*
Ingredients					
Ruby port		1 pt	2 qt	*5 dl*	*2 l*
Orange juice		6 oz	1 ½ pt	*18 cl*	*75 cl*
Orange zest		1 strip	4 strips	*1 strip*	*4 strips*
Strong brown stock or chicken stock		1 ½ pt	3 qt	*75 cl*	*3 l*
Butter		4 oz	1 lb	*125 g*	*500 g*
Salt					
Pepper					

Procedure:

1. Combine the port, juice, and zest. Boil until well reduced and syrupy.

2. Add the stock. Reduce by one-half.

3. Just before service, strain the sauce and stir in the butter. Season to taste.

BROWN SAUCE FOR GAME

		U.S.		Metric	
YIELD:		**1 pt**	**2 qt**	**5 dl**	**2 l**
Ingredients					
Red wine vinegar		4 oz	1 pt	*12 cl*	*5 dl*
Strong brown stock or demiglaze		1 pt	2 qt	*5 dl*	*2 l*
Red currant jelly		4 oz	1 lb	*125 g*	*500 g*
Salt					
Pepper					
Lemon juice					

Procedure:

1. Reduce the vinegar over high heat until it is syrupy, nearly dry.

2. Add the demiglaze. Bring to a boil and reduce by one-fourth.

3. Stir in the jelly and simmer until it is melted and well blended in.

4. Season to taste with salt, pepper, and lemon juice.

Variation

To make this sauce for a sautéed or roasted item, use the vinegar to deglaze the pan. Then proceed as usual. Strain the finished sauce.

Sauces with Cream

Use of cream in sauces, including a general procedure for making reduced cream sauces, is discussed in detail in the first part of this chapter. Reread pages 32–33 if necessary before beginning production of any of the recipes in this section.

The first recipe in the section is for crème fraîche, which is discussed on page 33. It can be used in place of heavy cream in most sauces, with very good results. Actually, this homemade crème fraîche is not the same as that which you would find in Europe, but it is a reasonable substitute.

One of the following sauce recipes (plus its variations) consists entirely of reduced cream plus flavorings. The others contain other liquids as well, usually reductions of stock or wine.

CRÈME FRAÎCHE

		U.S.		Metric	
YIELD:		**1 pt**	**2 qt**	**5 dl**	**2 l**
Ingredients					
Heavy cream		1 pt	2 qt	5 dl	2 l
Buttermilk		1 ½ tbsp	3 oz	25 ml	1 dl

Procedure:

Combine the milk and buttermilk. Let stand in a warm (not hot) place until slightly thickened. This takes from 6 to 24 hours, depending on the temperature.

CREAM SAUCE WITH FINES HERBES

		U.S.		Metric	
YIELD:		**1 pt**	**2 qt**	**5 dl**	**2 l**
Ingredients					
Crème fraîche or heavy cream		1 ½ pt	3 qt	75 cl	3 l
Lemon juice		1 oz	4 oz	3 cl	12 cl
Fresh chopped herbs: mixture of parsley, tarragon, chives, and chervil		¼ cup	1 cup	6 cl	25 cl
Salt					
White pepper					

Procedure:

This sauce should be made as close to serving time as possible.

1. Bring the cream to a boil and reduce by one-third.

2. Add the lemon juice and boil another 30 seconds.

3. Add the herbs.

4. Season to taste with salt, pepper, and additional lemon juice if necessary.

Variations

Sorrel Cream Sauce

Fresh sorrel leaves, cleaned and shredded	2–4 oz	8–16 oz	*60–125 g*	*250–500 g*

Substitute the sorrel for the herbs. Either add the sorrel directly to the sauce, or sweat it first in a little butter. Since the sorrel is tart, you may want to use less lemon juice.

Basil Cream Sauce

Fresh basil, shredded	2 oz	8 oz	*60 g*	*250 g*

Substitute the basil for the mixed herbs.

Watercress Sauce

Watercress	8 oz	2 lb	*250 g*	*1 kg*

Remove large stems from the watercress. Blanch in boiling water for 30 seconds. Squeeze out excess moisture and chop. Substitute for the mixed herbs in the basic recipe.

Walnut Sauce

Walnuts, ground	3 oz	12 oz	*90 g*	*375 g*

Substitute the ground walnuts for the herbs.

SAUCE AMERICAINE

This sauce is the one that results from the preparation of Lobster à l'Americaine (page 253).

CREAM BROWN SAUCE

		U.S.		Metric	
YIELD:		**1 pt**	**2 qt**	**5 dl**	**2 l**
Ingredients					
Strong brown stock		1 qt	1 gal	*1 l*	*4 l*
Crème fraîche or heavy cream		1 pt	2 qt	*5 dl*	*2 l*
Butter (optional)		½ oz	2 oz	*15 g*	*60 g*
Salt					
Pepper					
Fresh chives or tarragon					

Procedure:

1. Reduce the stock by three-fourths over moderately high heat.

2. Add the cream. Boil until the sauce is reduced by about one-third and has a slightly syrupy consistency.

3. Off the heat, stir in the butter. Adjust the seasoning.

4. If you are using them, add the fresh herbs at the last minute.

Variation

Wild Mushroom Sauce

Dried wild mushrooms, such as morels or cèpes	1–2 oz	4–8 oz	*30–60 g*	*125–250 g*
Water, to cover				

Soak the dried mushrooms in hot water to cover until soft. Drain and squeeze out the water; add the soaking liquid to the reduced brown stock. Reduce again to original volume. Add the mushrooms and then the cream. Continue as in the basic recipe. Do not strain the finished sauce.

CREAM SAUCE FOR FISH

		U.S.		Metric	
YIELD:		**1 pt**	**2 qt**	*5 dl*	*2 l*
Ingredients					
Shallots, chopped		1 oz	4 oz	*30 g*	*125 g*
Butter		½ oz	2 oz	*15 g*	*60 g*
Fish stock		1 pt	2 qt	*5 dl*	*2 l*
Dry white wine		8 oz	1 qt	*25 cl*	*1 l*
Parsley stems		4	16	*4*	*16*
Bay leaf		½	2	*½*	*2*
Heavy cream		1 pt	2 qt	*5 dl*	*2 l*
Lemon juice					
Salt					
White pepper					

Procedure:

1. Sweat the shallots in butter until soft.

2. Add the stock, wine, and herbs. Reduce by three-fourths over moderate or high heat.

3. Add the cream and bring to a boil. Boil for 1 or 2 minutes, until reduced to a saucelike consistency.

4. Season to taste with lemon juice, salt, and pepper.

5. Strain.

Variations

Alternative Method: Instead of sweating the shallots in butter, simply add them to the stock and wine, and reduce.

Note: The procedure in these recipes can be used for finishing poached items. Use the mixture of stock, wine, shallots, and herbs as the poaching liquid. When the item is cooked, remove it from the liquid. Then make the sauce.

Cream Sauce for Poultry and Meat

Substitute chicken stock or white veal stock for the fish stock.

Herbed Cream Sauce

Garnish the sauce with appropriate fresh herbs, such as tarragon, chives, or parsley.

Sorrel Sauce

Sorrel, shredded	4 oz	1 lb	*125 g*	*500 g*
Butter	½ oz	2 oz	*15 g*	*60 g*

Sweat the sorrel in butter until wilted. Add to sauce.

Mustard Cream Sauce

Dijon-style mustard or grainy mustard	2 oz	8 oz	*60 g*	*250 g*

Add the mustard to the reduction before adding the cream.

Saffron Sauce

Saffron threads	½ tsp	2 tsp	*2.5 ml*	*1 cl*
Optional garnish:				
Fresh tomato cut into small dice and drained	6–8 oz	1 ½–2 lb	*180–250 g*	*750–1000 g*

Add the saffron to the stock mixture before reducing. If desired, mix the diced, well-drained tomatoes into the sauce just before serving.

Port Wine Cream Sauce

Port wine	12 oz	3 pt	*4 dl*	*1.5 l*
Butter	4 oz	1 lb	*125 g*	*500 g*

Omit the stock and white wine. Instead, use ruby port. Reduce only by one-half. After straining the sauce, and just before serving, stir in the raw butter.

Cream Sauce with Mushrooms

Add sautéed sliced mushrooms (quantity to taste) to the sauce.

Cream Sauce with Morels

Dried morels	1–2 oz	4–8 oz	*30–60 g*	*125–250 g*
Hot water, to cover				

This variation is appropriate only for the sauce made with chicken or veal stock. Soak the dried morels in hot water to cover until soft. Remove the morels from the liquid and squeeze them out gently. Strain this liquid, add it to the stock, and proceed with the recipe. Add the morels at the same time as you add the cream.

Chipotle Cream Sauce

Chipotle peppers	2	8	*2*	*8*

Use chicken stock in the basic recipe, and substitute additional chicken stock for the wine. Add the chipotle peppers (smoked, dried jalapeño peppers) to the stock. Simmer the stock slowly, not rapidly, to reduce it, to allow the peppers time to flavor the reduction. Add the cream. Reduce and strain as in the basic recipe. Discard the peppers.

Roquefort Sauce

Roquefort cheese	4 oz	1 lb	*125 g*	*500 g*

Add the crumbled cheese (before straining the sauce) to the version made with chicken or veal stock. Stir until melted and blended in.

SHELLFISH SAUCE

		U.S.		Metric	
	YIELD:	**1 pt**	**2 qt**	*5 dl*	*2 l*
Ingredients					
Shellfish shells (see note)		1 lb	4 lb	*500 g*	*2 kg*
Leeks, trimmed		4 oz	1 lb	*125 g*	*500 g*
Onions		2 oz	8 oz	*60 g*	*250 g*
Celery		2 oz	8 oz	*60 g*	*250 g*
Carrots		2 oz	8 oz	*60 g*	*250 g*
Garlic		1 clove	4 cloves	*1 clove*	*4 cloves*
Butter		1 oz	4 oz	*30 g*	*125 g*
Bay leaf		½	2	*½*	*2*
Tarragon		¼ tsp	1 tsp	*0.25 g*	*1 g*
Brandy		1 oz	4 oz	*3 cl*	*12 cl*
White wine		4 oz	1 pt	*12 cl*	*5 dl*
Tomato paste		½ oz	2 oz	*15 g*	*60 g*
Fish stock		1 pt	2 qt	*5 dl*	*2 l*
Heavy cream		1 pt	2 qt	*5 dl*	*2 l*
Lemon juice		1 tsp	4 tsp	*5 ml*	*2 cl*
Salt					
White pepper					

Note: Use lobster, crab, shrimp, or crayfish shells. Lobster shells can be from cooked lobsters, but shrimp shells should be raw to yield enough flavor. On the east coast, blue crabs are often inexpensive enough to use whole, meat and all; these make an excellent sauce.

Procedure:

1. Crush or break up the shells.
2. Clean and trim the vegetables. Chop fine.
3. Sauté the vegetables in butter for 2 to 3 minutes.
4. Add the shellfish shells, bay leaf, and tarragon. Cook another 2 to 4 minutes, stirring a few times.
5. Add the brandy and boil for 1 minute to evaporate the alcohol.
6. Add the wine, tomato paste, and stock. Simmer 20 minutes.
7. Strain. Press down on the vegetables and shells in the strainer to press out all liquid.
8. Bring the liquid to a boil and reduce by one-half.
9. Add the cream and reduce by one-third. Partway through the cooking, add the lemon juice.
10. Adjust the seasoning.

Variations

For a sauce that is less rich, do not reduce the liquid as much in step 8. Use less cream and thicken the sauce as necessary with beurre manié.

For a more concentrated sauce, reduce the liquid by three-fourths in step 8. Add one-half the amount of cream.

Warm Butter Sauces

The basic recipe in this section is for beurre blanc. Please note that two different procedures for incorporating the butter are given (see step 2 in the recipe). The basic theory of making beurre blanc is discussed on page 31. Please reread this section if necessary.

Innumerable variations on the basic beurre blanc are possible. Several of these are suggested in the variations that follow the main recipe. Perhaps you can think of others.

Beurre blanc doesn't hold well, because the emulsion is unstable. However, if it is kept in a warm, not hot, place and given a few beats with a wire whip every now and then, it can sometimes be kept in good condition for up to 1 hour or more. A safer practice is to make it just before serving. Because it is quickly and easily made, this usually poses no difficulties.

Because of the slight acidity of beurre blanc, it should not be held in aluminum containers. The acid will react with the metal. Stainless steel, ceramic, and glass containers are suitable.

BEURRE BLANC

		U.S.		Metric	
	YIELD:	1 pt	2 qt	5 dl	2 l
Ingredients					
Dry white wine		8 oz	1 qt	25 cl	1 l
White wine vinegar		1½ oz	6 oz	45 ml	18 cl
Shallots, chopped		1 oz	4 oz	30 g	125 g
Cold butter, cut into small pieces		1 lb	4 lb	500 g	2 kg
Salt					

Procedure:

1. Combine the wine, vinegar, and shallots in a saucepan. Reduce heavily, that is, more than three-fourths, but not au sec.

2. Incorporate the butter by one of two methods:
   a. Set the pan over high heat. Add the butter all at once and beat vigorously with a wire whip. When the butter is about three-fourths melted, remove from the heat and continue to whip until the sauce is smooth.
   b. Set the pan over low heat. Add the butter a few pieces at a time, whipping constantly. When each addition is nearly melted, add a few more pieces. Continue until all the butter is added.

3. Pass the sauce through a fine strainer.

4. Hold the sauce in a warm, not hot, place until served. Stir or whip it from time to time.

Variations

Beurre Blanc with Cream I

Heavy cream or crème fraîche		2 oz	8 oz	6 cl	25 cl

Add the cream to the finished sauce.

Beurre Blanc with Cream II

Heavy cream or crème fraîche		8 oz	1 qt	25 cl	1 l

When you have completed step 1 in the basic recipe, add the cream to the reduction. Reduce by one-half and then proceed with step 2.

Beurre Rouge (Red Butter Sauce)

Use dry red wine instead of white wine. For good color in the sauce, use a young, bright red wine.

Beurre Blanc with Stock

White stock (fish, chicken, or veal) or vegetable cooking liquid	6 oz	1 ½ pt	*18 cl*	*75 cl*
White wine	2 oz	8 oz	*6 cl*	*25 cl*

Substitute the above quantities of stock and wine for the wine and vinegar in the basic recipe.

Tomato Beurre Blanc

Flavor the beurre blanc with about one-fourth its quantity of thick, seasoned tomato purée.

Saffron Beurre Blanc

Saffron	¼ tsp	1 tsp	*1 ml*	*5 ml*

Add the saffron to the wine mixture before making the reduction. If desired, use lemon juice in place of the vinegar.

Mustard Beurre Blanc

Dijon-style mustard	2 oz	8 oz	*60 g*	*250 g*

Add the mustard to the reduction. Use only one-half the quantity of vinegar in the recipe.

Herbed Butter Sauce I

Use an herbed compound butter (see page 76) in place of the plain raw butter. Appropriate fresh herbs for the compound butter include parsley, tarragon, chives, chervil or dill. For a stronger green color, include some spinach or watercress. Strain the sauce for a smooth, uniformly green sauce, or leave it unstrained.

Herbed Butter Sauce II

Add your choice of fresh herbs to the finished sauce.

Beurre blanc flavored with spices or herbs: To add just the essence of one of the more flavorful herbs (rosemary, tarragon, sage, thyme, bay leaf, etc.), include a small quantity of the herb in the reduction. Spicy sauces can also be made this way, by reducing the liquid with an appropriate spice, such as coriander, peppercorns, fresh or dried ginger, curry powder, or sichuan pepper.

Other garnished and flavored beurres blancs: Finished beurre blanc can be flavored or garnished with a great variety of ingredients. The following are a few suggestions.

Fresh herbs	Brunoise of vegetables
Sorrel	Green peppercorns
Diced tomato	Glace de viande
Chopped sundried tomato	Ginger juice
Sweet red pepper purée or other flavorful vegetable purée	Orange or lime zest, julienne

SABAYON

		U.S.	Metric
APPROX. YIELD:		**12 oz**	*3.5 dl*
Ingredients			
Egg yolks		6	*6*
White stock, fish stock, or vegetable cooking liquid (see note)		4 oz	*12 cl*
White wine		2 oz	*6 cl*
Heavy cream		1 oz	*3 cl*
Butter		3 oz	*90 g*
Salt			
White pepper			

Note: Use liquid appropriate to the dish the sauce is served with. In the case of vegetable cooking liquid, you might, for example, use asparagus cooking water if the sauce is to be served with asparagus or with a dish that is garnished with asparagus.

Procedure:

1. Whip the egg yolks with all the liquids in a stainless steel bowl.

2. Set the bowl over very low heat or over a hot water bath. Whip constantly until the sauce is thickened and foamy. Do not let it get too hot, or the eggs will curdle.

3. Whip in the raw butter.

4. Adjust the seasonings.

Cold Sauces

The four major families of sauces in this section are vinaigrette, mayonnaise, compound butter, and flavored oil. The discussion here is intended to broaden the skills you already have by showing some of the many varied applications that are possible with these basics.

Vinaigrette and mayonnaise are, of course, familiar to you as salad dressings. You may not have thought of them as sauces, but that is what salad dressings are. (The French term for salad dressing is translated as "salad sauce.") They can be served with a wide variety of foods, not just the traditional salads.

Vinaigrette. Vinaigrette is also known as oil-and-vinegar dressing and French dressing. At its simplest, it is nothing more than a mixture of oil and vinegar seasoned with salt and pepper. Many variations can be made by using different kinds of oil and vinegar, and by adding various flavoring ingredients to the basic mixture. A number of these possibilities are suggested in the variations following the basic recipe.

Vinaigrettes have become widely used as sauces for hot meat, poultry, and fish items, instead of the more traditional sauces based on stocks, cream, and so on. Because of their intense flavors, they can be used in small quantities.

When vinaigrettes are served as salad dressings, it is usual to shake or whip them just before serving to blend the oil and vinegar together. On the other hand, when they are used as sauces for meats and other hot items, they are often served unblended, so that the separate swirls of oil and vinegar make a pattern on the plate.

The standard ratio of oil to vinegar in vinaigrette is three to one, that is, three parts oil to one part vinegar. However, this ratio can be varied, depending on what the sauce is to be used for. For a bland salad, such as a cold white-bean salad, you might want to increase the proportion of vinegar in order to perk up the taste of the salad. On the other hand, in some cases you might want to increase the oil from three parts to four parts. For example, for a walnut-oil dressing for a simple green salad or for a warm poultry salad (see pages 132–133), you might want to emphasize the taste of the oil and also have a dressing that is not too tart.

Decide which flavors you want to emphasize in the sauce, then select other ingredients that have more neutral flavors. For example, if you want the flavor of a special, delicate vinegar to be the most predominant, then you had best not use a strong-flavored oil, strong herbs, and a powerful mustard in the sauce. Or if you want the vinaigrette to taste mostly of hazelnut oil, then don't overwhelm it with strong vinegar and strong herbs and other flavoring ingredients. Simplicity often produces the best results.

Some specialty vinegars are over 6 percent acidity, which is quite strong. To keep the vinaigrette from being too acidic for your purpose, you may want either to increase the ratio of oil in the dressing or to dilute the vinegar with water before mixing the sauce. This second method dilutes the vinegar's flavor as well as its acidity, but it is the best method if you want to keep the vinaigrette from becoming too oily.

Mayonnaise. Although mayonnaise and vinaigrette appear to be very different, in fact mayonnaise can be described as a vinaigrette that is emulsified with egg yolks (see page 29 for a discussion of emulsions). Also, mayonnaise has a much higher proportion of oil.

As suggested by the variations following the main recipe, mayonnaise, like vinaigrette, can be used as the base for a great variety of sauces. These sauces are served with all sorts of cold foods, including salads, vegetables, meats, poultry, and fish items. They are invaluable on the cold buffet table and in the preparation of hors d'oeuvres.

Compound Butters. Compound butters are made by softening raw butter and mixing flavoring ingredients into it. You have no doubt used these before and are familiar with several of the familiar ones. The following variations include the more common compound butters, as well as some that you may not be familiar with. The only ones that may be somewhat difficult are those based on shellfish, since the shells must be removed from the butter after contributing their flavor.

VINAIGRETTE

		U.S.		Metric	
YIELD:		1 pt	2 qt	5 dl	2 l
Ingredients					
Wine vinegar		4 oz	1 pt	12 cl	5 dl
Salt		1 ½ tsp	2 tbsp	8 g	30 g
White pepper		½ tsp	2 tsp	1 g	4 g
Salad oil		12 oz	3 pt	4 dl	1.5 l

Procedure:

1. Combine the vinegar, salt, and pepper. Stir to dissolve the salt.

2. Slowly whip in the oil in a thin stream.

3. Taste for seasonings and adjust if necessary.

Variations

Vinaigrette with special oils and vinegars: In place of those indicated, use special oils (olive, walnut, hazelnut, etc.) or vinegars (balsamic vinegar, sherry vinegar, raspberry vinegar, etc.) or lemon juice. Or use a blend of ingredients, such as one-half olive oil and one-half salad oil.

For the following variations, only ingredients are given. Use the same procedure as in the basic recipe, adding the seasoning ingredients to the vinegar in the first step. In some instances, egg yolk is included. Such vinaigrettes are like thinned-out mayonnaise; add the oil slowly, as when making mayonnaise, to preserve the emulsion.

Mustard Vinaigrette

Wine vinegar	3 oz	12 oz	1 dl	4 dl
Dijon-style mustard	1 oz	4 oz	30 g	125 g
Salt	1 ½ tsp	2 tbsp	8 g	30 g
White pepper	½ tsp	2 tsp	1 g	4 g
Garlic (mashed with the salt), optional	1 clove	4 cloves	1 clove	4 cloves
Salad oil or olive oil	12 oz	3 pt	4 dl	1.5 l

Thick Vinaigrette

Vinegar	4 oz	1 pt	12 cl	5 dl
Egg yolk	1 oz (about 1 ½ yolks)	4 oz	30 g	125 g
Salt	1 ½ tsp	2 tbsp	8 g	30 g
White pepper	½ tsp	2 tsp	1 g	4 g
Oil	12 oz	3 pt	4 dl	1.5 l

Vinaigrette for Warm Meat Salads

Wine vinegar	2 oz	8 oz	*6 cl*	*25 cl*
Strong reduced stock or deglazing liquid	2 oz	8 oz	*6 cl*	*25 cl*
Salad oil	12 oz	3 pt	*4 dl*	*1.5 l*
Salt				
Pepper				

Tomato Dill Vinaigrette

Lemon juice	4 oz	1 pt	*12 cl*	*5 dl*
Salt	2 tsp	8 tsp	*10 g*	*40 g*
White pepper	½ tsp	2 tsp	*1 g*	*4 g*
Fresh dill	¼ cup	1 cup	*15 g*	*60 g*
Olive oil	12 oz	3 pt	*4 dl*	*1.5 l*
Garnish:				
Fresh tomatoes, very small dice, well drained	8 oz	2 lb	*250 g*	*2 kg*

Thick Sherry Walnut Vinaigrette with Mustard

Sherry vinegar	3 oz	12 oz	*1 dl*	*4 dl*
Dijon-style mustard or grainy mustard	1 ½ oz	6 oz	*5 cl*	*2 dl*
Egg yolks	1 ½ oz	6 oz	*50 g*	*200 g*
Salt	1 ½ tsp	2 tbsp	*8 g*	*30 g*
White pepper	¼ tsp	½ tsp	*0.5 g*	*2 g*
Walnut oil	6 oz	1 ½ pt	*2 dl*	*8 dl*
Salad oil	6 oz	1 ½ pt	*2 dl*	*8 dl*

Thick Walnut Vinaigrette

In the above recipe, use white or red wine vinegar instead of sherry vinegar. Garnish the finished dressing with chopped toasted walnuts.

Mixed Herb Vinaigrette

Chopped parsley	½ cup	2 cups	*30 g*	*125 g*
Thyme	1 tsp	4 tsp	*1 g*	*4 g*
Rosemary, crumbled	½ tsp	2 tsp	*0.5 g*	*2 g*
Tarragon	1 tsp	4 tsp	*1 g*	*4 g*

Add the herbs to any basic vinaigrette.

Truffle Vinaigrette

Sherry vinegar	2 oz	8 oz	*6 cl*	*25 cl*
Truffle juice	4 oz	1 pt	*12 cl*	*5 dl*
Salad oil	8 oz	2 pt	*25 cl*	*1 l*
Walnut or hazelnut oil	4 oz	1 pt	*12 cl*	*5 dl*
Garnish: minced truffle				

Note: Canned truffle juice and truffles are available from specialty purveyors.

MAYONNAISE

		U.S.		Metric	
	YIELD:	**1 pt**	**2 qt**	**5 dl**	**2 l**
Ingredients					
Egg yolks		2	8	2	8
Vinegar		1 ½ tsp	1 oz	8 ml	3 cl
Dijon-style mustard		½ tsp	2 tsp	3 g	10 g
Salt		½ tsp	2 tsp	3 g	10 g
Cayenne		small dash	large dash	small dash	large dash
Salad oil or olive oil		14 oz	3 ½ pt	45 cl	1.8 l
Vinegar		½ oz	2 oz	15 ml	6 cl
Lemon juice		¼–½ oz	1–2 oz	8–15 ml	3–6 cl

Procedure:

1. Whip the egg yolks with the first quantity of vinegar, the mustard, salt, and cayenne.

2. Very slowly, whip the oil into the mixture, adding it in a thin stream and whipping constantly. When the mixture becomes very thick, thin it out with a little of the remaining vinegar and lemon juice. Gradually beat in the remaining oil alternately with the remaining vinegar and lemon juice. Adjust the seasoning, tartness, and consistency with additional salt and lemon juice as needed.

Variations

Aioli

Garlic		½–1 oz	2–4 oz	15–30 g	60–125 g

Mince the garlic and mash it with the salt in the recipe. Add this to the egg yolks. Use olive oil, or one-half olive oil and one-half salad oil.

Andalouse Sauce

Thick tomato purée		4 oz	1 pt	12 cl	5 dl
Pimiento, julienne		½ oz	2 oz	15 g	60 g

Add to the mayonnaise.

Remoulade Sauce

Dijon-style mustard	1 oz	4 oz	30 g	125 g
Chopped capers	½ oz	2 oz	15 g	60 g
Chopped sour pickles	½ oz	2 oz	15 g	60 g
Chopped parsley	1 tbsp	4 tbsp	4 g	8 g
Tarragon	½ tsp	2 tsp	0.5 g	2 g
Anchovy paste	1 tsp	4 tsp	5 g	20 g

Add to the mayonnaise.

Sauce Verte (Green Sauce)

Spinach leaves	2 oz	8 oz	60 g	250 g
Watercress	2 oz	8 oz	60 g	250 g
Parsley	1 oz	4 oz	30 g	125 g
Tarragon (fresh)	1 oz	4 oz	30 g	125 g
Hot pepper sauce, to taste				

Wash the greens and herbs; blanch them for a few seconds in boiling water. Drain, cool in cold water, then drain very well, pressing out excess moisture. Purée the blanched greens and herbs. (If fresh tarragon is not available, use one-fourth the quantity of dried, and add it at this point.) Mix with the mayonnaise, then force through a fine sieve. Season with hot pepper sauce.

Flavored Mayonnaise

Many ingredients can be added to mayonnaise. The following are a few suggestions:

Fresh herbs
Sorrel, shredded and sautéed until wilted
Dijon or grainy mustard
Parmesan cheese
Blue cheese
Pesto (see page 81)
Red pepper purée (see page 53)
Chopped sundried tomatoes

ROUILLE

		U.S.		Metric	
YIELD:		12 oz	3 pt	4 dl	1.5 l
Ingredients					
Dried hot, red chiles		2–4	8–16	2–4	8–16
Garlic cloves, chopped		2	8	2	8
White bread, crustless		1 ½ oz	6 oz	45 g	175 g
Pimiento		2 oz	8 oz	60 g	250 g
Salt		1 tsp	4 tsp	5 g	20 g
Black pepper		¼ tsp	1 tsp	0.5 g	2 g
Egg yolks		1	4	1	4
Olive oil		8 oz	2 pt	25 cl	1 l

Procedure:

1. Pulverize the peppers and garlic in a mortar, a blender, or a food processor.
2. Soak the bread in water and squeeze dry. Add the bread and the pimiento to the peppers and garlic and blend until smooth.
3. Add the salt, pepper, and egg yolks. Again blend well.
4. Little by little, beat in the oil, as for making mayonnaise. This can be done by hand or in the blender or food processor.

COMPOUND BUTTER

		U.S.		Metric	
Ingredients					
Flavoring ingredients, as required					
Butter		4 oz	1 lb	125 g	500 g

Procedure:

1. Prepare the flavoring ingredients as directed in the specific recipe.
2. Soften the butter by working it in a mixer or food processor.
3. Blend in the flavoring ingredients.
4. Roll the butter into a cylinder about 1 inch (2.5 cm) thick in a sheet of parchment, wax paper, or plastic film. Chill until firm. Slice off portions as needed.

Variations

The following are just a few of the many possibilities for making flavored butters. As different foods come in and out of fashion, you will want to experiment with other flavors.

Anchovy Butter

Anchovy fillets	½–1 oz	2–4 oz	*15–30 g*	*60–125 g*
Butter	4 oz	1 lb	*125 g*	*500 g*

Rinse excess salt off the anchovies. Mash to a paste. Blend with the butter.

Garlic Butter

Garlic, mashed to a paste	¼ oz	1 oz	*8 g*	*30 g*
Butter	4 oz	1 lb	*125 g*	*500 g*

Maître d'Hôtel Butter

Chopped parsley	1–2 tbsp	4–8 tbsp	*4–8 g*	*15–30 g*
Lemon juice	4 tsp	3 oz	*2 cl*	*8 cl*
White pepper	small pinch	large pinch	*small pinch*	*large pinch*
Butter	4 oz	1 lb	*125 g*	*500 g*

Escargot Butter

Garlic, mashed to a paste	¼ oz	1 oz	*8 g*	*30 g*
Maître d'hôtel butter	4 oz	1 lb	*125 g*	*500 g*

Shrimp Butter

Cooked shrimp, including shells	2 oz	8 oz	*60 g*	*125 g*
Butter	4 oz	1 lb	*125 g*	*500 g*

Grind shrimp very fine. Mix with butter. Force through a fine sieve to remove shells.

Crayfish Butter

Follow the instructions for shrimp butter, substituting crayfish for the shrimp.

Lobster Butter

Follow the instructions for shrimp butter, substituting lobster for the shrimp. Include the cooked red roe if possible.

Mustard Butter

	U.S.		Metric	
Dijon-style mustard	1 oz	4 oz	30 g	125 g
Butter	4 oz	1 lb	125 g	500 g

Foie Gras or Liver Pâté Butter

Foie gras or good quality liver pâté	4 oz	1 lb	125 g	500 g
Butter	4 oz	1 lb	125 g	500 g

Herb Butter

Fresh herbs, to taste				
Butter	4 oz	1 lb	125 g	500 g

COLD TOMATO SAUCE

		U.S.		Metric	
YIELD:		1 pt	2 qt	5 dl	2 l
Ingredients					
Tomato, peeled, seeded, and chopped		8 oz	2 lb	250 g	1 kg
Shallots, chopped fine		1 tsp	4 tsp	3 g	10 g
Red wine vinegar		½ oz	2 oz	15 ml	6 cl
Tarragon (optional)		½ tsp	2 g	0.5 g	2 g
Egg yolks		1	4	1	4
Olive oil, or part olive oil and part salad oil		8 oz	1 qt	25 cl	1 l
Hot red pepper sauce or cayenne, to taste					
Salt					
Pepper					

Procedure:

1. Combine the tomato, shallots, vinegar, and tarragon in a blender and purée to a smooth consistency.

2. Add the egg yolks and blend in well.

3. With the machine running, add the oil in a thin stream.

4. If necessary, thin out the sauce with a little water or vinegar. Season with hot pepper, salt, pepper, and extra vinegar if necessary.

SHALLOT OIL

		U.S.		Metric	
YIELD:		1 pt	2 qt	5 dl	2 l
Ingredients					
Shallots, chopped		2–3 tbsp	8–12 tbsp	30 g	125 g
Flavorless oil, such as canola, corn, safflower, grapeseed		1 pt	2 qt	5 dl	2 l

Procedure:

1. Combine the chopped shallots and the oil in a jar. Shake well.

2. Let stand for 30 minutes. Refrigerate.

3. The oil will be ready to use as soon as it has taken on the desired flavor, which may be in 1 or 2 hours. After 2 days, strain the oil through a paper coffee filter. Store in the refrigerator.

Variations

Ginger Oil or Horseradish Oil

Substitute ginger root or horseradish for the shallots in the basic recipe. For best results, chop the ginger or horseradish very fine in a food processor or grate with a fine-holed grater.

Garlic Oil

Substitute garlic for the shallots in the basic recipe. Substitute olive oil for the flavorless oil, if desired.

Lemon Oil or Orange Oil

		U.S.		Metric	
Grated lemon or orange zest		3–4 tbsp	12–16 tbsp	30 g	125 g

Substitute the above quantity of grated zest for the shallots in the basic recipe.

Rosemary Oil, Sage Oil, Thyme Oil, or Oregano Oil

		U.S.		Metric	
Chopped fresh rosemary, sage, thyme, or oregano		¾–1 cup	3–4 cups	100 g	400 g

Substitute the above quantity of herbs for the shallots in the basic recipe.

COLD WATERCRESS SAUCE

		U.S.		Metric	
YIELD:		**1 pt**	**2 qt**	*5 dl*	*2 l*
Ingredients					
Watercress		8 oz	2 lb	*250 g*	*1 kg*
Mayonnaise		8 oz	2 pt	*25 cl*	*1 l*
Heavy cream		5 ½ oz	1 pt 6 oz	*17 cl*	*7 dl*
Salt					
White pepper					

Procedure:

1. Wash the watercress and drain well. Remove and discard the thick parts of the stems.
2. Put the cress in a food processor and process until chopped as fine as possible. Add about one-fourth of the mayonnaise and continue to purée.
3. Stir in the rest of the mayonnaise.
4. Just before serving, whip the cream and fold it into the sauce.
5. Adjust the seasoning.

Variation

Green Sauce

Omit the watercress and substitute one-half its quantity of blanched, squeezed spinach. Flavor the sauce well with your choice of fresh herbs.

WASABI OIL

		U.S.		Metric	
YIELD:		**1 pt**	**2 qt**	*5 dl*	*2 l*
Ingredients					
Wasabi powder (Japanese green horseradish)		3 tbsp	12 tbsp	*20 g*	*80 g*
Water (approximate)		1 tbsp	4 tbsp	*15 ml*	*60 ml*
Flavorless oil		1 pt	2 qt	*5 dl*	*2 l*

Procedure:

1. Mix enough water into the wasabi to make a smooth paste.

2. Transfer the mixture to a jar and add the oil. Shake well.

3. Let stand at room temperature for 1 day. Shake several times.

4. When the oil has taken on enough flavor, filter through a paper coffee filter. Store the oil in the refrigerator.

Variations

Cinnamon Oil, Cumin Oil, Curry Oil, Ginger Oil, Mustard Oil, or Paprika Oil

Substitute the desired powder for the wasabi in the basic recipe.

PESTO

		U.S.		Metric	
YIELD:		12 oz	3 pt	*4 dl*	*1.5 l*
Ingredients					
Fresh basil leaves		1 pt	2 qt	*5 dl*	*2 l*
Olive oil		6 oz	1 pt 8 oz	*2 dl*	*8 dl*
Pine nuts (pignoli) or walnuts		1 oz	4 oz	*30 g*	*125 g*
Garlic cloves		3	12	*3*	*12*
Salt		½ tsp	2 tsp	*3 g*	*10 g*
Parmesan cheese		2 oz	8 oz	*60 g*	*250 g*

Procedure:

1. Wash the basil leaves and drain well.

2. Put the basil, oil, nuts, garlic, and salt in a blender or food processor. Blend to a paste, but not so long that it is smooth. It should have a slightly coarse texture.

3. Transfer the mixture to a bowl and stir in the cheese.

Variation

When pesto is used as a pasta sauce, the cheese is included. For other purposes, it may be omitted if desired.

BASIL OIL

Ingredients

Fresh basil leaves, as needed
Olive oil

Procedure:

1. Drop the fresh basil leaves into boiling water. Blanch for 10 seconds. Drain and refresh under cold water. Drain again and pat the herbs dry with towels.

2. Put the herbs in a blender and add a small amount of olive oil. Blend to make a paste. If necessary to make a paste, add a little more oil.

3. Remove the paste from the blender and measure its volume. Put in a jar and add four times its volume of olive oil. Shake well and let stand.

4. After 30 minutes, put the jar in the refrigerator.

5. The next day, filter the oil through a paper coffee filter.

Variations

Parsley Oil, Tarragon Oil, Chervil Oil, or Cilantro Oil

Substitute the desired herb for the basil in the basic recipe. Use either olive oil or a flavorless oil.

Chive Oil

Substitute chives for the basil in the basic recipe. Use either a flavorless oil or olive oil. Chop the chives, but do not blanch them. Blend the chopped chives to a paste in a blender with a little oil. Continue as in the basic recipe. Filtering is optional.

LOBSTER OIL

		U.S.		Metric	
	YIELD:	**12 oz**	**3 pt**	*35 cl*	*7 dl*
Ingredients					
Flavorless oil		2 oz	8 oz	*60 ml*	*25 cl*
Crushed lobster shells (see note)		1 lb	4 lb	*450 g*	*1.8 kg*
Carrot, chopped		2 oz	8 oz	*60 g*	*225 g*
Onion, chopped		2 oz	8 oz	*60 g*	*225 g*
Celery, chopped		2 oz	8 oz	*60 g*	*225 g*
Bay leaf		1	4	*1*	*4*
Parsley stems		10	40	*10*	*40*
White wine		8 oz	1 qt	*25 cl*	*1 l*
Water		4 oz	1 pt	*125 ml*	*5 dl*
Flavorless oil		1 pt	2 qt	*5 dl*	*2 l*

Note: Either raw or cooked shells are acceptable, but raw shells are best.

Procedure:

1. Heat the first quantity of oil in a heavy saucepan or brazier over moderate heat. Add the shells, being careful not to spatter hot oil.

2. Turn the heat to high and cook the shells in the oil, stirring often, for 15 minutes.

3. Add the vegetables and herbs and stir well. Cook for another 1 or 2 minutes

4. Add the wine and water, being careful not to spatter it in the hot oil. Cook for 15 minutes, stirring often.

5. Reduce the heat to moderate. Add the large quantity of oil. Stir. Cook slowly, stirring occasionally, for about 30 minutes, until all the moisture has evaporated and only oil and solids remain in the pot.

6. Remove from heat and cover. Let stand until completely cool.

7. Strain the oil through a paper coffee filter. Refrigerate.

Variation

Shrimp Oil

Substitute shrimp shells for the lobster shells in the basic recipe.

CHAPTER

4

Soups

*S*tudents of the professional culinary arts are generally familiar with a wide variety of soups. Soup is one of the first subjects taught in detail to beginning students. There are several reasons for this. Many soups are easily made in quantity, are often inexpensive, and at the same time familiarize the students with many of the techniques that they will need in other areas of cooking. Making soups gives the students practice in making stocks, in using thickening agents, in trimming and cutting vegetables, in simmering meats, in puréeing foods, and in other cooking techniques.

In keeping with today's spirit of invention, modern chefs are creating many new and unusual soup recipes. Nevertheless, upon closer inspection, we can see that most of these soups aren't so drastically different after all. It is true that they are likely to be lighter and less thick and to feature many imaginative ingredients and combinations of ingredients; however, for the most part, the basic techniques are still the classical ones that you probably learned in your beginning studies.

Because of the importance of classical soup-making theory and techniques even today, we spend some time in this chapter reviewing those procedures. Then we discuss how these techniques are applied in modern kitchens, and we provide some recipes to illustrate the techniques.

CLASSICAL SOUPS

Modern soups are the direct descendants of the classic soups outlined by Escoffier at the beginning of the century. The basics are the same, even though some of the details have changed. Basic consommé hasn't changed much in decades, although many of the dozens of complicated consommé garnishes from the classical kitchen have been forgotten. Conversely, cooks today are applying the classical techniques to new ingredients and combinations of ingredients and flavors that Escoffier wouldn't recognize.

Escoffier divided soups into two basic categories: clear and thick. We still use this classification today when we talk about soup-making techniques. By clear soups, Escoffier meant consommés, with their various garnishes. Today we also include clear—that is, unthickened—vegetable soups and other clear soups in this category. The main types of thick soups today are cream soups and purée soups. Escoffier also included a type of soup called *velouté,* which we now consider a type of cream soup. The difference is explained in the section on thick soups (see page 91).

It is also necessary to have a general catchall category of soups for those recipes that don't fit into the two main ones. This group includes many home-style soups and chowders.

This section is a review of the procedures for making the basic soup types, including consommés and other clear soups, cream soups, and purée soups. Some of this material may be familiar to you, but there may be some items that are new to you. In any case, it is important to understand this section before moving on to the discussions of modern soups, because the same procedures are used.

Clear Soups: Consommés

The modern definition of a *consommé* is a clarified stock—that is, it is a stock that has been made perfectly clear by *clarification,* which is a procedure that removes all the tiny particles that make a stock cloudy. Unfortunately, this definition is too simple.

Any old clarified broth, no matter how thin, watery, and flavorless, might get served as consommé. And today it often does.

In classical kitchens, the most important part of the definition of a consommé was that it must be strong and flavorful. A good consommé should have a deep, mellow flavor with plenty of body from the natural gelatin content of the stock. To get this result, you must start with a good, strong stock. If your stock isn't strong enough, you must either reduce the stock first until it is strong enough or plan on simmering the consommé for extra time during the clarification process to reduce it.

How Clarification Works. As you should remember, clarification of stocks works because of the *coagulation of proteins*. During the procedure, proteins that we have added to the stock are cooked and coagulate or solidify. As the proteins solidify, they collect all the tiny particles that cloud the stock and hold them in a solid mass that floats to the top of the simmering soup. This mass is called a *raft*.

The mixture of ingredients that we add to clarify a stock is called a *clarification* or a *clearmeat*.

The main ingredients of a clarification are as follows:

Lean ground meat: provides proteins and flavor

Egg whites: major source of protein for clarification

Mirepoix and other flavoring ingredients: provide flavor; mirepoix helps give structure to the raft; not absolutely necessary but generally used

Acid ingredients: tomato products for beef or chicken consommé, lemon juice or white wine for fish; acids help coagulate protein; not absolutely necessary but often used

It is possible to clarify a stock using only egg whites. This is often done with fish stock. Great care is necessary, however, because the raft is very fragile when only egg whites are used.

A general procedure for clarifying a consommé follows. A detailed recipe is included in Appendix 1 (see page 615).

Procedure for Clarifying Consommé

1. Start with a well-flavored, cold, strong stock or broth.
2. Combine the clearmeat ingredients in a heavy stock pot and mix them vigorously.
3. Gradually add the cold, degreased stock and mix well with the clearmeat.
4. Set the pot over moderately low heat and let it come to a simmer. Stir the contents occasionally so that the clearmeat ingredients circulate through the stock and don't stick to the bottom.
5. When the simmering point is approached, stop stirring.
6. Move to a lower heat so that the liquid maintains a slow simmer. Do not cover.
7. Let simmer 1½ hours, without disturbing the raft.
8. Carefully strain the consommé through a china cap lined with cheesecloth. Do not stir the raft or press on it in the china cap.
9. Degrease and adjust seasonings.

Special Essences. Ordinary consommé is usually made from brown veal or beef stock, although white stock could also be used. Logically, consommés of chicken, fish, or game are made from chicken, fish, or game stock.

In addition to these major types of basic consommé, special flavors can be created by adding ingredients to the clarification mixture. For example, by adding extra celery to the clarification, you make essence of celery consommé. Other traditional essences made in the same way include mushroom, tomato, and pimiento. Essence of tomato consommé is called *consommé madrilène.* Modern menus also list some less traditional essences, such as asparagus or fennel. These are made in precisely the same way, except that essences of delicate vegetables such as asparagus often work best when made with white stock rather than brown stock.

In elegant classical kitchens, special game essences are sometimes made by adding roasted quails or partridges to the clarification. Usually the breast meat is removed first and saved to use for garnish or for a cold dish.

Consommé Garnishes. Consommés served hot are almost always garnished. To garnish a consommé means to add a small quantity of a particular item or items, usually when the soup is served. The soup is then given a name that indicates the garnish. For example, consommé brunoise is a consommé that is garnished with vegetables cut into brunoise shape (tiny dice). Consommé Douglas, to name a less familiar example, is garnished with slices of sweetbreads, slices of artichoke bottoms, and asparagus tips.

The classical repertoire contains over 100 garnished consommés, each with its own name. Most of these, especially the more complicated and exotic ones, are rarely served today, and many of them have been completely forgotten.

A general list of the preparations used as garnish for the classic consommés follows. For extensive listings of classic consommés with their detailed garnish and proper names, you should consult such references as Escoffier and *Le Répertoire de la Cuisine* (see Bibliography, page 623).

Vegetables, cut various ways

Cooked meat and poultry

Fresh herbs

Rice

Tapioca

Truffles

Tiny ravioli and other pasta products

Crêpes, cut julienne

Profiterolles (tiny cream puffs) filled with savory purées

Quenelles

Royale

Garnishes are traditionally used in small quantities, usually about 1 to 2 tablespoons per portion.

Simple vegetable garnishes are used for such presentations as consommé brunoise and consommé julienne. Such vegetable garnishes are most often used because they are the least complicated.

There are two important things to remember about vegetable garnishes. First, they should be cut neatly and uniformly. Second, they usually should be cooked slowly in butter before being simmered in a little consommé to finish them. This procedure allows some of the butter to be absorbed by the vegetables, so that they develop a mellower, richer flavor. (There are some exceptions to this second rule; for example, peas and green beans usually are not cooked in butter from the raw state.)

Two other garnish items from the list require special explanation, namely quenelles and royale.

Quenelles. Small balls of cooked (usually poached) forcemeat are called *quenelles*. A *forcemeat* is a mixture of finely ground meat, poultry, or fish, usually raw, combined with other ingredients for flavoring, binding, and enriching (such as eggs, cream, and starch products). Quenelles are made by shaping the forcemeat into balls or other shapes by rolling it by hand, by shaping it with a pastry bag, or by molding it with a spoon. The forcemeat shapes are then poached in stock or other liquid. The quenelles may be made in any size, although when used for soup garnish they must be quite small.

Larger quenelles may be served with a sauce as an appetizer or luncheon dish. Chapter 6 provides more information on quenelles. These procedures are applied to meat and poultry quenelles as well. Recipes for forcemeats are on pages 259 and 307.

Royale. A type of savory or unsweetened custard that is sliced, cut into small shapes, and used as a consommé garnish is called a *royale*. At its simplest, royale is made by beating together a liquid (such as consommé or cream) and eggs, pouring the mixture into small containers, and cooking in a water bath until the custard is firm. Flavored royales contain purées of vegetables, meats, or fish, plus eggs and liquids such as cream or béchamel sauce.

After the cooked custard has cooled completely, it is cut into slices. These slices are then cut into small shapes with fancy cutters or with a knife. The cut pieces are added to consommé at serving time.

Royales were once an important part of classical service, but they are not often made today, perhaps because consommés themselves are not as popular. Many cooks do not consider all the effort worthwhile just to make tiny pieces of soup garnish. Nevertheless, this technique is still considered by classically trained cooks to be a necessary part of a chef's skills.

Recipes for royales are included in the recipe section of this chapter (see pages 99–100). The basic recipe for consommé is included in Appendix 1 (see page 615).

Clear Soups: Vegetable Soups and Home-Style Soups

Soups in this category originated with peasant-style soups in which any available vegetables, meats, and starches were tossed into the soup pot to make a robust, one-dish meal, perhaps accompanied only by some bread and cheese. Like consommés, they can be said to consist of broth plus garnish. However, they are much heartier than consommés. In general, there are two main differences between these soups and consommés:

- The broth or stock is not clarified and doesn't need to be as concentrated.
- The proportion of garnish (that is, solid ingredients) is much higher. In general, you will use about 12 to 16 ounces of vegetables and meats per quart of liquid (375 to 500 grams per liter).

Nearly any vegetable or meat can be used, as long as the combination is harmonious. Hearty, inexpensive vegetables such as onions, carrots, celery, turnips, cabbage, and potatoes are especially popular. Meats, when used, are usually added in smaller quantities than vegetables are. On average, you might use 2 to 4 ounces of cooked meat per quart of liquid (60 to 125 grams per liter).

Since these are considered informal, home-style soups, there is not a detailed procedure that will apply to all of them. In general, the preparation of these soups is not complicated. Most are made simply by simmering the vegetables in stock until done. However, just because these soups are relatively simple doesn't mean they should be prepared haphazardly. The care in preparation is reflected in the quality of the finished product.

Briefly let us review some guidelines for preparing quality vegetable soups:

1. Start with a clear, flavorful stock.
2. Select vegetables and other ingredients whose flavors go well together.
3. Cut vegetables uniformly.
4. Cook vegetables slowly in a little butter before combining with a liquid in order to improve their flavor.
5. Cook starches such as grains and pasta separately and add to the soup later.
6. Observe differences in cooking times (add long-cooking vegetables first, short-cooking ones later) and do not overcook.

Thick Soups: Cream Soups

A *cream soup* could be described as a diluted béchamel or velouté sauce flavored with a purée of the ingredient for which the soup is named. In the kitchens of Escoffier's day, there were two kinds of soups that fit this description: cream soups and velouté soups. The difference between these is as follows:

- Velouté soups consist of velouté sauce, a puréed flavoring ingredient, white stock to dilute, and an egg-yolk-and-cream liaison to finish.
- Cream soups consist of béchamel sauce, a puréed flavoring ingredient, milk or white stock to dilute, and cream to finish.

Today, we usually refer to both these types as cream soups. However, you will sometimes see a soup containing an egg-yolk-and-cream liaison referred to as a velouté, in keeping with classical tradition. In order to avoid confusion, you should use the name *velouté* for a soup only if it contains a liaison.

There are three variations of the method for making cream soups. The first variation is the classical method; if you already have velouté or béchamel sauce on hand, this is perhaps the easiest method. It gives you the most control over the cooking and thickening, and it produces excellent results.

The other two variations are closely related. The main difference is that the starch thickener is added at different times. Table 4.1 illustrates the similarities and differences. If you are familiar with only one or two of these methods, you should pay special attention to the others, so that you understand all three.

Procedures for Making Cream Soups

Method 1.

1. Prepare velouté sauce or béchamel sauce, using roux.
2. Prepare main flavoring ingredients (vegetables and/or meats). Sweat vegetables in butter to develop flavor.
3. Combine flavoring ingredients with prepared sauce and simmer until tender. Skim the surface as needed during cooking.
4. Purée the soup.
5. Thin out with hot white stock or milk.
6. Adjust seasonings.
7. Add cream or liaison at service time.

TABLE 4.1. **Structure of Cream Soups: Three Methods**

Method 1	Method 2	Method 3
Butter Vegetables	Butter Vegetables Flour	Butter Vegetables

Velouté or
  béchamel
  (liquid plus roux)
	Liquid	Liquid

		Beurre manié or roux
Additional liquid (stock or milk)		
Cream or liaison	Cream or liaison	Cream or liaison

Method 2.

1. Prepare flavoring ingredients. Sweat vegetables in butter.
2. Add flour to vegetables and butter and make a roux.
3. Add white stock, whipping to combine it with the roux.
4. Add other flavoring ingredients, if any.
5. Simmer until ingredients are tender, skimming as needed.
6. Purée the soup.
7. Thin out with hot milk or stock if necessary.
8. Adjust seasonings.
9. Add cream or liaison at service time.

Method 3.

1. Prepare flavoring ingredients. Sweat vegetables in butter.
2. Add hot white stock.
3. Add other flavoring ingredients, if any.
4. Simmer until ingredients are tender, skimming as needed.
5. Thicken with beurre manié, roux, or other starch.
6. Purée the soup.
7. Thin out with hot milk or stock.
8. Adjust seasonings.
9. Add cream or liaison at service time.

Standards of Quality for Cream Soups

Thickness: about the consistency of heavy cream; not too thick.

Texture: smooth; no graininess or lumps (except garnish, if any).

Taste: distinct flavor of main ingredient; no taste of uncooked starch.

Thick Soups: Purée Soups

Purée soups are made by simmering vegetables in stock or water and then puréeing the cooked mixture. There are three basic types of purée soups, which are determined by the type of vegetable used:

1. Purées of dried vegetables (such as dried beans, lentils, and peas) require no thickening or binding ingredient.
2. Purées of starchy fresh vegetables (such as potatoes) require no binding ingredient because of the starch in the main ingredient.
3. Purées of other fresh vegetables must usually contain a binding ingredient to keep the vegetable purée from separating out.

Some starch content is necessary for a purée soup to achieve the proper consistency. In the case of fresh vegetables that do not have enough of their own starch, an additional starchy ingredient is added. The three basic binders for purée soups are as follows:

Potato

Rice

Bread (usually sliced or diced and fried in butter)

It is possible to use a roux to bind purée soups. Many chefs argue, however, that the soup is then no longer a true purée soup, but is more like a cream soup. It is perhaps best to rely on the traditional binders. At least there is less danger of ending up with a soup that is too starchy.

Please note: The main difference between cream soups and purée soups is the binding agent. Cream soups are bound with roux or beurre manié or are made with a roux-bound béchamel or velouté sauce. Purée soups are bound with the vegetable's natural starch, with rice, or with bread.

Potatoes are the most commonly used binding ingredient in fresh vegetable purées. Rice is perhaps less common, but it is just as easy and versatile to use. Some cooks feel that rice makes the purée too heavy, but that is only if too much is used. You should need no more than 2 or 3 ounces per pound of vegetables (125 to 200 grams per kilogram).

Fresh bread browned in butter is an ancient binding technique that has been rediscovered by modern chefs. The browned bread gives a special, mellow flavor to the soup. The use of this technique is illustrated in the recipe on page 114.

Procedure for Making Purée Soups

1. Sweat mirepoix or other fresh vegetables in fat.
2. Add liquid.
3. Add dried or starchy vegetables; add any other binding ingredient.
4. Simmer until vegetables are tender.
5. Purée the soup.
6. Dilute to proper consistency with white stock, if necessary.
7. Adjust seasonings. Finish with cream or raw butter if desired.

Bisques. A purée soup or a cream soup made with shellfish is called a *bisque.* If a bisque is thickened with rice or with bread browned in butter, it can be considered a purée soup and is made like other purée soups. If it is thickened with roux or made with fish velouté, it can be considered a cream soup, and it is made by the same methods used for other cream soups. In Escoffier's kitchen, all these methods were used.

In classical cooking, some of the meat of the shellfish was set aside for garnish, and the rest was puréed with the soup. This method gives a great deal of flavor and body to the soup. Today, because of the high cost of most shellfish, it is perhaps more common to rely more heavily on the shells to provide flavor and to use just enough shellfish meat to serve as garnish.

Bisques actually belong to the cream soup and purée soup categories. However, because they employ special ingredients and sometimes special techniques, they are often given a special category of their own. Because they are so popular, many students learn to make a bisque early in their training. Nevertheless, they are generally considered advanced recipes, so we include one in this chapter (see page 111).

Coulis. A purée soup or cream soup made from poultry, game, or fish is called a *coulis*. Or, to put it another way, a coulis is the same as a bisque, except it is made from meat or fish instead of shellfish. (Both the singular and plural forms of the word *coulis* are spelled the same way, and both are pronounced "koo lee.")

This type of soup was important in classical cuisine, but it is rarely seen today. The term *coulis* is now used for almost any kind of purée, especially purées of fresh vegetables. For example, the recipe for fresh tomato sauce on page 50 is often called tomato coulis.

MODERN SOUPS

As in other areas of cooking, modern cooks tend to be much less systematic in their approach to soups than were the chefs of Escoffier's day. They often pay little attention to categories or families of recipes and instead are busy experimenting with different ingredients and with novel combinations.

Part of this is due to the size of modern kitchens and of modern menus, both of which tend to be smaller than those of years ago. For example, classical cream soups and velouté soups were based on béchamel and velouté sauces. When every kitchen routinely prepared large quantities of the basic sauces, it was a simple matter to convert some of them into a different selection of soups each day.

Today, except in some large, traditional kitchens, the situation is quite different. Production is often organized differently. Furthermore, soups play a less important role in most diets. At one time, a soup course was a part of most formal dinners. Today, it is more likely to be just one of a number of first-course choices.

Nevertheless, modern soups, even the most innovative or unusual ones, generally follow the classical or traditional patterns (even if the inventor of the recipe doesn't realize it). Such modern, stylish concoctions as Corn and Chili Cream Soup and Cream of Black Walnut Soup are made the same way as such old stand-bys as Cream of Celery Soup. Merely using different ingredients doesn't change the basic procedure.

This is why we have spent so much time reviewing the basics of traditional soup making. The more you understand the basic patterns, the easier it is to deal with innovations. Each new recipe isn't entirely new; it is merely a different application of something you already know.

The recipes included in this chapter are primarily new and sometimes unusual ones. For the most part, you will not find traditional recipes that you probably have already learned. In each section, we discuss how the recipes follow the classic procedures reviewed earlier. We also discuss what makes them different.

Unthickened Soups

With renewed interest in healthful foods, clear or unthickened soups are perfect candidates for stardom on modern menus. Loaded with fresh vegetables and lacking cream or thickening agents, unthickened soups can be light, nutritious, and satisfying starters for lunches or dinners.

You can give new vitality to clear soups in a number of ways. The following tips will help you produce lively soups:

1. *Do not overcook.* Pay close attention to all the rules of vegetable cookery that you have learned. Just because vegetables are to be part of a soup rather than to be served as side dishes is no reason to be careless with them. Properly cooked soups have better flavor, texture, and color.

2. *Do not hold soups too long in the steam table.* This is related to the first guideline. Even perfectly cooked soups will become overcooked if they stand too long at serving temperature. Instead, heat small batches every 30 minutes or so. Or, if your production schedule permits it, heat portions to order for the ultimate in freshness.

3. *Try new ingredients and combinations.* Innovative cooks are constantly experimenting with ingredient combinations that are not traditional. But more familiar ingredients can also give new interest to the soup menu. Duck, wild rice, and snow peas, for example, are not exactly new items; however, they are not often used in soups, so they draw attention when they are.

4. *Pay attention to appearance.* Cutting solid ingredients neatly and uniformly will make the soup look like it was carefully made, not just thrown together. Also, for clear soups, the liquid base should be as clear as possible. Ingredients that will make the soup cloudy, such as pasta and grains, should be cooked separately.

The classical technique of sweating vegetables in butter before simmering them in the soup is not always used, partly because of the emphasis on health and dieting. Although it is true that cooking the vegetables in butter first creates a richer, mellower flavor, sometimes chefs want the vegetables to have a crisper texture and a fresher "garden" flavor. In such cases, the raw vegetables are added directly to the simmering soup. The method you use will depend on the results you want to achieve.

Vegetable Broths. Vegetable broths may be used in place of stocks as bases for soups. The use of these broths was pioneered by vegetarian cooks, but the broths have also become popular with other chefs as well as with diners.

Vegetable broths are made like stocks, only without bones or meat products, of course. Because there is no need to extract gelatin from bones, cooking times are much shorter. Also, keeping the cooking time as short as 30 minutes results in fresher vegetable flavors.

A basic recipe for a mixed vegetable broth is included in this section (see page 101). Broths flavored with individual vegetables are made in a similar fashion, as indicated in the variations that follow the main recipe.

Consommés. It is strange that the renewal of interest in light, healthful, low-fat foods should have occurred at the same time as the near-disappearance of consommés from menus. Certainly there are few soups that are lighter or lower in calories per portion.

To most people, consommé is nothing more than a plain broth; therefore, it is rather boring. This is no doubt the reason for its decline. But the poor reputation of this classic soup must be due to the fact that it has so often been poorly prepared, with little flavor or body. A good consommé must be concentrated and have a full, rich flavor. When well made, consommés deserve their status as the most elegant and sophisticated of classical soups.

To make the most of consommés, review the discussion of special essences on page 88. This technique will enable you to make a variety of attractive and unusual soups. Also, pay attention to the various garnishes discussed. In this section you will find a recipe for royale garnish. Quenelles, another elegant garnish, are explained on page 90. Although some garnishes (such as royales) are not exactly low in fat, they are used in such small quantities that they add little fat to the total diet. For a basic consommé recipe, refer to page 615.

Consommé Service. Consommés are traditionally served in cups, with garnish traditionally used in small quantities. Modern chefs, however, have found that increasing the amount of garnish increases the appeal of the soup. Consequently, the service of consommés in broad soup plates with large pieces of garnish attractively arranged has become widely practiced.

For example, an essence of mushroom consommé might be served as follows: Arrange three large mushroom ravioli in a soup plate. Place a broiled shiitake mushroom cap in the center. Arrange some pieces of carrot, leek, and snow peas, all cut into diamond shapes, around the ravioli. Place the soup plate, on an underliner, in front of the diner. Bring the soup to the dining room in a tureen and ladle a portion of the soup over the garnish.

When a soup is served in this way, the garnish assumes greater importance; the soup takes on almost the role of a light sauce that moistens the garnish.

This style of service—that is, presenting the diner with a soup plate containing attractively arranged garnish and ladling the soup over the garnish at the table—can be used for other soups besides consomeés, such as cream soups and purées.

Thickened Soups

Cream soups and purée soups are reviewed in detail in the first part of this chapter. The classical procedures for preparing these types of soups are used to make not only the traditional soups but also many new and innovative soups.

The major difference between modern and traditional thickened soups is the ingredients that are used; the production methods are basically the same. This fact becomes clear when you analyze the modern recipes by breaking them down into their basic steps. Even when cooks don't realize it, they tend to follow tried-and-true patterns. When a recipe doesn't follow the classic method, it can often be improved by changing it so that it does. The main reason for stressing the classical methods is that they simplify your learning and your work by making it systematic.

Despite the many similarities between modern recipes and classical ones, some things have changed since Escoffier's day. You should be aware of these changes in order to deal with the range of soup preparations you will find today.

1. The term *cream soup* is now used for almost any soup that contains cream. This is contrary to classical practice, in which *cream soup* means something very specific. Today, the term is used not only for the classical cream soups but also for velouté soups and purée soups containing cream.

2. Cream soups are not always puréed. Instead, they may contain a variety of solid ingredients. This type of soup is similar to classic chowders, such as New England clam chowder.

3. Thickening ingredients are used less systematically. Often, no starch thickener is used at all. Potage Germiny (see page 116) is an example of a traditional or classical soup that contains no starch binder, only a liaison. Today, this technique is often used to make lighter soups. In keeping with the less systematic terminology (see number 1 in this list), something called a cream soup may be thickened with a starch, a purée, a liaison, or nothing at all. As explained earlier (see page 93), the ancient technique of thickening with bread is being revived.

4. Unusual or nontraditional combinations of ingredients are often used to create menu interest or to draw the diner's attention. When you are using such recipes, make sure that they are well tested and that the flavors work together. Sometimes unusual combinations work, but sometimes they are just strange.

5. Fish soups are becoming more popular, just as fish is becoming more popular as a main course because of the interest in healthful foods. Unless the fish is going to be puréed, be careful not to overcook it. Most fish items need only to be added at the last minute and heated through to be cooked. Overcooking makes them dry and tough or crumbly.

6. Remember that most cream soups can be served cold as well as hot. Cold soups are especially popular in hot weather. Check the seasoning after chilling, because cold temperatures dull tastes. Also, soups usually become thicker when chilled. Check the consistency carefully.

Uncooked Cold Soups

Cold soups are often treated as a separate category; however, most cold soups are simply chilled versions of hot soups. Cream soups in particular are popular when served chilled during hot weather. Cold cream of cucumber soup, for example, was very fashionable for several years.

Naturally, cold versions of hot soups are not a special category and call for no new techniques. However, two points need attention:

- Soups usually require more seasoning when chilled than when served hot. Check the seasoning carefully *after* the soup is chilled.

- Soups become thicker when chilled. This is especially true if the soup is based on a gelatinous stock. You may need to reduce the quantity of thickening agent

There is another variety of cold soup—those that are not cooked. This type of soup is usually made by simply mixing together the various ingredients. The mixture may or may not be puréed. The fact that the soup mixture is not cooked makes these soups quick and easy to prepare.

The classic uncooked, puréed soup is the Spanish soup gazpacho, which has become so popular that it is found in most beginning cooking texts and nearly any collection of soup recipes. Gazpacho is often called a liquid salad because it is a purée of raw vegetables, usually flavored with a little olive oil and vinegar. Gazpacho has inspired many similar puréed cold vegetable soups, such as the one found on page 117. Similar soups can be made quickly by simply adding some diced vegetables or other solid ingredients to plain tomato juice or other vegetable juice.

Besides tomatoes, other vegetables and even fruits can be the basis of uncooked soups. If the vegetables are not juicy enough, other liquids, such as cold stock, may be added to thin out the purée and also add other flavors.

Incidentally, the term *uncooked soup* means that the soup mixture itself is not cooked, not that all the ingredients must be raw. Cooked meats, fish, and vegetables may be added to uncooked soups.

Hearty and Substantial Soups

Most soups are served as a light appetizer or first course or as a luncheon dish in combination with a salad or sandwich. However, a number of popular soups are so full of meats, fish, and/or vegetables that they are substantial enough to be full meals by themselves.

Many, if not most, of these hearty soups are, or are derived from, unsophisticated, rough-and-ready peasant dishes or country soups or one-pot meals. Such dishes are made by taking advantage of whatever fresh ingredients are available and combining them in a flavorful mixture. Thus each region of the world develops its own characteristic hearty soups, because each region harvests a different combination of foods. In seacoast areas, favorite soups are often made with seafood, while inland regions use more meat and poultry or possibly freshwater fish if there are lakes and rivers nearby. In southern areas, soups are more likely to contain such ingredients as tomatoes and peppers, while colder regions make more use of hardy root vegetables and cabbages.

Native soups often become popular outside their native region and are adopted into the classic or international cuisine. It is not unusual to find what was originally a peasant dish on the menus of elegant restaurants.

Sometimes these peasant dishes become modified and refined over the years and turn into elegant dishes. The classic soup called *petite marmite* (see recipe on page 118) is an example of this kind of change. This dish began as a simple pot of broth called *pot-au-feu.* This name literally means "pot on the fire"; we could translate it as "stock pot." Pot-au-feu is basically a French home-style dish in which meat and vegetables are simmered in water. The broth is served as a soup, and the cooked meat and vegetables are the main part of the meal.

Chefs adapted this dish to the professional kitchen, took special care with it so that the broth was as rich as a fine consommé, and presented the dish, somewhat "dressed up," in a small earthenware pot called a *petite marmite.* In this form, the soup has been a basic part of classical cuisine since well before Escoffier's time.

Today, chefs are carrying the change one step further. They are making light soups from clear stock or consommé, a few colorful vegetables, and two or three kinds of meat, poultry, and/or fish, cooking them quickly rather than simmering them for hours, and calling them *petite marmite.* An example is the "petite marmite" of scallops and chicken on page 120.

There is no exact dividing line between the simple soups discussed earlier in this chapter and these hearty soups. Petite marmite, for example, could just as well be included with clear soups. However, chefs generally think of hearty soups as a special category because their substantial nature and the number of ingredients they contain often makes the procedures for making them longer and more complex. In general, you should be aware not only of the basic soup-making procedures dicussed earlier in this chapter, but also of the basic procedures for preparing and cooking meats, poultry, fish, and vegetables. If necessary, you should review the meat, poultry, fish, and vegetable chapters of your basic cookbooks and of this book before preparing some of the more complex soups.

PLAIN ROYALE FOR CONSOMMÉS

		U.S.		Metric	
	YIELD:	*12 oz*	*24 oz*	*350 g*	*700 g*
Ingredients					
Whole eggs		2	4	*2*	*4*
Egg yolks		3	6	*3*	*6*
Consommé, hot		8 oz	1 pt	*2.5 dl*	*5 dl*

Procedure:

1. Beat the eggs and egg yolks together.

2. Gradually pour the consommé into the eggs, beating constantly.

3. Pass the mixture through a fine sieve.

4. Butter well some flat-bottomed pans or custard cups. Pour in the royale mixture.

5. Bake in a water bath at 300°F (150°C) until set. Let cool completely.

6. Unmold and cut into desired shapes (see Figure 4.1).

Variations

Cream Royale

Substitute light cream or part milk and part cream for the consommé. Season with salt and a little nutmeg.

Herbed Royale

Add some herbs, such as tarragon or parsley, to the hot consommé. Let steep about 20 minutes before proceeding with the recipe.

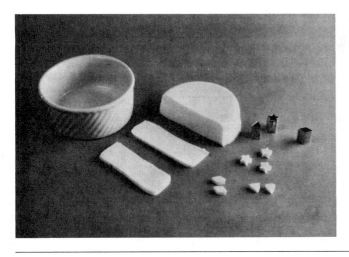

FIGURE 4.1. **To make royales for consommé garnish, unmold the cooled custard, slice, and cut with small cutters.**

FLAVORED ROYALES

		U.S.		Metric	
	YIELD:	**12 oz**	**24 oz**	*335 g*	*675 g*
Ingredients					
Flavoring ingredient (see variations)		3½ oz	7 oz	*100 g*	*200 g*
Béchamel sauce, cold		1½ oz	3 oz	*45 g*	*90 g*
Milk or cream		3 oz	6 oz	*1 dl*	*2 dl*
Whole eggs		1	2	*1*	*2*
Egg yolks		3	6	*3*	*6*
Salt					

Procedure:

1. Purée the flavoring ingredient with the béchamel by forcing them through a fine sieve.

2. Combine with the remaining ingredients and mix well.

3. Continue as you would for plain royales.

Note: If the flavoring ingredient is too dry to purée easily, you may purée it first in a food processor, combine with the liquid and egg, and then force this mixture through a sieve. If the flavoring ingredient is very liquid, an additional egg or eggs may be needed.

Variations

Chicken Royale

Use cooked chicken breast as the flavoring ingredient.

Fish Royale

Use cooked white fish, such as sole, as the flavoring ingredient.

Game Royale

Use cooked game as the flavoring ingredient. Substitute espagnole sauce or demiglaze for the béchamel.

Vegetable Royale

Use any appropriate vegetable, such as carrots, green peas, celery, leeks, tomato purée, or spinach. Cook the vegetable by stewing it in butter until tender, taking care not to brown it.

VEGETABLE BROTH

		U.S.		Metric	
Ingredients	YIELD:	1 qt	1 gal	1 l	4 l
Onion		4 oz	1 lb	125 g	500 g
Leeks		8 oz	2 lb	250 g	1 kg
Carrots		8 oz	2 lb	250 g	1 kg
Celery		4 oz	1 lb	125 g	500 g
Garlic cloves		½	2	½	2
Mushrooms		8 oz	2 lb	250 g	1 kg
Tomatoes		4 oz	1 lb	125 g	500 g
Water		3 pt	6 qt	1.5 l	6 l
Bay leaf		¼	1	¼	1
Peppercorns		2	8	2	8
Thyme		pinch	½ tsp	pinch	0.5 g
Parsley stems		4	16	4	16

Procedure:

1. Wash and trim the vegetables and chop coarsely.

2. Combine all ingredients in a stock pot. Bring to a boil. Reduce the heat and simmer, uncovered, about 30 minutes.

3. Strain and cool.

Variations

If desired, sweat the vegetables in butter before adding the water.

For a brown vegetable stock, sauté the onions until caramelized. Add the remaining vegetables and proceed as in the basic recipe.

Broths flavored with individual vegetables are made by the same procedure. Use a large quantity of the desired vegetable and omit the remaining vegetables in the basic recipe. Add fresh herbs and peppercorns as desired. In the case of mushroom broth and shallot broth, brown the vegetable well in butter before adding the water.

RAGOUT OF SHELLFISH WITH VEGETABLES

	YIELD:	U.S.		Metric	
		1 qt	**1 gal**	*1 l*	*4 l*
Ingredients					
Butter		½ oz	2 oz	*15 g*	*60 g*
Onion		2 oz	8 oz	*60 g*	*250 g*
Carrot		2 oz	8 oz	*60 g*	*250 g*
Turnip		1 oz	4 oz	*30 g*	*125 g*
Savoy cabbage		1 oz	4 oz	*30 g*	*125 g*
Garlic		small clove	large clove	*small clove*	*large clove*
Fish stock or vegetable stock		1 pt	2 qt	*5 dl*	*2 l*
Canned tomatoes, drained		2 oz	8 oz	*60 g*	*250 g*
Sea scallops		4 oz	1 lb	*125 g*	*500 g*
Small shrimp		5 oz	1 lb 4 oz	*150 g*	*600 g*
Butter					
Mussels or small clams		8	32	*8*	*32*
White wine		2 oz	8 oz	*60 ml*	*2.5 dl*
Snow pea pods		8–16	32–64	*8–16*	*32–64*
Salt					
White pepper					

Mise en Place:

1. Cut the onion, carrot, and turnip into small dice.
2. Shred the cabbage.
3. Mince the garlic.
4. Dice the tomato.
5. Cut the scallops into quarters.
6. Peel and devein the shrimp.
7. Clean the mussels or clams. Steam them in the wine until they open. Remove them from the shells and reserve them. Strain and reserve the liquid.
8. Clean the snow peas. Blanch them in boiling water for a few seconds. Drain and cool under cold water. Drain and reserve.

Cooking/Finishing:

1. Heat the butter in a soup pot. Add the onion, carrot, and turnip and cook them slowly for a few minutes. Add the cabbage and garlic. Cook another few minutes.
2. Add the stock, tomato, and the liquid from the mussels or clams. Bring to a boil and then reduce the heat to a simmer. Simmer until the vegetables are tender.
3. Meanwhile, sweat the scallops and shrimp in a little butter just until they are firm.
4. At the last minute, add the scallops, shrimp, mussels, and peas to the soup. Season.

MUSHROOM SOUP

		U.S.		Metric	
YIELD:		**1 qt**	**1 gal**	*1 l*	*4 l*
Ingredients					
Mushrooms		12 oz	3 lb	*375 g*	*1.5 kg*
Butter		½ oz	2 oz	*15 g*	*60 g*
Onion		2 oz	8 oz	*60 g*	*250 g*
Leek		2 oz	8 oz	*60 g*	*250 g*
Carrot		2 oz	8 oz	*60 g*	*250 g*
Celery		1 oz	4 oz	*30 g*	*125 g*
Butter		½ oz	2 oz	*15 g*	*60 g*
Strong brown stock		1 ½ pt	3 qt	*7.5 dl*	*3 l*
Madeira or sherry		1 oz	4 oz	*30 ml*	*125 ml*
Salt					
Pepper					
Chopped parsley, chives, or chervil		1 tbsp	4 tbsp	*4 g*	*15 g*

Mise en Place:

1. Chop the mushrooms fine.
2. Cut the rest of the vegetables brunoise.

Cooking/Finishing:

1. Sauté the mushrooms in the butter until all the liquid has evaporated and the mushrooms are dry.
2. In a separate pot, sweat the vegetables in butter.
3. Add the mushrooms and the stock. Simmer 15 to 20 minutes.
4. Add the madeira and season to taste.
5. Just before serving, add the chopped herbs.

Variations

In place of some or all of the plain cultivated mushrooms, use an assortment of wild or exotic mushrooms. See Chapter 10 for information on mushroom varieties.

Purée and strain the soup if desired.

Add cream to the soup just before serving, if desired. Use about 4 oz per quart of soup (12 cl per liter).

Use chicken velouté, thinned out with a little chicken stock, in place of the brown stock.

Mushroom Soup with Cèpes

Mushrooms	8 oz	2 lb	*250 g*	*1 kg*
Dried cèpes	1 oz	4 oz	*30 g*	*125 g*

Reduce the mushrooms to the quantity indicated. Soak the cèpes in hot water until soft. Drain. Strain the liquid and chop the cèpes. Add them and the liquid to the simmering soup.

MOREL AND LIVER PÂTÉ SOUP

		U.S.		Metric	
YIELD:		**1 qt**	**1 gal**	*1 l*	*4 l*
Ingredients					
Onions		1 oz	4 oz	*30 g*	*125 g*
Celery		1 oz	4 oz	*30 g*	*125 g*
Carrot		1 oz	4 oz	*30 g*	*125 g*
Butter		½ oz	2 oz	*15 g*	*60 g*
Dried morels		½ oz	2 oz	*15 g*	*60 g*
Hot water		4 oz	1 pt	*125 ml*	*5 dl*
Pâté de foie gras or other good-quality, firm, smooth, mild liver pâté		3 oz	12 oz	*100 g*	*400 g*
Strong consommé or chicken stock		1 qt	1 gal	*1 l*	*4 l*

Mise en Place:

1. Cut the vegetables neatly into brunoise.

2. Soak the morels in hot water until they are soft. Simmer them in their soaking liquid a few minutes until they are tender. Drain them, squeeze them out gently, and reserve them. Strain and reserve the soaking liquid.

3. Cut the pâté into ½-inch (1-cm) dice.

Finishing/Presentation:

1. Bring the consommé to a boil. Add the mushroom liquid. Adjust the seasoning of the liquid.

2. Divide all the solid ingredients among hot soup cups or soup plates. Add the hot consommé and serve.

Variations

Mushroom and Pâté Soup

Use part dried mushrooms and part fresh cultivated mushrooms sliced and sautéed in butter.

Morel or Mushroom and Foie Gras Soup

Use fresh foie gras instead of the pâté.

Truffle Soup

Omit the morels and add fresh, sliced black truffles to the soup.

Morel or Mushroom and Giblet Soup

Use cooked giblets of chicken or other poultry in place of the pâté. Increase the quantity of meat as desired. Flavor with a dash of madeira.

Morel or Mushroom and Duck Soup

Use cooked duck meat in place of the pâté. Increase the quantity of meat as desired. Flavor with a dash of madeira.

CREAM OF EGGPLANT SOUP

		U.S.		Metric	
YIELD:		**1 qt**	**1 gal**	*1 l*	*4 l*
Ingredients					
Onion		2 oz	8 oz	*60 g*	*250 g*
Garlic		1 oz	4 oz	*30 g*	*125 g*
Butter		2 oz	8 oz	*60 g*	*250 g*
Flour		1 ½ oz	6 oz	*45 g*	*180 g*
Chicken stock		1 ½ pt	3 qt	*7.5 dl*	*3 l*
Eggplant		1 lb	4 lb	*500 g*	*2 kg*
Milk		4 oz	1 pt	*125 ml*	*5 dl*
Heavy cream		4 oz	1 pt	*125 ml*	*5 dl*
Salt					
White pepper					
Lemon juice					

Mise en Place:

1. Chop the onion and garlic fine.
2. Peel the eggplant. Cut into small dice.

Cooking/Finishing:

1. Cook the onion and garlic in butter until soft. Do not let them brown.
2. Stir in the flour to make a roux. Cook the roux but keep it white.
3. Whip in the stock and bring to a boil.
4. Add the eggplant. Simmer until tender.
5. Purée and strain the soup.
6. Heat the milk and cream. Stir them into the soup.
7. Season to taste with salt, pepper, and lemon juice.

Variation

Curried Cream of Eggplant Soup

Ground coriander		¼ tsp	1 tsp	*0.5 g*	*2 g*
Ground cumin		¼ tsp	1 tsp	*0.5 g*	*2 g*
Turmeric		¼ tsp	1 tsp	*0.5 g*	*2 g*
Cayenne		pinch	½ tsp	*pinch*	*1 g*

Sauté the spices with the onion and garlic.

CREAM OF BLACK WALNUT SOUP

		U.S.		Metric	
	YIELD:	**1 qt**	**1 gal**	*1 l*	*4 l*
Ingredients					
Onion		2 oz	8 oz	*60 g*	*250 g*
Butter		2 oz	8 oz	*60 g*	*250 g*
Flour		1 oz	4 oz	*30 g*	*125 g*
Chicken stock or vegetable broth		1 pt 12 oz	7 pt	*9 dl*	*3.5 l*
Black walnuts		6 oz	1 ½ lb	*200 g*	*750 g*
Milk		6 oz	1 ½ pt	*2 dl*	*7.5 dl*
Heavy cream		6 oz	1 ½ pt	*2 dl*	*7.5 dl*
Salt					
White pepper					
Garnish:					
Walnut pieces		1–2 oz	4–8 oz	*30–60 g*	*125–250 g*
Chives		1 tbsp	4 tbsp	*15 ml*	*3 cl*

Mise en Place:

1. Chop the onion.
2. Toast the walnuts in a hot oven for a few minutes. Cool and grind them.

Cooking/Finishing:

1. Cook the onion slowly in the butter without letting it brown.
2. Add the flour to make a roux. Cook the roux but keep it white.
3. Whip in the stock. Bring to a boil. Add the ground walnuts and simmer 20 minutes.
4. Strain the soup through cheesecloth. Squeeze the solids in the cheesecloth to extract all liquid.
5. Reheat the soup. Heat the milk and cream and add them to the soup. Season.
6. Add the garnish to each serving.

Variations

Other nuts, such as hazelnuts, pecans, or English walnuts, can be substituted for the black walnuts.

CREAM OF ASPARAGUS AND MOREL SOUP

		U.S.		Metric	
YIELD:		**1 qt**	**1 gal**	*1 l*	*4 l*
Ingredients					
Asparagus		1 lb 12 oz	7 lb	*800 g*	*3.5 kg*
Dried morels		⅓ oz	1 ⅓ oz	*10 g*	*40 g*
Hot water		4 oz	1 pt	*125 ml*	*5 dl*
Shallots		1 oz	4 oz	*30 g*	*125 g*
Butter		½ oz	2 oz	*15 g*	*60 g*
Flour		4 tsp	1 ⅓ oz	*10 g*	*40 g*
Chicken stock		1 pt	2 qt	*5 dl*	*2 l*
Heavy cream		4 oz	1 pt	*125 ml*	*5 dl*
Salt					
White pepper					

Mise en Place:

1. Trim off the hard bottoms of the asparagus. Wash the asparagus and cut into 1-inch pieces.

2. Soak the morels in hot water until soft. Squeeze out the morels, reserving the soaking water. Rinse the morels in cold water. Squeeze dry and set aside. Carefully strain the soaking water through cheesecloth and set aside.

3. Peel and mince the shallots.

Cooking/Finishing:

1. Sweat the shallots in butter until soft.

2. Stir in the flour to make a roux. Do not brown.

3. Add the chicken stock and bring to a boil. Add the asparagus and the mushroom liquid. Simmer until the asparagus is about half cooked.

4. Set aside one mushroom per portion as garnish, choosing the best-looking ones, and add the rest of the mushrooms to the soup. Continue to cook until the asparagus is tender.

5. Remove a little of the liquid from the soup and simmer the mushrooms reserved for garnish. They will take only a few minutes to cook. When tender, drain the mushrooms and set aside. Return the liquid to the soup.

6. Purée the soup. Force it through a fine sieve so that the soup is perfectly smooth.

7. Heat the cream and add it to the soup.

8. Season to taste with salt and white pepper.

9. When serving, garnish each portion with one morel.

Variation

If you do not desire to force the soup through a sieve, the asparagus should be peeled so that there are no bits of fibrous peel in the soup. The total yield will be slightly greater if the soup is not strained.

STILTON CHEESE SOUP

		U.S.		Metric	
YIELD:		1 qt	1 gal	1 l	4 l
Ingredients					
Onion, chopped		2 oz	8 oz	60 g	250 g
Leek, white part, chopped		2 oz	8 oz	60 g	250 g
Garlic, minced		1 tsp	4 tsp	2 g	8 g
Butter		2 oz	8 oz	60 g	250 g
Flour		1 ½ oz	6 oz	45 g	180 g
Chicken stock		1 ½ pt	3 qt	7.5 dl	3 l
White wine		2 oz	8 oz	60 ml	2.5 dl
Stilton cheese, crumbled		8 oz	2 lb	250 g	1 kg
Heavy cream		8 oz	1 qt	2.5 dl	1 l
Salt					
White pepper					

Procedure:

1. Cook the vegetables slowly in the butter without browning.
2. Add the flour to make a roux.
3. Whip in the stock and the wine. Bring to a boil.
4. Add the cheese and stir until it is melted. Simmer the soup 10 to 15 minutes.
5. Strain the soup through a fine sieve. Press down on the solids to extract all the liquid.
6. Reheat the soup. Heat the cream and add it to the soup. Season.

Variations

For slightly different flavors, other blue cheeses can be used in place of the stilton.

Stilton and Cheddar Cheese Soup

Use half stilton and half cheddar cheese.

CURRIED CREAM SOUP WITH APPLES

		U.S.		Metric	
YIELD:		**1 qt**	**1 gal**	*1 l*	*4 l*
Ingredients					
Onion		4 oz	1 lb	*125 g*	*500 g*
Celery		2 oz	8 oz	*60 g*	*250 g*
Garlic		1 clove	4 cloves	*1 clove*	*4 cloves*
Butter		2 oz	8 oz	*60 g*	*250 g*
Curry powder		2 tbsp	½ cup	*15 g*	*60 g*
Flour		1 ½ oz	6 oz	*45 g*	*180 g*
Chicken stock		1 ½ pt	3 qt	*7.5 dl*	*3 l*
Tomatoes, fresh or canned		8 oz	2 lb	*250 g*	*1 kg*
Bay leaf		1	4	*1*	*4*
Apples		4 oz	1 lb	*125 g*	*500 g*
Heavy cream		4 oz	1 pt	*125 ml*	*5 dl*
Salt					
White pepper					

Mise en Place:

1. Chop the onion, celery, and garlic.
2. Chop the tomatoes, reserving the juices.
3. Peel and core the apple and cut into small dice.

Cooking/Finishing:

1. Cook the onion, celery, and garlic slowly in the butter without browning.
2. Add the curry powder and cook another minute.
3. Add the flour to make a roux.
4. Whip in the stock and bring to a boil. Add the tomato and bay leaf. Simmer until the vegetables are tender.
5. Remove the bay leaf. Purée and strain the soup.
6. Add the apples and bring the soup to a boil. Simmer a few minutes, until the apples are cooked but still slightly crisp.
7. Heat the cream and stir it in. Season.

Variation

Senegalese Soup

Omit the tomatoes and substitute additional chicken stock. Omit the apples and add desired quantity of cooked chicken cut into dice. If desired, finish the soup with an egg-yolk-and-cream liaison instead of the cream.

SHRIMP BISQUE

	YIELD:	U.S.		Metric	
		1 qt	**1 gal**	*1 l*	*4 l*
Ingredients					
Onions		1 oz	4 oz	*30 g*	*125 g*
Carrots		1 oz	4 oz	*30 g*	*125 g*
Butter		½ oz	2 oz	*15 g*	*60 g*
Small shrimp, shells on		8 oz	2 lb	*250 g*	*1 kg*
Bay leaf		small piece	½	*small piece*	*½*
Thyme		pinch	½ tsp	*pinch*	*½ tsp*
Parsley stems		3	12	*3*	*12*
Tomato paste		1 tbsp	2 oz	*15 g*	*60 g*
Burnt brandy (see Mise en Place, step 3)		1 oz	4 oz	*30 ml*	*125 ml*
White wine		3 oz	12 oz	*1 dl*	*3.5 dl*
Fish velouté		1 pt	2 qt	*5 dl*	*2 l*
Fish stock		8 oz	1 qt	*2.5 dl*	*1 l*
Heavy cream		4 oz	1 pt	*125 ml*	*5 dl*
Salt					
White pepper					

Mise en Place:

1. Chop the onions and carrots very fine.
2. Rinse and drain the shrimp. Do not peel them.
3. To prepare burnt brandy, heat brandy in a small pan and flame it to burn off the alcohol.

Cooking/Finishing:

1. Sauté the onions and carrots lightly in butter.
2. Add the shrimp, bay leaf, thyme, and parsley stems. Sauté until the shrimp turn red.
3. Stir in the tomato paste.
4. Add the brandy and wine. Simmer until reduced by half.
5. Remove the shrimp. Peel and devein them. Return the shells to the saucepan. Cut the shrimp into small dice and reserve for garnish.
6. Add the velouté and stock to the pan. Simmer 10 to 15 minutes.
7. Strain the soup and reheat it. Heat the cream and add it to the soup. Season to taste.
8. Add the diced shrimp.

Variations

Other shellfish, such as lobster or crab, can be used instead of shrimp.

Instead of using fish velouté, you can use all stock. Thicken the soup with beurre manié or with a little rice cooked with the soup and puréed.

Paprika can be used instead of tomato paste to color the soup. If you have red lobster roe, this can be forced through a sieve and added to the soup.

PURÉE OF SWEET POTATO SOUP

		U.S.		Metric	
YIELD:		**1 qt**	**1 gal**	*1 l*	*4 l*
Ingredients					
Onion		2 oz	8 oz	*60 g*	*250 g*
Carrot		2 oz	8 oz	*60 g*	*250 g*
Butter		½ oz	2 oz	*15 g*	*60 g*
Chicken stock		1 ½ pt	3 qt	*7.5 dl*	*3 l*
Sweet potatoes		1 lb	4 lb	*500 g*	*2 kg*
Heavy cream		4 oz	1 pt	*125 ml*	*5 dl*
Nutmeg					
Salt					
White pepper					

Mise en Place:

1. Chop the onion and carrot.
2. Peel and dice the sweet potatoes.

Cooking/Finishing:

1. Cook the onion and carrot slowly in the butter without letting them brown.
2. Add the stock and sweet potatoes. Bring to a boil and simmer until the vegetables are tender.
3. Purée the soup.
4. Heat the cream and add it to the soup. If the soup is too thick, thin it out with a little hot stock or water.
5. Season with a dash of nutmeg and with salt and pepper.

COLD CORN AND CHILI CREAM SOUP

		U.S.		Metric	
YIELD:		**1 qt**	**1 gal**	*1 l*	*4 l*
Ingredients					
Onion		2 oz	8 oz	*60 g*	*250 g*
Butter		2 oz	8 oz	*60 g*	*250 g*
Flour		1 oz	4 oz	*30 g*	*125 g*
Chicken stock		1 ½ pt	3 qt	*7.5 dl*	*3 l*
Fresh corn kernels (see Mise en Place, step 2)		8 oz	2 lb	*250 g*	*1 kg*
Jalapeño peppers		½–1 oz	2–4 oz	*15–30 g*	*60–125 g*
Salt					
White pepper					
Heavy cream		6 oz	1 ½ pt	*2 dl*	*75 cl*
Garnish:					
Corn kernels		1 oz	4 oz	*30 g*	*125 g*
Jalapeño pepper					

Mise en Place:

1. Chop the onion.

2. To prepare the fresh corn, cut the kernels from the cob. Scrape the cob with the back of the knife to get the milky residue of the kernels. Reserve some of the best whole kernels for the garnish. Weigh the remaining kernels and the scraped residue for cooking with the soup.

3. Steam the corn for the garnish (not for the soup) for a minute or two to cook it.

4. Cut the jalapeño in half lengthwise and remove the stem end, seeds, and membranes. Cut a little of the pepper into neat brunoise for the garnish; you will need less than ½ tsp per portion. Chop the remainder of the pepper.

Cooking/Finishing:

1. Cook the onions slowly in the butter. Add the flour to make a roux.

2. Whip in the stock. Add the corn and jalapeño. Season with a little salt and pepper. Simmer until the vegetables are tender, about 15 minutes.

3. Purée and strain the soup. Chill the soup.

4. Just before serving, add the cream. Taste carefully and adjust the seasoning.

5. Garnish each portion by sprinkling it with a few corn kernels and a bit of the jalapeño.

PUMPKIN SOUP

		U.S.		Metric	
	YIELD:	**1 qt**	**1 gal**	*1 l*	*4 l*
Ingredients					
Onions		4 oz	1 lb	*125 g*	*500 g*
Carrots		2 oz	8 oz	*60 g*	*250 g*
Butter		½ oz	2 oz	*15 g*	*60 g*
White wine		2 oz	8 oz	*6 cl*	*25 cl*
Chicken stock		1 ½ pt	3 qt	*75 cl*	*3 l*
Pumpkin meat		10 oz	2 lb 8 oz	*300 g*	*1.2 kg*
French bread		2 oz	8 oz	*60 g*	*250 g*
Butter		1 oz	4 oz	*30 g*	*125 g*
Heavy cream		2–4 oz	½–1 pt	*6–12 cl*	*25–50 cl*
Garnish:					
Additional croutons (see Mise en Place, step 3)					

Mise en Place:

1. Chop the onions and carrots.
2. Dice the pumpkin meat.
3. Slice the bread and fry the slices in butter until golden brown on both sides. If desired, prepare additional croutons for garnishing the soup.

Cooking/Finishing:

1. Cook the onions and carrots slowly in butter without browning.
2. Add the wine and chicken stock. Bring to a boil.
3. Add the pumpkin and the browned croutons. Simmer until the vegetables are tender.
4. Purée the soup.
5. Heat the cream and add it to the soup.
6. At service time, garnish each portion with one or two croutons.

Variations

Winter Squash Soup

Substitute winter squash (such as butternut, hubbard, or buttercup) for the pumpkin.

Summer Squash Soup

Yellow summer squash	1 lb	4 lb	*500 g*	*2 kg*

Substitute the indicated quantity of summer squash for the pumpkin. Omit the carrots.

Mixed Winter Vegetable Soup

Turnip	2 oz	8 oz	*60 g*	*250 g*
Celery root	4 oz	1 lb	*125 g*	*500 g*
Leeks	3 oz	12 oz	*90 g*	*375 g*
Cauliflower, cabbage, or kohlrabi	2 oz	8 oz	*60 g*	*250 g*
Parsnips	2 oz	8 oz	*60 g*	*250 g*

Omit the pumpkin and add these vegetables to the soup at the same time that you add the onions and carrots. (You may need a little additional butter to cook them.) Increase the amount of stock, if necessary, to thin the soup to proper consistency.

Chestnut Soup

Substitute canned or fresh whole chestnuts (peeled) for the pumpkin. Use only half the quantity of bread croutons for thickening the soup.

HONEYDEW MELON SOUP

		U.S.		Metric	
YIELD:		**1 qt**	**1 gal**	*1 l*	*4 l*
Ingredients					
Honeydew melon		4 lb	16 lb	*2 kg*	*8 kg*
Sugar		2 ½ oz	10 oz	*75 g*	*300 g*
Dry sherry		3 oz	12 oz	*1 dl*	*4 dl*
Lime juice		¾ oz	3 oz	*25 ml*	*1 dl*

Procedure:

1. Cut open the melons, discard the seeds, and cut out all the flesh from the rind (you should get about 50 percent yield).
2. Purée the melon with the remaining ingredients. Strain.

Variation

Canteloup Soup

Substitute canteloup for the honeydew melon.

CHILLED HERB SOUP

		U.S.		Metric	
	YIELD:	**1 qt**	**1 gal**	*1 l*	*4 l*
Ingredients					
Butter		½ oz	2 oz	*15 g*	*60 g*
Sorrel, shredded		2 oz	8 oz	*60 g*	*250 g*
Parsley, chopped		2 tbsp	½ cup	*30 ml*	*125 ml*
Fresh tarragon, chopped		2 tbsp	½ cup	*30 ml*	*125 ml*
Fresh basil, shredded		2 tbsp	½ cup	*30 ml*	*125 ml*
Chives, chopped		2 tbsp	½ cup	*30 ml*	*125 ml*
Chicken stock		1 ½ pt	3 qt	*7.5 dl*	*3 l*
Liaison:					
Egg yolks		4	16	*4*	*16*
Heavy cream		8 oz	1 qt	*2.5 dl*	*1 l*
Salt					
White pepper					

Procedure:

1. Heat the butter in a saucepan. Add the sorrel and other herbs. Cook until they are wilted.

2. Add the stock and bring to a boil. Reduce the heat to a bare simmer.

3. Beat the egg yolks and cream together. Temper with a little of the hot soup. Carefully stir this into the soup. Heat gently until the soup is slightly thickened. Do not let it boil or it will curdle.

4. Season the soup well. Chill it.

5. When the soup is cold, taste for seasonings and adjust if necessary.

Variations

This soup is best if only fresh herbs are used, but you can still make it if one or two of the fresh herbs are not available. If only dried herbs are available, use one-third of the quantity listed in the recipe.

Potage Germiny

Sorrel	3 oz	12 oz	*90 g*	*375 g*
Egg yolks	6	24	*6*	*24*

Increase the sorrel and the egg yolks to the quantities indicated. Omit the rest of the herbs. Serve the soup hot.

COLD TOMATO SOUP

		U.S.		Metric	
	YIELD:	**1 qt**	**1 gal**	*1 l*	*4 l*
Ingredients					
Ripe tomatoes		2 lb	8 lb	*1 kg*	*4 kg*
Celery, diced		2 oz	8 oz	*60 g*	*250 g*
Tomato paste		1 oz	4 oz	*30 g*	*125 g*
Olive oil		1 oz	4 oz	*30 ml*	*125 ml*
Sugar		¼ tsp	1 tsp	*1 g*	*4 g*
Salt					
White pepper					
Brown stock or chicken stock (optional)		4 oz	1 pt	*125 ml*	*5 dl*
Red pepper, small dice		2 oz	8 oz	*60 g*	*250 g*
Green pepper, small dice		2 oz	8 oz	*60 g*	*250 g*

Procedure:

1. Peel, core, and quarter the tomatoes.
2. Purée the tomatoes, celery, tomato paste, olive oil, and sugar in a blender or food processor. Pass through a strainer.
3. Season to taste.
4. If desired, add some cold stock to the soup to thin it out slightly and to add another flavor dimension.
5. Add the diced peppers.

Variations

If the tomatoes are bland and not acidic enough, add a few drops of lemon juice or red wine vinegar to the soup to liven up the taste.

Tomato Yogurt Soup

Plain yogurt		8 oz	1 qt	*2.5 dl*	*1 l*

Add the yogurt to the soup.

Curried Tomato Soup

Plain yogurt		8 oz	1 qt	*2.5 dl*	*1 l*
Curry powder		1 ½ tsp	2 tbsp	*3 g*	*12 g*

Add the yogurt and curry powder to the soup.

Moroccan Tomato Soup

Garlic, minced	1 tsp	4 tsp	5 g	20 g
Paprika	1 ½ tsp	2 tbsp	3 g	12 g
Ground cumin	1 tsp	4 tsp	2 g	8 g
Cayenne	pinch	¼ tsp	pinch	0.5 g
Olive oil	1 tbsp	2 oz	15 ml	60 ml

Stir the garlic and spices into the olive oil in a small sauté pan. Cook over low heat just until aromatic. Remove from the heat, cool slightly, and add to the tomato soup.

PETITE MARMITE

		U.S.		Metric	
PORTIONS:		4	16	4	16
Ingredients					
Beef shank meat		1 ½ lb	6 lb	750 g	3 kg
Chicken parts or stewing hen parts		1 lb	4 lb	500 g	2 kg
White or brown stock		3 pt	6 qt	1.5 l	6 l
Salt					
Pepper					
Carrots		4 oz	1 lb	125 g	500 g
Turnips		3 oz	12 oz	90 g	375 g
Leeks, white part		4 oz	1 lb	125 g	500 g
Celery		2 oz	8 oz	60 g	250 g
Cabbage		8 oz	2 lb	250 g	1 kg
Marrow bones		4 pieces	16 pieces	4 pieces	16 pieces
Small toast slices					

Mise en Place:

1. Leave the meat whole or in large pieces. Blanch it by placing it in cold water, bringing it to a boil, then draining and rinsing. The purpose of this is to remove impurities that would cloud the broth.

2. Blanch the hen or chicken.

3. Cut the marrow bones into 2- or 3-inch (5 to 7 cm) pieces, so that you have one piece per portion. Wrap the bones in pieces of cheesecloth to hold the marrow in as it cooks.

4. Prepare the vegetables by cutting them into neat shapes for serving. Carrots and turnips for this dish are traditionally tournéed (cut into oval or olive shapes). Leave the leek in relatively large pieces so that it will not fall apart. The cabbage should be in wedges.

Cooking/Finishing:

1. Place the meat in a stock pot. If you are using stewing hen, add it to the pot; but if you are using tender chicken, do not add it yet.

2. Add the stock and bring to a simmer. Season very lightly with salt and pepper. Do not add too much, because the liquid will be reduced and the salt will be concentrated.

3. Simmer slowly as though you were making stock, skimming the surface regularly.

4. Continue cooking very slowly until the meat is almost tender. Depending on the meat, this may take from 2 to 4 hours.

5. Add the tender chicken, if you are using it, and all the vegetables except the cabbage. Continue cooking until all ingredients are tender.

6. In a separate pot, steam the cabbage with a little of the broth.

7. In a separate pot, poach the marrow bones with a little of the broth.

8. Remove the meat and vegetables from the broth and keep them warm. Cut the meat into smaller pieces for serving.

9. Strain the broth through cheesecloth into another pot. Degrease the broth as necessary (traditionally, the broth is not degreased completely but is served, like hearty peasant fare, with a few drops of fat floating on it). If necessary, boil the broth until it is reduced to about 8 to 12 oz (25 to 40 cl) per portion. Adjust the seasoning.

Presentation:

Serve the meat, vegetables (except cabbage), and broth in earthenware pots or casseroles. Use either large ones, to be portioned in the dining room, or small individual casseroles. On separate plates or platters, serve the marrow bones, the cabbage, and the slices of toast (which are to be eaten with the marrow).

"PETITE MARMITE" OF SCALLOPS AND CHICKEN

		U.S.		Metric	
YIELD:		3 pt	6 qt	1.5 l	6 l
Ingredients					
Carrots		4 oz	1 lb	125 g	500 g
Turnips		2 oz	8 oz	60 g	250 g
Green beans		2 oz	8 oz	60 g	250 g
Scallions		1 oz	4 oz	30 g	125 g
Butter		½ oz	2 oz	15 g	60 g
Tarragon		1 tsp	4 tsp	1 g	4 g
Chicken breast		6 oz	1 ½ lb	200 g	750 g
Scallops		6 oz	1 ½ lb	200 g	750 g
Chicken stock, hot		1 qt	1 gal	1 l	4 l
Salt					
White pepper					
Chopped parsley or chives					
Sour cream or crème fraîche					

Mise en Place:

1. Cut the carrots and turnips into julienne.

2. Trim the green beans (preferably very young, slender ones) and cut into 2-inch (5-cm) lengths.

3. Cut the scallions diagonally into ¾-inch (2-cm) lengths; include some of the green part.

4. In separate pans, boil (or steam) the carrots, turnips, green beans, and scallions until they are cooked but still crisp. Drain and cool quickly under cold water.

5. Cut the chicken meat into strips about 2 inches (5 cm) long and ¼ inch (6 mm) thick.

6. If you are using bay scallops, leave them whole or cut them in half, depending on their size. If you are using sea scallops, slice them across the grain ¼ inch (6 mm) thick.

Cooking/Finishing:

1. Heat the butter in a saucepan or soup pot and add the vegetables and tarragon. Cook slowly for about a minute, coating them well with butter.

2. Add the chicken and scallops. Stir and cook until they are about half cooked.

3. Add the hot chicken stock. Bring just to a simmer. Cook slowly for a minute or two, until the scallops and chicken are cooked.

4. Season to taste.

Presentation:

Serve in broad soup plates. Sprinkle with the chopped herbs. Serve the cream on the side, to be added by the diner.

GULYAS

		U.S.		*Metric*	
YIELD:		**1 ½ qt**	**1 ½ gal**	*1.5 l*	*6 l*
Ingredients					
Pork fatback or bacon		1 oz	4 oz	*30 g*	*125 g*
Onions		4 oz	1 lb	*125 g*	*500 g*
Beef chuck or shank		12 oz	3 lb	*375 g*	*1.5 kg*
Garlic cloves		1	4	*1*	*4*
Caraway seeds		¼ tsp	1 tsp	*0.5 g*	*2 g*
Hungarian paprika		1 tbsp	4 tbsp	*6 g*	*25 g*
Tomato paste (optional)		1 ½ tsp	2 tbsp	*8 g*	*30 g*
Water or brown stock, hot		2 ½ pt	5 qt	*1.25 l*	*5 l*
Potatoes		8 oz	2 lb	*250 g*	*1 kg*
Salt					
Pepper					

Mise en Place:

1. Cut the fatback into fine dice or grind it.

2. Cut the onions, beef, and potatoes into medium dice.

3. Mince the garlic.

Cooking/Finishing:

1. Render the fatback in a heavy pot. Add the onions and sauté them without browning.

2. Add the beef and cook it with the onions over low heat for about 10 minutes.

3. Add the garlic, caraway seeds, paprika, and tomato paste. Stir them in well.

4. Add the liquid. Simmer until the beef is almost tender. This may take about 1 hour or more, depending on the type and quality of the meat.

5. Add the potatoes and simmer until done. Season to taste.

Variation

Diced green peppers are often cooked in a traditional gulyas.

FISH SOUP MARSEILLES STYLE

		U.S.		Metric	
PORTIONS:		**4**	**16**	**4**	**16**
Ingredients					
Fish stock		1 qt	4 qt	1 l	4 l
White wine		4 oz	1 pt	125 ml	5 dl
Parsley stems		6	24	6	24
Thyme		¼ tsp	1 tsp	0.5 g	2 g
Bay leaf		½	2	½	2
Fennel seeds		½ tsp	2 tsp	1 g	4 g
Orange peel		1 strip	4 strips	1 strip	4 strips
Olive oil		1 oz	4 oz	30 ml	125 ml
Onion, chopped fine		2 oz	8 oz	60 g	250 g
Leek, white part, chopped fine		2 oz	8 oz	60 g	250 g
Garlic, minced		1 tsp	4 tsp	5 g	20 g
Saffron		1 pinch	1 tsp	1 pinch	1 g
Crushed red pepper		¼ tsp	1 tsp	0.5 g	2 g
Tomatoes, peeled, seeded, and chopped fine		6 oz	1 lb 8 oz	175 g	700 g
Salt					
Whole fish, assorted (see note)		2–3 lb	8–12 lb	1–1.5 kg	4–5 kg
Toasted french bread slices					
Garlic mayonnaise (aioli)(p. 74)					
Rouille (p. 76)					

Note: Select at least three or four varieties of fresh fish, depending on what is best in the market. The more varieties of fish chosen, the more flavorful the soup will be. Whole fish, with heads, are traditional, but fish steaks and dressed fish can also be used. If steaks and dressed fish are selected, use a smaller quantity, since the edible portion will be greater. The following are possible choices of fish: red snapper, monkfish, tilefish, sea bass, porgy, haddock, eel, grouper, and rockfish. If desired, shellfish (such as lobster and shrimp) can also be included.

Mise en Place:

1. Combine the fish stock, wine, parsley stems, thyme, bay leaf, fennel seeds, and orange peel. Simmer 15 minutes. Strain.

2. Clean and prepare the fish as necessary.

Cooking:

1. Heat the olive oil in a brazier or other pot large enough to hold all the fish. Add the onion, leek, and garlic to the oil and sweat.

2. Add the saffron and red pepper. Stir in and cook for a few seconds.

3. Add the tomatoes and the prepared broth. Simmer 5 or 10 minutes, until the flavors are well blended. Season to taste with salt. If desired, purée the broth and vegetables.

4. Add the fish. Simmer gently until the fish is just cooked.

Presentation:

1. The soup can be presented in either of two ways: (1) present the fish and broth together in a large bowl or tureen or (2) remove the fish and serve it on a platter and present the broth in a separate bowl. Either way, the diners serve themselves at the table

2. Present each diner with an empty, hot soup plate on an underliner. Place a basket of toasted and sliced french bread, a bowl of garlic mayonnaise, and a bowl of rouille on the table. The diners place a few slices of toast in the soup plate, add a few pieces of fish, and ladle some soup over the top. Garlic mayonnaise and rouille are stirred into the soup to taste.

SOUTHWESTERN CORN TOMATO CHOWDER

		U.S.		*Metric*	
YIELD:		**1 qt**	**1 gal**	*1 l*	*4 l*
Ingredients					
Oil		½ oz	2 oz	*15 ml*	*6 cl*
Onion, small dice		4 oz	1 lb	*125 g*	*500 g*
Green pepper, small dice		2 oz	8 oz	*60 g*	*250 g*
Garlic, chopped		1 tsp	4 tsp	*2 g*	*8 g*
Ground coriander		½ tsp	2 tsp	*1 g*	*4 g*
Cayenne		¼ tsp	1 tsp	*0.5 g*	*2 g*
Tomatoes (canned or fresh) with juice, chopped		1 lb	4 lb	*500 g*	*2 kg*
Chicken stock		1 pt	2 qt	*5 dl*	*2 l*
Corn kernels		8 oz	2 lb	*250 g*	*1 kg*
Salt					
Garnish:					
Sour cream		2 oz	8 oz	*60 ml*	*2.5 dl*
Grated cheddar cheese		1 oz	4 oz	*30 g*	*125 g*

Procedure

1. Heat the oil in a soup pot and sauté the onion, green pepper, garlic, coriander, and cayenne.

2. Add the tomatoes and stock. Bring to a boil and simmer about 20 minutes.

3. Add the corn and simmer another few minutes. Season to taste.

4. Immediately before serving, top each portion with a spoonful of sour cream and a sprinkling of cheese.

Variations

Chili Corn Chowder					
Chili powder		1 tbsp	4 tbsp	*8 g*	*15 g*

Add the chili powder in step 1.

Corn, Zucchini, and Tomato Chowder

| Zucchini, small dice | 4 oz | 1 lb | 125 g | 500 g |

Add the zucchini at the same time that you add the corn.

CHAPTER

5

Salads, Pastas, and Other First Courses

Not many years ago, the appetizer section of the typical American restaurant menu listed the usual standards: shrimp cocktail, chicken liver pâté, tomato juice cocktail, fruit cocktail, onion soup, and so on. First courses were often seen as nothing more than a way to keep the customer occupied while the cooks prepared the main course.

By contrast, many of today's chefs see the first course as the best place to display their creativity. And diners are often willing or even eager to try something unusual to start their meals, even when they may prefer a more traditional meat (or fish) item with vegetables and starch for their main course. For the chef, this enhanced receptivity means more opportunity to work with a variety of ingredients, including new and unusual ones, and to try innovative combinations.

Two popular types of first-course dishes that have received much attention are salads and pastas. Modern salads far exceed traditional bounds and may include various warm, freshly cooked meats and seafoods as well as vegetables and dressings in innovative combinations. Many of today's pasta creations are distinctly modern and have little in common with old standbys such as spaghetti with tomato sauce or any classic Italian dishes.

The bulk of this chapter concentrates on a variety of specialty salads and pasta dishes. Additional attention is given to a number of other popular hot and cold first courses. Other first-course items, including soups and pâtés, are discussed in other chapters.

Many of the recipes in this chapter call for cooked poultry, meats, seafood, and so on. These recipes rely on your understanding of basic cooking techniques for these items and on cooking techniques discussed in other chapters of this book. These procedures are not repeated in this chapter.

TYPES OF FIRST COURSES

The modern approach to the first course suggests that almost anything goes. There are few limits on what kinds of preparations may appear at the beginning of a meal—that is, many of the techniques and recipes explained throughout this book apply to first courses as well as to main dishes and accompaniments.

First-Course Ideas from Other Chapters

The following types of preparations may be used as first courses. Most of these preparations are discussed in other chapters of this book. To make this list a more complete catalog of first courses, however, items from this chapter are included as well.

Soups. Soups are perennial favorites as first courses and appear on virtually every restaurant menu. Hearty and substantial soups are also offered frequently as luncheon dishes, perhaps accompanied by a salad. Soups are the subject of Chapter 4.

Salads. Modern salads go well beyond a simple serving of lettuce and dressing and may incorporate a variety of meats, seafood, vegetables, cheese, and so on. Innovative presentations as well as nutritional value have made salads one of the most popular types of first courses. Salads are discussed in this chapter, and salad dressings are included with other sauces in Chapter 3.

Pasta dishes. At appropriate portion sizes, pasta dishes are widely popular both as first courses and as main courses. A variety of pasta preparations are included in this chapter.

Vegetable dishes. Although such items as artichoke vinaigrette have long been staples on appetizer menus, most vegetables were long relegated to the role of side dishes. Few people would think of a dish of peas and carrots, for example, as an ideal first course. Today, however, creative cookery and nutritional concerns have combined to make vegetable dishes regular features of the first-course menu. For example, the following types of preparations, as discussed in Chapter 10, are appropriate as first courses. (The last two items in the list, which are based on grains, are often classified with pastas.) In addition, many of the other individual recipes in Chapter 10 can be used as the basis for appetizers.

Grilled vegetables. These are often served in an assortment with a vinaigrette or other appropriate sauce.

Vegetable ragouts and other mixtures. These are especially appropriate in more elaborate presentations such as *en feuilleté* (with puff pastry).

Vegetable gratins. Extra garnish may be desirable to transform gratins from side dishes to first courses. For example, garnish the top of asparagus gratin (see page 528) with slices of thick-cut bacon and thin slices or shavings of parmesan cheese.

Timbales. These are usually served with an appropriate sauce, such as a beurre blanc or a liquid purée of a contrasting vegetable.

Potato galettes, vegetable pancakes (see page 517), chips, or other flat items, stacked or layered with other vegetable preparations or with various hot or cold meat and seafood items. The galettes are used like the layers of puff pastry in a napoleon or like the bread or pastry serving as the base of a tart or pizza. (See, for example, the Napoleon of Salmon Tartare on page 175.)

Risottos.

Polentas.

Seafood dishes. Seafood is generally perceived as lighter than meat or poultry and is often used for appetizers. Nearly any recipe in Chapter 6 can be used as a first course, although in many cases it will be desirable to reduce the portion sizes. Some of the recipes, in fact, are almost always used as first courses rather than main courses. Examples include various oyster dishes and raw-fish items such as Salmon Carpaccio.

Meat, poultry, game, variety meat, and sausage dishes. Meats and poultry are often thought of as "heavy," at least when compared to fish and vegetables. Nevertheless, they can play a role in first courses. Diners who choose a light seafood dish as a main course, for example, often like to start their meals with something meaty.

Among poultry items, grilled duck breast, duck confit, smaller poultry (such as quail and squab), and chicken quenelles are possibilities, especially when served with salad greens or attractive vegetables.

Delicate meat and game dishes, especially those in which vegetables play an important part, are other choices. For example, a few slices of Oriental Beef Steamed in Cabbage Leaves or Roast Saddle of Rabbit Stuffed with Vegetables and Herbs, appropriately garnished, can be attractive first courses.

Sausages are often rich and fatty; however, in small portions and presented in combination with vegetables or greens, they make good appetizers. The recipe on page 452 is one example.

Variety meats such as sweetbreads and kidneys have long played a role on the appetizer menu, while liver is most often used as a main-course item.

Preparation and cooking information for these various food items is found in Chapters 7, 8, and 9.

Pátés, terrines, and other cold appetizer items. Chapter 11 is devoted to a discussion of these dishes, both classic and modern.

Specialty items. Foie gras, caviar, and smoked salmon are natural favorites as appetizers For many people, the best way to serve these delicacies is as simply as possible, with no elaborate accompaniments, garnish, or sauces to detract attention from their basic flavor. Because portion sizes are generally small, the first course is perhaps the most suitable place to enjoy such expensive products.

Planning First Courses

As the preceding discussion implies, no precise distinction can be made between first and main courses. A first course sometimes becomes so elaborate and substantial that it seems just like a main course. The term *appetizer* may no longer be appropriate, because the first course satiates rather than stimulates. It overwhelms and makes the main course less satisfying.

This potential pitfall can be avoided and well-balanced menus can be created through careful planning. The following guidelines aid in developing attractive first courses.

- First courses should be light and stimulating, not heavy and filling. Portion sizes should be generally smaller than for the main course.
- Low-fat foods are less filling than those high in fat. Fats satisfy the appetite quickly. If the first course is too satiating, it detracts from the main course.
- When using high-fat ingredients in first courses, keep the quantities small.
- Flavorful, well-seasoned foods stimulate the appetite more than bland foods do. Fresh herbs and piquant ingredients, such as vinaigrettes and mustard, stimulate the taste buds. Be careful, however, not to overwhelm or deaden the palate with excessively spicy foods.
- To add variety and interest, offer some complex items that combine two or more preparations on one plate—for example, a small portion of a fish item, such as seafood sausage (page 262), garnished with an arrangement of fresh spring vegetables. Remember, however, to keep the items light and the portions fairly small so that they do not look like main courses.
- Attractively presented foods are more appetizing, so pay careful attention to the plating and garnish. The items should look fresh and should be served at the proper temperature.
- Maintain balance and harmony between the first-course selections and the rest of the menu. Main-course selections consisting of large portions of meats and fish can be balanced with appetizing salads or vegetable items as the first course.

SALADS

It is perhaps easier to recognize a salad when you see one than it is to define the term. Modern salads are so varied that it is difficult to frame a definition that includes all of them. But even among more traditional salads we can find exceptions to most definitions.

Do salads necessarily include lettuce or other greens? Do they always contain raw ingredients? Must they contain vegetables? We need look no further than old-fashioned chicken and tuna salads, bean salads, and fruit salads to find exceptions. Are they always cold? Classic hot German potato salad is but one exception from the traditional repertoire.

It might be suggested that salads are different from other foods in that they are served with a salad dressing. But this characteristic fails to distinguish a salad from a cold seafood platter with mayonnaise, for example, or from a meat or fish main course served with a vinaigrette (a popular modern alternative to a more customary sauce based on stock, cream, or tomato purée).

In the absence of any adequate definition, perhaps the only safe route is to define a salad as "anything the chef calls a salad."

Presentation

The essence of salads is freshness. The first and most important rule of salad preparation is to use the best, freshest, and most attractive ingredients possible. A green salad composed of fresh, bright, crisp greens that look as though they have just been picked is one of the most appetizing of first courses. Even when greens are used only in a small quantity as a garnish, they should be selected and handled with care. Other vegetables, cooked or raw, should be fresh and bright. Meats, seafood, and other ingredients should also look fresh, not dry and discolored as though they have been sitting in the refrigerator for days.

Except in such classic preparations as caesar salad, in which romaine is the only lettuce to be used, an assortment of greens is usually most effective. A variety of textures and colors, including shades of green from pale to dark and the reds, yellows, and whites of specialty lettuces, makes for an appetizing salad even with no garnish or additional ingredients.

An assortment of greens can be made into a more substantial course by adding one, two, or three other items, such as meat or seafood items, cheese, vegetables, or nuts. A popular example from many bistro menus is the country salad made of robust greens, such as chicory, and garnished with blue cheese, chunks of crisp slab bacon, and garlic croutons.

Use restraint with salad dressings. A salad dressing is a sauce and, like other sauces, should be used as a seasoning to enhance the flavor of a dish; it should not be used as a main ingredient to dominate or cover up the flavors of the other ingredients. The modern trend with sauces is to make them lighter and to use less of them. With salads, a vinaigrette is nearly always a good choice. A light hand with dressings is also good from a nutritional standpoint, because most dressings are high in fat content.

Salad Greens

Common salad greens such as romaine, Boston, bibb, escarole, chicory, Belgian endive, spinach, watercress, and loose-leaf lettuces (such as oak-leaf) are familiar to most cooks and are readily available in most markets. In addition, some formerly scarce specialty items have become more widely used in recent years:

Arugula—also known as rugula, rocket, and roquette. Related to mustard and watercress, this green has a mustardlike bite. It is tender when young, with a pleasantly spicy, pungent flavor, but it becomes bitter and more fibrous when too mature. Often sandy, it requires careful washing.

Frisée (pronounced "free-zay")—also known as chicorée frisée, which means curly chicory. Frisée is none other than the familiar curly endive or chicory, except it is grown in the French manner to make it more tender and less bitter. Except for the outside layer, the leaves are thinner, more feathery, and are pale yellow with a tinge of green, unlike the heavy, fibrous, dark green leaves of the more familiar American chicory. While retaining some of the distinctive bitterness of the chicory family frisée is mild and tender enough to be eaten without mixing with other greens.

Mâche (pronounced "mahsh")—also known as corn salad, lamb's lettuce, lamb's tongue, or field salad. This expensive green consists of small, very tender, spoon-shaped leaves with a delicate, rather nutty flavor. Because it is so delicate in texture and mild in flavor, it is best used by itself, with a very light dressing so that its exquisite flavor can be best appreciated. If it is mixed with other greens, use only the mildest and most tender; bibb lettuce is a good choice.

Mâche comes to market as whole, tiny plants with the roots attached. Since the leaves are so small, for most purposes it is best to trim off the roots but leave the leaves attached to each other. Wash gently but thoroughly to flush soil from the base of the leaf stalks.

Radicchio (pronounced "ra-dik-ee-oh")—also known as red chicory. Radicchio is available in two forms: (1) a round-headed variety that slightly resembles a small head of red cabbage and (2) a variety with elongated, spear-shaped leaves called radicchio de Treviso, named after the Italian city that is its home. The round variety is generally available here, while the Treviso type is rarely seen. Radicchio leaves have a striking red color with creamy white veins or ribs. The flavor is slightly bitter, and the texture is crisp and somewhat waxy. While it is expensive, it is often used in small quantities to give both color and flavor to mixed salads.

Mesclun—This is not a type of lettuce; it is a mixture of various lettuces and other greens picked when they are only a few inches high. Mesclun may include any of the common or specialty lettuces as well as more unusual items such as edible flowers. (Nasturtiums are perhaps the most commonly used edible flowers; their leaves, which resemble small water lily pads and have a spicy, pungent flavor, may also be added to salads in small quantities.) Even robust, strong-flavored greens will be more tender and delicate if picked when they are small. While mesclun mixtures have become fashionable and are available on the market, many chefs prefer to buy individual types of greens and make their own mixtures.

The quantity of greens to be used in salads is variable. For salads consisting of greens alone or for those with only a small garnish, allow 2 to 3 ounces (60 to 90 g) per portion. If the greens function more as a garnish or as a bed for other items, allow 1 to 2 ounces (30 to 60 g) per portion.

Warm Salads

Considered unusual and innovative not long ago, warm salads are now served in an increasing number of restaurants—informal bistros as well as the most elegant establishments. A typical warm salad may consist of an assortment of greens, dressed with an appropriate vinaigrette, and plated with a just-cooked portion of meat, poultry, or seafood. Other warm salads may feature such items as baked goat cheese, grilled vegetables, or sautéed slices of foie gras.

Note that these are called warm salads, not hot salads. (In French, such a salad is referred to as a *salade tiède*, meaning "tepid.") Although the warm meat or other item is cooked or heated just before service, common practice is to allow it to stand for a few minutes before plating it with the greens. If the item is too hot, it is likely to wilt the greens quickly, with unpleasant results.

The best dressings for warm salads are vinaigrette variations. Mayonnaise-based dressings or other thick, creamy dressings are sometimes used on some special items but are not as versatile. Vinaigrette-type dressings may incorporate a little of the cooking fat from the warm meat item or some of the deglazing juices from the pan. Chapter 3 includes more information on dressings for warm salads (see page 71).

In addition to those in this chapter, other warm salad recipes can be found on pages 422 and 452.

QUAIL SALAD

(Color Plate 1)

		U.S.		Metric	
PORTIONS:		*4*	*16*	*4*	*16*
Ingredients					
Quails		4	16	*4*	*16*
Madeira wine		1 oz	4 oz	*30 ml*	*125 ml*
Lemon juice		1 tsp	4 tsp	*5 ml*	*20 ml*
Pepper		¼ tsp	1 tsp	*0.5 g*	*2 g*
Thyme		½ tsp	2 tsp	*0.5 g*	*2 g*
Salt		¼ tsp	1 tsp	*1 g*	*5 g*
Olive oil		2 oz	8 oz	*60 ml*	*2.5 dl*
Mixed greens		8 oz	2 lb	*250 g*	*1 kg*
Artichoke bottoms, cooked		2	8	*2*	*8*
Asparagus tips, cooked		12	48	*12*	*48*
Sherry vinaigrette made with olive oil or walnut oil (p. 72)		6 oz	1 pt 8 oz	*175 ml*	*7 dl*
Cherry tomatoes		4	16	*4*	*16*
Oyster mushrooms		8	32	*8*	*32*
Butter		1 tsp	4 tsp	*5 g*	*20 g*
Chicken stock or brown stock (optional; see Cooking, step 2)		4 oz	1 pt	*125 ml*	*5 dl*

Mise en Place:

1. Remove the backbones from the quails and flatten the quails.
2. Mix together the madeira, lemon juice, pepper, thyme, salt, and olive oil. Add the quails to the mixture and turn them so that they are coated. Let them marinate for several hours or overnight.
3. Trim, wash, and drain the salad greens.
4. Slice the artichoke bottoms. Combine with the asparagus tips and toss with one-third of the vinaigrette. (This should be done as close as possible to service time to avoid discoloring the asparagus.)
5. Cut the cherry tomatoes in half.
6. Trim and clean the mushrooms as necessary.

Cooking:

1. Remove the quails from the marinade. Cook them by grilling or sautéing.
2. If the quails are sautéed, deglaze the pan with the stock and reduce until syrupy. Drizzle the reduced deglazing liquid over the quails.
3. While the quails are cooking, sauté the mushrooms lightly in butter.

Presentation:

1. Toss the salad greens with another one-third of the vinaigrette (that is, half of the remaining vinaigrette). Arrange the greens on plates.
2. Let the quails cool for a minute or two so that they are warm, not hot. Place one quail on top of each plate of greens.
3. Arrange the remaining vegetables around the quail.
4. Sprinkle the remaining vinaigrette over the salads (about ½ oz or 15 ml per portion).

Variations

For a simpler salad, plate the quail with the greens but omit the vegetable garnish.

Squab Salad

Substitute squab for the quail in the basic recipe, using one-half squab per portion. Cook the squab as desired, by roasting, grilling, or sautéing. For each portion, serve one half of the breast meat, removed from the bone, and one leg.

Other meats or poultry, such as sliced, grilled duck breast, lamb loin, or beef tenderloin, can be substituted for the quail.

FOIE GRAS SALAD WITH PEARS

		U.S.		Metric	
PORTIONS:		*4*	*16*	*4*	*16*
Ingredients					
Pears, bosc or bartlet		2	8	*2*	*8*
White wine		2 oz	8 oz	*60 ml*	*2.5 dl*
Water		4 oz	1 pt	*125 ml*	*5 dl*
Sugar		2 oz	8 oz	*60 g*	*250 g*
Balsamic vinegar		1 oz	4 oz	*30 ml*	*125 ml*
Peppercorns		2	8	*2*	*8*
Thyme		¼ tsp	1 tsp	*0.25 g*	*1 g*
Fresh, raw foie gras (see note)		6–8 oz	1 ½–2 lb	*175–225 g*	*700–900 g*
Salt					
Pepper					
Flour					
Butter					
Small, tender spinach leaves		3 oz	12 oz	*90 g*	*375 g*
Watercress or arugula		2 oz	8 oz	*60 g*	*250 g*
Mustard vinaigrette made with balsamic or red wine vinegar and flavored with chives (p. 72)		3 oz	12 oz	*90 ml*	*3.5 dl*

Note: See pages 598–599 for product and handling information on foie gras.

Mise en Place:

1. Peel the pears, cut them in half, and remove the cores.
2. Combine the wine, water, sugar, vinegar, peppercorns, and thyme in a saucepan. Bring to a boil. Add the pear halves and poach until tender, about 20 to 30 minutes.
3. Cool and store the pears in the poaching liquid until ready for use.
4. Trim, wash, and drain the greens.

Cooking and Presentation:

1. Cut the pear halves into thin slices.
2. Place about a teaspoonful (5 ml) of vinaigrette on the bottom half of each plate. Fan the slices of pear out on top of the vinaigrette, using one-half pear per portion.
3. Toss the spinach and arugula with the remaining vinaigrette. Place the greens on the top half of the plate, mounding them.
4. Cut the foie gras, which should be chilled, into slices ½ inch (1 cm) thick. Season the slices and dredge them in flour.
5. Heat a sauté pan over moderately high heat. Add the butter and sauté the foie gras very quickly, about 10 to 30 seconds on each side. Because the foie gras has a very high fat content, it must be cooked and removed from the pan very quickly to prevent too much of the fat from melting out and being lost.
6. Immediately remove the foie gras slices from the pan and arrange them on the plates, leaning them up against the mound of greens. Serve immediately.

DUCK CONFIT SALAD

		U.S.		Metric	
PORTIONS:		4	16	4	16
Ingredients					
Duck confit, legs (p. 321)		4	16	4	16
Chicory frisée		4 oz	1 lb	125 g	500 g
Romaine or other robust, dark green lettuce		4 oz	1 lb	125 g	500 g
Mustard vinaigrette made with olive oil (p. 72)		4 oz	1 pt	125 ml	5 dl
Garlic croutons for garnish (see Mise en Place, step 2)					

Mise en Place:

1. Trim, wash, and drain the greens.
2. Prepare the garlic croutons by sautéing some small slices of bread in olive oil until crisp and then rubbing them with cut cloves of garlic.

Cooking and Presentation:

1. Heat the confit in a little of its own fat in a sauté pan until it is hot and the skin is crisp.
2. Toss the greens with the vinaigrette and place on plates.
3. Put one duck leg on each plate. Drizzle the salad with a little of the fat from the pan.
4. Garnish the salad with the garlic croutons.

STEAK AND POTATO SALAD

		U.S.		Metric	
PORTIONS:		**4**	**16**	*4*	*16*
Ingredients					
Boneless beefsteak, about ½ inch (12 mm) thick		12–16 oz	3–4 lb	*350–450 g*	*1.4–1.8 kg*
Thyme		¼ tsp	1 tsp	*0.25 g*	*1 g*
Salt					
Pepper					
Lemon juice		1 tbsp	2 oz	*15 ml*	*60 ml*
Olive oil		1 oz	4 oz	*30 ml*	*125 ml*
Vegetable oil, for cooking					
Small boiled potatoes		8 oz	2 lb	*250 g*	*1 kg*
Salt					
Pepper					
Vegetable oil, for cooking					
Mixed salad greens, preferably firm, robust greens					
Brown stock		3 oz	12 oz	*90 ml*	*3.5 dl*
Balsamic or red wine vinegar		1 oz	4 oz	*30 ml*	*125 ml*
Olive oil		3 oz	12 oz	*90 ml*	*3.5 dl*
Salt					
Pepper					

Mise en Place:

1. Trim the beef of all fat and sinews.

2. Rub the beef with thyme, salt, pepper, lemon juice, and olive oil. Let stand 30 to 60 minutes.

3. Peel and slice the cooked potatoes.

4. Trim, wash, and drain the greens.

Cooking and Presentation:

1. In a sauté pan, sear the steak in a thin film of oil until rare but well browned.

2. At the same time, brown the potatoes lightly in a little oil in a separate pan. Season with salt and pepper.

3. Arrange the greens on plates.

4. Slice the steak across the grain into thin strips.

5. Arrange the meat and potatoes on top of the greens.

6. With the brown stock, deglaze the sauté pan used for cooking the meat. Reduce by one-half.

7. Add the vinegar and olive oil. Season to taste with salt and pepper.

8. Pour the dressing over the salads and serve at once.

SALAD OF SMOKED GOOSE BREAST, GREEN BEANS, AND SUNDRIED TOMATOES

		U.S.		Metric	
PORTIONS:		4	16	*4*	*16*
Ingredients					
Sherry vinegar		4 tsp	16 tsp	*20 ml*	*160 ml*
Mustard, dijon-style		1 tsp	4 tsp	*5 ml*	*20 ml*
Olive oil		2 oz	8 oz	*60 ml*	*125 ml*
Salt					
Pepper					
Sage, crumbled or minced		small pinch	large pinch	*small pinch*	*large pinch*
Smoked goose breast (or substitute smoked duck breast)		12 oz	3 lb	*350 g*	*1.4 kg*
Mixed greens		4 oz	1 lb	*125 g*	*500 g*
Green beans, cooked		12 oz	3 lb	*350 g*	*1.4 kg*
Sundried tomatoes, oil-packed		1 oz	4 oz	*30 g*	*125 g*

Mise en Place:

1. Make a vinaigrette by mixing together the vinegar, mustard, and oil. Season with salt, pepper, and sage.

2. Slice the goose breast.

3. Rinse and drain the greens.

4. Cut the tomatoes into julienne.

Finishing:

1. Just before serving, mix the vinaigrette well to make an emulsion.

2. Toss the beans with about one-fourth of the vinaigrette to coat them very lightly.

3. Plate the greens and arrange the beans and sliced meat on top of them.

4. Scatter the julienne of dried tomato over the salads.

5. Drizzle the remaining dressing over the salads.

LOBSTER SALAD WITH AVOCADO

		U.S.		Metric	
PORTIONS:		**4**	**16**	*4*	*16*
Ingredients					
Tomato, peeled and seeded		4 oz	1 lb	*125 g*	*500 g*
Vinaigrette (p. 72) made with lemon juice and hazelnut oil		6 oz	1 ½ pt	*2 dl*	*7.5 dl*
Mushroom caps		2 oz	8 oz	*60 g*	*250 g*
Lobsters, about 1 ½ lb (750 g) each		2	8	*2*	*8*
Avocados, small		1	4	*1*	*4*
Belgian endive leaves		4 oz	1 lb	*125 g*	*500 g*
Watercress		1 bunch	4 bunches	*1 bunch*	*4 bunches*

Mise en Place:

1. Cut the tomato into small dice. Drain briefly in a strainer and then place in a bowl. Add about one-fourth of the vinaigrette and mix gently.

2. Cut the mushrooms into julienne. Toss with a little of the vinaigrette, just enough to coat them and keep them from discoloring.

3. Steam the lobsters for 10 minutes. Cool. Remove the tails from the shells and cut into slices ¼ inch (6 mm) thick. Moisten with a little of the vinaigrette. Use the claws to garnish the salads or reserve for another purpose.

4. Pit and peel the avocados. Cut the avocados into medium dice. Moisten with a little of the vinaigrette to keep from discoloring.

5. Cut the Belgian endive leaves crosswise into julienne. Remove the stems from the watercress. Toss the endive and watercress together.

Finishing:

1. Toss the greens with the remaining vinaigrette. Place the greens in a mound in the center of each plate.

2. Top the greens with the mushrooms.

3. Arrange the slices of lobster around the mound of greens, leaning them up against it.

4. Place 4 small spoonfuls of tomato dice around the outside of the plate. Place 4 spoonfuls of avocado dice in between the mounds of tomato.

Variations

Shrimp Salad with Avocado

Prepare as in the basic recipe, substituting cooked shrimp for the slices of lobster tail.

Salade Riche

Omit the avocado. Sauté slices of fresh foie gras, following the procedure in the recipe on page 134. Add the slices of foie gras to the salads, using 3 or 4 slices per portion. If desired, top each slice of foie gras with a slice of black truffle.

GRILLED HAM SALAD

	U.S.		Metric	
PORTIONS:	4	16	4	16
Ingredients				
Red onion	2 oz	8 oz	60 g	250 g
Olive oil	4 oz	1 pt	125 ml	5 dl
Red wine vinegar	2 oz	8 oz	60 ml	2.5 dl
Salt				
Pepper				
Watercress, with coarse stems removed	4 oz	1 lb	125 g	500 g
Chicory frisée	4–6 oz	1–1 ½ lb	125–185 g	500–750 g
Flavorful ham, smoked or unsmoked, such as Smithfield, black forest, or Westphalian, in thin slices	6 oz	1 ½ lb	185 g	750 g

Mise en Place:

1. Cut the onion into very thin slices. Mix with the olive oil and let stand several hours or overnight.

2. Remove the onion from the oil and reserve. Make a vinaigrette with the oil and the vinegar. Season it with salt and pepper, but don't add too much salt if the ham is very salty.

3. Wash and drain the watercress and frisée.

Finishing:

1. Grill the ham for a few seconds to heat it and to make light grill marks.

2. Immediately remove it from the grill, place it on a platter, and pour the vinaigrette over it. Let stand for a few minutes to absorb a little of the dressing.

3. Drain the ham and toss the greens with the vinaigrette.

4. Plate the greens and arrange the ham on top. Arrange a small mound of the marinated onion on top of the ham.

SHRIMP AND KASHA SALAD

		U.S.		Metric	
	PORTIONS:	**4**	**16**	*4*	*16*
Ingredients					
Kasha, whole granulation		¼ cup	1 cup	*60 ml*	*250 ml*
Water		4 oz	1 pt	*125 ml*	*5 dl*
Olive oil		1 tbsp	2 oz	*15 ml*	*60 ml*
Lemon juice		1 tsp	4 tsp	*5 ml*	*20 ml*
Salt					
Pepper					
Small to medium peeled, cooked shrimp		8 oz	2 lb	*250 g*	*1 kg*
Tomato dill vinaigrette (p. 73)		4 oz	1 pt	*125 ml*	*5 dl*
Roasted bell peppers, red, green, or yellow (p. 521)		4 oz	1 lb	*125 g*	*500 g*
Tender salad greens		6 oz	1 lb 8 oz	*175 g*	*700 g*

Mise en Place:

1. Put the kasha in a heavy saucepan or braising pan. Set the pan over moderately high heat until it is hot. Add the water, cover, and move to low heat. Simmer slowly until the kasha is tender and the water is completely absorbed.

2. Transfer the kasha to a bowl and toss with the olive oil and lemon juice. Add salt and pepper to taste.

3. Combine the shrimp with the vinaigrette and marinate for an hour or two.

4. Cut the roasted peppers into wide strips.

5. Trim, wash, and drain the salad greens.

Finishing:

1. Line salad plates with the mixed greens.

2. Arrange the peppers on top of the greens.

3. Place a mound of the kasha in the center of the plates.

4. Remove the shrimp from the vinaigrette and arrange on top of the kasha. Spoon the vinaigrette over the tops of the salads.

Variation

Lima Bean Salad with Shrimp				
Lima beans	12 oz	3 lb	*375 g*	*1.5 kg*

Omit the kasha from the basic recipe. Cook the lima beans, cool slightly, mix with the vinaigrette, and cool completely. Plate the beans, with the vinaigrette, on top of the greens and peppers. Garnish the salads with a few shrimp, using about 1 oz (30 g) per portion.

COLD EGGPLANT SALAD

		U.S.		*Metric*	
PORTIONS:		**4**	**16**	*4*	*16*
Ingredients					
Eggplant, preferably small Japanese or Italian eggplants		1 lb 8 oz	6 lb	*750 g*	*3 kg*
Sesame paste (tahini)		2 oz	8 oz	*60 g*	*250 g*
Lemon juice		1 ½ oz	6 oz	*45 ml*	*175 ml*
Olive oil		1 oz	4 oz	*30 ml*	*125 ml*
Cayenne		¼ tsp	1 tsp	*0.5 g*	*2 g*
Turmeric		¼ tsp	1 tsp	*0.5 g*	*2 g*
Fresh chives, chopped		1 tbsp	4 tbsp	*3 g*	*10 g*
Salt					
Pepper					
Tomatoes, peeled, seeded, and diced		4 oz	1 lb	*125 g*	*500 g*

Mise en Place:

1. Trim the eggplants. Peel them if they are large. Steam until tender, about 20 to 25 minutes. Cool.

2. Mix together the sesame paste, lemon juice, olive oil, cayenne, turmeric, and chives. Add salt and pepper to taste.

3. Mix the dressing with the eggplant. Hold in refrigerator until ready for service.

Finishing:

1. About 30 minutes before serving, add the tomatoes to the eggplant and toss gently.

2. Serve the salad plain and unadorned or, if desired, on a bed of lettuce.

GOAT CHEESE AND WALNUT SALAD

		U.S.		Metric	
PORTIONS:	4	16	4	16
Ingredients				
Belgian endive or radicchio	2 oz	8 oz	60 g	250 g
Arugula	3 oz	12 oz	90 g	375 g
Bibb lettuce	2 oz	8 oz	60 g	250 g
Romaine lettuce	3 oz	12 oz	90 g	375 g
Bread crumbs, dry	⅓ cup	1 ⅓ cup	75 ml	300 ml
Thyme	1 tsp	4 tsp	1 g	4 g
Basil, dried	1 tsp	4 tsp	1 g	4 g
Black pepper	½ tsp	2 tsp	1 g	4 g
Fresh goat's milk cheese, preferably in log shape	8 oz	2 lb	250 g	1 kg
Walnut pieces	1 ½ oz	6 oz	45 g	175 g
Vinaigrette made with red wine vinegar and olive oil	2–3 oz	8–12 oz	60–90 ml	250–375 ml

Mise en Place:

1. Trim, wash, and drain the salad greens. Tear into bite-size pieces. Toss together.
2. Mix together the crumbs, herbs, and pepper.
3. Slice the cheese into 1-oz (30-g) pieces. Roll the pieces in the seasoned crumbs to coat them. Arrange the pieces on a baking sheet.

Finishing:

1. Bake the cheese at 450°F (230°C) for 10 minutes.
2. At the same time, toast the walnuts in a dry sauté pan or in the oven with the cheese.
3. Toss the greens with the vinaigrette and place on plates. Top each plate of greens with 2 pieces of cheese and sprinkle with a few walnut pieces.

Variations

Salad with Goat Cheese in Phyllo

Prepare the salad according to the basic recipe, but prepare the cheese as follows. For each 8 oz of cheese, cut 2 sheets of phyllo pastry in half. Brush one half sheet with melted butter, sprinkle with a few bread crumbs, and top with another half sheet. Repeat until 4 sheets thick. Place the cheese logs end to end at one edge of the pastry and roll up. Using a serrated knife, score the phyllo log into portions to make it easier to cut after baking. Bake at 400°F (200°C) until browned. Cool slightly, cut into portions, and plate with the salads.

Blue Cheese Salad with Walnuts

Omit the goat cheese and herbed crumbs from the basic recipe. Instead, sprinkle the salads with crumbled stilton, gorgonzola, roquefort, or other blue cheese.

Roast Beet Salad with Walnuts *(Color Plate 2)*

Omit the goat cheese and seasoned crumbs. Prepare roast beets with walnut vinaigrette according to the directions on page 509, omitting the beet greens. Make the green salad as in the basic recipe, except make the vinaigrette with walnut oil. Plate the green salad with the beets and sprinkle with the walnuts.

TABBOULEH

	U.S.		Metric	
PORTIONS:	*4*	*16*	*4*	*16*
Ingredients				
Bulgur (processed cracked wheat), fine or medium texture	4 oz	1 lb	*125 g*	*500 g*
Cucumber	6 oz	1 lb 8 oz	*175 g*	*700 g*
Coarse salt	½ tsp	2 tsp	*2 g*	*8 g*
Chopped parsley	½ oz	2 oz	*15 g*	*60 g*
Scallions, sliced thin	½ oz	2 oz	*15 g*	*60 g*
Tomato, peeled, seeded, and chopped	2 oz	8 oz	*60 g*	*250 g*
Lemon juice	1 oz	4 oz	*30 ml*	*125 ml*
Olive oil	1 oz	4 oz	*30 ml*	*125 ml*
Salt				
Pepper				
Lettuce, as desired				

Mise en Place:

1. Place the bulgur wheat in a bowl. Pour over it about twice its volume of boiling water. Cover and let stand until completely cool. The bulgur should have absorbed most or all of the water and should be tender enough to eat. If any liquid remains, drain it and squeeze out gently. Fluff the bulgur with a fork.

2. Peel the cucumbers and quarter them lengthwise. Scoop out and discard the seeds. Slice the cucumbers ¼ inch (5 mm) thick. Toss with the coarse salt in a bowl and let stand 30 minutes. Rinse, drain, and pat dry.

Finishing

1. Mix together all ingredients except the lettuce. Taste for seasonings and add additional salt, pepper, lemon juice, and olive oil if necessary.

2. Serve plain or on lettuce bases.

WARM SALAD OF ASPARAGUS AND MUSHROOMS

	U.S.		Metric	
PORTIONS:	4	16	4	16
Ingredients				
Mixed salad greens	6 oz	1 lb 8 oz	*175 g*	*700 g*
Asparagus	1 lb	4 lb	*450 g*	*1.8 kg*
Mushrooms (see note)	8 oz	2 lb	*225 g*	*900 g*
Butter	½ oz	2 oz	*15 g*	*60 g*
Mustard vinaigrette (p. 72) made with hazelnut oil	4 oz	1 pt	*125 ml*	*5 dl*

Note: Morels are the best choice for this recipe; their flavor makes a perfect combination with asparagus. However, they are expensive. Reconstituted dried morels may also be used. Shiitakes or oyster mushrooms are also good choices for this recipe. Regular white cultivated mushrooms may also be used.

Mise en Place:

1. Trim, wash, and drain the salad greens.
2. Trim off the bases of the asparagus stalks. Peel the lower parts of the stalks and cut the asparagus into pieces about 1 ½ inches (4 cm) long.
3. Clean and trim the mushrooms. Leave them whole if they are small; or cut them into halves or quarters if large. If large shiitakes are used, discard the stems and cut the caps into strips.

Finishing:

1. Arrange the salad greens on plates.
2. Boil the asparagus until cooked but al dente. Drain.
3. At the same time, sauté the mushrooms in butter.
4. Remove the mushrooms from the heat and add the asparagus.
5. Add the vinaigrette to the vegetable mixture and mix. Taste and adjust the seasonings.
6. Immediately spoon the vegetables over the salad greens and serve at once.

Variation

Salad of Grilled Scallops with Asparagus and Mushrooms

Top the basic salad with a few large grilled scallops. Reduce the quantities of vegetables as desired.

ORIENTAL NOODLE AND VEGETABLE SALAD

	U.S.		Metric	
PORTIONS:	4	16	4	16
Ingredients				
Fresh Chinese noodles, Japanese udon, or fettuccine	4 oz	1 lb	125 g	500 g
Vegetable oil	1 tsp	4 tsp	5 ml	20 ml
Dressing:				
Grated fresh ginger	½ tsp	2 tsp	2 g	8 g
Japanese soy sauce	1 oz	4 oz	30 ml	125 ml
Red wine vinegar	1 oz	4 oz	30 ml	125 ml
Sugar	1 tsp	4 tsp	4 g	15 g
Chinese chili paste with garlic	1 tsp	4 tsp	5 g	20 g
Vegetable oil	1 oz	4 oz	30 ml	125 ml
Oriental sesame oil	1 tbsp	2 oz	15 ml	60 ml
Snow peas	2 oz	8 oz	60 g	250 g
Scallions, sliced thin	2	8	2	8
Carrots, grated	2 oz	8 oz	60 g	250 g
Bean sprouts	2 oz	8 oz	60 g	250 g
Water chestnuts, sliced, or jicama, cut julienne	2 oz	8 oz	60 g	250 g
Toasted sliced almonds	1 oz	4 oz	30 g	125 g
Chopped cilantro	1 tbsp	4 tbsp	3 g	12 g
Shredded Chinese cabbage	6 oz	1 lb 8 oz	175 g	700 g

Mise en Place:

1. Boil the noodles until tender. Drain and cool under cold water. Drain again and toss with the vegetable oil.
2. Mix together all the ingredients for the dressing.
3. Trim, blanch, and chill the snow peas.

Finishing:

1. In a large bowl, combine the noodles, dressing, and vegetables (except for the Chinese cabbage). Mix.
2. Line plates with the shredded cabbage and place the noodle and vegetable mixture on top.

Variations

Cooked chicken or duck can be added to the salad.

BLACK AND WHITE BEAN SALAD WITH FENNEL AND PINE NUTS

		U.S.		Metric	
PORTIONS:		**4**	**16**	*4*	*16*
Ingredients					
Frisée or other robust salad greens		6 oz	1 lb 8 oz	*175 g*	*700 g*
Small, tender fennel bulbs, trimmed, quartered, and cored		4 oz	1 lb	*125 g*	*500 g*
Red wine vinegar		1 oz	4 oz	*30 ml*	*125 ml*
Salt		½ tsp	2 tsp	*3 g*	*10 g*
White pepper		¼ tsp	1 tsp	*0.5 g*	*2 g*
Shallot, minced		½ oz	2 oz	*15 g*	*60 g*
Walnut oil		1 ½ oz	6 oz	*45 ml*	*175 ml*
Heavy cream		½ oz	2 oz	*15 ml*	*60 ml*
Cooked black beans, well drained and cooled		4 oz	1 lb	*125 g*	*500 g*
Cooked cannellini beans or other white beans, well drained and cooled		4 oz	1 lb	*125 g*	*500 g*
Chopped parsley		1 tbsp	4 tbsp	*3 g*	*12 g*
Toasted pine nuts		1 oz	4 oz	*30 g*	*125 g*

Mise en Place:

1. Trim, wash, and drain the salad greens.
2. Cut the fennel into thin slices.
3. Make the dressing. Mix together the vinegar, salt, pepper, and shallot. Beat in the oil and then the cream.
4. Mix together the beans, dressing, and chopped parsley.

Finishing:

1. Mix the fennel into the beans. Taste the mixture and add more salt and pepper if necessary.
2. Line salad plates with the greens.
3. Spoon the bean mixture onto the plates.
4. Top with the pine nuts.

Variations

Other types of cooked dried beans may be substituted for the black and white beans. Flageolets are especially good in this recipe.

Other nuts may be used instead of the pine nuts.

PASTA DISHES

In the past decade or two, pasta dishes have risen in popularity more rapidly than perhaps any other category of food. There are relatively few restaurants that do not have some sort of noodle dishes on their menus, and "pasta of the day" is a common feature in simple neighborhood cafés and elegant "continental" dining establishments.

Authorities on Italian cuisine regularly remind the public, in books, magazines, and newspaper articles, that there is nothing Italian about many of the pasta items often favored by restaurant-goers. This is no doubt true. It is also true that there is nothing Chinese or Japanese about many of those dishes, to name but two other cuisines with indigenous noodle traditions. "Is it good?" is perhaps a more important question to ask about a dish than "Is it authentic?"—unless, of course, the restaurant claims to offer authentic ethnic cuisine.

The recipes in this section are examples of the kinds of pasta dishes made in modern American kitchens. No claims are made about their being authentic Italian (or Chinese or Japanese) dishes. Rather, they are popular dishes with appeal to the American palate.

Nevertheless, American cooks can take some hints from Italian traditions to improve the quality of their own offerings. In an Italian pasta dish, pasta is the main ingredient. When the pasta is of good quality, with a firm, resilient texture and a pronounced, wheaty flavor, less sauce is needed. The sauce and other ingredients are a seasoning and an enhancement, and the pasta retains its own identity.

In second-rate pasta dishes, on the other hand, the pasta becomes more of a filler, providing little more than bulk, while the sauce and other ingredients overwhelm the dish. Lasagne, as it is often served, is hardly a pasta dish at all. The sheets of noodle dough serve merely to keep the layers separate and to provide inexpensive volume.

Fortunately, American chefs are paying more attention to the quality of the noodles they serve. They are buying better quality factory-made pastas (for spaghetti, linguine, and so on) made of pure semolina, and are often making their own egg pastas (for fresh-noodle products such as fettuccine, lasagne, ravioli, and so on). Having made this investment in time and money, they prefer to highlight the quality of these products rather than drown them with lots of other ingredients.

Fresh versus Dried

Although many people think that fresh pasta is necessarily better than factory-made dried spaghetti and macaroni, such a comparison is meaningless. They are two different products, like apples and oranges. Factory-made pasta is made of flour and water. The flour (at least for the best pasta) is a hard-wheat flour called semolina. The dough is mixed, then extruded through dies into spaghetti, rigatoni, and other shapes. It is then dried under controlled conditions in the factory.

Fresh pasta, on the other hand, is made of flour and eggs, sometimes with the addition of water, oil, or other ingredients. In Italy, semolina is *not* used for fresh egg pasta, with perhaps a few exceptions. A softer flour is considered more suitable to achieve the proper texture. The dough is not extruded but is rolled out into sheets and cut into various shapes. In most cases, fresh pasta is best cooked and served soon after it is made, while still soft and pliable, rather than dried.

The best factory pasta is as good as the best handmade fresh pasta and certainly better than mediocre egg noodles. Italians use fresh and dried pastas in different ways, with specific recipes for each type.

Making Fresh Pasta Variations

The recipe on page 153 gives the ingredients and basic procedure for making and rolling fresh egg pasta. The first procedure given is for mixing the dough by hand. When large quantities are being made, however, it is quicker to make the dough with a mixer or food processor. The procedures are simple and involve putting all the ingredients in the bowl of the machine and running it until the dough forms. More details are given in the variations following the basic recipe.

Ingredients for basic egg pasta may vary somewhat. The recipe given here includes olive oil and salt. Many cooks feel that eggs and flour should be the only ingredients, while other cooks permit salt as a third ingredient but no oil. Still others argue that a little oil improves the texture by tenderizing the gluten slightly and making the dough more pliable. Both the oil and salt may be omitted from the basic recipe if desired.

Adding a small amount of puréed, cooked spinach or other vegetable to pasta dough to color it is a traditional Italian technique. Most of these additions add little if any detectable flavor; their contribution is primarily to appearance.

Picking up this technique and modifying it, American and European cooks have developed a staggering variety of colored and flavored pastas. Some of these utilize strong-flavored spices, herbs, and other ingredients that give the pasta a distinctive taste. In some other cases, such as pasta sheets containing whole herb leaves, the addition is primarily for appearance.

A sampling of flavored pastas is included in the variations following the basic recipe.

Adding Flavoring Ingredients. Many of these additions to basic egg noodle dough have a high moisture content. This changes the ratio of flour to moisture in the basic recipe, so adjustments may have to be made.

- If the addition is a vegetable purée, it is often best to cook the purée over low heat to evaporate some of the water before adding it. With some other vegetables, such as spinach, the moisture content can be reduced by squeezing it out.
- The proportion of moisture can be further adjusted by increasing the quantity of flour or by decreasing the egg content.
- If the flavoring ingredient is dry, such as mushroom powder, a very small amount of additional egg or water may be necessary, or the quantity of flour can be reduced.

In all cases (unless otherwise instructed), add the flavoring ingredients to the flour and eggs at the beginning of the mixing period. An important exception to this rule is the herb pasta in which whole leaves are sandwiched between two sheets of pasta, which are then passed again through the roller (see page 154).

Filled Pastas

One important use of fresh egg pasta is to make filled pastas such as ravioli and tortellini. Making filled pastas by hand is labor-intensive, but the results are very popular and allow for a wide variety of presentations, both in the filling and in the sauce.

Filled pastas are best served with simpler, lighter sauces so that the flavor and texture of the fillings can be enjoyed. Often the best way to dress or sauce ravioli or other stuffed pastas is simply with a little butter or cream and parmesan cheese, a well-seasoned broth, a light sauce made of vegetable juice (see page 34), or a few drops of flavored oil (see page 36).

Stuffed pastas can be classified as small and large. An overview of some of the most important filled pastas of both categories follows.

Small Filled Pastas. Small pastas are usually about 2 inches (5 cm) or less in diameter, although the sizes may vary. Because of their small size, it is generally not practical to fill them with solid or chunky ingredients. Fillings are pastes, purées, or finely ground mixtures of cheese, meats, seafood, vegetables, or a combination of any of these. Recipes for a number of such fillings are on page 156.

Unlike plain pastas such as spaghetti and fettuccine, filled pastas should not be cooked at a rolling boil. Lower the heat to a simmer to avoid breaking or bursting open the pastas.

In Italy, names for stuffed pastas vary from region to region. What are called "tortelli" in one locale may be called "ravioli" elsewhere. Consequently, it is impossible to give a definitive listing of these items. The following, however, are some widely used terms.

Ravioli are small squares or circles consisting of two layers of pasta with a filling between them. The two layers of pasta are sealed around the edges. The procedure for making ravioli is illustrated in Figure 5.1.

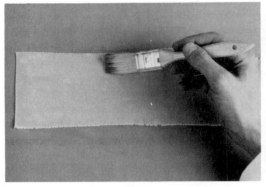

FIGURE 5.1. **Making ravioli.**
(a) **Brush a sheet of fresh pasta with water or egg wash to help make a good seal. This step may not be necessary if the dough is moist.**

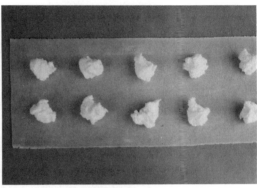

(b) **Drop evenly spaced spoonfuls of filling onto the dough.**

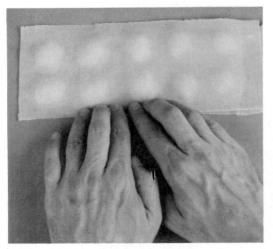

(c) **Top with a second sheet and press well around and between the mounds of filling to expel air bubbles and seal the two layers of dough together.**

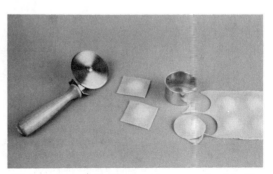

(d) **Cut out ravioli with a cutter or a wheel knife.**

The term *tortelli* is sometimes used interchangeably with ravioli. An alternative meaning for tortelli is small circles of pasta folded in half to enclose a filling, forming half-moon shapes. The procedure is the same as the first stage of shaping tortellini, below (see Figure 5.2c). Another name for small, half-moon-shaped, filled pastas is *agnolotti*.

Tortellini are small circles of dough folded in half to enclose the filling, then twisted around the finger into a loop. The procedure is illustrated in Figure 5.2.

The term *cappelletti* is often used interchangeably with tortellini, but it is sometimes used to specify small pastas made from squares rather than circles of dough. The squares are folded into a triangle to enclose the filling and then are twisted into a loop around the finger the same way as tortellini.

Large Filled Pastas. Of course, if stuffed pastas are made larger, they can hold a greater volume of filling. Consequently, fillings can be more complex and are not limited to the pastes and ground mixtures used to fill tortellini and similar items.

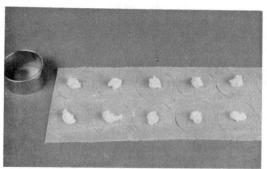

FIGURE 5.2. **Making tortellini.**
(a) **Cut out circles, using a 2-inch (5-cm) round cutter, from a sheet of fresh pasta. Place a small spoonful of filling in the center of each circle.**

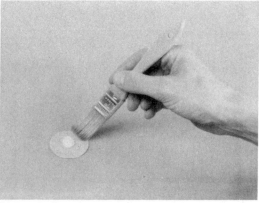

(b) **Brush the edges of the circle with water or egg wash to help make a good seal. This may not be necessary if the dough is moist.**

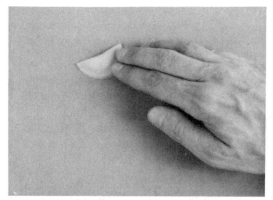

(c) **Fold the dough in half, making a half-moon shape, to enclose the filling. Press out all air bubbles and seal the edges well. Filled pastas in this shape are called tortelli or agnolotti.**

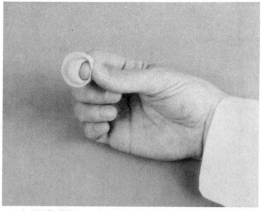

(d) **Twist the dumpling into a loop around a finger tip and seal the two ends together.**

Ravioli are often made as large as 4 inches (10 cm) in diameter. Ravioli this large can enclose interesting assortments of solid ingredients, and many modern chefs like to experiment with different combinations. The recipes for lobster ravioli with zucchini (page 160) and vegetable ravioli in ginger broth (page 158) are examples of this type of preparation.

Such large ravioli are usually served only 3 to 5 per portion as an appetizer. Because the emphasis is on the filling, the sauce should be light. Of course, any garnishes should be compatible with the filling.

In addition to large ravioli, other large filled pastas include the following. Unlike traditional ravioli and other filled pastas, which are made of raw pasta dough and boiled after filling, the types listed here are made with cooked sheets of pasta. Because the filling is not sealed inside the dough, they are not boiled after filling, although they may be baked or gratinéed. Of course, fully cooked or ready-to-eat fillings must be used if the assembled pasta is to be served without further cooking.

Cannelloni are filled tubes made by rolling up a filling in a rectangle of cooked pasta. The recipe on page 162 illustrates the method for making this type of item.

Open ravioli might be described as ravioli that are not sealed. Two sheets of cooked pasta enclose the filling but are not sealed together. This type of pasta is assembled just before serving, using the following procedure:

1. Lay a sheet of cooked pasta on a plate. Squares or rectangles about 4 or 5 inches (10 or 12 cm) on a side are most often used.
2. Place the filling, freshly cooked and hot, on top of the pasta sheet.
3. Place a second sheet of pasta on top. This sheet may be placed slightly askew— that is, at a different angle from the first sheet or even slightly to one side to show some of the filling.
4. Add garnish or sauce as desired. Serve at once.

To enhance the appearance of open ravioli, the dish may be made with various colored and flavored pastas. Two contrasting colors may be used for the top and bottom sheet. Pasta with whole herbs (see page 154) makes an especially attractive top layer for open ravioli. The recipe on page 163 illustrates the method for making open ravioli.

Lasagne is a dish consisting of sheets of cooked pasta layered with other ingredients. The term *lasagne* also refers to the broad sheets of noodle dough used to make the dish.

According to this definition, open ravioli could also be called lasagne, because it consists of layers of pasta with fillings in between. As the two terms are usually used, however, open ravioli requires two sheets of pasta with the filling enclosed between them, whereas lasagne may be made with any number of sheets. Usually the term refers to three or more sheets of pasta layered with fillings, but it may also be used for a single sheet of pasta—remember that the term *lasagne* also refers to the noodle itself—placed on a plate and topped with a sauce or other ingredients. These aren't rules, however; merely a description of how the words are often used.

Note that the above discussion says nothing about baking the assembled lasagne. Although most people understand lasagne as a baked casserole, that need not be the case. It may also be assembled and served immediately, like open ravioli. In Italian, baked lasagne is distinguished by the term *lasagne al forno* ("forno" means "oven").

Pasta Substitutes

Various items may be used in place of fresh pasta to make some of the products described earlier.

Thin wonton skins, dumpling skins, or spring roll skins are especially useful for making large ravioli. Wonton skins are a type of noodle dough, so using them to make large ravioli gives excellent results and saves a great deal of labor.

The procedure for making large ravioli is the same as when using regular pasta. Place the filling on one round wonton skin. Brush the edges with water or egg wash. Top with another skin and seal the edges. Cutting may not be necessary, but you might wish to trim the edges by using a round cutter slightly smaller than the size of the skin.

Wonton skins may also be used to make canneloni. Of course, like regular noodle dough, they must first be cooked (by boiling).

Egg roll skins are sometimes used like wonton skins, but they are thicker and therefore do not make delicate pasta dishes.

Crèpes (or, in Italian, *crespelle*) may be used in place of pasta sheets to make cannelloni. This is a traditional Italian practice.

The Recipes

The following pasta recipes include examples of several of the stuffed or filled pastas discussed earlier.

The section opens with a basic recipe for egg pasta, followed by a number of flavoring variations. For some of the flavored pastas, recipes are included later in the section; for some others, serving suggestions are described.

Due to variations in moisture content, some adjustments may be required when making any of the flavored pastas. Read the discussion on page 148 for an explanation of moisture adjustment.

Following the recipes for pasta doughs are recipes for various stuffings or fillings for small pastas such as tortellini. Follow the procedures described on pages 149–150 to make stuffed pastas with these fillings.

When a fresh pasta dough product, such as fresh fettuccine, is specified in any of the recipes, the quantities indicated are for soft, freshly made dough. If dried egg noodles are being used, use about 25 percent less by weight—that is, if 1 pound of fresh fettuccine is called for, use about 12 ounces of dried noodles. (If the noodles are partially dried, use an intermediate figure.)

In the recipes for filled pastas, such as large ravioli, the quantities of pasta dough needed are approximations. The exact amounts will vary, depending on how thin the pasta is rolled and how it is cut.

FRESH EGG PASTA

		U.S.		Metric	
YIELD:		1 lb 8 oz	6 lb	*700 g*	*2.7 kg*
Ingredients					
Bread flour		1 lb	4 lb	*450 g*	*1.8 kg*
Eggs, lightly beaten		5	20	*5*	*20*
Olive oil		½ oz	2 oz	*15 ml*	*60 ml*
Salt		pinch	½ tsp	*pinch*	*3 g*

Procedure:

1. Put the flour in a mound on a work surface. Make a well in the center and add the eggs, oil, and salt.
2. Working from the center outward, gradually mix the flour into the eggs to make a dough.
3. When the dough is firm enough, begin kneading it, incorporating more of the flour. If the dough is still sticky when all of the flour has been incorporated, add more flour a little at a time. Knead well until the dough becomes elastic and fairly smooth.
4. Cover the dough and let it rest for at least 30 minutes.
5. Cut the dough into pieces about 6 to 8 oz each (175 to 250 g). Set the rollers of a pasta machine at the widest opening. Working with one piece of dough at a time, pass the dough through the machine. Fold the dough into thirds, then pass it through the rollers again without resetting the width. Continue rolling and folding, using the widest opening, until the dough is smooth. If the dough is sticky after rolling, dust it lightly with flour as needed. Repeat this procedure with the remaining pieces of dough.
6. Again working with one piece of dough at a time, decrease the width between the rollers by one notch and pass the dough through them again. Dust the dough with flour as necessary to keep it from sticking. Repeat the rolling procedure, decreasing the width by one notch each time, until the dough is as thin as desired.

Variations

The olive oil or the salt or both may be omitted from the basic recipe if desired.

Mixing with a mixer

Fit the mixer with a dough hook. Place all ingredients in the bowl of the mixer. Run the mixer at medium speed until the dough forms a ball and pulls away from the sides of the machine. Let the dough rest before rolling out, as in the basic procedure.

Mixing with a food processor

Fit the processor with the steel blade. Place all ingredients in the bowl. Process until the ingredients are uniformly blended and look like coarse meal. Remove from the machine and gather into a ball. Knead a few times and then let rest as in the basic procedure.

Fettuccine or Tagliatelli

Roll the dough thin and cut with the wide cutting rollers.

Papardelle

Roll the dough thin. Cut by hand, using a fluted cutting wheel, into long noodles about ¾ inch (2 cm) wide.

Filled or Stuffed Pastas

Follow the procedures described on pages 149–150.

Flavored and Colored Pastas

For each of the following variations, quantities of eggs and flavoring additions are indicated for each pound (450 g) of flour. The oil and salt remain the same as in the basic recipe, or they may be omitted. Unless instructed otherwise, add the flavoring ingredients at the beginning of mixing (that is, at step 1 of the basic recipe).

Spinach Pasta

For each pound (450 g) of flour, use 4 eggs and 4 oz (110 g) of cooked, squeezed, and chopped spinach.

Herb Pasta

Arrange whole herb leaves, such as flat-leaved parsley, chervil, or tarragon, at intervals on a sheet of rolled-out pasta. Top with another sheet and press down firmly. Pass the double sheet again through the rollers.

Jalapeño Cilantro Pasta

For each pound (450 g) of flour, use 4 eggs, 4 tbsp (15 g) of chopped cilantro, and 6 fresh jalapeño peppers that have been cored, stemmed, seeded, and minced.

Chile Pasta I

For each pound (450 g) of flour, use 5 eggs and 5 tbsp (75 ml) of chili powder.

Chile Pasta II

Soak dried ancho or New Mexico chiles, which have been cored and seeded, in boiling water until soft. Drain and purée in a blender. For each pound (450 g) of flour, use 4 eggs and 1 ½ to 2 oz (45 to 60 g) of this chile purée.

Red Beet Horseradish Pasta

For each pound (450 g) of flour, use 3 eggs, 1 oz (30 g) of fresh grated horseradish, and 5 oz (150 g) of cooked, chopped red beets. Using a food processor, process the beets and horseradish with the flour before adding the eggs.

Serving suggestion: This pasta goes well with various poached fish items. For example, poach halibut in white wine, such as Alsatian riesling, and serve with beurre blanc and thin beet noodles.

Lemon Pasta

Add 3 to 4 teaspoons (7 to 10 g) of grated lemon zest to the basic recipe.

Lemon noodles make an excellent accompaniment for fish dishes.

Saffron Pasta

Add a generous pinch of saffron to 2 oz (60 ml) of dry white wine. Reduce the wine over moderate heat to ½ oz. Cool completely. For each pound (450 g) of flour, use this mixture plus 4 eggs.

Wild Mushroom Pasta

For each pound (450 g) of flour, use 5 eggs and 1 to 1½ oz (30 to 45 g) of dried porcini or other wild mushrooms, ground to a fine powder. If the dough is too dry, add an additional egg yolk or two or a little beaten egg.

Serving suggestion: Toss mushroom fettuccine with a little heavy cream that has been reduced by one-third with a little salt. Add diced tomato and cooked shrimp, crayfish, or crabmeat. Or use to make ravioli and stuff with wild mushroom filling (page 137). See also the recipe on page 161.

Black (Squid Ink) Pasta

For each pound (450 g) of flour, use 5 eggs and 2 to 3 tsp (10 to 15 ml) of squid ink, or enough to color the pasta a deep black. (*Note:* Squid ink is available from seafood purveyors in various packages, for example, in cellophane packets of 4 g each.)

Properly made black pasta is flavorful and should be served very simply. For example, toss with a little fresh tomato lightly cooked in olive oil and garnish with some cooked seafood, such as mussels, squid, or shrimp.

FILLINGS FOR TORTELLINI AND OTHER SMALL PASTAS

Cheese Filling

		U.S.		Metric	
YIELD:		**10 oz**	**2 lb 8 oz**	*300 g*	*1.2 kg*
Ingredients					
Ricotta cheese		7 oz	1 lb 12 oz	*200 g*	*800 g*
Egg yolks		2	8	*2*	*8*
Parmesan cheese		1 ½ oz	6 oz	*50 g*	*200 g*
Chopped parsley					
Salt					
White pepper					
Nutmeg					

Mix together the ricotta, egg yolks, and parmesan. Add a generous quantity of chopped parsley. Season to taste with salt, pepper, and nutmeg.

Spinach and Cheese Filling

YIELD:		**1 lb 2 oz**	**4 lb 8 oz**	*550 g*	*2.2 kg*
Ingredients					
Spinach		1 lb 8 oz	6 lb	*750 g*	*3 kg*
Ricotta cheese		6 oz	1 lb 8 oz	*185 g*	*750 g*
Eggs		1	4	*1*	*4*
Egg yolks		1	4	*1*	*4*
Parmesan cheese		3 oz	12 oz	*90 g*	*375 g*
Chopped parsley					
Salt					
Pepper					
Nutmeg					

Trim the spinach, discarding the stems and coarse ribs. Wash well. Blanch in boiling water, drain, and cool under cold water. Squeeze dry and chop fine. Mix with the remaining ingredients and season to taste.

Chard and Cheese Filling

Substitute swiss chard for the spinach in the preceding recipe.

Meat Filling

	YIELD:	10 oz	2 lb 8 oz	*300 g*	*1.2 kg*
Ingredients					
Cocked lean pork		1 ½ oz	6 oz	*50 g*	*200 g*
Cocked chicken		2 oz	8 oz	*60 g*	*250 g*
Prosciutto		½ oz	2 oz	*15 g*	*60 g*
Ricotta cheese		5 oz	1 lb 4 oz	*150 g*	*600 g*
Parmesan cheese		1 oz	4 oz	*30 g*	*125 g*
Egg yolk		1	4	*1*	*4*
Salt					
Pepper					
Nutmeg					

Chop or grind the pork, chicken, and prosciutto very fine. Mix with the remaining ingredients and season to taste.

Gorgonzola Filling

	YIELD:	1 lb	4 lb	*500 g*	*2 kg*
Ingredients					
Gorgonzola cheese		8 oz	2 lb	*250 g*	*1 kg*
Ricotta cheese		6 oz	1 lb 8 oz	*185 g*	*750 g*
Egg yolks		4	16	*4*	*16*
Parmesan cheese		1 oz	4 oz	*30 g*	*125 g*
Salt					
Pepper					

Mash the gorgonzola. Mix with the remaining ingredients. Season to taste.

Mushroom Filling I

	YIELD:	8 oz	2 lb	*250 g*	*1 kg*
Ingredients					
Mushrooms, trimmed		10 oz	2 lb 8 oz	*300 g*	*1.2 kg*
Dried porcini mushrooms		½ oz	2 oz	*15 g*	*60 g*
Butter		½ oz	2 oz	*15 g*	*60 g*
Shallots, minced		1 oz	4 oz	*30 g*	*125 g*
White wine		4 oz	1 pt	*125 ml*	*5 dl*
Heavy cream		4 oz	1 pt	*125 ml*	*5 dl*
Salt					
Pepper					

Chop the mushrooms as fine as possible. Soak the porcini in hot water until soft. Squeeze them out and chop fine. Strain and reserve the soaking liquid. Heat the butter in a sauté pan. Add the shallots and sauté briefly. Add the mushrooms and porcini. Sauté over medium heat until dry. This will take some time, as a great deal of liquid will cook out of the mushrooms. When dry, add the wine and the soaking liquid from the porcini. Reduce until dry. Add the heavy cream and simmer until the mixture is thick. Season to taste. Cool.

Mushroom Filling II

	YIELD:	8 oz	2 lb	250 g	1 kg
Ingredients					
Dried porcini or morels		½ oz	2 oz	15 g	60 g
Gruyère cheese		3 oz	12 oz	90 g	375 g
Crushed garlic		¼ tsp	1 tsp	1 g	5 g
Parmesan cheese		1–2 oz	4–8 oz	30–60 g	125–250 g
Chopped parsley		1 tbsp	4 tbsp	3 g	12 g
Heavy cream					
Salt					

Soak the mushrooms in hot water until soft. Drain and squeeze out excess liquid. Purée the mushrooms, gruyère cheese, and garlic in a food processor. Mix in the parmesan and parsley. Add enough heavy cream to make a smooth paste. Salt to taste. (*Note:* If a leaner filling is desired, use stock or mushroom-soaking liquid instead of the heavy cream.)

VEGETABLE RAVIOLI IN GINGER BROTH

		U.S.		Metric	
	PORTIONS:	4	16	4	16
Ingredients					
Chinese cabbage		6 oz	1 lb 8 oz	175 g	700 g
Scallions		3	12	3	12
Shiitake mushroom caps		2 oz	8 oz	60 g	250 g
Snow peas		2 oz	8 oz	60 g	250 g
Vegetable oil		1 oz	4 oz	30 g	125 g
Grated fresh ginger		¼ tsp	1 tsp	1 g	5 g
Sherry (optional)		2 tsp	8 tsp	10 ml	40 ml
Chinese oyster sauce		1 tsp	4 tsp	5 ml	20 ml
Chinese sesame oil		½ tsp	2 tsp	3 ml	10 ml
Cilantro, chopped		1 tbsp	4 tbsp	3 g	12 g
Salt					
Fresh herb pasta dough, in thin sheets		8 oz	2 lb	250 g	1 kg
Water or egg wash, as needed					
Chicken stock		10 oz	2 pt 8 oz	3 dl	12 dl
Fresh ginger slices		6–8	24–32	6–8	24–32
Salt					
Cilantro for garnish					

Mise en Place:

1. Prepare the vegetables: Shred the cabbage. Cut the scallions into thin slices. Cut the mushrooms into thin julienne. Trim the snow peas and cut diagonally into julienne.

2. Heat the oil in a sauté pan over moderate heat. Add the vegetables and ginger. Sauté until the vegetables are wilted.

3. Add the sherry and the oyster sauce. Continue to cook until the vegetables are tender and there is no liquid in the pan.

4. Remove from the heat and cool. Add the sesame oil and the cilantro. Season with salt.

5. Lay out half the pasta sheets on the worktable. Place mounds of the vegetable mixture about 3 to 4 inches (8 to 10 cm) apart on the pasta, using about ½ oz (15 g) for each mound.

6. Brush the exposed pasta with water or egg wash. Top with the remaining sheets of pasta. Press the two layers of pasta together to seal them, at the same time pressing around the vegetable mounds to eliminate air bubbles. Cut into round or square ravioli.

7. In a saucepan, simmer the stock with the ginger slices until reduced by half. Strain and season with salt.

Finishing:

1. Drop the ravioli into boiling salted water. Reduce the heat and simmer about 3 minutes, until the pasta is cooked.

2. Remove the ravioli with a skimmer and drain well.

3. Arrange the ravioli in broad soup plates and pour the ginger-flavored stock over them. Garnish with a few leaves of cilantro.

Variations

Vegetable broth or a fresh vegetable juice can be substituted for the chicken stock.

Wonton skins may be used instead of pasta sheets, as in the recipe on page 160.

LOBSTER RAVIOLI WITH ZUCCHINI

		U.S.		Metric	
PORTIONS:		**4**	**16**	*4*	*16*
Ingredients					
Lobsters, about 1 ¼ lb (600 g) each		2	8	*2*	*8*
White wine		½ oz	2 oz	*15 ml*	*60 ml*
Zucchini, medium, as needed					
Crème fraîche or heavy cream		3 ½ oz	14 oz	*1 dl*	*4 dl*
Tomato paste		2 tsp	8 tsp	*10 g*	*40 g*
Tarragon		¼ tsp	1 tsp	*0.25 g*	*1 g*
Chives, chopped		½ tsp	2 tsp	*0.5 g*	*2 g*
Salt					
Cayenne					
Wonton skins (see note)		40	160	*40*	*160*
Egg yolks, thinned with an equal volume of water		1	4	*1*	*4*
Shellfish sauce (p. 66)		6 oz	1 pt 8 oz	*2 dl*	*8 dl*
Crème fraîche		2 oz	8 oz	*60 ml*	*2.5 dl*

Note: Fresh pasta dough, rolled out very thin, may be used instead of wonton skins. See pages 149 and 151 for information on making ravioli.

Mise en Place:

1. Steam the lobsters for 5 minutes. Cool. Remove the meat from the shells. Use the shells to make the sauce or save for another purpose.

2. Cut the lobster meat into thin slices. Toss with the white wine.

3. Cut the zucchini into slices about ⅛ inch (3 mm) thick. You will need 5 slices per portion. Blanch the slices in boiling salted water for about 30 seconds. Drain and cool under cold water.

4. Mix together the crème fraîche or heavy cream, tomato paste, tarragon, and chives. Add salt and cayenne to taste. Whip the mixture until it holds a soft shape.

5. Drain the lobster. Lay out half of the wonton skins on the worktable. Place a piece of zucchini in the center of each one. Top each with ½ oz (15 g) of lobster and then with 1 tsp (5 ml) of the cream mixture.

6. Brush the edges of each of the skins with the egg yolk mixture. Top with the remaining wonton skins. Press the edges together well to seal, taking care to press out any air bubbles.

Finishing:

1. Drop the ravioli into boiling salted water. Reduce the heat to a simmer. Simmer for 3 minutes.

2. Remove the ravioli from the water with a skimmer. Drain well.

3. Plate the ravioli, allowing 5 per portion.

4. Ladle a ribbon of shellfish sauce around and over each portion. Drizzle with 1 tbsp (15 ml) of crème fraîche that has been warmed slightly.

Variations

Other sauces may be used to dress the ravioli. For example, use 1 to 2 oz (30 to 60 ml) of carrot juice sauce (page 56) per portion or about ½ oz (15 ml) of lobster oil (page 83) per portion. Other options include herbed or saffron beurre blanc.

WILD MUSHROOM FETTUCCINE WITH GORGONZOLA, WALNUTS, AND TOMATO CREAM

	U.S.		*Metric*	
PORTIONS:	**4**	**16**	***4***	***16***
Ingredients				
Tomatoes, peeled, seeded, and chopped	6 oz	1 lb 8 oz	*175 g*	*700 kg*
Salt	¼ tsp	1 tsp	*1 g*	*5 g*
Butter	1 oz	4 oz	*30 g*	*125 g*
Heavy cream	4 oz	1 pt	*125 ml*	*5 dl*
Gorgonzola cheese, crumbled	4 oz	1 lb	*125 g*	*500 kg*
Marjoram	pinch	½ tsp	*pinch*	*0.5 g*
Fettuccine made from wild mushroom pasta (p. 155)	12 oz	3 lb	*350 g*	*1.4 kg*
Walnuts, toasted, and coarsely chopped	3 oz	12 oz	*90 g*	*350 g*
Heavy cream	2–4 oz	8–16 oz	*60–125 ml*	*2.5–5 dl*
Parmesan cheese	2–3 oz	8–12 oz	*60–90 g*	*250–375 g*
Salt				

Procedure:

1. Mix the tomatoes with the salt. Place in a strainer and let drain.

2. In a sauté pan large enough to hold the cooked pasta, heat the butter and cream until the butter is melted. Add the gorgonzola and marjoram and remove from the heat.

3. Drop the fettuccine into boiling salted water. As soon as the fettuccine is al dente (which should be about 1 minute after the water returns to a boil), drain it.

4. Put the fettuccine into the pan with the gorgonzola mixture. Add the tomatoes and two-thirds of the walnuts. Set over moderate heat and toss until well combined. Add additional cream as needed so that the pasta is smooth and creamy, not dry and sticky.

5. Mix in the parmesan cheese. Check for seasonings and add salt if necessary. Plate and sprinkle the top with the remaining walnuts. Serve at once.

CANNELLONI OF FRESH GREENS AND DUCK CONFIT

		U.S.		Metric	
PORTIONS:		4	16	4	16
Ingredients					
Butter		½ oz	2 oz	15 g	60 g
Spinach, stems removed		2 oz	8 oz	60 g	250 g
Arugula, stems removed		2 oz	8 oz	60 g	250 g
Tender lettuce, such as Boston or bibb		2 oz	8 oz	60 g	250 g
Chopped parsley		2 tbsp	½ cup	7 g	25 g
Fresh tarragon, chopped		1 tbsp	4 tbsp	3 g	12 g
Duck meat from confit (p. 321)		4 oz	1 lb	125 g	500 g
Salt					
White pepper					
Fresh egg pasta or spinach pasta		6 oz	1 lb 8 oz	175 g	700 g
Parmesan cheese		1 oz	4 oz	30 g	125 g
Butter or fat from confit, for baking dish					
Brown stock or duck stock		8 oz	2 pt	2.5 dl	1 l
Parmesan cheese		1 oz	4 oz	30 g	125 g
Spinach, stems removed		4 oz	1 lb	125 g	500 g

Mise en Place:

1. Heat the butter in a sauté pan over moderate heat. Add the spinach, arugula, lettuce, parsley, and tarragon. Cook until wilted. Remove from the pan. Squeeze out excess moisture. Chop fine. Cool.

2. Pull the duck meat apart into shreds.

3. Mix the duck with the chopped greens. Season to taste with salt and pepper.

4. Roll out the pasta as thin as possible. Cut into rectangles 3 by 4 inches (8 by 10 cm). You will need 4 rectangles per portion.

5. Drop the pasta into boiling salted water. When the water returns to the boil, drain at once and cool under cold water. Spread the rectangles out on trays or on a work surface.

6. Sprinkle the pasta lightly with parmesan cheese.

7. Place about 2 tbsp of the duck mixture along one short edge of each rectangle. Roll up.

8. Select a baking pan or dish just large enough to hold the cannelloni. Grease it with butter or fat from the confit. Arrange the cannelloni in it. Hold for service.

Finishing:

1. Add enough stock to the cannelloni to come about halfway up to the tops of the cannelloni. Sprinkle the tops with parmesan cheese. Heat in a moderate oven.

2. Meanwhile, blanch the spinach leaves in boiling salted water. Drain and press out excess moisture, but do not squeeze dry.

3. Arrange a few spinach leaves on each serving plate. Top with 4 hot cannelloni. Spoon a little of the stock around them and serve at once.

OPEN RAVIOLI WITH SCALLOPS   *(Color Plate 3)*

		U.S.		Metric	
PORTIONS:		4	16	*4*	*16*
Ingredients					
Spinach pasta		3 oz	12 oz	*90 g*	*375 g*
Herb pasta (see note)		3 oz	12 oz	*90 g*	*375 g*
Olive oil		½ oz	2 oz	*15 ml*	*60 ml*
Tomatoes, peeled, seeded, and diced		8 oz	2 lb	*250 g*	*1 kg*
Fresh basil, chopped		1 tbsp	4 tbsp	*3 g*	*12 g*
Fresh rosemary, chopped		1 tsp	4 tsp	*1 g*	*4 g*
Garlic, chopped		1 tsp	4 tsp	*5 g*	*20 g*
Salt					
Cayenne					
Sea scallops		12 oz	3 lb	*350 g*	*1.4 kg*
Olive oil					
Salt					
Basil oil (p. 82)		1 oz	4 oz	*30 ml*	*125 ml*
Paprika oil (p. 81)		1 oz	4 oz	*30 ml*	*125 ml*

Note: If it is necessary to avoid making two separate batches of pasta, the dish can be made with all one kind.

Mise en Place:

1. Roll out the pasta very thin. Cut into squares about 4 to 5 inches (10 to 12 cm) across. You will need one square of each kind per portion.
2. Heat the olive oil in a sauté pan. Add the tomatoes, herbs, and garlic. Cook until well reduced and there is no juice. Season well with salt and cayenne.
3. If the scallops are large, cut them in half crosswise.

Finishing:

1. For service, reheat the tomato mixture if necessary.
2. Have ready a pot of boiling water to cook the pasta.
3. Heat a sauté pan until very hot. For each portion, add a little olive oil and brown 3 oz (90 g) of scallops on both sides. Season with salt.
4. Drop a square of spinach pasta into the boiling water. Cook 1 minute and remove with a skimmer. Place in the center of a plate.
5. Place a spoonful of the tomato mixture in the center of the square. Spread it around a little with the spoon.
6. Arrange the scallops on top of the tomato mixture.
7. Cook a square of herb pasta in the same way and place it on top of the scallops.
8. Drizzle a tablespoon of each of the oils decoratively around the ravioli.

RED AND GREEN CHILE FETTUCCINE WITH GRILLED CHICKEN

		U.S.		Metric	
PORTIONS:		**4**	**16**	*4*	*16*
Ingredients					
Chicken breasts, boneless and skinless		8 oz	2 lb	*250 g*	*1 kg*
Chili powder					
Salt					
Olive oil or corn oil					
Sour cream		2 oz	8 oz	*60 ml*	*2.5 dl*
Lime juice		½ oz	2 oz	*15 ml*	*60 ml*
Tomatoes, peeled, seeded, and chopped		6 oz	1 lb 8 oz	*175 g*	*700 g*
Garlic, minced		½ tsp	2 tsp	*2 g*	*10 g*
Olive oil or corn oil		1 oz	4 oz	*30 ml*	*125 ml*
Mild green chiles or green bell peppers, roasted, peeled (p. 521), and cut into small strips		2 oz	8 oz	*60 g*	*250 g*
Salt					
Fettuccine made from red chile pasta (p. 154)		5–6 oz	20–24 oz	*150–175 g*	*600–700 g*
Fettuccine made from jalapeño cilantro pasta (p. 154)		5–6 oz	20–24 oz	*150–175 g*	*600–700 g*
Monterey jack cheese, grated		4 oz	1 lb	*110 g*	*450 g*
Sliced avocado		3 oz	12 oz	*90 g*	*350 g*

Mise en Place:

1. Season the chicken breasts lightly with chili powder and salt. Coat with oil. Let marinate in the refrigerator until ready to cook.
2. Mix together the sour cream and lime juice.

Finishing:

1. Warm the tomatoes and garlic gently in the oil. Add the pepper strips. Season to taste with salt.
2. Grill the chicken.
3. Cook the pastas in boiling water. They can be cooked together if they are both freshly made; however, if one pasta is drier than the other, it is best to boil them separately.
4. Drain the pastas and immediately toss together with the tomato mixture.
5. Add the cheese and toss lightly. Check for seasonings and add more salt if necessary. Put into serving plates or pasta bowls.
6. Slice the grilled chicken. Arrange the sliced chicken and sliced avocado on top of the pasta.
7. Drizzle with the sour cream mixture. Serve at once.

Variation

To serve as a main course, increase the quantity of chicken as desired.

FUSILLI WITH MIXED-HERB PESTO AND TOMATO

		U.S.		Metric	
PORTIONS:		4	16	4	16
Ingredients					
Fresh basil leaves, chopped		2 tbsp	½ cup	7 g	25 g
Fresh chives, chopped		1 tbsp	4 tbsp	2 g	10 g
Fresh marjoram or oregano, chopped		1 tbsp	4 tbsp	3 g	12 g
Fresh thyme, chopped		2 tsp	8 tsp	2 g	10 g
Fresh parsley, chopped		1 tbsp	4 tbsp	3 g	12 g
Garlic, chopped		1 tsp	4 tsp	5 g	20 g
Olive oil		2 oz	8 oz	60 ml	2.5 dl
Tomatoes, peeled, seeded, and diced		4 oz	1 lb	125 g	500 g
Olive oil		½ oz	2 oz	15 ml	60 ml
Salt					
Fusilli		8 oz	2 lb	250 g	1 kg
Parmesan cheese		2 oz	8 oz	60 g	250 g
Salt					
Pepper					

Mise en Place:

Using a food processor, blender, or preferably a mortar and pestle, combine the herbs, garlic, and olive oil and work them to a coarse paste.

Finishing:

1. Heat the tomatoes in the olive oil just until warm. Sprinkle with a little salt.
2. Boil the fusilli in salted water until al dente. Drain and transfer to a heated bowl.
3. Add the herb pesto to the fusilli and toss to coat. Add the cheese and season to taste. Toss again.
4. Transfer the fusilli to pasta bowls. Place a spoonful of the warm tomatoes in the center. Serve at once.

BLACK PASTA WITH GRILLED SHRIMP   *(Color Plate 4)*

		U.S.		Metric	
PORTIONS:		**4**	**16**	*4*	*16*
Ingredients					
Jumbo shrimp		16	64	*16*	*64*
Olive oil		1 oz	4 oz	*30 ml*	*125 ml*
Lemon juice		½ oz	2 oz	*15 ml*	*60 ml*
Salt					
Pepper					
Black (squid ink) pasta dough		12 oz	3 lb	*350 g*	*1.4 kg*
Olive oil		2 oz	8 oz	*60 ml*	*250 ml*
Garlic, minced		1 clove	4 cloves	*1 clove*	*4 cloves*
Tomatoes, peeled, seeded, and chopped		8 oz	2 lb	*250 g*	*1 kg*
Additional olive oil, if needed					
Basil sprigs		4	16	*4*	*16*

Mise en Place:

1. Peel and devein the shrimp.
2. Combine the olive oil, lemon juice, salt, and pepper. Add the shrimp and marinate for 15 minutes.
3. Roll out the pasta dough to the same thickness as the width of the narrow cutting roller. Cut with the narrow cutting roller to make a pasta that resembles square spaghetti.

Finishing:

1. Heat the second quantity of olive oil in a sauté pan. Add the garlic and sauté briefly without browning. Add the tomatoes and sauté another minute.
2. Remove the shrimp from the marinade. Grill or broil just until cooked.
3. At the same time, drop the pasta into boiling salted water. Boil until al dente. Drain.
4. Toss the pasta with the tomato mixture. Add additional olive oil if needed. Taste for seasonings and add salt if necessary.
5. Plate the pasta in spaghetti bowls. Top each portion with 4 grilled shrimp and garnish with a sprig of fresh basil.

Variations

Omit the shrimp and toss the pasta with some steamed, shelled mussels.

For extra flavor, toss the cooked pasta with additional squid ink before the sauce is added. Use about ¼ tsp (1 g) per portion.

SPAGHETTI WITH FRESH SARDINES

		U.S.		Metric	
PORTIONS:		4	16	*4*	*16*
Ingredients					
Olive oil		1 oz	4 oz	*30 ml*	*125 ml*
Fresh sardines		12	48	*12*	*48*
Garlic cloves		1	4	*1*	*4*
Fennel seed		1 tsp	4 tsp	*2 g*	*8 g*
Hot red pepper flakes, to taste					
Spaghetti		8 oz	2 lb	*250 g*	*1 kg*
Chopped parsley		2 tbsp	½ cup	*7 g*	*25 g*
Additional olive oil, as needed					
Salt					
Black pepper					

Mise en Place:

1. Fillet the sardines.
2. Peel and chop the garlic cloves.

Finishing:

1. Heat the olive oil in a sauté pan over moderate heat. Add the sardine fillets, garlic, fennel seed, and hot pepper. Sauté until the sardines are cooked. Remove from the pan and keep warm. Leave the oil and spices in the pan.
2. Boil the spaghetti in salted water until al dente. Drain.
3. Immediately add the spaghetti to the sauté pan set over low heat. Add the chopped parsley and toss to coat the spaghetti with oil and spices. Add additional olive oil if necessary. Adjust the seasonings with salt and pepper.
4. Place the spaghetti in pasta bowls and top with the sardine fillets.

Variation

Spaghetti with Fresh Tuna

Fresh tuna steak		8 oz	2 lb	*250 g*	*1 kg*
Tomatoes, peeled, seeded, and chopped		6 oz	1 lb 8 oz	*175 g*	*700 g*

Omit the fennel in the basic recipe. Cut the tuna into medium dice. Proceed as in the basic recipe, except use high heat; the tuna should be rare but well seared on the outside. After removing the tuna from the pan, add the tomatoes and cook just until heated through. Finish the spaghetti as in the basic recipe by tossing it in the pan, plating it, and topping with the diced tuna. If desired, substitute chopped fresh basil for the parsley.

RIGATONI OR PENNE WITH CLAMS AND SAUSAGE

		U.S.		Metric	
PORTIONS:		**4**	**16**	*4*	*16*
Ingredients					
Olive oil		½ oz	2 oz	*15 ml*	*60 ml*
Italian sausage, cut into ½-inch (1-cm) slices		4 oz	1 lb	*125 g*	*500 g*
Onion, chopped		2 oz	8 oz	*60 g*	*250 g*
Green bell pepper, diced		2 oz	8 oz	*60 g*	*250 g*
Red bell pepper, diced		2 oz	8 oz	*60 g*	*250 g*
Tomatoes, peeled, seeded, and chopped		3 oz	12 oz	*90 g*	*350 g*
Saffron		pinch	½ tsp	*pinch*	*0.3 g*
Hot red pepper flakes, to taste					
Littleneck clams, well scrubbed		12	48	*12*	*48*
Salt					
Pepper					
Rigatoni or penne		8 oz	2 lb	*250 g*	*1 kg*
Chopped parsley					

Procedure:

1. Heat the oil in a sauté pan. Add the sausage and sauté until just cooked. Remove with a slotted spoon.
2. Add the onion and diced peppers to the fat in the pan. Sauté briefly until just starting to get tender.
3. Add the tomatoes, saffron, and hot pepper. Simmer about 5 minutes.
4. Meanwhile, add the penne or rigatoni to boiling salted water and boil until al dente.
5. Shortly before the pasta is cooked, return the sausage to the pan with the vegetable mixture. Set over moderately high heat. Add the clams and cover. Cook just until the clams open. Do not overcook or they will be tough. Season with salt and pepper.
6. Drain the pasta and immediately transfer to pasta bowls for serving.
7. Top with the contents of the pan, dividing the clams, sausage, and vegetables evenly among the servings.
8. Sprinkle with chopped parsley. Serve immediately.

Variations

Mussels may be substituted for clams. Adjust the quantity as desired. If neither clams nor mussels are available, the dish can be made with shrimp, although the flavor and character of the dish will be quite different.

Rigatoni or Penne with Sausage, Peppers, and Tomatoes

Omit the seafood from the recipe and double the quantity of sausage.

OTHER FIRST COURSES

The final section of this chapter presents an assortment of first-course recipes not covered elsewhere in this book. Some of the recipes include specialty items such as caviar and cured salmon. As an introduction to the recipes, some background information on several of these products is provided.

Caviar

Caviar is the salted roe, or eggs, of the sturgeon. In the United States, any product labeled simply "caviar" must come from sturgeon. Roe from any other fish must be labeled as such (for example, "whitefish caviar").

The most important caviar-producing countries are Russia and Iran, both of which border on the Caspian Sea, where the sturgeon are harvested. Sturgeon live in other waters as well, including North American waters. Production of American caviar has been growing in recent years, although it is not large enough to compete seriously with caviar from the Caspian Sea.

To categorize it further, caviar is given the name of the species of sturgeon it is taken from. The beluga is the largest and scarcest sturgeon, and it yields the largest and most expensive eggs. Next in size are osetra and sevruga.

Although the larger eggs are generally more expensive, size or price alone does not necessarily indicate quality. All three types of caviar vary considerably in quality. The only sure way to determine the quality of a particular tin or jar of caviar is to taste it.

Good-quality caviar should be made up of shiny, whole eggs, with few if any broken eggs. It should not have a strong, fishy smell, nor should it look watery or oily.

Caviar that is made with a relatively low proportion of salt is labeled "malossol," which means "little salt." Malossol caviar is generally considered to be of better quality than the more highly salted varieties. Of interest to those who must restrict their intake of sodium, there is no such thing as low-sodium caviar. Even malossol is salty.

Caviar is either fresh or pasteurized. Fresh caviar in an unopened tin will keep for a few weeks, as long as it is kept cold. Once opened it begins to deteriorate quickly and should be eaten the same day, if possible. Pasteurized caviar, because it has been heat-treated, is of somewhat lesser quality but will keep much longer unopened. When opened, however, it too should be eaten as quickly as possible, although it may keep reasonably well for a few days.

Other Caviars. Caviar from American sturgeon has been made as long ago as colonial times, but only recently the American caviar industry has begun to grow anew. Because it is still growing and changing, it is difficult to make definitive statements about the products available. American-made sturgeon caviars of varying grades and qualities are available, and some of them are excellent.

Roe from other fish, including trout, salmon, whitefish, and lumpfish, is also salted to make caviar. Once again, quality varies considerably, ranging from good to nearly inedible. Those of better quality are useful alternatives to more expensive sturgeon caviar. Among them are the following types:

• Salmon caviar—large, red eggs, often paired with smoked salmon or other salmon products in appetizer dishes.

- Bleak roe—tiny, mild-tasting, orange eggs from a fish native to the Baltic. Long popular in Scandinavia, it is now becoming more widely available in the United States. It sometimes appears under its Swedish name, *löjrom* (pronounced, approximately, "loy-roam").
- Tobiko—tiny, orange eggs from Japanese flying fish. Tobiko was introduced to this country by sushi restaurants, and adopted for other dishes by American chefs.

Serving Caviar. The best caviar should be served ice-cold and as simply as possible. Some say that the only thing to serve alongside caviar is a spoon. The traditional caviar accompaniments of chopped onion, lemon, chopped egg, and sour cream may be all right for inexpensive roes, but they overwhelm the delicate flavor of top-quality beluga, osetra, and sevruga. Spoons for eating caviar should be made of bone, porcelain, mother of pearl, or even plastic. However, the spoons should not be made of metal, because metal reacts with the salty caviar and gives it an unpleasant taste.

For more elaborate presentations, caviars a notch or two below the best quality are better choices. Other foods for which caviar is to be used as a garnish should be fairly mild or delicate, so that they will harmonize with the caviar. Such items as mild smoked salmon, oysters, and potatoes are often used successfully. The recipe on page 177 is an example of this type of presentation.

Caviars from sturgeon and other fish vary considerably in color, from gold to orange to red to various shades of grey and black. Chefs often take advantage of this color variation by making attractive presentations of two or more different colors of caviar.

Caviar does not take well to heating and should not be cooked. If it is to be used in a sauce, the sauce should be warm rather than hot and the caviar should not be added until the last moment. Similarly, avoid topping piping-hot foods with a spoonful of caviar. Let the food cool until it is just warm.

Gravlax and Other Cured Fish

Gravlax, also called gravad lax, is salt-cured salmon. It is a traditional Scandinavian dish that has achieved international popularity. Just as ham is made by curing pork with salt (or a salt brine), gravlax is made by coating fresh salmon fillets with salt and letting it stand (in the refrigerator) until the cure is complete.

Because a pure salt cure would dry out the fish too much, the salt is mixed with sugar because sugar helps retain moisture. (Sugar is also used in cures for meats; see pages 353–354.) To give the item its special flavor, a generous quantity of fresh dill is packed over the fish after it receives its coating of salt and sugar. The recipe explaining the complete procedure is on page 172.

Although dill is the traditional flavoring for gravlax, other herbs and spices may be used to create variations on the basic theme.

Other firm, meaty fish, such as halibut and cod, may be cured by the same process. Some restaurants offer a cured fish sampler as a first course, comprising, for example, salmon, halibut, and cod, cured with different spices and plated with appropriate garnishes. Other cured fish should not be called gravlax, since "lax" means salmon.

Gravlax should be sliced like smoked salmon, as explained in the next section.

Cured fish is almost always served uncooked; it can, however, be cooked, but special care is necessary. Fish loses moisture when it is cured, and, of course, cooking dries it out more. It is best to cure it for only a short time and then to cook it very lightly. An example of this type of preparation is included with other fish recipes in Chapter 6 (see page 231).

Smoked Salmon

The smoked salmon regularly served in thin slices as an appetizer is, technically speaking, cold-smoked—that is, it is exposed to smoke at a low temperature so that it does not cook. Before being smoked, it must be cured, much the same way that gravlax is cured. As a result, the textures of these two products are similar, although they differ in flavor; one tastes of dill and the other of wood smoke. (Salmon can also be hot-smoked, but because this process cooks the fish, the result is entirely different.)

Although the price of salmon has come down in recent years due to increased supply, smoked salmon still commands high prices on menus because it is seen as a luxury food. Excellent quality smoked salmon, both domestic and imported, is available in a wide range of prices. Flavors range from lightly smoked to heavily smoked. Some chefs have set up their own small-scale smokehouse operations and are smoking their own salmon.

Smoked salmon should be cut on a sharp diagonal—that is, with the knife almost parallel to the table—into broad, paper-thin slices, as shown in Figure 5.3. The best knife for the purpose is a long slicing knife with a thin blade. Knives made specifically for smoked salmon are available.

Salmon and Tuna Tartare

Raw fish was not commonly seen on American restaurant menus until Japanese restaurants offering sashimi and sushi became popular. Smoked salmon and gravlax, of course, are exceptions, but because they are processed, people tend not to think of them as raw. Currently, however, items such as salmon or tuna carpaccio (included in Chapter 6) and tartare are frequently served. Carpaccio consists of paper-thin slices of the raw product, while tartare is made of chopped raw fish (or meat), preferably chopped by hand for the best texture.

Salmon and tuna are the usual choices for serving raw because they are flavorful and tender, and they have a richness or oiliness that makes them especially suitable for this treatment.

There are two schools of thought regarding fish tartares. Some chefs feel that the chopped fish should be mixed with the bare minimum of seasonings and condiments, perhaps only some oil and salt, so that the natural flavor of the fish can shine through. Others feel that a tartare needs more piquant ingredients, like mustard and lime juice, to liven it up. The recipe and variations on page 174 present both these alternatives. Another approach is to chop gravlax or other cured or smoked fish for tartares.

FIGURE 5.3. **Slice smoked salmon on the diagonal into paper-thin slices. Cut toward the tail end.**

GRAVLAX

		U.S.	Metric
	YIELD:	**1 lb 14 oz**	*850 g*
Ingredients			
Salmon fillet, skin on		2½ lb	*1.2 kg*
Coarse salt		4 oz	*125 g*
Sugar		4 oz	*125 g*
White pepper		¼ tsp	*0.5 g*
Fresh dill sprigs		2 oz	*60 g*
Sauce	YIELD:	**9 oz**	*265 ml*
Dijon-style mustard		2 oz	*60 ml*
Red wine vinegar		1 oz	*30 ml*
Sugar		1 tsp	*5 g*
Vegetable oil		6 oz	*175 ml*
Chopped fresh dill to taste			

Note: The recipe may be multiplied as necessary. If two fillets are to be cured at the same time, follow the procedure indicated in step 4. The yield indicated is for the edible portion—that is, without skin.

Procedure:

1. Pass the fingertips over the surface of the salmon fillet to locate any bones. Pull them out with a needlenose pliers.

2. Mix together the salt, sugar, and white pepper.

3. Select a stainless steel, glass, ceramic, or other nonreactive pan to hold the salmon for curing. Sprinkle a little of the salt mixture on the bottom of the pan and lay the salmon on it skin side down. Cover the flesh side of the fillet completely with a layer of the salt mixture. Then top with the dill, again covering the fillet completely.

4. If curing two fillets, salt the second fillet in the same manner as the first and invert it on top of the first, so that the dill is sandwiched between the two fillets and the skin side of each fillet is toward the outside.

5. Cover the pan well and refrigerate for one day. Turn the fillet or fillets over and refrigerate for another day (for a total of two days). *Note:* Some instructions say to place a weight on the fish during the cure. This is optional. Weighting the fish produces a slightly drier, firmer finished product.

6. After two days, drain off any liquid that has accumulated in the pan. Carefully scrape all the dill and curing mixture from the fish.

7. To serve, cut in thin slices like smoked salmon (see page 171). Accompany each portion with a spoonful of the mustard dill sauce.

Variations

To make the flavor a little spicier, substitute 1 ½ tsp (3 g) of crushed white peppercorns for the white pepper in the basic recipe.

Other spices and herbs may be used instead of dill (for example, a mixture of fennel seeds and crushed black peppercorns).

Cured Halibut

White peppercorns, crushed	1 ½ tsp	*3 g*
Mustard seeds, crushed	1 tsp	*2 g*
Ground allspice	¼ tsp	*0.5 g*

Use halibut fillets instead of salmon. Omit the ground white pepper and dill from the basic recipe and mix the above spices with the salt and sugar.

Cured Salmon with Oriental Flavors

Grated fresh ginger	2 oz	*60 g*
Chopped lemon grass (optional)	1 oz	*30 g*
Soy sauce	8 oz	*2.5 dl*
Hoisin sauce	4 oz	*125 ml*

Omit the dill in the basic recipe and mix the ginger and lemon grass with the salt and sugar. After curing, scrape off the curing mixture and marinate the salmon for one day in the soy sauce and hoisin sauce, which have been mixed together. Serve with two sauces: (1) a mustard sauce made by mixing dry mustard to a thin paste with water and (2) hoisin sauce.

SALMON TARTARE

		U.S.		Metric	
	PORTIONS:	4–6	16–24	4–6	16–24
Ingredients					
Salmon fillets, skinless		12 oz	3 lb	350 g	1.4 kg
Shallots, minced		2 tbsp	2 oz	15 g	60 g
Parsley, chopped		1 tbsp	4 tbsp	3 g	12 g
Fresh tarragon, chopped		1 tbsp	4 tbsp	3 g	12 g
Lime juice		½ oz	2 oz	15 ml	60 ml
Dijon-style mustard		½ oz	2 oz	15 ml	60 ml
Olive oil		1 oz	4 oz	30 ml	125 ml
Salt					
White pepper					

Procedure:

1. Remove all bones and sinews from the salmon. In addition, cut away and discard the dark, fatty tissue that runs down the centerline of the fillet.

2. Mince the fish with a knife. The most effective way to do this is to cut the fillet into thin slices, cut the slices into thin strips, and cut the strips into very small dice. (The fish may also be chopped with a food processor, pulsing the machine and being careful not to process the fish to a paste. Do not pass the fish through a grinder; this produces an undesirable texture.)

3. Mix the chopped fish with the remaining ingredients shortly before serving, seasoning to taste with salt and pepper.

4. Salmon tartare may be served very simply mounded on a small plate or in more elaborate ways. Some other presentations are included in the following variations.

Variations

Omit the shallots, parsley, tarragon, lime juice, and mustard. Add some chopped chives and a dash of hot pepper sauce.

Cure the salmon for one day as in the recipe for Gravlax (page 172), but without the dill. Chop the fish and mix with a little spicy mayonnaise or with sour cream, mustard, and lemon juice.

Tuna Tartare

Substitute tuna for salmon in the basic recipe or the first variation.

Presentation suggestions:

Place a round biscuit cutter in the center of a plate. Fill it with the tartare and spread the top with a layer of sour cream or crème fraîche. Remove the cutter. Place a fresh herb leaf (such as chervil) or a dab of caviar on top. Or top with the herb and place spoonfuls of caviar around the salmon, as in the recipe on page 177.

Pack into timbale molds (or into cutter) a layer of tartare, a layer of peeled, seeded, and diced cucumber that has been salted, drained, and mixed with fresh dill, and another layer of tartare (see Figure 5.4).

Napoleon of Salmon Tartare	*(Color Plate 5)*

Prepare gaufrette potatoes, potato chips, or fried chips of other vegetables. Stick one chip to the center of a plate with a dab of sour cream. Top with a spoonful of fish tartar. Continue stacking chips and tartare, making three layers of each. Garnish the plate as desired, such as with spoonfuls of caviar as in the recipe on page 177.

FIGURE 5.4. **Using a round cutter to shape a portion of salmon tartare with cucumber.**
(a) After filling the cutter with a layer of salmon, a layer of cucumber, and a final layer of salmon, smooth the top layer with a spatula.

(b) Carefully remove the cutter.

CRAB CAKES

		U.S.		Metric	
PORTIONS:		**4**	**16**	*4*	*16*
Ingredients					
Crabmeat (see note)		12 oz	3 lb	*350 g*	*1.4 kg*
Fresh bread crumbs		1 oz	4 oz	*30 g*	*125 g*
Mayonnaise		3 tbsp	6 oz	*45 g*	*175 g*
Eggs, beaten		1	4	*1*	*4*
Prepared mustard		½ tsp	2 tsp	*3 g*	*10 g*
Worcestershire sauce		½ tsp	2 tsp	*3 g*	*10 g*
Salt		½ tsp	2 tsp	*3 g*	*10 g*
White pepper		pinch	½ tsp	*pinch*	*1 g*
Chopped parsley		2 tsp	8 tsp	*2 g*	*8 g*
Scallions, chopped fine		2	8	*2*	*8*
Butter, for sautéing					
Lemon wedges					

Note: Meat from cooked crabs is used for this recipe. To save the labor of picking crabmeat from cooked crabs, tinned crabmeat, usually from blue crabs, is generally used. The best-quality packaged crabmeat must be kept refrigerated even when unopened, since it is not processed enough to make it shelf-stable.

Mise en Place:

1. Pick over the crabmeat to remove any bits of shell.
2. Mix together the remaining ingredients, except the butter and lemon wedges. Fold in the crabmeat.
3. Form by hand into round cakes. For each portion, allow 1 large cake, about 4 oz (125 g) or 2 small cakes, about 2 oz (60 g) each. (*Note:* This mixture has very little bread filler, so it may be somewhat difficult to handle. If desired, add more bread crumbs to make a firmer mixture that will pack more easily into cakes. The texture of the crabmeat may also affect the texture of the cakes and the quantity of bread crumbs needed.)

Cooking and Presentation:

1. Sauté the cakes in butter until browned on both sides and cooked through. (As an alternative, the cakes can be breaded and deep-fried.)
2. Serve with lemon wedges.

Variations

Serve small crab cakes as part of a warm salad with greens and a vinaigrette.

Other ingredients and seasonings may be used, such as chives, paprika, sherry, and minced green pepper.

Fish Cakes

Substitute cooked, flaked fish, such as salmon or codfish, for the crabmeat.

Crab Cakes with Shrimp Mousseline

Omit the crumbs, mayonnaise, and egg from the basic recipe. Prepare enough shrimp mousseline (page 230) to equal the weight of the crabmeat. Season the mousseline with the mustard, worcestershire sauce, salt, pepper, parsley, and scallions from the basic recipe. Combine the crab and mousseline and form into cakes. Coat lightly in fresh bread crumbs. Sauté and serve as in the basic recipe.

Duck Cakes

Substitute chopped, cooked duck meat for the crabmeat in the basic recipe. Proceed as in the basic recipe, except add the following additional ingredients, to taste, for seasoning and texture: cayenne, thyme, diced bell pepper (any color), and chopped toasted almonds. Depending on the texture and moistness of the duck, it may be necessary to increase the quantity of crumbs or egg. Serve the cakes with tomato beurre blanc (page 69).

SMOKED SALMON WITH THREE CAVIARS

	U.S.		Metric	
PORTIONS:	4	16	4	16
Ingredients				
Smoked salmon, in paper-thin slices	8 oz	2 lb	250 g	1 kg
Salmon caviar	1 oz	4 oz	30 g	125 g
Golden caviar	1 oz	4 oz	30 g	125 g
Black caviar	1 oz	4 oz	30 g	125 g
Crème fraîche	2 oz	8 oz	60 ml	2.5 dl
Horseradish oil (p. 79), optional	1 oz	4 oz	30 ml	125 ml
Dill sprigs	4	16	4	16

Presentation:

1. For each portion, roll 2 oz (60 g) of salmon into a rosette and place in the center of a plate. Garnish it with a small dill sprig.
2. At three equal intervals around the salmon, place 1 tsp (5 ml) of crème fraîche.
3. Top each dab of cream with ⅓ oz (10 g) of one of the caviars.
4. Drizzle with 1½ tsp (7 ml) of the flavored oil.

Variations

Spread the salmon out in a thin layer to cover the plate. Top with a potato galette (page 540) placed in the center. On top of the galette, place 1, 2, or 3 spoonfuls of caviar, each on top of a dab of crème fraîche.

For the basic recipe, if only two kinds of caviar are available, plate 2 spoonfuls of each on alternating quadrants of the plate.

CASSOLETTES OF ESCARGOTS

		U.S.		Metric	
PORTIONS:		**4**	**16**	**4**	**16**
Ingredients					
Court bouillon:					
Carrot, sliced		1 oz	4 oz	*30 g*	*125 g*
Onion, sliced		1 oz	4 oz	*30 g*	*125 g*
Shallot, sliced		½ oz	2 oz	*15 g*	*60 g*
Parsley stems		6	25	*6*	*25*
Bay leaf		½	2	*½*	*2*
Peppercorns		3	12	*3*	*12*
Thyme		pinch	½ tsp	*pinch*	*0.5 g*
Dry white wine		4 oz	1 pt	*125 ml*	*5 dl*
Water		4 oz	1 pt	*125 ml*	*5 dl*
Salt		¼ tsp	1 tsp	*1 g*	*5 g*
Snails, canned		24	96	*24*	*96*
Escargot butter (p. 77)		2 oz	8 oz	*60 g*	*250 g*
Toasted hazelnuts, chopped fine, then crushed		1 tbsp	4 tbsp	*10 g*	*40 g*

Mise en Place:

1. Combine the ingredients for the court bouillon and bring to a boil. Simmer 15 minutes, partially covered to prevent evaporation.

2. Drain the snails, rinse under cold water, and add to the court bouillon. Simmer very gently for 30 minutes.

3. Remove the snails with a slotted spoon. Strain the court bouillon and divide it in half. Return the snails to half the liquid and refrigerate until needed. Reserve the other half of the liquid to make the sauce.

4. Blend together the snail butter and nuts.

Finishing:

1. Reheat the snails in their broth.

2. Reheat the reserved liquid in a second saucepan. Whip in the seasoned butter, as for making beurre blanc. Taste and adjust the seasonings if necessary.

3. With a slotted spoon, transfer the snails to small individual serving casserole dishes. Pour the sauce over them.

4. Place the casserole dishes on underliners. Serve with bread for soaking up the sauce.

Variations

Ragout of Escargots

Demiglaze	2 oz	8 oz	*60 ml*	*2.5 dl*
Tomatoes, peeled, seeded, and chopped	2 oz	8 oz	*60 g*	*250 g*
Sautéed, diced mushrooms, preferably chanterelles	2 oz	8 oz	*60 g*	*250 g*
Cooked carrots, brunoise	1 oz	4 oz	*30 g*	*125 g*
Fresh herbs, as desired				

Do not reduce the liquid for the sauce (see Finishing, step 2, in the basic recipe). Add the demiglaze and tomatoes. Bring to a simmer and add the reheated snails, the mushrooms, the carrots, and a generous quantity of herbs. Finish with the escargot butter as in the basic recipe or with fresh raw butter. Serve each portion over a thin crouton in a soup plate.

Feuilleté of Snails

Prepare either the basic recipe or the variation. Serve with puff pastry. Use the procedure in the recipe on page 182, substituting the snail mixture for the vegetable mixture.

GRILLED VEGETABLES WITH ROMESCO SAUCE

	U.S.		Metric	
YIELD OF SAUCE:	1 pt	4 pt	5 dl	2 l
Ingredients				
White bread	1 oz	4 oz	30 g	125 g
Olive oil	½ oz	2 oz	15 ml	60 ml
Blanched almonds	3 oz	12 oz	90 g	375 g
Garlic, chopped	2 tsp	8 tsp	10 g	40 g
Tomatoes, peeled	10 oz	2 lb 8 oz	300 g	1.2 kg
Spanish paprika	2 tsp	8 tsp	4 g	16 g
Cayenne	⅛ tsp	½ tsp	0.25 g	1 g
Red wine vinegar (see steps 5–6)	1 ½ oz	6 oz	50 ml	2 dl
Olive oil	3–4 oz	12–16 oz	90–125 ml	3.5–5 dl
Salt				
Pepper				
Assorted grilled vegetables (pp. 491–492)				

Procedure:

1. Sauté the bread in olive oil until golden.

2. Toast the almonds in an oven (350°F or 175°C for about 15 minutes) or in a skillet over moderately low heat until light golden not dark brown. Remove from the pan as soon as they are golden, so that they do not brown further.

3. Combine the bread, almonds, and garlic in a food processor. Grind until fine.

4. Add the tomatoes, paprika, and cayenne. Process to a paste.

5. With the machine running, gradually add the vinegar and then the oil in a slow stream.

6. Adjust the seasonings with salt and pepper. Also add more vinegar if required. The sauce should not be too acidic but should have a definite sharpness.

7. Prepare a selection of grilled vegetables (see the discussion in Chapter 10). Arrange them on individual plates or on a serving platter. Serve the sauce on the side, drizzled over the vegetables, or in a pool in the center of the plate. Allow 2 to 4 oz (60 to 125 ml) of sauce per portion.

LEEK TART

	U.S.		Metric	
YIELD (8-INCH/20-CM TARTS):	**1**	**4**	*1*	*4*
Ingredients				
Tart pastry (p. 616)	8 oz	2 lb	*225 g*	*900 g*
Leeks, white part plus a little of the green	12 oz	3 lb	*350 g*	*1.4 kg*
Butter	1 oz	4 oz	*30 g*	*125 g*
Heavy cream or crème fraîche	2 oz	8 oz	*60 ml*	*2.5 dl*
Milk	2 oz	8 oz	*60 ml*	*2.5 dl*
Eggs	1	4	*1*	*4*
Salt				
White pepper				
Nutmeg				

Procedure:

1. Line tart pans or pie pans with the pastry. The pastry should be rolled out as thin as possible. There is relatively little filling in this tart, so if the pastry is too thick there will be too much bottom crust in proportion to the filling.

2. Quarter the leeks lengthwise and wash them well. Slice thin.

3. Sweat the leeks in butter until tender; do not brown. Cool thoroughly.

4. Spread the leeks in the bottom of the tart shell(s). This is intended to be a very light tart, so there will be only a thin layer of leeks. The tarts can be prepared ahead up to this point and refrigerated, to be baked to order at serving time.

5. Beat together the remaining ingredients and pour into the shell(s).

6. Place in a 375°F (190°C) oven on the bottom shelf or, if using a deck oven, directly on the deck. Bake until the filling is set and the pastry is golden brown, about 25 to 30 minutes. Serve warm.

Variation

Onion Tart

Substitute sliced onions for the leeks. Brown slowly until golden and greatly reduced in volume. Flavor with a dash of sherry.

FEUILLETÉ OF VEGETABLES

		U.S.		Metric	
PORTIONS:		**4**	**16**	*4*	*16*
Ingredients					
Puff pastry (p. 616)		8 oz	2 lb	*225 g*	*900 g*
Egg wash					
Mushrooms		3 oz	12 oz	*90 g*	*350 g*
Oil, as needed					
Tomatoes, peeled, and seeded		3 oz	12 oz	*90 g*	*350 g*
Salt		¼ tsp	1 tsp	*1 g*	*5 g*
Butter		½ oz	2 oz	*15 g*	*60 g*
Shallot		½ oz	2 oz	*15 g*	*60 g*
Artichokes		1	4	*1*	*4*
Carrots, peeled		3 oz	12 oz	*90 g*	*350 g*
Tender green beans		2 oz	8 oz	*60 g*	*225 g*
Zucchini		3 oz	12 oz	*90 g*	*350 g*
Water		1 oz	4 oz	*30 ml*	*125 ml*
Butter, cut into pieces		1 ½–2 oz	6–8 oz	*45–60 g*	*175–225 g*
Chopped parsley		1 tsp	4 tsp	*1 g*	*4 g*
Tarragon		pinch	½ tsp	*pinch*	*0.5 g*
Toasted pine nuts or sliced almonds		½ oz	2 oz	*15 g*	*60 g*
Lemon juice, to taste					
Salt					

Mise en Place:

1. Prepare the feuilletés. Roll out the puff pastry about ³⁄₁₆ inch (5 mm) thick. Cut out 3-by-5 inch (8-by-12 cm) rectangles, 5-inch (12-cm) ovals, or 4-inch (10-cm) circles; cut one piece of pastry per portion. Arrange on sheet pans and brush with egg wash. Refrigerate for 30 minutes. Bake at 400°F (200°C) until browned and crisp. If the pastries brown too quickly before being done in the middle, lower the heat to 350°F (175°C) to continue baking. Cool on a rack.

2. Trim and cut the vegetables. Quarter the mushrooms if they are small. Cut them in half and then slice them if they are large. Dice the tomatoes. Mince the shallot. Trim the artichokes to their bases and cut the bases into thin slices; reserve in water containing some lemon juice. Cut the carrots into batonnets. Cut the green beans into 1 ½-inch (4-cm) lengths. Cut the zucchini into batonnets.

Cooking:

1. Sauté the mushrooms very briefly in a little oil. Place in a strainer.

2. Toss the tomatoes with salt and add to the mushrooms in the strainer. Let drain.

3. Heat the butter in a sauté pan and add the shallot, artichokes, carrots, and green beans. Cover and cook over low heat until the vegetables are crisp-tender.

4. Add the mushrooms, tomatoes, and zucchini. Cook over moderately high heat for about 2 more minutes. At this point, all the vegetables should be sufficiently cooked If necessary, cook 1 or 2 more minutes.

5. Add the water. Remove from the heat and add the raw butter. Swirl it around until it is melted and blended with the vegetables. Stir in the herbs and nuts. Season to taste with a little lemon juice and salt. Do not return to the heat. The butter and juices form a sauce similar to beurre blanc; the butterfat may separate if the mixture is heated too much.

Presentation:

Cut the tops off the pastry cases. If there is soft, doughy pastry in the center, scoop it out. Place the pastry bottoms on plates. Spoon in the vegetable mixture, letting it overflow onto the plates. Replace the pastry tops. Serve at once.

Variations

Substitute other vegetables in season.

In place of the puff pastry, use layers of baked phyllo pastry, as in the recipe on page 184.

In place of the final quantity of raw butter, which forms the sauce for the vegetables, substitute a mild balsamic vinaigrette.

NAPOLEON OF COUNTRY HAM WITH FIGS (Color Plate 5)

		U.S.		Metric	
PORTIONS:		**4**	**16**	*4*	*16*
Ingredients					
Phyllo sheets		3	12	*3*	*12*
Melted butter		1 oz	4 oz	*30 g*	*125 g*
Heavy cream		4 oz	1 pt	*125 ml*	*5 dl*
Lime juice		½ oz	2 oz	*15 ml*	*60 ml*
Vegetable oil		2 tsp	8 tsp	*10 ml*	*40 ml*
Sugar		pinch	½ tsp	*pinch*	*3 g*
Mace		dash	pinch	*dash*	*pinch*
White pepper					
Country ham (see note)		4 oz	1 lb	*125 g*	*500 g*
Tart apples		½	2	*½*	*2*
Lime juice, as needed					
Chopped pecans		1 oz	4 oz	*30 g*	*125 g*
Fresh figs		4	16	*4*	*16*
Lime wedges (or other decorative cut of lime)		4	16	*4*	*16*
Additional chopped pecans for garnish					

Note: If country ham is not available, use another flavorful ham, such as Westphalian, black forest, or prosciutto.

Mise en Place:

1. On a cutting board, lay out one sheet of phyllo dough. Brush very lightly with butter. It is not necessary to cover the surface thoroughly with butter; use a light hand. Top with a second and third layer, buttering each layer lightly. Cut the pastry into squares about 3 ½ inches (9 cm) on a side. Three squares per portion are needed. Repeat the procedure as necessary until you have enough squares.
2. Arrange the squares on baking sheets. Bake at 400°F (200°C) until brown, about 5 minutes.
3. Whip the cream lightly, then whip in the lime juice, oil, sugar, and seasonings.
4. Cut the ham into thin slices and then into julienne.

Finishing:

1. Shortly before serving, peel and core the apple and cut into brunoise. Toss with a little lime juice to keep it from darkening.
2. Mix together the lime cream, ham, apple, and nuts.
3. Layer the ham mixture with the pastries, spooning two layers of ham mixture in between three layers of pastry.
4. For each portion, place a napoleon on one side of the plate. Cut a fig into quarters lengthwise and arrange on the other side of the plate, cut side up. For garnish, add a wedge of lime and sprinkle with a few nuts. (If available, a few red currants or other small berries scattered around the plate make an attractive garnish instead of the nuts.)

Variations

Substitute Asian apple pears, papaya, lychees, or other fruit for the figs, depending on availability.

POTATO RAVIOLI WITH MUSHROOM FILLING

	U.S.		Metric	
YIELD (PIECES):	20–30	80–120	*20–30*	*80–120*
Ingredients				
Large russet (baking) potatoes	1	4	*1*	*4*
Vegetable oil, as needed				
Egg wash				
Mushroom pasta filling (p. 158)	3 oz	12 oz	*90 g*	*350 g*

Procedure:

1. Peel the potatoes. Using a mandoline or an electric slicer, cut lengthwise into paper-thin slices, as for making potato chips.

2. Oil a baking sheet and arrange the potato slices on the sheet in a single layer.

3. Bake at 400°F (200°C) until soft and still white, about 3 to 5 minutes. The object is to make them pliable enough to be folded without breaking. Remove from the oven and let cool but do not let them dry out.

4. Brush the potatoes with egg wash. Put 1 tsp of filling in the center of each slice and fold over to enclose the filling. Press down to seal the edges and to eliminate any air bubbles.

5. Deep-fry at 350° to 375°F (175° to 190°C) until golden brown.

6. Serve immediately in a basket or a folded napkin.

Variations

Many other fillings, from chopped vegetables to truffles and foie gras, may be used in place of the mushroom filling. The filling should not be too moist or the ravioli will not fry properly.

TARTELETTES OF FETA CHEESE, NEW POTATOES, AND PEPPERS

		U.S.		Metric	
PORTIONS:		4	16	4	16
Ingredients					
Phyllo sheets		4	16	4	16
Olive oil					
Small red-skinned potatoes		4 oz	1 lb	125 g	500 g
Garlic, chopped		1 clove	4 cloves	1 clove	4 cloves
Olive oil					
Grilled or roasted peppers, skinned, cored, and seeded (p. 521)		4 oz	1 lb	125 g	500 g
Scallions		2	8	2	8
Feta cheese		3–4 oz	12–16 oz	90–125 g	375–500 g
Brine-cured black olives, such as Greek or calamata, pitted		½ oz	2 oz	15 g	60 g
Balsamic vinegar		2 tsp	8 tsp	10 ml	40 ml
Parmesan cheese		2 tbsp	½ cup	10 g	40 g

Mise en Place:

1. Stack up 4 sheets of phyllo. Brush the top layer with olive oil. Cut out 4 circles, 6 inches (15 cm) in diameter. Repeat as necessary to make one circle of pastry per portion. Place on baking sheets. Bake at 400°F (200°C) for about 5 minutes, until light brown.
2. Without peeling the potatoes, cut them into thin slices (about $\frac{3}{16}$ inch (5 mm) thick). Brush a baking sheet with olive oil and sprinkle with chopped garlic. Place the potato slices on the sheet in a single layer. Brush them with oil. Bake at 400°F (200°C) until soft but not browned, about 10 minutes.
3. Cut the peppers into large dice.
4. Cut the scallions into thin slices.
5. Crumble the feta cheese.
6. Chop the olives coarsely into chunks.

Cooking:

1. Brush the top of the pastry circles with additional olive oil. Arrange the potatoes on top of the pastry and add the peppers. Sprinkle the scallions, feta cheese, and olives on top. Drizzle a few drops of balsamic vinegar over each tartelette and top with the parmesan cheese.
2. Bake at 400°F (200°C) for 8 to 10 minutes. Serve at once.

Variation

Use baked puff pastry circles in place of the phyllo circles for the bases of the tartes.

CHICKEN AND SWEET POTATO BEIGNETS
WITH WASABI SAUCE
(Color Plate 6)

	U.S.		Metric	
PORTIONS:	**4**	**16**	*4*	*16*
Ingredients				
Chicken meat, boneless and skinless	8 oz	2 lb	*250 g*	*1 kg*
Soy sauce	1 oz	4 oz	*30 ml*	*125 ml*
Grated fresh ginger	½ tsp	2 tsp	*2 g*	*10 g*
Sweet potatoes	4 oz	1 lb	*125 g*	*500 g*
Soy sauce	2 oz	8 oz	*60 ml*	*2.5 dl*
Chicken stock, thoroughly degreased	4 oz	1 pt	*125 ml*	*5 dl*
Radishes, trimmed	4	16	*4*	*16*
Reconstituted wasabi (see note)	2–3 tsp	8–12 tsp	*10–15 g*	*40–60 g*
Egg yolks	1	4	*1*	*4*
Ice-cold water	6½ oz	1 pt 10 oz	*2 dl*	*8 dl*
Flour, sifted	3 oz	12 oz	*90 g*	*350 g*
Flour for dredging				

Note: Wasabi is a type of green Japanese horseradish available in powder form. Reconstitute by mixing in just enough water to make a very thick paste.

Mise en Place:

1. Cut the chicken into thin strips. Mix with the soy sauce and ginger. Marinate for 30 minutes.
2. Peel the sweet potatoes. Cut into julienne. Drop into cold water and hold until needed.
3. Mix the soy sauce and chicken stock together.
4. Grate the radishes.

Cooking:

1. Heat the mixture of soy sauce and chicken stock just until warm. Hold for service.
2. Beat the egg yolks with the cold water. Add the flour all at once and stir briefly to make a loose, rather lumpy batter. Do not overmix.
3. Drain both the chicken and sweet potatoes. Pat dry with clean towels. Mix together.
4. Dust the chicken mixture lightly with flour and toss to coat. Add about three-fourths of the batter and mix gently. If the mixture is dry, add the rest of the batter.
5. Have ready deep-frying fat heated to 350°F (175°C). Drop small spoonfuls of the chicken mixture into the fat and fry just until light golden brown. Remove from the fat and drain well.

Presentation:

Arrange the fritters on plates. On each plate place a small mound of grated radish and a small mound of wasabi. Serve the soy sauce mixture in a small dish on the side. The diner mixes the radish and wasabi to taste into the soy and chicken stock mixture to make a dipping sauce.

CHAPTER

6

Fish and Other Seafood

The popularity of seafood has increased enormously in recent years. This is due to many factors. Modern refrigeration and transportation methods make it possible to ship many varieties of fish to and from all over the world. Popularity of ethnic cuisines has made Americans interested in trying new dishes that they had not even heard of a few years ago. Perhaps most importantly, increased interest in health, diet, and physical fitness has stimulated people to eat more fish, which is perceived as being more healthful.

For the restaurateur, this means that more people are ordering fish from the menu, partly because they are less likely to cook fish at home than they are to cook their familiar meat and chicken standbys. There are more restaurants that specialize in seafood today, and more restaurants that have more fish dishes on their menus than they once did. For all these reasons, it is important for cooks to devote some effort to learning the fine points of fish cookery.

In this chapter, we start by examining cooking methods. Building on the basic methods already learned, we look at the ways these methods can be used to create variety and interest on a menu. We give special attention to the details you need to know in order to have complete control over the cooking processes, so that the finished dish will be of high quality.

In the second half of the chapter, we explain some specialized techniques for handling, preparing, and presenting various seafood items. Included is a sampling of recipes illustrating the range of techniques discussed.

BASIC PREPARATION AND COOKING TECHNIQUES

The first section of this chapter explores the general cooking methods for fish, as they are applied to more advanced or more refined dishes. Rather than concentrate on the basic procedures for sautéing, poaching, deep-frying, and so on, procedures that you already know, we review these procedures briefly while looking at some of the finer points and some useful variations of these basic procedures.

Because of the special nature of fish products, it is extremely important that you learn how to control cooking procedures precisely. *Fish cooks very quickly, because it has very little connective tissue.* When you are cooking many meat items, part of the purpose of cooking is to break down the connective tissue to make the product tender. Fish, however, is naturally tender. The object of cooking is not to break down connective tissue but to bring the fish just to the point of doneness, while at the same time preserving natural moistness and flavor.

What we call "doneness" is caused by the coagulation of proteins. If fish is cooked too long, the proteins shrink too much and the product becomes dry. In addition, because too much connective tissue is broken down, most types of fish tend to fall apart if they are overcooked.

The texture changes that take place in fish as it is cooked can be described in general as follows. Raw fish is relatively soft and yielding to the touch. As heat is applied, it gradually becomes firmer and begins to release moisture. At the same time, what little connective tissue there is begins to dissolve. When it reaches the point of doneness, the protein is just uniformly coagulated and still retains considerable moisture. The connective tissue has broken down enough so that the fish just separates into flakes.

If cooking continues, more connective tissue is broken down and the fish begins to fall apart. The protein continues to shrink and become firmer. As it does, it loses more moisture and becomes drier.

Testing for Doneness. The most common error in fish cooking is *overcooking*. This is partly due to the fact that most books and recipes say that fish is done when it "flakes easily." Cooks often interpret this as meaning "nearly falling apart." Since fish continues to cook in its own retained heat after it is removed from the fire, it is often dreadfully overcooked when it reaches the customer.

To avoid these problems, use the following tests for doneness:

1. The fish *just separates* into flakes; that is, it is beginning to flake, but does not yet fall apart easily.

2. If bone is present, the flesh separates from the bone, and the bone is no longer pink.

3. The flesh has turned from translucent to opaque (usually white, depending on the kind of fish).

Toughness. As we have said, fish is usually tender and therefore requires little cooking. Our problem in cooking is to avoid breaking down too much connective tissue.

Toughness, when it occurs, is often the result of overcooking. That is, it is caused not by too much connective tissue, but by proteins that have toughened because of too high heat or too long a cooking time. Some fin fish, such as cod, are rather tough and chewy if overcooked. On the other hand, many kinds of fish, such as flounder, have shorter, more delicate protein fibers. They do not get tough when overcooked. Rather, they get dry and fall apart.

Toughness is often a problem with shellfish. Lobsters and shrimp, for example, become quite rubbery if cooked too long. And trying to chew a cherrystone clam that has boiled or steamed too long is like trying to chew a wad of rubber bands. Therefore, most shellfish should be cooked for the shortest possible time. For example, small and medium shrimp should be sautéed just until they turn opaque, only a minute or so. Longer cooking toughens them.

There are a few exceptions to this rule. A few seafood items, notably octopus (especially large ones) and conch (pronounced "konk," a large shellfish from the Gulf of Mexico and Caribbean region, something like a big ocean snail) are naturally tough. Such items need long, slow simmering in order to become tender.

Small squid can be tender if cooked only for a few seconds and removed from the heat before they get tough. Or, like their relative the octopus, they can be given a long, slow simmer.

Fat Fish and Lean Fish. In most recipes, many types of fish are interchangeable. For example, in a typical recipe for baked haddock fillets, you might substitute such fish as cod, sea bass, grouper, or weakfish. In order to make such a substitution, you must make judgments based on your knowledge of the fish. First you must decide which fish are appropriate for substituting. Then you must decide if the recipe or procedure should be modified to allow for differences in flavor, texture, and cooking qualities. In making such judgments, there is no substitute for personal experience.

One of the most important characteristics of a fish is its fat content. While the fat content of different kinds of fish varies over a broad range (from about 0.5 percent to 20 percent), in general, fish fall into two categories, fat and lean. Lean fish, those low in fat, include cod, sole, flounder, red snapper, pike, porgy, halibut, and perch. Fat fish, those high in fat, include salmon, tuna, swordfish, pompano, mackerel, and bluefish.

Lean fish are most easily overcooked, because they have little fat content to protect them from drying out. They are best suited to moist heat cooking methods, such as poaching, and to cooking in fat, such as sautéing and frying. If a dry heat method like broiling is used, lean fish should be basted well with fat to protect them from drying. In all cases, watch cooking times carefully; even the slightest overcooking can dry out these fish.

Fat fish are usually more resistant to drying out because of their fat content. Nevertheless, overcooking can ruin fat fish, too. For example, overcooked salmon can be so dry—in spite of its fat content—that it is almost impossible to swallow. In general these fish take well to moist heat methods, and they are better suited to dry heat methods than lean fish are. Broiled salmon and swordfish steaks are very popular. As for cooking with fat, smaller and more delicately flavored fish like trout are often cooked in fat, but more strongly flavored ones like mackerel usually are not.

Cooking in Liquid or Steam

Moist-heat cooking methods are well suited to almost all kinds of seafood, including fat fish and lean fish. By poaching or steaming, it is possible to cook even the most delicate products, while protecting them from the kind of agitation that would break them up. The methods are flexible enough so that you can season and flavor the fish in a variety of ways, either by varying the cooking liquid or by using a marinade, or you can cook the fish without added ingredients to emphasize the natural flavor of the fish.

Furthermore, moist-heat methods are especially good for items that are to be served with a sauce. In many cases, the cooking liquid itself is used as the base for the sauce.

It is not true, as many believe, that cooking with moisture is a way to guarantee that the fish will not dry out. When a protein food is overcooked, the proteins contract and moisture is squeezed out like water out of a sponge. Thus, even fish that is cooked completely submerged in liquid can have a dry texture when served. In addition, overcooked fish may be too fragile to be drained and plated without breaking up. No matter what cooking methods you use, you must guard against overcooking.

Using low temperatures is the best guarantee of moistness. Salmon poached at 160°F (70°C) until just done, for example, retains a tender, moist, almost buttery texture.

There are three basic methods for cooking fish in moisture:

- Poaching in court bouillon—the cooking liquid is usually not made into a sauce or served with the item.
- Poaching in stock and wine—the cooking liquid is usually made into a sauce that is served with the item.
- Steaming—the item is cooked in steam without being submerged in a liquid.

These three categories give us a convenient way to talk about these methods, but in fact there are many variations on the basics, and sometimes these categories overlap. We will discuss these methods separately and explain many of the possible variations.

Guidelines for Poaching Fish in Court Bouillon. A *court bouillon* (French for "short broth") is a quickly made seasoned liquid, usually used for cooking fish. The simplest cooking liquid is salted water, often used for cooking lobster and other shellfish. More commonly, the cooking liquid is flavored with other ingredients, including spices (such as pepper), herbs (such as parsley and bay leaf), mirepoix, and wine, vinegar, or lemon juice. Two fairly typical recipes for court bouillon are included in this chapter (see pages 224–225).

Following are some guidelines for cooking fish in a seasoned liquid:

1. Fish cooked in court bouillon are often called "boiled fish," but *fish should never be boiled.* The best cooking temperatures are 160° to 180°F (70° to 80°C), well below boiling. Cooking at these lower temperatures reduces the danger of overcooking. Also, the rapid bubbling of a boiling liquid may cause fish to break up.

2. Shellfish such as lobsters, crabs, and shrimp should not be boiled, either. Because they are not as fragile as fin fish, they may be *simmered* at a slightly higher temperature than more delicate products. However, boiling temperatures may toughen them.

3. Cooked fish is delicate and easily broken. Therefore you should use cooking equipment that will allow you to remove the fish from the liquid easily without breakage. Fish poachers with removable racks are best. Other techniques for removing fish from court bouillon include wrapping it in cheesecloth before cooking or placing a large strip of foil under it. The ends of the cheesecloth or foil can then be grasped to lift the fish.

4. Start large fish in cold liquid. This is especially important for large whole fish that are to be decorated and presented cold on a buffet. Lowering the fish into hot liquid causes the skin to contract suddenly and split, spoiling the appearance.

5. Start fish steaks and other portion-size items in hot liquid, in order to cook the fish quickly and retain flavor.

6. Start crustaceans (lobsters, crabs, etc.) by dropping them into boiling liquid. When the liquid returns to the simmer, adjust heat so that it maintains a slow simmer and does not boil.

7. When it is done, fish will feel firm, not mushy, at its thickest part, and the backbone, as seen inside the cavity, will no longer be pink. You can also check doneness by using a meat thermometer. Look for a temperature of about 160°F (70°C) in the middle of the thickest part. In general, cooking time will be about 8 to 10 minutes for each inch (2.5 cm) of thickness, depending on the cooking temperature.

8. If the item is to be served cold, remove it from the heat before the fish is done and let it finish cooking in the retained heat, or else stop the cooking by dropping ice into the liquid. Cool the fish in the liquid to retain moisture and flavor.

9. If the item is to be served hot, remove from the court bouillon when it is cooked, and serve it immediately.

10. If the pieces of fish are small enough, they can be cooked by simply heating the liquid to 160° to 170°F (70° to 77°C), putting in the fish, removing the pan from the heat, and letting it stand for 10 to 15 minutes or so. The retained heat is sufficient to cook the fish to doneness. Because the heat is low, the fish stays moist and tender.

11. Be sure to drain poached fish very well. If it is not drained properly, the excess liquid may dilute the sauce that is served with the fish, or it may run across the serving plate and spoil the vegetable and starch accompaniments.

Guidelines for Poaching Fish in Stock and Wine. This technique involves cooking fish gently in a small amount of liquid, which is then used to make a sauce that accompanies the fish. The most commonly used liquids for this procedure are fish fumet, white wine, or both.

This is one of the most important preparations in fish cookery, and the dishes made this way include some of the finest preparations in classic and modern cuisines. The most basic dish is fillets of sole (or other fish) au vin blanc, meaning "in white wine" (see recipe on page 226). For this dish, the poaching liquid of fumet and wine is reduced, thickened, finished with butter or cream, and served as a sauce with the fillets.

By using different liquids, garnishes, and flavoring ingredients, the cook can produce a great many variations. We explore some of these variations later. First, we examine the basic method more closely.

1. Cooking time is very short in most cases. Items being poached are usually small, single-portion pieces such as fillets and steaks. Since small pieces of fish cook in only a few minutes, the cook must watch cooking times closely. The advantage of short cooking times is that such items are well adapted to a la carte cooking and service.

2. Heat must be gentle to avoid damaging or overcooking delicate fish.

3. Use a small amount of cooking liquid, no more than is necessary to make the sauce. Using too much liquid results in diluted flavors, and excessive reduction of the liquid will then be needed to make a good sauce.

4. Use a shallow cooking utensil just large enough to hold the fish in a single layer. If you use a pan that is too large, you will need to use excess liquid.

5. Because of the delicacy of the flavors, this preparation requires good quality fish and well made stock, and the wine should have good flavor. Using a cheap, bad-tasting wine will spoil the dish.

6. Because only a small amount of liquid is used, the fish is often not completely covered by the liquid. To ensure even cooking, you must cover the fish, either with a pan lid or a paper cover or, best of all, both. A paper cover—you can use buttered parchment, wax paper, or aluminum foil, cut to fit inside the cooking utensil—is placed directly on top of the fish items, in contact with them. This technique works well because steam is trapped closely around the fish and helps to cook it more evenly. It also helps keep the top of the fish from drying out.

7. Fish can be poached on top of the stove or in the oven. The oven is usually preferable, because the item is heated evenly from all sides, not just the bottom. Cooking can thus be quicker and at the same time more gentle. It requires less attention from the cook, and the range top is free for other purposes.

   To poach fish in the oven, first heat the pan containing the fish and liquid on top of the stove, just until the liquid barely begins to simmer. Then transfer it to the oven to complete the cooking.

Basic Procedure for Poaching Fish in Fumet and Wine

The following procedure illustrates this cooking method in its most basic form. A broad range of variations can be produced by using different kinds of fish, cooking liquids, flavoring ingredients, garnish, and sauce-making techniques. Many such variations are illustrated by the recipes included in this chapter.

1. Butter the bottom of the pan and sprinkle with chopped shallots or other ingredients called for in the recipe.

2. Season the fish portions lightly and arrange them in the pan in a single layer.

3. Add enough fish fumet and white wine to almost cover the fish.

4. Cover the fish with a piece of buttered paper and cover the pan with a lid.

5. Bring the liquid to a simmer and transfer the pan to the oven to finish cooking.

6. Drain the liquid into a wide pan and keep the fish warm.

7. Reduce the liquid and finish the sauce as directed in the recipe. The usual method is to thicken the liquid with fish velouté or beurre manié, and/or to enrich the sauce with butter or cream.

8. Adjust the seasoning and consistency of the sauce and strain it.

9. Plate the fish, nap with the sauce, and serve immediately.

Variations of Moist-heat Procedures. The procedures we have just discussed are the basic, classic methods for poaching fish in court bouillon and wine, but they are not the only ways to cook seafood in liquid. We can use the basic principles as our guide, but vary some of the details—such as flavoring ingredients, cooking liquids, and techniques for finishing sauces—to create a great variety of fish dishes.

While it is impossible to list every conceivable variation, we can discuss the major types. Consult the recipes in this chapter for illustrations of these techniques.

Substitutions for Basic Poaching Liquids. When fish is poached in wine, the poaching liquid is used to make a sauce. White wine and fish fumet are not the only liquids that can be used for poaching. Although red wine is not usually associated with fish, it can be used for poaching fish. Even some recipes in the classical cuisine called for red wine in fish cookery (see page 235).

Today, many cooks are experimenting with unusual combinations. Not only red wine but other ingredients such as chicken stock, brown stock, orange juice, clam juice, tomato sauce, the liquid left from soaking dried wild mushrooms, and many other liquids that might be used in a sauce, find their way into a poached fish recipe. For an example, see the recipe on page 229.

It should be no surprise that many of the sauce-making techniques popular today, as discussed in Chapter 3, are applied to poached fish dishes. Traditionally, fish-poaching liquids have been made into sauces based on velouté sauce. However, other types of sauces can also be made. For example, you could use a minimum of poaching liquid and then, after the fish is cooked, reduce the liquid and use it as the base for one of the *beurre blanc* variations (page 68) or cream sauce variations (pages 61 and 64). Or you could combine it with a fresh tomato sauce variation (page 50).

Fish cannot usually be poached in a starch-thickened sauce, because the liquid that cooks out of the fish would dilute the sauce too much and spoil its consistency. However, on rare occasions, a sauce is used as a cooking liquid. In these instances, the seafood products are very delicate items like oysters, that are not so much being cooked as merely being warmed gently in the sauce.

When fish is poached in court bouillon, the cooking liquid is usually not served with the fish. Court bouillon is often made with vinegar or large quantities of salt and is not particularly tasty by itself. However, if a flavorful liquid is used for a court bouillon, the fish item may be served with some of the liquid. Such a preparation is generally served in a soup plate and is referred to as *à la nage* (pronounced "ah la nahj"). This French term means "swimming" (see page 252).

Poaching liquids can be simple and mildly flavored, such as lightly salted fish stock, or they can be more spicy and robust, such as a combination of stock and tomatoes, highly seasoned with herbs and spices. This technique allows you to create an unlimited variety of dishes.

Milk is sometimes used as a poaching liquid, especially for smoked fish such as finnan haddie (smoked haddock). The fish may be served with a little of the poaching liquid to moisten it, or it may be drained completely and served with a cream sauce or other sauce.

For cooking shellfish like lobsters and crabs, simple salted water is the most frequently used cooking liquid. To create variety and add flavor and piquancy to shellfish, spices may be added to the water. For example, court bouillons for cooking shrimp and crawfish in Louisiana contain such spices as hot pepper sauce, dry mustard, allspice, pepper, thyme, bay leaves, and cloves.

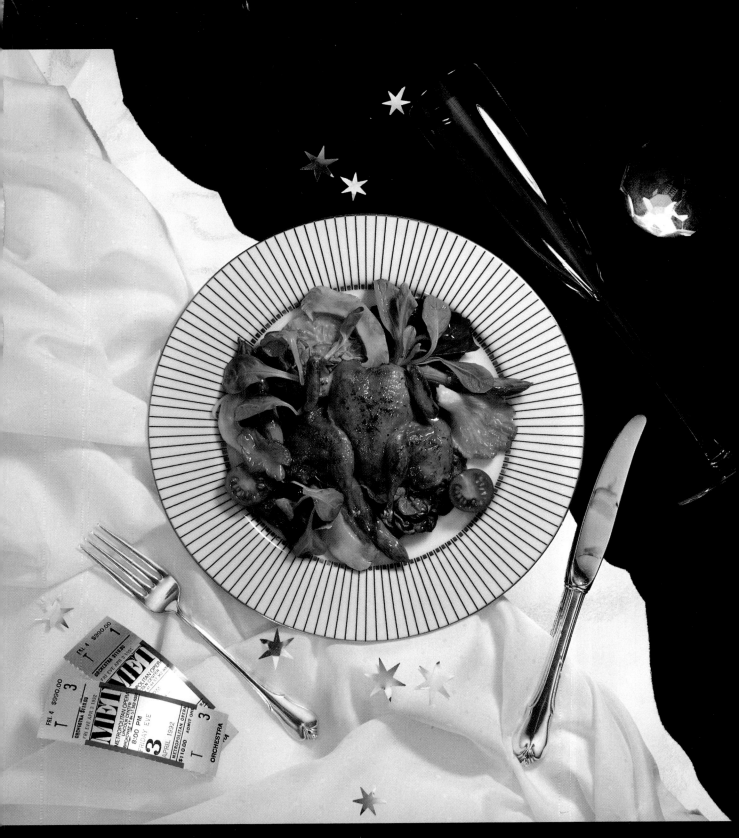

Color Plate 1   Quail Salad

Color Plate 2   Roast Beet Salad with Walnuts

Color Plate 3   Open Ravioli with Scallops

Color Plate 4   Black Pasta with Grilled Shrimp

Color Plate 5   Napoleon of Country Ham with Seckel Pears

Color Plate 6 Chicken and Sweet Potato Beignets
with Wasabi Sauce

Color Plate 7   Grilled Red Snapper Mediterranée

Color Plate 8   Ragout of Seafood: Two interpretations

Fish Soups and Stews. What, you might ask, is the difference between a fish served "à la nage" and a fish soup or stew? In practice, there is very little difference, except perhaps that a fish soup or stew has a little larger proportion of liquid.

It might be objected that in a soup or stew the fish should be cut into smaller pieces. But this is not always the case. For example, the classic Mediterranean fish stew called bouillabaisse is often made with whole fish, at least in its home territory of Marseille, France. (See the fish stew recipe on page 122.)

In other words, there are no clear-cut rules about when you should call something "poached fish" and when you should call it "fish stew." The important thing to remember is that the basic procedures are essentially the same. Follow the guidelines for poaching fish. Use low heat, and do not overcook.

Substitutions for Garnish and Flavoring Ingredients. Just as the poaching liquids can be varied, so can other ingredients that are cooked or presented with the fish.

In classical cuisine, there are dozens of variations on the basic fillets of sole in white wine sauce (au vin blanc). Many of these variations are made by adding different items to the fish before cooking it, or by garnishing it with different items after it is cooked. For example, sole bonne femme is prepared like sole au vin blanc, except that sliced mushrooms are cooked with the fish. Sole argenteuil is made like sole au vin blanc except that after the fish is cooked it is garnished with asparagus tips.

Several of these traditional variations are included with the recipes in this chapter. For extensive lists of the many classical variations, consult reference works like Escoffier and *Le Répertoire de la Cuisine.*

Today, as many cooks are experimenting with new combinations of flavors, new recipes are appearing. As examples of such untraditional preparations, see the recipe for Fillets of Sole à l'Orange on page 229. It is helpful to note that, while the combinations of ingredients in these kinds of recipes are new, the basic procedures are based on the classic methods. This again is an important reason for learning the classic cuisine well.

Whenever you cook another ingredient with poached fish, you must know how quickly it will cook. If its cooking time is longer than the fish, you should partially cook it ahead of time. If its cooking time is shorter, it may be better to cook it separately and use it to garnish the fish after the fish is cooked.

Of course, if the ingredient is used only for flavoring and will not be served with the fish, these precautions may not be necessary.

Braising Fish. Traditional chefs classify braising as a distinct category of fish cookery, although in practice it turns out to be a combination of poaching and baking. The procedure is similar to poaching in wine and fumet, except for the following differences:

1. Whereas poaching in wine is used mostly for fillets or other small items, braising is generally applied to large whole fish, or sometimes to large pieces.

2. For braised fish, the bottom of the cooking pan is covered with a thick layer of mirepoix or other aromatic vegetables, and the fish is laid directly on this layer or on a rack above it.

3. Equal parts of fish fumet and white or red wine are added to the pan, just until the liquid covers one-half to three-fourths the thickness of the fish.

4. The liquid is brought to a boil on top of the stove and the pan is then placed in the oven. It should be covered only loosely, so that some of the liquid can evaporate during cooking. While it cooks, the fish is basted frequently with the liquid. Toward the end of cooking, remove the cover and continue to baste. This frequent basting while the liquid is reducing is intended to give the fish a shiny glaze.

When the fish is cooked, it is drained. As in the case of poached fish, the liquid is used to make a sauce; it is strained, degreased, reduced, and finished according to the instructions in the particular recipe.

As you can see, this procedure is almost like the procedure for braising large cuts of meat, except that the fish is not browned in fat first.

Clearly, braising is inherently a longer cooking method, because of the basting and glazing procedure. It is difficult to cook small fish items this way without overcooking them. Braising is more suited to home-style cooking, where large items are cooked, and is not as well adapted to food service use.

Presentation of Poached Fish. Keep the following guidelines in mind when you are plating poached fish:

1. Drain the fish well, so that excess liquid will not dilute the sauce or spoil the presentation.

2. Fish poached in court bouillon is usually served with a sauce that is prepared separately. Appropriate sauces include butter sauces such as hollandaise, beurre blanc, and beurre noisette; white sauces based on fish velouté, béchamel, or cream; and miscellaneous sauces such as light tomato sauce. See Chapter 5 for recipes.

3. Fish poached in wine and fumet is served with a sauce made from the poaching liquid. If the fish is to be napped with the sauce, be sure that the sauce has the proper consistency so that it will lightly coat the fish. It should not be too thick or too thin.

4. If several portions of poached fish are being arranged on a platter for presentation in the dining room, coat the platter with a little of the sauce before placing the fish on it. This makes it easier to lift the portions off the platter for individual plating.

5. After poached fish is plated and coated with a sauce, it is sometimes placed under a broiler or salamander until the top is browned. Since this technique involved both poaching and broiling, it is discussed in the section on mixed cooking methods (see page 208).

Steaming. To steam means to cook a food by exposing it to hot steam. Since all foods contain moisture, steam is present whenever foods are cooked, even if they are cooked by a dry-heat method such as broiling or roasting. However, when we are speaking of basic cooking methods, we use the term steaming only if the steam is somehow trapped around the food, such as by cooking the food with a cover or in an enclosed steamer.

In practice, poaching is often partly steaming. Remember that when fish is poached in wine, it is usually not completely covered by the liquid. The top part of the fish is cooked by steam that is trapped underneath the cover.

In other words, steam has a role in several different types of cooking techniques. Some cooking methods we might call "pure steaming," because the heat that cooks the food is carried to it only by steam, not by simmering liquid, hot fat, or other source. These methods involve cooking the food in various types of steamers.

In some other cooking methods, we do not use steam from an outside source to cook the fish, but steam that is created from the moisture content of the fish and other ingredients. By cooking the foods in closed containers, we trap this steam around the fish, and this steam helps to cook the fish. This will become clearer as we discuss these methods in more detail.

"Pure" Steaming in a Steamer. The simplest type of steamer is nothing more than a regular cooking pot fitted with a rack to hold the foods a few inches off the bottom of the pot. A little water is poured into the pot and set over heat. Steam rises through the rack and cooks the food.

A large fish poacher is convenient to use for steaming. Set over low heat on the range top, it is always ready whenever an order is called in. To use a fish poacher for steaming, you must support the removable rack so that it is several inches above the bottom of the poacher. This allows enough room for an inch or inch and a half of water below the rack.

Another simple steamer, one that works the same way, looks like a double boiler, except that the bottom of the top section is perforated. Water is boiled in the bottom section, and foods to be steamed are placed in the top section.

Compartment steamers, of course, are widely used, especially in high-volume operations, because of their speed and efficiency.

The following guidelines are applicable both to compartment steamers and to simpler steamers:

1. Watch cooking times very carefully. Steam is very hot, and therefore it cooks fish quickly.

2. Convection or nonpressure steaming is better for fish than pressure steaming. The high temperatures in a pressure steamer can overcook fish in a matter of seconds. Items like lobster can easily become tough and rubbery.

3. Gentle steaming is an excellent way to cook many types of fish, especially fish with delicate flavor and texture. There is less danger of damaging the fish, because it is not agitated by bubbling liquid. Also, because it is not sitting in a liquid, less flavor is dissolved out of the fish into the cooking liquid.

4. Steaming is also a good method for cooking shellfish like lobsters and crabs. Although lobster lovers do not always agree, many argue that steaming is better than simmering in salted water, because they feel that steamed lobster is less watery and therefore more flavorful. However, as we said, you must take care not to overcook steamed shellfish.

5. Steaming is a good method to use if you want to preserve the pure flavor of the fish without adding the extra flavors of a court bouillon.

6. If you want to flavor the fish, you must of course season the fish directly, since there is no cooking liquid. For extra flavor penetration, season the fish ahead of time, or marinate it. See page 236 for an example of marination.

7. Use solid steamer pans to retain the juices that cook out of the fish, and use the juices for sauces and soups.

8. For fish that is very fragile when cooked, place the fish portions on pieces of parchment before placing them in the steamer. When the fish is cooked, the parchment makes it easier to remove the fish from the pan without breaking it.

Other Types of Steaming. As we said earlier, poached fish is often cooked partly by steam, because the fish is not completely covered by the poaching liquid. Nevertheless, the liquid is still the primary cooking medium, so we do not call this method steaming.

On the other hand, some recipes call for adding only a very small amount of liquid, and most of the fish is cooked by the steam that is created when this liquid is heated. For example, in the recipe for Mussels Marseille-style on page 256, there is not enough liquid to actually poach the mussels. Rather, the mussels are cooked by steam.

In some preparations, no liquid is added. Instead, the fish or shellfish is sautéed in a little fat and then covered. The trapped steam from the fish's own juices completes the cooking. The French term *étuver* (pronounced "ay too vay") is used for this kind of procedure. The word is usually translated as "stew," but this is misleading. More precisely, it means "to cook or steam in its own juices," or "to sweat." This is practically the same procedure that is often used to cook vegetables (see page 493).

In almost all cases, when fish is cooked by these methods, the flavorful juices are served with the fish. The juices may be left as they are, as in the mussel recipe we used as an example; or the fish may be removed and the liquid reduced, thickened, or enriched like a sauce.

One precaution is important. Since these techniques often involve strong bottom heat, there is a danger of uneven cooking. When cooking delicate fish, use low heat to avoid overcooking the bottom before the top is done. In the case of shellfish, shake the pot (while holding on the cover) occasionally to ensure even cooking.

Cooking en Papillote. A specialized version of cooking in a closed container to trap steam is called cooking *en papillote* (pronounced "on poppy-yote"), or in paper. All ingredients are tightly enclosed in a piece of parchment so that steam does not escape. When it is heated, the item steams in its own moisture. All the juices, flavors, and aromas are held inside the paper, which is not opened until it is placed before the diner. The procedure for enclosing foods in parchment is illustrated in Figure 6.1.

Aluminum foil is sometimes used instead of parchment. The advantage of foil is that it is easier to seal, but it does not make an attractive presentation for the diner. However, foil can be used if the fish is removed from the foil and plated in the kitchen.

Some cooks feel that foil should not be used because it will affect the flavor of the food. However, this is rarely a problem when cooking fish. Cooking times are so short (or should be!) that there is not enough time for the aluminum to react with food acids.

Sometimes a starch-thickened sauce is used in cooking fish en papillote. In this case the fish is usually precooked so that it will not exude juices that will dilute and spoil the sauce. The problem with this method is that the fish is often overcooked by the time it reaches the customer.

Sautéing and Frying

Cooking fish and seafood in fat is quick and convenient. Because such cooking methods allow fresh foods to be cooked at the last minute and presented to the diner hot out of the sauté pan or fryer, frying and sautéing have always been popular in restaurants. Fried or sautéed seafood can be simple or complex, and many variations are possible.

Since cooking in fat involves high temperatures, special care must be taken with fish and seafood, since it usually cooks faster than meat and poultry. Also, because of the high temperatures and rapid cooking, these cooking methods are usually used for small items—fillets and pieces of fillets, fish steaks, small whole fish like trout, and whole small shellfish like shrimp and scallops. Larger pieces do not cook evenly when fried or sautéed. For more even cooking, they may be browned in fat and then finished in the oven.

Cooking in fat is especially appropriate for lean fish. Fat fish are not often sautéed, although there are some exceptions, such as trout, whitefish, and small cuts of salmon. The more strongly flavored fat fish can sometimes be fried or sautéed, but you should take care that the fish does not become too greasy.

FIGURE 6.1. **Preparing foods en papillote.**
(a) Cut out a heart-shaped piece of parchment. This is done by folding a sheet of parchment in half and cutting half a heart from the folded side. Oil or butter the parchment on both sides.

(b) Place the fish fillet or other item plus any sauce, topping, or seasoning on one side of the heart.

(c) Fold over the other half of the heart. Starting at the top of the fold, make a small crimp in the edge as shown.

(d) Continue crimping around the edge. Each crimp holds the previous one in place.

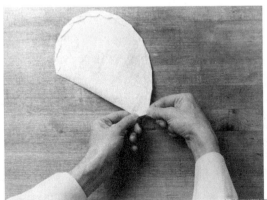

(e) When you reach the bottom of the heart, fold the point under to hold it in place. The papillote is now ready for cooking. Place it in a hot pan and bake in a hot oven until the parchment is puffed and the fish is cooked.

Sautéing. There are a number of basic ways of sautéing and panfrying seafood. The following general guidelines apply to most of these preparations:

1. Sautéed fish is often given a coating of flour, breading, or other starchy product before being cooked. This forms a crust that browns attractively, enhances the flavor, and helps prevent sticking to the pan.

2. Fish may be soaked briefly in milk or marinated in lemon juice and seasonings before being sautéed. Soaking in milk before dredging in flour helps the flour form a better crust.

3. Small items such as shrimp and scallops are sautéed over high heat. Larger items are cooked over low heat so that they cook evenly and do not brown too much.

4. Cook the presentation side first for the most attractive appearance. In the case of fillets, the presentation side is usually the side that was against the bone, not the skin side.

5. Prepare sauces and garnishes in advance, as far as possible, so that the fish can be finished and served as quickly as possible.

Various sauté preparations are discussed below, beginning with the preparation that is considered the basic sauté method in classical cuisine.

Sauté à la Meunière. Cooking fish *à la meunière* (pronounced "mun yair") is usually applied to small whole fish and to fillets and steaks of fish. The product is dredged in flour and sautéed in clarified butter or oil. It is then plated and sprinkled with lemon juice and chopped parsley. Freshly prepared, hot beurre noisette (page 30) is then poured over the fish. When the hot butter hits the lemon juice and parsley, it sizzles and creates a froth. The fish must then be served immediately. The plate is usually garnished with lemon wedges, slices, or halves.

This preparation is one of the simplest yet most delectable ones for fish. It is well suited to many of the finest fish, such as Dover sole and trout, and it can also be used for less expensive fish, especially lean, white fish.

With different garnish, you can produce variations of fish meunière, such as the following:

Fish Doré—omit the lemon juice, chopped parsley, and beurre noisette; top the fish with lemon slices (skinned) or garnish with lemon wedges.

Fish Amandine—top with browned almond slices.

Fish Doria—garnish with cucumber cut into the shape of garlic cloves and cooked.

Fish Grenobloise—garnish with capers and skinned lemon segments.

Fish Meunière aux Cèpes or *aux Morilles*—garnish with sautéed cèpes (bolete mushrooms) or morels.

Fish Meunière à l'Orange—omit lemon juice and parsley, and top the fish with thin slices of peeled orange before pouring on the beurre noisette.

Fish Murat—in addition to the lemon juice and parsley, sprinkle the fish with a little melted meat glaze (glace de viande); garnish with a mixture of diced, sautéed potato and diced, cooked artichoke bottoms.

Other Coatings. For cooking à la meunière, fish is coated with flour. For other preparations, other coatings can be used, such as the following:

1. Standard breading procedure. The basic breading (flour, egg wash, and bread crumbs) can be used for sautéing or panfrying fish as well as for deep-frying it. The French term for "breaded" is *pané* (pronounced "panay"). Breaded items are sometimes referred to as *à l'Anglaise.*

2. Nut breading. In place of the breadcrumbs in the standard breading, you can use chopped pecans, walnuts, filberts, macadamia nuts, or other nuts, or—more economically—a mixture of nuts and crumbs.

3. Egg coating. The product is dredged in flour, then dipped in egg, then placed in a hot sauté pan.

   This preparation is sometimes noted on menus as *à la française* (pronounced "fran sez") or, in Italian, *francese* (pronounced "fran chay zeh"). However, do not confuse this with *deep-frying à la française,* which refers to a coating only of flour (see page 204).

4. Other starch products. In place of flour, other products like cornmeal, fine oatmeal, and cracker or bread crumbs can be used. Cornmeal is a popular coating for catfish and similar regional American specialties. Any of these items may be mixed with various herbs and spices to create different flavors.

   In general, any of these items used alone will give a lighter, more delicate and more fragile coating than standard breading, because the egg in the standard breading makes the coating thicker and firmer. As we mentioned earlier, dipping the fish in milk before applying the starch coating usually makes a better crust.

Sautéing Without a Coating. While fish to be sautéed is often given a coating of flour or other material, it can also be sautéed without a coating. This is especially true in the case of small items. Shrimp, for example, are rarely sautéed with a starch coating. Fish scaloppine (thin slices of fillets) are often seared very quickly in a hot sauté pan without a flour coating, for a light, delicate effect (see page 242).

If a liquid ingredient is added to a sautéed item to finish it, a starch coating may absorb some of the liquid and gelatinize; it may thicken the sauce more than you want. Depending on the recipe or on the effect you want to create, you have the choice of sautéing the item with or without breading, flour, or other material added.

In general, the *disadvantages* of sautéing fish without first breading it or dredging it in flour or other material are as follows:

- It browns less easily. Of course, if you do not want to brown it, this is not a problem.
- It is more likely to stick to the pan. In the case of shrimp or other very firm items, this is not a problem, but with more delicate fish, it may be.
- It does not have the starch coating to help hold it together. Again, this applies primarily to the more delicate fish.

Liquid Ingredients. Liquid ingredients are incorporated with sautéed fish items in one of two ways:

1. The fish is fully cooked by sautéing and removed from the pan. Then the pan may be deglazed for completing a sauce, or a sauce and garnish may be prepared separately and combined with the fish on the plate. For à la carte service, sauces and garnish that are made separately are best prepared in advance.

2. Liquid ingredients (including juicy ingredients like tomatoes) may be added to an item while it is still sautéing in the pan, and all ingredients are cooked together briefly. In this case, take care not to sauté the fish item until done in the first stage of cooking, because it will cook further when it simmers with the liquids.

If the item is seared only briefly in hot fat, and cooked primarily in simmering liquid, the cooking process is more like the braising of meats, so we do not treat it as a sautéed item. This procedure is discussed in the section on mixed methods (page 208).

Stir-frying. The Chinese technique of stir-frying is similar to sautéing, except that the ingredients are stirred and tossed with spatulas or other utensils, while in sautéing, the food is tossed by flipping the pan. This technique can also be used with American ingredients. Because of the vigorous flipping and tossing and the short cooking times, it is suitable primarily for small, firm items like shrimp and scallops. More delicate fish would be broken up.

Deep-frying. Small fish and small pieces of fish are most suitable for frying. Large fish do not cook evenly, because the outside is overcooked by the time the heat penetrates to the interior.

Sometimes whole fish is deep-fried even if it is rather thick. To facilitate the penetration of heat to the center, several deep gashes are cut in the side of the fish. This technique is not necessary if the fish is small.

Deep-frying is not the most subtle cooking method, and it is not subject to as many variations and applications as sautéing or other cooking methods. Nevertheless, there are several different styles of deep-fried fish in classical and modern kitchens. They are similar to the styles of sautéed fish, discussed above.

A brief review of frying styles follows. It is assumed that you are familiar with the fundamentals of deep-frying, so the techniques are not explained in detail. In all of the following styles of frying, the fish may be marinated in lemon juice, salt, pepper, and herbs for a short time before coating and frying.

1. *Breaded.* The fish is passed through seasoned flour, egg wash, and breadcrumbs, and it is then fried. This style is referred to in French as *à l'anglaise* (English-style) or *pané* (breaded).
2. *Battered.* The fish is dredged in flour, then in batter, and then fried. The item must be dropped into the frying fat carefully, so that it does not hit the submerged fryer basket before a crust forms on the batter. If this happens, it will stick to the basket. Batter-fried fish fillets may be called *à l'orly,* or Orly-style if they are served with tomato sauce and garnished with deep-fried parsley.
3. *Floured.* The fish is dipped in milk (optional) and, immediately before frying, dredged in flour. It should not be floured ahead of time, or the flour will absorb moisture from the fish and become pasty. Fish cooked in this way is sometimes called *à la Française* (French-style).
4. *Coated in egg.* The fish is dredged in flour, then dipped in beaten egg or egg wash, and fried. For a heavier, more batterlike coating, the fish may be dipped in flour a second time, after the egg wash. This method is not used as often as the first three.

After frying, the fish must be drained well before being plated.

Baking, Broiling, and Grilling

The cooking methods discussed in this section all involve subjecting the fish to dry heat. Because the fish is cooked in neither fat nor liquid, there is more danger of drying out the fish than there is with other cooking methods. Therefore, these dry-heat cooking methods are in some ways the most difficult to use for fish, and special precautions must be taken.

Coating or topping the seafood product with some material is a useful way to reduce the loss of moisture. Fat is most often used. With few exceptions, baked or broiled fish is coated with oil or butter before cooking and basted with fat during cooking. Flour, crumbs, and other coatings and toppings can also be used to preserve moisture and at the same time add flavor and variety.

Broiling and Grilling. Although these two terms are often used interchangeably, in this book—in order to avoid confusion—we use the term *grilling* to mean cooking on an open grid *above* a heat source, and *broiling* to mean cooking *below* a heat source.

While broiling and grilling are, for the most part, used for the same purposes, there are some differences that determine the uses to which they can be put.

Since the heat source is above the food in a broiler, the food can be cooked either directly on the open grid or on a solid pan. This is important for delicate fish that might break up and fall through an open grill. Furthermore, a broiler can be used to brown the top of a food that cannot be turned over, such as a food with a sauce or topping. Obviously, this cannot be done with a grill.

A grill, on the other hand, can give foods a "charcoal-broiled" flavor in a way that broilers cannot. This flavor is caused by smoke from fats that drip onto the heat source. Special woods and charcoals, such as hickory and mesquite, can be used in grills to create flavors that are desirable in some styles of cooking. Hearty steaks of such fish as salmon and swordfish grilled over mesquite, fruitwood, or hickory, and perhaps served with an herb butter, mustard sauce, or light vegetable garnish, are some of the most popular foods in modern American restaurants.

Guidelines for Grilling and Broiling Fish

1. Because of the intense heat of a broiler or grill, only small items are suitable for broiling or grilling, such as steaks, fillets, and sometimes small whole fish.

2. In most cases, fish should be dipped in oil or melted butter before cooking and basted with one of these fats during cooking, in order to avoid drying the fish out. Oiling the fish also helps to keep it from sticking to the grill.

3. Fish may be dredged in flour before being dipped in butter or oil. The flour forms a flavorful crust which browns nicely and helps retain moisture in the fish. As an alternative, you may instead brush the fish with butter or oil and then dip it in breadcrumbs or cornmeal.

4. Fat fish is usually better for these cooking methods because it does not dry out as readily. Lean fish can also be used, as long as it is basted well and not overcooked.

5. Instead of using plain butter or oil to baste the fish, you can create different flavors by basting with other liquids, such as herb butters, various vinaigrette sauces, and barbecue sauce.

6. In general, the thicker the piece, the farther it should be from the heat in order to cook evenly.

7. Thick fish steaks or other thick items must usually be cooked on both sides in order to cook evenly. Use only items that are firm enough to be turned over without breaking.

8. Thin fillets can be arranged on a buttered or oiled pan, placed under a broiler, and broiled on one side only. This is especially helpful if the item is too delicate to be turned.

9. A two-sided gridiron can be used in a broiler or grill. The fish items are enclosed in the metal grid and the whole thing can be turned easily without damaging the fish (see Figure 6.2).

10. Small, whole fish can be broiled or grilled, but they are difficult to cook evenly because the tail section is usually thinner and cooks more quickly. If the heat in

FIGURE 6.2. **A gridiron holding fish for grilling.**

your equipment is uneven, arrange the fish so that the tail is in a cooler area. Another technique is, after the whole fish is initially seared, to slow down the cooking of the tail section by putting a piece of potato or other item under it (on a grill) or to protect it from the heat with a piece of foil (either on a grill or under a broiler).

11. Whole fish are often scored lightly with the point of a knife before broiling or grilling. This helps the heat to penetrate the fish more quickly and to prevent the skin from bursting and spoiling the appearance of the fish. For the most attractive results, make the gashes neatly, either in a diamond pattern or in parallel lines.

12. Just as for other cooking methods, fish for broiling and grilling may be marinated for a short time before cooking, in order to season and flavor it. Do not marinate too long in a strongly acidic marinade, however, or the fish will be "cooked" by the acid.

Baking. When we refer to baking as a cooking method, we mean a dry-heat cooking method that is performed by *surrounding the food with hot, dry air.*

The term *baking* is also used in a more general way to mean any kind of cooking that is done in an oven; this more general usage would also include braising and poaching in an oven. Please note that in this section we are using the term only in its narrower sense, as defined in the preceding paragraph. Thus, even though a fish product may be cooked in an oven, if it is being cooked with a liquid (such as stock or wine), or if the pan is covered to retain steam, we classify the procedure as a moist-heat cooking method, such as poaching or steaming. These methods are discussed earlier in this chapter.

It should be noted that in classical French cuisine baking is not recognized as one of the cooking methods for fish, while braising is classified as a separate method. In this book, we discuss braising as a type of moist-heat cooking (see page 197).

Baking is best suited for fish fillets and steaks, for small whole fish, and for shellfish such as stuffed clams and oysters. While large, whole fish may be baked, this is usually not practical in food service, where uniform individual portions are the goal.

Fat fish are best for baking because their fat content helps them to resist drying out. Lean fish also may be baked, although their leanness requires extra care in basting with fat and avoiding overcooking. Because baking is a dry-heat cooking method, many of the guidelines and precautions listed above for broiling and grilling also apply to baking.

Baking at Moderate Heat. The basic procedure for baking fish is straightforward:

1. Oil or butter a baking pan or suitable dish.
2. Place the fish on the pan and brush or baste with oil or butter.
3. If desired, add toppings such as seasoned breadcrumbs or vegetable garnish.
4. Bake until the fish is done.
5. Baste with fat, if necessary, during cooking.

Variations in flavor and presentation are created by using different seasonings, toppings, accompaniments, and garnish. Anything placed on top of the fish, in addition to the fat used for basting, will help to prevent moisture loss.

Appropriate sauces or seasoned butters are often served with baked fish.

Whole fish are sometimes stuffed before baking. If possible, bone the fish before stuffing to make eating easier (see page 211 for some special techniques). Stuffing will increase the cooking time.

The normal range of temperatures for baking fish is about 350° to 425°F (175° to 220°C). In general, larger pieces are baked at lower temperature than small pieces, for even cooking.

Cooking time depends on the thickness of the fish. At a temperature of 400°F (200°C), cooking will take about 10 to 12 minutes per inch (2.5 cm) of thickness at the thickest point. At 350°F (175°C) the cooking time will be several minutes longer per inch (2.5 cm) of thickness.

Low-Temperature Baking. Just as poaching at a low temperature helps maintain a moist texture in fish (see page 193), so does baking at a low temperature. At 225° to 250°F (110° to 120°C), small pieces of fish cook in 10 to 20 minutes. Larger items are not as well suited to cooking at such low temperatures, because of the extended cooking times that would be required.

A word of caution may be necessary here. Unfortunately, overcooked fish is so common that some people assume that if fish is juicy it has not been properly cooked. Fish baked at a low temperature may seem unusually moist and tender to people accustomed to dry, flaky baked fish, and they may need to be assured that the fish is indeed fully cooked and not raw.

Flash Baking. Baking in a very hot oven is a useful technique that can often be used in place of broiling or sautéing. There are several advantages to high-heat baking. Because the heat is not as intense as that of a broiler, the cooking is easier to control; yet the cooking is almost as fast. Also, fragile pieces of fish can easily be cooked and plated, without danger of sticking to a grill or sauté pan or of breaking up and falling through a grill, or without having to be turned over halfway through the cooking time.

This procedure works best for slices or fillets ½ inch thick or less. It is ideal for scaloppine of fish (see page 214); such thin slices are easily broken, so the less they have to be handled, the better.

For an example of a recipe using this technique, see page 242.

Procedure

1. Preheat the oven to very hot: 500° to 550°F (260° to 290°C).
2. Butter a baking sheet well.
3. Arrange thin slices or fillets of fish on the buttered baking sheet. For best results, use pieces that are no thicker than ½ inch (12 mm).

4. To protect the tops of the fish pieces from drying out during cooking, do one of the following:
   a. Just before baking, brush the tops with water. (Wine, fish stock, or other liquid could also be used.)
   b. Brush the tops with butter, seasoned butter, oil, or other fat.
   c. Cover each piece with a leaf of lettuce.
5. Bake until done, about 1 to 2 minutes.
6. Plate and serve immediately.

Mixed Methods

We use the term *mixed methods* to refer to procedures that involve more than one cooking method. For example, a food might be partially cooked by sautéing, then finished by simmering in stock.

The classic example of using a combination of cooking methods for cooking fish is gratinéing, in which the product is partially or completely cooked by another method (usually poaching), then finished in a hot oven or broiler in order to brown the top.

Recipes that use cooked fish (including leftovers) to make casseroles and other items also fall into this category.

In addition, we also discuss raw fish preparations in this section.

Gratinéing and Glazing.

In classical French cooking, gratinéing is classified as one of the basic cooking methods for fish. An item that is prepared this way may be referred to on the menu as "au gratin." There are several variations on this technique, but what they all have in common is a crusted or browned top, created by putting them under a salamander or broiler or in a hot oven for a few moments, just before serving.

To gratiné a fish or seafood item, you normally start by poaching it until almost done. Be careful not to overcook it, because it will be cooked again briefly before being served. It is then placed in a dish, covered with a product that will brown easily, and set to brown in a salamander.

Various combinations of topping ingredients are used. The basic ones are as follows:

- Breadcrumbs and melted butter
- Grated cheese and melted butter
- Breadcrumbs, grated cheese, and melted butter
- A sauce enriched with any or all of the following: egg yolks, butter, cream, cheese
- An enriched sauce plus a sprinkling of grated cheese

These items are used because they brown easily. Note that butter (or something containing butterfat and milk solids, such as cream or cheese) is common to all the variations.

The last two items in this list, the ones including sauces, are by far the most widely used in fish cookery. When a sauce is used as the browned topping, we call the technique *glazing,* and on the menu the item may be referred to as *glazed* or, in French, *glacé* (pronounced "glah say"). A sauce used for glazing is called a *glaçage* (pronounced "glah sahj").

A glaçage may be based on a standard white sauce, such as white wine sauce or cream sauce. So that it will brown, it is enriched as indicated in the list above. The enriching agents may be hollandaise sauce (page 613), sabayon (page 70), a liaison (page 29), whipped heavy cream, or a combination of these. Cheese can also be added to the sauce, or you can use Mornay sauce as the base.

Hollandaise-type sauces used by themselves are good glaçages, as are other sauces rich in egg yolks and butter or cream, such as sabayon. Mousseline sauce, a mixture of hollandaise and whipped cream, is also widely used for glazing.

Guidelines for Gratinéing or Glazing Fish

1. When poaching a fish to be gratinéed, do not cook it until it is completely done, because it will cook further when browned.

2. For the best quality, fish and seafood should be poached just before they are gratinéed. However, if your production schedule does not permit you to do this, the fish may be cooked ahead of time. Firm items like shrimp and lobster tails suffer less from being cooked ahead than do delicate items like sole.

3. Butter the bottom of the gratin dish or, if the item is to be glazed, spread some of the sauce on the bottom of the dish before placing the fish in it.

4. Other items, such as vegetables, may be combined with the fish in the gratin dish. For example, you might cover the fish with chopped cooked mushrooms before coating with the glaçage, or you might put the fish on a bed of cooked spinach.

5. Before using a glaçage, test it to make sure that it will brown. Ladle a little onto a plate and run it under the salamander. If it does not brown, you will have to enrich it more.

6. Make sure the sauce is thick enough to coat the fish item.

7. Do not glaze or gratiné an item until immediately before it is to be served. Serve it immediately after it is browned.

Other Preparations Using Cooked Fish. In addition to gratinéed dishes, various other preparations use cooked fish. Most of these dishes are made by combining the fish or seafood with a sauce. Among the most popular dishes of this type are casseroles, filled crêpes, puff pastry preparations such as patty shells and vol-au-vents, and simple sauced mixtures such as curries and blanquettes or fricassées.

Croquettes and similar fried items are, of course, also made with cooked fish.

Several of these preparations are illustrated in the recipe section of this chapter, and in the recipes for crab cakes and fish cakes in Chapter 5.

Stewed Seafood. Stewing is, of course, a moist-heat cooking method. In fish cookery, it is for the most part the same as poaching or simmering. However, sometimes the seafood is sautéed or browned in fat briefly before the liquids are added and poaching begins. This technique is the same as the braising or stewing of meat.

Although there are exceptions, this method is used primarily for firmer seafoods, especially shellfish, rather than for delicate fillets, because firm fish will better survive the agitation of being both sautéed and simmered.

To be successful with these recipes, observe the guidelines for both sautéing and poaching, discussed earlier in this chapter. For an example of this kind of preparation, see the recipe for Lobster à l'Americaine on page 253.

Seafood Served Raw. The popularity of Japanese sushi and sashimi in this country has led chefs to experiment with different ways to prepare and serve raw fish. Most raw fish preparations fall into one of the following categories:

1. Very thin slices of fish, served with a sauce; inspired by the Italian carpaccio, consisting of paper-thin slices of raw beef, usually served with a piquant sauce (see the recipe on page 243).

2. Slices or pieces of fish, often with a dipping sauce; inspired by Japanese sashimi and sushi.

3. Fish tartare, or chopped raw fish mixed with various condiments; based, of course, on beef tartare. A recipe is included in Chapter 5 (see page 174).

4. Marinated raw fish. If the marinade is very acidic, the preparation is basically the same as the familiar Mexican dish *ceviche*. In this dish, the acid coagulates the fish protein, giving it the appearance and texture of cooked fish.

Unfortunately, pollution of fishing waters has become a major concern, and many health officials warn against the consumption of raw fish, especially raw shellfish. Nevertheless, raw oysters and other raw fish items remain popular, especially if they are from reliable sources. If you decide to serve any of these items, observe the following guidelines.

1. Use only the freshest possible fish.

2. Use only saltwater fish and seafood from clean waters. Freshwater fish often contain parasites that can infect the eater.

3. Buy the fish from a reliable purveyor.

4. Keep the fish cold, and handle as quickly as possible. Observe the strictest sanitation procedures.

RECIPES AND SPECIAL TECHNIQUES

Most of the cooking methods and their variations discussed in the first part of this chapter are illustrated by the recipes that follow. The recipes were selected to give you a representative sample not only of various classic dishes, but also of the variety of new fish preparations that are popular today.

As stated in Chapter 5, fish dishes are often used as first courses or appetizer courses. Most of the recipes in this chapter are suitable for first courses, for luncheon main dishes, and for dinner main dishes. In most cases, the portion size of first courses and luncheon dishes is smaller than the portion size of main dinner dishes. With a few exceptions, the quantities and portions indicated in the recipes in this chapter are for dinner portions. The quantities listed for four portions, for example, are sufficient to make six or eight appetizer or luncheon portions. Recipes in this chapter that are more suitable for appetizers than for dinner main courses are Salmon Carpaccio and the various oyster recipes.

Chapter 3 contains recipes for many sauces that are particulary good with fish. While only a few of these sauces are called for in the recipes in this chapter, you are of course not limited to these few. Using the cooking skills that you have learned by now, you should be able to cook most kinds of fish by one or more of the cooking methods we have discussed, and combine it with an appropriate sauce from Chapter 3. You have the resources to create an almost unlimited variety of seafood dishes.

Fin Fish Dishes

Since you should know how to dress and filet both round fish and flat fish, we will not review these basic techniques here. Some other special techniques are needed for the recipes in this chapter and for other preparations that you will encounter. These are explained here.

Boning Fish Through the Back. The basic procedure for dressing fish calls for slitting the belly and removing the entrails through this opening. However, in some preparations in which the fish is stuffed, the belly skin is left intact and the fish is boned and gutted through the back. Preparing the fish in this way makes the fish easier to eat and also makes more room for stuffing.

This procedure is illustrated and explained in Figure 6.3.

Gutting Through the Gills. In some special instances, you might want to keep a fish as whole and intact as possible. In such cases, a fish may be gutted through the gill opening, without cutting open the belly.

In theory, this can be done with any fish, but in practice it is done only with fish that have reasonably large gills. If the gill openings are small, this technique is difficult enough to be impractical. (Even with large-gilled fish, this is not often done, but it may nevertheless be handy to know this trick.)

FIGURE 6.3. **Boning a fish through the back.**
(a) Begin by making a cut against the backbone, just to one side of the dorsal fin, as though starting to fillet the fish.

(b) Repeat the cut on the other side of the backbone. Continue cutting along the bone around the rib bones and toward the stomach of the fish to expose the skeleton, but leave the fillets attached at the tail and gill ends. Hold the knife against the bones to avoid cutting into the flesh.

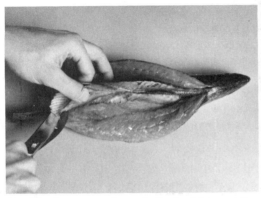

(c) With shears, cut through the backbone at the tail end.

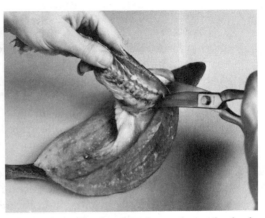

(d) Repeat at the head end to release the backbone.

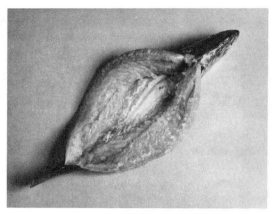

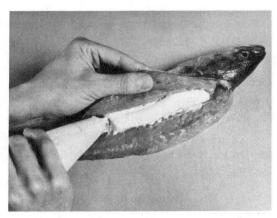

FIGURE 6.3. (Continued)

(e) The boned fish, a trout in this case, is ready to be stuffed.

(f) The quickest way to stuff the fish with mousseline is with a pastry bag.

(g) In this illustration, a boned whiting is being filled with a larger quantity of mousseline in a decorative style.

To gut fish through the gills, first open the gill slits and, with shears, detach the gills at the top and bottom; pull them out. Reach through the opening and pull out the entrails, and rinse the cavity well.

Preparing Sole for Colbert and for Stuffing. In classical cuisine, a special preparation of breaded, deep-fried sole is called Sole Colbert. To prepare the fish for breading, the fillets on one side are first partially separated from the backbone. This is done so that, after frying, the backbone can be easily removed before the fish is presented at the table. After the bones are removed, a slice of maître d'hôtel butter (page 77) is placed in the opening, and the fish is served.

This cutting technique is illustrated in Figure 6.4. The same procedure is used to bone whole sole or other flatfish for stuffing, as shown in the illustration.

Making Paupiettes with Mousseline Filling. Rolling sole fillets and other flat fillets into paupiettes is a basic technique that cooks learn early in their training. An elaboration of this technique that is often used in classical cuisine is to spread the fillets with a layer of fish mousseline (page 259) before rolling them up. The mousseline may be of a contrasting flavor to give added interest to the dish.

This procedure is illustrated in Figure 6.5.

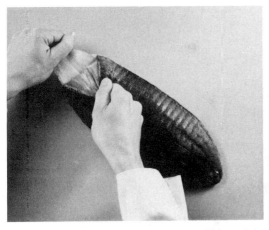

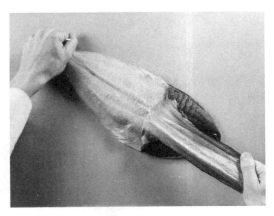

FIGURE 6.4. **Preparing a Dover sole for frying à la Colbert.**
(a) Skin the top or dark side of the sole by making a slit near the tail and pulling the skin loose.

(b) Pull the skin off down to the head end.

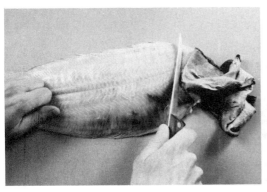

(c) Cut off the head and gut the fish.

(d) With shears or a heavy knife, cut away the bones at the sides of the fish, keeping at least ¼ inch (6 mm) away from the fillets.

(e) With the skinned top side of the fish up, make a cut from head to tail just to one side of the center line, down to the backbone.

(f) Turn the knife so that it is almost parallel to the table. Cut horizontally against the backbone toward the outer edge of the fish to partially release the fillet, but leave the fillet attached at the side of the fish and at both ends. Repeat on the other half of the top side of the fish.

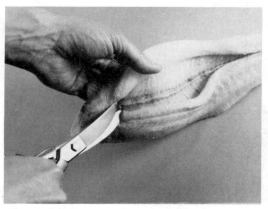

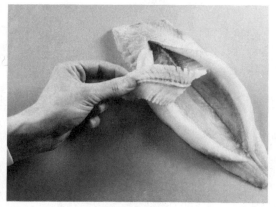

FIGURE 6.4. (Continued)
(g) Break the backbone at both ends and in the middle, or cut through it with shears, being careful not to damage the flesh. For sole à la Colbert, the fish is now breaded and fried. The backbone is removed after the fish is cooked.

(h) For sole to be stuffed, the backbone can be removed from the uncooked fish.

Cutting Scaloppine of Fish. A number of preparations, such as flash-baked fish (page 207), call for very thin slices of fish. These slices are cut the same way that scaloppine of veal and other meats are cut. The technique is explained in Figure 6.6.

Preparing Skate. Skate (sometimes called by its French name, "raie") is an unusual fish that is unlike other fin fish. Even if you have not handled this fish in the kitchen, you are probably familiar with it from underwater films, where the fish is usually called "stingray."

Like its relative the shark, skate has no bones but instead has a skeleton made entirely of cartilage. Only the two triangular "wings" are prepared and eaten (see Figure 6.7).

Skate is often soaked in salted water for several hours before it is cooked. This soaking helps whiten the fish by drawing out blood that would darken when cooked.

Skate can be filleted or it can be cooked without filleting. Filleting and skinning a skate wing is done the same way as filleting and skinning a regular fish, by run-

FIGURE 6.5. Paupiettes, or rolled fillets of sole, can be spread with a fish mousseline before rolling. Spread the mousseline on the skinned side of the fillet.

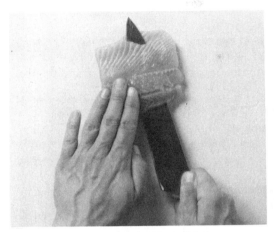

FIGURE 6.6. **Cutting scaloppine of fish.**
(a) Holding the knife parallel or nearly parallel to the fish fillet, cut a thin slice.

(b) The cut slice. Several slices can be cut from the fillet, depending on its thickness.

ning the knife between the bones—or in this case, cartilage—and holding the edge of the blade against the bone to keep from cutting into the flesh. Similarly, to skin, place the fillet skinside down on the work surface and slide the knife between the skin and flesh, while holding onto the edge of the skin. Skate fillets must be handled very carefully after cooking to keep them from falling apart.

Whole, unfilleted skate wings must be skinned before they are served. It is possible but difficult to shave the skin from a raw wing with a sharp knife. Another method is to skin it after it is poached (the skin will come off easily), or to blanch the skate in boiling water for two minutes, then scrape the skin off with the back of a knife (it will slide off without difficulty). Blanched, skinned skate can then be chilled and cooked to order.

The classic method for cooking skate is to poach it in salted water or court bouillon and serve it with brown butter or black butter (page 30). But, like other fish, it can also be steamed, poached in wine, sautéed à la meunière, and seasoned and garnished in a variety of ways.

FIGURE 6.7. **Skate.**
(a) The underside of a small skate wing, left, and the top side of a large wing, right.

(b) Skate can be filleted like other fish, by cutting against the cartilage "bones."

Shellfish Dishes

Basic techniques for preparing shellfish include opening clams and oysters, splitting lobsters, and peeling and deveining shrimp. These can be reviewed in many basic cookbooks and are not repeated here. Some additional special techniques are useful for preparing specialty seafood dishes. A few of these techniques are explained here. You will need them in some of the recipes in this chapter.

Cleaning Soft-shell Crabs. Soft-shell crabs are ordinary blue crabs that have been caught just after molting, before their new shells have hardened. Except for the gills, they are completely edible. Sautéed or fried, they are a popular delicacy in the spring, when they are in season.

To prepare soft-shell crabs for cooking, follow the procedure explained in Figure 6.8.

Cleaning Squid. Although biologists classify squids as mollusks, along with clams and oysters, this classification has no practical meaning for the cook, since they are handled so differently. Because they have no external shell, they of course do not have to be opened like clams. The procedure for cleaning squid is relatively simple, as shown in Figure 6.9.

Cutting Lobster for Sautés. Lobster sautés, such as Lobster à l'Americaine, require live lobsters that have been cut up a special way. This procedure is shown in Figure 6.10.

Miscellaneous Items

This section includes techniques for items that do not fit neatly into the two main categories of fin fish and shellfish. The most important group of items in this section are those based on fish forcemeats and mousselines. These mixtures may be made with fin fish, shellfish, or a mixture of the two.

In addition, we also include a brief discussion of frog legs. Although frogs are neither fish nor shellfish, they are usually classified by cooks as a seafood item.

Forcemeats and Mousselines. A *forcemeat,* as defined in Chapter 11, is a mixture of seasoned, ground meats or fish used as a stuffing or filling. The garde manger department uses forcemeats in the preparation of cold pâtés and terrines. The hot kitchen also uses forcemeats in the preparation of various appetizer, main dish, and garnish items. Some of the most delicate and delectable of these are made from fish and seafood.

There are two basic types of fish forcemeats, the ordinary forcemeat and the mousseline forcemeat.

Ordinary Forcemeats. Ordinary forcemeats are a mixture of ground fish or meat, some form of fat (such as butter or cream), and a cooked starch binder called a *panade,* (pronounced "pah nahd"). There are several kinds of panades, the most common of which are:

• Flour panade is made from flour, water, and butter. The procedure for making it is the same as the first stage in making pâte à choux, or cream puff paste.
• Frangipan panade is made from flour, egg yolks, butter, and milk. The procedure for making it is like the procedure for making pastry cream, except of course that the panade is not sweetened.
• Bread panade is made by boiling equal weights of milk and fresh bread crumbs until the mixture forms a paste.

FIGURE 6.8. **Preparing soft shell crabs.**
(a) Soft shell crabs, seen from the top and bottom.

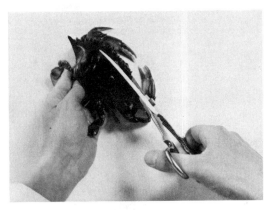

(b) Cut off the head just behind the eyes.

(c) Pull out the stomach sac.

(d) Pull back one side of the soft top shell to reveal the feathery gills.

(e) Pull out the gills. Repeat on the other side.

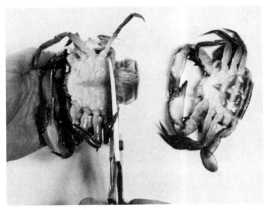

(f) Cut or pull off the apron on the underside. The wide apron indicates that this is a female crab. Males have a much narrower apron.

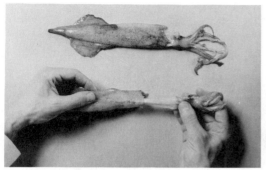

FIGURE 6.9. **Cleaning squid.**
(a) Pull off the head; the interior organs will come out with it.

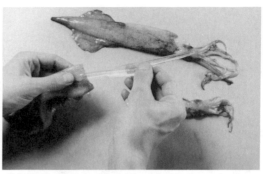

(b) Pull out the plasticlike "quill" from the body sac. Rinse out the sac to clean it well.

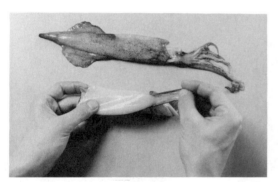

(c) Pull off the skin.

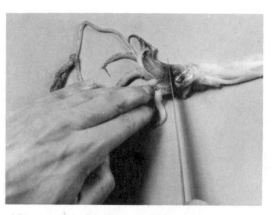

(d) Cut off the tentacles just above the eyes. Discard the head, organs, and "beak," which is found at the center of the tentacle cluster.

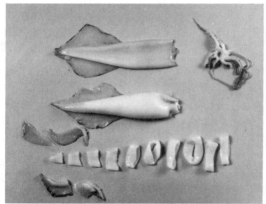

(e) From top to bottom: cleaned whole body sac and tentacles; stuffed squid, fastened with a pick; and squid sac sliced into rings.

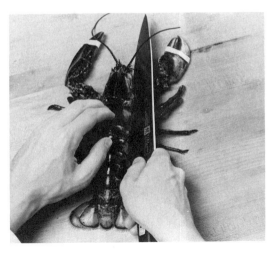

FIGURE 6.10. **Cutting lobster for sautés and stews.**
(a) Place the lobster on the cutting board. Pierce the head with a firm thrust of the knife point to kill the lobster quickly.

(b) Cut off the legs and claws.

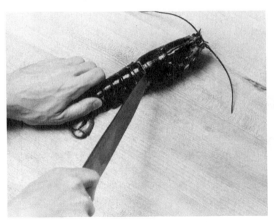

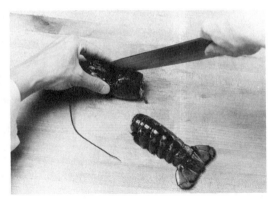

(c) Remove the tail section from the thorax, either by breaking it off or by inserting a knife behind the thorax as shown and cutting through the flesh.

(d) Cut the thorax in half lengthwise.

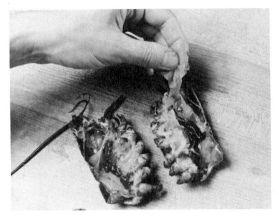

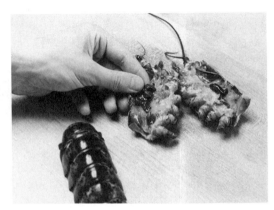

(e) Remove and discard the stomach, a sac just behind the eyes.

(f) Remove the tomalley and coral for use in the sauce to accompany the lobster.

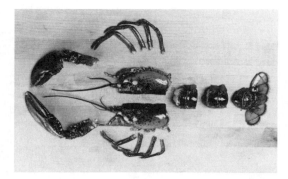

FIGURE 6.10. (Continued)
(g) Cut the tail into pieces where the segments join. This is a small lobster. Large tails should be cut into more pieces (at least 4 or 5) so that each piece is not too large.

(h) The cut-up lobster, ready to cook.

A recipe for flour panade is on page 257. We do not include a recipe for frangipan panade, since the flour panade is a little easier to use and will suffice for most purposes. A recipe for bread panade is not necessary, since the description above gives you enough information to make this product if you need it.

Mousseline Forcemeats. Mousseline forcemeats are made of ground fish or meat, heavy cream, and usually a small quantity of egg to serve as a binder. Egg whites are most often used, but some recipes call for whole eggs. Because they contain no starch binder, mousseline forcemeats are the most delicate of the forcemeats.

Ingredient proportions in mousseline forcemeat depend on the qualities of the fish being used. The albumin protein of the egg white makes the mousseline firm when it is cooked. If the fish that you are using has a high albumin content, however, you may be able to reduce the quantity of egg white, or in some cases you may not need any egg white. Similarly, the amount of cream you can add depends on the firmness of the fish. The more cream that is added, the softer the mousseline becomes. In general, lean, firm fish require less egg white and can absorb more cream, while soft fish need more egg white.

Making and Handling Fish Forcemeats. Keep the mixture and the ingredients cold at all times. This is especially important when you are adding the cream to a mousseline. The cream will not be absorbed properly if the mixture is not cold.

A well-made fish forcemeat has a perfectly smooth, light, delicate texture. In order to achieve this, the fish must be ground to a fine purée. In the old days, this was done by pounding the fish in a mortar. Modern food processors simplify this task greatly. To be sure of a smooth texture with no sinews or connective tissue, rub the fish through a fine sieve after puréeing it (see the illustration of the drum sieve in Chapter 10 on page 496). This step may not be necessary if the fish is well trimmed and the processor blade is sharp.

To test the texture and seasonings of the finished (raw) forcemeat, poach a small quenelle in water and taste it. This gives you the opportunity to make any adjustments, if necessary, before using the forcemeat.

A classic use of forcemeats is to make them into *quenelles,* which are forcemeat dumplings. There are several methods for shaping quenelles, as illustrated in Figure 6.11. The choice of method depends on the firmness of the forcemeat. One based on flour panade may be firm enough to roll by hand, while mousseline forcemeats are too soft for this method.

FIGURE 6.11. **Preparing quenelles from ordinary and mousseline forcemeats.**
(a) For ordinary forcemeat made with a panade, dust the worktable with flour and roll the forcemeat into a long cylinder.

(b) Cut the cylinder diagonally into pieces as shown.

(c) Roll each piece into an oval shape on the worktable under the palm of the hand.

(d) For small mousseline quenelles, the mousseline forcemeat can be piped directly into a buttered pan with a pastry bag. Hot water, court bouillon, or stock is added to poach the quenelles.

(e) To make oval quenelles, pick up a portion of mousseline with a spoon.

(f) With a second spoon, pick up the mousseline from the first spoon as shown.

FIGURE 6.11. (Continued)
(g) This procedure forms the forcemeat into an oval shape.

(h) Carefully drop the quenelle into the poaching liquid.

(i) Vary the size of the quenelle by using spoons of a different size.

Other uses of fish forcemeats include making them into hot or cold terrines or timbales, stuffing them into sausage casings, and using them as stuffings for fish fillets. The forcemeats may be used plain or combined with solid ingredients and garnish. Several of these uses are illustrated in the recipes in this chapter.

Frog Legs. Frog legs are a tender, mild-flavored delicacy that are popular in many parts of the world, but not widely favored in America. Nevertheless, they are frequently encountered on the menus of French restaurants in this country, as well as on the menus of restaurants that feature various regional cuisines. On French menus they are called *cuisses de grenouilles* (pronounced "kweese duh grenwee"), or simply grenouilles.

Frog legs usually come from the market in pairs, fully cleaned, skinned, and ready to cook. A half pound (250 g) makes an ample serving for one person. Since they vary greatly in size, the number in a half pound may range from two pairs to six or more pairs.

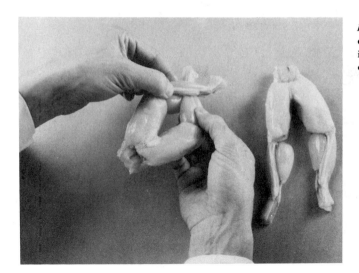

FIGURE 6.12. **To keep frog legs more compact for cooking, one leg can be inserted between the muscle and bone of the other leg.**

For cooking, a pair of legs may be left intact, or the two legs may be cut apart. If a pair is left intact, one leg can be drawn through the other, as shown in Figure 6.12. This makes it more compact and easier to handle when cooking.

Frog legs are usually cooked by poaching, sautéing, or deep-frying. In general, many of the recipes for scallops and shrimp may be used for frog legs (except that frog legs are usually dredged in flour before sautéing, while shrimp are not).

Since many standard preparations for various seafood can be applied easily to frog legs, we include in this chapter only one recipe for them to serve as an example. Among the popular treatments for frog legs are the following:

Sauté à la meunière (see page 202)

Breaded or battered and deep-fried

Poached in white wine with mushrooms and shallots and served with poulette sauce (page 43) or gratinéed with mornay sauce (page 39)

You should be able to prepare any of these by referring to the appropriate procedures and sauce recipes.

ORDINARY COURT BOUILLON FOR FISH

		U.S.		Metric	
YIELD:		**2 qt**	**2 gal**	*2 l*	*8 l*
Ingredients					
Water		2 qt	2 gal	*2 l*	*8 l*
White vinegar, wine vinegar, or lemon juice		4 oz	1 pt	*125 ml*	*5 dl*
Onions, sliced		4 oz	1 lb	*125 g*	*500 g*
Celery, sliced		2 oz	8 oz	*60 g*	*250 g*
Carrots, sliced		2 oz	8 oz	*60 g*	*250 g*
Salt		1 oz	4 oz	*30 g*	*125 g*
Peppercorns, crushed		¼ tsp	1 tsp	*0.5 g*	*2 g*
Bay leaves		½	2	*½*	*2*
Thyme		pinch	½ tsp	*pinch*	*0.5 g*
Parsley stems		5–6	20–25	*5–6*	*20–25*

Procedure:

1. Combine all ingredients in a stock pot or saucepan and bring to a boil.

2. Reduce heat and simmer 30 minutes.

3. Strain and cool.

COURT BOUILLON WITH WHITE WINE

		U.S.		Metric	
	YIELD:	**2 qt**	**2 gal**	*2 l*	*8 l*
Ingredients					
Water		1 qt	1 gal	*1 l*	*4 l*
White wine		1 qt	1 gal	*1 l*	*4 l*
Onions, sliced		2 oz	8 oz	*60 g*	*250 g*
Celery		2 oz	8 oz	*60 g*	*250 g*
Leeks		2 oz	8 oz	*60 g*	*250 g*
Bay leaf		½	2	*½*	*2*
Peppercorns, crushed		¼ tsp	1 tsp	*0.5 g*	*2 g*
Thyme		¼ tsp	1 tsp	*0.25 tsp*	*1 tsp*
Parsley stems		5–6	20–25	*5–6*	*20–25*
Cloves		1	4	*1*	*4*
Salt		1 tbsp	2 oz	*15 g*	*60 g*

Procedure:

1. Combine all ingredients in a stock pot or saucepan and bring to a boil.

2. Reduce heat and simmer about 20 minutes.

3. Strain and cool.

FILLETS OF SOLE AU VIN BLANC

		U.S.		Metric	
PORTIONS:		4	16	4	16
Ingredients					
Sole fillets		1 lb	4 lb	*500 g*	*2 kg*
Salt					
White pepper					
Butter		½ oz	2 oz	*15 g*	*60 g*
Shallots		½ oz	2 oz	*15 g*	*60 g*
White wine		2 oz	8 oz	*60 ml*	*2.5 dl*
Fish stock (quantity variable; see Cooking, step 2)		4 oz	1 pt	*125 ml*	*5 dl*
Fish velouté		8 oz	1 qt	*2.5 dl*	*1 l*
Heavy cream		2 oz	8 oz	*60 ml*	*2.5 dl*
Salt					
White pepper					
Lemon juice					

Mise en Place:

1. Season the fillets with salt and pepper. Fold them in half so that the skin side is on the inside of the fold.
2. Mince the shallots.
3. Prepare the fish velouté. Have it ready and hot at service time.

Cooking/Finishing:

1. Butter the inside of a baking pan or other suitable pan for poaching the fish. Sprinkle the shallots on the bottom, then lay the fillets on top of the shallots in a single layer.
2. Add the white wine and enough fish stock to almost cover the fish. Cover the fish with a piece of buttered paper and cover the pan with a lid.
3. Bring the liquid to a simmer, then transfer the pan to a moderate oven to finish cooking. Watch it closely, since it will take only a few minutes to finish. For best results, undercook it slightly, so that it will not become overcooked as it stands.
4. Drain the cooking liquid into a wide pan and keep the fish warm.
5. Reduce the liquid over high heat by three-fourths.
6. Add the velouté and cream. Reduce to bring to a good sauce consistency.
7. Season to taste with salt, white pepper, and lemon juice. Strain. (If desired, the sauce may be finished with a little raw butter.)

Presentation:

Plate the fillets and coat each portion with 2 oz (60 ml) of the sauce.

Variations

Alternative method: Poach the fish as in the basic method. As soon as it is cooked, plate it and coat it with a prepared white wine sauce (page 41). The poaching liquid can be saved to cook additional orders of fish and then saved and used to make a future batch of white wine sauce.

Other lean, white fish may be used instead of sole.

Instead of white wine sauce, any sauce appropriate for fish can be used. The following are some suggestions (see Chapter 3 for recipes):

Mornay sauce	Shrimp sauce
Nantua sauce	Diplomate sauce
Cardinal sauce	Venetian sauce
Curry sauce	Cream sauce for fish
Mushroom sauce	Sorrel sauce
Bercy sauce	Saffron sauce
Herb sauce	Shellfish sauce
Normandy sauce	Beurre blanc and variations

Glazed Poached Fish

Refer to page 208 for the guidelines and procedure for glazing fish.

Poached Paupiettes of Sole

Instead of folding the fillets in half, lay them on the table with the skin side up and roll them up. If desired, they may be coated with fish mousseline (see Figure 6.5) before rolling. Cook and finish them as in the basic recipe or variations.

Fillets of Sole Argenteuil

Prepare as in the basic recipe. Garnish with cooked asparagus tips.

Fillets of Sole Bercy

Poach as in the basic recipe. Reduce the cooking liquid by two-thirds and add some chopped parsley. Omit the velouté and cream, but add a few drops of lemon juice and enrich the sauce with raw butter. Glaze the fish before serving; see page 208 for glazing procedure.

Fillets of Sole Bonne Femme

Mushrooms	4 oz	1 lb	*125 g*	*500 g*

Slice or mince the mushrooms and sprinkle them on the bottom of the baking dish with the shallots. Poach and finish as in the basic recipe, but do not strain the sauce. If desired, the sauce may be enriched with butter and the dish glazed.

Fillets of Sole Diplomate

Poach the sole as in the basic recipe. Drain and plate it, and coat it with diplomate sauce (page 43). Garnish with a few truffle slices.

Fillets of Sole Dugléré

Tomato, peeled, seeded and diced	4 oz	1 lb	*125 g*	*500 g*
Parsley, chopped	2 tsp	3 tbsp	*4 g*	*115 g*
Butter	1 oz	4 oz	*30 g*	*125 g*

Add the tomato and parsley to the pan when poaching the fish. Poach as in the basic recipe. Omit the heavy cream and instead add the raw butter to the sauce. Do not strain.

Fillets of Sole Fermière

Mirepoix:				
Onion	1 oz	4 oz	*30 g*	*125 g*
Celery	½ oz	2 oz	*15 g*	*60 g*
Carrot	½ oz	2 oz	*15 g*	*60 g*
Red wine	6 oz	1 ½ pt	*2 dl*	*7.5 dl*
Beurre manié, as needed				
Butter	2 oz	8 oz	*60 g*	*250 g*
Garnish:				
Sliced mushrooms sautéed in butter				

Add finely chopped mirepoix to the pan. Omit the white wine and fish stock and poach the fish in red wine. When the fish is cooked, reduce the cooking liquid by half and thicken with beurre manié. Finish the sauce with raw butter. Plate the fish, garnish with sliced mushrooms, coat with the sauce, and glaze briefly.

Fillets of Sole Florentine

Cook as in the basic recipe. Put the fillets on a bed of cooked, buttered spinach. Coat with mornay sauce that has been enriched for glazing (see page 208). Brown lightly under the salamander.

Fillets of Sole Marguery

Cook the fish as in the basic recipe. Plate the fish and garnish it with cooked, shelled mussels and cooked shrimp, arranging them in a border around the fish. Enrich the sauce with butter, coat the fish and garnish, and glaze lightly under the salamander.

Fillets of Sole Mornay

Cook as in the basic recipe. Plate the fish, coat it with mornay sauce, and sprinkle with grated parmesan and gruyère cheeses. Brown under the salamander.

Fillets of Sole Nantua

Cook as in the basic recipe. Plate the fish, place some cooked shrimp or crayfish tails around it, and coat with nantua sauce. Decorate with a few slices of truffle.

Fillets of Sole Parisienne

Prepare as in the basic recipe, but add some mushroom trimmings to the cooking liquid for flavor. Garnish the finished dish with sliced truffles, sliced mushrooms, and a few crayfish or shrimp.

FILLETS OF SOLE À L'ORANGE

		U.S.		Metric	
PORTIONS:		**4**	**16**	**4**	**16**
Ingredients					
Leek, white part		3 oz	12 oz	*90 g*	*375 g*
Carrot		3 oz	12 oz	*90 g*	*375 g*
Butter		1 oz	4 oz	*30 g*	*125 g*
Fillets of sole		1 ½ lb	6 lb	*700 g*	*2.8 kg*
Salt					
White pepper					
Orange juice		8 oz	1 qt	*2.5 dl*	*1 l*
White wine		8 oz	1 qt	*2.5 dl*	*1 l*
Butter		1 oz	4 oz	*30 g*	*125 g*
Oranges		1	4	*1*	*4*

Mise en Place:

1. Cut the leek and carrot julienne.

2. Season the sole fillets with salt and pepper; set them aside.

3. With a knife, peel and section the oranges.

Cooking/Finishing:

1. Sweat the leeks and carrots in butter until they are cooked but still slightly crisp.

2. Poach the fillets in the orange juice and wine.

3. Remove the fillets and keep them warm. Reduce the cooking liquid by two-thirds. Stir in the raw butter.

Presentation:

1. For each portion, spoon a little of the sauce onto the center of the plate. Place the fillets on top of the sauce. Top the fillets with the julienne vegetables.

2. Surround the fillets with some orange sections.

Variations

Fillets of Sole Sauté à l'Orange

Sauté the fish *doré* (see page 202). Serve it with the same garnish and sauce as in the basic recipe.

FINNAN HADDIE WITH CELERY

		U.S.		Metric	
PORTIONS:		**4**	**16**	**4**	**16**
Ingredients					
Celery root, peeled		6 oz	1 lb 8 oz	*150 g*	*600 g*
Butter		1 oz	3 oz	*25 g*	*80 g*
Water		1 oz	4 oz	*25 ml*	*1 dl*
Finnan haddie (smoked haddock) fillets		1 lb 8 oz	6 lb	*600 g*	*2.5 kg*
Milk		8 oz	1 qt	*2 dl*	*8 dl*
Celery		1 oz	4 oz	*25 g*	*100 g*
Beurre manié:					
Butter		1 oz	4 oz	*25 g*	*100 g*
Flour		1 tbsp	1 oz	*6 g*	*25 g*
Heavy cream		2 oz	8 oz	*50 ml*	*2 dl*
Salt					
White pepper					

Mise en Place:

1. Cut the celery root into small batonnet.

2. Cut the stalk celery into small dice.

3. Prepare the beurre manié.

Cooking/Finishing:

1. Brown the celery root in butter. Add the water, cover, and steam gently until the celery root is cooked but still somewhat crisp.

2. Put the finnan haddie in a pan and add the milk and diced celery. Poach the fish until it is done.

3. Remove the fish from the milk and keep the fish warm.

4. Bring the milk to a simmer and thicken lightly with the beurre manié, adding it a little at a time. Do not thicken the sauce too much; it should have the consistency of heavy cream. Add the cream and season with salt and pepper. Strain the sauce and discard the diced celery.

Presentation:

1. For each portion, ladle 2 oz (50 ml) of the sauce onto a plate. Place a portion of fish in the center of the plate, and distribute the celery root randomly around the fish.

2. This dish should be accompanied by small boiled potatoes.

SAUTÉED LIGHTLY CURED COD WITH MASHED POTATOES

		U.S.		Metric	
	PORTIONS:	4	16	*4*	*16*
Ingredients					
Cod fillets, about 6 oz each		4	16	*4*	*16*
Sugar		½ oz	2 oz	*15 g*	*60 g*
Coarse salt		1 oz	4 oz	*30 g*	*125 g*
White pepper		¼ tsp	1 tsp	*0.5 g*	*2 g*
Olive oil		1 oz	4 oz	*30 ml*	*125 ml*
Soft mashed potatoes flavored with garlic and olive oil (p. 544)		12 oz	3 lb	*375 g*	*1.5 kg*
Chive oil (p. 82)		2 oz	8 oz	*60 ml*	*2.5 dl*

Mise en Place:

1. Coat the fish with a mixture of the sugar, salt, and white pepper. Refrigerate for 1 to 2 hours, no longer.
2. Remove from the refrigerator and wipe off the salt mixture. Put the fish in a clean container and refrigerate until ready to cook.

Cooking and Presentation:

1. Heat the olive oil in a sauté pan. Sauté the fish on both sides until browned and just cooked.
2. Place each fillet on a bed of mashed potatoes on a dinner plate.
3. Drizzle a little chive oil onto the plate around the cod and mashed potatoes.

Variations

The sautéed cod can be presented in many other ways. The following are a few suggestions:

In place of the potatoes, serve the cod on a bed of white bean purée.

Use another flavored oil, such as basil oil, in place of the chive oil.

Omit the oil and use a light vinaigrette.

Top the cod with a handful of crisp, fried julienne of leeks.

SKATE WITH BROWN BUTTER

		U.S.		Metric	
PORTIONS:		4	16	4	16
Ingredients					
Skate wings		3 lb	12 lb	1.25 kg	5 kg
Water, as needed					
Salt		1 ½ tbsp	6 tbsp	20 g	80 g
Wine vinegar		2 oz	8 oz	50 ml	2 dl
Salt					
White pepper					
Parsley, chopped		4 tbsp	1 cup	15 g	60 g
Capers, drained		4 tbsp	1 cup	25 g	100 g
Wine vinegar		2 tsp	8 tsp	10 ml	40 ml
Butter		3 oz	12 oz	75 g	300 g

Mise en Place:

1. Cut the skate into individual portions.
2. The skate may be skinned ahead of time or after cooking. Refer to page 214 for details on handling skate.

Cooking/Finishing:

1. Poach the skate in a simple court bouillon consisting of water, salt, and wine vinegar (or use the ordinary court bouillon on page 224).
2. If the skate has not been skinned, skin it after it is cooked. The skinned skate may be served as is or boned out.

Presentation:

1. Drain the skate well and plate it. Season each portion to taste with salt and white pepper, and sprinkle it with parsley, capers, and a little wine vinegar.
2. Brown the butter (beurre noisette) and immediately pour the butter over the skate. Serve at once.
3. A good accompaniment for the skate is small boiled or steamed potatoes.

Variations

This is by far the most common skate preparation, but it is not the only possible one. Skate can be filleted and substituted for other fish fillets in many recipes (see page 214). For example, you may substitute skate fillets in the various preparations of fish poached in wine (see page 226), in a sauté meunière (see page 202), or in marinated, steamed fillets (see page 199).

POACHED OR BAKED FISH WITH TOMATO GARLIC SAUCE

		U.S.		Metric	
PORTIONS:		4	16	4	16
Ingredients					
Fish stock		12 oz	3 pt	3.5 dl	1.5 l
Chopped tomatoes		4 oz	1 lb	125 g	500 g
Garlic, crushed		1 clove	4 cloves	1 clove	4 cloves
Anchovy paste		¼ tsp	1 tsp	0.5 g	2 g
Grated orange zest		¼ tsp	1 tsp	0.5 g	2 g
Fillets of red snapper, sea bass, or similar white, firm, ocean fish, 6 oz (175 g) each		4	16	4	16
Aioli (p. 74)		3 oz	12 oz	90 g	350 g
Salt					
White pepper					
Optional garnish: chopped parsley					

Mise en Place:

1. Combine the stock, tomatoes, garlic, anchovy paste, and orange zest.
2. Simmer slowly for about a half hour. Reserve.

Cooking/Finishing:

1. Put the fillets in a baking pan just large enough to hold them in a single layer. Pour the hot stock mixture over them.
2. Bake at 450°F (230°C) until done.
3. Drain the fillets and keep them warm.
4. Reduce the cooking liquid by half. Whip in the aioli. Do not boil after the aioli has been added, or the emulsion will break. Season the sauce to taste with salt and pepper.

Presentation:

1. Plate the fillets and pour the sauce over them.
2. Sprinkle with chopped parsley if desired.

MATELOTE OF TROUT WITH ZUCCHINI FEUILLETÉ

		U.S.		Metric	
PORTIONS:		4	16	4	16
Ingredients					
Small trout		4	16	4	16
Fish mousseline (p. 259)		12 oz	3 lb	350 g	1.4 kg
Mirepoix		8 oz	2 lb	225 g	450 g
Anchovy fillets		4	16	4	16
Red wine		1 pt	2 qt	5 dl	2 l
Fish stock		8 oz	1 qt	2.5 dl	1 l
Strong brown veal stock or demiglaze		8 oz	1 qt	2.5 dl	1 l
Beurre manié, as needed					
Heavy cream		3 oz	12 oz	90 ml	3.5 dl
Salt					
Pepper					
Butter		1–2 oz	4–8 oz	30–60 g	110–225 g
Garnish (see Mise en Place):					
Puff pastry rectangles, about 2 by 4 inches (5 by 10 cm)		4	16	4	16
Tomato concassé		4 oz	1 lb	125 g	500 g
Shallots, minced		¼ oz	1 oz	7 g	30 g
Olive oil					
Zucchini		8 oz	2 lb	250 g	1 kg
Carrots		6 oz	1 lb 8 oz	175 g	700 g
Potatoes		6 oz	1 lb 8 oz	175 g	700 g
Salt					
Butter					

Mise en Place:

1. Bone and gut the trout through the back, as shown in Figure 6.3. Do not make the opening too large; the fish will be less likely to fall apart if not cut too much.

2. With a pastry bag, stuff each fish with mousseline.

3. Chop the mirepoix and anchovies finely.

4. Prepare the elements of the garnish as directed in the following steps. Please note that the quantities given are only suggestions. You may modify them to suit your needs.

5. Bake the puff pastry rectangles (see the recipe for Feuilleté of Vegetables, page 182, for the procedure for making puff pastry rectangles, or feuilletés).

6. Sauté the tomato concassé with the minced shallots in a little olive oil. Season.

7. Cut the zucchini into batonnets, discarding the interior seedy part. Salt them and let them stand in a strainer for 15 minutes to draw off some excess moisture.

8. Tourné the carrots and potatoes into small, elongated olive shapes.

9. Cook the vegetables: Steam the zucchini and carrots separately in a little butter, keeping them a little crisp. Steam or boil the potatoes.

Cooking/Finishing:

1. Place the fish upright (that is, back side up) on top of the mirepoix and anchovies in a shallow baking pan; add the wine and stock. *Note:* The pan should be small enough so that the liquid comes at least halfway up the sides of the fish.

2. Cover the fish with a piece of buttered parchment and set the pan in a 450°F (230°C) oven. Cook for 10 to 15 minutes, basting frequently with the liquid, until the fish and mousseline are cooked.

3. Carefully remove the fish from the pan and keep them warm.

4. Reduce the cooking liquid by three-fourths over high heat. Add the demiglaze, bring to a boil, and reduce slightly.

5. Thicken the sauce lightly with a little beurre manié if necessary. Strain the sauce.

6. Add the heavy cream and season to taste with salt and pepper. Finish the sauce with raw butter.

7. Reheat the vegetables for the garnish as necessary.

Presentation:

1. For each portion, ladle about 3 oz (90 ml) of sauce onto a plate. Carefully set the fish across the bottom half of the plate.

2. Split a puff paste rectangle in half horizontally and remove the top. Spoon a little of the tomato onto the bottom half. Set this on the plate above the fish. Spoon some of the zucchini on top and replace the top of the pastry.

3. Arrange a few pieces of carrot and potato on either side of the puff pastry.

Variations

Other small fish may be substituted for the trout. Whiting is especially easy to bone out for this preparation because it has no rib bones, but it is very delicate when cooked; extra care is needed to keep it from falling apart.

For a simpler but also very attractive production, use meaty fish fillets, such as salmon, instead of whole small fish. Top with a thick layer of fish mousseline; either use a pastry bag to make a decorative topping, or apply the mousseline with a spatula and smooth it. Cook as in the basic recipe, adjusting the cooking time as necessary.

Traditional Matelote

The main recipe is not a traditional matelote but a modern adaptation. A traditional matelote is a fish stew made with red or white wine and usually with freshwater fish. To make it, follow the general procedure of the above recipe with the following modifications. Use one or several kinds of whole fish and cut them crosswise into pieces. Add a clove of garlic to the mirepoix. Simmer the fish in the wine and stock until done, either in the oven or on top of the stove. Reduce the cooking liquid only by one-third and thicken it with beurre manié. Omit the demiglaze or veal stock and the cream. Omit the garnish at the end of the recipe and, instead, garnish with small whole cooked onions and button mushrooms and with croutons fried in butter.

Salmon Steaks in Red Wine

Cook salmon steaks as in the basic recipe, in place of the stuffed whiting. Prepare the sauce as in the basic recipe but omit the cream.

Note: This recipe is similar to the classical dish called *Salmon Chambord,* except that Salmon Chambord is served with a complicated garnish consisting of quenelles, truffles, crayfish, fried smelts, and other items.

MARINATED STEAMED TROUT WITH ONION COMPOTE

	U.S.		Metric	
PORTIONS:	**4**	**16**	*4*	*16*
Ingredients				
Marinade:				
Olive oil	1 oz	4 oz	*30 ml*	*125 ml*
Lemon juice	1 oz	4 oz	*30 ml*	*125 ml*
White wine	1 oz	4 oz	*30 ml*	*125 ml*
Salt	½ tsp	2 tsp	*2.5 g*	*10 g*
White pepper	pinch	½ tsp	*pinch*	*1 g*
Trout fillets, 4–6 oz (125–175 g) each	4	16	*4*	*16*
Onion compote (p. 520)	6 oz	1 lb 8 oz	*180 g*	*725 g*
Tomato sauce for fish (p. 51)	3 oz	12 oz	*1 dl*	*3.5 dl*

Mise en Place:

1. Combine the marinade ingredients.

2. Dip the fillets in the marinade so that they are moistened on all sides. Marinate for 1 to 2 hours. Do not marinate too long or the fish will become "cooked" by the acidity.

Cooking/Finishing:

Steam the fillets until they are just done.

Presentation:

1. For each portion, spoon 1 ½ oz (45 g) of onion compote onto a plate. Place a fillet on top of the onion.

2. Put a spoonful of tomato sauce alongside the fish.

Variations

The fish may be flash baked (see page 207) or sautéed instead of steamed.

Omit the tomato sauce and drizzle a little parsley oil around the fish.

Other fish, such as salmon or bluefish fillets, may be substituted for the trout.

GRILLED TUNA OR SWORDFISH
WITH CILANTRO BALSAMIC VINAIGRETTE

		U.S.		Metric	
PORTIONS:		4	16	*4*	*16*
Ingredients					
Balsamic vinegar		1 tbsp	2 oz	*15 ml*	*60 ml*
Water		1 tsp	4 tsp	*5 ml*	*20 ml*
Cilantro leaves, chopped		1 tbsp	4 tbsp	*3 g*	*12 g*
Fresh chives, chopped		1 tbsp	4 tbsp	*3 g*	*12 g*
Salt		¼ tsp	1 tsp	*1 g*	*5 g*
White pepper		pinch	½ tsp	*pinch*	*1 g*
Olive oil		1 ½ oz	6 oz	*45 ml*	*2 dl*
Tuna or swordfish steaks, 5–6 oz (about 150 g) each		4	16	*4*	*16*
Salt					

Mise en Place:

Make a vinaigrette with the vinegar, water, herbs, salt, pepper, and olive oil. (*Note:* Do not make the vinaigrette more than a few hours in advance or the herbs will begin to lose color.)

Cooking/Finishing:

1. Season the steaks with a little salt and brush them very lightly with some of the vinaigrette.

2. Grill the fish on both sides until nearly cooked, though still juicy. Do not cook until well done or the fish will be dry.

Presentation:

1. Plate the fish.

2. Spoon a little of the vinaigrette over the steaks, spreading it with the back of the spoon to coat the tops with the herbs and oil.

GRILLED RED SNAPPER MEDITERRANÉE   *(Color Plate 7)*

	U.S.		Metric	
PORTIONS:	*4*	*16*	*4*	*16*
Ingredients				
Red snapper fillets	1–1 ½ lb	4–6 lb	*400–600 g*	*1.6–2.4 kg*
Salt				
Pepper				
Olive oil				
Carrots, peeled	2 oz	8 oz	*50 g*	*200 g*
Fennel, trimmed	2 oz	8 oz	*50 g*	*200 g*
Snow peas	2 oz	8 oz	*50 g*	*200 g*
Wine vinegar	2 oz	8 oz	*50 ml*	*2 dl*
Tomato, peeled, seeded, and chopped	4 oz	1 lb	*100 g*	*400 g*
Olive oil	4 oz	1 pt	*1 dl*	*4 dl*
Lemon juice	1 tsp	4 tsp	*4 ml*	*20 ml*
Green peppercorns	2 tsp	3 tbsp	*5 g*	*20 g*
Capers	2 tsp	3 tbsp	*5 g*	*20 g*
Thyme	¼ tsp	1 tsp	*0.25 g*	*1 g*
Rosemary	¼ tsp	1 tsp	*0.25 g*	*1 g*
Basil	¼ tsp	1 tsp	*0.25 g*	*1 g*
Salt				

Mise en Place:

1. Cut the fish fillets into individual portions of 4 to 6 oz (100 to 400 g) each.
2. Cut the carrots and fennel into batonnet, about 2 inches (5 cm) long. Cook them separately until they are cooked through but still crisp.
3. Trim the ends of the snow peas. Blanch them for about a minute in boiling water, until they are just cooked but still crisp.
4. Reduce the vinegar by half over moderate heat. Remove from the heat and add the remaining ingredients, seasoning to taste with salt.

Cooking/Finishing:

1. Season the fish fillets with salt and pepper and brush them with olive oil. Grill them on both sides until they are done.
2. Heat the mixture of vinegar, oil, and seasonings (from step 4 of mise en place) until simmering. Add the carrots, fennel, and peas and simmer just until the vegetables are heated.

Presentation:

1. For each portion, place a portion of fish skin side up in the center of the plate.
2. Spoon the vegetable mixture all around the fish, so that the solids are evenly and randomly distributed.

GRATIN OF SEA BASS WITH MUSTARD AND TARRAGON

		U.S.		Metric	
PORTIONS:		4	16	*4*	*16*
Ingredients					
Black sea bass fillets, 4–5 oz (125–155 g) each		4	16	*4*	*16*
Lemon juice		1 oz	4 oz	*30 ml*	*125 ml*
Salt					
Pepper					
Butter, melted		1 ½ oz	6 oz	*45 g*	*175 g*
Grainy mustard		1 oz	4 oz	*30 g*	*125 g*
Egg yolks, beaten		2	8	*2*	*8*
Lemon juice		1 tsp	4 tsp	*5 ml*	*20 ml*
Tarragon		1 tsp	4 tsp	*1 g*	*4 g*
Crème fraîche		2 oz	8 oz	*60 ml*	*2.5 dl*

Mise en Place:

1. Arrange the fish fillets skin side down on a buttered baking sheet.
2. Mix together the mustard, egg yolks, lemon juice, and tarragon.

Cooking/Finishing:

1. Sprinkle the fish with lemon juice, salt, and pepper. Brush them with melted butter.
2. Cook the fillets until they are half done, either under the broiler or in a 400°F (200°C) oven. Remove them from the heat.
3. While the fish is cooking, whip the cream and fold it into the mustard mixture.
4. When the fish is half cooked, spread the mustard mixture over the fillets so that they are completely coated.
5. Run them under the broiler until the top is nicely browned.

Presentation:

1. Remove the fillets from the baking sheet with a spatula, plate them, and serve them immediately.
2. It is not necessary to serve a sauce with this item, but if desired, you could serve a small spoonful of fresh tomato sauce or red pepper sauce (page 53) on the side.

ROASTED MONKFISH WITH WHITE BEANS

		U.S.		Metric	
PORTIONS:		4	16	4	16
Ingredients					
Monkfish tails, boned, skinned, and trimmed, about 6–8 oz (175–250 g) each		4	16	4	16
Garlic cloves		2–4	8–16	2–4	8–16
Flour					
Salt					
Pepper					
Butter		1 oz	4 oz	30 g	125 g
Olive oil		1 oz	4 oz	30 ml	125 ml
White wine		4 oz	1 pt	125 ml	5 dl
Cooked white kidney beans or navy beans		12 oz	3 lb	350 g	1.4 kg
Additional butter or olive oil, as needed					
Chopped parsley					

Mise en Place:

Cut the garlic cloves into slivers. Make slits in the monkfish with the point of a paring knife and insert the garlic pieces in them.

Cooking:

1. Dust the fish lightly with flour. Season with salt and pepper.
2. Heat the butter and oil in a sauté pan. Brown the monkfish tails well on all sides.
3. Add the wine and transfer the sauté pan to an oven heated to 400°F (200°C). Roast for 4 to 5 minutes, until the fish is cooked. (*Note:* The sauté pan must not be too large, or too much liquid will evaporate.)
4. Remove the fish from the pan and keep warm. Add the beans to the pan and set over moderate heat. Cook until the beans are hot and the liquid, if any, is reduced so that the beans are quite moist but without excess liquid. Adjust the seasonings. Add a little butter or olive oil or both to the beans if desired.

Presentation:

Spoon the beans onto dinner plates. Leave the fish pieces whole or slice into medaillons, as desired, and arrange on top of the beans. Sprinkle with a little chopped parsley.

Variation

Omit the beans. Use the cooking liquid to make a beurre blanc; serve with the fish.

BAKED HADDOCK WITH WALNUTS

		U.S.		*Metric*	
PORTIONS:		**4**	**16**	***4***	***16***
Ingredients					
Walnuts		4 oz	1 lb	*100 g*	*400 g*
Garlic		1 clove	4 cloves	*1 clove*	*4 cloves*
Basil		16 leaves fresh or 2 tsp dried	½ cup (packed) fresh or 8 tsp dried	*16 leaves fresh or 2 g dried*	*50 g fresh or 10 g dried*
Butter		½ oz	2 oz	*12 g*	*50 g*
Haddock fillets, 5–6 oz (150 g) each		4	16	*4*	*16*
Salt					
Pepper					
Butter, melted					

Mise en Place:

1. Chop the nuts coarsely.
2. Mince the garlic.
3. If using fresh basil, remove any coarse stems and chop the leaves.
4. Heat the butter in a sauté pan. Add the nuts and garlic and sauté until lightly colored. Add the basil and sauté another 30 seconds. Remove from the heat and reserve.

Cooking/Finishing:

1. Season the fish with the salt and pepper.
2. Place the fillets in a buttered baking pan, skinned side down, and brush them with melted butter. Top them with the nut mixture.
3. Bake at 450°F (230°C) until the fish is cooked, about 10 minutes per inch of thickness.
4. Plate and serve immediately.

SALMON SCALOPPINE WITH GINGER AND LIME BEURRE BLANC

		U.S.		Metric	
PORTIONS:		4	16	4	16
Ingredients					
Salmon fillet		12–16 oz	3–4 lb	375–500 g	1.5–2 kg
Fresh ginger root		¾ oz	3 oz	22 g	90 g
Lime juice		½ tsp	2 tsp	2.5 ml	10 ml
Lime zest		of ½ lime	of 2 limes	of ½ lime	of 2 limes
Beurre blanc:					
Lime juice		½ oz	2 oz	15 ml	60 ml
White wine		1 ½ oz	6 oz	45 ml	2 dl
Shallot, chopped		½ oz	2 oz	15 g	60 g
Lime zest, grated		½ tsp	2 tsp	1 g	4 g
Fresh ginger root, chopped		¼ tsp	1 tsp	0.5 g	2 g
Butter, cold		4 oz	1 lb	125 g	500 g

Mise en Place:

1. Cut the salmon fillets into thin scaloppine (see Figure 6.6). Each portion may consist of one large slice or 2 or 3 overlapping slices.
2. Peel the ginger root. Grate it and squeeze out the juice. Mix the juice with the lime juice and water.
3. Cut the lime zest into fine julienne.
4. As close as possible to serving time, make the beurre blanc out of the indicated ingredients, using the lime juice, wine, shallot, lime zest, and ginger for the reduction. Refer to Chapter 3 for complete instructions on making beurre blanc. Strain the sauce and keep it warm.

Cooking/Finishing:

1. Arrange the scaloppine on a well-buttered baking sheet. Brush the tops with the ginger juice/lime juice mixture. Sprinkle with the julienne of lime zest.
2. Flash bake the fish in an oven at 500°F (260°C) for 2 or 3 minutes, until the fish is just cooked.

Presentation:

Carefully plate each portion in the center of a plate and spoon a little of the sauce over it.

Variations

The scaloppine may be sautéed instead of flash baked. In this case, marinate them in the ginger juice mixture for about 30 minutes, then dry them before sautéing. Use a well-seasoned pan or a no-stick pan and cook them very briefly over high heat. If cooked too long, they are likely to break up. For this reason, it is also advisable to cut them a little thicker than you might for flash baking.

Salmon with Sorrel Sauce

Omit the seasonings for the fish and simply flash bake the fish as in the basic recipe, first brushing the tops of the slices with water to prevent drying. (You can also sauté the fish, as in the preceding variation.) Ladle sorrel sauce (page 62 or 65) onto plates. Place the fish slices on top.

Other appropriate sauces may be used instead of sorrel sauce. A flavorful vegetable juice sauce, such as fennel or red beet (page 56), goes well with salmon.

SALMON CARPACCIO

	U.S.		Metric	
PORTIONS:	4	16	*4*	*16*
Ingredients				
Salmon fillet	12–16 oz	3–4 lb	*300–400 g*	*1.2–1.6 kg*
Well-seasoned herb vinaigrette made with lemon or lime juice, or herbed mustard vinaigrette	3–4 oz	12–16 oz	*80–100 ml*	*3–4 dl*
Garnish (see Presentation)				

Preparation:

1. Run your fingers across the surface of the fillet to make sure there are no bones in it. If there are, pull them out carefully with needlenose pliers.

2. Holding the knife almost horizontally, slice the salmon into very thin, broad slices. The slices should be so thin as to be almost transparent. If any are too thick, put them between two sheets of plastic film; gently and carefully flatten them to an even thickness.

Presentation:

1. Arrange the slices on cold plates so that they are in a single layer with the edges just overlapping, covering the whole plate.

2. Immediately before serving, spoon the vinaigrette on top.

3. Garnish each portion by arranging three or four small, appropriate items around the edge of the plate. Some suggestions are as follows:

a slice or two of avocado
a small mound of chopped tomatoes mixed
  with a little hazelnut oil
a dab of caviar
small Belgian endive leaves or mâche leaves

fresh basil leaves
lemon or lime wedges
a small mound of capers
radish slices
chives

MONKFISH WITH SUNDRIED TOMATOES AND GARLIC

		U.S.		Metric	
PORTIONS:		**4**	**16**	*4*	*16*
Ingredients					
Olive oil		1 oz	4 oz	*30 ml*	*125 ml*
Garlic cloves		2	8	*2*	*8*
Monkfish fillets		1 lb	4 lb	*450 g*	*1.8 kg*
Salt					
White pepper					
Sundried tomatoes packed in oil, drained		4 oz	1 lb	*115 g*	*450 g*
Lemon juice		4 tsp	2 ½ oz	*20 ml*	*80 ml*
Parsley, chopped		1 tbsp	4 tbsp	*4 g*	*15 g*
Butter		2 oz	8 oz	*60 g*	*225 g*

Mise en Place:

1. Slice the garlic.

2. Slice the fish on the diagonal into small medaillons.

3. Cut the tomato into julienne.

4. Cut the raw butter into pieces.

Cooking/Finishing:

1. Heat the olive oil in a sauté pan over high heat. Add the garlic and sauté about 30 seconds, but do not let it brown.

2. Season the fish with salt and white pepper. Add the fish to the pan and sauté on one side for about 1 minute.

3. Turn the pieces of fish over and add the tomato strips. Sauté about two minutes.

4. Add the lemon juice and parsley. Cook another few minutes, turning the fish over.

5. Add the raw butter and swirl it in the pan just until it melts.

Presentation:

1. Arrange the fish pieces neatly on plates.

2. Spoon the tomatoes and pan juices over the top.

SOFT-SHELL CRABS WITH CAVIAR AND BEURRE BLANC

		U.S.		Metric	
PORTIONS:		*4*	*16*	*4*	*16*
Ingredients					
Soft-shell crabs		8	32	*8*	*32*
Salt					
White pepper					
Flour (optional), as needed					
Butter, for sautéing					
Black caviar		2 tsp	8 tsp	*10 g*	*40 g*
Red caviar		2 tsp	8 tsp	*10 g*	*40 g*
Beurre blanc		6 oz	1 ½ pt	*2 dl*	*7.5 dl*

Mise en Place:

Clean the crabs as illustrated in Figure 6.8.

Cooking/Finishing:

1. Season the crabs with salt and pepper. If desired, dredge them lightly in flour for sautéing.

2. Sauté them in butter on both sides until done.

Presentation:

1. For each portion, ladle 1 ½ oz (45 ml) beurre blanc onto a plate.

2. Place two crabs on the plate, upside-down and facing outward.

3. Place a dab of red caviar on top of one crab and black caviar on the other.

Variations

If you have very small crabs, serve three per portion. Top the third one with a dab of golden caviar.

Substitute carrot juice sauce (page 56) for the beurre blanc. Omit the caviar and plate the crabs rightside up. Drizzle with a little cinnamon oil (page 81).

STUFFED SQUID BRAISED WITH TOMATOES

		U.S.		Metric	
PORTIONS:		4	16	4	16
Ingredients					
Squid, small to medium		8	32	8	32
Olive oil		1 oz	4 oz	30 ml	125 ml
Onion, chopped fine		3 oz	12 oz	90 g	350 g
Garlic cloves, chopped		1	4	1	4
Instant couscous		1 oz	4 oz	30 g	125 g
Dry white wine		1 oz	4 oz	30 ml	125 ml
Water		1 oz	4 oz	30 ml	125 ml
Eggs, beaten		1	4	1	4
Chopped parsley		2 tbsp	½ cup	7 g	30 g
Olive oil		½ oz	2 oz	15 g	60 g
Shallots		½ oz	2 oz	15 g	60 g
Tomatoes, canned or fresh		8 oz	2 lb	250 g	1 kg
Dry white wine		4 oz	1 pt	125 ml	5 dl
Salt					

Mise en Place:

1. Clean the squid, as shown in Figure 6.9.
2. Chop the tentacles very fine.
3. Heat the first quantity of oil in a sauté pan. Add the chopped tentacles, onions, and garlic. Sauté over moderate heat until the juices that exude from the tentacles and onions have evaporated.
4. Add the wine and water and bring to a simmer. Stir in the instant couscous, cover, remove from the heat, and let stand until the couscous has absorbed the liquid and is soft. Remove from the pan and cool completely.
5. Mix in the beaten egg and chopped parsley. Adjust the seasonings if necessary.
6. Fill the squid sacs about three-fourths full of the couscous mixture. Fasten the openings shut with picks.
7. Chop the shallots very fine. Chop the tomatoes coarsely.

Cooking/Finishing:

1. Heat the second quantity of oil in a pan just large enough to hold the squid in a single layer. Add the shallots and sauté for a few seconds.
2. Add the squid, tomatoes, and wine. Bring to a boil, cover, and place in a 325°F (160°C) oven. Bake about 45 minutes, until the squid are tender firm to the touch.
3. Remove the squid from the cooking liquid and keep them warm.
4. Reduce the cooking liquid and tomato mixture if necessary to adjust the consistency. Purée the mixture in a blender or pass it through a food mill.
5. Season the tomato mixture to taste with salt.

Presentation:

1. Spoon a little of the tomato sauce onto the centers of warm plates.

2. Remove the picks from the squid. Cut the squid crosswise into ½-inch-thick (1 cm) slices. Arrange the slices neatly in a circle on top of the sauce. (If desired, sprinkle with chopped parsley.)

Variations

Dry bread crumbs may be substituted for the instant couscous.

BAKED OYSTERS NORMANDE

		U.S.		Metric	
PORTIONS:		4	16	4	16
Ingredients					
Oysters		24	96	24	96
Normandy sauce (p. 43)		12 oz	3 pt	375 ml	1.5 l
Butter		½ oz	2 oz	15 g	30 g
Fresh bread crumbs		1 cup	1 qt	2.5 dl	1 l
Chopped parsley		2 tbsp	½ cup	7 g	30 g

Mise en Place:

1. Shuck the oysters and reserve the bottom halves of the shells. Drain the liquid (use it to prepare the normandy sauce).

2. Heat the butter in a small sauté pan. Add the crumbs and parsley. Sauté until the crumbs begin to brown lightly.

Cooking/Finishing:

1. Arrange the oyster shells, hollow side up, in a baking pan. Put one oyster in each shell. Spoon 1 tbsp (15 ml) sauce over each oyster. Sprinkle with the bread crumbs.

2. Bake at 450°F (230°C), or run under the broiler, until the oysters are hot and the crumbs are lightly browned. This will take about 8 to 10 minutes in the oven and only 1 to 2 minutes under the broiler. Do not overcook the oysters.

Variations

Many other appropriate sauces may be substituted for the normandy sauce. Also, other toppings, such as grated parmesan or gruyère cheese, may be used instead of or in addition to the crumbs.

OYSTERS WITH CUCUMBERS AND TWO SAUCES

		U.S.		Metric	
PORTIONS:		*4*	*16*	*4*	*16*
Ingredients					
Cucumbers, large		½	2	*½*	*2*
Coarse salt		1 ½ tsp	2 tbsp	*6 g*	*25 g*
Watercress sauce (cream sauce variation, p. 62)		5 oz	1 pt 4 oz	*1.5 dl*	*6 dl*
Beurre blanc, made with lemon juice		4 oz	1 pt	*125 ml*	*5 dl*
Oysters		16	64	*16*	*64*
White wine		2 oz	8 oz	*60 ml*	*2.5 dl*
Watercress for garnish					

Mise en Place:

1. Peel the cucumbers. Cut in half lengthwise and scoop out the seeds. Cut into julienne. Toss with the salt and let stand for 30 minutes. Drain and rinse briefly. Taste and, if they are too salty, rinse again. Drain and pat dry.

2. Purée the watercress sauce in a blender, then strain, in order to get a uniform green color.

3. Prepare the beurre blanc as close as possible to service time.

4. Shuck the oysters. Drain and reserve the liquid.

Cooking:

1. Combine the oyster liquid and wine. Bring to a simmer.

2. Add the oysters. Cook gently, just until the edges of the oysters curl. Remove with a slotted spoon. Reserve the liquid for another use.

Presentation:

1. Place four small mounds of cucumber on a plate, one on each quadrant of the plate.

2. Place a small bouquet of watercress in the center of the plate.

3. Place a drained, warm oyster on top of each mound.

4. Coat each oyster with a small spoonful of beurre blanc.

5. Drizzle the watercress sauce around the plate.

OYSTERS WITH SORREL

		U.S.		Metric	
PORTIONS:		4	16	*4*	*16*
Ingredients					
Sorrel leaves, trimmed		2 oz	8 oz	*60 g*	*250 g*
Butter		¼ oz	1 oz	*7 g*	*30 g*
Oysters		20	80	*20*	*80*
Heavy cream		8 oz	2 pt	*2.5 dl*	*1 l*
Lemon juice		2 tsp	1 ½ oz	*10 ml*	*40 ml*
Whipped cream		2 tbsp	8 tbsp	*30 ml*	*125 ml*
Sorrel leaves, cut into fine shreds		2–4	8–16	*2–4*	*8–16*

Mise en Place:

1. Wash, drain, and shred the sorrel. Sweat in butter until wilted.
2. Shuck the oysters. Drain and reserve the liquid. Discard the flat top shells but reserve the hollow bottom shells.

Cooking and Presentation:

1. Place the oyster shells on sheet pans and warm briefly in the oven to take the chill off them. They should be just slightly warm to the touch.
2. Combine the heavy cream and oyster liquid. Bring to a boil. Add the lemon juice and simmer gently until slightly thickened.
3. Add the oysters to the liquid. Poach gently just until the edges curl.
4. For each serving, arrange five shells on a plate. If seaweed is available, arrange the shells on a bed of seaweed to hold them steady. Place about ½ tsp (3 g) of sorrel purée in each shell.
5. Remove the oysters from the cream sauce with a slotted spoon. Place one oyster in each shell.
6. Strain the sauce. Return it to a pan and reheat it if necessary. Taste and correct the seasonings if necessary.
7. Fold the whipped cream into the sauce. This step is optional, but it gives the sauce an attractive foamy appearance.
8. Immediately top the oysters with the sauce. Sprinkle each oyster with a few shreds of raw sorrel.

Variation

Substitute watercress purée for the sorrel purée.

SCALLOPS WITH CABBAGE EN PAPILLOTE

		U.S.		Metric	
PORTIONS:		4	16	4	16
Ingredients					
Savoy cabbage		12 oz	3 lb	375 g	1.5 kg
Shallots		1 oz	4 oz	30 g	125 g
Rosemary, crumbled		¼ tsp	1 tsp	0.25 g	1 g
Butter		1 oz	4 oz	30 g	125 g
Salt					
White pepper					
Scallops		1 lb	4 lb	500 g	2 kg
White wine (optional)		1 oz	4 oz	30 ml	125 ml
Butter		1 ½ oz	6 oz	45 g	180 g
Salt					

Mise en Place:

1. Cut the cabbage into wedges. Blanch in salted water 5 minutes. Drain, cool under cold running water, and squeeze out excess moisture. Shred the cabbage.

2. Mince the shallots. Sauté the shallots and rosemary in the butter for a minute. Add the cabbage and sauté until it is coated with butter. Season with salt and pepper. Cool and reserve it.

3. If the scallops are large, cut them in half. Otherwise, leave them whole.

4. Cut out a parchment papillote for each portion, as shown in Figure 6.1.

Cooking/Finishing:

1. For each portion, place a portion of cabbage on one side of a papillote that has been lightly buttered. Place a portion of scallops on top of the cabbage.

2. Sprinkle with a little wine and season the scallops with a little salt. Top with a pat or two of butter. Fold and seal the papillote as shown in the illustration.

3. Place on a baking sheet and bake at 450°F (230°C) for 5 to 8 minutes.

Presentation:

The papillote may be opened and the fish plated in the kitchen, but it is preferable to place the closed papillote on a plate, send it to the dining room, and open it in front of the customer, so that the customer can enjoy the released aroma as the package is opened. After opening it, the waiter may remove the food from the papillote and place it on a clean plate so that it is easier to eat.

Variations

Other firm-textured seafood items, such as shrimp or slices of monkfish, may be substituted for the scallops.

Scallops with Leeks en Papillote

Substitute leeks for the cabbage. Do not blanch the leeks, but slice them and sweat them in butter until tender.

SPICY SHRIMP WITH ROSEMARY

		U.S.		Metric	
PORTIONS:		4	16	4	16
Ingredients					
Butter		1 oz	4 oz	25 g	100 g
Peeled, deveined shrimp, preferably small to medium size		1 ½ lb	6 lb	600 g	2.4 kg
Rosemary		1 ½ tsp	2 tbsp	1.5 g	6 g
Worcestershire sauce		1 oz	4 oz	25 ml	1 dl
Lemon juice		½ oz	2 oz	12 ml	50 ml
Hot pepper sauce		1 tsp	4 tsp	5 ml	20 ml
Salt					
White or black pepper					
Butter		2 oz	8 oz	50 g	200 g
Parsley, chopped		2 tbsp	½ cup	7 g	30 g

Procedure:

1. Heat the butter in a sauté pan. Add the shrimp and rosemary. Sauté until the shrimp is about half done.
2. Add the worcestershire sauce, lemon juice, and pepper sauce. Continue to sauté until the shrimp is cooked. Season to taste.
3. Immediately before serving, swirl in the raw butter and add the parsley.

Presentation:

Plate the shrimp and garnish as desired; lemon slices or wedges are appropriate. Plain white rice is a recommended accompaniment for this dish.

SCALLOPS AND SHRIMP À LA NAGE

		U.S.		Metric	
PORTIONS:		4	16	4	16
Ingredients					
Carrots, trimmed and peeled		3 oz	12 oz	75 g	300 g
Leeks, trimmed and cleaned		3 oz	12 oz	75 g	300 g
Celery, trimmed		2 oz	8 oz	50 g	200 g
Butter		½ oz	2 oz	12 g	50 g
Court bouillon with white wine (p. 225), strained		1 pt	2 qt	4 dl	16 dl
Shrimp, peeled and deveined		8 oz	2 lb	200 g	800 g
Scallops		8 oz	2 lb	200 g	800 g
Salt					

Mise en Place:

Cut the vegetables into julienne, small dice, or any other neat, small shapes.

Cooking/Finishing:

1. Sweat the vegetables gently in the butter for a few minutes. Add the court bouillon. Simmer until the vegetables are cooked but still slightly crisp.
2. Bring the court bouillon to a simmer. Add the shrimp and scallops. Poach them gently until they are just cooked, about 5 minutes.
3. Remove the seafood and vegetables with a slotted spoon and keep them warm.
4. Bring the court bouillon to a boil and reduce by one-third.
5. Season and strain it through cheesecloth or a fine chinois.

Presentation:

1. Divide the shrimp, scallops, and vegetables among broad soup plates or other appropriate dishes for service.
2. Pour the hot court bouillon over them and serve immediately.

Variation

A small amount of crème fraîche or heavy cream may be added to the reduced court bouillon.

LOBSTER À L'AMERICAINE

		U.S.		Metric	
PORTIONS:		**4**	**16**	*4*	*16*
Ingredients					
Live lobster, about 1 ½ lb (700 g) each		2	8	*2*	*8*
Butter, softened		2 oz	8 oz	*60 g*	*250 g*
Oil		2 oz	8 oz	*60 ml*	*2.5 dl*
Shallot, chopped fine		½ oz	2 oz	*15 g*	*60 g*
Garlic, chopped fine		1 tsp	4 tsp	*2 g*	*8 g*
Brandy		4 oz	1 pt	*125 ml*	*5 dl*
White wine		12 oz	3 pt	*3.5 dl*	*1.5 l*
Fish stock		8 oz	1 qt	*2.5 dl*	*1 l*
Tomato concassée (or use half as much tomato purée)		8 oz	2 lb	*250 g*	*1 kg*
Chopped parsley		2 tbsp	½ cup	*7 g*	*30 g*
Tarragon		pinch	½ tsp	*pinch*	*0.5 g*
Cayenne, to taste					

Mise en Place:

1. Cut up the lobster as shown in Figure 6.10.
2. Remove the tomalley (liver) and coral (if any). Mash them in a small bowl with the soft butter.

Cooking/Finishing:

1. Heat the oil in a sauté pan and add the lobster pieces. Sauté over high heat until the shells turn red.
2. Drain off the oil by tilting the pan and holding the lobster in with the pan lid.
3. Add the shallot and garlic to the pan. Sauté for a few seconds.
4. Remove from the heat (to avoid burning yourself if the brandy flares up) and add the brandy. Return to the heat and add the wine, fish stock, tomato, chopped parsley, tarragon, and cayenne. Cover the pan and simmer until the lobster is cooked, about 10 minutes.
5. Remove the lobster from the cooking liquid and place it on large plates or in broad soup plates. The meat may be left in the shell or removed from the shell, as desired.
6. Reduce the cooking liquid over high heat until there is about 3 oz (1 dl) per portion. Remove from the heat and stir in the mixture of butter, tomalley, and coral. Heat the sauce gently for 1 minute; do not let it boil or it will curdle. Adjust the seasonings. Strain the sauce and pour it over the lobster.

FEUILLETÉ OF SEAFOOD CARDINALE

		U.S.		Metric	
PORTIONS:		**4**	**16**	*4*	*16*
Ingredients					
Assorted seafood, such as crabmeat, scallops, shelled shrimp, shelled lobster, flaked or diced white fish or salmon		1 lb	4 lb	*500 g*	*2 kg*
Baked puff pastry rectangles, cases, or patty shells (p. 182)		4	16	*4*	*16*
Cardinal sauce (p. 40)		8 oz	1 qt	*2.5 dl*	*1 l*

Procedure:

1. Cook each type of seafood separately by poaching or steaming. If necessary, cut into bite-size pieces.

2. Combine the seafood with the sauce. Warm the mixture gently until the fish and sauce are hot.

Presentation:

1. Remove the tops from the feuilletés, if any. Place the bases on dinner plates.

2. Spoon the seafood mixture over the bases, letting it spill over the sides. Replace the pastry tops.

Variations

Substitute any appropriate sauce for the cardinal sauce, such as nantua sauce, white wine sauce, normandy sauce, diplomate sauce, mushroom sauce (made with fish stock), or one of the many cream sauce variations. If a very rich sauce is used, such as beurre blanc or a sauce based on heavily reduced cream, you may want to decrease the quantity of sauce somewhat.

Napoleon of Seafood

Instead of filling puff pastry cases, stack the seafood with two or three thin sheets of baked puff pastry. As an alternative, use sheets of baked phyllo dough (see recipe on page 184 for procedure) or potato galettes (page 540).

Ragout of Seafood   *(Color Plate 8)*

Omit the puff pastry and use an appropriate sauce containing some cream. Mix in a colorful assortment of young, tender vegetables, cooked separately, such as peas, pearl onions, mushrooms, green beans, and carrots.

Seafood Crêpes

Make a mixture of sauce and seafood as in the basic recipe. Enclose the seafood mixture in crêpes. Coat with hollandaise sauce or a glaçage and brown under the salamander.

Seafood Cassolette

This dish is appropriate for an appetizer course. Prepare a mixture of sauce and seafood as in the basic recipe. Put it in little ceramic cassolettes just large enough to hold single portions. Top with a spoonful of hollandaise or glaçage and brown under the salamander. Serve on an underliner.

MUSSELS MARSEILLE-STYLE

		U.S.		Metric	
PORTIONS:		4	16	4	16
Ingredients					
Mussels		3 lb	12 lb	1.2 kg	5 kg
Olive oil		3 tbsp	6 oz	45 ml	1.5 dl
Onion		1 oz	4 oz	25 g	100 g
Leek, white part		1 oz	4 oz	25 g	100 g
Garlic		1 clove	4 cloves	1 clove	4 cloves
Fennel seeds		½ tsp	2 tsp	1 g	4 g
Dry white wine		6 oz	1 ½ pt	1.5 ml	6 dl
Tomatoes, fresh or canned		4 oz	1 lb	100 g	400 g
Saffron		¼–½ tsp	1–2 tsp	1–2 ml	4–8 ml
Black pepper		pinch	½ tsp	pinch	1 g
Cayenne		pinch	½ tsp	pinch	1 g
Chopped parsley		2 tbsp	½ cup	7 g	30 g

Mise en Place:

1. Scrub and debeard the mussels.

2. Mince the onion, leek and garlic. Chop the tomatoes coarsely.

3. If desired, the cooking broth may be prepared ahead of time (see Cooking, steps 1 and 2).

Cooking/Finishing:

1. In a pot large enough to hold the mussels, heat the oil and sauté the onion, leek, garlic, and fennel seeds. Do not let them brown.

2. Add the wine, tomatoes, saffron, pepper, cayenne, and parsley. Bring to a rapid boil.

3. Add the mussels, cover and steam the mussels until they open, about 5 minutes. Shake the pot once or twice during cooking to make sure that all the mussels cook evenly.

Presentation:

Serve the whole mussels and broth in large soup plates. Accompany with crisp-crusted French bread for dunking in the broth.

Variations

Mussels Marinière

Omit the olive oil, leek, garlic, fennel, tomato, saffron, and cayenne. Steam the mussels in wine flavored with minced onion (or shallot), a few parsley stems, and pepper. When the mussels are steamed, finish the cooking liquid with a little butter and season with a few drops of lemon juice. Add the chopped parsley.

Mussels in Cream

Steam mussels in white wine as for mussels marinière. Remove the mussels, and reduce the cooking liquid by half over high heat. Finish with crème fraîche or heavy cream (about 1 oz or 25 ml per portion), or with a liaison of cream and egg yolks.

FLOUR PANADE FOR QUENELLES

		U.S.		Metric	
	YIELD:	**1 lb**	**4 lb**	*500 g*	*2 kg*
Ingredients					
Water		10 oz	2½ pt	*3 dl*	*1.2 l*
Butter		2 oz	8 oz	*60 g*	*240 g*
Salt		¼ tsp	1 tsp	*1 g*	*5 g*
Flour, sifted		5 oz	1 lb 4 oz	*150 g*	*600 g*

Procedure:

1. Combine the water, butter, and salt in a saucepan. Bring to a full boil.

2. Add the flour all at once. Stir vigorously over the heat until the mixture forms a stiff ball and pulls away from the sides of the pan.

3. Cool the paste, then chill it. Keep it covered so that it does not form a skin on the surface.

FISH FORCEMEAT FOR QUENELLES

		U.S.		Metric	
YIELD:		**1 ½ lb**	**6 lb**	*750 g*	*3 kg*
Ingredients					
Firm, fresh, white fish fillets, such as sole or pike		8 oz	2 lb	*250 g*	*1 kg*
Flour panade, cold		8 oz	2 lb	*250 g*	*1 kg*
Egg whites (see note)		2	8	*2*	*8*
Salt		1 tsp	4 tsp	*5 g*	*20 g*
White pepper		pinch	½ tsp	*pinch*	*1 g*
Nutmeg		small dash	¼ tsp	*small dash*	*0.5 g*
Butter, soft		8 oz	2 lb	*250 g*	*1 kg*

Note: If desired, substitute 1 whole egg and 1 yolk for each 2 egg whites.

Procedure:

1. Purée and sieve the fish in the same way as for fish mousseline (page 259).

2. Put the panade in a bowl, and beat in the egg whites and seasonings until the mixture is smooth.

3. Beat in the fish purée until the mixture is smooth.

4. Beat in the butter until the mixture is smooth.

5. Keep the mixture cold and covered until needed.

FISH MOUSSELINE FORCEMEAT

		U.S.		Metric	
APPROX. YIELD:		1 lb 12 oz	7 lb	875 g	3.5 kg

Ingredients

	U.S.		Metric	
Firm, fresh, white fish fillets, such as sole or pike	1 lb	4 lb	500 g	2 kg
Egg whites	2	8	2	8
Heavy cream (approximate quantity)	12 oz	3 pt	375 ml	1.5 l
Salt				
White pepper				
Cayenne				

Procedure:

1. Purée the fish in a food processor. *Note:* It is important to keep all ingredients and equipment cold throughout the production process. If the material becomes too warm at any time, set it in the refrigerator and proceed only when it is chilled.

2. Add the egg whites and process until they are well blended in.

3. Force the purée through a fine sieve to remove any bits of sinew, bone, or skin. This step is sometimes omitted, but it much improves the texture.

4. Put the fish purée in a stainless steel bowl, and set the bowl in another bowl of crushed ice, so that the mixture stays cold.

5. Little by little, blend in the cream with a wooden spoon. The amount of cream you can add depends on the firmness and type of fish used. The finished mousseline should be light and fluffy but still hold its shape.

6. Season to taste with salt, pepper, and a dash of cayenne. (A little nutmeg may also be added.)

7. Test the consistency and seasoning of the mixture by poaching a small quenelle in salted water. Adjust the seasoning if necessary. If the cooked quenelle is too firm, add a little more cream. If it is not firm enough, add a little more egg white.

8. Keep the mixture cold and covered until needed.

Variations

If desired, substitute an equal weight of whole egg for the egg whites. One egg white weighs about 1 oz (25–30 g).

Special mousseline forcemeats may be made out of other fish and seafood, such as salmon, shrimp, and scallops.

Green, herbed mousseline can be made by adding a mixture of puréed herbs and spinach to the forcemeat. See the recipe for sauce verte on page 75 for an example of such a mixture.

QUENELLES AU GRATIN

		U.S.		Metric	
	PORTIONS:	4	16	4	16
Ingredients					
Mornay sauce		8 oz	1 qt	2 dl	8 dl
Egg yolks		1	4	1	4
Heavy cream		1 tbsp	2 oz	12 ml	50 ml
Quenelle forcemeat		1 lb 4 oz	5 lb	500 g	1 kg
Duxelles (see note)		6 oz	1 ½ lb	150 g	600 g
Gruyère or Swiss cheese, grated		2 oz	8 oz	50 g	200 g
Melted butter		1 oz	4 oz	25 g	100 g

Note: Duxelles consists of finely chopped mushrooms sautéed in butter with chopped shallots until all moisture has evaporated.

Mise en Place:

1. Prepare the mornay sauce and finish it with a liaison of egg yolks and cream.

2. If using a panade forcemeat, the quenelles can be made ahead. Shape the quenelles as shown in Figure 6.11. Poach in salted water about 5 minutes. Drain and chill.

    If using a mousseline forcemeat, you can cook the quenelles ahead of time, but the quality will not be as good. It is better to cook them as close as possible to serving time.

Cooking/Finishing:

1. If the quenelles were not cooked ahead of time, shape them (see Figure 6.11) and poach them for 5 minutes in salted water. Drain well.

2. Spread a layer of duxelles on the bottom of buttered gratin dishes.

3. Arrange the quenelles on top of the duxelles.

4. Coat the top with mornay sauce. Sprinkle with grated cheese and melted butter.

5. Place the dishes in a hot oven or under a salamander until the top is browned. If the quenelles were cooked ahead of time and are cold, it is better to start the dish in an oven to make sure it heats through. If necessary, it can be finished for a few seconds under the salamander to brown the top.

Variations

Instead of gratinéeing the quenelles with mornay sauce, they can be simply served with any other appropriate sauce.

FROG LEGS WITH GARLIC AND HERBS

		U.S.		Metric	
	PORTIONS:	*4*	*16*	*4*	*16*
Ingredients					
Frog legs		2–2½ lb	8–10 lb	*0.8–1 kg*	*3.6–4 kg*
Milk, as needed					
Salt					
Pepper					
Flour, for dredging					
Oil, for sautéing					
Chopped parsley		2 tbsp	½ cup	*7 g*	*30 g*
Lemon juice		1–2 tsp	4–8 tsp	*5–10 ml*	*20–40 ml*
Butter		2 oz	8 oz	*50 g*	*200 g*
Garlic, minced		2 tsp	3 tbsp	*4 g*	*15 g*

Mise en Place:

1. Either prepare the frog legs as shown in Figure 6.12 or separate the two halves of each pair by cutting them apart at the hip.
2. Soak the legs in milk for a half hour.

Cooking/Finishing:

1. Remove the frog legs from the milk. Season them with salt and pepper. Dredge them in flour.
2. Sauté them in hot oil until they are browned and cooked through.
3. Place them on plates or on a serving platter. Sprinkle them with chopped parsley and lemon juice.
4. Brown the garlic in the butter. Pour the mixture over the frog legs and serve immediately.

Variation

Frog Legs Provençale					
Tomato concassée		4 oz	1 lb	*100 g*	*400 g*

Add the tomato to the garlic mixture after it is browned and cook another 1 or 2 minutes before pouring the mixture over the frog legs. Also, substitute olive oil for the cooking oil and the butter.

SEAFOOD SAUSAGE
(Color Plate 9)

		U.S.		Metric	
PORTIONS:		**4**	**16**	*4*	*16*
Ingredients					
Fish mousseline (see note)		12 oz	3 lb	*375 g*	*1.5 kg*
Shrimp or lobster meat, small dice		3 oz	12 oz	*90 g*	*375 g*
Salmon fillets, small dice		3 oz	12 oz	*90 g*	*375 g*
Chopped parsley		2 tsp	3 tbsp	*2 g*	*10 g*
Hog casings, as needed					

Note: If the sausages are to be served hot and skinned, the mousseline must be firmer than usual; use less cream and/or more egg in the mixture. If they are to be served cold, or if the casings are to be left on, a more delicate mixture will work.

Procedure:

1. Mix together the mousseline, diced seafood, and parsley.
2. Stuff the mixture into the sausage casings and tie the sausage off into portion-size links.
3. Poach in salted water.

Presentation:

The sausages can be served hot or cold. If you serve them hot, remove the casings only if they are firm enough to be peeled without breaking up. Serve them with an appropriate sauce, such as sauce americaine, nantua sauce, saffron sauce, port wine cream sauce, herb sauce, venitienne sauce, or a beurre blanc. Cold, they may be sliced and served as part of a cold appetizer or as part of an elegant salad.

Variations

For larger sausages, use larger casings, or roll the mousseline mixture up in a buttered sheet of foil. Thicker sausages can be sliced into medaillons and served hot or cold.

Solid ingredients can, of course, be varied or even omitted, and the sausages can be made from mousseline forcemeats based on other fish or seafood.

Hot Fish Mousselines

Instead of filling sausage casings, use the mixture to fill buttered timbale molds. For varied presentation, you can fill them with layers of two or three different mousseline mixtures. Solid ingredients, if used, can be mixed with the mousseline forcemeats, or they can be arranged in the molds between layers of forcemeat. Cover the molds and bake them in a hot water bath in a moderate oven until the forcemeat is firm, about 15 minutes. Unmold onto plates and serve with an appropriate sauce, as for seafood sausages.

Fish Terrines

Fish terrines, made with mousselines, are discussed in Chapter 11.

Poultry and Feathered Game

*L*ike seafood, poultry items are enjoying increased popularity on menus across the country. This may be partly because chicken and turkey are seen as being leaner and therefore more healthful than red meats. But there must be other reasons as well. After all, one of the items showing up more often on menus is duck, which is especially high in fat.

Another reason for the interest in poultry dishes is the creativity of today's chefs. Not only are modern cooks experimenting with new recipes for chicken, turkey, and duckling to stimulate our interest and attract our business, they are also turning back to the methods of classical cuisine to find techniques that they can borrow and adapt to today's tastes. Thus, on the same menu we might find a modern dish such as mesquite-grilled chicken with cilantro and jalapeño peppers, listed next to a confit of duck and a salmis of squab, both borrowed from traditional French cooking.

A second reason is the increased availability of such items as farm-raised quail, partridge, pheasant, and other game birds. Clearly, today's chefs have a lot to work with, both in raw materials and in techniques.

In this chapter we will explore some of the complexities of the basic cooking techniques and look at some procedures that you may not have encountered before. We will then discuss some specialized techniques for handling specific poultry products, with particular attention to the ways that chicken parts can be used, and will provide guidelines for handling duck and game birds.

PRIMARY COOKING METHODS

Poultry items are popular and versatile in all styles of cooking, from the simplest to the most complex. You have undoubtedly had varied experience cooking many types of poultry dishes, and you should be familiar with all the basic cooking methods as they are applied to poultry, especially to chicken.

In the first part of this chapter, we will explore a number of variations on the basic cooking techniques. These variations will enable you to expand your repertory to include a broader range of dishes, as well as to exercise more control over the quality, flavor, and appearance of finished dishes.

The basic cooking methods are essentially the same for poultry as for other classes of foods. These include the dry-heat methods (roasting, grilling, and broiling), the dry-heat methods using fat (sautéing and frying), and the moist-heat methods (simmering, poaching, steaming, and braising).

The theory and practice of cooking is, of course, based on these distinct cooking methods. The foundation of your professional training consists of learning how to perform these methods and how to apply them to various food items.

As you come to understand more of the complexities of cooking, however, you will realize that not everything fits neatly into these categories. There are many gray areas where one method or technique blends into another or where a particular preparation calls for a combination of several techniques borrowed from two or more of the basic cooking methods. In such cases, it becomes impossible to say whether a particular dish is roasted, sautéed, or braised. We will touch on this subject again later.

Roasting

Roasting has always been one of the most important ways of cooking poultry. Everything from large turkeys to tiny quail are cooked by this method in food-service operations. As you would expect, however, the exact procedure for roasting a quail differs in several respects from the procedure for roasting a turkey. In fact, there are many variables to determine before roasting any given kind of bird—what temperature to use, whether or not to use a rack, how to arrange the bird in the pan, when and how often to turn the bird, how often to baste it, and so on. Chefs often disagree about these matters.

Our purpose is not to settle those disagreements; that would be impossible anyway. After all, two chefs who disagree may both produce excellent results. Instead, the aim of this chapter—as it is of the rest of the book—is to show you various methods that can be used effectively. Then, with experience, you will be able to make up your own minds about what works best for you.

Low-temperature Roasting. For large items such as turkeys and capons, roasting at a continuous low temperature (250° to 350°F, or 120° to 175°C) results in a tender, juicy product with the most uniform doneness and with the least shrinkage or cooking loss.

With turkeys and large chickens, cooking times are long enough so that the skin browns nicely, even though the oven temperature is low. Generally speaking, for the most even cooking and browning, the larger the bird is, the lower the temperature should be (within the limits of your production schedule).

While this method can in theory be used for any size poultry, in practice it is not often used for the smallest birds. This is because small birds cook more quickly, so the skin doesn't have enough time to brown. A browned skin is not necessary for doneness, but it greatly enhances both flavor and eye appeal. Also, because small birds have much more surface area per pound, they are more likely to dry out too much if they have to spend a long time in the oven. Therefore, one of the next two methods is usually preferred for small poultry.

Low-temperature roasting is best suited for volume cooking, as well as for home-style cooking. In à la carte restaurants and clubs, where the emphasis is on portion-size items and on cooking to order, the following methods are more often used.

High-temperature Roasting. Small items can be roasted with good results at temperatures of 400°F (200°C) and above. The cooking time for small birds is so short that they do not dry out, unless of course they are overcooked. In principle, this method is in some ways similar to broiling, because both methods use intense dry heat for a short time. For another similar technique, read the discussion of flash-baking of fish on page 207.

The skin of a small chicken roasted at 450°F (230°C) will be attractively brown and crisp, especially if it has been basted well with butter and with the drippings in the pan. Furthermore, because of the short cooking times at these high temperatures, it is possible to roast birds to order and send them to the dining room at their peak of quality.

Roasting with high heat requires great care. At temperatures above 400°F (200°C), small birds can become overcooked rapidly. Be constantly alert, and remove the item from the oven as soon as it is cooked. Remember, too, to allow for carryover cooking. The item will continue to cook slightly while you let it rest after roasting and while you keep it warm during finishing procedures (such as deglazing the pan and finishing the sauce).

Roasting After Preliminary Browning. For small birds such as quail and squab, roasting even at high heat may not brown the skin as much as you might want. In that case, you can brown the bird in butter or oil on top of the stove before putting it in the oven. First season and truss the item for roasting, then brown it in a sauté pan over moderately high heat, turning it as necessary so that it browns evenly on all sides. You can then either transfer it to a roasting pan or simply roast it right in the sauté pan.

This method is frequently used for small game birds like partridge and quail. Of course, the browning procedure partially cooks the items, so the roasting time is reduced accordingly. For example, quail that have been browned may need only ten minutes or less in the oven.

Larger items, like chickens and ducklings, can also be browned before roasting. The procedure is exactly the same as for small items. It is less often done with these larger birds, but the results can be exceptional. For example, a number of elegant, expensive French restaurants list on their menus what appears to be simple roast chicken. What makes the dish special is that its skin is well browned, crisp, and nicely seasoned, and it is cooked to order and roasted to the exact point of doneness.

Duckling can also be browned before roasting, but you must take care to drain off the large amount of rendered fat as it collects in the pan. (More on roasting duck later.)

Browning poultry on top of the stove before roasting is closely related to the traditional *searing method* of roasting. In this method, the food item is started in a very hot oven (400° to 450°F or 200° to 230°C). After about 15 minutes, the temperature is reduced, and roasting is completed at a lower temperature. The degree of browning is not as great when this method is used, but it is a useful alternative to the browning-in-fat method. (Another reason this searing method has long been used is that it was thought that the searing seals in the meat's juices. Even though this myth has been repeatedly disproven over the years, it still persists.)

In all of these roasting methods, you will usually want to use the pan drippings for preparing a sauce or gravy. If necessary, review the appropriate parts of Chapter 3, where the basic principles of sauce making are discussed, including the incorporation of pan drippings.

Spit Roasting. Roasting on a spit or rotisserie has been a popular cooking technique since primitive people first started roasting meat over a fire. Even though the method is ancient, it is still an important one and, in fact, has some advantages over oven roasting. First, since the food item is constantly turning in front of the heat source, it is cooked more evenly and uniformly. Second, because of this turning motion, melting fats provide a continuous basting as they wash over the surface of the revolving meat.

Third, roasting is supposed to be a dry-heat method, but in an enclosed oven, some steam from the food is always present, inhibiting browning. In an unenclosed rotisserie (as well as in a convection oven), steam is not trapped around the cooking poultry or meat. Thus, it is usually easier to get a well-browned, crisp skin when poultry is cooked on a spit than when it is roasted in a conventional oven.

Procedure for Spit Roasting Poultry

1. If desired, marinate or season the poultry ahead of time.
2. Truss the poultry so that the legs and wings are held firmly against the body.
3. Insert the spit lengthwise through the bird and fasten in place tightly with the holding forks or brackets. If you are putting more than one bird on a single spit, leave an inch or two between them to allow the heat to circulate between them. Then install the spit on the rotisserie unit. Follow the manufacturer's directions.

4. Make sure drip pans are in place to catch fat that drips off the cooking food.

5. Roast the poultry until done. Cooking times and temperatures will vary, depending on your equipment. Manufacturers will usually supply charts of suggested cooking times.

6. Basting is not necessary, but you may want to baste with flavored butter, marinade, barbecue sauce, or other flavoring ingredient. Remember that sauces or marinades containing sugar or tomato will burn easily, so it is best to use these only during the last half hour of the cooking time.

Barbecuing. According to the federal government's legal definition, to barbecue means to cook with dry heat created by the burning of hardwood or by the hot coals of this wood. In other words, barbecuing is a roasting or grilling technique requiring a wood fire. (In this section we are concerned with roasting techniques. Grilling is discussed in the next section.)

Authentic, traditional American barbecue is done in wood-burning ovens or pits, but these are not really practical for the average restaurant that wants to add some barbecued items to the menu. So today, most barbecuing is done in specially designed smoke ovens or cookers. In principle, these units work like regular ovens, except that they also have devices that heat small pieces of hardwood to produce smoke. Technically, the foods cooked in these units cannot be said to be barbecued, since the heat is created by electric or gas burners. But because of the wood smoke, the results can be nearly identical.

Most of these units work automatically once you have set the controls for the cooking time and the cooking and holding temperatures. Foods should be placed on racks or suspended in some way so that the smoke and heat can circulate freely. In other respects, cooking in these ovens is much like roasting in regular ovens. In some units, basting is not really feasible when the equipment is operating with smoke, because opening the door would release the smoke. In certain other units, however, the smoke is forced out a vent when the door is opened, so that basting can be done.

A spicy sauce is often served with barbecued foods, and the foods are sometimes basted with this sauce while cooking.

Broiling and Grilling

Broiled and grilled foods have become increasingly popular, especially with health-conscious diners who view this method of cooking as a way of preparing succulent, well-browned foods without added fat. The availability of hardwoods such as hickory and mesquite to add a smoky tang to grilled foods has also contributed to this popularity.

As we said earlier, grilling and broiling are in some ways similar to high-temperature roasting. All these methods cook foods by subjecting them to intense heat without using added moisture or fat (except for basting or marinating). This is especially true for small items. For example, whether you roast a quail in a very hot oven or split it and broil it, the results are similar. The main difference is that, because the temperature on a grill or under a broiler is much higher than in an oven, there is usually more browning, and the food cooks faster.

Broiling and grilling are thus well suited to establishments that specialize in cooking to order. The methods are quick, and they are most appropriate for individual portions. However, because of the high heat, they demand more attention from the cook.

Broiling chicken and other poultry usually requires lower heat than broiling red meat. When you are broiling a steak to the rare stage, you usually need high heat to get a well-browned surface on the meat before it gets too well done. On the other hand, when you are broiling chicken, you must be careful to keep the heat low enough so that you do not char the skin too much before the meat is cooked through. Poultry skin browns quickly.

Large or thick poultry items are not well suited to broiling and grilling, because it would take so long for the heat to penetrate to the center and cook them through. For example, turkey thighs could be broiled if you kept the heat low enough, but in practice this is rarely done. On the other hand, if you boned them out and flattened them lightly with a cutlet mallet, you would make them more suitable for broiling and grilling.

Grilled meat and poultry items are fairly simple, straightforward dishes, without the variety of ingredients and components that you find in, for example, stews. However, there are a number of ways you can give variety to your grill menu:

- *Marinate the poultry or rub it with seasonings before cooking.* Keep in mind that marinade ingredients such as sugar and tomato burn easily, so use these with care. Also, herbs on the surface of the poultry burn easily. Charred rosemary can give a pleasant aroma to the food, but herbs such as parsley, if used in large quantity and allowed to burn, may end up tasting like burnt leaves.

- *Use different hardwoods in your grill to add smoky flavors.* Suitable woods include mesquite, hickory, oak, maple, and fruitwoods such as apple and cherry.

- *Baste with seasoned butter, marinade, or other flavorings during broiling.* Again, be careful with ingredients that burn easily. Use them only toward the end of cooking.

- *Serve with an appropriate sauce or seasoned butter.* Flavored butters can be placed on top of the grilled poultry, but sauces should be underneath or on the side so that they don't detract from the crisp, browned skin.

- *Select vegetable garnishes for variety and interest.* Well-chosen and carefully plated garnishes should be thought of as part of the whole presentation, not just as something served on the side.

Sautéing and Frying

The French verb *sauter* means "to jump" or "to make jump." This term refers to the way small pieces of food are tossed in hot fat in the pan when they are being cooked by this method.

This definition explains the instruction "toss in butter" that you will often see in translations of French cookbooks. This direction means to sauté, not simply to mix with melted butter.

The classic explanation of sautéing, as given by Escoffier, can be summarized as follows:

- A sauté is made with small cuts of poultry or meat. They are cooked dry, that is, with a fat such as butter or oil, but with no added moisture. The cooking is completed in the sauté pan or in the oven, uncovered.

- When fully cooked, the items are removed from the pan so that the pan can be deglazed. If the items are put back into the sauce or mixed with moist garnish, they are left there only long enough to reheat. They should not cook in the liquid.

Note that Escoffier's explanation covers both sautéing and the procedure we call panfrying. There is, of course, no exact dividing line between the two, and Escoffier doesn't really make the distinction.

The basic procedures for sautéing and panfrying foods, as well as the various guidelines to follow in order to ensure the quality of the finished product, are probably familiar to you. Rather than repeat these here, we will look at some of the variations that are possible with sautéed poultry items.

Classical Sautés. In the classical kitchen, meat and poultry are sautéed according to the procedure described earlier. Breaking the procedure down into its basic steps, the method is as follows:

1. Heat a small amount of fat in a sauté pan over high heat. Add the food items and sear quickly on all sides. Depending on the individual recipe, the food may be browned heavily or only lightly.

2. Small pieces of poultry, such as pounded, boneless chicken breast or slices of chicken breast, can be sautéed to doneness very quickly, but larger pieces must continue to cook more slowly so that they cook through without browning too much on the outside. There are two basic ways to do this:
   a. Lower the heat and continue to sauté until done.
   b. Transfer the sauté pan, uncovered, to the oven to finish the cooking, and baste the item from time to time.

3. When the poultry is done, remove it from the pan. Discard excess fat from the pan.

4. Deglaze the pan with wine, stock, or other liquid as indicated in the recipe. Use this deglazing liquid to complete the sauce.

5. Either plate the poultry item immediately and serve the sauce with it, or return the poultry item to the pan *briefly* to reheat in the sauce. Do not let it actually cook in the sauce.

In step 5, note that if the poultry is actually cooked in the sauce rather than merely warmed, it becomes a braised item. This creates a certain amount of confusion in terminology, because such braised dishes are also called sautés. Escoffier, however, says about these dishes, "Preparations of a mixed nature, which partly resemble *sautés* and partly *braisings,* are also called *sautés.* Stews, however, is their most suitable name."

To partly avoid this confusion, some chefs refer to the true sautéing procedure as *sauter à la minute,* or quick sautéing, in order to distinguish these dishes from the braised dishes that are also called sautés. This latter kind of preparation is discussed in the section on braising.

Another difference between sautés and braised stews is that sautés are often served with much less sauce than stews. This is not a strict rule, but it is often the case.

Various Types of Sautéed Poultry Dishes. As we pointed out at the beginning of this chapter, there are not always such clear boundaries between cooking methods, and sometimes it is difficult to say where one method stops and another begins. For example, when you are heating a sautéed item with its sauce in the procedure that we just discussed, at exactly what point does it stop being a sautéed item and become a braised item? It's hard to say for sure, but most chefs have, with experience, developed an instinctive feel for these procedures, and they understand that the character of the dish changes if it is heated too long with the sauce.

Another example of this mixing of cooking methods can be seen in step 2 of the sautéing procedure. Note that the second method of cooking until done—that is, finishing the item in the oven—actually changes the procedure from sautéing to roasting. Since it is still a dry-heat cooking method, however, the basic character of the dish is not changed, and we still refer to the dish as a sauté.

Similarly, in our discussion of roasting, we said that poultry is sometimes browned by sautéing before being put in the oven. In other words, if you finish a sauté by putting it in the oven, the actual procedure is almost exactly one of the roasting procedures that we discussed.

The point of this long discussion is not to confuse you but to emphasize that the reality of cooking is not necessarily as straightforward as the primary cooking methods themselves are. As suggested at the beginning of this chapter, the basic cooking methods are not used in such rigid and definite ways as might be suggested by a beginning cooking course. Often a mixture of techniques is used, and for any given set of methods, there are many variables.

We can think of sautéing, then, as a tool that we can use to prepare various kinds of poultry dishes—whether or not we call those dishes "sautés." The following are examples of cooking procedures in which sautéing plays a part:

1. Straight sautéing until done.
2. Sautéing until partially done, then finishing in the oven, uncovered.
3. Sautéing and then finishing with a sauce. The item is sautéed until done and removed from the pan. The pan is deglazed and a sauce is made. The item may then be rewarmed in the sauce.
4. Braising. The item is only partially cooked by sautéing and then finished by simmering with liquid ingredients or with a completed sauce.
5. Sautéing until browned or until partially done and then finishing covered, either on top of the stove or in the oven. Although no liquid is added, this can also be considered braising, because steam is trapped in the pan, making this a moist-heat method. If desired, a sauce may be made from the pan juices.

Poaching, Simmering, and Steaming

Poaching, simmering, and braising (discussed in the next section) are similar in that they all involve cooking in contact with a liquid, such as water or stock. A fourth method, steaming, is related to these three methods because it also involves cooking with moisture. In this case, the moisture takes the form of steam rather than a liquid.

The results of cooking poultry and meats with moist heat are different from the results of the dry-heat methods that we have been discussing. With dry-heat methods, we are usually concerned with producing a properly browned, crisped surface and with cooking just to the right point of doneness so that the meat is as juicy as possible. This may mean stopping the cooking while the interior is still pink or even rare. We are usually cooking tender meats that do not require long, slow cooking.

With moist-heat cooking methods, the objects are somewhat different. Except in the case of braising, we are not concerned with browning and crisping. Even in braising, the browning is not for the purpose of crisping the poultry skin or surface, because the moisture softens it anyway. Furthermore, moist-heat methods may be used to tenderize tough products, such as stewing hen, by long, slow simmering. Even with tender poultry, the product is usually cooked to the well-done stage, and the texture is different from that of roasted, sautéed, or grilled poultry.

With moist-heat methods, developing the flavor of the cooking liquid is often an important part of the cooking process. So we are concerned not just with the flavor and doneness of the poultry but also with the flavor, texture, and character of the cooking medium. This cooking liquid may be served with the poultry without any further changes, or it may be made into a sauce after the poultry is cooked.

The importance of careful attention to the cooking liquids is emphasized by the fact that Escoffier classified these cooking methods in the same category as sauce making. Your sauce-making skills are very important, particularly for braised dishes.

We will review briefly the basic moist-heat cooking methods as they are applied to poultry, with special attention to some special variations. Then, in the next section, we give somewhat more attention to various braising methods.

Poaching. To *poach* means to cook in a minimum amount of liquid at a temperature that is well below boiling. It is used for small, tender poultry items that do not require long simmering. The poultry items that are most commonly poached are boneless chicken breasts, often called *suprêmes,* and small dumplings called *quenelles.* (See page 220 for a discussion of fish quenelles. Poultry quenelles are made the same way, and a recipe for the forcemeat is included in this chapter.)

For practical purposes, the procedure for poaching poultry is basically the same as that for poaching fish. While poaching is one of the most important methods of fish cookery, however, it is used much less often for cooking poultry.

Please review the guidelines for poaching fish listed in Chapter 6. Most of these apply to poultry as well. Of course, there are some differences. Poultry items are usually not as fragile and delicate as fish fillets, so they don't demand the same kind of care in handling. Also, cooking liquids differ. For poultry, the cooking liquid is usually a flavorful chicken stock, which then may be used to make a sauce for the poultry.

Note that there is another cooking technique that is sometimes called "poaching in butter." This method uses no added liquid as in true poaching, but is actually related to another method called "poêlé," discussed on pages 276–278.

Simmering. Poaching and simmering are very nearly the same thing. The difference is mostly one of degree. In simmering, the cooking time is usually longer, more liquid is used, and the temperature may be a little higher, although still below boiling. While poaching is usually done in shallow, flat pans with the poultry in a single layer, simmering may be done in large pots or kettles, with enough liquid to cover the items.

Simmering may be done for one or more of several purposes:

- To tenderize tough poultry, such as stewing hen.
- To cook large pieces, whole poultry, or large quantities of poultry.
- To enhance the flavor of poultry by cooking it in a flavorful liquid, such as stock or water well seasoned with herbs and aromatic vegetables.
- To cook poultry to be served cold, such as in salads.
- To prepare certain types of stews.

Note that the term *stew* is also used for certain braised dishes. The difference is that in a braised stew, such as a *fricassée,* the poultry is lightly seared or browned in fat before being simmered in a liquid, while in a simmered stew, such as a *blanquette,* it is not.

Simmering is an excellent method for cooking poultry to be used in cold dishes. While it is true that cold dishes such as salads are a convenient way to use leftovers, the meat from leftover roasts and other items is often somewhat dry. By simmering poultry just to the point of doneness in a flavorful liquid and then cooling the product in the cooking liquid, you can have juicy, flavorful poultry that makes excellent salads and cold dishes.

As pointed out in the last chapter, cooking in liquid does not guarantee that meat will not become dry. Even simmered poultry can be dry if it is overcooked. As always, careful attention to doneness is essential.

Steaming. Steaming is a moist-heat cooking method in which the product does not come in contact with a cooking liquid but is instead cooked by contact with steam.

Steaming is used to cook poultry for the same purposes as poaching and simmering, except that steamed poultry cannot be flavored or seasoned by a flavorful cooking liquid. Some cooks champion steaming as a way of preserving the natural flavor of the food. On the other hand, for those who feel that the flavor of a plain, steamed chicken breast is pretty boring, the chicken can of course be seasoned or marinated before cooking, and it can be served with a flavorful sauce.

The two most important uses of steaming are:

- In à la carte operations, as a substitute for poaching, to cook such items as suprêmes of chicken and poultry quenelles.
- In high-volume cooking, as a substitute for simmering, to cook bulk quantities of poultry.

Procedures and guidelines for steaming poultry are essentially the same as for steaming fish. Please refer to pages 198–200 for this information.

Braising

Braising is one of the most important methods for cooking poultry. It has some of the advantages of both dry-heat and moist-heat cooking methods because it is a combination of both. From dry-heat methods, braising borrows the flavor and appearance of browned or seared meat. From moist-heat methods, it incorporates a wide variety of tasty cooking liquids, sauces, and other moist ingredients, such as vegetable garnishes cooked along with the poultry.

The extensive variety of braised poultry dishes is due not only to the many different kinds of ingredients that can be used, but also to variations on the basic procedures.

In modern cooking, braising is normally defined as a mixture of dry-heat and moist-heat cooking whereby the food is first seared or browned by a dry-heat method such as sautéing, then cooked to doneness by a moist-heat method such as simmering.

In classical cooking, the term *braising* was used only for a very specific, rather complicated procedure. In fact, most of the items we now refer to as braised would not fit Escoffier's definition. For a more detailed discussion of the classical procedure, see the discussion of braised meats in the next chapter.

The basic technique of braising—first searing or browning and then simmering—can of course be applied to whole birds of any size, to disjointed poultry, or to cut-up, boneless meat from chicken, turkey, or other kind of poultry. This is different from the terminology of Escoffier's day, when the term *braising* was reserved primarily for whole poultry or large cuts of meat.

The complicated history of braising and the close relationship with sautéing (see page 272) and with simmering and stewing have led to the current situation in which the term braising is applied to several different procedures. In general, we can say that modern cookery includes the following types of braised poultry dishes.

Braised "Sautés" and Miscellaneous Stews. These terms almost always refer to preparations made with cut-up or disjointed poultry.

In an earlier section, we noted the relationship between the classical sauté procedure and the braising procedure. If the poultry is allowed to cook in the sauce rather than just to be warmed (step 5 in the procedure on page 272), the dish becomes a braised item.

If a tender poultry or meat item is partly or mostly cooked during the browning or searing stage of the procedure and is then braised for a relatively short time in the liquid, the dish is still often called a "sauté." On the other hand, if the food is cooked only briefly in fat and then simmered for a longer time in the liquid, it is usually given another name, such as "stew" or "fricassée." Tougher items, as well as tender items, can be "stewed," because the long, moist cooking helps to tenderize them.

Depending on the ingredients you are using and on the exact nature of the dish you want to create, the procedure for braising cut-up chicken varies from recipe to recipe. Most of the commonly used procedures resemble one of the following variations.

Also, for any given recipe, you may be directed to brown the poultry well or only to sear it lightly without too much browning:

Various Procedures for Braising "Sautés" and Stews

1. Sear or brown the poultry. Add any vegetable garnish, if required. Cover the pan and finish cooking in the oven without any added liquids. When the poultry is cooked, deglaze the pan and prepare the sauce as directed in the recipe.
2. Sear or brown the poultry. Add vegetable garnish, if required. Add liquids, such as stock or wine. With the pan covered, cook the poultry in the liquid until done. When the poultry is cooked, remove it from the cooking liquid, and prepare the sauce from the cooking liquid.
3. Sear or brown the poultry and remove it from the pan. Deglaze the pan and make a sauce. Return the poultry to the pan and cook it in the sauce. When the poultry is cooked, degrease the sauce and finish it as required.

A dish consisting of pieces of poultry or meat lightly cooked in fat without browning and then simmered in a sauce is called a *fricassée*. The sauce is usually a white or blond sauce finished with cream.

Braised Whole Poultry. The procedure for braising whole birds is the same as for braising large cuts of white meat, such as a leg or rump of veal. Since this procedure is dealt with in the next chapter, there is no need to repeat it here.

Please note the explanation of *glazing* on page 344. This is an optional procedure for whole braised items, and it is often done when whole poultry is braised.

Poêlés. One special technique for whole poultry and some cuts of meat is called *poêlé* (pronounced "pwah lay"; see the introduction to the glossary at the end of the book regarding the use of French words). We can define this term as cooking in an enclosed casserole with butter for basting, but with no added liquids, usually on a bed of aromatic vegetables. While this technique was classified as a separate cooking method in classical cookery, many modern chefs think of it as a type of braising. Variations of this cooking method are still often used today, even though they may not be called by this name. In particular, small poultry such as young chickens and pheasants are well suited to be cooked this way.

The name of this cooking method is derived from a type of traditional French casserole or pot, called a *poêle* (pronounced "pwall"). Because poêlé means to cook in a pot, European-trained chefs sometimes call this method *pot roasting*. This sometimes leads to confusion, since the term *pot roast* has long been used in America to refer to regular braised items, especially large cuts of beef or other meats. We will avoid using the term *pot roast* in this book. (To add to the confusion, French chefs may also use the term *poêlé* to mean panfry or sauté; we will avoid this usage also, but you may see it elsewhere, especially in foreign cookbooks.)

This cooking method is suitable only for tender poultry and meats. Tougher items should be cooked by the regular braising methods so that they can be tenderized by slow cooking in liquid. In the case of poultry, young chickens, cornish hens, and pheasant are most often poêléed. Other young game birds such as squab and partridge can also be used.

When you read the following procedure, you will see that a poêlé is very much like a roast, except that it is cooked covered. The cover holds in the steam and changes the cooking from a dry-heat method to a moist-heat method.

Procedure for Poêléing Poultry

1. Select a casserole just large enough to hold the poultry item to be cooked. Butter the inside of the casserole lightly, and cover the bottom with finely chopped mirepoix mixed with a little minced ham, a pinch of thyme, and a piece of bay leaf.
2. Season and truss the poultry as for roasting. Lean poultry, such as game birds, may be barded if desired (see page 295).
3. Place the bird in the casserole and brush generously with melted butter. As a general guideline, you will need about ½ ounce (15 g) of butter per portion.
4. Cover the casserole tightly and cook in a low to moderate oven (325° to 350°F or 160° to 175°C). Baste frequently with butter during the cooking.
5. If light browning is desired, uncover the casserole near the end of the cooking period to allow the poultry to color.
6. When it is done, remove the poultry from the casserole. Cover it and keep it warm.
7. Deglaze the casserole with brown veal stock or demiglaze (about 2 to 4 oz, or 60 to 125 ml, per portion, depending on the amount of sauce desired). Or, if desired, deglaze with a little red or white wine or madeira, and then add the stock or demiglaze. Boil gently to reduce by one-half. Strain and degrease the sauce. Serve in a sauceboat to accompany the poultry.

Poêlé Variations. The basic idea of a poêlé is a relatively simple one—that is, baking a food with butter in a casserole covered to retain moisture. Like many basic ideas, it can be given many variations, some simple and some complex. Some of the common variations—both classical and modern—of the basic method are as follows:

• Poêlés that are cooked and served in an earthenware casserole, especially if prepared without vegetables, are traditionally called *en casserole* on the menu. A traditional style of casserole used for this purpose is shown in Figure 7.1. By contrast, ordinary poêlés are served on a platter or plate like a roast.
• Poêlés served "en casserole" with a variety of vegetables and other garnishes are known as *en cocotte* (a cocotte is a type of casserole dish). Commonly used garnishes for en cocotte dishes include carrots, turnips, potatoes, chestnuts, small onions, mushrooms, artichoke hearts, and lardons (bacon cut batonnet). Potatoes

FIGURE 7.1. **A cocotte or traditional casserole for presentation at the table.**

and root vegetables are usually tournéed or cut into other neat, uniform shapes. Vegetables for garnish may be cooked separately, but it is preferable, when possible, to cook them partially in butter and then add them to the casserole toward the end of cooking, so that they finish cooking with the poultry or meat.

- Sauces may be varied as desired. It is not necessary to restrict your ingredients to wine and brown stock or demiglaze, which are indicated in the basic procedure. The casserole may be deglazed and the sauce finished in many of the ways that you would finish a sauce for a roast or sauté. Review Chapter 3 for deglazing and sauce-making techniques.

- The poultry may be browned in fat before being poêléed, just as in regular braising. This technique is popular and widely used, both with traditional *en cocotte* dishes and with recent innovations. See the recipe on page 332 for an example of this kind of preparation.

- By extension, any item that is cooked in a covered container with a little fat and no liquid can be considered to be a type of poêlé. Thus, you can use this method to cook poultry parts as well as whole poultry. Boneless chicken breasts (called *suprêmes*; see page 280) are often prepared this way, and they are sometimes referred to as "poached in butter." The procedure follows.

Procedure for "Poaching" Chicken Suprêmes in Butter

1. Select a pan with a tight cover and just large enough to hold the pieces of chicken in a single layer. Coat the bottom of the pan with melted butter.

2. Season the chicken breasts and roll them in the butter so that they are completely coated. Sprinkle on a few drops of lemon juice, if desired.

3. Cover the pan tightly and place in a very hot oven until done. This should take only a few minutes, depending on the quantity being cooked and the exact temperature of the oven. The chicken breasts should still be springy to the touch. Do not overcook, or they will be dry and hard.

4. Plate the chicken. If desired, deglaze the pan and prepare an appropriate sauce to serve with the chicken.

HANDLING AND PREPARING VARIOUS POULTRY

Primary skills familiar to experienced cooks include knowing how to truss poultry for roasting, how to split chicken and other birds for broiling, how to cut it up into quarters and eighths, both bone-in and semiboneless, and how to cut boneless breasts. This material is covered in basic cookbooks and is not reviewed here, but you may want to review your basic cookbooks to refresh your memory.

This section introduces some additional specialized techniques that are necessary for certain, more elaborate poultry dishes. In addition, it offers some guidelines for cooking and handling a variety of poultry items.

Handling Lean Poultry: Chicken and Turkey

Chicken is, of course, the most widely used poultry item. Not only is it inexpensive, but it is adaptable to an extremely broad range of preparations, from delicately-flavored, elegant dishes, to hearty, country-style preparations.

Turkey was at one time rarely served except as a holiday roast, but as cooks became aware of its versatility, it was adapted to many other types of preparations. While it may not be as versatile as chicken, it can indeed be cut up and used in sautés, stews, grills, and braised dishes to bring variety to the menu.

Types. The following types of chicken are the most useful for à la carte restaurant service:

1. Broilers of about 1½ to 2½ lb (0.7 to 1.1 kg) are, naturally, useful for broiling and grilling. One-half chicken makes a portion. They are also excellent for roasts and for classic sautés, because they are small enough to be cooked to order. In the case of roasts, they are normally listed on the menu as serving two people.

2. Larger chickens of 3 to 4 lb (1.4 to 1.8 kg) can also be used for roasts and sautés, but because of their larger size are not quite as adaptable to à la carte service when cooked by these methods. On the other hand, they are well suited to two uses in particular:
    a. Braised items, stews, and fricassées. One chicken yields four portions.
    b. Separate parts, for example, boneless breasts, legs for stuffing, and so on. Parts from smaller chickens are not usually big enough to be full portions.

3. Rock cornish hens, from ¾ to 1½ lb (350 to 700 g) are small enough to be served one per portion. They can be cooked by virtually any method.

4. Young chickens called *poussin* (pronounced "poo-san") are popular in Europe; they weigh about 1 lb (450 g). In English, they are referred to as "squab chickens" (do not confuse them with squabs, which are young pigeons). Since they are not widely available in the United States and are expensive when they are, you can substitute rock cornish hens in recipes calling for poussin.

In the case of turkeys, the youngest, smallest birds, generally called *fryer-roasters*, are the most adaptable for à la carte service. These are turkeys under 16 weeks old, weighing from 4 to 9 lb (1.8 to 4 kg). They can be cut up for braising, sautéing, or even broiling and grilling.

Larger turkeys are useful because they yield large pieces of boneless breast meat which can be cut into cutlets and scaloppine. The leg meat can be used for stews, for grinding into sausage meat, and for other applications.

Special Cutting, Boning, and Other Preparation Techniques. As you know, there are two basic ways of cutting up chicken. For traditional American-style fried chicken and for home-style dishes, chickens are generally left completely bone-in and simply cut into quarters or eighths. For most restaurant dishes, however, chickens are disjointed by separating the legs from the carcass at the hip joint and by cutting the breast meat off the rib cage. The remaining carcass, consisting of the rib cage, breast bone, backbone, and hip, is used for making stock.

Turkey can be cut up the same ways. While there are fewer traditional recipes using turkey parts, modern chefs are frequently experimenting with ways to prepare and serve this versatile product.

Chicken and turkey lend themselves to a number of special preparations, including the following:

Chicken Parts. Chicken breasts and legs are versatile items that can be made into simple or elaborate dishes.

1. Breasts can be used in the following forms:
   a. Completely boneless and skinless. In this form, they are called *suprêmes.* This form is widely used, especially in more elegant preparations. Boneless, skinless chicken breasts are especially good poached, steamed, poêléed, and sautéed, but they can also be fried, grilled, or braised.
   b. Skinless, but with the wing bone left in. For better appearance, the knobby end of the wing bone may be chopped off with a heavy knife. This is a traditional form, often used in classical preparations. It is called a *cutlet* or, in French, *cotelette.* The wing bone gives shape and identity to the cut.
   c. Either of the two above forms, but with the skin left on. These are used mostly for sautéing and broiling.
2. Chicken breasts in any of the above forms can be used in several ways, depending on the recipe:
   a. Cooked as is, just as they are cut from the carcass.
   b. Flattened with a meat mallet.
   c. Flattened and rolled around a stuffing.
   d. Cut as shown in Figure 7.2 to form a pocket, and stuffed.

FIGURE 7.2. **Cutting and stuffing a pocket in a chicken breast.**
(a) Insert the tip of a boning knife in the edge of the chicken breast at its thickest part.

(b) Push the knife into the breast and move the tip from side to side to enlarge the pocket without enlarging the opening. Be careful not to cut through to the surface, making a hole.

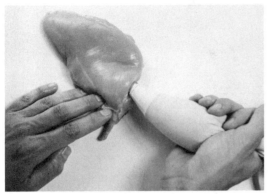

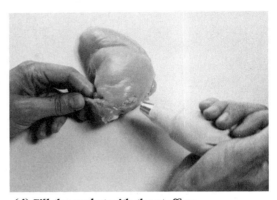

FIGURE 7.2. (Continued)
(c) Fill a pastry bag with mousseline or other filling and insert the tip into the hole made by the knife.

(d) Fill the packet with the stuffing.

3. Chicken legs can be cooked as is, or they can be boned or partially boned and stuffed. (*Note:* According to the terminology used in this book, a *leg* of poultry consists of two joined parts, the *thigh* and the *drumstick*. This terminology is fairly standard, although you will sometimes see a drumstick referred to as a leg.)
   a. Partially boned and stuffed, as shown in Figure 7.3, the item is sometimes called a *ballotine* (from the French word *ballot,* meaning bundle).
   b. The leg can also be completely boned and stuffed (see Figure 7.4). When prepared this way, the cooked item can be sliced into rounds for serving.

Whole Boned Chicken. Whole chickens can be boned out prior to stuffing. This technique is especially useful for small chickens, such as cornish hens, which may be served one per portion. There are two basic methods:

1. Starting by cutting through the skin at the backbone, as shown in Figure 7.5. This method is the easier of the two. After the chicken is stuffed, the bird must be held together, such as by fastening the seam with skewers or by wrapping the bird (in cheesecloth, for example, or in thin slices of pork fatback) and tying it. (A similar method is used for making chicken galantines, explained in Chapter 11.)
2. Leaving the skin intact and removing the bones through the neck opening, as shown in Figure 7.6.

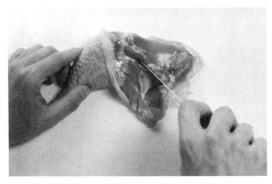

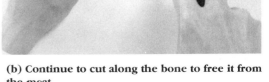

FIGURE 7.3. **Making a ballotine from a partially boned chicken leg.**
(a) Make a shallow cut along the thigh bone.

(b) Continue to cut along the bone to free it from the meat.

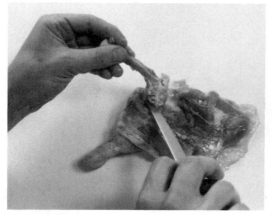

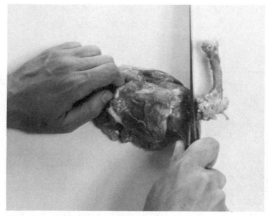

FIGURE 7.3. (Continued)
(c) Separate the entire thigh bone and the knee joint from the meat.

(d) The thigh bone can be simply cut off at the joint, but cutting through the leg bone to remove the entire joint section makes more room for stuffing. Chop through the bone with the heal of a heavy knife or with a cleaver.

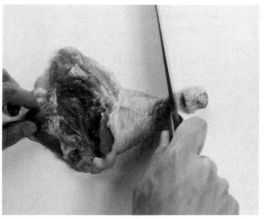

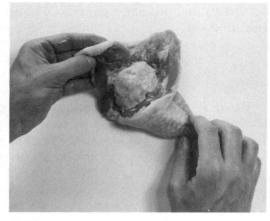

(e) For a neater appearance, also cut off the end of the drumstick bone. This leaves only the center section of the drumstick bone in the leg.

(f) Place a portion of stuffing in the space where the bone was. Fold the meat over the stuffing to enclose it.

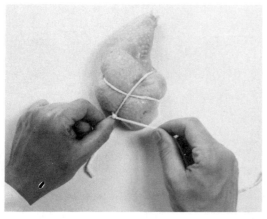

(g) Tie the ballotine securely.

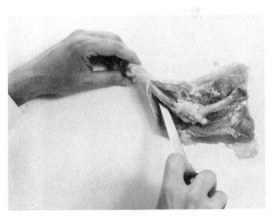

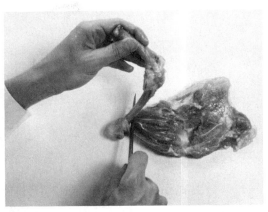

FIGURE 7.4. **Stuffing a fully boned chicken leg.** (a) Begin as though boning the leg for a ballotine (see Figure 7.3), except make the cut along the entire length of the leg to expose all the bone.

(b) Remove the bone completely from the meat.

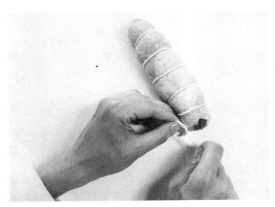

(c) Place a sausage-shaped portion of stuffing on the meat and roll the leg up into a cylinder to enclose the stuffing.

(d) Tie securely.

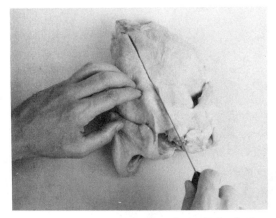

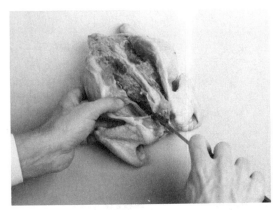

FIGURE 7.5. **Boning a chicken through the back.** (a) Make a cut the length of the backbone, cutting to, but not through, the bone.

(b) Carefully cut the meat away from the rib cage and other bones, holding the blade against the bones to avoid cutting into the flesh.

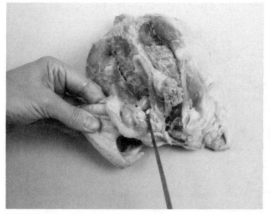

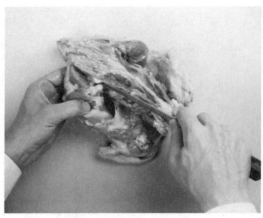

FIGURE 7.5. (Continued)
(c) Separate the wing bones from the shoulder by cutting through the joint.

(d) Separate the thigh bone from the hip by cutting through the hip socket joint.

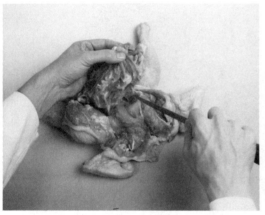

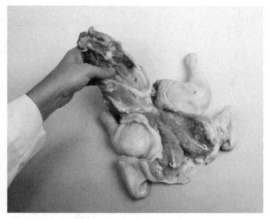

(e) Continue to work the knife against the bones to separate them from the meat.

(f) Remove the bones.

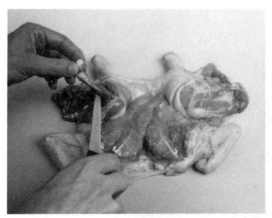

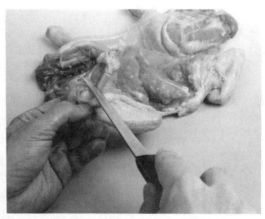

(g) The leg bones may be left in to help give shape to the chicken, or they may be removed as shown.

(h) The wing bones may also be removed by stripping the meat away from the bone.

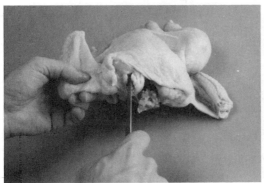

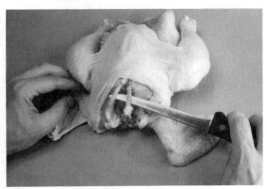

FIGURE 7.6. **Boning a chicken through the neck. (a) Begin by separating the wing bone from the shoulder by cutting through the joint.**

(b) The wishbone may also be removed at this point.

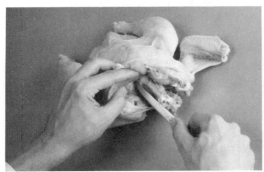

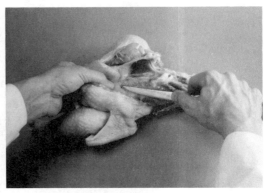

(c) Inserting the point of the boning knife through the neck opening, carefully begin stripping the meat away from the bone, holding the edge of the blade against the bone to avoid cutting into the flesh.

(d) As you cut more flesh away from the rib cage and other bones, peel the meat back to expose more of the bone.

(e) Continue to work back toward the legs and hip section.

(f) Separate the end of the leg or thigh bone from the hip at the socket joint. When the legs are separated from the hips, the bones of the body can be pulled completely out.

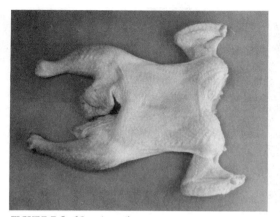

FIGURE 7.6. (Continued)
(g) This is the appearance of the boned chicken, with the leg and wing bones left in place.

(h) The leg and wing bones can be removed by stripping the meat away from the bone.

Turkey Parts. Turkey breasts, legs, and wings can also be prepared in a number of ways.

1. Turkey breast can be sliced and cooked like veal. Sliced very thin, the slices are often called scaloppine. Cut into thicker, larger slices, they are called cutlets.

2. Turkey tenderloins are the small muscles inside the breast, lying against the rib cage. These commonly weigh from 3 to 8 ounces (90 to 225 g), depending on the size of the turkey. They can be cooked like chicken suprêmes and served one or two per portion.

3. Turkey legs and wings are ideal for braising. In addition, the legs from small, tender birds can be boned, flattened, and grilled, or they can be cut up for sautéed items or for broiling on skewers.

4. Turkey wings, especially those from larger turkeys, make good luncheon dishes when braised. Most braised poultry recipes and even veal stew recipes can be applied to them. Use only the two large sections of the wings and cut them apart at the joint. The tip section has hardly any meat, but it can be used for stock.

Note About Cooking and Overcooking. Chicken and turkey breasts are relatively low in fat and in connective tissue. This can be both an advantage and a disadvantage. On the one hand, they cook quickly, are naturally tender, have a delicate flavor and texture, and appeal to those who wish to eat less fat for dietary reasons. On the other hand, they are easily overcooked, with a resulting loss in quality. Overcooked chicken breast becomes dry and rubbery. Turkey breast can get so dry that it is difficult to swallow.

It is important to guard against overcooking when preparing chicken and turkey breast items. When sautéing or grilling them, cook only briefly. They should be removed from the fire when they still yield to pressure from the fingertips. If they are firm and hard, they are already overcooked and dry.

When poaching or braising them, do not let the cooking liquid boil. This will give them a rubbery texture. It is better to leave them slightly undercooked, since they will continue to cook in their retained heat during the time that you finish the sauce or garnish, plate them, and send them to the dining room.

Because the legs are higher in connective tissue and fat, they suffer less from overcooking. First, they take longer to cook. Second, the fat and gelatine content keep them moister even if they are cooked too long. Nevertheless, for the best quality, they should not be overcooked either.

Roasting whole birds presents a problem, since the breast is likely to be done before the legs. Most chefs agree that it helps to turn the poultry from time time during roasting so that it cooks as evenly as possible on all sides. What they don't agree on, however, is the exact procedure. There are many different versions that produce good results. Most of them have one thing in common: they call for roasting the bird breast up for only part of the cooking time. Basting is called for to help brown the skin.

The following are some typical roasting procedures for chicken, as used by different chefs; see also the recipes in this chapter. These are applied to both high-heat and low-heat methods. When you have the opportunity, you can experiment to determine which methods you prefer.

- Roast the chicken on one side for one-third of the cooking time; on the second side for one-third of the time, and finally breast up for the last third of the time. Baste regularly.
- Roast breast up at high heat until browned. Then turn the chicken on its side and roast it at a lower temperature, first on one side, then on the other, until done. Baste regularly.
- Roast breast down for about two-thirds of the cooking time. Then roast breast side up until the chicken is done and breast is browned.

Handling Fat Poultry: Duck and Goose

Duckling is becoming more and more popular in restaurants, and chefs are experimenting with different ways to cook it. Although at one time roast duck, usually with orange sauce, was the only form of this poultry you ever saw on most menus, it is now common to see such items as grilled duck breast and warm duck salad on menus across the country.

Goose is similar to duck in composition and flavor, although it is of course larger. Because it is very rarely used in restaurants and is served mostly as a roast at family dinners, we mention it only briefly. For the most part, it is handled much like duck, except that cooking times are longer.

Types of Ducks. Most ducks raised in the United States, including the well-known Long Island duck, are a breed called White Pekin. This is a mild-flavored duck with a large quantity of fat under the skin.

A second variety raised here is the Muscovy duck or musk duck. This bird is also found in France, where it is called Barbary duck. It has a more pronounced flavor than the White Pekin, but cooks disagree about its quality. Some feel that the flavor is strong and disagreeable. Others say that it has a rich, full flavor, and that the more common Pekin is bland by comparison.

Therefore, it is not possible to make an absolute claim about these varieties. It is a fact, however, that the quality of domestic duck varies greatly from grower to grower and from market to market. The best ducks are meaty, flavorful, with good texture and not too much fat. The poorest have little meat, are too bland and fatty, and have a mushy or stringy texture.

A third type of duck occasionally seen here is the mullard (sometimes spelled mulard or moulard). This is a hybrid duck that has thick, meaty breast meat and good flavor. Unfortunately, it is not often seen in this country, although a similar type is common in Europe.

Comparison with French Ducks. It is important to know something about French ducks, because you may often have opportunity to see recipes from French chefs, and you may want to use them. Unfortunately, French ducks are somewhat different from ours, and the recipes may not work the same way.

The most famous is the Rouen duck. This is a fine-quality duck that is killed without being bled. The blood stays in the flesh, giving the meat a red or reddish-brown color and a pronounced taste.

The second major type is the Nantes duck. This variety is killed and bled normally.

Both these types are meatier and less fatty than ours. Thus, they have better yield per pound and are easier to roast, grill, and sauté, because the cook doesn't have to worry about cooking off so much fat.

Breast of mullard or moulard duck, known as *magret* (pronounced "ma-gray"), is a popular item in European restaurants. The French version is large and meaty, looking almost like a beefsteak. Breasts of American ducks can be used in the same ways, but they make a smaller portion.

Roasting Duck and Goose. The heavy layer of fat under the skin of duck and goose makes roasting them somewhat different from roasting chicken. Most people like duck with crisp, browned skin. Unfortunately, many cooks are so concerned with cooking the bird long enough to crisp the skin that the meat ends up dry and stringy, and even then a lot of fat remains under the skin.

A major objective in roasting duck (as well as goose) is to cook the bird just to the desired point of doneness, while at the same time rendering as much fat as possible. Most cooks have their favorite roasting methods and other techniques for reaching this goal. Chefs even report success with procedures that are completely the opposite of one another. For example, some cooks roast ducks at a low temperature to allow plenty of time for the fat to cook off. Others prefer to start ducks at a high temperature to brown the skin as quickly as possible before the meat becomes overcooked.

The following are some techniques that can be applied to roasting duck and goose. Keep in mind that these are individual techniques. It isn't expected that you use all of them at one time.

1. Before and during roasting, prick the skin all over with the point of a knife to help release rendered fat. Be careful to pierce the skin only; do not pierce the meat, or juices will be lost.
2. Brown the duck in a sauté pan before roasting (see page 269), to crisp the skin and render fat.
3. Since the breast is done before the legs, roast just until the breast is done. Cut off the legs and roast or grill them for a few more minutes. (The legs can also be reserved for another purpose.)
4. Carve the duck in the kitchen. Cut off and discard the fatty parts of the skin, leaving on only the parts of the skin that have browned well. In addition, the skin on the breast pieces can be removed, the fat scraped off the underside of the skin, and the skin replaced.
5. Keep the duck rare. Carve the duck and put the pieces under the broiler to brown the skin. (*Note:* The meaty ducks of France, especially the Rouen duck with its red flesh, are commonly served rare. In this country, because people have come to enjoy rare grilled duck breast, the idea of rare—or at least pink—roast duck is becoming more and more accepted. Like any meat, it retains more moisture and flavor if not cooked until well done. Of course, the carved duck can also be left under the broiler until it is no longer rare.)

Below are some typical roasting procedures for duck. Since each of them is used by successful chefs, we don't claim that one of them is better than the others.

Caution: A single duck may release more than 8 ounces (225 g) of fat as it cooks. No matter what roasting method you use, it is important to drain off rendered fat from the roasting pan as it accumulates. A pan full of hot fat can easily spatter or spill and burn you or start a fire.

Total roasting times depend on the size of the duck, the temperature of the oven, and the desired doneness.

Typical Procedures for Roasting Duck

Method 1.
1. Heat the oven to 325°F (165°C). Roast the duck breast up for 40 to 45 minutes.
2. Raise the heat to 500°F (260°C). Roast breast up until done, about 10 to 20 minutes.

Method 2.
1. Preheat the oven to 300°F (150°C). Place the duck on its side and roast for 30 minutes.
2. Raise the heat to 350°F (175°C). Turn the duck to its other side and roast 30 minutes.
3. Raise the heat to 400°F (200°C). Turn the duck breast up and roast until done, about 15 to 20 minutes.

Method 3.
1. Roast the duck breast up at 450°F (230°C) for 15 minutes.
2. Reduce the heat to 350°F (175°C) and roast until done.

Method 4.
1. Preheat the oven to 425°F (220°C).
2. Roast the duck at a constant temperature until done. Either leave it breast up or turn it over every 15 minutes.

For roasting goose, the techniques are similar, except that the cooking times are longer and the oven temperatures are usually a little lower. For example:

- Roast breast down at 400°F (200°C) for 1 hour. Reduce the heat to 350°F (175°C) and roast breast up until done.
- Roast at a constant 325°F (165°C) until done, about 4 to 5 hours.

Because of its cooking time, duck presents a problem for restaurants that want to roast them to order. If they are cooked ahead of time and reheated, they are usually lower in quality. To get around this difficulty, chefs often brown them at high heat and roast them until half done. They can then be finished to order in a relatively short time.

Cooking Duck Parts. Cooking duck parts separately extends the range of dishes that a restaurant can include on its menu. Another reason for the popularity of duck parts among chefs is that they cook more quickly than whole duck, so it is easier to cook them to order and serve them at their peak of quality.

Grilled or sautéed boneless duck breast is perhaps the most popular item. It should be cooked for most or all of the cooking time with the skin side toward the heat, in order to render the fat and to crisp the skin. Duck breast should be served slightly rare.

Be careful when broiling or grilling them. They release a lot of fat, which can cause flare-ups of the fire. When sautéing them, drain off the fat from the pan frequently.

Another way of serving duck breast is to cut off the legs of the duck and use them for another purpose. Roast the duck rare. Carve the breast meat by cutting it into long, thin slices and arrange them on a plate with the selected sauce and garnish. Such long, thin slices are known as *aiguillettes* (pronounced "egwee-yet").

Duck legs, like chicken legs, can be cooked by broiling, sautéing, and braising. Since they are sometimes a little tough, especially if they are from larger ducks, a slow cooking method like braising is perhaps the most satisfactory method.

An excellent and popular method for cooking cut-up duck and goose is a very old preparation called *confit* (pronounced "con-fee", a French term meaning "preserved"). This technique was developed as a means of preserving the meat before the days of modern refrigeration. The duck or goose parts are stewed slowly in their own rendered fat. They are then packed into a container and the melted fat is poured in to cover them completely. The fat seals the meat off from the air so that it will keep for long periods.

Today, with modern refrigeration, we are interested not in preserving the duck and goose but in its flavor and texture. Properly made confit has a rich flavor and is almost as tender as butter. (See page 321 for recipe and serving suggestions.)

Duck with Fruit. Perhaps the most well-known duck dish is roast duck à l'orange. Fruit sauces are classic accompaniments to duck because the acidity of the fruit goes well with the fattiness of the duck. A common error, however, is to make fruit sauces for duck too sweet. They should be only slightly sweet, and the sweetness should be balanced by acidity.

The standard base for a fruit sauce for duck is a mixture of caramel and vinegar, called a *gastrique* (pronounced "gas-treek"). As illustrated in the recipe on page 318, the procedure is to caramelize some sugar, then add vinegar and simmer until the caramel is dissolved. Some chefs prefer to combine the sugar and vinegar at the beginning, and then cook until the sugar caramelizes. The results are somewhat different, since much of the acidity of the vinegar is cooked off by the time the sugar caramelizes. The gastrique is combined with brown sauce or stock, fruit, and other ingredients to finish the sauce.

This method can be applied to many different fruits. You may need to vary the proportions of sugar and vinegar, depending on the sweetness or tartness of the fruit.

Pressed Duck and Related Dishes. The celebrated dish called *canard à la presse* is especially suited to the Rouen duck (see page 288) because of its high blood content. (The English term "pressed duck" is not really accurate, since it is only the skeleton that is pressed, not the whole duck.) The general procedure is as follows. Except for the roasting, the preparation is usually done in the dining room. There are many variations, but this gives you the basic outline.

Procedure for Preparing Duck à la Presse

1. Roast the duck, keeping it rare.
2. Cut off the legs and send them to the grill for further cooking.
3. Carve the breast into thin slices. Arrange them on a hot, buttered platter.
4. Chop up the carcass and put it in the duck press. Add some red wine to it, and press the juices out of the carcass.

5. In the dish's simplest form, these juices are simply sprinkled over the duck with some more butter, and it is heated briefly and served. Often, however, one or both of the following are added:
   a. Demiglaze sauce.
   b. A raw duck liver, puréed by forcing it through a sieve.
6. Heat the sauce gently, but do not let it boil. The duck liver and the blood in the juices will coagulate to bind the sauce, but it will break or curdle if boiled.

Variation

Press the carcass without the wine, and simply add the juices to a prepared Rouennaise Sauce (page 47).

Since we do not have Rouen ducks in the United States and since few establishments have a duck press, which is very expensive, this material is primarily of theoretical interest. Nevertheless, it helps us to understand a number of related dishes and gives ideas that can be applied in other ways.

Duck à la presse is usually classified as a *salmis* (pronounced "sal-mee"). A salmis is a dish, usually of game or poultry, prepared by roasting the item part way and finishing it in a sauce. The sauce is usually made with red or white wine and flavored by adding the juices from the carcass or by simmering the carcass with the sauce. The meat may then be simply reheated with the sauce or simmered in it for a longer time.

Salmis techniques work better with wild duck or with other game birds than with our fatty domestic ducks. With farm-raised game birds becoming more widely available, salmis of various sorts are showing up on many menus. A recipe for a typical modern salmis is on page 328.

Handling Other Domestic Birds and Game Birds

In recent years, the availability of such birds as quail and squab has increased dramatically, and they are seen regularly on restaurant menus across the country.

While most of these (except for guinea fowl) are classified as game birds, the fact is that all of the items discussed in this chapter are raised domestically. While farm-raised pheasants and partridge lack the full gamy flavor of their wild cousins, they do have a richer, somewhat gamelike taste, especially when compared with chicken. With bland, factory-raised chickens dominating the market, cooks and eaters are turning more and more to various exotic poultry and are willing to pay the higher price.

Traditionally, true wild game is hung and allowed to age, usually before plucking and dressing. The purpose is essentially the same as that of aging beef, namely to allow the natural enzymes in the meat to tenderize it and to develop flavor. Often, game is hung until it becomes "high," to the point where spoiled meat is mistaken for aged meat. With today's farm-raised game birds, this procedure is not really appropriate. Anyway, most people prefer a fresh taste to a strong, gamy one.

The types of birds available include:

1. *Quail*
   a. Size: 4 to 5 oz (110 to 140 g) each. A normal portion is two birds.
   b. Comments: Perhaps the most popular and widely available of the small birds. They have meaty breasts for their size, but there is not much meat on the legs. Richly flavored without being really gamy. The French name is *caille*.

2. *Squab*
   a. Size: 12 to 20 oz (340 to 565 g); the smaller ones are generally more tender.
   b. Comments: A squab is a young, domestic pigeon. Widely available and favored for its moist, meaty dark flesh, with a faintly gamy flavor. Often considered to be the best all-purpose "game" bird, although technically it is not game. The French name for squab is *pigeonneau;* for mature pigeon the name is *pigeon.*

3. *Partridge*
   a. Size: about 1 lb (450 g).
   b. Comments: Important to look for young, tender birds, because partridge is often tough. Excellent flavor, but not as delicate as squab or pheasant. French names are *perdreau* (young partridge) and *perdrix* (mature patridge).

4. *Guinea fowl*
   a. Size: Wide range of sizes, from less than 1 lb (450 g) to about 3 lb (1350 g). Commonly around 2 lb (900 g).
   b. Comments: These are not game birds but are always raised domestically. Often compared to the pheasant, but the guinea fowl is not as delicate and has darker meat. Females (hens) are preferred to the males, because the hens are more tender. French names are *pintadeau* (young guinea) and *pintade* (mature guinea).

5. *Pheasant*
   a. Size: 2 to 2 ½ lb (900 to 1200 g). Young pheasants of 1 lb (450 g) or less are also available.
   b. Comments: Delicate, light-colored meat with subtle flavor. Can be very dry if overcooked. The French name is *faisan.*

6. *Wild duck*
   a. Size: 1 ½ to 3 lb (700 to 1400 g).
   b. Comments: Many varieties of wild ducks are eaten, but mallard is the most common. Farm-raised mallards are available. Unlike domestic duck, wild duck is very lean. It has dark, flavorful flesh.

Preparing and Cutting. Handling game birds is easy if you remember that their structure is basically the same as the structure of chickens. All the cutting and trussing techniques that you already know for chicken can be applied to these other birds.

Since most of these birds are small, they are not often cut up for sautés like chicken is, except for older, tougher birds that require braising. Most often they are prepared in one of the following ways:

- Left whole and trussed. For roasting or poêléing. Sometimes the legs are cut off and saved for another use; the rest of the bird is roasted and the breast is carved and served.
- Split open by cutting out the backbone, spread open, and flattened. The rib bones may be removed for easier eating. For grilling or sautéing; especially for squab, quail, and small guinea hens.
- Split open as above, but cut into halves through the center of the breast.
- Completely or partially boned. May be split open for grilling or sautéing or left intact and stuffed.

Quails are especially good when boned and stuffed. Because of their size, they can be served whole without looking too big and awkward on the plate. The technique is exactly the same as for boning whole chickens (Figures 7.5 and 7.6), but because they are so small, they are a little more difficult to do. Figures 7.7 and 7.8 show you the same procedures again, this time performed on quails.

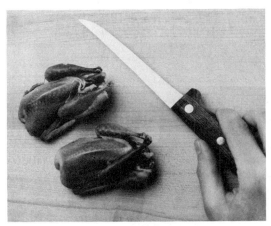

FIGURE 7.7. **Boning a quail through the back.**
(a) Quails are boned like chickens, but because they are much smaller, greater care is required.

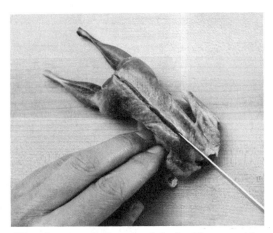

(b) Make a cut the length of the backbone, cutting to, but not through, the bone.

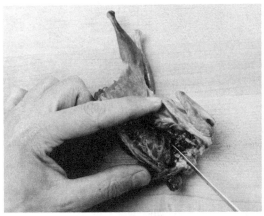

(c) Carefully cut the meat away from the rib cage and other bones, holding the blade against the bones to avoid cutting into the flesh.

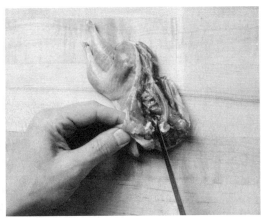

(d) Separate the wing bones from the shoulder by cutting through the joint.

(e) Separate the thigh bone from the hip by cutting through the hip socket joint.

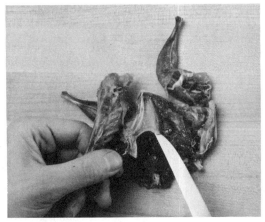

(f) Remove the central bones completely. Be careful not to cut or tear the skin and flesh near the breast bone, where the bone is very close to the surface.

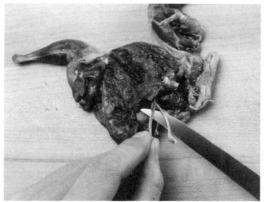

FIGURE 7.7. (Continued)
(g) Remove the wishbone if it is still in place.

(h) The leg bones may be left in to help give shape to the quail, as shown.

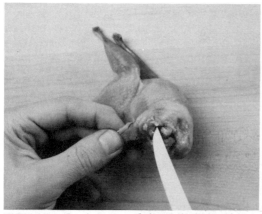

FIGURE 7.8. Boning a quail through the neck.
(a) Begin by separating the wing bone from the shoulder by cutting through the joint.

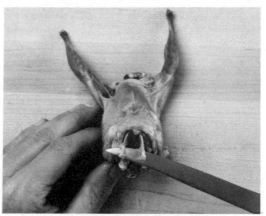

(b) The wishbone may also be removed at this point.

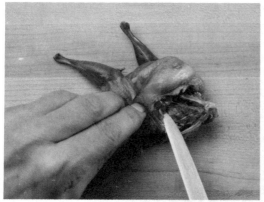

(c) Inserting the point of the boning knife through the neck opening, carefully begin stripping the meat away from the bone, holding the edge of the blade against the bone to avoid cutting into the flesh.

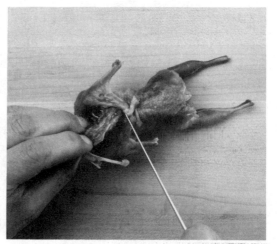

(d) As you cut more flesh away from the rib cage and other bones, peel the meat back to expose more of the bone. Continue to work back toward the legs and hip section.

294

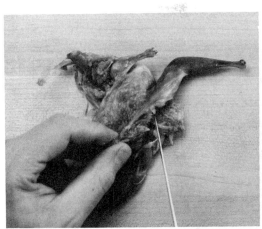

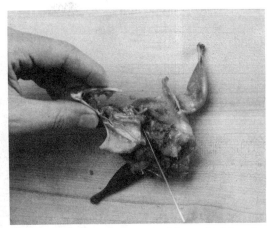

FIGURE 7.8. (Continued)
(e) Separate the end of the leg or thigh bone from the hip at the socket joint.

(f) When the legs are separated from the hips, the bones of the body can be pulled completely out.

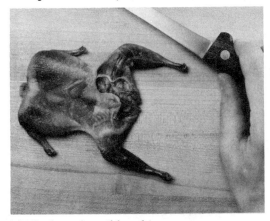

(g) The boned quail has this appearance.

Cooking. Young, tender birds are roasted, sautéed, broiled, grilled, barbecued, and sometimes poêléed, poached, and steamed. Older, tougher birds (which are almost never served in American restaurants) are braised in order to tenderize them.

The most important thing to remember about game birds is that they are usually very lean. Therefore, they are best served slightly rare. If cooked to well done they become dry. This is especially true of wild duck, which is almost inedible if overcooked. Wild duck is usually left rarer than the other birds discussed here; its meat is then red and juicy.

Pheasant is also very dry if well done. Its light-colored meat is best if still slightly pink at the bone.

Squab and quail don't become quite as dry, but they too have the best flavor and texture if served slightly rare.

The breast meat of all game birds is drier and leaner than the legs. To protect it during cooking, the breast is often *barded.* This means that thin slices of pork fatback or bacon are tied over it to supply fat and to reduce drying. Figure 7.9 illustrates.

To avoid overcooking the breasts of game birds when roasting, remove the birds from the oven when the breasts are done. Cut off the legs and, if they are too rare, return them to the oven or broil them for a few more minutes.

Game birds are usually roasted at high heat so that they brown well. Often they are browned in a sauté pan before roasting (see page 269). At 450°F (230°C), quails will

FIGURE 7.9. **To bard a trussed bird, tie a thin sheet of fatback over the breast as shown.**

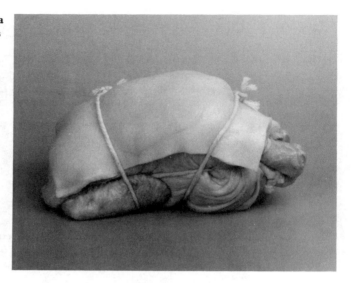

roast in about 10 to 15 minutes, squab and partridge in 20 to 35 minutes, and larger birds in less than 1 hour. If they are browned on top of the stove first, the cooking times will, of course, be less.

Imaginative chefs have devised many appealing recipes for all these birds. Nevertheless, many people prefer a simple roast so that they can savor the bird's own special taste by itself. For such customers, the ultimate game bird recipe is as follows:

1. Season the bird with salt and pepper (and possibly a few fresh herbs).
2. Roast until slightly rare.
3. Degrease the roasting pan and deglaze it with a little stock, preferably made with the bones of the same kind of bird.
4. Reduce this juice and serve as a sauce.

In addition to the game-bird recipes in this chapter, a recipe for quail salad appears in Chapter 5.

POACHED CHICKEN BREAST WITH WATERCRESS SAUCE

(Color Plate 10)

		U.S.		Metric	
PORTIONS:		4	16	4	16
Ingredients					
Chicken breasts, boneless, skinless		4	16	4	16
Chicken stock, as needed					
Salt					
White pepper					
Watercress Sauce (p. 54 or p. 62)		8 oz	1 qt	2.5 dl	1 l
Vegetable garnish:					
Carrots					
Turnips					
Leeks					
New potatoes					

Mise en Place:

1. Trim and clean the vegetables for garnish. Tourné the carrots and turnips or cut them into any neat, uniform shapes. Quarter the leeks lengthwise and cut into 2-inch (5-cm) lengths. If the potatoes are small, cut a strip of peel off each one. If they are large, halve or quarter them.
2. Steam the vegetables separately until just cooked.
3. Season the stock well.

Cooking/Finishing:

1. Poach the chicken breasts in the stock.
2. Rewarm the vegetables. If desired, coat them with a little butter.

Presentation:

1. For each portion, ladle 2 oz (60 ml) of the sauce onto the center of each plate.
2. Slice the chicken breast on the diagonal. Arrange the slices in the shape of a fan on top of the sauce.
3. Arrange the vegetables attractively around the chicken.

Variations

Instead of poaching, the chicken breast can be cooked by sautéing, baking, poêléing (poaching in butter), broiling, or grilling, or the chicken can be roasted (minus the legs) and the breast sliced from it.

Turkey breast slices or other suitable poultry items can be substituted.

In place of the watercress sauce, a vegetable juice sauce (page 34), such as one made from asparagus or broccoli, is a good accompaniment to this dish.

ROAST CHICKEN WITH TARRAGON

		U.S.		Metric	
PORTIONS:		4	16	4	16
Ingredients					
Small chickens, 2 lb (900g) each (see note)		2	8	2	8
Salt					
Pepper					
Tarragon (see note)		2 tsp	8 tsp	2 g	8 g
Oil					
Butter		2 oz	8 oz	60 g	250 g
Carrots		1 oz	4 oz	30 g	125 g
Celery		1 oz	4 oz	30 g	125 g
Shallots		½ oz	2 oz	15 g	60 g
Garlic		½ clove	2 cloves	½ clove	2 cloves
Chicken stock		8 oz	1 qt	2.5 dl	1 l

Note: One large chicken can be used instead of two small ones. Dried tarragon is assumed; if you have fresh, use three times as much.

Mise en Place:

1. Season the chickens inside and out with salt and pepper, and rub half the tarragon inside the cavities.
2. Truss the chickens.
3. Chop the carrot, celery, shallot, and garlic coarsely.

Cooking/Finishing:

1. In one or more sauté pans, brown the chickens well in oil on all sides.
2. Remove the chickens from the pan and rub the skin carefully with the remaining tarragon.
3. Discard the oil from the pans. In the same pans or in roasting pans, melt the butter. Add the chopped vegetables to the pans.
4. Put the chickens in the pans on their sides. Roast at 425°F (220°C) for 10 minutes.
5. Turn the chickens to the other side and roast 10 minutes. Turn them breast up and roast until done, another 5 to 15 minutes. Baste frequently with the butter in the pan throughout the roasting period.
6. When the chickens are done, tip them up to drain the juices in the cavity into the roasting pans. Set the chickens aside in a warm place.
7. Discard excess fat from the pans but keep the vegetables and juices in the pans. Deglaze with the stock and reduce by one-half.
8. Strain and degrease the sauce. Taste for seasonings and, if necessary, add more salt, pepper, and tarragon.

Presentation:

1. Carve the chicken, cutting the breast off the bones, and cutting the drumstick and thigh apart at the joint. Serve one piece of breast, one thigh, and one drumstick per portion, with a spoonful of the sauce.

2. Accompany with desired vegetable garnish.

Variations

Roast the chicken without browning it first. Increase the oven temperature to 450°F (230°C), and increase the roasting time as necessary (about 5 to 15 minutes).

Other herbs can be used instead of or in addition to tarragon, especially if fresh ones are available.

Omit the herbs and serve the roasted chicken with an appropriate sauce (see Chapter 5). For example:

Suprême
Ivory
Diable
Perigueux
Cream Sauce with Morels
Wild Mushroom Sauce

GRILLED CHICKEN WITH GARLIC AND GINGER

		U.S.		Metric	
PORTIONS:		**4**	**16**	*4*	*16*
Ingredients					
Chicken parts or halves, or whole cornish hens		3–4 lb	12–16 lb	*1.4–1.8 kg*	*5.5–7 kg*
Lemon or lime juice		3 oz	12 oz	*1 dl*	*4 dl*
Vegetable oil		1 oz	4 oz	*30 ml*	*125 ml*
Fresh ginger, grated		½ oz	2 oz	*15 g*	*60 g*
Garlic, chopped fine		1 tsp	4 tsp	*2 g*	*8 g*
Salt					
Pepper					
Melted butter, as needed					
Ginger Oil (p. 79), optional					

Mise en Place:

1. Cut the chickens into parts or halves for broiling. If using cornish hens, split down the back and flatten, or cut into halves.

2. Combine the lemon or lime juice, oil, ginger, garlic, and salt and pepper to taste, to make a marinade.

3. Marinate the chicken for 3 to 4 hours.

Cooking/Finishing:

1. Remove the chicken from the marinade. Grill or broil the chicken until done. Baste with the marinade several times during cooking.

2. Shortly before the chicken is done, brush the pieces once or twice with melted butter.

3. If desired, drizzle a few drops of ginger oil around the chicken after plating.

Variations

Substitute any of the following for the chicken parts in the above recipe or in any of the following variations:

Chicken or turkey brochettes: cubes of boneless meat on skewers
Boneless chicken breast
Turkey cutlets: thick slices of turkey breast
Turkey paillards: broad slices of turkey breast pounded thin
Chicken or turkey thighs boned out and lightly pounded

Southwestern Grilled Chicken

Tomato, puréed	2 oz	8 oz	*60 g*	*250 g*
Jalapeño pepper, chopped very fine	2 tsp	8 tsp	*4 g*	*15 g*
Fresh cilantro, chopped	2 tbsp	½ cup	*7 g*	*30 g*
Red wine vinegar	1 ½ oz	6 oz	*45 ml*	*2 dl*

Substitute the above ingredients for the marinade in the basic recipe.

Spicy Barbecue-Style Grilled Chicken

Worcestershire sauce	1 oz	4 oz	*30 ml*	*125 ml*
Red wine vinegar	1 tbsp	2 oz	*15 ml*	*60 ml*
Paprika	2 tsp	8 tsp	*5 g*	*20 g*
Chili powder	1 tsp	4 tsp	*2.5 g*	*10 g*
Dry mustard	½ tsp	2 tsp	*1 g*	*4 g*
Garlic, crushed	½ tsp	2 tsp	*1 g*	*4 g*
Black pepper	¼ tsp	1 tsp	*0.5 g*	*2 g*
Powdered bay leaf	¼ tsp	1 tsp	*0.5 g*	*2 g*
Salt	½ tsp	2 tsp	*2.5 g*	*10g*

Substitute the above ingredients for the marinade in the basic recipe. Toss the chicken pieces by hand so that the pieces are all coated.

Grilled Chicken Oriental Style

Soy sauce	4 oz	1 pt	*125 ml*	*5 dl*
Rice wine or sherry	1 oz	4 oz	*30 ml*	*125 ml*
Chicken stock or water	1 oz	4 oz	*30 ml*	*125 ml*
Lemon juice	½ oz	2 oz	*15 ml*	*60 ml*
Sugar	1 tsp	4 tsp	*4 g*	*16 g*
Fresh ginger, grated	2 tsp	8 tsp	*5 g*	*20 g*

Substitute the above ingredients for the marinade in the basic recipe. Brush the chicken with the marinade frequently during grilling.

Grilled Chicken Marinated in Yogurt and Spices

Unflavored yogurt	4 oz	1 pt	*125 ml*	*5 dl*
Onion, grated	1 oz	4 oz	*30 g*	*125 g*
Garlic, crushed	¼ tsp	1 tsp	*0.5 g*	*2 g*
Fresh ginger, grated	¼ tsp	1 tsp	*0.5 g*	*2 g*
Ground cumin	½ tsp	2 tsp	*1 g*	*4 g*
Ground cardamom	¼ tsp	1 tsp	*0.5 g*	*2 g*
Mace	pinch	½ tsp	*pinch*	*1 g*
Cayenne	¼ tsp	1 tsp	*0.5 g*	*2 g*
Black pepper	¼ tsp	1 tsp	*0.5 g*	*2 g*
Salt	½ tsp	2 tsp	*2.5 g*	*10 g*

Substitute the above ingredients for the marinade in the basic recipe. Marinate the chicken overnight.

POULET SAUTÉ PORTUGAISE

		U.S.		Metric	
PORTIONS:		4	16	4	16
Ingredients					
Chickens, 2–2 ½ lb (900–1100 g) each (see note)		2	8	2	8
Salt					
Pepper					
Oil or butter		1 oz	4 oz	25 g	100 g
Onions, cut brunoise		1 ½ oz	6 oz	40 g	160 g
Garlic, minced		½ tsp	2 tsp	1 g	4 g
Mushrooms, sliced		2 oz	8 oz	50 g	200 g
Tomato, peeled, seeded, and diced		4 oz	1 lb	100 g	400 g
Chopped parsley		1 tsp	4 tsp	1 g	4 g
Garnish: Tomato halves filled with rice pilaf					

Note: If necessary, use larger chickens. One 3 ½ lb (1.6 kg) chicken will make four portions. Increase cooking time as necessary.

Mise en Place:

1. Disjoint the chickens, cutting them into eighths. Season the pieces with salt and pepper.

2. Prepare the onions, garlic, mushrooms, tomato, and parsley and have them ready.

3. Peel and hollow out small tomato halves for the garnish. Shortly before service time, prepare the pilaf for the garnish.

Cooking/Finishing:

1. Brown the chicken well in hot oil or butter. Since the chicken pieces are small, they should be at least half cooked by the time they are browned.

2. Cover the pans and place in a 375°F (190°C) oven until done, approximately 15 minutes.

3. When the chicken is cooked, remove it from the pans and keep it warm. (The breast and wing pieces will be done first; so remove them from the pans when they are done and continue to cook the leg pieces.)

4. Discard excess fat from the pans. (If there is moisture in the pans, first set them over heat to evaporate the moisture; the solids in the drippings will solidify on the bottom of the pan so that you can discard the fat without losing the flavor of the juices.) In the fat remaining in the pans (or in some fresh butter, if desired) sauté the onions and garlic until soft. Add the mushrooms and sauté. Add the tomatoes and cook rapidly to reduce the moisture. Add the parsley. Adjust the seasonings.

5. Optional: Heat the chicken in the sauce briefly if desired.

Presentation:

1. Arrange the chicken on plates or on a platter. Spoon the sauce over the chicken.

2. Arrange the prepared garnish around the chicken.

3. If desired, sprinkle with a little additional chopped parsley.

Variations

For the following chicken sautés, proceed as in the basic recipe, except when otherwise directed. (In some cases, the chicken is to be sautéed lightly without browning.) Omit the ingredients above, except for the chicken, salt, pepper, and oil or butter. Substitute the ingredients listed for each preparation.

The quantity of sauce in these recipes is usually small. It is intended to be an accent or seasoning for the chicken. If more sauce is desired, simply double the ingredients for the sauce.

Poulet Sauté Arlésienne

White wine	4 oz	1 pt	*1 dl*	*4 dl*
Garlic, crushed	¼ tsp	1 tsp	*0.5 g*	*2 g*
Demiglaze	2 oz	8 oz	*50 ml*	*2 dl*

Garnish:
  Fried, sliced onions
  Fried eggplant slices
  Tomato concassé sautéed in butter

When the chicken is cooked, deglaze the pan with the wine. Add the garlic and demiglaze; reduce to a light sauce consistency. Arrange the garnish in small heaps around the chicken, and spoon the sauce over the chicken to moisten it.

Poulet Sauté Bordelaise

Demiglaze or strong chicken stock	4 oz	1 pt	*1 dl*	*4 dl*

Garnish:
  Sliced potatoes cooked in butter
  Fried, sliced onions
  Fried parsley

Arrange the garnish around the cooked chicken. Deglaze the pan with the demiglaze or stock, reduce by about one-half, and sprinkle the chicken with this liquid.

Poulet Sauté Bretonne

Leek, white part	3 oz	12 oz	*75 g*	*300 g*
Onion	1 oz	4 oz	*25 g*	*100 g*
Butter, as needed				
Mushrooms	2 oz	8 oz	*50 g*	*100 g*
Chicken velouté	2 oz	8 oz	*50 ml*	*2 dl*
Heavy cream	3 oz	12 oz	*75 ml*	*3 dl*

Sauté the chicken lightly, without browning. Slice the leek and onion, and stew in butter until half cooked. Add them to the chicken and finish the cooking in the oven. Chop the mushrooms very fine and sauté lightly in a little butter. Add to the chicken 5 minutes before it is done. When the chicken is done, remove it from the pan, but leave the vegetables in the pan. Add the velouté and cream; reduce by half. Pour the sauce and vegetables over the chicken.

Poulet Sauté Chasseur

White wine or chicken stock	1 oz	4 oz	*25 ml*	*75 ml*
Chasseur sauce	6–8 oz	1 ½–2 pt	*2 dl*	*8 dl*

Deglaze the pan with the wine or stock. Add the sauce. Pour the sauce over the chicken.

Poulet Sauté Hongroise

Onion, brunoise	2 oz	8 oz	*50 g*	*100 g*
Hungarian paprika	1 tsp	4 tsp	*2 g*	*8 g*
Hongroise sauce	6–8 oz	1 ½–2 pt	*2 dl*	*8 dl*
Heavy cream	2 oz	8 oz	*50 ml*	*2 dl*
Garnish:				
Rice pilaf				

Sauté the chicken with the onion and paprika, but do not let it brown. When the chicken is cooked, remove it from the pan and add the sauce and cream. Reduce slightly. Coat the chicken with the sauce and serve with rice pilaf.

Poulet Sauté Lyonnaise

Onions, sliced	8 oz	2 lb	*200 g*	*800 g*
Butter	1 oz	4 oz	*25 g*	*100 g*
Demiglaze	3 oz	12 oz	*75 ml*	*3 dl*
Chopped parsley	1 tsp	4 tsp	*2 g*	*8 g*

Brown the onion in butter and add the chicken when it is about two-thirds cooked. When done, remove the chicken but leave the onions in the pan. Add demiglaze; reduce slightly; pour over chicken. Sprinkle with chopped parsley.

Poulet Sauté Marengo

White wine	2 oz	8 oz	*50 ml*	*2 dl*
Tomato, peeled, seeded, and chopped	2 oz	8 oz	*50 g*	*200 g*
Garlic, minced	¼ tsp	1 tsp	*0.5 g*	*2 g*
Small mushrooms	2 oz	8 oz	*50 g*	*200 g*
Demiglaze	2 oz	8 oz	*50 ml*	*2 dl*

Garnish:
    Heart-shaped croutons fried in
      butter
    Fried eggs, neatly trimmed
    Poached crayfish
    Chopped parsley

Deglaze the pan with the wine. Add the tomato, garlic, and mushrooms and cook briefly. Add the demiglaze and bring to a boil. Spoon the sauce over the chicken and surround it with the garnish.

Poulet Sauté Provençale

White wine	2 oz	8 oz	*50 ml*	*2 dl*
Provençale sauce	4 oz	1 pt	*1 dl*	*4 dl*
Pitted black olives	8–10	30–40	*8–10*	*30–40*
Basil	¼ tsp	1 tsp	*0.25 g*	*1 g*

Deglaze the pan with the wine. Add the remaining ingredients and simmer a few minutes. Spoon the sauce over the chicken.

TURKEY SCALOPPINE WITH GRAPEFRUIT

		U.S.		Metric	
PORTIONS:		4	16	4	16
Ingredients					
Turkey breast, boneless and skinless		1 lb	4 lb	*500 g*	*2 kg*
Salt					
White pepper					
Flour					
Oil					
Grapefruit zest, cut julienne		2 tbsp	½ cup	*10 g*	*40 g*
Grapefruit juice		1 oz	4 oz	*30 ml*	*125 ml*
Honey		1 tsp	4 tsp	*5 ml*	*20 ml*
Chicken stock or turkey stock		4 oz	1 pt	*125 ml*	*5 dl*
Butter, cut in pieces		1–2 oz	4–8 oz	*30–60 g*	*125–250 g*

Mise en Place:

1. Cut the turkey diagonally across the grain into broad, thin slices. Pound them lightly so that they are less than ¼ inch (6 mm) thick.

2. Blanch the grapefruit zest by simmering in water for about 3 minutes. Drain and set aside.

3. Mix the grapefruit juice and honey. Set aside.

Cooking/Finishing:

1. Just before cooking, season the turkey scaloppine with salt and pepper and dredge in flour.

2. Heat the oil in a sauté pan or pans large enough to hold them in a single layer (or do in several batches). Brown the turkey lightly on both sides. This will take only a few seconds; do not overcook.

3. Remove the turkey from the pan and keep warm. Drain off excess oil from the pan.

4. Add the stock to the pan and deglaze. Add the grapefruit juice and honey mixture and half the julienne zest. Reduce by one-half. Monter au beurre and check the seasonings.

5. Return the turkey to the pan to rewarm it and coat it with the sauce.

Presentation:

Place the scaloppine on plates. Spoon the remaining sauce over them. Top with remaining zest.

Variations

Other citrus fruits make interesting variations. Substitute any of the following for the grapefruit juice and zest:

Lemon
Lime
Orange
Tangerine

A few drops of orange liqueur may be added to the orange sauce variation.

CHICKEN MOUSSELINE

		U.S.		Metric	
YIELD (APPROX.):		**1 ½ lb**	**6 lb**	**750 g**	**3 kg**
Ingredients					
Chicken meat		1 lb	4 lb	500 g	2 kg
Egg whites		2	8	2	8
Heavy cream		12 oz	3 pt	375 ml	1.5 l
Salt					
White pepper					
Nutmeg					

Procedure:

1. Review the guidelines for making mousselines on page 220.
2. Dice the meat and put into the container of a food processor. Process until puréed.
3. Add the egg whites and process until blended in.
4. Force the purée through a sieve to remove sinews.
5. Put the purée into a stainless steel bowl that is nested in another bowl of crushed ice. Chill until the meat is very cold.
6. Gradually blend in the cream by hand. Season with salt, pepper, and just a dash of nutmeg.
7. Test the seasoning and consistency by poaching and tasting a small quenelle. Adjust as necessary.

CHICKEN BALLOTINES ALBERT

		U.S.		Metric	
PORTIONS:		**4**	**16**	*4*	*16*
Ingredients					
Large chicken legs (thigh and drumstick in one piece)		4	16	*4*	*16*
Salt					
Pepper					
Chicken Mousseline (p. 307)		4 oz	1 lb	*100 g*	*400 g*
Prosciutto or smoked ham		1 oz	4 oz	*25 g*	*100 g*
Oil, as needed					
Butter		½ oz	2 oz	*12 g*	*50 g*
Carrot		1 oz	4 oz	*25 g*	*100 g*
Onion		1 oz	4 oz	*25 g*	*100 g*
Celery		1 oz	4 oz	*25 g*	*100 g*
Thyme		pinch	½ tsp	*pinch*	*0.5 g*
Bay leaf		¼	1	*¼*	*1*
Madeira or sherry		1 oz	4 oz	*25 ml*	*1 dl*
Strong chicken stock		8 oz	1 qt	*2 dl*	*8 dl*
Salt					
Pepper					
Optional: butter or beurre manié					

Mise en Place:

1. Remove the thigh bone and knee joint of each leg, as shown in Figure 7.3, and cut off the end of the leg bone. Season with salt and pepper.

2. Chop the prosciutto very fine and mix with the mousseline. Stuff the legs with this mixture and tie them up.

3. Cut the carrot, onions, and celery into brunoise (fine dice).

Cooking/Finishing:

1. Brown the chicken legs lightly in hot oil. Remove them from the pan and degrease the pan.

2. Add the butter to the pan and sauté the vegetables lightly. Add the herbs and deglaze with the madeira or sherry.

3. Transfer the vegetable mixture to a braising pan just large enough to hold the chicken legs. Put the chicken on top. Cover and bake at 350°F (175°C) until done, about 30 minutes.

4. Remove the chicken from the pan and keep it warm.

5. Add the stock to the braising pan and reduce by one-third over high heat. Strain and degrease the sauce. Adjust the seasoning. If desired, finish the sauce with a little butter or beurre manié.

Presentation:

1. Remove the trussing strings from the chicken ballotines. Place the chicken on serving plates. If desired, you can display the stuffing by cutting a few neat slices off the ballotine and arranging them attractively alongside the rest of the piece.

2. Moisten with an ounce (30 ml) of sauce.

Variations

Other ingredients may be added to the mousseline, in place of the prosciutto, such as:

Chopped blue cheese (roquefort, stilton, etc.) plus finely chopped walnuts or diced apple

Minced truffle

Thin slices of foie gras (not mixed with the mousseline, but used in addition to the mousseline)

Fresh sage leaves

Dried morels, soaked in hot water, squeezed dry, and chopped

Blanched, chopped sorrel or watercress

Diced lobster, crab, or shrimp

CHICKEN BREAST WITH ONION PURÉE AND LEEKS

		U.S.		Metric	
PORTIONS:		**4**	**16**	*4*	*16*
Ingredients					
Chicken cutlets (wing bone in) or boneless chicken breasts, skin on		4	16	*4*	*16*
Chicken mousseline		4 oz	1 lb	*100 g*	*400 g*
Stewed Leeks (p. 516)		4 oz	1 lb	*100 g*	*400 g*
Onion Purée (p. 532)		4 oz	1 lb	*100 g*	*400 g*
Salt					
Pepper					
Clarified butter		1 oz	4 oz	*25 g*	*100 g*
Shallots, chopped		½ oz	2 oz	*12 g*	*50 g*
Sherry vinegar		1 oz	4 oz	*25 ml*	*1 dl*
Strong chicken stock		8 oz	1 qt	*2 dl*	*8 dl*
Salt					
Pepper					
Garnish:					
Small rissolé potatoes					
Buttered julienne of carrots					
Seasonal green vegetable(s)					

Mise en Place:

1. Prepare the chicken breasts. Cut a pocket in each one, as shown in Figure 7.2.

2. Mix *half* of the cooked leeks (cooled) with the mousseline. Stuff the chicken breasts with this mixture.

3. Mix the rest of the leeks with the onion purée.

Cooking/Finishing:

1. Heat the clarified butter in a sauté pan. Put the chicken breasts in the pan skin side down. Brown them lightly.

2. Without turning the chicken pieces over, cover the pan and put in an oven heated to 350°F (175°C). Bake until done, about 10 minutes.

3. Remove the chicken breasts from the pan and keep them warm.

4. Set the sauté pan over moderate heat and reduce the juices until all the moisture has evaporated and the solids have browned on the bottom of the pan. Discard the excess fat from the pan. Add the shallots and cook lightly. Deglaze the pan with the vinegar. Add the stock and reduce by one-half. Strain and adjust the seasonings.

5. Reheat the onion purée mixture.

Presentation

1. For each portion, place a small spoonful of the onion purée just to one side of the center of a plate.
2. Place a chicken breast, skin side up, on top of the onion purée.
3. Arrange small groups of the vegetable garnish around the chicken. Spoon the sauce over or around the chicken.

Variations

Steamed chicken breast: Prepare as in basic recipe, except remove the skin from the chicken first. Steam rather than braise. Spoon the sauce over the chicken.

Other stuffings may be substituted if desired.

Other appropriate sauces may be served with the chicken (see Chapter 3). Since the mousseline filling is rich, it is best to use a sauce that is not too rich, and to use only a small quantity.

STUFFED CHICKEN LEGS WITH PECAN BUTTER

		U.S.		*Metric*	
PORTIONS:		4	16	*4*	*16*
Ingredients					
Large chicken legs (drumstick and thigh in one piece)		4	16	*4*	*16*
Salt					
Pepper					
Shallots		1 oz	4 oz	*25 g*	*100 g*
Garlic, small cloves		1	4	*1*	*4*
Butter		½ oz	2 oz	*12 g*	*50 g*
Pecans		2 oz	8 oz	*50 g*	*200 g*
Butter, soft		2 oz	8 oz	*50 g*	*200 g*
Parsley, chopped		1 tbsp	4 tbsp	*3 g*	*15 g*
Salt					
Pepper					
Oil or butter, as needed					
Chicken stock		4 oz	1 pt	*1 dl*	*4 dl*
Salt					
Pepper					

Mise en Place:

1. Bone the chicken legs completely (see Figure 7.4). Season them with salt and pepper.

2. Mince the shallot and garlic. Sauté lightly in the first quantity of butter without letting them brown. Cool.

3. Chop the pecans fine.

4. Mix the shallots, garlic, pecans, soft butter, and salt and pepper to taste.

5. Stuff the legs with the pecan mixture. Roll and tie as shown in Figures 7.4c and 7.4d.

Cooking/Finishing:

1. Brown the chicken legs well in the oil or butter. Cover the pan and cook over low heat or in a slow oven until done, about 15 minutes.

2. Remove the cooked legs from the pan and keep warm. Degrease the pan and deglaze it with the stock. Reduce by one-half. Strain and season.

Presentation:

1. Remove the trussing strings from the chicken. Slice the meat on the diagonal.

2. Arrange the slices overlapping each other on the plates. Moisten each portion with about ½ oz (15 ml) of the pan juices.

Variations

Chicken breasts can be used instead of the legs. Use either suprêmes (boneless) or cutlets (with the wing bone left in). Flatten the breasts with a meat mallet, stuff, and roll up starting from a long side.

Many different mixtures can be used for stuffing in place of the pecan butter. The following are a few suggestions:

Mushroom duxelles.

Mixture of dried fruits, such as prunes and apricots, soaked and simmered until soft, mixed with browned almond slices and sautéed minced onion.

Chopped smoked ham, flavored with shallots and sage.

Poached sweetbreads, marinated in brandy, cut into batonnet to fit the legs, and well seasoned with mixed herbs.

Lightly steamed mixed vegetables julienne or brunoise, seasoned with tarragon or with a pinch of cayenne and nutmeg, and moistened with a few drops of heavy cream or mixed with grated parmesan cheese.

Cooked wild rice mixed with chopped sautéed mushrooms (domestic or wild, such as morels or cèpes) and chives.

CHICKEN WITH SHELLFISH

		U.S.		Metric	
PORTIONS:		**4**	**16**	*4*	*16*
Ingredients					
Chicken parts		2 lb 4 oz	9 lb	*1 kg*	*4 kg*
Salt					
Pepper					
Shallots, chopped		½ oz	2 oz	*15 g*	*50 g*
Oil		1 oz	4 oz	*25 ml*	*1 dl*
Tomato, crushed		2 oz	8 oz	*50 g*	*200 g*
Chicken stock		4 oz	1 pt	*1 dl*	*4 dl*
Shellfish, preferably raw, without shells (see note)		8 oz	2 lb	*225 g*	*900 g*
Shellfish Sauce (p. 66) or Sauce Americaine (p. 62)		8 oz	1 qt	*2.5dl*	*1l*

Note: Use lobster, shrimp, scallops, crab, crayfish, or a mixture of any of these. You may name the dish after whatever shellfish you use, such as "Chicken with Lobster."

Mise en Place:

1. Cut up the chicken for sautéing. Season with salt and pepper.
2. Prepare the shellfish if necessary (clean, shell, etc.).
3. Prepare the sauce. Have it hot at service time.

Cooking/Finishing:

1. Brown the chicken lightly in oil. Remove the chicken from the pan and discard the fat.
2. Add the shallots to the pan and sauté 1 minute.
3. Add the tomato and stock. Return the chicken to the pan, cover, and cook over low heat or in the oven until almost done.
4. Remove the chicken from the pan. Strain and degrease the cooking liquid. Reduce it over moderate heat until nearly dry.
5. Return the chicken to the pan and add the sauce and shellfish. Heat gently just until the shellfish and chicken are cooked through.

Presentation:

Serve on a large plate with steamed rice or in a small cassolette.

Variation

Chicken Breast with Shellfish

Instead of braising a disjointed chicken, simply sauté or poach chicken suprêmes or cutlets, and serve them with the sauce and shellfish garnish.

CHICKEN BRAISED WITH VINEGAR

		U.S.		Metric	
PORTIONS:		**4**	**16**	*4*	*16*
Ingredients					
Chicken parts		2½–3 lb	10–12 lb	*1250 g*	*5 kg*
Oil					
Butter		½ oz	2 oz	*12 g*	*50 g*
Shallots		2 oz	8 oz	*50 g*	*200 g*
Carrots		2 oz	8 oz	*50 g*	*200 g*
Onion		2 oz	8 oz	*50 g*	*200 g*
Garlic		½ oz	2 oz	*12 g*	*50 g*
Tomato paste		½ oz	2 oz	*12 g*	*50 g*
Red wine vinegar		3 oz	12 oz	*75 ml*	*3 dl*
Tarragon		¼ tsp	1 tsp	*0.25 g*	*1 g*
Salt					
Pepper					
Demiglaze or strong chicken stock		4 oz	1 pt	*1 dl*	*4 dl*
Butter (optional)		1 oz	4 oz	*25 g*	*50 g*

Mise en Place:

1. Cut up the chicken for sautéing.

2. Mince the shallots, carrots, onion, and garlic.

Cooking/Finishing:

1. Brown the chicken in the oil. Remove the chicken and degrease the pan.

2. Add the butter to the pan and sauté the vegetables lightly.

3. Add the tomato paste, vinegar, tarragon, and salt and pepper. Return the chicken to the pan. Cover and braise until done.

4. Remove the chicken from the pan. Reduce the liquid by two-thirds over high heat.

5. Add the demiglaze. Simmer to reduce slightly and thicken the sauce. Strain the sauce and, if desired, monter au beurre. Adjust the seasonings.

Presentation:

Serve the chicken and sauce with buttered noodles.

Variations

Fricassée of Chicken with Tomato Cream

Tomato sauce	6 oz	1 ½ pt		*1.5 dl*	*6 dl*
Heavy cream	4 oz	1 pt		*1 dl*	*4 dl*

Omit the vinegar and tarragon from the basic recipe. Add the indicated quantity of tomato sauce to the braising liquid (see Cooking, step 3). After the chicken is cooked, do not reduce the cooking liquid by two-thirds, but only enough to get a saucelike consistency. In place of the raw butter, add the indicated quantity of heavy cream to the sauce and simmer a few minutes to thicken.

BRAISED TURKEY WITH SAUSAGES

		U.S.		Metric	
PORTIONS:		**4**	**16**	*4*	*16*
Ingredients					
Turkey parts (see note)		2 ½ lb	10 lb	*1125 g*	*4.5 kg*
Butter		1 oz	4 oz	*30 g*	*125 g*
Garlic		1 clove	4 cloves	*1 clove*	*4 cloves*
White wine		4 oz	1 pt	*125 ml*	*5 dl*
Demiglaze		8 oz	1 qt	*2.5 dl*	*1 l*
Tomato purée		4 oz	1 pt	*125 ml*	*5 dl*
Salt					
Pepper					
Italian pork sausages		4 oz	1 lb	*125 g*	*500 g*
Mushrooms		4 oz	1 lb	*125 g*	*500 g*
Butter					
Parsley, chopped					

Note: If you buy whole turkeys and use the breast meat for other purposes, this is a good way to use the wings and legs. The quantities indicated are for bone-in parts from young birds. You can also bone out the turkey and cut the meat into large dice. In this case, use about two-thirds of the quantities of turkey indicated.

Mise en Place:

1. Mince the garlic.

2. Brown the sausages and cut them into ½-inch (1-cm) slices.

3. If the mushrooms are small, leave them whole. Otherwise, cut them into halves or quarters.

Cooking/Finishing:

1. Brown the turkey in the butter.

2. Add the garlic and sauté a minute.

3. Add the white wine and reduce slightly. Add the demiglaze, tomato purée, and salt and pepper to taste. Cover and braise in a 325°F (165°C) oven.

4. After 15 minutes, add the sausages to the pan.

5. Brown the mushrooms in a little butter and add them to the pan so that they cook with the turkey for about the last 10 minutes of cooking time.

6. When the turkey is tender, remove the solids with a slotted spoon and keep them warm. Degrease the sauce and reduce over high heat to thicken to a sauce consistency. Adjust the seasonings.

7. Return the turkey, sausages, and mushrooms to the sauce. When plating, top each portion with a little chopped parsley.

Variations

Other ingredients or combinations of ingredients can be used instead of or in addition to the sausages and mushrooms, such as:

Green and red peppers, in large dice

Small onions, browned

Whole braised chestnuts (substitute for the mushrooms, but use twice as many)

Carrots, large dice or tournéed, glazed

Bacon lardons

Cooked artichoke hearts (added at the end)

Turkey with Sage

Omit the tomato purée, sausages, and mushrooms. Double the quantity of white wine and add a generous quantity of sage. As an option, substitute strong turkey or chicken stock for the demiglaze and, if desired, thicken the sauce with a little beurre manié.

ROAST DUCK WITH MANGOES

		U.S.		Metric	
PORTIONS:		4	16	4	16
Ingredients					
Mangoes, large		1	4	*1*	*4*
Sugar		1 tbsp	2 oz	*15 g*	*60 g*
Brandy or water		1 oz	4 oz	*30 ml*	*125 ml*
Lemon juice		1 tbsp	2 oz	*15 ml*	*50 ml*
Sugar		1 oz	4 oz	*30 g*	*125 g*
Red wine vinegar		1 oz	4 oz	*30 ml*	*125 ml*
Demiglaze or strong brown stock (see note 1)		8 oz	1 qt	*2.5 dl*	*1 l*
Red currant jelly		1 tbsp	4 tbsp	*15 g*	*60 g*
Salt					
Pepper					
Lemon juice					
Ducks, 5 ½ lb each (see note 2)		1	4	*1*	*4*
Salt					
Pepper					
Oil					
Stock (chicken, duck, or veal) or white wine		2 oz	8 oz	*60 ml*	*2.5 dl*

Note 1: If possible, use brown duck stock or demiglaze made with brown duck stock, or brown duck bones and trimmings and simmer them with regular demiglaze to give it a duck flavor.

Note 2: Instead of one large duck for four portions, you may use two small ones.

Mise en Place:

1. Peel the mangoes and cut them into thick slices as neatly and uniformly as possible. Simmer the slices slowly, covered, with the sugar, brandy or water, and lemon juice, for about 5 minutes, until tender but still firm and not mushy. Drain and reserve the juice.

2. Heat the sugar in a small saucepan over low heat until the sugar melts and caramelizes—do not let it get too dark. Remove from the heat and add the vinegar, keeping your face away from the pan. Add the demiglaze and the juice from the mangoes. Simmer until all the caramel has dissolved and the sauce is reduced slightly. Add the jelly. Adjust the seasonings with salt, pepper, and lemon juice. (*Note:* If the sauce is too thin, you can thicken it with a little cornstarch dissolved in cold stock.)

Cooking/Finishing:

1. Season the ducks inside and out and truss them for roasting.

2. Brown the ducks well on all sides in hot oil. As often as necessary, drain off the fat as it renders and accumulates in the pans.

3. Roast the ducks at 375°F (190°C) until done. Do not overcook.

4. Optional step: The ducks may be glazed during the last 5 or 10 minutes of roasting time. Make an extra quantity of sauce (about 4 oz or 125 ml per duck). Place the ducks on clean pans and baste them often with this extra sauce until they take on a shiny glaze.

5. Let the ducks stand in a warm place while you finish the sauce. Degrease the roasting pans and deglaze them with stock or wine. Strain the liquid into the sauce.

Presentation:

1. Carve the duck by cutting off the legs, cutting apart the thigh and drumstick, and slicing the breast.

2. For each portion, spoon a little of the sauce onto the plate. Top with some of the breast and some of the leg. Arrange a few warm mango slices around the duck.

Variations

The base of the sauce in this recipe is the foundation for many fruit sauces, both traditional and modern, that can be served with roast duck. In addition to the variations that follow, you can use the same procedure to make sauces flavored with such fruits as tangerine, grapefruit, raspberries, and cherries.

Roast Duck à l'Orange

Orange zest, julienne	of 2 oranges	of 8 oranges	*of 2 oranges*	*of 8 oranges*
Orange juice	3 oz	12 oz	*90 ml*	*3.5 dl*
Orange liqueur (optional)	1 oz	4 oz	*30 ml*	*125 ml*

Omit the mangoes in the basic recipe, as well as the sugar and liquids used to cook them. Blanch the julienne zest 2 to 3 minutes and drain. Add the zest, juice, and liqueur to the sauce base. Season with lemon juice as needed.

Roast Duck with Apples

Apples	3	12	*3*	*12*
Butter	1 oz	4 oz	*30 g*	*125 g*
Sugar	1 oz	4 oz	*30 g*	*125 g*
Calvados	2 oz	8 oz	*60 ml*	*2.5 dl*

Omit the mangoes and the sugar and liquids used to cook them. Sauté the apples in butter and sugar until golden brown. Drain the juice and add it and the calvados to the sauce base.

Roast Duck with Figs

Sugar	2 oz	8 oz	*60 g*	*250 g*
Red wine vinegar	1 ½ oz	6 oz	*45 ml*	*2 dl*
Fresh figs	6	24	*6*	*24*

Omit the mangoes and the sugar and liquids used to cook them. Increase the sugar and vinegar used to make the *gastrique* to the quantities indicated above. Chop two-thirds of the figs and add them to the caramelized sugar when making the *gastrique,* then add the vinegar. Add the demiglaze and simmer 30 minutes. Strain through a fine sieve. Omit the currant jelly, and season to taste with salt, pepper, and lemon juice. Quarter or slice the remaining figs and serve as garnish. They can be served raw or glazed by sautéing lightly in a little butter and sugar.

Roast Duck with Cassis

Crème de cassis or cassis syrup	1 ½ oz	6 oz	*45 ml*	*2 dl*

Omit the mangoes and the sugar and liquids used to cook them. Add the cassis to the sauce base. Adjust the seasonings.

Roast Duck with Port

Omit the fruit and sauce and serve the roast duck with Port Wine Sauce (page 59). If desired, garnish the duck with a few orange sections, raspberries, or other appropriate fruit.

Grilled or Sautéed Duck with Fruit Sauce

Grill or sauté duck breast or cut-up duck and serve each portion with about 1 ½ oz (45 ml) of any of the above sauces.

DUCK OR GOOSE CONFIT

		U.S.		Metric	
PORTIONS:		**4–6**	**16–24**	*4–6*	*16–24*
Ingredients					
Duck or goose parts, preferably legs		4 lb	16 lb	*1.8 kg*	*7.2 kg*
Salt		½ oz	2 oz	*15 g*	*60 g*
White pepper		½ tsp	2 tsp	*1 g*	*4 g*
Nutmeg		¼ tsp	1 tsp	*0.5 g*	*2 g*
Powdered bay leaf		¼ tsp	1 tsp	*0.5 g*	*2 g*
Ground cloves		pinch	½ tsp	*pinch*	*1 g*
Extra duck or goose fat as needed					

Procedure:

1. Trim off excess fat from the duck or goose and reserve.

2. Rub the duck or goose pieces with the salt, herbs, and spices. Refrigerate overnight.

3. Render the trimmed fat, plus as much extra fat as needed. You will need enough rendered duck or goose fat to completely cover the poultry pieces.

4. Put the duck or goose and the rendered fat in a brazier, large saucepan, or casserole. Simmer gently in the fat over low heat or in a 300°F (150°C) oven until very tender, about 1 ½ to 2 hours for duck, 2 to 3 hours for goose.

5. Remove the cooked poultry from the fat and pack into a clean crock or other container. Pour the melted fat over the meat so that it is completely covered, but be careful not to pour in any of the juices. (The degreased juices may be used for another purpose, such as cooking beans.)

6. Remove pieces of meat and use as needed. For best storage, remaining pieces must be kept covered by the fat. The confit can be used in Cassoulet (pages 448–450), or it may be browned in a little of the fat until heated through and served with such accompaniments as braised cabbage, cooked white beans, or sautéed potatoes with garlic, or on a bed of salad greens that have been wilted with a little of the hot fat.

DUCK BREAST WITH SALSIFY (Color Plate 11)

		U.S.		Metric	
PORTIONS:		**4**	**16**	*4*	*16*
Ingredients					
Sugar		2 oz	8 oz	*60 g*	*250 g*
Sherry vinegar		2 oz	8 oz	*60 ml*	*2.5 dl*
Strong brown stock or brown duck stock		8 oz	1 qt	*2.5 dl*	*1 l*
Salt					
Salsify		10 oz	2 ½ lb	*300 g*	*1.2 kg*
Butter, as needed					
Boneless duck breasts, skin on		4	16	*4*	*16*
Salt					
Pepper					
Brown stock		4 oz	1 pt	*125 ml*	*5 dl*
Butter		2 oz	8 oz	*60 g*	*250 g*

Mise en Place:

1. Caramelize the sugar in a small saucepan. Add the vinegar and the first quantity of brown stock. Simmer until the caramel is dissolved and the sauce is reduced by one-half. Season to taste.
2. Blanch the salsify in boiling water for 2 to 3 minutes. Drain, peel, and cut into 1-inch (2.5-cm) lengths. Brown the salsify slowly in butter, then add to the sauce and simmer until tender. Remove the salsify from the sauce and keep the salsify and sauce separately. Keep them warm or reheat them to order.

Cooking/Finishing:

1. Season the duck breasts with salt and pepper.
2. In a heavy sauté pan over moderate heat, cook the duck breasts skin side down until the skin is well browned. Keep the meat rare. Drain off the fat as it accumulates in the pan.
3. Turn the breasts over and brown the other side for about 30 seconds. Remove them from the pan and keep them warm.
4. Degrease the pan and deglaze with the second quantity of brown stock. Strain into the sauce, and reduce the sauce to its original volume. Stir in the raw butter to finish the sauce. (If desired, you may thicken the sauce with a little beurre manié, but it should not be too thick.)

Presentation:

1. For each portion, put an ounce (25 ml) of sauce on a plate. Slice the duck breast on the diagonal and fan out the slices on the lower half of the plate.
2. Place a few pieces of the salsify above the duck slices. Garnish with a selection of vegetables, as desired.

Variations

For the preceding recipe or any of the following variations, you may grill the breasts instead of sautéing them, or you may use other duck parts.

Duck breast or other parts for sautéing or grilling can be rubbed with herbs or spices mixed with a little salt. Let them stand several hours or overnight before cooking to allow the seasonings to penetrate. Some suggestions:

Rub with thyme, sage, powdered bay leaf, crushed garlic, and black pepper. Serve as in the basic recipe or the green peppercorn variation, or with a red wine sauce.

Rub with allspice, pepper, and a pinch of cinnamon. Serve with one of the fruit sauces (mango, orange, etc.) in the roast duck recipe.

Rub with ground sichuan pepper and star anise. Serve with chicken stock flavored with soy sauce and lightly thickened with cornstarch.

Duck Breast with Sweet Potatoes

Omit the salsify. Steam whole sweet potatoes (enough for about 2 oz or 60 g per portion) until about half done. Peel and slice. Cook the slices in butter until lightly browned and cooked through. Prepare the sauce as in the basic recipe, but use red wine vinegar instead of sherry vinegar. (Do not cook the sweet potatoes in the sauce.)

Duck Breast with Turnip, Carrots, or Celery Root

Substitute one of the above vegetables, cut batonnet or tournéed, for the salsify.

Duck Breast with Roasted Shallots

Omit the salsify. Garnish the finished dish with Roasted Shallots (page 522).

Duck Breast with Mustard

Dijon-style mustard	1 oz	4 oz	30 g	125 g

Substitute red wine vinegar for the sherry vinegar, and use only one-half the quantity. Add the above quantity of mustard to the sauce.

Duck Breast with Green Peppercorns

For each portion, add 1 tsp (2 g) green peppercorns to 1 ½ oz (45 ml) of one of the following sauces: Red Wine Sauce (page 58), Red Wine Sauce with Garlic (page 58), or Brown Sauce Thickened with Vegetable Purée (page 55). If desired, add a pinch of sugar or a dash of port wine to the sauce. Serve with sautéed or grilled duck breast.

BRAISED DUCKLING WITH PEAS

		U.S.		Metric	
PORTIONS:		4	16	4	16
Ingredients					
Salt pork or slab bacon		4 oz	1 lb	125 g	500 g
Pearl onions, peeled		4 oz	1 lb	125 g	500 g
Butter		2 oz	8 oz	60 g	250 g
Whole ducklings		2	8	2	8
Brown stock or duck stock		4 oz	1 pt	125 ml	5 dl
Demiglaze		8 oz	1 qt	2.5 dl	1 l
Thyme		¼ tsp	1 tsp	0.25 g	1 g
Parsley stems		5–6	20	5–6	20
Bay leaf		½	2	½	2
Peas		12 oz	3 lb	375 g	1.5 kg
Salt					
Pepper					

Mise en Place:

1. Cut the salt pork or bacon into batonnet. Blanch by putting it into cold water, bringing to a boil, and draining.

2. Brown the pork in butter. Remove with a slotted spoon. Brown the onions in the same fat. Drain and save a little of the fat for browning the duck.

3. The ducklings may be left whole or cut into quarters.

4. Tie the herbs in a piece of cheesecloth.

Cooking/Finishing:

1. Brown the duck well on all sides and discard the rendered fat.

2. Deglaze the pan with the stock. Return the duck to the pan and add the demiglaze, herbs, and browned pork or bacon, and braise in a 325°F (165°C) oven until tender, about 1 hour.

3. After about 30 minutes of cooking time, add the onions and braise them with the duck. *Note:* If you are braising whole ducks, you may glaze them if you wish (see page 344).

4. When the duck is tender, remove it from the pan. Remove the pork and onions with a slotted spoon and keep them warm with the duck.

5. Strain and degrease the liquid. Add the peas. Boil to cook the peas and reduce the liquid by one-half. Adjust the seasonings.

6. Combine all ingredients and serve.

Variations

Braised Duckling with Turnips

Omit the peas and bacon in the basic recipe. Tourné some turnips and brown them slowly in butter. Add them to the duck at the same time as the onions.

Braised Duckling with Olives

Pit some good-quality green olives (about 2 oz or 60 g per portion) and blanch them in boiling water for 1 to 2 minutes to eliminate the briny taste. Prepare the duck as in the basic recipe, but omit the peas and use white wine instead of the brown stock. Just before serving, add the olives.

Braised Duckling with Cabbage

Omit the peas and instead use an equal quantity of shredded savoy cabbage. Prepare the duck as in the basic recipe, but omit the onions and demiglaze. While the duckling is cooking, sauté the cabbage in a little of the rendered duck fat. Moisten with a little stock to keep it from scorching, and braise the cabbage until tender but still bright green. To serve, moisten the cabbage with some of the duck cooking liquid. Serve the remainder of the liquid as a sauce for moistening the duck.

ROAST SQUAB WITH MUSHROOMS

		U.S.		Metric	
PORTIONS:		**4**	**16**	**4**	**16**
Ingredients					
Stuffing:					
Bacon		2 oz	8 oz	*50 g*	*200 g*
Squab livers		4	16	*4*	*16*
Carrots		2 oz	8 oz	*50 g*	*200 g*
Onion		4 oz	1 lb	*100 g*	*400 g*
Garlic cloves		2	8	*2*	*8*
Rosemary		1 tsp	4 tsp	*1 g*	*4 g*
Butter		1 oz	4 oz	*25 g*	*100 g*
Squabs		4	16	*4*	*16*
Salt					
Pepper					
Butter for browning and roasting the squabs					
Mushrooms		4 oz	1 lb	*100 g*	*400 g*
Shallots		1 oz	4 oz	*25 g*	*100 g*
Butter		1 oz	4 oz	*25 g*	*100 g*
White stock		1 pt	2 qt	*4 dl*	*16 dl*
Butter		1 oz	4 oz	*25 g*	*100 g*
Salt					
Pepper					
Garnish:					
Watercress					

Mise en Place:

1. Chop all the stuffing ingredients fine and sauté them together lightly in the butter. Reserve.

2. Season the squabs inside and out. Stuff them with the stuffing mixture and truss them for roasting. *Caution:* If you are not stuffing the birds immediately before cooking, the stuffing must be completely cooled to avoid spoilage.

3. Cut the mushrooms and shallots into small dice.

Cooking/Finishing:

1. In a sauté pan, brown the squabs on all sides in butter.

2. In a roasting pan or in the same sauté pan, put the squabs on their sides and brush with some fresh butter. Put into a very hot oven (500°F or 260°C) and roast them for 5 minutes on one side. Turn them to the other side and roast another 5 minutes, then turn them breast up for a final 5 to 6 minutes. Baste regularly with butter during the roasting period.

3. Remove them from the oven. They should be slightly rare. Cut off the legs (and if they are too rare, return them to the oven for another minute). Cut off each side of the breast in one piece, keeping the skin intact. Cover and keep warm.

4. While the squab is roasting, sauté the mushrooms and shallots in butter until nearly dry. Reserve.

5. Chop the carcass and put the carcass and stuffing into a pan with the stock. Boil for 5 minutes, pressing down on the solids to help extract flavors.

6. Strain through a fine sieve, pressing down on the solids to squeeze out as much liquid as possible. Degrease the liquid and reduce by one-half. Monter au beurre with the last quantity of butter and adjust the seasonings.

Presentation:

1. For each portion, spoon a little of the mushrooms onto the center of the plate.

2. Arrange the breast pieces and legs of the squab symmetrically on top of the mushrooms.

3. Spoon the sauce around the squab.

4. Garnish with a bunch of watercress at the top of the plate.

SALMIS OF PARTRIDGE

		U.S.		Metric	
PORTIONS:		**4**	**16**	*4*	*16*
Ingredients					
Partridges, about 1 lb (500 g) each		2	8	*2*	*8*
Salt					
Pepper					
Butter, for roasting					
Shallots		1 oz	4 oz	*30 g*	*125 g*
Butter		½ oz	2 oz	*15 g*	*60 g*
Peppercorns, crushed		3–4	12–15	*3–4*	*12–15*
Red wine		10 oz	2½ pt	*3 dl*	*12 dl*
Demiglaze		4 oz	1 pt	*125 ml*	*5 dl*
Butter		2 oz	8 oz	*60 g*	*250 g*

Mise en Place:

1. Season and truss the partridges for roasting.

2. Chop the shallots.

Cooking/Finishing:

1. Brush the partridges with butter and roast them in a hot oven (475°F or 250°C), keeping them rare.

2. Cut off the legs. Put them under the broiler for a few minutes with the insides toward the heat.

3. Remove the skin from the breasts and carve them in long, thin slices. Arrange them on a platter and keep them warm.

4. Chop the carcass. Sauté it with the shallots in a little butter.

5. Add the peppercorns and wine. Reduce by two-thirds.

6. Add the demiglaze and bring to a boil. Strain through a fine sieve, pressing down on the solids to squeeze out as much liquid as possible. Adjust the seasonings of the sauce and monter au beurre.

Presentation:

Coat the slices of breast meat with the sauce. Place the legs around the outside of the platter and heat for 1 or 2 minutes in the oven. Serve at once.

Variations

This recipe can be prepared with any of the following in place of the partridge. The number of birds to use will depend on their size.

Pheasant
Squab
Wild duck
Guinea hen

This recipe can be prepared using white wine instead of red wine.

Salmis Rouennaise

Strictly speaking, a salmis Rouennaise is made with Rouen ducks (see page 288). Nevertheless, you can make a salmis in a similar style using other birds. Three methods are suggested:

1. Follow the basic recipe above, but add the birds' puréed livers to the sauce (see page 291).

2. Follow the basic recipe, but omit the demiglaze and pepper and use only half the wine. Reduce the wine (see Cooking, step 5) and strain it into a prepared Rouennaise Sauce (page 47).

3. If a duck press is available, press the carcass with a little red wine. Add this liquid to Rouennaise sauce.

SAUTÉED SQUAB WITH HAZELNUTS

		U.S.		Metric	
PORTIONS:		4	16	4	16
Ingredients					
Squabs		4	16	4	16
Brandy		3 oz	12 oz	75 ml	3 dl
Bay leaves		6	24	6	24
Garlic cloves, chopped		1	4	1	4
Salt					
Pepper					
Oil					
Butter		1 oz	4 oz	25 g	100 g
Hazelnuts		2 oz	8 oz	50 g	200 g
Glace de viande		1 oz	4 oz	25 g	100 g
Butter		1 oz	4 oz	25 g	100 g
Salt					
Pepper					
Lemon juice					

Mise en Place:

1. Cut the squabs into halves or quarters. Marinate overnight with the brandy, bay leaves, garlic, and salt and pepper to taste.

2. Skin the hazelnuts by toasting them on a tray in a moderate oven for 10 to 15 minutes, then rubbing off the skins in a towel. Chop them coarsely.

Cooking/Finishing:

1. Remove the squab and bay leaves from the marinade. Sauté the squab with the bay leaves in hot oil until they are done. (Or, if preferred, brown them in the oil and finish them in the oven, uncovered.)

2. Remove them from the pan and keep them warm. Degrease the pan.

3. Put the butter in the pan. Return the bay leaves to the pan and add the nuts. Brown them lightly.

4. Add the reserved brandy marinade to the pan and flame it. Remove the bay leaves. Add the glace de viande and let it melt. Immediately before serving, stir in the last quantity of butter. Season this nut/butter mixture to taste with salt, pepper, and a few drops of lemon juice.

Presentation

1. Plate the squabs and spoon the nut butter over the tops of them.

2. Serve with your choice of vegetables on the plate. Potatoes browned in butter make an excellent accompaniment to this dish.

Variations

Sautéed Quail with Hazelnuts

Substitute two quail for each squab. Bone the quail as shown in Figure 7.7. Prepare as in basic recipe, but reduce the cooking time accordingly—the boned quail will cook to doneness in only a few minutes.

Other poultry, such as small chickens and cornish hens, can also be used in this recipe.

The squabs or other poultry may be broiled or grilled instead of sautéed, or they may be left whole and roasted. Do not broil the bay leaves from the marinade with the birds, but use them in the preparation of the nut butter (see Cooking, steps 3 and 4).

Other nuts, such as walnuts, may be substituted for the hazelnuts.

PHEASANT EN COCOTTE

		U.S.		Metric	
PORTIONS:		4	16	4	16
Ingredients					
Pheasant (see note for quantities)					
Salt					
Pepper					
Fresh pork fatback or bacon, for barding					
Butter		1 oz	4 oz	25 g	100 g
Optional: brandy		1 oz	4 oz	25 ml	1 dl
Tiny white onions		4 oz	1 lb	100 g	400 g
Small new potatoes		8 oz	2 lb	200 g	800 g
Butter		½ oz	2 oz	15 g	50 g
Brown stock or demiglaze		4 oz	1 pt	1 dl	4 dl

Note: Pheasants vary considerably in size. A large pheasant of around 3 pounds (1.4 kg) will make 4 portions, although such large birds may not be of the best quality. Pheasants of around 2 pounds (900 g) are large enough for 2 portions, while baby pheasants may make 1 portion.

Mise en Place:

1. Season and truss the pheasants. Bard with thin slices of pork fat or bacon (see Figure 7.9). If you are using bacon, first soak it for several hours in water to extract some of the salt and smoky flavor.

2. Peel the onions and potatoes. Brown them in the second quantity of butter, then cover them and let them steam over low heat until they are about half cooked. They will finish cooking with the pheasant.

Cooking/Finishing:

1. In a casserole just large enough to hold the birds, brown the pheasants well in butter over moderate heat, making sure that all sides are browned.

2. If the butter has burned during the browning, wipe out the casserole or transfer the birds to a clean casserole and add a little fresh butter.

3. Add the brandy, if it is being used. Also add the onions and potatoes. Cover tightly and place in a 375°F (190°C) oven. Cook until done, about 30 to 45 minutes for larger birds, 15 to 30 minutes for smaller ones. Halfway through the cooking time, remove the barding fat and baste the birds with butter.

4. When the pheasant is done, remove it from the casserole and keep it warm. Deglaze the casserole with the stock and reduce it slightly.

Presentation:

The pheasant, with its vegetable garnish and sauce, may be sent to the dining room in its own casserole, to be carved and plated by the dining room staff. Or it can be carved in the kitchen. Cut off the legs and, if they are large, cut the thighs and drumsticks apart. For small pheasants, cut off each side of the breast in one piece; for large pheasants, slice the breasts. Plate the pheasant with the vegetable garnish and moisten it with a spoonful of the sauce. This is a hearty dish which, with its garnish, should fill out the plate.

Variations

Poêléed Pheasant

For a regular poêlé, refer to the procedure on page 277.

Other birds, such as partridges, guinea hens, small chickens, or cornish hens, may be prepared according to this recipe.

Other garnishes may be used in place of the onions and potatoes, such as:

Mushrooms
Cabbage, blanched and sautéed in a little pork fat
Whole chestnuts, cooked separately
Peas
Sliced artichoke bottoms

QUAIL BAKED WITH PROSCIUTTO AND HERBS

		U.S.		Metric	
PORTIONS:		4	16	4	16
Ingredients					
Butter		1 oz	4 oz	30 g	125 g
Sage, crumbled		2 tsp	3 tbsp	2 g	10 g
Rosemary, crumbled		½ tsp	2 tsp	0.5 g	2 g
Parsley, chopped		1 tbsp	4 tbsp	3 g	15 g
Salt					
Pepper					
Quails		8	32	8	32
Prosciutto, sliced paper-thin		8 slices	32 slices	8 slices	32 slices
Optional sauce:					
Balsamic vinegar or red wine vinegar		1 oz	4 oz	30 ml	125 ml
Chicken stock		2 oz	8 oz	60 ml	2.5 dl

Mise en Place:

1. Melt the butter. Add the herbs and seasonings.
2. Brush the quails heavily with the herb butter. Wrap each quail in a slice of prosciutto.

Cooking/Finishing:

1. Place the quails in a covered casserole just large enough to hold them. Cover and bake at 400°F (200°C) until done, about 30 minutes.
2. When they are done, remove the quails from the casserole and keep them warm. Without degreasing it, deglaze the pan with the vinegar and reduce *au sec*. Add the chicken stock and bring to a boil.

Presentation:

For each portion, place a tablespoon of the sauce on the plate. Set two quail on top. Garnish with your choice of vegetable accompaniment—braised fennel is an excellent choice.

Variations

Chicken, squab, and guinea hens can be cooked using this recipe. Cut them into pieces and wrap each piece with a slice of prosciutto. If desired, the skin can be removed before the pieces are brushed with the herb butter.

Stuffed Quail Baked with Prosciutto and Herbs

Bone the quails as shown in Figure 7.8. Stuff with cooked, buttered wild rice mixed with sautéed, chopped mushrooms and shallots.

GLAZED QUAIL WITH GARLIC TIMBALE

		U.S.		Metric	
PORTIONS:		4	16	*4*	*16*
Ingredients					
Quail		4	16	*4*	*16*
Butter, for cooking, as needed					
Carrot, chopped		2 oz	8 oz	*60 g*	*250 g*
Onion, chopped		2 oz	8 oz	*60 g*	*250 g*
Leeks, chopped		2 oz	8 oz	*60 g*	*250 g*
Honey		2 tbsp	½ cup	*30 ml*	*125 ml*
Garlic, chopped		½ clove	2 cloves	*½ clove*	*2 cloves*
Red wine vinegar		1½ oz	6 oz	*50 ml*	*2 dl*
Soy sauce		1 oz	4 oz	*30 ml*	*125 ml*
Chicken stock		1 pt	2 qt	*5 dl*	*2 l*
Lemon juice					
Salt					
Garlic Timbales (p. 535)		4	16	*4*	*16*

Mise en Place:

1. Bone the quail following the procedure illustrated in Figure 7.7. Chop the bones coarsely.

2. Heat enough butter to cover the bottom of a saucepan. Add the chopped carrot, onion, and leeks and the chopped quail bones. Brown lightly.

3. Add the honey and continue to brown the vegetables and bones until well caramelized. Be careful not to let them burn.

4. Add the garlic, vinegar, and soy sauce to deglaze the pan. Add the chicken stock and bring to a simmer. Simmer until the liquid is reduced by two-thirds.

5. Strain. Season with lemon juice and salt.

Cooking:

1. In a sauté pan, brown the quail on both sides in butter, until about half cooked.

2. Baste the quail with a little of the sauce. Continue to cook the quail, turning and basting with additional sauce, until they are cooked to desired doneness and well browned and glazed.

Presentation:

1. Plate the quail, skin side up. Garnish each plate with a garlic timbale.

2. Serve the remaining sauce separately.

Variation

The portion size of this recipe makes it more appropriate for a first course, a luncheon dish, or one of the courses in a multicourse dinner. For a larger dinner portion, double all quantities and serve two quail per portion.

Squab can be cooked and served using the same procedure.

CHAPTER

8

Beef, Lamb, Pork, and Veal

We began the two previous chapters by noting that the consumption of fish and poultry has increased markedly in this country, due in part to a concern with health and diet. In addition, greater availability of many kinds of fish and poultry has attracted attention on restaurant menus. As a result, Americans are eating less meat than they once did.

Nevertheless, we are still primarily a nation of meat eaters. Chefs have responded to consumer demands not by abandoning meats but by applying to them the same imagination and creativity that they apply to fish and poultry. Meat selections on menus are more varied. Lighter treatment is the hallmark of many of the new-style dishes; portions are smaller, and sauces, seasonings, and garnish are used in more innovative ways. At the same time, cooks have been taking a new look at many classic preparations and have been finding ways to present them, refreshed and reawakened, on modern menus.

Rather than dwell at length on basic cooking methods that are already familiar to you, we will look at some special procedures and concentrate on various techniques and recipes that are particularly useful for today's menus.

TOUGHNESS AND MOIST-HEAT COOKING METHODS

Preparation and cooking techniques suitable for various cuts of meat depend in large part on the composition and structure of meat in general and of the individual cuts in particular. This is why it is helpful to understand such details as connective tissue, fat content and distribution, and the reaction of protein to heat, as well as the related subjects of inspection, grading, aging, and identification of standard cuts. One of these topics, the reaction of protein to heat, perhaps needs a little clarification before we begin to consider preparation and cooking techniques.

The heat of cooking, you will recall, affects tenderness in two ways:

1. It shrinks and toughens protein. This process, called coagulation, also results in loss of moisture. Even naturally tender cuts are toughened by overcooking.
2. It tenderizes collagen, if moisture is present. Even the toughest cuts, such as beef shank, can be made tender and moist by proper cooking.

Collagen is one of two kinds of connective tissue found in meats; the other is elastin. Because collagen can be broken down by proper cooking, tougher cuts of meat can be made tender, but only if they are cooked correctly. (Elastin is not broken down by cooking, but it is usually found concentrated in tendons that can be cut away, and is not as well distributed through the meat tissue as collagen is.)

The usual explanation of this process is that *moist heat*, applied over a relatively long period of time, breaks down the connective tissue, converting it to gelatin and water. This is essentially correct for nearly all practical applications. Technically, however, it is not totally accurate.

Meat is about 75 percent water. This means that we are not really saying anything meaningful if we say that heat breaks down collagen in the presence of moisture. Moisture is always present, whether we are using a moist-heat method, such as simmering or braising, or a dry-heat method, such as roasting or broiling.

This means that it is the *length of time that meat is subjected to heat* that affects how much connective tissue is broken down—no matter what cooking method is used. This has been confirmed by laboratory tests. It is long, slow cooking, rather than moist-heat cooking methods, that enables us to prepare tough meats so that they are tender.

Of course, the cooking methods requiring long cooking times are, for the most part, moist-heat methods, namely, braising, stewing, and simmering. To put it another way, the so-called moist-heat methods involve *both* long, slow cooking and the presence of moisture around, not just inside, the meat.

Dry-heat methods, such as broiling, frying, and sautéing, on the other hand, are quick cooking methods. The reason for this is obvious. Foods would dry out if cooked by these methods for very long.

The case of roasting is a little more complicated. The length of time needed to roast a piece of meat to a given degree of doneness depends upon its thickness. The thicker the meat, the longer it takes for heat to penetrate to the interior. Remember, however, that heat toughens and drives out moisture from proteins at the same time that it tenderizes collagen. This is why small, tough pieces of meat, such as lamb shanks, would become shrunken and dried out in the oven long before they ever had a chance to become tender.

By contrast, a 40-pound steamship round of beef, which requires many hours in the oven, makes a magnificent roast, even though beef round has more connective tissue than the really tender cuts. If you cut that same piece of beef into small steaks, they would be too chewy for first-class eating. Furthermore, cutting meat into smaller pieces creates more surface area, which means more area from which moisture can escape.

In theory, if we had a 40-pound lamb shank, we could probably roast it successfully, too. Unfortunately, it's not likely that we will have a chance to actually try it, unless animal breeders are able to develop an extraordinarily large sheep.

Rather than simply recommending moist-heat cooking for certain meats, let us take the following two-step approach to the problem:

1. If a meat is naturally tough due to a high collagen content, it can be made tender by long, slow cooking.
2. The smaller the cut of meat, the more likely it is to dry out over a long exposure to dry heat. It is then necessary to use a procedure that will preserve or add moisture. There are two basic techniques for cooking small, tough cuts of meat without drying them out:
   a. Use a liquid cooking medium.
   b. Cook in a closed container to prevent the evaporation of moisture.

JUICINESS

There are three main factors that determine the juiciness, or more accurately the *perception* of juiciness, in cooked meat. Despite the myths about basting with stock and about searing meat to "seal in the juices," the following are the only factors that have any significant effect on juiciness.

1. *Internal Fat*

Fat makes meat taste juicy. This is why well-marbled meats taste juicier than lean meats. We understand the health effects of too much fat in the diet; however, there is no getting around the fact that high fat content makes meat taste juicier. When lean meats are cooked, other measures (such as using sauces and especially avoiding overcooking) are used to increase palatability.

2. *Gelatin*

This factor is most important in braised meats. Gelatin, converted from connective tissue, helps to bind water molecules and hold them in the meat. Also, the texture of the gelatin improves the texture of the meat in the mouth. This is why braised beef shank tastes so much juicier than braised bottom round.

3. *Protein Coagulation*

As you know, as protein coagulates or is cooked, it breaks down and begins to lose water. The more it is cooked, the more it contracts and forces out moisture. No matter how much you try to "sear to seal in the juices," this moisture will be lost. The only way to minimize this loss is to avoid overcooking.

COOKING LARGE CUTS

There are many ways of classifying meat cooking techniques: by cooking method, by type of meat, and so on. One classification used by many chefs trained in the classical traditions is to divide all meat preparations into large meat dishes and small meat dishes. This classification has its origins in the structure of nineteenth-century banquet menus, in which small meat and poultry items (called *entrées*), large braised cuts, and roasts were served as separate courses.

Today this classification is still a useful one for professional cooks because, for the most part, it distinguishes between those dishes that can be cooked to order, one portion at a time, and those that must be cooked a little ahead of time and then cut to order.

Dishes such as stews don't quite fit this pattern because the meat cuts are small while the cooking times are long. Nevertheless, since stew making shares many techniques with the preparation of other small meat dishes, we will follow the traditional classification in our discussion.

In the finer restaurants, large meat dishes are less prominent on the menu than in the past. Foods cooked to order are seen as being more in tune with today's cooking styles and thus get most of the attention. Nevertheless, one or two well-selected roasts or braised items, perhaps offered as daily specials, can help round out the menu and take a little of the pressure off the kitchen during peak hours. Of course, large meat items will always play an important role on banquet and party menus.

The information in this section is intended to supplement understanding of the basic cooking methods for large meat items—namely roasting, braising, and simmering. First, we will discuss the technique of braising as it was practiced in classical kitchens earlier in this century. Next we will examine miscellaneous other topics related to roasting, braising, and simmering.

Classical Braising

The term *braising* usually means to brown or partially cook by a dry-heat method, generally with fat, and then to cook in a covered pan in a small amount of liquid until done. In classical cuisine, however, the braising process is more complicated. There are several versions of classical braising, but the following procedures describe the general pattern.

It is interesting to review these procedures from a historical standpoint, but there is a practical as well as theoretical purpose for reexamining these classical procedures. All too often in today's kitchens, braised dishes are not considered as "glamorous" as grilled and sautéed dishes. By understanding the care and attention that was once devoted to braised meats, we can perhaps raise the quality and menu appeal of our own braisings.

Classical Procedure for Braising Red Meats

1. *Lard the meat if it is lean.*

Larding, the insertion of strips of fat into the meat, is explained on page 350. Well-marbled meats, such as ribs of beef, do not need to be larded; they already have enough interior fat to keep them moist. On the other hand, such cuts as beef round and leg of lamb are leaner, and they are more likely to become dry when braised. Larding can improve the palatability of the product.

2. *Prepare the aromatics for the braising.*

The aromatics consist of a mirepoix lightly browned in fat and the desired herbs tied into a bouquet garni or a cheesecloth sachet.

3. *Season the meat with salt and pepper and then marinate it for several hours or longer.*

This step is sometimes omitted, but it is recommended. A marinade for classical braised meats consists of red or white wine plus the aromatics from step 2. See page 352 for more information.

4. *Remove the meat from the marinade, drain it, and dry it well.*

5. *Select a braising pan just large enough to hold the meat and the aromatics. Heat some oil or meat fat in the pan and brown the meat well on all sides.*

It is important to use a braising pan that is the right size. If it is too big, you will need to add too much braising liquid. The flavor of the sauce then will be too diluted, resulting in a mediocre dish.

6. *If the meat is lean, you may bard it at this point.*

Barding, which means covering the meat all around with thin sheets of fat and tying it, protects the meat from drying. This is the same technique often used to protect the breast meat of lean poultry during roasting (see page 295).

7. *Put the aromatics from the marinade on the bottom of the braising pan and lay the meat on top of them. Pour in the wine from the marinade.*

If you have not marinated the meat, you can sauté a fresh mirepoix in the braising pan after browning the meat. Add a bouquet garni and return the meat to the pan. In place of marinade, add a small amount of wine or substitute brown stock.

8. *Set the pan over moderate heat. Reduce the wine to a glaze, basting the meat frequently with the liquid as it reduces.*

The instructions of Escoffier and other classic authorities are to cover the pan during this operation so that the heat surrounds the meat and it doesn't cook just from the bottom. Naturally, the cover should be a loose-fitting one; if the pan is covered tightly, the liquid can't reduce.

9. *Add a rich brown stock to the pan.*

The amount of stock added should be based on the amount needed for the sauce. Since the stock will be reduced by about one-half during cooking, this means that you need 3 to 4 oz (1 dl) of stock per portion. If you have used the proper size pan (see step 5), this amount of stock will cover the meat by one-third or more.

10. *Cover the pan and put it in an oven at about 300°F (150°C). Let it cook until there are no traces of red blood in the juices that appear when the meat is pierced deeply with a skewer. Baste the meat occasionally as it cooks.*

11. *Remove the meat from the cooking liquid. Strain and degrease the liquid.*

At this point, you may either proceed directly to step 12, or you may enrich the braising liquid as follows: Reduce it by one-half and then bring it back to its original volume by adding some demiglaze, plain espagnole sauce, or espagnole to which a little tomato purée has been added.

12. *Put the meat and the liquid in a clean braising pan and return it to the oven. Let it cook, basting frequently, until the meat is tender.*

13. *If desired, the meat may be glazed, as explained in the procedure on page 344.*

14. *Remove the meat from the sauce again. Finish the sauce.*

Strain and degrease it again. Adjust the consistency by reducing it slightly, by thickening it with a roux or other thickening agent, or, if it is too thick, by adding a little stock. Check for seasoning. Hold the sauce separately, serving it with the meat when it is sliced.

Classical Procedure for Braising White Meats

The braising of white meats—veal and pork, as well as poultry—is nearly the same as the braising of red meats, except that the second stage of cooking in the sauce (step 12 in the preceding procedure) is omitted. The reason for this is that white meats are usually more tender than red meats used for braising, so this extended braising is unnecessary.

1. *Season the meat. Brown it in butter or other fat.*
   White meats are usually browned only lightly.

2. *Remove the meat from the pan. In the same pan, lightly brown the mirepoix.*

3. *Add a bouquet garni or herb sachet to the pan and put the meat on top of the mirepoix and herbs.*

4. *Add a little brown veal stock to the pan. Reduce the stock over moderate heat, while basting the meat, until the stock is reduced to a glaze.*

Note that this step corresponds to the reduction of the wine marinade in the procedure for braising red meats. If desired, white wine can be used instead of or in addition to the veal stock in the procedure for white meats.

5. *Add a little more stock and again reduce to a glaze, continuing to baste the meat.*
   This step is often omitted.

6. *Add enough stock to serve as the braising liquid, cover the pan, and set it in a moderate oven to braise.*

Less stock is used for braising white meats than for braising red meats. White meats are often glazed (see the section that follows), and a smaller quantity of concentrated liquid makes this operation easier. Furthermore, the cooking time for white meats is generally less, so the liquid has less time to reduce.

7. *Baste the meat occasionally while it is cooking. The meat is done when the juices run clear, not red or pink, when the meat is pierced with a skewer.*

8. *Shortly before it is done, the meat may be glazed, if desired.*

See the section that follows.

9. *Remove the meat from the pan. Strain and degrease the braising liquid and finish the gravy or sauce as desired.*

Reduce the liquid or add stock as necessary, thicken it as desired, and adjust the seasoning.

Glazing Braised Meats. Braised meats can be glazed after cooking. *Glaze* is a thin coating of the reduced, gelatinous cooking liquid. It is applied by basting the meat repeatedly with the cooking liquid, so that the moisture evaporates, leaving a layer of *glace de viande* on the meat.

The main purpose of glazing is to enhance the appearance of braised meats; it is especially effective with white meats. Glazed meats look nicely browned, shiny, and juicy. This procedure is used most often for meats that are presented and carved in the dining room.

The glazing operation will work well only if a good, strong, gelatinous stock was used for the braising liquid.

Procedure for Glazing Braised Meats

1. During the last stage of braising, when the meat is nearly done, remove the cover from the braising pan. If the braising liquid is well reduced, you can leave the meat and liquid in the same pan. However, if the liquid covers most of the meat, either remove most of the liquid from the pan or put the meat in another pan. This exposes the surface of the meat so that it can be basted.

2. Leaving the meat in the oven, baste it well with the cooking liquid.

3. Repeat this basting every few minutes, until the meat is nicely glazed.

4. Remove the meat from the oven and keep it warm for service.

5. With the remaining braising liquid, prepare the sauce or gravy as in the basic braising procedures.

Poêléing Meats. The technique of *poêléing* or poêlage could be said to be somewhere in between braising and roasting. Poêléed meats are cooked slowly in a covered container; however, unlike braising, no liquid is added to the pot. This procedure is intended only for fine quality, tender meats. Poêléing is discussed in detail in chapter 7 (see page 277 for the procedure).

Roasting

Roasting is generally defined as a dry-heat cooking method in which the food is surrounded by hot, dry air, usually in an oven. As we have discussed in earlier chapters, there is no exact dividing line between roasting and other dry-heat methods. The effects of roasting at a high temperature, for example, are similar to those of broiling, even though the heat sources are different.

For our purposes, the term *roast* means the same as *bake*. The basic method for baking meat loaves and other hot meat terrines is essentially the same as for roasting whole meat cuts.

Roasting is generally explained as relatively pure technique, in which a meat is cooked from the raw state to doneness. Roasting or baking can also be used as a partial cooking technique, however. For example, a boiled ham can be finished by baking or roasting it in an oven while applying a glaze, or smaller meat cuts that have been broiled or sautéed to partial doneness can be finished in the oven.

The basic roasting techniques explained in Chapter 7 are applied to meats as well as to poultry. If necessary, review the following methods as explained on pages 268–270:

1. Low-temperature roasting
2. High-temperature roasting
3. Roasting after preliminary browning
4. Spit roasting
5. Barbecuing

Variables in Roasting Methods. While the basic methods for roasting meats are the same as for roasting poultry, there are a number of special concerns pertaining to meats.

Heat Intensity and Uniformity of Doneness. If you compare the directions from various sources for roasting rack of lamb, for example, you will find many variations. One source may say to brown the racks first, and then roast at 325°F (160°C) for 20 minutes. Another may say to brown the lamb and then roast it at 400°F (200°C) for 6 to 8 minutes. Which method is best? How do we determine roasting temperature?

In the case of poultry, the oven temperature depends to a large extent on the size of the roast—the bigger the bird, the lower the temperature. In the case of red meats, however, especially those that are roasted rare or medium, heat intensity can be used to control uniformity of doneness.

What this means is that a piece of meat roasted at high heat (for example, a whole beef tenderloin) will show a strong gradation of doneness and color, from well done and brown near the outside to rare and red in the middle. If you continue to roast it until medium in the center, a large proportion of the meat will be well done. The same piece of meat roasted at low heat will show more uniform doneness throughout. Any of these results could be desirable, depending on the particular dish and the effect you want to create.

In other words, by controlling oven temperature, you can get exactly the results you would like. Of course, a cook's ability to use this technique with skill and accuracy is developed with experience. Reading about it in a book can point the cook in the right direction, but it can't substitute for the essential experience.

Temperature and Connective Tissue. High-temperature roasting is appropriate only for the most tender cuts. For less-tender cuts, a medium or low temperature is needed, so that the cooking time will be long enough for some connective tissue to break down. On the other hand, if a cut is naturally very tender, too long a roasting time at low temperature may break down more connective tissue than is desirable. This results in a tender but mealy texture. Therefore, the most tender cuts are usually roasted at a medium to high temperature.

Basting. A great deal of misunderstanding exists about the practice of basting meats while roasting. Many books and recipes talk about the necessity of basting, but they never explain why. At best, they might suggest, misleadingly, that basting makes a roast juicy. The following points can be made:

1. Basting with *fat only* can help reduce moisture loss by creating a thin coating of fat that slows down evaporation, but its effect is limited. Well-marbled meats and

meats with a natural fat covering can usually remain moist by themselves, and such basting is not needed.

2. Basting with moist drippings or stock does not make a roast juicier. In fact, it may increase drying as it washes away a protective film of fat. Juices used for basting will not soak into the meat.

3. Basting with drippings or juices may be used to increase the appetite appeal of the roast because it enhances browning. Gelatin and other solids dissolved in the juices are deposited on the surface of the meat, helping to form a flavorful brown crust. This does not increase the juiciness of the meat, however. Some cookbooks claim that basting forms a waterproof coating that seals in juices, but this is not the case.

4. Basting sometimes produces more tender roasts for an unexpected reason: frequent basting interrupts and slows down the cooking. Every time the oven door is opened, the temperature in the oven drops considerably, so the roasting time is longer and more connective tissue breaks down. Thus, it is not the basting but the lower temperature that increases tenderness.

In summary, basting can improve flavor and appearance, but by itself it has little to do with juiciness.

Roasting Veal and Pork. It has long been the practice to advise against roasting veal and pork. Instead, braising is recommended, either a traditional braise (with liquid or sauce) or a pôélé (with little or no liquid; see page 276). This is because when these white meats are roasted until well done, as they usually are, they are often dry and unpalatable.

It is interesting to note that when recipes for veal and pork "roasts" are given in many books, they are often not roasts at all. Typical instructions call for adding mirepoix and covering the pan during the last part of cooking. The cover, of course, holds in steam, changing the procedure to a moist-heat cooking method.

Today, the rule that one should braise rather than roast veal and pork is generally good advice but is not ironclad. Diners today are more likely than they were 10 or 20 years ago to prefer roast veal that is not well done and dry but still somewhat pink and juicy.

In the case of pork, roasts that are cooked to an internal temperature of 160°F (71°C) are safe from danger of trichinosis yet are still juicy. They need not be cooked until dry to be safe to eat.

Center loin cuts from today's leaner pork have so little fat that they are difficult to keep moist when roasted, but slightly fattier cuts such as butt and leg (fresh ham) can make succulent roasts.

Simmering

Simmering is not a method that is often used to cook meat, except for cured meats such as corned beef and smoked ham, less tender cuts such as beef brisket ("boiled beef"), and white stews or blanquettes. Techniques for preparing these items should already be familiar to you.

Two special topics will be considered briefly in this section.

Simmering Tender Cuts. Because simmering is useful for breaking down connective tissue, simmering is most often used to cook less tender cuts, such as beef brisket, in order to make them palatable. Of course, such meats are always cooked until well done, or actually beyond well done.

Contrary to what you might expect, the simmering method is also used occasionally to cook tender cuts of beef and lamb to the rare or medium stage of doneness. Tender veal may also be cooked this way, but it is cooked to a medium-well–done stage.

A meat thermometer should be used to check for doneness, just as if the meats were roasted. Because simmering liquid is a very efficient conductor of heat, it is important to monitor the cooking closely to avoid overcooking.

The recipe for Boeuf à la Ficelle (page 366) illustrates the procedure for simmering tender meat to a rare or medium-done stage. This recipe is a modern, stylish interpretation of old-fashioned boiled beef. The recipe in this book utilizes beef tenderloin, which, because it is cooked rare, resembles a roast when it is sliced and plated. An advantage of this technique, as the recipe shows, is that it can produce healthful dishes that have no added fat but that can fit the most elegant menus.

The simmering method can also be used to cook tender meats that are to be served cold, as in the recipe for Cold Beef Tenderloin (page 367). The meat may be removed from the cooking liquid when done and then cooled, or, for maximum flavor and moistness, it can be cooled in the cooking liquid (such as stock). In this case, it should be removed from the heat when slightly underdone, because the retained heat of the liquid will continue to cook the meat.

Preparing Country Hams. Country hams present more challenges for the cook than regular hams do. This is because of the heavy curing and long aging that they undergo. The hams are dry-cured rather than brine-cured, and they are hung to age for 6 months to a year or longer. This results in a low moisture content and a very high salt content. The USDA requires that such hams have a salt content of 4 percent or more.

Because of the dry cure, the kitchen preparation needed by country hams is time-consuming, but the depth and complexity of flavor of these hams make them well worth the labor required. The difference between a fine, aged country ham and a simple boiled ham from the deli counter could be compared to the difference between a fine, aged wine from a great chateau and a simple, mass-produced jug wine.

Country hams are raw and therefore are cooked before being served. Some mild ham with a relatively low salt content is sometimes simply sliced and panfried. Strong as well as mild ham may be used in small quantities to contribute flavor to soups, dried bean dishes, casseroles, and other dishes. In most cases, however, it is first soaked to reduce the salt content; then it is usually cooked by simmering it in water. The following procedure explains the steps in preparation.

Procedure for Preparing Country Hams

1. Some aged hams have some mold on the surface. This is normal and not a sign of spoilage. Remove the mold by scrubbing the ham with a brush under cool or tepid running water.

2. Place the ham in a large stock pot or other container large enough for the ham to fit completely inside. Fill with enough cold water to cover the ham.

3. Soak the ham for 12 to 48 hours. Every 10 or 12 hours, discard the water and replace with fresh. The total amount of soaking required depends on how salty the ham is, how long it was aged, and how salty you want the finished product to be. In general, well-aged hams are saltier and require longer soaking.

4. After draining the final time, the ham is ready to be cooked. In most cases the preferred method is simmering, since it helps to draw out more of the salt. Place the ham in a large stock pot and add cold water to cover. Some mirepoix and

a bouquet garni may be added to the water if desired. Bring to a boil and then reduce the heat to a *slow simmer*. Cook until the meat is tender and the shank bone feels loose. This will take 20 to 30 minutes per pound (45 to 60 minutes per kilogram), or about 5 hours for a 12- to 14-pound (about 6 kg) ham. Be careful not to let the water boil. Slow cooking will produce a more tender and moist ham.

5. When the ham is done, remove it from the pot and discard the cooking liquid. Peel off the skin or rind and trim the surface fat to a thickness of about ½ inch (1 cm).

6. The ham may now be sliced and used as is, or it may be finished by baking it with a glaze, topping, or coating. Such a treatment not only improves the appearance of the ham when it is to be presented whole, but it also enhances the flavor of the ham and permits a number of seasoning variations. (See page 379 for glazed ham variations.)

COOKING SMALL CUTS

Small meat dishes comprise two categories of preparations: dishes that are cooked to order, which are usually single-portion sizes but sometimes for two to four portions; and stews, which are made of small cuts but which usually require longer cooking.

The basic cooking methods for small meat dishes may be classified as dry-heat methods and moist-heat methods. Dry-heat methods include those using fat (sautéing, panfrying, deep-frying) and those without fat (broiling, grilling, baking or roasting). Moist-heat methods are poaching and simmering, braising, and steaming.

Much of the information in Chapter 7 concerning cooking techniques for poultry applies to meats as well. If necessary, review the material on pages 270–278. Many of the techniques discussed in the sections of Chapter 7 indicated in the following list are particularly useful in meat cookery:

- Giving variety to grilled items through the use of marinades, basting ingredients, accompaniments, and so on (see "Broiling and Grilling," page 270).
- Using the technique of sautéing to create various types of dishes (see "Various Types of Sautéed Poultry Dishes," page 272).
- Using various ways of braising or stewing small meats (see "Braised Sautés and Miscellaneous Stews," page 275).
- Converting a baked or sautéed item to a poêlé by covering the pan (see "Poêlé Variations," page 277).

Instant Stews

This book has stressed throughout that there are no exact dividing lines between cooking techniques. This fact also enables us to make stews without actually stewing.

There are two basic steps in making a traditional browned stew:

1. Brown the meat, either lightly or heavily, as desired.
2. Add a liquid, such as a stock or sauce, and continue to cook.

Many of today's chefs, looking for new dishes to offer their customers, work variations on one or both of those steps to create untraditional menu items.

First, any dry-heat cooking method can be used to brown meats. While sautéing or panfrying is the normal method used to brown meat for stews, any of the other dry-heat methods can be used. For example, you might experiment with browning the meat by grilling it over a hardwood fire. (To make this possible, it may be necessary to grill the meat in large pieces and then cut it into smaller pieces for the stew after it is browned.) This can lend an intriguing flavor to a stew and often works well with tender meats.

Second, because old-fashioned stews are good ways of utilizing tougher cuts, slow cooking in liquid is necessary to tenderize them. But if top-quality tender cuts are used, this moist-heat cooking is unnecessary, and the dish is more like a classical sauté, as discussed on pages 271–272.

Some chefs carry this technique to its logical extreme, serving what might be called "instant stews." The technique often used is similar to the Chinese technique of stir-frying, a cooking method for quickly cooking a mixture of vegetables and meats.

Procedure for Making Instant Stews

1. Select only tender meats, such as those suitable for sautéing or broiling. Trim and cut up as desired.
2. Select appropriate vegetables for the stew. Trim and cut up as desired. Vegetables that can be cooked quickly may be prepared to order, but long-cooking vegetables should be precooked, chilled, and held for service.
3. Prepare desired sauce, broth, or other liquid medium. Hold for service.
4. Quickly brown the meat, cooking it to desired doneness.
5. Reheat or cook precut vegetables as necessary. Combine vegetables, meat, and sauce over heat. When the mixture is hot, serve immediately.

Of course, a dish cooked by such a method isn't actually a stew. Such dishes are often lighter and more elegant than real stews, which are generally more earthy and unrefined. It looks much like a stew, however, and to further the illusion, some chefs give these dishes names associated with stews, such as ragout or fricassée. An example of this type of dish can be found on page 404.

Steaming Meats

The technique of steaming foods has been discussed as it applies to fish (page 198) and to poultry (page 275). While steamed fish appears regularly on some menus, steamed poultry and meats have not been popular. Because of the demand for more healthful foods, however, many chefs have looked for ways to make steamed meats more interesting. Two successful techniques are listed here. Either one or both of these methods may be used for any particular preparation.

1. Season the meat well to give it a distinctive and noticeable flavor. This may be done by various methods, such as by marinating it or by coating it heavily with spices or other flavoring ingredients. Many chefs find that spicy or strongly flavored ingredients, such as those used in Mexican or Asian cuisines, are especially effective and popular with steamed meats, because the flavoring ingredients offset the blandness of the meat. After completing this procedure, either steam the meat as is or proceed with the second technique.
2. After seasoning, enclose the meat in an edible package, such as blanched cabbage or spinach leaves. Meats wrapped in this way can make attractive presentations. For further discussion of wrapping foods, see page 357.

To see how these techniques can be applied, see the recipe for Oriental Beef Steamed in Cabbage Leaves on page 394.

PREPARATION TECHNIQUES

Meats are prepared for cooking in a variety of ways. At the most basic level, preparation techniques include trimming, cutting, and seasoning. Some dishes require slightly more involved techniques such as marinating, larding, or barding. Restaurants that feature elegant presentations often use rather complex preparation techniques that enhance not only the flavor but also the appearance of the meat. Some of these techniques are explained in this section and are applied in a number of the recipes in this chapter.

Larding

Larding is the insertion of strips of fat into lean meats. Meats that are low in internal fat, or marbling, can become very dry when cooked. Braised beef bottom round, for example, is often so dry that it is almost inedible. The purpose of larding is to supply fat that the meat lacks so that the cooked meat tastes juicier.

Larding is especially beneficial for the less tender, lean red meats that are to be braised. Their long cooking times makes them especially prone to drying out. White meats, being more tender, are usually not larded.

In the case of roasting, the usefulness of larding depends on the degree to which the meat is roasted. Meats that are to be left quite rare retain most of their juice, so larding is not necessary. Besides, a piece of larding fat in the center of a rare roast will not even get warm enough to begin melting, so it serves no purpose. On the other hand, if a lean red meat—even a relatively tender cut—is to be cooked to the medium-well–done stage, larding will help to make up for lost moisture.

There are two types of larding, requiring two different kinds of larding needles:

1. The first type of larding, perhaps the most common, requires long strips of fat about ¼ inch (6 mm) thick and a large, hollow larding needle. A strip of fat is fitted into the groove of the needle, which is then inserted into the meat, parallel to the grain of the meat. When the needle is removed, the strip of fat is left in the meat. This process is repeated so that there are strips of fat about an inch (2.5 cm) apart throughout the meat. This procedure is illustrated in Figure 8.1.

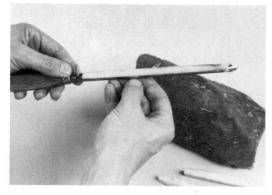

FIGURE 8.1. **Larding meat using a large needle.**
(a) **Cut a strip of fatback to fit inside the needle.**

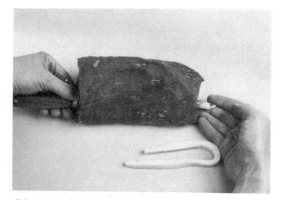

(b) **Insert the needle through the meat. Withdraw the needle, holding the strip of fat so that it stays in the meat.**

2. A second type of larding is used for smaller pieces of meat, especially those that are to be roasted.

As mentioned earlier, if a meat is not roasted until well done, larding fat in the center of the roast will not melt enough to be of any benefit. On the other hand, if thin strips of fat are inserted just under the surface, they will help to keep the outer part of the meat moist as it browns. At the same time, the ends of the strips of fat that are left protruding from the meat help to baste the surface as they melt.

A smaller needle is required for this technique. A small strip of fat is inserted in the end of the needle. It is then threaded into the meat as though you were stitching with a needle and thread. The two ends of the strip of fat are left protruding from the meat. This technique is sometimes referred to by its French name, *piquage* (pronounced "pee-kahzh"), from the verb *piquer* (pronounced "pee-kay"). The procedure is shown in Figure 8.2.

Other Types of Piquage. Other ingredients can be inserted beneath the surface of meat to flavor it. The most common example is slivers of garlic inserted into a leg of lamb before roasting it. Other items that are sometimes used this way in special preparations include slivers of black truffle, whole spices, and fresh herbs.

The usual technique is to poke small slits in the meat with the point of a knife and to push in the flavoring ingredient with the fingers.

Barding

To *bard* means to tie thin sheets or slices of fat, such as pork fatback, over meats with no natural fat cover to protect them while roasting. Barding is illustrated in Figure 7.9, on page 296. This technique can, of course, be used with meats as well as with poultry.

Meats that have been barded before roasting will not brown well. Therefore, the normal procedure is first to brown the meat on top of the stove and then to bard and roast it. An especially useful material for barding is *caul fat*. (See page 415 for a discussion of caul.)

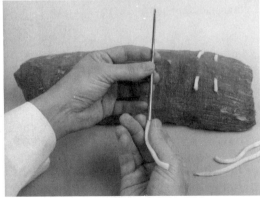

FIGURE 8.2. **Larding meat using a small or piqué needle.**
(a) **Insert a small strip of fat into the back end of the needle.**

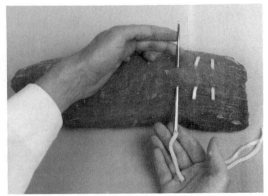

(b) **Push the needle under the surface of the meat and pull it through as though stitching, leaving the strip of fat in place.**

Marinating

To marinate means to soak a food in a seasoned liquid. It is a well-known technique, widely used for many kinds of foods. Historically, marination of meats has had three purposes:

1. Preserving

2. Tenderizing

3. Flavoring

Modern refrigeration has made the first of these obsolete. The second function is due to the slight acidity of a typical wine marinade, but the tenderizing action is only slight. Besides, meats today are considerably more tender than they were at the beginning of the century or earlier.

Today, flavoring is by far the most important purpose of marination. By choosing different marinades, the cook can create a variety of differently flavored dishes using the same cut of meat.

It must be pointed out, however, that marinated meats are not necessarily better than unmarinated meats; they're just different. In developing a recipe, you may choose instead to emphasize the plain, unadorned flavor of the meat or perhaps to contrast the natural flavor of an unmarinated meat with an interesting condiment or sauce on the plate. Especially if you are paying top prices for high-quality, flavorful meats, you probably will not want to alter their flavor too much with strong marinades. A compromise that is useful in many situations is a short marination lasting from 30 minutes to a few hours.

Traditional marinades are usually based on red or white wine, usually with the addition of herbs, spices, and aromatic vegetables. Other, less traditional marinades may be based on other liquids, such as fruit juices. In theory, any liquid food ingredient that can be used in cooking can also be used as a marinade, provided that its flavor will enhance the flavor of the meat. Similarly, nearly any ingredient that can be used to season or flavor meat can also be used to flavor a marinade.

Use caution when employing strong acids, such as vinegar or lemon juice, in a marinade. A marinade that is too acidic will partially coagulate the protein of the meat, making it seem partially cooked. When the meat is then cooked, its texture will not be as desirable. Strong acids can be used in marinades if they are used in small quantities or if the meat is marinated for only a few hours.

This chapter includes a number of recipes that use marinades of various types, some traditional and some not so traditional.

Game-Style Marinades. Wine marinades have long been used to marinate venison and other game (discussed in Chapter 9). In fact, part of the taste that many people associate with "gaminess" is actually due to the marinade.

Several traditional recipes involve marinating domestic meat, such as beef, in the type of marinade ordinarily used for venison or other game. After marinating and cooking, the meat tastes somewhat like game. When these dishes are made with beef or, occasionally, lamb, they are generally referred to as *en chevreuil* (pronounced, approximately, "on shev roy"), which means something like "in the style of venison." Pork dishes made to taste like wild boar are known as *en marcassin* (pronounced "on mar ka san"), meaning "in the style of boar."

A recipe for steak *en chevreuil* is on page 381.

Dry "Marinades." Strictly speaking, the term *marinade* refers to seasoned liquids used to soak foods in order to flavor them, but this term is also used frequently to refer to dry mixtures of salt, herbs, and spices. Moist ingredients, such as crushed garlic or fresh herbs, can be included in the mixture. The mixture should be rubbed evenly over the surface of the meat, which is then allowed to stand a few hours for small cuts such as chops, or as long as overnight for large cuts such as roasts.

Before cooking, the spice mixture may be scraped off the meat, or it can be left on, depending on how strongly you want to flavor the meat. In the case of chops or other small cuts, it is usually better to scrape it off so that the meat won't be too salty.

For examples of this technique, see the recipe for Roast Pork Loin Yucatan-style, on page 374.

Brines. Dry salt rubs have traditionally been used to cure hams and certain other meats. Many of the world's best hams are made this way. A disadvantage of this method, however, is that the cure takes a long time for a large cut of meat. A faster way to cure meat is to use a brine.

A *brine* is a solution of salt in water to which may be added nitrites, sugar, and spices. Brines are used for curing meats such as hams, corned beef, beef tongue, and any meat that is to be smoked. When meats are cured in brine, they are usually steeped in the salt mixture for a minimum of 3 days and for as long as 6 to 8 days, depending on the size of the meat.

The purpose of the nitrites is to help the meat maintain a red color when it is cooked (it also helps inhibit bacteria, and it helps keep meat fat from becoming rancid). Traditionally, saltpeter (potassium nitrate) has been used in home-cured meats, but it can be toxic, especially if used excessively. The purpose of the sugar is to help keep the meat moist, since salt used alone has a drying effect.

The subject of brines is included here because they can also be used for short marinations, particularly of pork. If a cut of pork is first marinated in a brine for 6 to 12 hours, the resulting meat tends to be juicier, more tender, and more flavorful.

Twelve hours or less in brine is much shorter than the time needed for curing, so the meat tastes more like fresh pork than cured pork. It is not too salty, and it is excellent for roasting and braising. On the other hand, if the meat is left in the brine longer, it becomes saltier and generally must be poached first to rid it of some of the excess salt.

Because we are concerned with brines used as marinades rather than as curing mediums, the method outlined here differs in four respects from the standard method for making and using brines:

1. The effect of nitrites or saltpeter in standard brines is to keep the meat pink or red, even after it is cooked. If we simply want to use the brine for a short marination, however, saltpeter is not particularly appropriate. We want the product to look like fresh meat, not like ham. Therefore, we omit the saltpeter.

2. Commercial operations that cure large quantities of meats use special instruments to determine the exact salt concentration in their brines. For our purposes here, this is not necessary.

3. Because the curing process takes many days, and because cured meats are often stored for longer periods than fresh meats are, special sanitation procedures are necessary to avoid contaminating the cure with organisms that can cause spoilage. For the purposes of short marinations, however, normal sanitary kitchen practices are generally sufficient. Always start with a freshly made brine; do not reuse a brine that has had meat in it.

4. The marinating brine described in the procedure that follows is not as strong as most curing brines. Typical formulas for French curing brine, called *saumure,* specify 1 pound (500 grams) of salt, plus an equal quantity of sugar, per gallon (4 liters) of water.

The following procedure is suitable not only for pork, but also for chicken, duck, and other poultry. Not much success has been reported with other meats, but you may want to do your own experimenting after you have become accustomed to its effects on pork.

Procedure for Short Marination in Brine

1. For each gallon (or 4 liters) of brine, assemble the ingredients that follow. This quantity of brine is enough to marinate about 5 or 6 pounds (about 2.5 kg) of meat. The herbs and spices listed are good for a general purpose brine, but they may be varied to taste.
   1 gal (4 l) water
   4 oz (125 g) kosher salt or sea salt
   3 oz (90 g) sugar
   2 bay leaves
   2 tsp (2 g) thyme
   4 whole cloves
   1 tbsp (9 g) whole peppercorns
2. Combine the water, salt, and sugar in a large pot. Bring to a boil, stirring to make sure that the salt and sugar are dissolved.
3. Tie the herbs and spices in a piece of cheesecloth and add to the brine. Simmer a minute, and then remove from the heat.
4. Let cool until completely cold. Remove the spice bag.
5. Put the meat to be marinated into the brine. The meat must be completely covered by the liquid. If it floats, weight it down to keep it submerged. Keep refrigerated while marinating.
6. For large cuts to be roasted or braised, marinate for at least 6 hours or overnight. For small pieces, such as chops and cutlets, marinate for 2 to 6 hours.
7. Remove the meat from the marinade, dry it, and proceed with your recipe, treating the brined meat like fresh meat. Cook the meat as is or, if desired, give it a short marination in a wine marinade or other flavoring preparation. Discard the used brine.

Trimming and Cutting Beef Tenderloin

While beef tenderloin can be roasted whole, it is more often cut into steaks and other cuts such as tournedos, filet mignon steaks, and chateaubriand. Before it is cut, external fat and silverskin is trimmed from the tenderloin. Procedures for trimming and cutting beef tenderloin are illustrated in Figure 8.3.

Preparing Tournedos of Beef. Of the cuts from the tenderloin that have just been described, the tournedos are often perceived as especially elegant and desirable. They have had an important place on menus since before the days of Escoffier.

In the classical repertoire, there are dozens of preparations for tournedos, all with their own standardized names. Each preparation involves, in most cases, simply sautéing or grilling the meat and serving it with the sauce and garnish indicated in the recipe. Modern cookery includes many new versions, but the basic procedures are generally based on the classical methods.

FIGURE 8.3. Trimming and cutting a beef tenderloin.

(a) A whole untrimmed tenderloin, covered with a thick layer of kidney fat or suet.

(b) Pull the large masses of fat from the meat, freeing them with a knife as necessary.

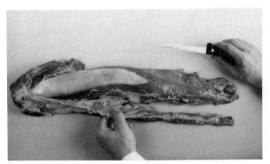

(c) Separate the strip of gristly meat, or chain, from the side of the tenderloin. Use this piece for ground meat.

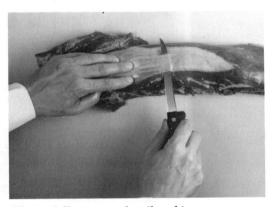

(d) Carefully remove the silverskin.

(e) The fully trimmed tenderloin before cutting.

(f) One of many ways to cut a tenderloin, depending on the types of cuts needed. From left to right: three fillet steaks; two large pieces for chateaubriand; three tournedos; and two filets mignons. In front, trimmings from both ends. This is a small tenderloin; larger ones yield more cuts.

The basic procedures for making tournedos dishes are explained in the following guidelines. Directions for a number of variations follow. Refer to other chapters as necessary for details regarding the preparation of sauces and vegetable and other garnishes.

Note: Both the singular and plural forms of tournedos are spelled with a final s, and both are pronounced "TOOR nuh doe." The word is derived from the French word *dos* (pronounced "doe"), which means the back section of the carcass between the neck and the loin or hip.

1. Tournedos are usually tied around their circumference with a piece of string before cooking. The purpose is to hold them in a neat round shape to enhance their appearance. The string must be removed before the meat is served.

2. A strip of fresh pork fat may be tied around the tournedos, instead of merely tying them with string. Bacon strips are sometimes used, but bacon is not as good as fresh pork fat for two reasons. First, the nitrites in the bacon discolor the beef. Second, the flavor of the bacon is too strong for the more delicate flavor of the beef, and it may not harmonize well with the sauce and garnish.

3. Cook the tournedos to desired doneness by grilling or by sautéing or panfrying in oil or butter, as directed in the specific recipe.

4. If the sides of the tournedos are wrapped in fat, remove the fat before serving and brown the sides of the meat.

5. Many recipes specify setting the tournedos on top of croutons, that is, slices of bread fried in butter, for serving. The croutons should be cut to the same size as the tournedos. The croutons serve two main purposes. First, they enhance the presentation by increasing the height of the tournedos on the plate or platter. Second, they absorb juices that may be released by the meat and ruin the appearance of the sauce. Some modern presentations substitute other foods for the croutons, such as potato cakes or small mounds of vegetables.

Tournedos Variations

- **Béarnaise**—Panfry the tournedos; set on croutons. Coat with a little glace de viande. Spoon a ribbon of béarnaise sauce around them or serve sauce separately. Garnish: small potatoes or potato balls browned in butter and sprinkled with chopped parsley.

- **Bordelaise**—Grill the tournedos. Top each with a slice of poached marrow. Serve with bordelaise sauce.

- **Castilian**—Panfry the tournedos in butter; set on croutons. Cook some peeled, seeded, chopped tomatoes in butter until thick. Place a spoonful of this tomato fondue in tiny tartlet shells and set one on each tournedos. Additional garnish: onions sliced into rings and fried in oil until brown. Sauce: deglaze sauté pan with white wine and reduce; add a little glace de viande or rich brown stock, reduced until somewhat thickened; stir in a little raw butter.

- **Chasseur**—Panfry the tournedos in butter. Serve with chasseur sauce.

- **Choron**—Panfry in butter; set on croutons. Garnish: artichoke bottoms filled with buttered peas or asparagus tips. Sauce: choron.

- **Henri IV**—Panfry in butter; set on croutons. Garnish: artichoke bottoms filled with very small potato balls browned in butter, set on top of tournedos. Sauce: béarnaise, in a ribbon around tournedos, or served separately.

- **Marechale**—Panfry in butter; set on croutons. Top with a slice of truffle. Garnish: asparagus tips.

- **Niçoise**—Panfry in butter. Garnishes: chopped tomato cooked in butter with a little chopped garlic; buttered green beans; small potatoes cooked in butter.
- **Rossini**—Panfry in butter; set on croutons. Top with a round slice of foie gras and a slice of truffle. Sauce: melted glace de viande or demiglaze or, as an alternative, Madeira sauce.
- **Vert-Pré**—Grill. Top with slice of maître d'hôtel butter. Garnishes: watercress and shoestring potatoes.

Boning and Handling Loins of Lamb, Veal, and Pork

Loins and rib sections of lamb, veal, and pork are frequently roasted whole or cut into bone-in chops. For more elegant presentations, however, many chefs prefer to bone out these cuts completely and use the trimmed eye muscles. These can then be cooked whole and sliced before plating, or they can be first cut into *medaillons* or *noisettes* and cooked like small steaks. A medaillon is, as the name implies, a round or oval slice. A noisette is a small round portion, generally no more than a few ounces, usually cut from the loin or rib eye.

A special advantage of the loin eye muscle is that it is fairly uniform from end to end. Therefore, if it is cooked whole, it will cook evenly. If it is cut into medaillons, it is easy to cut slices of uniform size.

This boning and trimming technique decreases the net yield (by weight) of a whole saddle or rack and consequently increases the per-ounce cost of an already expensive cut. Nevertheless, it allows a greater variety of plate presentations. Furthermore, it makes the dish easier to eat than bone-in cuts. This may not be an advantage in casual dining establishments, but it is an asset in luxury restaurants. Finally, the technique yields a greater quantity of bones for the stock pot.

Figure 8.4 illustrates how to bone out a section of veal loin. The same technique is used for lamb and pork. Figure 8.5 shows how to cut and handle a paillard of veal. This is a slice of veal loin that is flattened until it is thin and broad and cooked quickly on a grill. Figure 8.6 shows how to stuff, roll, and tie a boneless loin. In this illustration, a loin of pork is being prepared for the recipe for Roast Loin of Pork with Date and Gorgonzola Stuffing (page 372), but the same technique can be used for other meats and other stuffings.

Small Cuts Coated or Wrapped

A well-known dish called Beef Wellington was for many years a familiar attraction in restaurants nationwide. This preparation consists of a large cut of beef tenderloin, usually enough for two or more portions, partially roasted, cooled, coated with a seasoned liver pâté, wrapped in puff pastry, and baked until the pastry is cooked and browned and the meat is done to the desired degree. Modern chefs often reject this dish as being unnecessarily fussy and complicated and too heavy for today's lighter styles of cooking. Yet these same cooks often devise elaborate preparations of stuffed and wrapped meats that might be considered up-to-date versions of Beef Wellington.

In fact, there are many techniques that involve coating or wrapping meats to be cooked, and there may be many benefits to using them. Barding, for example, is a wrapping technique we have already discussed (page 351), and it is useful to help prevent moisture loss in meat. Other techniques are used not only to protect the surface of meat from drying but also to create variety of flavor and appearance, which lends interest to the menu.

FIGURE 8.4. **Boning a loin of veal.**
(a) A section from a loin of veal, showing the tenderloin to the left of the bone and the loin eye muscle to the right of the bone.

(b) Begin by cutting the tenderloin from the underside of the loin.

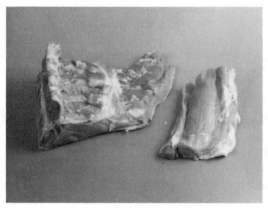

(c) The tenderloin is removed.

(d) Cut under the bones (called fingerbones) to separate them from the loin muscle.

(e) Turn the loin over and cut to one side of the spine down to the vertebrae to completely separate the loin muscle.

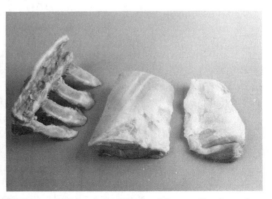

(f) From left to right: the backbone, the boneless loin, and the flank, which has been separated from the loin. The tenderloin is not shown.

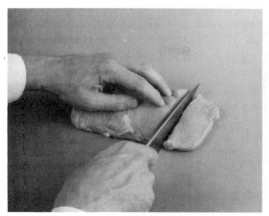

FIGURE 8.5. **Preparing a paillard of veal.**
(a) Cut a slice ½ inch (12 mm) thick from a well-trimmed boneless loin of veal.

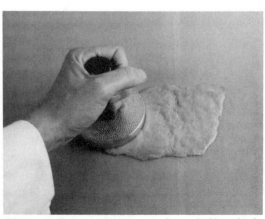

(b) Carefully pound it out until it is half as thick and much broader.

(c) Pounding the veal between two sheets of plastic film helps prevent tearing the meat or pounding holes in it.

Two points require special attention when coated or wrapped meats are prepared:

1. Meats that are wrapped or coated will not brown. Because the coating traps moisture around the meat, the meat actually steams in its own moisture. Even such a simple coating as a standard breading works this way. When a breaded cutlet is browned in a sauté pan, it is the breading that browns, not the meat.

   Sometimes, of course, the intention is to steam the meat, as discussed in the section on steaming (page 349). If we want browned meat, however, it must be browned before being wrapped. This is a normal procedure for barded meats (see page 351), as well as for the Beef Wellington just described.

2. Meat may release considerable moisture when cooked, and most of this moisture may be trapped inside the coating or wrapping. Some coatings, such as breading, allow most of the moisture to escape. Heavy pastry wrappers, on the other hand, trap most of the moisture and may become soggy.

FIGURE 8.6. **Double butterfly of a boneless pork loin for stuffing.**
(a) Cut the boneless loin as for regular butterflying, holding the knife parallel to the table, but make the cut about one-third of the way up.

(b) Spread open the cut loin, and butterfly the thicker portion as shown, cutting from the center toward, but not through, the outside edge.

(c) Spread open this second cut. Spread the filling over the meat.

(d) The stuffed loin, rolled and tied.

To avoid this problem, the meat is usually partially cooked and then cooled before being wrapped. Meats that are not damaged by long cooking, such as sausages, may be cooked completely before being enclosed in pastry, but other meats must be undercooked in this first stage so that they will not be overcooked later. A disadvantage of this precooking process is that the finished meat dish may taste reheated, which, of course, it is.

Briefly, the following techniques are commonly used methods for coating or wrapping meats:

1. *Barding.*

This is discussed on page 351 of this chapter.

2. *Standard breading.*

This coating of flour, egg wash, and bread crumbs is extensively used for a wide array of foods. It gives foods an attractive golden appearance, crisp coating, and pleasant flavor. It protects the foods from the frying fat, and it increases the bulk of the food.

3. *Variety breadings.*

Other items, such as chopped nuts, may be mixed with the bread crumbs of a standard breading. To create even more unusual dishes, many chefs omit the bread crumbs and instead "bread" the meat with other items. Two examples in this book are the Lamb (or Beef) Noisettes in a Potato Crust (page 384) and the variation in which the meat is coated with chopped dried wild mushrooms.

Chefs who use this technique may not think of it as breading, but the technique is basically the same. As variations, sometimes only egg whites or yolks are used for the egg wash instead of whole eggs.

4. *Wrapping in pastry.*

For the reasons discussed previously meats baked in pastry are generally browned and partially cooked before being wrapped. Other ingredients, such as vegetable mixtures, are often included with the meat in the pastry crust. Puff pastry, brioche dough, and bread dough are among the materials used.

Baking temperature should be rather high, so that the crust browns and cooks thoroughly before too much heat penetrates to the center and overcooks the meat. For the same reason, the dough should not be too thick, so that it will not take too long to cook. This technique is represented by the recipe for Veal Medaillons with Artichokes en Croûte (page 386).

5. *Wrapping in leaves.*

This technique is used for steaming or other moist-heat methods, because dry heat would dry out and possibly burn the leaf coatings.

If the leaf wrappers are edible, such as cabbage or lettuce leaves, the leaves serve not only as wrappers but as a flavorful and nutritious part of the dish. An example is the recipe on page 394.

Inedible leaves, such as lotus leaves (in Chinese cooking), corn husks (for Mexican tamales), and banana leaves (many cuisines) are sometimes used. They serve primarily as wrappers for steaming but may contribute some flavor to the foods they enclose.

BOEUF À LA MÔDE (BRAISED BEEF IN RED WINE)

		U.S.		Metric	
PORTIONS:		4	16	*4*	*16*
Ingredients					
Pork fatback		4 oz	1 lb	*125 g*	*500 g*
Brandy		1 tbsp	2 oz	*15 ml*	*60 ml*
Salt					
Pepper					
Beef top round or rump, trimmed of excess fat		2 lb	8 lb	*1 kg*	*4 kg*
Salt					
Pepper					
Red wine		12 oz	3 pt	*4 dl*	*1.5 l*
Brandy		1 oz	4 oz	*30 ml*	*125 ml*
Bay leaf		1	2	*1*	*2*
Parsley stems		5	20	*5*	*20*
Thyme, dried		pinch	large pinch	*pinch*	*large pinch*
Butter or beef fat		1 oz	4 oz	*25 g*	*100 g*
Onion, chopped coarsely		2 oz	8 oz	*50 g*	*100 g*
Carrot, chopped coarsely		2 oz	8 oz	*50 g*	*100 g*
Calf's foot		1	4	*1*	*4*
Garlic cloves		2	8	*2*	*8*
Brown stock		1 pt	2 qt	*5 dl*	*2 l*
Carrots		8 oz	2 lb	*250 g*	*1 kg*
Pearl onions		8–12	32–48	*8–12*	*32–48*

Mise en Place:

1. Cut the fatback into strips ¼ inch (6 mm) across and at least as long as the piece of beef.

2. Sprinkle the fatback strips with brandy, salt, and pepper (omit the salt if you are using salted fatback). Marinate for 2 hours.

3. Lard the beef with the fatback strips (see Figure 8.1).

4. Rub the beef with salt and pepper. Combine the red wine and brandy. Tie the herbs into a cheesecloth bag and add to the wine. Marinate the beef overnight in the wine mixture.

Cooking:

1. Remove the meat from the marinade and dry it. Remove the herb bag from the marinade and set it aside.

2. Heat the butter or beef fat in a heavy braising pan. Brown the meat well in the fat.

3. Remove the meat from the pan. Brown the chopped onion and carrot in the pan.

4. Return the meat to the pan. Add the marinade. Set the pan over moderate heat. Cook until the marinade is reduced by one-half. Baste the meat with the marinade occasionally.

5. Add the calf's foot, garlic, stock, and reserved herb bag to the pan. Bring to a simmer, cover, and place in an oven heated to 300°F (150°C). The meat should cook slowly at a very gentle simmer.

6. Braise the meat until there are no traces of red blood in the juices that appear when the meat is pierced deeply with a skewer. Baste the meat occasionally as it cooks.

7. Remove the beef and the calf's foot from the cooking liquid. Strain and degrease the liquid.

8. Put the meat, calf's foot, and liquid in a clean braising pan. Cover the pan and return it to the oven. Let it cook, basting frequently, until the meat is tender. Total cooking time, starting with step 4, will be about 4 hours.

9. While the meat is cooking, prepare the carrot and onion garnish. Cut and trim the carrots into uniform pieces about 1 ½ inches (4 cm) long. Blanch them in boiling salted water for 3 to 4 minutes. Peel the pearl onions and brown slowly in butter in a sauté pan. About 1 hour before the meat is done, add them to the braising pan and let them finish cooking with the meat.

10. Remove the foot from the pan. Bone it out, being careful to remove all the tiny bones. Cut the meat and rind from the foot into half-inch (1-cm) squares. (*Note:* It is traditional to serve the diced calf's foot with the meat, but it may be discarded if desired. The main purpose of cooking the foot with the meat is that the foot enriches the liquid with its high gelatin content.)

11. Remove the meat and vegetable garnish from the cooking liquid. Strain and degrease the liquid. There should be about 2 oz (60 ml) of liquid per portion, and it should be rich and somewhat syrupy. If necessary, reduce the liquid over moderate heat to reach the proper volume. If it is not rich enough, add additional stock and reduce again. Adjust the seasonings. The finished braising liquid serves as a sauce for the meat.

Presentation:

Slice the meat. Arrange it on a platter or on dinner plates with the garnish of carrots, pearl onions, and diced foot (if desired). If the meat is presented on a platter, serve the sauce on the side in a sauceboat. If the meat is presented on dinner plates, the sauce may be served on the side or ladled over the meat.

A green salad is a good accompaniment for this dish.

Variations

If calves' feet are not available, pig's feet may be used instead. Substitute 2 pig's feet for each calf's foot required.

Beef crossrib or other cut from the chuck may be substituted for the round.

This dish is eaten cold as well as hot. To serve cold, slice the meat and arrange it in a terrine or deep casserole. Arrange the vegetable garnish neatly on top. Carefully pour the strained braising liquid over the meat and vegetables; there should be enough liquid to cover the vegetables. Chill. The calf's foot should have supplied enough gelatin to gel the liquid.

ROAST LAMB OR BEEF CLOAKED IN GARLIC, THYME, AND PEPPER PASTE

		U.S.		Metric	
PORTIONS:		**4**	**16**	*4*	*16*
Ingredients					
Boneless lamb from the leg, *or* beef tenderloin, trimmed		1 lb 8 oz	6 lb	*700 g*	*2.8 kg*
Garlic cloves		1	4	*1*	*4*
Thyme, dried		¼ tsp	1 tsp	*¼ g*	*1 g*
Crushed black peppercorns		1 tsp	4 tsp	*1 g*	*4 g*
Butter		1 ½ tbsp	3 oz	*25 g*	*100 g*
Flour		1 tbsp	4 tbsp	*8 g*	*30 g*
Salt		1 tsp	4 tsp	*5 g*	*20 g*
Spinach, AP		1 lb 8 oz	6 lb	*700 g*	*2.8 kg*
Butter					
Salt					
White pepper					
Celery root, pared		4 oz	1 lb	*125 g*	*500 g*
Butter					
Salt					
White pepper					
Lemon juice					
White stock (optional)		4 oz	1 pt	*125 ml*	*5 dl*

Mise en Place:

1. Trim external fat and silverskin from the meat. Please note that the quantities specified are for total amounts. Six pounds of boneless lamb, for example, may be in several pieces.

2. Blend the crushed garlic, thyme, pepper, butter, flour, and salt into a paste.

3. Dry the meat thoroughly so that the seasoning paste will adhere. Rub the paste over the surface of the meat.

4. Pick over the spinach, removing all stems and discarding any spoiled or discolored leaves. Wash in several changes of water.

5. Blanch the spinach in boiling salted water. Drain and rinse under cold water until the spinach is cold. Press out excess moisture and chop the spinach coarsely.

6. Cut the celery root into brunoise (fine dice). Stew the celery brunoise in a little butter until tender, seasoning it as it cooks with salt, white pepper, and a few drops of lemon juice to keep it white. Remove from the heat and cool.

Cooking:

1. Preheat the oven to 450°F (230°C). Roast the meat on a rack until it is rare or medium rare. Roasting time will vary greatly, depending on the thickness of the meat. A small piece of tenderloin may take less than 20 minutes, while a large piece of leg of lamb may take more than 45 minutes. Watch carefully for proper doneness, since the meat can quickly become overcooked in a hot oven.

2. When the meat is done, remove it from the oven and let it rest in a warm place for 10 to 15 minutes.

3. If a sauce is desired, degrease the roasting pan and then deglaze it with the white stock. Reduce by one-half, strain, and season with salt if necessary.

4. Heat the spinach in a little butter. Season with salt and white pepper.

5. Reheat the celery root in a small pan.

Presentation:

1. Place a small spoonful of the celery root onto the center of each plate. With the back of the spoon spread it out slightly into a thin layer.

2. Arrange the spinach in a circle around the celery root.

3. Slice the meat. Arrange the slices in the center of each plate so that they cover the celery root and some of the spinach. Some of the spinach should be visible around the outer edge of the meat arrangement.

4. If desired, moisten each portion of meat with ½ oz (15 ml) of sauce.

Variation

Roast Lamb with Smoky Eggplant Purée

Prepare and roast lamb as in the basic recipe. Omit the celery root and spinach preparations. Prepare Smoky Eggplant Purée (page 529), making enough for 2 oz (60 g) per portion. Spoon purée onto plate. Arrange lamb slices on top. Sprinkle lightly with chopped parsley and garnish with parsley, black olives, a wedge of lemon, and sautéed cherry tomatoes or fresh tomato wedges.

BOEUF À LA FICELLE

		U.S.		Metric	
PORTIONS:		4	16	*4*	*16*
Ingredients					
High-quality beef such as tenderloin or top butt, well trimmed		1 lb 4 oz	5 lb	*600 g*	*2.4 kg*
Fatback for larding, optional		as needed		*as needed*	
Brown stock		1 qt	4 qt	*1 l*	*4 l*
Salt					
Pepper					
Vegetable garnish as desired (see Mise en Place, step 3)					
Cornichons (small sour pickles)					
Dijon-style mustard					

Mise en Place:

1. Trim all external fat from the meat. If you are cooking a large quantity, cut the meat into uniform pieces no larger than about 3 lb (1.4 kg). Tie the meat pieces as though trussing a roast, leaving a length of twine attached to each piece.

2. If desired, the beef may be larded. This will be only of minor benefit for beef that is to be served rare, but for well-done or medium-well–done beef it will contribute moistness (see page 350).

3. Choose and prepare the vegetable garnish. Three to six fresh vegetables should be served as part of this dish. Select several vegetables that can be cooked in stock, such as carrots, turnips, leeks, celery, and celery root. Other possibilities include boiled or steamed potatoes, grilled tomatoes, and artichoke bottoms. Hard vegetables or vegetables that have a long cooking time may be precooked, chilled, and held for service.

Cooking:

1. Bring the stock to a boil in a stock pot or other pot large enough to hold the stock and the beef.

2. Lower the meat into the stock. Tie the loose end of the twine onto the pot handle so that the beef is suspended in the stock and does not rest on the bottom. This will allow slower, more even cooking.

3. Cook at a very slow simmer until the meat reaches the desired doneness, as determined by a meat thermometer. The temperature at the center of the meat should be 110°F (43°C) for rare, 115°F (46°C) for medium. Cooking time will be about 20 to 30 minutes for rare, slightly longer for medium.

4. Remove the meat from the liquid and let rest in a warm place about 15 minutes.

5. While the meat is cooking and resting, cook or reheat the desired vegetables as necessary.

6. Taste the cooking stock and reduce as necessary to make a rich, flavorful liquid. Set aside enough stock for 2 to 4 oz (60 to 125 ml) per portion. Season with salt and pepper. Use the remaining liquid for another purpose.

Presentation:

1. Slice the meat and place it on large dinner plates or shallow soup plates.

2. Arrange the vegetables on the plates with the meat.

3. Ladle the seasoned stock onto the plates or serve it in a sauceboat on the side.

4. Serve cornichons and mustard on the side.

Variations

Cold Beef Tenderloin

When the meat is done, remove it from the pot and place in a smaller container. Add just a small amount of the stock to help keep the meat moist, and cool. When the meat is completely cool, remove from the stock and chill. To serve, slice and arrange on top of a few lettuce leaves or other greens. Serve with a flavorful vinaigrette or with a mayonnaise-based sauce such as Sauce Verte (page 75) or Andalouse Sauce (page 74).

Poached Stuffed Beef Tenderloin

Stuff the tenderloin as shown in Figure 8.6, using any appropriate stuffing. One suggestion is to prepare the stuffing for Braised Rolled Breast of Veal (page 376) but omit the lemon zest. Substitute thyme for the sage and rosemary and add a generous quantity of chopped parsley. Roll the stuffed loin in caul fat (see page 415) or cheesecloth and tie securely. Poach as in basic recipe. Serve hot as in the basic recipe or cold as in the previous variation.

SADDLE OF LAMB WITH CHESTNUTS AND WILD MUSHROOMS

		U.S.		Metric	
PORTIONS:		*4*	*16*	*4*	*16*
Ingredients					
Lamb loin, bone-in, trimmed		2 ½–3 lb	10–12 lb	*1.1–1.4 kg*	*5 kg*
Black peppercorns, crushed		¼ tsp	1 tsp	*½ g*	*2 g*
Juniper berries, chopped		½ tsp	2 tsp	*1 g*	*4 g*
Thyme		¼ tsp	1 tsp	*¼ g*	*1 g*
Coarse salt		1 tsp	4 tsp	*4 g*	*15 g*
Dried wild mushrooms (see note)		1 oz	4 oz	*30 g*	*125 g*
Chestnuts		12–16	50–60	*12–16*	*50–60*
Butter		¼ oz	1 oz	*10 g*	*30 g*
Shallots, minced		1 oz	4 oz	*30 g*	*125 g*
Red wine		4 oz	1 pt	*1 dl*	*5 dl*
Demiglaze, rich brown stock, or lamb stock		8 oz	1 qt	*2.5 dl*	*1 l*
Raw butter (optional)		1 tbsp	2 oz	*15 g*	*60 g*

Note: A variety of dried mushrooms may be used, such as porcini or cèpes (boletus), chanterelles, or shiitake. If they are available, fresh mushrooms such as chanterelles, shiitake, or oyster mushrooms may be used; the quantity of fresh mushrooms should be about 4 times the weight of dried, or about 1 oz (30 g) per portion. If necessary, regular cultivated button mushrooms may be substituted for up to one-half the quantity of wild or exotic mushrooms.

Mise en Place:

1. Make sure the lamb is well trimmed of excess fat, leaving only a thin coating of fat on top. See Figure 8.7 for instructions on preparing saddle of lamb for roasting.

2. Mix together the crushed peppercorns, chopped juniper berries, thyme, and coarse salt. Rub this mixture over the meat.

3. If dried mushrooms are being used, soak them in warm water until they are soft. Squeeze them out and chop them coarsely. Strain the soaking liquid to remove grit and sand. Combine the mushrooms and liquid in a small saucepan. If necessary, add enough additional water to cover the mushrooms. Simmer 5 minutes. Strain and gently squeeze out the mushrooms. Reserve the mushrooms and liquid separately.

4. If fresh mushrooms are being used, chop them coarsely or slice them. Sauté them briefly in a little butter, then cool and reserve.

5. If fresh chestnuts are used, slit the shells with the point of a knife and simmer them about 15 minutes. Drain and cool slightly and then shell and peel them. If canned chestnuts are being used, merely set aside the proper quantity.

Cooking:

1. To cook the lamb, either roast in a preheated 450°F (230°C) oven until rare or medium (30 to 45 minutes) or cook on a grill or under a broiler. When the lamb is cooked to desired doneness, remove it from the heat and let it rest in a warm place for 15 minutes.

2. Heat the butter in a saucepan and sweat the shallots slowly until they are soft.

3. Add the red wine and reduce to a glaze.

4. Add the mushroom liquid (if you are using dried mushrooms) and reduce by two-thirds.

5. Add the demiglaze or stock and bring to a boil.

6. Add the mushrooms and chestnuts. Simmer about 15 minutes or longer, uncovered, until the liquid is reduced to a rich sauce consistency. (*Note:* The chestnuts will break up into smaller pieces during cooking. If any chestnuts remain whole, break them into two or three pieces.)

7. If desired, finish the sauce by swirling in a little raw butter just before serving.

Presentation:

1. Slice the lamb as shown in Figure 8.8.

2. Arrange the slices, overlapping, on one side of the plate. Spoon the mixture of mushrooms, chestnuts, and sauce along the edge of the meat. Garnish the other side of the plate with desired vegetables.

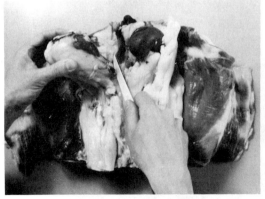 

FIGURE 8.7. **Preparing a whole loin or saddle of lamb for roasting.**
(a) Pull the kidneys from the underside of the loin, if they are still attached.

(b) Trim fat and silverskin from the tenderloin area.

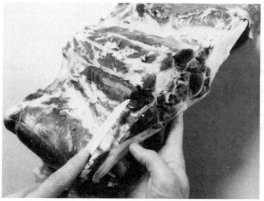

FIGURE 8.7. (Continued)
(c) The point of the knife shows the location of the tenderloins.

(d) Trim off the ends of the flanks, leaving enough attached to cover the tenderloins.

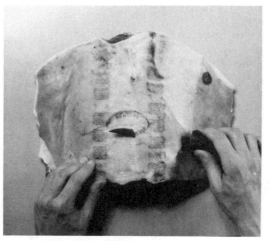

(e) Remove the rib bones (the thirteenth ribs) from the rib end of the loin.

(f) Turn the loin right side up and trim off excess fat, leaving a thin layer to protect the meat during roasting.

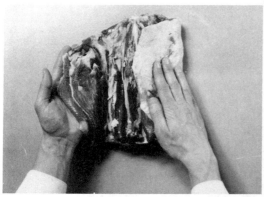

(g) Turn the loin over again, and fold the flanks over the tenderloin.

(h) Tie the loin for roasting.

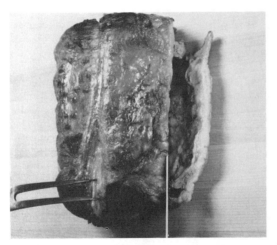

FIGURE 8.8. Carving roast saddle of lamb.
(a) Begin by cutting off the flanks from the sides of the roast.

(b) One method of carving the loin begins by making a cut below the loin muscle parallel to the table.

(c) Holding the knife vertically and parallel to the backbone, cut thin slices from the loin muscle.

(d) A second method begins by making a cut just to one side of the backbone, as shown. (Note that the cutting board has been turned around in this photo, so that the right side of the loin in Figure 8.8c is now on the left.)

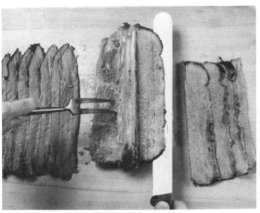

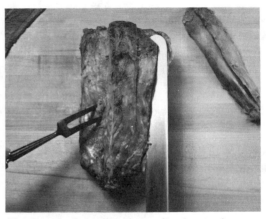

(e) Holding the knife parallel to the table, cut thin slices from the loin.

(f) When the loins have been sliced, turn the roast over and remove the tenderloins.

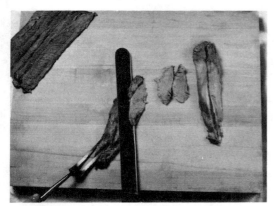

FIGURE 8.8. (Continued)
(g) Slice the tenderloins as desired.

ROAST LOIN OF PORK WITH DATE AND GORGONZOLA STUFFING ON A BED OF ONION FONDUE

		U.S.		Metric	
PORTIONS:		**4**	**16**	*4*	*16*
Ingredients					
Pitted dates, chopped		3 oz	12 oz	*90 g*	*350 g*
Butter		½ tsp	2 tsp	*2 g*	*8 g*
Rosemary		pinch	¼ tsp	*pinch*	*¼ g*
Water		1 ½ oz	6 oz	*50 ml*	*2 dl*
Gorgonzola cheese		1 oz	4 oz	*30 g*	*125 g*
Pork loin, center cut, bone in		2 ½ lb	10 lb	*1.1 kg*	*4.5 kg*
Optional: curing brine (p. 354)					
Salt					
Pepper					
Ground coriander					
Onions		1 ½ lb	6 lb	*700 g*	*3 kg*
Butter		1 oz	4 oz	*30 g*	*125 g*
Demiglaze or rich brown stock		4 oz	1 pt	*1 dl*	*4 dl*
White wine		2 oz	8 oz	*60 ml*	*2.5 dl*
Salt					
Pepper					

Mise en Place:

1. In a saucepan, briefly cook the chopped dates in butter until slightly softened. Add the rosemary and water. Cook until the mixture forms a thick paste. Cool.

2. When the date mixture is completely cool, add the gorgonzola and blend in well.

3. Trim excess fat from the pork loin, leaving only a thin covering. Either bone out completely or remove only the chine and featherbones, leaving the rib bones attached to give shape and definition to the slices when the meat is served.

4. If desired, give the loin a short marination in brine, about 4 to 6 hours. Follow the procedure on page 354.

5. Remove the meat from the brine, if used. Dry the surface of the meat well.

6. Stuff the meat. This can be done in either of two ways.
   a. Butterfly the meat as shown in Figure 8.6, spread the date mixture inside, refold the meat to cover the stuffing, and tie the meat well.
   b. Poke a hole lengthwise through the center of the loin with a thick wooden spoon handle (make sure that the spoon handle is clean and sanitary). Force the date mixture into the hole so that it fills the hole completely.

7. Season the surface of the meat lightly with salt, pepper, and ground coriander. Hold in refrigerator until ready to cook.

8. The onion fondue may be prepared ahead of time or while the pork is roasting. Peel and cut the onions into thin slices. Cook slowly in butter, uncovered, until evenly browned and greatly reduced in volume. This will take about 30 minutes. The onions must cook slowly enough so that they brown evenly and do not scorch. Add the demiglaze or stock and reduce until the mixture is thick and no liquid separates from the onions.

Cooking:

1. Preheat the oven to 425°F (220°C). Place the roast in the oven. After 10 minutes, turn the heat down to 325°F (160°C). (The initial roasting at high temperature is optional; its purpose is to help brown the roast.) Continue to roast until done (internal temperature 165°F or 74°C). This will take 1½ to 2½ hours, depending on the size of the meat and whether or not it has been boned. When the meat is done, remove it from the heat and let it rest 15 minutes in a warm place.

2. While the roast is cooking, reheat the onions if they were cooked in advance or cook them as directed in Mise en Place, step 8.

3. While the finished roast is resting, degrease the roasting pan. Deglaze the pan with the wine and reduce by one-half. Add this liquid to the onions. Season the onion mixture with salt and pepper. (Note: If the pork was brined, the sugar from the brine may have caramelized on the bottom of the pan. If it is burned, be careful when deglazing to avoid getting a burned taste in the sauce, or omit this step entirely.)

Presentation:

Slice the meat. Serve on a bed of onion fondue.

Variations

For a more robust garlic flavor, rub the meat with a paste made of crushed garlic, salt, pepper, and ground coriander before roasting.

Instead of roasting the pork, brown it well and then braise it with the onion fondue, using a little white wine to moisten the braising.

ROAST PORK LOIN YUCATAN-STYLE

		U.S.		Metric	
PORTIONS:		**4**	**16**	*4*	*16*
Ingredients					
Ground cumin		¼ tsp	1 tsp	*½ g*	*2 g*
Oregano		¼ tsp	1 tsp	*¼ g*	*1 g*
Black pepper		¼ tsp	1 tsp	*½ g*	*2 g*
Ground allspice		⅛ tsp	½ tsp	*¼ g*	*1 g*
Garlic cloves, crushed		2	8	*2*	*8*
Paprika		1 tsp	4 tsp	*2 g*	*8 g*
Salt		1 tsp	4 tsp	*5 g*	*20 g*
Orange juice		1 tbsp	2 oz	*15 ml*	*60 ml*
Lemon juice		1 tbsp	2 oz	*15 ml*	*60 ml*
Boneless pork loin		1 ½ lb	6 lb	*700 g*	*3 kg*
Sauce:					
Scallions, sliced thin		¾ oz	3 oz	*25 g*	*100 g*
Jalapeño pepper, minced		1 tbsp	4 tbsp	*15 g*	*60 g*
Salt		¼ tsp	1 tsp	*1 g*	*5 g*
Orange juice		2 tbsp	4 oz	*30 ml*	*125 ml*
Lemon juice		2 tbsp	4 oz	*30 ml*	*125 ml*

Mise en Place:

1. Mix together the first set of ingredients (spices, garlic, salt, and juices) into a thin paste.
2. Trim excess fat from the pork loin.
3. Rub the spice mixture over the pork.
4. Wrap the meat in plastic film. Let it marinate overnight in the refrigerator.
5. Mix together the sauce ingredients. Cover and hold in the refrigerator. (If the sauce is being made within 1 hour before serving, it may be held at room temperature.)

Cooking and Presentation:

1. Roast the pork in an oven preheated to 325°F (160°C) until the internal temperature is about 160°F (70°C).
2. Remove the roast from the oven and let stand in a warm place for 15 minutes.
3. Slice the meat and plate it. Top each portion with about 1 ounce (30 g) of the sauce or serve the sauce in a small cup on the side.

PORK LOIN BRAISED IN APPLE CIDER

		U.S.		*Metric*	
	PORTIONS:	**4**	**16**	*4*	*16*
Ingredients					
Boneless pork loin		1 ½ lb	6 lb	*700 g*	*3 kg*
Sage, crumbled		2 tsp	8 tsp	*2 g*	*8 g*
Black pepper		½ tsp	2 tsp	*1 g*	*4 g*
Salt		2 tsp	8 tsp	*10 g*	*40 g*
Oil					
Onion, chopped		4 oz	1 lb	*125 g*	*500 g*
Garlic		1 clove	2–4 cloves	*1 clove*	*2–4 cloves*
Apples, peeled, chopped		4 oz	1 lb	*125 g*	*500 g*
Apple juice or cider		6 oz	1 ½ pt	*2 dl*	*8 dl*
Garnish:					
Apples		2	6–8	*2*	*6–8*
Butter					

Mise en Place:

1. Trim excess fat from the pork loin.

2. Combine the sage, pepper, and salt. Rub the mixture over the meat. Refrigerate overnight.

Cooking and Presentation:

1. Dry the surface of the meat. In a braising pan, brown the meat well in oil. Remove the meat from the pan.

2. Add the onion and garlic to the pan. Brown lightly.

3. Add the chopped apple and sauté for a few minutes.

4. Return the meat to the pan. Add the apple juice and bring to a boil.

5. Cover and braise in a low oven (325°F or 160°C) for 45 to 60 minutes, until the meat is done.

6. Prepare the garnish: Peel and core the apples. Cut into thick wedges or rings. Sauté in butter over moderate heat until tender and lightly browned. Keep warm.

7. When the meat is done, remove it from the pan and keep it warm. Degrease the cooking liquid and reduce as necessary. Strain. There should be about 1 to 2 oz (30 to 60 ml) per portion. Adjust the seasoning of the sauce.

8. Slice the meat. Plate and garnish with apple slices. Serve with the sauce spooned over the meat or in a sauceboat.

BRAISED ROLLED BREAST OF VEAL WITH PINE NUTS

		U.S.		Metric	
PORTIONS:		**4**	**16**	*4*	*16*
Ingredients					
Veal breast, bone-in		3 lb 8 oz	14 lb	*1.5 kg*	*6 kg*
Stuffing:					
Olive oil		½ oz	2 oz	*15 ml*	*60 ml*
Onion, minced		1 oz	4 oz	*30 g*	*125 g*
Garlic, minced		1 clove	3–4 cloves	*1 clove*	*3–4 cloves*
Carrot, grated		½ oz	2 oz	*15 g*	*30 g*
Sage, crumbled		¼ tsp	1 tsp	*¼ g*	*1 g*
Rosemary, crumbled		¼ tsp	1 tsp	*¼ g*	*1 g*
Pine nuts, toasted		½ oz	2 oz	*15 g*	*30 g*
Fresh bread crumbs		½ oz	2 oz	*15 g*	*30 g*
Parmesan cheese, grated		1 oz	4 oz	*30 g*	*125 g*
Lemon juice		1 tsp	4 tsp	*5 ml*	*20 ml*
Grated lemon zest		pinch	¼ tsp	*pinch*	*½ g*
Salt					
Pepper					
Oil, as needed					
Butter		½ oz	2 oz	*15 g*	*60 g*
Onion, chopped		2 oz	8 oz	*60 g*	*250 g*
Carrot, chopped		1 oz	4 oz	*30 g*	*125 g*
White wine		2 oz	8 oz	*60 ml*	*2.5 dl*
Brown veal stock		2 oz	8 oz	*60 ml*	*2.5 dl*
Brown veal stock		2 oz	8 oz	*60 ml*	*2.5 dl*
Brown veal stock		6 oz	1 ½ pt	*2 dl*	*8 dl*

Mise en Place:

1. Remove all bones and cartilage from the veal breast. Trim well of fat. Set aside in refrigerator.
2. Heat the olive oil in a sauté pan. Add the onion, garlic, and carrot. Sauté gently until softened but not browned.
3. Add the sage and rosemary. Remove from heat and cool.
4. Add the nuts, crumbs, cheese, lemon juice, and lemon zest. Mix well. Season with salt and pepper.
5. Spread the veal breast out on the workbench. The inside—that is, the side where the rib bones were—should be on top.
6. Season the meat with salt and pepper. Spread the stuffing evenly over the meat.
7. Roll up the meat into a cylinder and tie it tightly so that it will hold its shape and the stuffing will remain inside.

Cooking:

1. Heat the oil in a braising pan. Brown the veal lightly on all sides.

2. Remove the meat from the pan and discard any oil remaining in the pan.

3. Add the butter to the pan. Add the chopped onion and carrot. Brown lightly.

4. Return the meat to the pan and add the wine and the first quantity of stock. Cook over moderate heat until the wine is reduced to a glaze. Baste the meat occasionally with the liquid as it is reducing.

5. Add the second quantity of stock and repeat the basting and reducing procedure.

6. Add the last quantity of stock. Cover the pan and place in a low oven (about 325°F or 160°C). Braise until the meat is tender. This will take about 2 hours.

7. If desired, the meat may be glazed after it is cooked. Follow the procedure on page 344 for glazing braised meats.

8. When the meat is done, remove it from the pan and keep it warm. Strain and degrease the braising liquid. If necessary, reduce the liquid over moderate heat until there is about 1 oz (30 ml) sauce per portion. Adjust the seasonings.

Presentation:

1. Remove the twine from the meat. Cut the meat into slices with a very sharp slicing knife, handling the meat carefully so that the pieces hold together and the stuffing does not fall out.

2. Plate the meat. Ladle an ounce (30 ml) of the sauce around the edge of the meat, or in a ribbon across the top, but do not disguise the meat by pouring sauce all over the top.

3. Since this is a hearty dish rather than a delicate one, the plate should be finished off with robust portions of vegetables and starch.

Variations

Braised or Roast Stuffed Loin of Veal

Prepare the stuffing as in the basic recipe. Prepare and stuff the veal loin using the same procedure as described for Roast Loin of Pork with Date and Gorgonzola Stuffing (page 372). Either braise the loin as in the basic recipe or roast it, deglaze the roasting pan with veal stock, and serve the roast with the pan juices.

Braised Rump or Shoulder of Veal

Braise rump or shoulder of veal as in the basic recipe but omit the stuffing. Allow about 2 to 2¼ lb (1 kg) raw veal for 4 portions or 8 to 9 lb (4 kg) for 16 portions.

BRAISED HAM WITH MADEIRA

	U.S.	Metric
PORTIONS:	**20–25**	**20–25**

Ingredients

Ham (see Mise en Place for information on selecting a ham)	1 whole, 10–12 lb	*1 whole, 4.5–5.5 kg*
Onion, diced	4 oz	*125 g*
Carrot, sliced	4 oz	*125 g*
Celery, sliced	2 oz	*60 g*
Madeira wine (preferably Sercial)	8 oz	*2.5 dl*
Demiglaze	1 qt	*1 l*
Bay leaf	1	*1*
Parsley sprigs	6–8	*6–8*
Cornstarch or arrowroot	as needed	*as needed*
Optional garnish for sauce:		
Mushrooms, sliced	1 lb	*500 g*
Butter	2 oz	*60 g*

Mise en Place:

1. Select a mildly cured but flavorful ham for this recipe. Most hams on the U.S. market are fully cooked and are suitable for this dish if they are not too bland and watery. Uncooked hams may also be used, but they will require a longer cooking time (see Cooking, step 4). Aged country hams are not suitable for this recipe; their pronounced flavor is best enjoyed on its own and does not blend well with the flavor of the wine sauce. Furthermore, their salt content is likely to make the sauce inedibly salty.

2. Remove the rind from the ham. Trim off the fat, leaving a fat covering only about ¼ inch (6 mm) thick. Reserve about 1 oz (25 g) of the fat for cooking the mirepoix.

Cooking:

1. Render the reserved fat in a braising pan large enough to hold the ham. Remove the solids, leaving the rendered fat in the pan.

2. Add the onions, carrots, and celery to the pan. Sauté over moderate heat until the vegetables begin to soften.

3. Place the ham in the pan. Add the wine, demiglaze, bay leaf, and parsley. Bring the liquid to a boil.

4. Cover the pan and place in an oven preheated to 300°F (150°C). If it is a fully cooked ham, braise until the internal temperature registers 130°F (55°C); this will take about 15 minutes per pound. If it is an uncooked ham, braise until the internal temperature registers 160°F (70°C); this will take about 20 minutes per pound.

5. Remove the ham from the pan. If it is to be glazed or coated with a topping, follow the directions in the Variations section following the main recipe. If it is to be served as is, set it in a warm place while the sauce is finished.

6. Degrease and strain the braising liquid. Measure it and taste it for seasonings. If it is undersalted, reduce it over moderately high heat to 3 cups (7 dl), taste again, and adjust the seasonings. If it is sufficiently salted, merely reserve 3 cups of it. Reducing it would make it too salty. In a saucepan, thicken the sauce slightly, if desired, with a little cornstarch or arrowroot mixed with cold stock, water, or Madeira.

7. If desired, sauté the mushrooms in butter and add to the sauce.

Presentation:

The finished ham is sliced and served as desired with the sauce on the side. A whole glazed ham is especially attractive when presented on a buffet and carved to order. For best eating, cut the slices very thin and serve several per portion, rather than serving one or two thick slices.

Variations

Braised Ham à la Crème

Substitute white wine for the Madeira in the basic recipe. Substitute chicken stock for the demiglaze. To finish the sauce, reduce the braising liquid with an equal quantity of heavy cream until lightly thickened.

Glazed Hams

The following glazes and toppings can be used with any baked ham, braised ham, or simmered country ham. Before applying the glaze or topping, score the fat in a diamond pattern. This contributes to the appearance of the finished ham and also helps the glaze adhere.

Simple sugar glaze: Sprinkle top of the ham with powdered sugar from a sieve or shaker. Place the ham in a hot oven until the sugar caramelizes.

Baste-on glaze: Melt preserves or jelly (such as red currant, apple cranberry, orange marmalade, apricot, pineapple, peach) and, if desired, dilute with a little rum, brandy, bourbon, sweet wine, or apple juice. Brush over the ham. Place the ham in a hot oven, basting occasionally with more of the mixture, until the surface is well glazed.

Mustard–brown sugar glaze. Mix 8 oz (250 g) of brown sugar with 2 oz (60 g) of prepared mustard. Mix in enough honey or molasses to make a paste. Brush over the ham. Bake until the ham is glazed.

Crumb topping: Mix together 4 oz (125 g) of brown sugar, 1 pt (5 dl) of fresh bread crumbs, and 1 tsp (2 g) or more of dry mustard. Pat onto the surface of the ham. Bake until the crumbs are well browned. (For a nonsweet variation, omit the brown sugar.)

STEAK HACHÉ WITH FENNEL   *(Color Plate 12)*

		U.S.		Metric	
PORTIONS:		**4**	**16**	*4*	*16*
Ingredients					
Ground beef		1 ½–2 lb	6–8 lb	*700–900 g*	*3–3.5 kg*
Cold brown stock		2 oz	8 oz	*60 ml*	*2.5 dl*
Pepper		¼ tsp	1 tsp	*½ g*	*2 g*
Salt		1 tsp	4 tsp	*5 g*	*20 g*
Fennel seeds		½ tsp	2 tsp	*1 g*	*4 g*
Rosemary		½ tsp	2 tsp	*½ g*	*2 g*
Bulb fennel, trimmed		12 oz	3 lb	*350 g*	*1.4 kg*
Olive oil		1 tbsp	2 oz	*15 ml*	*60 ml*
Water or chicken stock		as needed		*as needed*	
Tomato, peeled, seeded, coarsely chopped		10 oz	2 ½ lb	*300 g*	*1.2 kg*
Garlic, chopped		1 tsp	4 tsp	*4 g*	*15 g*
Thyme		¼ tsp	1 tsp	*¼ g*	*1 g*
Salt					
Pepper					
Optional: maître d'hôtel butter, garlic butter, or escargot butter					

Mise en Place:

1. Lightly mix together the beef, stock, pepper, and salt. Form into patties 1 ½ inches (3 to 4 cm) thick. Handle gently and do not pack the meat.

2. Crush the fennel seeds and rosemary together. Sprinkle this mixture on both sides of the meat patties and pat it so that it adheres.

3. Cut the bulb(s) of fennel in half through the root end. Cut out and discard the root ends. Cut the fennel into 1-inch (2.5-cm) dice.

4. (*Note:* The vegetable mixture can be cooked ahead of time and held in the refrigerator, or it can be cooked just before serving.) Sweat the fennel in olive oil over low heat. Cover and let simmer in its own moisture until almost tender, about 20 minutes. If the vegetable becomes too dry and in danger of scorching, add a little water or chicken stock as necessary. When the fennel is almost tender, uncover and, if there are juices in the pan, reduce until nearly dry.

5. Add the tomato, garlic, and thyme. Raise the heat and cook rapidly until the garlic has softened and the mixture is only slightly juicy. The vegetables should retain their separate identities—that is, the mixture should look like chunks of fennel and tomato, not fennel in tomato sauce. Season with salt and pepper.

Cooking:

1. Grill or panbroil the steaks to desired doneness.
2. Reheat the vegetable mixture if necessary.

Presentation:

1. Place each steak in the center of a plate.
2. Spoon the vegetable mixture around the steak.
3. If desired, top each steak with a slice of flavored butter. (A sprig of fennel top could also be used to garnish the top of the steak.)

Variations

Mix some minced onion, cooked in a little butter and cooled, into the meat mixture.

Ground lamb can be prepared using the same recipe.

STEAK EN CHEVREUIL

		U.S.		Metric	
	PORTIONS:	4	16	4	16
Ingredients					
Beef steaks, size and type (tenderloin, strip, sirloin, etc.) as desired		4	16	4	16
Marinade for Venison (p. 460)		1–1½ pt	2–3 qt	5–7.5 dl	2–3 l
Poivrade Sauce (p. 46)		8 oz	1 qt	2.5 dl	1 l

Mise en Place:

1. Trim steaks as necessary.
2. Place the steaks and marinade in a stainless steel or other nonreactive container. Refrigerate for 1 or 2 days. Turn the steaks several times so that they will marinate evenly.
3. On the day of cooking, remove the steaks from the marinade and return them to the refrigerator. Use the marinade to prepare the poivrade sauce, or use an already prepared sauce. Have the sauce hot at service time.

Cooking and Presentation:

1. Dry the steaks before cooking. Grill or sauté them to desired doneness.
2. Plate the steaks as desired. Serve the sauce in a separate sauceboat on the side or ladle it around the steaks.

TENDERLOIN STEAK WITH GREEN PEPPERCORNS

		U.S.		Metric	
PORTIONS:		4	16	4	16
Ingredients					
Beef tenderloin steaks, trimmed, 6 oz (170 g) each		4	16	4	16
Salt					
Green peppercorns (packed in brine or water), drained		1 tbsp	4 tbsp	10 g	20 g
Oil, as needed					
Brandy		2 oz	8 oz	60 ml	2.5 dl
Rich brown stock or demiglaze		8 oz	1 qt	2.5 dl	1 l
Raw butter		1 oz	4 oz	30 g	125 g
Salt					
Garnish: additional green peppercorns, as desired					

Mise en Place:

1. Check over the steaks to be sure that they have been completely trimmed of external fat and silverskin.
2. Season the steaks with salt.
3. Rinse the peppercorns in cold water and drain well. Crush the peppercorns with the side of a knife blade and spread them onto both sides of each steak.

Cooking:

1. Heat a film of oil in a heavy sauté pan over moderately high heat.
2. Place the steaks in the pan and cook them on both sides to desired doneness.
3. Remove the steaks from the pan and keep them warm. Degrease the pan.
4. Deglaze the pan with the brandy. Reduce au sec.
5. Add the stock or demiglaze. Reduce by one-half.
6. Finish the sauce by swirling in the raw butter. Season to taste with salt.

Presentation:

1. Ladle pools of sauce onto dinner plates, using about 1 oz (30 ml) of sauce per portion.
2. Place a steak in the center of each pool of sauce.
3. Sprinkle a few green peppercorns around each steak to garnish.

Note: As a variation, you might plate the steaks and then ladle the sauce over them. This presentation might be best if the tops of the steaks are not as well browned or as attractive as they should be.

VEAL NOISETTES WITH ARMAGNAC AND SICHUAN PEPPERCORNS

		U.S.		Metric	
PORTIONS:		**4**	**16**	*4*	*16*
Ingredients					
Veal noisettes, 2 oz (60 g) each (see Mise en Place, step 1)		8	32	*8*	*32*
Salt					
White pepper					
Oil or clarified butter for cooking					
Sichuan peppercorns		1 tsp	4 tsp	*1 g*	*5 g*
Shallot, peeled		1 oz	4 oz	*30 g*	*125 g*
Armagnac (see note)		2 oz	8 oz	*30 ml*	*2.5 dl*
Demiglaze		8 oz	1 qt	*2.5 dl*	*1 l*
Raw butter		2 oz	8 oz	*60 g*	*250 g*

Note: If armagnac is not available, substitute another type of brandy and change the name of the recipe.

Mise en Place:

1. To prepare veal noisettes from loin of veal, bone out the loin and trim away all fat and silverskin. Cut the loin into 4-oz (125-g) slices and then cut each slice in half crosswise. Noisettes may also be cut from the tenderloin.

2. Mince the shallot.

Cooking:

1. Heat the oil in a sauté pan. Season the veal with salt and pepper and add them to the pan. Add the sichuan peppercorns to the pan at the same time. Cook the veal on both sides over moderate heat until well browned and cooked to desired doneness.

2. Remove the noisettes from the pan and keep them warm. Pour off any fat remaining in the pan, leaving only a thin film. Leave the sichuan peppercorns in the pan.

3. Add the shallots to the pan and sauté briefly.

4. Deglaze with the armagnac. Reduce by one-half.

5. Add the demiglaze and bring to a boil. Reduce by one-fourth.

6. Finish the sauce by swirling in the raw butter. Strain and adjust the seasoning.

7. Plate the veal and ladle the sauce (1 ½ oz or 50 ml per portion) around or over the noisettes.

LAMB NOISETTES IN A POTATO CRUST

		U.S.		Metric	
PORTIONS:		4	16	*4*	*16*
Ingredients					
Starchy potatoes		8 oz	2 lb	*500 g*	*2 kg*
Lemon juice					
Sweet red bell pepper, brunoise		1 oz	4 oz	*30 g*	*125 g*
Shallots, minced		½ oz	2 oz	*15 g*	*60 g*
Chopped parsley		1 tbsp	4 tbsp	*3 g*	*14 g*
Basil leaves, fresh, chopped		3–4	12–15	*3–4*	*12–15*
Boneless loin of lamb, trimmed of all fat and silverskin		1 lb	4 lb	*500 g*	*2 kg*
Salt					
Pepper					
Egg whites		2	6–8	*2*	*6–8*
Olive oil					
Balsamic vinegar		1 oz	4 oz	*30 ml*	*125 ml*
Water		½ oz	2 oz	*15 ml*	*60 ml*
Glace de viande		1 ½ oz	6 oz	*50 g*	*200 g*
Raw butter		½ oz	2 oz	*15 g*	*60 g*
Zucchini timbales (small) with gruyère cheese (p. 534)		4	16	*4*	*16*

Mise en Place:

1. Peel the potatoes. Grate them into a bowl containing water with a little lemon juice (use about 2 tbsp lemon juice per pint of cold water, or 30 ml per 5 dl). The purpose of the lemon water is to keep the potatoes white.

2. Have ready the red pepper, shallot, parsley, and basil.

3. Shortly before cooking, drain the liquid from the potatoes. Squeeze out excess moisture and dry the potatoes with clean towels. Mix with the red pepper, shallot, parsley, and basil.

4. Cut the lamb into noisettes (small, thick slices) about 2 oz (60 g) each. Flatten them slightly so that they are all the same thickness. Season them with salt and pepper.

5. Beat the egg whites slightly (do not whip to a foam). One by one, dip the lamb noisettes into the egg white, and then coat them with the potato mixture. Handle them carefully so that the potato doesn't fall off.

Cooking:

1. In a heavy skillet, preferably a nonstick skillet, heat a generous quantity (about ¼ inch, or 6 mm) of olive oil or vegetable oil. Carefully place the potato-coated lamb pieces in the hot oil. Cook on both sides until the potatoes are well browned and the lamb is cooked to desired doneness. Remove from the pan and drain well.

2. Degrease the pan. Deglaze it with the vinegar and reduce au sec. Add the water and glace; heat and mix. Finish by swirling in the raw butter.

Presentation:

1. Place two noisettes and one zucchini timbale on each plate.

2. Balance out the plate with a small quantity of fresh vegetables—the selection depends on seasonality and availability.

3. Dribble a little of the deglazing sauce (about ½ oz or 15 ml per portion) onto the plate around the meat.

Variations

Pork, beef, and veal noisettes from the tenderloin or loin can be prepared the same way. You may omit the red pepper and substitute an appropriate herb for the parsley and basil, such as tarragon for veal or sage for pork.

Lamb Noisettes with a Coating of Wild Mushrooms

In place of the potato mixture, coat the meat with minced dried mushrooms prepared as follows: Soak the mushrooms in warm water until soft, squeeze out moisture, and chop fine. Porcini (boletes or cèpes) or black trumpet mushrooms are especially appropriate for this dish.

VEAL MEDAILLONS WITH ARTICHOKES EN CROÛTE

		U.S.		Metric	
PORTIONS:		**4**	**16**	**4**	**16**
Ingredients					
Artichokes, large		1	4	*1*	*4*
Lemons, as needed					
Onion, peeled		1 oz	4 oz	*30 g*	*125 g*
Garlic, minced		1 tsp	4 tsp	*4 g*	*15 g*
Olive oil		2 tsp	8 tsp	*10 ml*	*40 ml*
White wine		1 oz	4 oz	*30 ml*	*125 ml*
Tomato concassé		1 oz	4 oz	*30 g*	*125 g*
Chopped parsley		large pinch	1 tbsp	*large pinch*	*3 g*
Salt					
Pepper					
Boneless loin of veal, trimmed		1 lb	4 lb	*500 g*	*2 kg*
Salt					
White pepper					
Flour					
Butter, for cooking					
Italian fontina or taleggio cheese		4 oz	1 lb	*125 g*	*500 g*
Grated parmesan cheese		½ oz	2 oz	*15 g*	*60 g*
Puff pastry (p. 616; approximate measure)		1 lb	4 lb	*500 g*	*2 kg*
Egg yolks		1	2	*1*	*2*
Cold water		2 tsp	4 tsp	*10 ml*	*20 ml*
Sauce, any one of the following: Bercy Sauce (p. 44) Perigueux Sauce (p. 46) Brown Sauce Thickened with Vegetable Purée (p. 55) Cream Brown Sauce (p. 63)		4–8 oz	1–2 pt	*1–2.5 dl*	*5–10 dl*

Mise en Place:

1. Trim the artichokes down to the bases. Rub them with cut lemon as necessary to keep them from darkening. Cut them into small (¼-inch or 5-mm) dice. Put them into a bowl of water containing lemon juice.

2. Cut the onion brunoise.

3. Drain the artichoke dice. Sweat the artichoke, onion, and garlic in olive oil. Add the wine, cover, and cook slowly until tender.

4. Add the tomato to the artichoke mixture and cook, uncovered, until the mixture is dry. Add the parsley and season with salt and pepper.

5. Cut the veal into 4-oz (125-g) medaillons and flatten them slightly with a meat mallet.

6. Dry the medaillons. Season them with salt and white pepper, then dredge them in flour. Shake off the excess.

7. Brown them well in butter, about 2 minutes on each side. They must remain somewhat rare, since they will cook more later. Cool them and then chill them well.

8. Cut about two-thirds of the taleggio cheese into thin slices. Grate the rest and mix it with the parmesan cheese.

9. On a lightly floured surface, roll out about one-third of the puff pastry into a very thin rectangle, about ⅛ inch (3 mm) thick. Cut out ovals or rectangles somewhat larger than the veal medaillons; they must be large enough to leave a generous border around the veal when a medaillon is placed on top. Cut out one piece of pastry for each medaillon. These pieces are the bottoms of the pastry cases.

10. For the tops of the pastry cases, roll out the remaining pastry into a rectangle only slightly thicker (about 3/16 inch or 4 mm). Cut out ovals or rectangles slightly larger than those for the bottoms. They must be larger so that they will cover the mound of meat, vegetables, and cheese.

11. Place the pastry bottoms (the thin pieces) onto baking sheets. Beat the egg yolk with the cold water. Brush the borders of the pastry pieces with the egg wash.

12. Center a veal medaillon on each piece of pastry. Place the sliced cheese on top of the meat.

13. Mix the grated cheese with the artichoke mixture. Place a small mound of this mixture on top of each piece of veal.

14. Top with the thicker pastry pieces, smoothing it down gently over the meat (do not stretch the pastry) and pressing it firmly against the pastry bottoms to seal. Trim off the edges of the pastry neatly to leave a border about ½ inch (1 cm) wide. Place the trays in the refrigerator and chill for at least 20 minutes.

15. Prepare the desired sauce.

Cooking:

1. Preheat an oven to 425°F (220°C). Egg wash the tops of the pastries. Bake the veal medaillons en croûte until the pastry is golden brown, about 15 to 20 minutes.

2. Reheat the sauce as necessary.

Presentation:

1. Plate the veal en croûte. Spoon about 1 oz (25 ml) of the sauce around the veal.

2. If desired, serve additional sauce in a sauceboat.

VEAL POJARSKI

		U.S.		Metric	
PORTIONS:		4	16	4	16
Ingredients					
Fresh bread crumbs		4 oz	1 lb	100 g	400 g
Milk, as needed					
Lean veal, trimmed of all fat and sinew		1 lb	4 lb	400 g	1.6 kg
Butter, softened		4 oz	1 lb	100 g	400 g
Salt		1 tsp	4 tsp	5 g	20 g
White pepper		pinch	¼ tsp	pinch	½ g
Nutmeg		pinch	¼ tsp	pinch	½ g
Flour					
Butter, for cooking					

Note: The U.S. measures yield generous portions of 6 oz each; for smaller portions, reduce quantities proportionately. The metric measures yield slightly smaller portions of 150 g each.

Mise en Place:

1. Place the crumbs in a bowl and add enough milk to moisten them thoroughly. Let them soak until soft. Press out the excess milk.

2. Chop the veal very fine or grind it. Mix it gently but thoroughly with the butter, crumbs, and seasonings.

3. Scale the meat mixture into equal 6-oz or 150-g portions. (For each portion, you may make two small patties or one large one.) Shape the meat into oval patties or into the shape of chops. For a traditional and elegant presentation, make mock rib chops by molding the meat onto fresh, raw rib-chop bones. Place the meat in pans in one layer and chill well.

Cooking:

1. Dredge the meat patties in flour and shake off the excess.

2. Sauté them on both sides in butter over moderate heat until golden brown and completely cooked but not dry (if they are overcooked, the butter will begin oozing out and the texture will suffer).

Variations

An appropriate herb, such as tarragon, can be added to the meat mixture.

Instead of dredging the meat patties in flour, coat them lightly with fresh bread crumbs. It is also possible to give them a standard breading (flour, egg wash, and bread crumbs), but this is not advisable, since the breading may be too heavy for the delicate meat.

VEAL PAILLARD WITH CHILI BUTTER

		U.S.		Metric	
PORTIONS:		4	16	4	16
Ingredients					
Powdered ancho chiles, or commercial chili powder		1 tbsp	4 tbsp	5 g	20 g
Butter		2 oz	8 oz	60 g	250 g
Lime juice		½ tsp	2 tsp	2 ml	10 ml
Salt, to taste					
Boneless veal loin, trimmed of all fat and silverskin		1 ½–2 lb	6–8 lb	700–900 g	2.8–3.6 kg
Salt					
Pepper					
Vegetable oil					
Vegetable oil, as needed					
Butter		1 tbsp	2 oz	15 g	60 g
Lime wedges		4	16	4	16
Lemon wedges		4	16	4	16

Mise en Place:

1. Blend together the chili powder, butter, lime juice, and salt. Roll the flavored butter into a cylinder shape in a piece of plastic wrap and refrigerate overnight.
2. Cut the veal loin across the grain into slices (one slice per portion) about ½ inch (12 mm) thick. With a meat mallet, very carefully pound the cutlets until they are a uniform ¼ inch (6 mm) thick or slightly less. Be careful not to tear the meat. See Figure 8.5 for the technique.

Cooking:

1. Preheat a grill or broiler until it is very hot. Extremely high heat is necessary to cook the paillards properly.
2. Season the veal with salt and pepper. Brush both sides of each piece lightly with oil to help prevent sticking.
3. Place each piece of veal diagonally on the grill. Cook about 10 seconds, then give it a quarter turn to make diamond-shape grill marks on the first side. Cook another 10 seconds. Turn the veal over and repeat the grill-marking procedure on the second side. Total cooking time depends on the degree of heat and the thickness of the veal, but will generally be about 45 seconds. Watch the cooking very closely, because the meat will become overcooked and dry very quickly in this intense heat.

Presentation:

1. Immediately plate the paillards. Rub the top of the meat with a little butter to give it a shine.
2. Place a slice of chili butter in the center of each paillard.
3. Garnish each plate with a wedge of lime and a wedge of lemon.

PORK MEDAILLONS WITH BLACK BEAN SAUCE

		U.S.		Metric	
PORTIONS:		**4**	**16**	**4**	**16**
Ingredients					
Black turtle beans		4 oz	1 lb	*125 g*	*500 g*
Water, as needed					
Chicken stock		12 oz	3 pt	*375 ml*	*1.5 l*
Bay leaf		1	2	*1*	*2*
Onion, peeled and quartered		1 small	1 large	*1 small*	*1 large*
Olive oil		1 oz	4 oz	*30 ml*	*125 ml*
Red onion, small dice		2 oz	8 oz	*60 ml*	*2.5 dl*
Jalapeño pepper, seeded and cut brunoise		1	4	*1*	*4*
Tomatoes (fresh or canned), peeled, seeded, chopped		4 oz	1 lb	*125 g*	*500 g*
Salt					
Pepper					
Lime juice or red wine vinegar		2 tsp	8 tsp	*10 ml*	*40 ml*
Boneless pork loin or tenderloin		1–1 ½ lb	4–6 lb	*500–700 g*	*2–2.7 kg*
Marinade:					
Chopped cilantro		1 tbsp	4 tbsp	*3 g*	*15 g*
Garlic, chopped		1 tsp	4 tsp	*3 g*	*10 g*
Olive oil		2 oz	8 oz	*60 ml*	*2.5 dl*
Lime juice		1 tbsp	2 oz	*15 ml*	*60 ml*
Salt		½ tsp	2 tsp	*3 g*	*10 g*
Chopped cilantro		1 tbsp	4 tbsp	*3 g*	*15 g*
Cilantro sprigs for garnish					

Mise en Place:

1. Pick over the beans and rinse them thoroughly. Soak them overnight in cold water or speed soak them as follows: Place them in a saucepan with cold water to cover by 2 inches (5 cm); bring to a boil, cover, and let stand 1 to 2 hours.

2. Drain the beans. Combine them with the stock, bay leaf, and quartered onion. Bring to a boil, cover, and simmer until the beans are tender. If necessary, add a little additional stock or water during cooking to prevent drying and scorching. There should be very little liquid remaining in the pan when the beans are tender.

3. Heat the olive oil in a saucepan and sauté the onion and jalapeño pepper for a few minutes.

4. Add the tomato and simmer 5 minutes.

5. Add the cooked beans and simmer another 5 minutes. Season with salt and pepper and add the lime juice or vinegar.

6. Cut the pork into medaillons; they may be large or small as desired, but they should be of fairly uniform size. Flatten them slightly with a meat mallet.

7. Combine the marinade ingredients. Add the marinade to the pork cutlets and toss gently so that all the meat surfaces are lightly coated with the marinade. Marinate 2 to 4 hours.

Cooking:

1. Brush any marinade solids from the pork medaillons and dry the meat.

2. Cook the medaillons by grilling, broiling, or sautéing, as desired.

3. Reheat the black bean mixture and add the chopped cilantro.

Presentation:

1. Spread a layer of the bean mixture on dinner plates.

2. Arrange the medaillons in the center of the plates.

3. Garnish the top of the meat with a few leaves of cilantro.

LAMB "LONDON BROIL" WITH ROSEMARY, GARLIC, AND ANCHOVY SAUCE

		U.S.		Metric	
PORTIONS:		*4*	*16*	*4*	*16*
Ingredients					
Boneless, trimmed lamb from the leg		1 ½ lb	6 lb	*700 g*	*2.8 kg*
Marinade:					
Rosemary, fresh, chopped (see note)		1 ½ tsp	2 tbsp	*1.5 g*	*6 g*
Pepper		¼ tsp	1 tsp	*½ g*	*2 g*
Salt		¼ tsp	1 tsp	*1 g*	*5 g*
Lemon juice		1 tbsp	2 oz	*15 ml*	*60 ml*
Olive oil		3 tbsp	6 oz	*50 ml*	*2 dl*
Sauce:					
Olive oil		1 oz	4 oz	*30 ml*	*125 ml*
Anchovy fillets, chopped		3–6	12–24	*3–6*	*12–24*
Rosemary		1 tsp	4 tsp	*1 g*	*4 g*
Garlic cloves, sliced		1	4	*1*	*4*

Note: The quantities indicated for rosemary are for the fresh herb. If using dried rosemary, use one-third the quantity.

Mise en Place:

1. Seam and trim the lamb, removing all silverskin. If necessary, butterfly the piece or pieces of meat or cut them in half horizontally so that the meat is about 1 inch (2.5 cm) thick.

2. Combine the crushed rosemary, pepper, and salt and rub the mixture into the meat. Combine the lemon juice and olive oil and coat the meat on all sides with the mixture. Marinate the meat 3 or 4 hours, refrigerated.

Cooking:

1. Preheat a grill or broiler. Broil the lamb on both sides to a rare or medium-rare stage of doneness. Remove the meat from the heat and let it rest in a warm place for a few minutes.

2. Make the sauce immediately before serving. Heat the olive oil in a small pan. Add the anchovy, rosemary, and garlic and sauté a minute or two, until the garlic begins to turn golden brown. Be careful when adding the anchovies to the pan; the oil may spatter, especially if it is too hot.

Presentation:

1. Holding a slicing knife at a sharp angle in order to make broader slices, slice the meat into very thin slices across the grain. Arrange the slices, overlapping each other like shingles, on dinner plates.

2. Spoon a little (about 1 to 1 ½ tsp or 5 to 7 ml per portion) of the sauce, including the solids, over each portion.

3. Garnish the plate with any appropriate vegetable and potato.

Variation

The anchovies may be omitted if desired.

ORIENTAL BEEF STEAMED IN CABBAGE LEAVES

(Color Plate 13)

		U.S.		Metric	
PORTIONS:		**4**	**16**	*4*	*16*
Ingredients					
Beef tenderloin		1 lb	4 lb	*500 g*	*2 kg*
Chinese chili paste		1 oz	4 oz	*30 g*	*125 g*
Lemon juice		1 tbsp	2 oz	*15 ml*	*60 ml*
Sherry wine		1 tbsp	2 oz	*15 ml*	*60 ml*
Fresh ginger root, grated		½ tsp	2 tsp	*2 g*	*10 g*
Salt, to taste					
Savoy cabbage, as needed					
Scallions		4	16	*4*	*16*
Toasted unsweetened coconut		2 tsp	8 tsp	*2 g*	*10 g*
Oriental sesame oil		2–3 tsp	3–4 tbsp	*10–15 ml*	*40–60 ml*
Ginger Oil (p. 79)		2–3 tsp	3–4 tbsp	*10–15 ml*	*40–60 ml*
Cooked brown rice or wild rice					

Mise en Place:

1. Make sure that the beef is trimmed of all fat and silverskin. Cut the beef into 4-oz (125-g) portions about 3 to 4 inches long and 1½ inches wide (8 to 10 cm long, 4 cm wide).

2. Mix together the chili paste, lemon juice, sherry, ginger, and salt. (If you are using a type of chili paste containing whole soybeans, mash them.) Toss the beef pieces with this mixture until they are well coated. Let them marinate 1 to 2 hours.

3. Cut out the core of the cabbage and carefully pull off the leaves of the outer part of the cabbage without tearing them. These leaves are used to form wrappers for the meat. Save the inner part of the cabbage for another purpose. You will need 4 to 6 leaves per portion. Blanch the leaves for 2 minutes in boiling water, drain, and cool them under cold water. Shave off the thick part of the center rib of each leaf so that it will lie flat.

4. Cut the scallions into thin slices.

5. Arrange 3 to 4 cabbage leaves on a work surface so that they overlap each other to form a square or rectangle 8 to 10 inches (20 to 25 cm) on each side. See Figure 8.9 for an illustration of the technique.

6. Place one piece of beef centered along one edge of the cabbage rectangle. Do not wipe any of the marinade off the beef; for maximum flavor, it should be lightly coated with the chili paste mixture. Sprinkle the beef with some sliced scallions and a little toasted coconut. Fold the two sides of the cabbage rectangle over the beef and then roll it up like an egg roll. To secure the roll and keep it from coming apart, you can tie it with a piece of twine or with a blanched scallion, or you can wrap it tightly in heat-proof plastic film. Repeat this procedure with each portion of beef.

Cooking:

Arrange the beef rolls in a steamer on a rack or in a perforated pan. Steam for 10 minutes. Remove from the steamer and keep warm and covered for another 5 minutes.

Presentation:

1. Untie or unwrap the beef and cabbage rolls. Cut them crosswise into 3 or 4 slices.

2. Arrange the slices, cut side up, on dinner plates with the cooked brown rice or wild rice. Drizzle a few drops of sesame oil and the ginger oil over and around the beef rolls.

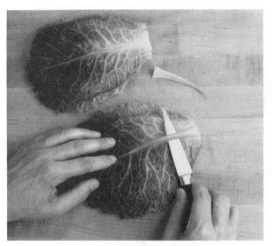

FIGURE 8.9. **Preparing Oriental Beef Steamed in Cabbage Leaves.**
(a) Trim the thick ribs of the blanched leaves so that they will roll easily.

(b) Arrange three or four leaves, depending on their size, into a square or rectangle. Place the piece of the marinated tenderloin toward one edge of the cabbage square and sprinkle with sliced scallions and toasted coconut.

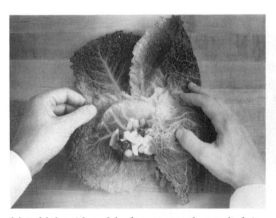

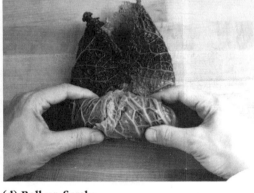

(c) Fold the sides of the leaves over the tenderloin.

(d) Roll up firmly.

(e) The roll is ready for steaming.

SPICED BEEF OR LAMB STEWED WITH SAFFRON AND ONIONS

		U.S.		Metric	
PORTIONS:		**4**	**16**	**4**	**16**
Ingredients					
Onions		1 lb	4 lb	*500 g*	*2 kg*
Vegetable oil		2 oz	8 oz	*60 ml*	*250 ml*
Beef or lamb shank, shoulder, or chuck, boned and trimmed of fat and sinews		1 ½ lb	6 lb	*700 g*	*2.8 kg*
Bay leaves		1	3	*1*	*3*
Cardamom pods		6	25	*6*	*25*
Black peppercorns		½ tsp	2 tsp	*1 g*	*4 g*
Whole cloves		4	16	*4*	*16*
Yogurt		2 oz	8 oz	*60 ml*	*250 ml*
Brown stock, white stock, or water		12 oz	3 pt	*3.5 dl*	*1.5 l*
Saffron threads		large pinch	1 tsp	*large pinch*	*¼ g*
Cayenne		pinch	large pinch	*pinch*	*large pinch*
Salt					
Heavy cream or sour cream		3 oz	12 oz	*1 dl*	*4 dl*

Mise en Place:

1. Cut the onions into very thin slices. Over moderate heat, cook them in the oil, stirring often, until they are well browned. Drain and squeeze out the excess oil. Reserve both the onions and the oil.
2. Cut the meat into large cubes.

Cooking:

1. Heat the reserved onion oil in a braising pan. Add the meat cubes and brown well. Remove the meat from the pan with a slotted spoon.
2. Add the bay leaves, cardamom, peppercorns, and cloves to the pan and cook them briefly, until the bay leaves are brown. Add a little more oil if necessary. Remove the spices from the pan and tie them in a piece of cheesecloth.
3. Return the meat and spice bag to the pan. Add the yogurt, stock or water, saffron, cayenne, and salt to taste. Bring to a simmer, cover, and simmer until the meat is tender.
4. When the meat is tender, remove the meat from the pan with a slotted spoon. Remove and discard the spice bag.
5. Degrease and reduce the braising liquid as necessary.
6. Add the browned onions, the cream, and the meat to the sauce. Simmer 5 to 10 minutes to blend the flavors. Do not let it boil.
7. Season to taste with salt.

ESTOUFFADE OF BEEF AND PORK PROVENÇALE

		U.S.		Metric	
PORTIONS:		**4**	**16**	*4*	*16*
Ingredients					
Beef chuck, boneless, well trimmed		12 oz	3 lb	*350 g*	*1.4 kg*
Pork shoulder or butt, boneless, well trimmed		12 oz	3 lb	*350 g*	*1.4 kg*
White wine		12 oz	3 pt	*4 dl*	*1.5 l*
Olive oil		1 oz	4 oz	*30 ml*	*125 ml*
Salt					
Green olives, pitted		3 oz	12 oz	*100 g*	*400 g*
Meaty slab bacon		2 oz	8 oz	*60 g*	*250 g*
Olive oil		1 ½ oz	6 oz	*50 ml*	*2 dl*
Brown stock		12 oz	3 pt	*4 dl*	*1.5 l*
Onions, sliced		4 oz	1 lb	*125 g*	*500 g*
Sachet:					
Whole cloves		1	4	*1*	*4*
Bay leaves		½	2	*½*	*2*
Thyme		¼ tsp	1 tsp	*¼ tsp*	*1 tsp*
Parsley stems		6	25	*6*	*25*
Orange peel		1 small strip	2 strips	*1 small strip*	*2 strips*
Peppercorns		6	25	*6*	*25*
Tomato paste		1 oz	4 oz	*30 g*	*125 g*
Salt					

Mise en Place:

1. Cut the beef and pork into large cubes.
2. Combine the wine and olive oil. Salt the meat lightly and add it to the wine mixture. Cover and marinate overnight, refrigerated.
3. Blanch the olives as follows: In a saucepan, add enough cold water to the olives to cover. Bring to a simmer, simmer 2 minutes, drain, and rinse under cold water.
4. Cut the bacon into ½-inch (1-cm) dice. Blanch as follows: Add enough cold water to the bacon to cover. Bring to a simmer, simmer 5 minutes, drain, and rinse under cold water.

Cooking:

1. Remove the meat from the marinade and pat it dry.
2. Heat the oil in a braising pan and brown the meat well on all sides.
3. Drain off excess fat from the pan. Add the marinade, stock, onions, sachet, tomato paste, and blanched bacon. Bring to a boil, cover, and braise in an oven at 325°F (160°C) for 1 hour.
4. Add the olives and continue to braise until the meat is tender.
5. Degrease the sauce and reduce it slightly, if necessary, to thicken it. Season to taste.

PORK CHOPS WITH PRUNES

		U.S.		Metric	
PORTIONS:		4	16	4	16
Ingredients					
Thick pork chops		4	16	4	16
Carrot, chopped		2 oz	8 oz	60 g	250 g
Onion, chopped		2 oz	8 oz	60 g	250 g
Celery, chopped		1 oz	4 oz	30 g	125 g
Butter		½ oz	2 oz	15 g	60 g
Red wine vinegar		1 oz	4 oz	30 ml	125 ml
Red wine		12 oz	3 pt	4 dl	1.5 l
Sachet:					
Parsley stems		6	25	6	25
Bay leaf		¼	1	¼	1
Thyme		pinch	½ tsp	pinch	½ g
Whole cloves		1	4	1	4
Peppercorns		4	16	4	16
Prunes		6 oz	24 oz	175 g	700 g
Water, as needed					
Salt					
Pepper					
Vegetable oil					
Beurre manié					

Mise en Place:

1. Trim off excess fat from the edges of the chops.

2. If desired, chops may be marinated in brine for a few hours (see page 354 for procedure).

3. Sweat the onion, carrot, and celery in butter. Add the vinegar, wine, and sachet. Simmer slowly about 20 minutes, uncovered, until the liquid is reduced by one-third. Strain, pressing on the vegetables to extract all the liquid. Discard the solids and reserve the liquid.

4. Soak the prunes for a few hours in just enough water to cover. Then simmer gently until the prunes are soft and plump. Reserve both the prunes and the liquid.

Cooking:

1. Season the chops with salt and pepper. Brown on both sides in hot oil in a braising pan.

2. Add the reserved wine sauce and a little of the prune liquid (about ½ oz or 15 ml prune liquid per portion). Cover and braise the chops until they are tender.

3. Remove the chops from the cooking liquid and keep them warm. Degrease the sauce, reduce it by about one-third, and strain. Thicken the sauce lightly with a little beurre manié. Adjust the seasoning.

4. Add the prunes to the sauce to heat them up. Serve the sauce and prunes with the chops.

Variations

For additional flavor, soak and poach the prunes in red wine with a dash of brandy added.

Finish the sauce with a little crème fraîche or heavy cream, if desired.

Noisettes of Pork with Prunes

Bone out the chops and use only the eye muscle or cut noisettes from a boned pork loin.

Pork Chops with Prunes in White Wine

Substitute white wine for red wine in the basic recipe. Finish the sauce with cream and a little red currant jelly.

RAGOUT OF VEAL WITH SHERRY VINEGAR

	U.S.		Metric	
PORTIONS:	**4**	**16**	*4*	*16*
Ingredients				
Boneless veal from shoulder or breast, trimmed of all fat	2 lb	8 lb	*1 kg*	*4 kg*
Butter, or part butter and part oil	1 oz	4 oz	*30 g*	*125 g*
Flour	1 tbsp	1 oz	*8 g*	*30 g*
Sugar	½ tsp	2 tsp	*3 g*	*10 g*
Onion	2 oz	8 oz	*60 g*	*250 g*
Brandy	1 oz	4 oz	*30 ml*	*125 ml*
White wine	3 oz	12 oz	*1 dl*	*4 dl*
Sherry vinegar	3 oz	12 oz	*1 dl*	*4 dl*
Garlic	½ oz	2 oz	*15 g*	*60 g*
Marjoram	½ tsp	2 tsp	*½ g*	*2 g*
Chicken stock or white veal stock	12 oz	3 pt	*4 dl*	*1.5 l*
Salt				
Brown sugar	2 tsp	8 tsp	*10 g*	*40 g*
Additional sherry vinegar, as needed				
Raw butter or beurre manié, as needed				

Mise en Place:

1. Cut the veal into 1-inch (2.5-cm) cubes.
2. Cut the onion into fine dice. Mince the garlic.

Cooking:

1. In a sauté pan, brown the veal in the butter or butter/oil mixture.

2. When the veal is brown, sprinkle the flour and sugar over the meat and stir it in. Cook, stirring occasionally, until the flour is lightly browned. Remove the meat with a slotted spoon and put it in a braising pan or casserole.

3. If necessary, add a little more fat to the sauté pan and add the onion; sauté for about 30 seconds. Be careful not to burn the cooking residue that remains on the bottom of the pan.

4. Leaving the onion in the pan, deglaze the pan with the brandy and reduce au sec.

5. Add the wine and simmer 2 minutes.

6. Add the sherry vinegar, garlic, and marjoram. Simmer until the liquid is reduced by one-half.

7. Add the stock and bring to a boil.

8. Pour the contents of the sauté pan into the braising pan with the veal. Add a little salt, but underseason because the salt will be concentrated when the liquid reduces later.

9. Cover the pan and place in an oven heated to 325°F (160°C). Cook until the veal is tender, about 1 to 1 ½ hours.

10. Remove the meat with a slotted spoon and keep it warm in a separate container. Degrease the sauce and reduce it by about one-third to concentrate and thicken it. There should be about 1 ½ to 2 oz per portion (50 to 60 ml).

11. Add the brown sugar to the sauce; the sugar helps to bring out the taste of the sherry vinegar. Taste the sauce and, if necessary, add a few more drops of sherry vinegar. Add salt to taste.

12. If the sauce is too thin, thicken it with a little beurre manié or enrich it with a little raw butter.

13. Return the meat to the sauce.

BEEF OR LAMB STEW WITH ORANGE AND COCONUT MILK

	U.S.		Metric	
PORTIONS:	4	16	4	16
Ingredients				
Beef or lamb, boneless, lean, from shank, chuck, or shoulder	1 ½ lb	6 lb	700 g	2.8 g
Vegetable oil, as needed				
Garlic cloves	2	8	2	8
Jalapeño peppers	1	4	1	4
White veal stock, chicken stock, or lamb stock	1 pt	2 qt	5 dl	2 l
Grated orange zest	1 tsp	4 tsp	2 g	8 g
Salt				
Pepper				
Orange juice	6 oz	1 ½ pt	2 dl	8 dl
Unsweetened coconut milk	8 oz	1 qt	2.5 dl	1 l
Grated orange zest (approximate measure)	1 tsp	4 tsp	2 g	8 g
Steamed white rice				
Optional garnish:				
Orange wedges or slices				
Unsweetened shaved coconut or toasted coconut				

Mise en Place:

1. Cut the meat into large dice.

2. Chop the garlic.

3. Cut the jalapeño peppers in half. Discard the interior membranes, seeds, and stem end. Cut the peppers into thin slices.

Cooking:

1. Brown the meat in oil in a braising pan.

2. Add the garlic and jalapeño. Cook them for a few minutes with the meat.

3. Add the stock, the first quantity of orange zest, and a little salt and pepper. Simmer, lightly covered, until the lamb is tender.

4. Remove the meat with a slotted spoon. Degrease the liquid and reduce it by about one-half.

5. Add the orange juice and coconut milk. Bring the mixture to a simmer and reduce by about one-third. Return the meat to the liquid.

6. Add additional grated orange zest to the mixture to taste; the orange flavor should be distinct but not overpowering. Adjust the seasoning with salt. Do not thicken the liquid; the finished dish should be rather soupy.

Presentation:

Serve the stew in broad soup plates. Just before serving, place a scoop of steamed white rice in each soup plate, a little to one side. The dish may be garnished with a wedge or slice of orange and a little unsweetened shaved coconut or toasted coconut.

Variation

Pork Stew with Orange and Coconut Milk

Substitute lean pork for the beef or lamb.

RAGOUT OF GRILLED VEAL AND BEEF WITH SPRING ONIONS

		U.S.		Metric	
PORTIONS:		**4**	**16**	*4*	*16*
Ingredients					
Veal loin, boneless, trimmed		8 oz	2 lb	*250 g*	*1 kg*
Tender, boneless beef, such as tenderloin, loin, or rib eye, trimmed		8 oz	2 lb	*250 g*	*1 kg*
Salt		¾ tsp	1 tbsp	*4 g*	*15 g*
Paprika		½ tsp	2 tsp	*1 g*	*4 g*
Dry mustard		¼ tsp	1 tsp	*½ g*	*2 g*
White pepper		¼ tsp	1 tsp	*½ g*	*2 g*
Sage, crumbled		¼ tsp	1 tsp	*¼ g*	*1 g*
Thyme		¼ tsp	1 tsp	*¼ g*	*1 g*
Ground cumin		⅛ tsp	½ tsp	*¼ g*	*1 g*
Cayenne		pinch	¼ tsp	*pinch*	*½ g*
Spring onions (see Mise en Place)		12	48	*12*	*48*
Butter, as needed					
Small red-skinned potatoes		6 oz	1 lb 8 oz	*175 g*	*700 g*
Tomato, peeled, seeded, and diced		4 oz	1 lb	*125 g*	*500 g*
Fava beans or lima beans, cooked		2 oz	8 oz	*60 g*	*250 g*
Rich demiglaze		4 oz	1 pt	*125 ml*	*5 dl*
Chicken stock		2 oz	8 oz	*60 ml*	*2.5 dl*
Raw butter (optional)		½ oz	2 oz	*15 g*	*60 g*
Salt, to taste					

Note: This dish is not a true ragout but an "instant stew" as discussed on page 348.

Mise en Place:

1. Make sure the meats are trimmed of all fat and silverskin. Cut the meat with the grain into strips about 1 to 1 ½ inches (3 to 4 cm) wide and the same thickness.

2. Combine all the ingredients in the spice mix. Toss the meat strips with the spice mix. Marinate for several hours or overnight.

3. Trim the spring onions (fresh onions that resemble scallions but have an enlarged, round bulb at the base) well, removing the roots and stems. Reserve a few of the best stems for garnish; cut them into thin slices.

Cooking:

1. Boil or steam the potatoes until tender. Cooking should be timed so that the potatoes are done, and still hot, when the finished dish is being assembled. They can be cooked ahead of time and reheated, but their flavor and texture will not be as good.

2. Dry the meat if necessary but leave as much of the spice mixture as possible on the surface of the meat. Grill or broil the meat to the desired doneness. Remove from the heat and let rest a few minutes.

3. While the meat is cooking and resting, brown the onions over low heat in a small amount of butter. The heat should be adjusted so that the onions are cooked through but still slightly crunchy by the time the outside is lightly browned.

4. Add the demiglaze and stock. Simmer a minute.

5. Add the tomato and simmer another few minutes.

6. Cut the potatoes into halves, quarters, or dice, depending on their size. (They may be peeled or not, as desired.) Add the potatoes and beans to the sauce mixture and heat.

7. If desired, enrich the sauce by stirring in a little raw butter.

8. Slice the meats and combine with the sauce and vegetables.

9. Adjust the seasoning, if necessary. Sprinkle with a few sliced onion tops and serve at once.

CHAPTER

9

Miscellaneous Meats

*B*utcher's cuts of beef, pork, lamb, and veal, in addition to poultry and fish, form the basis for the great majority of our meals. The specialty items that are the subject of this chapter are, by most people, eaten only occasionally, if they are eaten at all.

It has not always been this way. Variety meats have long been highly esteemed in other cultures and other times. Valued for their flavor and for their nutritional value, organ meats were important both in peasant kitchens and on the tables of aristocrats. Sausages are still an integral part of many cuisines around the world. They are a way not only of preserving meats, but also of converting trimmings and undesirable cuts into choice edibles. And, of course, game has been an essential source of food from prehistoric times until relatively recently.

Modern rediscovery of and renewed interest in good cooking has led to renewed demand for variety meats, sausage, and game. Connoisseurs looking for the unusual and the flavorful may often skip over the steaks and chicken on a restaurant's menu and zero in on the roast venison with chestnuts, the stewed tripe with tomatoes and garlic, braised rabbit with mustard, or the salad of duck sausage. Sometimes dishes of this sort become a restaurant's most popular offerings because they are seen as a special treat, as something out of the ordinary.

It is assumed that you already understand the fundamental techniques of meat cookery. This chapter presents an overview of basic product information and preparation techniques unique to variety meats, sausages, and game. A number of recipes are provided, while other dishes are described in sufficient detail to make it possible to produce them without explicit recipes.

VARIETY MEATS OR OFFAL

Variety meats include the various edible internal organs of meat animals, such as liver and kidneys, as well as various extremeties and other parts, such as tails and feet, that are not generally included among those cuts that we normally think of as butcher's meats.

For the most part, variety meats are not as well appreciated in the United States as they are in many other countries, where they are often prized as delicacies. Sweetbreads fetch high prices in some areas of the country, and liver is generally accepted nationwide, even if it is disliked by many people. Other glandular meats, however, are rarely eaten. Among the muscle meats, tongue and oxtail are commonly found, but there is a limited market for most other variety meats.

By contrast, cuisines as different as French and Chinese place high value on variety meats and have developed a vast array of recipes for them. In France, for example, sausages called *andouillettes*, made from pork or veal intestines, are almost as popular as hot dogs are in America, and rich, hearty tripe stews are normal features on bistro menus.

To people who appreciate them, variety meats are at the same time more delicate and more flavorful than popular cuts like steaks and chops. Furthermore, the nutritional value of many variety meats, such as liver, is extremely high. They are rich in protein as well as many vitamins and minerals. Unfortunately, some of them are also very high in cholesterol, especially brains, sweetbreads, liver, and kidneys. These items should perhaps be avoided by people with high blood cholesterol levels.

As already suggested, variety meats can be divided into two categories, glandular or organ meats, and muscle meats and other extremities.

Organ Meats

The most important glandular meats are liver, sweetbreads, kidneys, and brains. Other animal organs, such as lungs and pancreas, are sometimes eaten, but they have little commercial importance in the United States.

These meats do not consist of muscle tissue like regular meats, but instead are internal organs or glands. This fact is important for two reasons.

First, since they do not consist of bundles of muscle fibers, their texture is unlike that of regular meats. Because they are not muscles, they are naturally tender. They do not require long, slow cooking to be made tender, like some meat cuts do. If organ meats are tough or dry, it is usually because they have been overcooked. Liver, for example, becomes very dry and mealy if overcooked, and kidneys can become rubbery unless they are cooked only briefly.

Second, glandular meats are much more perishable than muscle meats. While some muscle meats, especially beef, benefit from aging, organ meats must be very fresh to be of the best quality. Liver, sweetbreads, and brains should be used within a day or two after purchase. If brains or sweetbreads must be kept longer, they should be blanched (procedures follow) so that they will keep another day or two.

Liver. Beef, pork, lamb, and calf's liver can all be eaten, but only calf's liver finds a regular place on restaurant menus. Beef liver is dark and has a rather strong flavor. Lamb liver can be tender and delicate if it comes from young animals, but it is not widely available. Pork liver is used mostly in sausages and patés.

Fine quality calf's liver is pink or light red and should not be confused with the darker "baby beef" liver, which is stronger in flavor and more like beef liver. Calf's liver is very tender and delicate, so it should be handled carefully.

Preparation. Starting with a whole liver, first peel off the thin membrane covering the outside. (Sometimes the liver and the membrane are so delicate that it is difficult to pull the membrane off; in this case, this step can be omitted.) Slice the liver on the bias into slices about ¼ inch (6 mm) thick for sautéing, about ½ inch (12 mm) thick for broiling. Remove any internal ducts from the slices; these will be tough.

Cooking. No matter what the cooking method, liver should not be cooked to the well-done stage (unless the customer requests it), because it will be dry and tough. Properly cooked calf's liver is pink inside and still retains some juices.

Liver is usually cooked by sautéing or panfrying. For most recipes, season it and dredge it in flour (or dredge in seasoned flour) before cooking. Sauté over moderate or moderately high heat; if the heat is too high, the liver may get too dark and crusty on the outside. Liver browns more quickly than most other meats because of its relatively high sugar content.

Create variety by deglazing the pan with different liquids (wine, stock, vinegars) to prepare different sauces, and by accompanying the liver with various garnishes.

Liver to be broiled should be sliced thicker than for sautéing, so that it can be handled on the grill or broiler. Season the liver and, if desired, dredge in flour. Brush with or dip in melted butter or oil before broiling. Watch carefully so that the liver doesn't burn or overcook. Serve with a flavored butter, an appropriate sauce, or a small amount (½ oz or 15 ml) of vinaigrette.

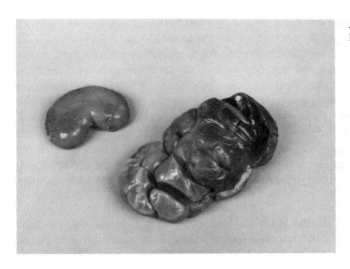

FIGURE 9.1. **Lamb kidney and veal kidney.**

Kidneys. Only veal and lamb kidneys (see Figure 9.1) are used with any frequency in American food service. Beef and pork kidneys are tougher and more strongly flavored.

Veal kidneys weigh about 8 to 12 oz (225 to 350 g) each. Lamb kidneys are very small, about 1 ½ to 3 oz (40 to 85 g) each. If you purchase whole lamb or veal carcasses, you will find a pair of kidneys inside the cavity, attached to the small of the back in the region of the tenderloin and surrounded by a heavy layer of fat or suet.

Preparation. If the kidney is encased in fat, pull the fat away from the kidneys with your hands, and use a knife to cut it away from the core area where the ducts emerge from the inside of the kidney.

In classical recipes for kidneys to be cooked whole, directions often call for cutting off the fat with a knife but leaving a thin protective layer. Today, kidneys are not often cooked whole, and modern dietary practices would dictate against leaving so much fat attached.

Lamb kidneys are usually broiled and served two or three per portion, or as part of a mixed grill. Butterfly them by splitting them almost in half, starting at the curved or convex side. Spread them open and skewer them to hold them open during cooking.

Veal kidneys can be broiled like lamb kidneys, but they are most often cut up, sautéed, and served in a sauce. To prepare them for sautéing, first split them in half. Remove the white ducts from the center. Then cut into large dice or thick slices.

Cooking. There are two main pitfalls encountered when cooking kidneys. First, they become tough and rubbery if overcooked. Properly cooked, they should be pink in the middle and still tender and juicy. Cooking time is very short.

Second, they have a high moisture content, which can interfere with proper sautéing. Make sure the sauté pan is very hot before adding the kidneys, and do not overcrowd the pan. Failure to do this will result in kidneys that are boiled in their juices rather than sautéed.

To avoid overcooking when sautéing over high heat, do not try to brown the kidneys too heavily. Brown them only lightly, and remove them from the pan when they are still somewhat rare. Set them aside while you deglaze the pan and prepare the sauce. During this time, some juices will be released from the kidneys. Drain this juice from the kidneys and add it to the sauce if desired, or discard it if you feel the flavor is too strong. Finally, add the kidneys to the sauce and warm them gently. Do not let them simmer long. Serve at once.

A second way to sauté kidneys is preferred by some chefs and is suitable for both veal and lamb kidneys. Leave lamb kidneys whole, and split veal kidneys in half. Because larger pieces are being cooked, lower heat is needed for even cooking. Sauté the kidneys on both sides over medium heat until rare or medium, about 6 minutes total cooking time for lamb kidneys, 10 to 12 minutes for veal kidneys. Remove from the pan and set aside. Deglaze the pan and prepare the sauce. Split the lamb kidneys in half, or slice the veal kidneys; discard the juices or add them to the sauce, as desired. Arrange the slices on plates or platters, and ladle the sauce over them.

To broil or grill kidneys, prepare for cooking as described above. Use high heat. Brush the kidneys with oil or melted butter before cooking, as well as several times during cooking. Cook until rare or medium, never well done. Cooking time is 3 to 5 minutes on each side.

Sweetbreads. Sweetbreads are the thymus glands of young animals. Because the gland, which is located in the neck area, disappears as the animal ages, there are no sweetbreads in mature animals. Only veal sweetbreads find widespread use in this country. When the term *sweetbreads* is used, it is understood that this means veal sweetbreads unless another kind (such as lamb sweetbreads) is specified. Sweetbreads have a mild flavor and delicate texture. They are considered a luxury food and usually command a high price.

Veal sweetbreads come in pairs, with a duct connecting the two halves of the pair. The so-called "heart sweetbread" is round and compact, while the "throat sweetbread" is somewhat elongated. The two halves are virtually identical in flavor, but the throat sweetbread is somewhat looser in texture. The heart sweetbread makes neater slices because of its compact shape.

Preparation. Sweetbreads should be soaked and blanched in advance. In addition, if they are to be sliced before final cooking, they should also be pressed after blanching. Pressing makes slicing easier and results in firmer slices that are less likely to break up. If they are to be diced and served in a sauce, pressing is not necessary, although it may be done.

Blanching makes the sweetbreads firmer. Membranes, connective tissue, and fat are easier to remove after blanching, and the sweetbreads are generally easier to handle. Also, blanching helps the extremely perishable sweetbreads keep an extra day.

1. Soak the sweetbreads in several changes of cold, salted water for several hours. This removes blood so that the sweetbreads will not darken when cooked.
2. Drain the sweetbreads and place in a saucepan with cold, salted water. Bring slowly to a simmer, and simmer about 5 minutes.
3. Drain. Rinse briefly under fresh cold water until cool.
4. Peel off membranes and connective tissue.
5. If the sweetbreads are to be pressed, place them between two trays and weight down the upper tray. Chill until cold and firm. The sweetbreads are now ready to be sliced. They can be split in half horizontally or sliced on the diagonal, depending on the recipe.

Cooking. The usual cooking methods for sweetbreads are sautéing, broiling, and braising.

1. *Sautéing.* Slice the sweetbreads horizontally or on the diagonal, as desired. Bread the slices by dipping them in flour, egg wash, and bread crumbs, or simply dredge them in flour. Sauté in butter until golden brown. Sauce and garnish as desired or as indicated in the recipe.

2. *Broiling.* Leave the pressed sweetbreads whole or slice them if they are thick. Season. Dip in melted butter and broil slowly, basting with additional butter as needed until lightly browned. Garnish as desired.

Sautéed and broiled sweetbreads are usually cooked after the preliminary blanching and pressing described above. Some chefs feel that sweetbreads are too bland to be prepared this way, however, and prefer to braise them first in order to give them more flavor. After braising, they are cooled, sliced, and sautéed or broiled.

3. *Braising.* Sweat a little finely diced mirepoix in butter in a casserole or braising pan just large enough to hold the sweetbreads. Add the sweetbreads and a splash of white wine (optional). Cook a few minutes, then add some rich demiglaze, brown stock, or white stock, enough to cover the sweetbreads by about half. Cover and cook slowly in the oven about 45 minutes. Baste occasionally.

Strain the sauce; reduce it and finish it as desired. Serve the sweetbreads with the sauce and with the desired vegetable garnish.

Sweetbreads may be braised from the raw state, or they may be first blanched and pressed.

Brains. Brains are the richest and most delicate of the variety meats. Their flavor is somewhat similar to that of sweetbreads, but they are softer and milder. Their texture is creamy and custardy.

While few people would object to the mild, delicate flavor of brains if they were to taste them, the mere thought of eating brains prevents most people from enjoying this delicacy. A more serious dietary consideration, however, bans them from the diets of many people: brains are extremely high in cholesterol. A 4-oz portion of poached brains contains more than 2000 mg cholesterol; that is more cholesterol than in an omelet made with six eggs. Nonetheless, for a small number of people they will always be a special treat, even if only a rare one.

Calf's brains are by far the most frequently used, although lamb's brains are sometimes available. Calf's brains weigh up to ½ lb (450 g); lamb's brains are only half that size, up to 4 oz (225 g) each.

Preparation. Brains should be soaked in cold water, like sweetbreads, to remove blood that would discolor them. Before or after soaking, peel off the thin membrane that surrounds them, being careful not to damage the fragile brains. Continue soaking, changing the water as necessary, to whiten the brains.

For most purposes, brains are then poached in a well-seasoned court bouillon containing about 1 ounce (30 ml) lemon juice or vinegar per quart (1 liter) water, plus a bouquet garni. Simmer gently for about 20 minutes. Drain and serve immediately, or cool in fresh cold water and refrigerate for later use.

Cooking. Brains may be served poached, sautéed, panfried, or deep-fried.

For poached brains, cook in court bouillon as described above. Drain them, put them on plates, and pour a little vinaigrette over them; serve additional vinaigrette on the side. Or, in place of the vinaigrette, dress the brains with beurre noir and garnish with capers.

For sautéed or fried brains, cut the poached, chilled brains into slices. Before sautéing or panfrying, dredge them in flour or bread them. Before deep-frying them, bread them or dip them in a batter. Serve with lemon wedges or with an appropriate sauce. Because they are so rich, they are usually served with lemon or with a sauce containing some acidity (such as lemon, tomato, or vinegar) to balance the richness and blandness of flavor. Deep-fried brains in batter are traditionally served with tomato sauce.

Other Variety Meats

Besides glands like liver and kidneys, many other parts of meat animals are classified as variety meats because they are not part of the regular dressed carcass. Some of these, like heart and tongue, consist almost entirely of muscle tissue. Since these are well-used muscles, these meats are tough and require long, slow cooking to be made tender.

Other meats in this category are extremities consisting of muscle tissue as well as skin, bone, cartilage, and so on. Examples of these are feet and tails. Except in some ethnic or international cuisines, most of these products are used primarily as supplementary ingredients rather than as main ingredients.

Tongue. Beef, veal, and lamb tongues are generally available, but beef tongue is the most widely used. Whether it is fresh, cured, or cured and smoked, cooked tongue is most often cooled, sliced, and used as a sandwich ingredient or as a component of cold-meat platters.

Like other tough meats, tongue requires long, slow cooking. Simmer it in court bouillon or salted water until tender; about 3 to 4 hours for beef tongue, somewhat less for veal or lamb tongues. Peel off the skin and cut away any gristle at the base of the tongue.

Oxtail. The tails of beef animals contain flavorful meat and a rich gelatin content, so they are highly desirable for soups and stews. Their only disadvantage is that they are labor intensive, since they contain a high proportion of bone, and the meat is usually removed by hand from the cooked tails in the preparation of soups.

Some cooks chop the tails into sections with a cleaver, but this may result in splintered bones. It is better to cut the sections apart at the joints; this can be done easily with a French knife.

Oxtails are braised or simmered like other stew meats.

Heart. The heart is a muscle that is in constant use; therefore, it is tough and lean. Beef and veal hearts are the most frequently used, but lamb and pork hearts are available as well.

To prepare a heart for cooking, wash it well and trim away the external fat and large blood vessels. Heart can be braised or simmered, or it can be ground and mixed with other ground meats.

Tripe. Tripe is the muscular stomach lining of meat animals. Although lamb and pork tripe are sometimes available, beef tripe is by far the most widely used. Because cattle have four stomachs, there are four kinds of beef tripe. Honeycomb tripe (see Figure 9.2), from the second stomach, is the kind generally available in the United States, and recipes often specify honeycomb tripe. Other kinds, however, can be substituted in recipes that call for honeycomb tripe. In France, another kind of beef tripe, known as *gras-double*, is popular; it is smooth rather than honeycombed.

Most tripe that comes from the market has been partially cooked, but it still requires several hours of simmering to be made tender. Undercooked tripe is chewy and somewhat rubbery, but tripe that has simmered long enough is tender, with a pleasant gelatinous texture.

Tripe may be an acquired taste, but the many people who like it are devoted to its texture and to its earthy taste. Although it is certainly not our most popular variety meat, it is well liked enough to be the basis of some classic regional dishes. Philadelphia pepper pot soup, in which tripe is a main ingredient, is widely known, for example, and pickled tripe is popular enough in some regions of the country to be found on the

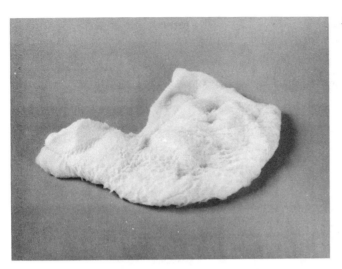

FIGURE 9.2. **Honeycomb tripe.**

menus of roadside diners. In addition, tripe dishes play an important role in the cuisines of such countries as France, Italy, and Spain.

Preparation and Cooking. First remove any lumps of fat from the tripe by pulling or cutting them off. Next, the tripe may be blanched if desired. Although it is already partially cooked when purchased, some cooks prefer to blanch it again to freshen it. To blanch, place it in a pot with cold, salted water. Bring to a boil, then simmer 5 to 10 minutes. Drain and rinse under cold water.

Tripe recipes may or may not call for preliminary simmering. In those that do not, the tripe is cut into pieces of the desired size, combined with other ingredients, and simmered or stewed until tender. The stew is then finished and served. An example of this type of preparation is Tripes à la Môde de Caen (Tripe Caen-Style) on page 428.

In those that do call for preliminary simmering, the tripe is first cut up and simmered in salted water until tender or nearly tender. It is then drained and combined with a sauce and/or other ingredients. An example of this type of recipe is Tripe Florentine-Style (page 426).

Intestines. The most common use for intestines is to make sausage casings. These are discussed in the sausage section of this chapter.

Chitterlings, popular in some parts of the country, are pork intestines that are treated like tripe. They are blanched or simmered, then braised or fried. Chitterlings are generally available in 10-pound pails. Because they shrink a great deal when simmered, this quantity will yield only 3 pounds or less of finished product.

Andouillettes (pronounced "on-dwee-yet") are chitterling sausages. They are popular in France and can be found in any meat market or charcuterie. They are made by simmering chitterlings until tender, seasoning them with a little mustard, salt, pepper, and chopped shallot sweat in butter and simmered in dry white wine. This mixture is then stuffed into casings.

Caul. Pig's caul (see Figure 9.3) is a fatty membrane covering the animal's stomach. It looks somewhat like a delicate piece of lace. Its main use is to line terrines, and to wrap forcemeats and other foods so that they hold their shape during cooking and do not dry out. Sliced fatback is also used for these purposes, but the advantage of caul is that it is so thin that it melts almost completely away during cooking.

FIGURE 9.3. **Caul.**

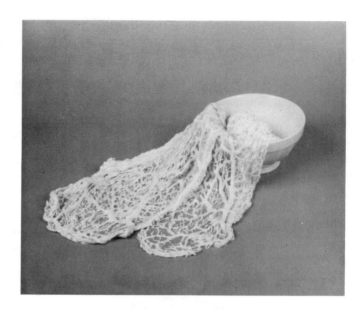

Feet. Feet are exceptionally rich in gelatin. For this reason, they are added to soups, stews, and stocks to add richness and body. Indeed, some stews made with feet, such as Tripes à la Môde de Caen, may be so rich in gelatin that not only will they solidify when cold, but they can even be unmolded and sliced like cold cuts.

Pig's feet are readily available and can be found in any supermarket. Calf's feet and ox feet are also available, but often only on the wholesale market. The feet from older animals have less gelatin.

If a recipe calls for a calf's foot, but none is available, in most cases you can substitute two pig's feet.

In France, where the feet are cut longer and consequently have more meat on them, pig's feet are a common luncheon dish. The feet are brined (see page 353), simmered until tender, coated with bread crumbs, and then sold at this stage in charcuteries. They need only be reheated in the oven and served with mustard and sour pickles on the side. The meat, skin, and gelatinous parts are all eaten.

ESCALOPES OF SWEETBREADS WITH MADEIRA SAUCE

		U.S.		Metric	
PORTIONS:		4	16	4	16
Ingredients					
Sweetbreads		1 lb 8 oz	6 lb	700 g	2.8 kg
Salt					
White pepper					
Flour					
Butter					

Madeira	2 oz	8 oz	*60 ml*	*2.5 dl*
Demiglaze (see note)	6 oz	1 ½ pt	*2 dl*	*8 dl*
Butter	1 oz	4 oz	*30 g*	*125 g*
Potato Galettes (p. 540) 5 inches (13 cm) in diameter	4	16	*4*	*16*
Carrots, cut julienne	2 oz	8 oz	*60 g*	*250 g*
Leeks, cut julienne	2 oz	8 oz	*60 g*	*250 g*
Butter				

Note: If necessary, use a good brown stock instead of demiglaze, and bind the sauce as required with beurre manié.

Mise en Place:

1. Prepare, blanch, and press the sweetbreads as indicated on page 412.
2. Cut each sweetbread lobe diagonally into 3 or 4 slices, so that you have 3 to 4 slices, totaling 4 to 5 oz (120 to 150 g), per portion.
3. Prepare the potato galettes as directed in the recipe.
4. Blanch the carrot and leek julienne briefly until cooked but still crisp. Chill and combine the two vegetables.

Cooking:

1. Season the sweetbreads with salt and pepper. Dredge them in flour and shake off the excess.
2. Sauté them in butter until lightly golden on both sides. Remove from the pan and keep warm.
3. Degrease the pan and deglaze it with Madeira. Add the demiglaze. Reduce slightly. Check the seasoning of the sauce and finish it with a little raw butter.

Presentation:

1. For each portion, place one of the potato galettes in the center of a plate. Arrange the sweetbread slices on top.
2. Pour about 1 to 1 ½ oz (30 to 45 ml) of Madeira sauce around the sweetbreads, not over them.
3. Toss the vegetable julienne with a little butter in a sauté pan to reheat. Top the sweetbreads with a small mound of the julienne.

Variations

Instead of making a Madeira sauce by deglazing the pan, prepare a standard Madeira sauce (page 45) in advance.

Other appropriate sauces can be substituted for the Madeira sauce.

Calf's Liver with Madeira Sauce

Season and flour calf's liver. Sauté in the normal manner. Serve with Madeira sauce as in the basic recipe.

CALF'S LIVER WITH SHERRY VINEGAR AND THYME

		U.S.		Metric	
PORTIONS:		**4**	**16**	*4*	*16*
Ingredients					
Calf's liver		1 lb	4 lb	*500 g*	*2 kg*
Salt					
Pepper					
Flour					
Butter, or part butter and part oil		1 oz	4 oz	*30 g*	*125 g*
Sherry vinegar		2 oz	8 oz	*60 ml*	*2.5 dl*
Fresh thyme leaves (see Mise en Place, step 2)		½ tsp	2 tsp	*½ g*	*2 g*
Butter		1 oz	4 oz	*30 g*	*125 g*
Garnish:					
Fresh thyme sprigs		4	16	*4*	*16*
Beet Greens with Browned Shallot (p. 509)		8 oz	2 lb	*250 g*	*1 kg*
Pears		1	4	*1*	*4*
Sugar, as needed					
Butter, as needed					

Mise en Place:

1. Cut the liver into slices about ¼ to ⅓ inch thick (1 cm).
2. If at all possible, use fresh thyme. If dried thyme must be used, measure one-third the quantity indicated.
3. Prepare the beet greens according to the recipe indicated. The quantity specified refers to the cooked greens.
4. As close as possible to serving time, prepare the pear garnish. Peel the pears, cut them in half, and remove the cores. Cut into thin slices lengthwise. Sauté briefly in butter, sprinkle with a little sugar, and continue to cook briefly to caramelize the sugar. Remove from the heat and set aside.

Cooking:

1. Season the liver with salt and pepper. Dredge in flour and shake off excess.
2. Heat the butter (or butter and oil) in a sauté pan. Sauté the liver over moderate heat until both sides are browned and the liver is cooked but still pink inside. Remove from the pan and keep warm.
3. Deglaze the pan with the vinegar and add the thyme at the same time. Reduce by about two-thirds.
4. Swirl in the butter to finish the sauce.

Presentation:

1. For each portion, place a slice of liver on one side of a plate and coat with a little of the sauce. Top with a sprig of thyme.

2. On the other side of the plate, arrange caramelized pear slices from one-fourth of a pear, overlapping the slices.

3. Place a small mound of beet greens on the plate to balance out the arrangement.

Variations

Other vinegars, such as balsamic, red wine, or raspberry vinegar, can be substituted for the sherry vinegar.

Calf's Liver with Capers

Use about 1 ½ tsp (6 g) of drained capers for each portion. Add the capers to the vinegar sauce before serving. Omit the thyme. Substitute other appropriate garnish as desired.

Calf's Liver with Country Ham

Prepare the liver according to the basic recipe, using sherry vinegar or balsamic vinegar for the deglazing. Using about 1 oz (30 g) cooked country ham per portion, cut the ham into thin slices, then into julienne. After saucing the liver, warm the ham julienne briefly in the sauté pan. Top the liver with the ham, either sprinkling it evenly over the liver or mounding it loosely in the center of the liver slice.

Calf's Liver Meunière

Season, flour, and sauté the liver as in the basic recipe. Plate it and sprinkle it with lemon juice and chopped parsley. Top the liver with hot browned butter (beurre noisette).

SESAME SWEETBREADS

		U.S.		Metric	
PORTIONS:		**4**	**16**	*4*	*16*
Ingredients					
Sweetbreads		1 lb 4 oz	5 lb	*600 g*	*2.4 kg*
Eggs		1	3	*1*	*3*
Soy sauce		1 tsp	1 tbsp	*1 tsp*	*1 tbsp*
Sesame seeds		2–3 oz or as needed	8–12 oz or as needed	*75 g or as needed*	*300 g or as needed*
Cornstarch					
Red bell pepper, cut julienne		6 oz	1 lb 8 oz	*175 g*	*700 g*
Jalapeño pepper, seeded, cut julienne or brunoise		1	4	*1*	*4*
Oriental sesame oil		2 tsp	8 tsp	*10 ml*	*40 ml*
Chicken stock		6 oz	1 ½ pt	*2 dl*	*8 dl*
Soy sauce		1 oz	4 oz	*30 ml*	*125 ml*
Sugar		1 tbsp	2 oz	*15 g*	*60 g*
Red wine vinegar		1 tbsp	2 oz	*15 ml*	*60 ml*
Cornstarch		2 tsp	8 tsp	*5 g*	*20 g*
Cold water		1 oz	4 oz	*30 ml*	*125 ml*
Cilantro (see note)		1–2 bunches	4–8 bunches	*1–2 bunches*	*4–8 bunches*

Note: If cilantro is not available, Italian parsley may be used instead, although its flavor is quite different.

Mise en Place:

1. Prepare, blanch, and press the sweetbreads as indicated on page 412. Break them into irregular chunks no larger than 2 inches (5 cm) across.
2. Beat the eggs with the soy sauce to make an egg wash. Set up a breading station with some cornstarch in the first bowl, the egg wash in a second bowl, the sesame seeds in a third bowl, and a layer of cornstarch on a tray or sheet pan.
3. Dip the sweetbread pieces in cornstarch, then in egg wash, then in sesame seeds. Place them on the tray of cornstarch and roll them around lightly. Leave them on the tray to dry.
4. Make the sauce. Sauté the red peppers and jalapeños slowly in sesame oil until slightly soft. Add the stock, soy sauce, sugar, and vinegar; bring to a boil. Mix together the cornstarch and cold water. Stir the cornstarch mixture a little at a time into the sauce over moderate heat to thicken it. Add just enough to thicken lightly; you may not need all the cornstarch.
5. Trim the stems from the cilantro and discard. Rinse the leaves and dry them well.

Cooking:

1. Deep-fry the sweetbreads until golden. Drain well.
2. Make sure the cilantro leaves are dry. Deep-fry them for a few seconds, until crisp. Drain well.

Presentation:

1. Heat the sauce and make a pool of sauce, with the pepper julienne, on dinner plates.

2. Distribute the sweetbreads on top of the sauce in the center of the plate.

3. Top with a generous mound of fried cilantro.

BROILED SWEETBREADS MAÎTRE D'HÔTEL

		U.S.		Metric	
PORTIONS:		**4**	**16**	*4*	*16*
Ingredients					
Sweetbreads		1 lb 8 oz	6 lb	*700 g*	*2.8 kg*
Melted butter					
Salt					
Pepper					
Maître d'Hôtel Butter (p. 77)		2 oz	8 oz	*60 g*	*250 g*

Mise en Place:

Prepare, blanch, and press the sweetbreads as indicated on page 412. Prepare the maître d'hôtel butter.

Cooking:

1. Depending on the thickness of the sweetbreads, either leave them whole or split them in half horizontally.

2. Dip them in melted butter and season with salt and pepper.

3. Broil slowly under moderate heat until hot and lightly browned. Brush with additional butter as necessary.

Presentation:

Plate the sweetbreads and top with a slice of maître d'hôtel butter. Garnish the plate as desired.

Variations

In place of the seasoned butter, broiled sweetbreads can be served with an appropriate sauce, such as Diable, Italian, or Robert.

Salad of Broiled Sweetbreads with Black Beans and Hazelnut Vinaigrette

Soak black turtle beans, about 1 ½ oz (45 g) per portion, overnight. Simmer in water until tender but still firm and whole, not mushy and broken. Drain. Sauté a little chopped shallot (1 to 2 tsp or 5 to 10 g per portion) and a pinch of chopped garlic in a little oil until tender. Add to the beans and mix well. Moisten and flavor by mixing in a little vinaigrette made with hazelnut oil and red wine vinegar or sherry vinegar. Season to taste. Garnish a dinner plate with some mixed greens, plate the grilled sweetbreads, and garnish with the bean salad. Drizzle the entire plate with a little more vinaigrette.

VEAL KIDNEYS WITH MUSHROOMS

		U.S.		Metric	
PORTIONS:		**4**	**16**	*4*	*16*
Ingredients					
Oil		1 oz	4 oz	*30 ml*	*125 ml*
Butter		1 oz	4 oz	*30 g*	*125 g*
Veal kidneys		2	8	*2*	*8*
Butter		1 oz	4 oz	*30 g*	*125 g*
Mushrooms		1 lb	4 lb	*500 g*	*2 kg*
Flour		1 tbsp	4 tbsp	*7 g*	*30 g*
Shallot, chopped		1 oz	4 oz	*30 g*	*125 g*
Butter		2 tsp	8 tsp	*10 g*	*40 g*
White wine		4 oz	1 pt	*125 ml*	*5 dl*
Cognac		3 oz	12 oz	*1 dl*	*4 dl*
Dijon-style mustard		1 tbsp	2 oz	*15 g*	*60 g*
White wine		1 oz	4 oz	*30 ml*	*125 ml*
Heavy cream		4 oz	1 pt	*125 ml*	*5 dl*
Salt					
White pepper					
Chopped parsley		2 tbsp	8 tbsp	*7 g*	*30 g*
White rice or puff pastry shells for serving					

Mise en Place:

1. Prepare the kidneys as indicated on page 411. Cut into ½-inch (12 mm) chunks.

2. Clean the mushrooms. Cut them into quarters or leave them whole if they are small.

3. Sauté the chopped shallot slowly in butter. When soft, add the white wine and reduce *au sec*.

Cooking:

1. Heat the oil and the first quantity of butter in a sauté pan until very hot. Add the kidneys and sauté quickly until about three-fourths done. Remove with a slotted spoon and set aside, leaving remaining fat in the pan.

2. Add additional butter and sauté the mushrooms over high heat for about a minute.

3. Sprinkle the flour over the mushrooms and stir in.

4. Add the cooked shallots to the pan.

5. Remove from the heat and add the cognac; return to the heat, being careful in case the cognac flames up. Reduce briefly.

6. Mix together the mustard and white wine. Stir this mixture into the mushrooms.

7. Drain the liquid that has accumulated under the kidneys. If desired, add this to the mushrooms, or discard it.

8. Add the cream and simmer briefly. Taste and adjust the seasonings with salt and pepper.

9. Add the kidneys to the mushrooms and sauce; simmer to reheat the kidneys.

10. Stir in the chopped parsley.

Presentation:

This dish must be served at once. The kidneys will become rubbery if the dish is held. Serve with steamed or boiled rice or in a puff pastry shell.

FRICASSÉE OF PORK AND SWEETBREADS WITH ASPARAGUS

(Color Plate 14)

	U.S.		Metric	
PORTIONS:	**4**	**16**	*4*	*16*
Ingredients				
Asparagus spears, medium thickness	12	48	*12*	*48*
Shiitake mushroom caps	2 oz	8 oz	*60 g*	*250 g*
Butter	2 tsp	3 tbsp	*10 g*	*40 g*
Pistachios, in shell	2 oz	8 oz	*60 g*	*250 g*
Chicken or veal mousseline forcemeat (p. 307)	6 oz	1 lb 8 oz	*175 g*	*700 g*
Butter	½ oz	2 oz	*15 g*	*60 g*
Shallots	1 oz	4 oz	*30 g*	*125 g*
Garlic cloves	1	4	*1*	*4*
Lean pork, well trimmed	8 oz	2 lb	*250 g*	*1 kg*
Veal sweetbreads	6 oz	1 lb 8 oz	*175 g*	*700 g*
Flour	1 tbsp	4 tbsp	*7 g*	*30 g*
White wine	3 oz	12 oz	*1 dl*	*4 dl*
White veal stock or white chicken stock	6 oz	1 ½ pt	*2 dl*	*8 dl*
Heavy cream, hot	1 ½ oz	6 oz	*50 ml*	*2 dl*
Salt				
White pepper				
Glace de viande	2 oz	8 oz	*60 g*	*250 g*

Mise en Place:

1. Cut off the top 2 to 2 ½ inches (5 to 6 cm) of the asparagus spears; reserve the bottoms for soups or for another purpose. Wash the asparagus spears, boil until al dente, cool under cold water, and drain. Cut them in half lengthwise.

2. Cut the mushroom caps into julienne. Sauté briefly in butter until tender. Cool.

3. Blanch and peel the skins from the pistachios. Chop the nuts coarsely.

4. Prepare quenelles in one of two ways.
   a. Using small spoons, make oval quenelles as shown in Figure 6.11e through h.
   b. Put the veal or chicken mousseline in a pastry bag fitted with a large tube. Make quenelles by forcing the mixture from the bag over simmering, salted water and cutting off 1-inch (2.5-cm) lengths. Simmer until cooked through. Remove with a slotted spoon and drop into ice water. Drain and keep the quenelles chilled.

5. Peel and mince the shallots and garlic.

6. Cut the pork into medium dice.

7. Prepare, blanch, and press the sweetbreads as indicated on page 412. Break into small pieces.

Cooking:

1. Heat the butter in a saucepan or braising pan over low heat. Add the shallot and garlic; sweat until tender. Do not brown.

2. Add the pork and sweetbreads. Sauté over medium heat but do not brown.

3. Sprinkle the flour over the meat and stir in. Cook 2 to 3 minutes.

4. Stir in the wine and stock. Bring to a simmer, stirring. Cover loosely and simmer until the pork is tender.

5. When the pork is tender, drain the liquid from the solids and check the quantity. There should be about 1 ½ oz (50 ml) per portion. If necessary, reduce the liquid over moderate heat, or if there is not enough liquid, add white stock.

6. Add the hot cream. Return the solids to the liquid. Also add the asparagus, mushrooms, and quenelles. Heat gently. Adjust the seasonings with salt and white pepper.

Presentation:

1. Arrange the fricassée on hot dinner plates or shallow soup plates. Concentrate the solids in the center of the plate, mounding slightly, and let the sauce flow toward the outside of the plates.

2. Drizzle a little hot glace de viande around the outside edge of the sauce. If desired, swirl it a bit with the point of a knife or the tines of a dinner fork.

3. Sprinkle the meat with chopped pistachios.

Variations

Another white meat, such as veal or chicken, can be used in place of the pork.

Fricassée of Pork and Sweetbreads en Feuilleté

Roll out puff pastry (p. 616) about ¼ inch (5 mm) thick or slightly less. Cut out desired shapes, such as rectangles or hearts, about 4 inches (10 cm) across. Glaze the tops with egg wash and bake. Split in half horizontally and, if necessary, scoop out any undercooked dough. Put the bottoms on plates and spoon in the stew, letting it spill over the sides. Put on the tops. Sprinkle the pistachios over the stew around the outside of the pastry.

TRIPPA ALLA FIORENTINA (TRIPE FLORENTINE)

	U.S.		Metric	
PORTIONS:	4	16	4	16
Ingredients				
Tripe	2 lb	8 lb	900 g	3.6 kg
Olive oil	2 oz	8 oz	60 ml	2.5 dl
Parsley sprigs, stemmed and chopped	5–6	20–25	5–6	20–25
Garlic cloves, chopped	1	4	1	4
Onion, chopped fine	2 oz	8 oz	60 g	250 g
Carrot, chopped fine	2 oz	8 oz	60 g	250 g
Celery, chopped fine	2 oz	8 oz	60 g	250 g
Rosemary	¼ tsp	1 tsp	¼ g	1 g
Tomatoes, fresh or canned, peeled and chopped, with juice	12 oz	3 lb	350 g	1.5 kg
White stock	8 oz	1 qt	2.5 dl	1 l
Salt				
Pepper				
Parmesan cheese	1 oz	4 oz	30 g	125 g

Procedure:

1. Simmer the tripe in salted water for 3 to 4 hours, until nearly tender. Drain, rinse, and cut into strips about ½ inch wide and 2 inches long (1 by 5 cm).

2. Heat the oil in a braising pan or other heavy pot. Add the parsley, garlic, onion, carrot, celery, and rosemary. Cook slowly about 10 minutes to soften the vegetables.

3. Add the tripe and cook slowly, uncovered, another 5 minutes.

4. Add the tomatoes, stock, salt, and pepper. Simmer slowly, loosely covered, about 1 to 2 hours, until the tripe is very tender and the mixture is no longer juicy but fairly thick. Taste and adjust the seasonings.

5. Serve very hot. Top each portion with grated parmesan cheese, or mix it in before serving. *Note:* Portion size is about 8 oz or 250 g, which tripe lovers will consider relatively modest. For larger portions, increase ingredient quantities proportionately.

Variation

Tripe with Beans

Dry white wine	4 oz	1 pt	*1 dl*	*5 dl*
Cooked white kidney beans or cannellini beans, drained	1 lb	4 lb	*500 g*	*2 kg*

Prepare as in the basic recipe, but with the following changes. Add the white wine at the same time as the stock. When the tripe is done but still a little juicy, add the cooked beans. Simmer together 10 minutes. Double the quantity of parmesan cheese and stir it in before serving.

Because of the quantity of beans, this variation increases the number of servings by 50 percent; for example, 6 portions instead of 4, 24 portions instead of 16.

TRIPES À LA MÔDE DE CAEN

		U.S.		Metric	
PORTIONS:		4	16	4	16
Ingredients					
Beef tripe		2 lb 4 oz	9 lb	1 kg	4 kg
Calf's foot (see note 1)		1	3	1	3
Onion, medium dice		4 oz	1 lb	125 g	500 g
Carrots, sliced		3 oz	12 oz	100 g	400 g
Leek, sliced		3 oz	12 oz	100 g	400 g
Sachet:					
Peppercorns, lightly crushed		6	25	6	25
Bay leaves		1	4	1	4
Parsley stems		6	25	6	25
Thyme		¼ tsp	1 tsp	¼ g	1 g
Whole cloves		2	8	2	8
Dry white wine (see note 2)		1 pt	2 qt	5 dl	2 l
White stock		8 oz	1 qt	2.5 dl	1 l
Salt					
Calvados (apple brandy)		2 oz	8 oz	60 ml	2.5 dl
Boiled potatoes		12 oz	3 lb	350 g	1.5 kg

Note 1: If calf's feet are not available, substitute twice the number of pig's feet. Do not omit, or the tripe stew will not have enough gelatin to give it the proper texture.

Note 2: This dish is from the Normandy region of France, famed for, among other things, its apples. The traditional recipe calls for hard cider, but white wine is an acceptable substitute.

Procedure:

1. Trim all fat from the tripe. Put the tripe in a pot of cold water and bring it to a boil. Simmer 5 minutes. Drain and rinse in cold water. Cut the tripe into 1 ½-inch (4-cm) squares.

2. Cut the feet into pieces as necessary, so that they fit into the braising pan.

3. Combine all the ingredients, except the calvados and potatoes, in a braising pan or other heavy pot. Salt lightly. Bring to a boil, cover tightly, and put in an oven at 325°F (160°C). Cook 5 hours or longer, until the tripe is very tender.

4. Remove the foot (or feet) and bone it out. Dice the skin and meat and return it to the pot. Discard the bone, fat, and connective tissue.

5. Stir in the calvados. Adjust the seasoning.

6. Serve very hot with boiled potatoes.

FRESH SAUSAGES

A sausage is a mixture of ground meat, usually pork, and seasonings, stuffed into a casing. The term "sausage" may also be used for the meat mixture itself, without the casing.

Reduced to its simplest form, sausage meat may be nothing more than ground pork seasoned with salt. Because salt as well as other traditional additives such as saltpeter have a preservative effect, the technique of sausage-making developed in ancient times in many different cultures as a way of preserving various meats without refrigeration. Today we have inherited a bewildering variety of sausages from around the world.

Although there are hundreds or even thousands of kinds of sausages, the majority of them are based upon the same few basic principles. These principles are simple enough that we can make a wide variety of sausages in the kitchen and not have to rely entirely on commercially made ones. Furthermore, it is not necessary to restrict ourselves to traditional sausage recipes. Many chefs are experimenting with different ingredients and seasonings to add variety to the menu.

Categories of Sausages

Sausages can be classified into three basic groups:

Fresh sausages
Cured sausages
Smoked sausages

A *fresh sausage*, by USDA definition, is one that contains no nitrates or nitrites. It is basically a mixture of ground meat, seasonings, and flavorings. Although they are usually raw, fresh sausages may contain cooked ingredients, or they may even be fully cooked before being sold. Any fresh raw sausage containing pork, of course, must be fully cooked before being served and eaten.

A *cured sausage* is one that contains nitrites or nitrates of sodium or potassium. (Sodium nitrite is the most important of these, commercially.) These chemicals help prevent spoilage and food-borne disease, and incidentally they also keep the meat red or pink, even when cooked. Cured sausages may be sold raw or cooked, soft and moist like fresh sausages, semidried and firm, or dried and hard like salami. Pork salamis, which are Italian in origin, and similar cured, dried sausages are raw, but the curing, aging and drying process renders them safe to eat.

Smoked sausages, in theory, may be cured or uncured. In practice, however, commercially made smoked sausages are usually cured. Smoking may be light or heavy, depending on the sausage. The sausage may be hot-smoked, and therefore cooked, or cold-smoked.

Making cured or smoked sausages in the kitchen is possible, but there are difficulties. Accurate measurement of the curing agent is critical. Using too much can be toxic, while not using enough can result in spoilage. Proper smoking requires investment in special equipment. For these reasons, discussion in this section is limited to making fresh sausages, which are within the capabilities of any kitchen.

Basic Sausages and Variations

The basic ingredients of sausage meat are the following:

Lean pork
Pork fat, preferably hard fatback, ground with the meat
Salt
Spices, herbs, and other seasonings and flavorings

Just as hundreds of varieties of cheeses are made from the same basic ingredients (milk plus a coagulating agent), so are hundreds of varieties of sausage made from this simple plan. Variations upon this basic plan are made in a number of ways. These techniques are outlined below. Examples of simple sausages as well as a number of variations are included in the recipe section, beginning on page 439.

Understanding these basics is important not only for making sausages from existing recipes. After all, if you can read the directions, it is simple enough to weigh the ingredients, grind the meats, mix the ingredients, and stuff the casings. But further understanding gives the cook the ability to vary or modify old recipes and to create new ones.

After reading this section, you may find it useful to turn to Chapter 11 and read the material on basic forcemeats for pâtés and terrines (pages 565–569). Sausages have much in common with pâtés, and many of the production techniques are the same.

Sausage variations are created by varying any of the following elements. Please note that this section refers to the ingredients and procedures for ground-meat sausages. Specialty sausages made according to other principles are discussed later.

1. The meat

Pork is the most commonly used meat in sausage making, but other meats or mixtures of meat may be used. Beef, veal, lamb, chicken, turkey, duck, liver, rabbit, and venison all find their way into sausages. Mixtures of pork plus one or more of these meats are often used. More exotic sausages may include such ingredients as sweetbreads or brains.

2. The fat

Pork fat, or other fat such as the beef fat used in all-beef sausages, is an important ingredient. Since our impression of juiciness in any cooked meat is largely due to the meat's fat content, some fat is included in sausage mixtures. Without it, the texture of the cooked sausage would be very dry.

In most traditional sausages, fat makes up 25 to 50 percent of the total weight, with 33 percent fat being the norm. In other words, proportions of fat to lean range from 3 parts lean plus 1 part fat (the leanest sausages) to 1 part lean plus 1 part fat (rich, fatty sausages). Varying the proportions changes the character of the sausage.

Hard fatback is preferred over other fats for pork sausage. Softer fats are more likely to melt out of the sausage during cooking. A quick and easy way to make pork sausages without worrying about the ratio of fat to lean is to use whole pork butt. The ratio of fat to lean in this cut is very good for sausages.

In today's diet-conscious atmosphere, it may make sense to try to create low-fat sausages. But be advised that extra care is required when making sausages with less than 25 percent fat. Lean sausages should never be overcooked, since overcooking makes them dry. Keep the meat mixture cold to avoid damage to the texture of the meat and fat. With care, it is possible to make tasty sausages with a fat content as low as 10 or 15 percent. One should not expect, however, that the eating qualities of lean sausages will be the same as those of fattier sausages.

Cereal ingredients and fillers (rice, barley, bread crumbs, and so on) can be used to help reduce the fat content. Because these starches absorb and retain moisture, they enhance the total moisture content of low-fat sausages.

3. *The grind*

The fineness or coarseness of the grind is an important characteristic of any sausage. For example, one identifying feature of Toulouse Sausages (page 440) is their coarse texture; the meat is chopped rather than ground. On the other hand, typical breakfast sausages have a fairly fine grind. In the finest-textured sausages, the meat is actually puréed to a smooth paste with a food processor or similar machine.

When following any recipe, adhere closely to the grinding and processing directions in order to achieve the proper texture and character of the sausage.

Additional textural variation can be created by mixing chunks or dice of meat or other ingredients into a more finely ground forcemeat, just as is often done in pâtés.

In almost all cases, the meat mixture must be kept cold during grinding. When the mixture gets too warm, the fat becomes soft and begins to lose its structure. As a result, the fat may melt out too readily when the sausage is cooked, resulting in excessive shrinkage, poor texture, and dryness. If the kitchen is warm, return the meat to the refrigerator to chill it thoroughly after cutting it up and before grinding it. If it must be ground more than once, return it to the refrigerator between grindings.

4. *Seasonings*

Herbs, spices, and other flavorings account for the primary differences among various sausages. Many if not most of the world's fresh sausages are made of nothing more than ground pork and seasonings. It is the seasonings that give them their characteristic flavor. A glance at the recipes in this section will confirm this.

Some of the major spices and herbs used in sausage making are the following:

Allspice
Caraway seeds
Cayenne or hot red pepper
Cinnamon
Cloves
Coriander
Cumin
Fennel seed
Ginger
Mace
Marjoram
Mustard
Nutmeg
Paprika
Parsley
Pepper, black and white
Sage
Tarragon
Thyme

Other important flavoring ingredients include the following:

Garlic

Onion

Shallots

Chives

Wine, white and red

Vinegar

Eggs

5. *Other ingredients*

A number of sausages are characterized by unusual or exotic ingredients. Some of these are traditional and time-honored, such as the black truffles included in some regional French sausages, or the chestnuts or the raisins in other specialty sausages.

Other unusual sausages are modern innovations by creative chefs. It is no longer uncommon, when reading today's restaurant menus, to come across sausages with such ingredients as sundried tomatoes or fresh vegetables like sweet bell peppers and spinach. In theory, there is no limit to what can be stuffed into sausage casings. The main requirement is that the ingredients complement or enhance one another, just as the meat, seasonings, and vegetable garnish on a dinner plate should complement one another.

Casings. Natural casings are made from the intestines of meat animals. Sheep casings are the smallest and are used for breakfast links, frankfurters, and similar sausages. At the opposite extreme are beef casings, used for large sausages. Hog casings are medium-sized, about 1 to 1½ inches, or 3 to 4 cm, wide. They are used for many popular fresh sausages, such as Italian sausages and fresh bratwurst. These casings are the most readily available on the retail market.

Natural casings are often sold packed in salt. Because of the preservative effect of the salt, the casings will keep indefinitely as long as they are refrigerated. Natural casings are easy to use if they are handled correctly. Before stuffing, they must be untangled, rinsed and flushed, and examined for holes according to the following procedure.

Procedure for Preparing Natural Casings

1. Carefully remove the casings, one at a time, from the salt pack and unravel them. Because a single casing may be 12 feet long, it is easiest to do this on a large workbench. Separate the individual lengths and keep them separate in their own little stacks on the bench. When unraveling them, do not pull hard, because this may cause knotting.

   Unravel slightly more casing than you think you will need. It is easier to return unused casings to the salt pack than it is to separate and flush additional casings when you run out before you have stuffed your whole batch of meat.

2. Partially fill a large bowl with clean water and set it in a sink under the faucet. Take hold of the end of one casing and drop the rest of it into the bowl of water. Open the end of the casing and run cold water into it, enough to fill about 12 inches (30 cm) of it. Holding the casing at both ends of this "water sausage," allow the water to flush through the casing from one end to the other.

   This accomplishes two purposes. It rinses out the inside of the casing, and it identifies any holes that might be present. Pinpoint-size holes are no problem, but if a large hole is found, simply cut the casing in two at that point. Short pieces may be discarded for the sake of efficiency.

3. If you are making a small quantity of sausages and stuffing them immediately, each casing can be put on the stuffing horn as it is rinsed. If this is not the case, they must be stored for later use. Select a container with a cover and fill it about three-quarters full with cold water. Drop in the casing and let one end hang over the edge.

   Repeat with remaining casings. Fill the container to the top with cold water, cover, and refrigerate until needed. By letting the ends of the casings hang over the edge, you can remove one at a time from the container without tangling them. If the end of the casing has dried out, simply cut it off.

Because the supply of natural casings is not nearly large enough to accommodate all the sausages produced, other types of casings have come into wide use. *Collagen casings* are molded from animal materials and are completely edible, like natural casings. Unlike natural casings, they are uniform in size, making portion control easier. Collagen casings must be refrigerated to keep them from becoming dry and brittle. To use, dip them in water for a few seconds to soften them if they are dry and then put them on the sausage stuffing nozzle.

Synthetic fibrous casings are made from a plastic material and are not edible. They are widely used for salamis and luncheon meats, and the casing is peeled off before or after slicing. These casings are nonperishable and need no refrigeration. They must be soaked in water before using to make them flexible. Soaking time varies, and the manufacturer should specify the recommended time.

Equipment. Most fresh sausages can be made with no special equipment other than a meat grinder and a device for getting the meat into the casings. The simplest stuffer resembles a funnel. The casings are pushed over the narrow end and the meat is pushed through the wide end by hand or with a wooden plunger. These are adequate for making a few pounds of sausage but are not suitable for larger batches.

Larger stuffers have detachable nozzles or horns of various sizes for different sizes of casings. The nozzle is attached to a cylindrical reservoir that holds the meat, which is pushed through by a piston. On smaller machines, the piston is simply pushed through by hand. These machines, such as that shown in Figure 9.4, are suitable for small-scale production such as might be done in a small to medium-size restaurant. For large-scale commercial production, larger machines are used. The piston in a large machine is operated by means of a crank and a sequence of gears.

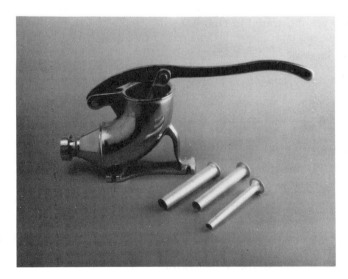

FIGURE 9.4. **A small sausage stuffer with nozzles. This stuffer holds 3 pounds of meat at a time and is suitable for small-scale production.**

FIGURE 9.5. Stuffing sausage.
(a) Flush out the casings with fresh cold water, while looking for holes.

(b) Slide the casings onto the proper size nozzle.

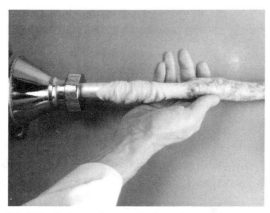

(c) With the nozzle attached to the stuffer, push the meat into the casings, using a hand to guide the casing as it slides off the nozzle.

Production. The following procedure is applicable to most standard kinds of sausages. Steps in the procedure are illustrated in Figure 9.5.

Procedure for Making Fresh Sausages

1. Weigh the meats and fat. Cut them into chunks small enough to fit into the grinder.
2. Measure the salt and spices.
3. Grind the meat and fat, following the directions in the recipe to achieve the proper fineness or coarseness of grind.
4. Chill the meat well. Ideally the meat should be chilled to 32° to 35°F (0° to 2°C) before mixing and stuffing.
5. Combine the meat, salt, and spices and mix thoroughly. This is best done by hand in a large tub or other container.

   If the recipe calls for cold water or other liquid, mix the salt and spices with the water first, then mix this combination with the meat. This facilitates a better distribution of the spices than mixing them dry with the meat.

Many recipes say to refrigerate the meat overnight after it is mixed, to allow the meat to absorb the seasonings and the flavors to blend. However, it is easier to stuff the sausages immediately after mixing. If the salted meat mixture is allowed to stand it becomes firmer, and thus it is harder to force through the stuffer. Stuffing immediately allows the casings to be filled more uniformly and with fewer air bubbles. Besides, the meat can absorb the seasonings just as well in the casings as in the meat tub.

6. Test for seasonings. Do not taste the raw meat. Rather, make a small ball or patty and cook it in a small sauté pan. Then cool the meat slightly and taste. If more salt or other seasoning is needed, add it to the sausage mixture.

7. Place the meat in the stuffer one handful at a time. Pack each handful firmly into the stuffer to eliminate air bubbles.

8. Slide the casings onto the nozzle. So that they slide on easily, moisten the stuffer nozzle with water, and also make sure the casings are wet.

9. Stuff the sausages, following the directions for your particular equipment. The sausages will pull the casings off the nozzle as the meat flows through it, but it is best to hold your hand at the end of the nozzle to help guide it. From time to time, as the casing is filled, it is necessary to push the bunched-up, unfilled casing toward the end of the nozzle so that it will slide off more easily. Do not stuff the casings too tightly. If the meat is packed too tightly, it will be difficult to twist the sausage into links.

10. After all the meat is stuffed into casings, twist the sausage into links of uniform size.

Other Kinds of Fresh Sausage

The kinds of fresh sausages we have been discussing up to this point, as different as many of them may be, are all made in essentially the same way and consist of the same basic ingredients, that is, ground meat and fat, salt, and seasoning or flavoring ingredients.

Several types of sausages are characterized by ingredients or points of technique that do not fit this basic pattern. The most important of these are briefly discussed here.

Sausages Made with Puréed Meats. In its simplest form, this type is a basic sausage mixture made with meat ground to a smooth texture. As an example, see the variation following the bratwurst recipe on page 443. Since the invention of the food processor, making this type of sausage is comparatively easy. After the meat is cut up or ground coarsely, it is necessary only to chill the meat well (because the puréeing process creates heat) and to process it until it is smooth.

More complex sausages of this type often contain liquid ingredients, such as milk, cream, eggs, brandy, and so on. Puréed meats can absorb more liquid than ground meats, so these ingredients are added in order to make the sausages more delicate and refined. The classic example of this is the white sausage, known as *boudin blanc* in France and *weisswurst* in Germany. White sausages are made with white meats, mainly pork, veal, or chicken or a combination of two or more of these, often with milk or cream, eggs, bread crumbs, and onions. A typical recipe is on page 446.

Texture can be varied by mixing solid ingredients such as diced meats, nuts, chopped vegetables, and so on into the meat purée before stuffing.

While purée-type sausages may be sold raw, they are often fully cooked (by poaching or steaming) after stuffing into casings. This makes them less perishable and easier to handle. For service, they need only be heated through by grilling, sautéing, or braising.

Mousseline Sausages. These sausages are also made with puréed ingredients but are even more delicate than the puréed sausages just discussed. In addition to the puréed main ingredient, the mixture contains eggs and a large proportion of heavy cream. It is the same mixture that is used to make quenelles of seafood, poultry, and meat. The techniques for making mousseline mixtures are discussed on pages 216–222 and 581.

A recipe for a seafood mousseline sausage can be found on page 259. Meat and poultry mousseline sausages are made in exactly the same way, using the recipe on page 307 to make the forcemeat. With this information, you should be able to make these sausages without requiring a separate recipe.

Note that the seafood sausage recipe contains solid ingredients mixed with the mousseline. As a general rule, appropriate solid ingredients are also included in meat and poultry sausages. Proportions can vary, but a useful rule of thumb is one part solid ingredients to two parts mousseline, by weight.

The variety of solid ingredients that can be used is limited only by the imagination. The following are some examples from restaurant menus:

Chicken mousseline sausage with diced red, yellow, and green peppers, flavored with ground cumin and coriander

Turkey mousseline sausage with sage, chopped nuts, and dried currants

Veal mousseline sausage with diced foie gras

Chicken mousseline sausage with cooked chicken livers, cut into fine dice, sautéed minced shallot, grated fresh ginger, and chives

Pork mousseline sausage with corn kernels, diced chili peppers, cumin, and cilantro

Veal and pork mousseline sausages with diced ham, diced sweetbreads, and pistachios

Blood Sausages. These are made of pig's blood, seasoned and mixed with various ingredients, often including diced fat, and poured through a funnel into casings. The sausages are then poached very slowly in water until the blood is completely coagulated; the sausages are then cooled and held for later use.

Because of the difficulty of obtaining fresh blood in the United States, these sausages are rarely made in the restaurant or home. They are, however, available commercially, although not in nearly the variety that they are in Europe. France alone has dozens of kinds, differing not only in seasoning but also in garnish (that is, the solid ingredients that are mixed with the blood). Depending on the region, garnishes may include chestnuts, apples, spinach, or onions. Other additions may include milk, cream, brandy, or eggs.

Blood sausages may be sold under various names: *boudin noir* (French), *blutwurst* (German), *black pudding* (English), *zungenwurst* (a German blood sausage with diced cured tongue), *morcilla* (Spanish), *kaszanka* (Polish blood sausage with buckwheat and liver).

Cooking Sausages

Preparation of sausages before cooking is minimal. In most cases, sausages may be considered ready to cook, or in the case of fully cooked sausages, ready to heat. Fresh, raw sausages containing pork must be fully cooked before serving, like other fresh pork products. If a fresh sausage contains no pork, such as the lamb sausage on page 444, it may be served somewhat less done. Removing it from the heat when still pink inside helps to retain juices.

Color Plate 9   Seafood Sausage; Tomato Cream Sauce;
Onion Purée with Leeks

Color Plate 14   Fricassée of Pork and Sweetbreads with Asparagus

Color Plate 15   Noisettes of Venison with Red Wine Sauce;
Pear Ginger Chutney; Polenta

Color Plate 16   Roast Saddle of Rabbit Stuffed
with Vegetables and Herbs

Fully cooked sausages need only be heated through before serving. Cooking times, however, are nearly the same as for raw sausages. In other words, the time it takes for the heat to penetrate to the center is about the same.

The following cooking methods are most often used for sausages:

1. *Simmering.*

    Place sausages in a pan with enough salted water to cover. Bring to a simmer, and simmer until completely cooked. Do not let the water boil. This is likely to make the sausages burst or shrink excessively.

    Time depends on the thickness of the sausage. Sausages in hog casings take about 20 minutes to cook; smaller ones may take as little as 10 minutes, larger ones 30 minutes or more.

    Raw sausages may be simmered until cooked through, then finished by one of the following methods, such as panfrying or grilling.

2. *Sautéing and panfrying.*

    Sausages are sautéed or panfried using the same techniques as for other meats. For many kinds of sausages, the browning that results makes them more appetizing than simmered ones.

    If the sausages are not raw, it is necessary only to cook them until they are lightly browned and heated through. If they are raw, lower heat is necessary so that they have time to become completely cooked by the time they are browned.

    Sautéing and panfrying are used not only for sausages in casings, but also for sausage patties and *crépinettes* which are sausage patties wrapped in caul fat (see page 415). Do not press on the patties with the spatula while cooking; this forces out juices and makes them dry.

3. *Braising.*

    Because fresh, raw sausages may require long cooking times, braising is often the preferred cooking method. The sausages are browned by sautéing over moderate heat for up to 5 minutes, then finished using a moist-heat cooking method. Cooking with moisture may take any of several forms, including the four methods listed below. These methods are suitable not only for fresh sausages but also for fully cooked and smoked sausages that are served hot.
    a. Covering the pan to hold in steam.
    b. Adding a small amount of liquid (water, stock, wine, and so on), covering the pan, and cooking until done.
    c. Glazing: adding a small amount of stock and continuing to cook. The pan may be covered or left uncovered at the beginning, but the last part of cooking takes place with the cover off. The sausages are basted with the stock as it reduces, giving them a glaze. Any stock remaining in the pan after the sausages are cooked will be reduced and thickened, and it may be served with the sausages as a sauce. This cooking method is especially suitable for patties and crépinettes.
    d. Cooking the sausages in a casserole or stew after they are browned. Sauerkraut, bean dishes such as Cassoulet (page 448), and gumbos are some examples.

4. *Broiling and grilling.*

    Brush the sausages with oil to prevent sticking, and broil or grill as for other meats. Moderate heat is usually best. High heat may brown the sausages too much before they are fully cooked and is more likely to cause splitting.

About the Sausage Recipes. Two kinds of recipes are included in this section: recipes for making homemade, fresh sausages, and recipes for various dishes employing cooked or heated sausages, both homemade and commercial.

With regard to the recipes for homemade sausages, please take note of these three points:

1. Refer to the general procedure for making sausages on page 434. Because this procedure has already been explained in detail, many of these points are not repeated in each recipe.

2. Ratios of fat to lean are not specified in the recipes. Refer to the explanation of fat/lean ratios on page 430, and adjust the amount of fat in the recipes as desired.

3. Grinding instructions in the recipes refer to the size of the holes in the plates used in meat grinders. In general, a coarse grind is achieved by one pass through a ¼-inch or ⅜-inch plate (that is, a plate with holes of those diameters). A finer grind is usually achieved by one pass through a ¼-inch or ⅜-inch plate, then one pass through a finer plate, ⅛-inch or ³⁄₁₆-inch.

Standardized spice mixtures are often used to season sausages, pâtés, and similar items. One of the most common of these is *quatre épices* (French for "four spices"), a mixture that exists in many versions. It can usually be obtained commercially, or it can be homemade, using recipes such as the first two that follow.

QUATRE ÉPICES I

		U.S.		*Metric*	
	YIELD:	**3 tbsp**	**4½ oz**	*37 g*	*135 g*
Ingredients					
White or black pepper, ground		2 tbsp	3 oz	*25 g*	*90 g*
Nutmeg		1 tsp	½ oz	*4 g*	*15 g*
Cloves, ground		1 tsp	½ oz	*4 g*	*15 g*
Cinnamon		1 tsp	½ oz	*4 g*	*15 g*

Procedure:

Combine ingredients and mix well. Store in a tightly closed container.

QUATRE ÉPICES II

		U.S.		Metric	
YIELD:		8 ½ tsp	4 ¼ oz	34 g	138 g
Ingredients					
White pepper, ground		5 tsp	2 ½ oz	20 g	80 g
Nutmeg		1 ½ tsp	¾ oz	6 g	25 g
Ginger		1 ½ tsp	¾ oz	6 g	25 g
Cloves, ground		½ tsp	¼ oz	2 g	8 g

Procedure:

Combine ingredients and mix well. Store in a tightly closed container.

FRENCH GARLIC SAUSAGE

		U.S.		Metric	
YIELD:		3 ½ lb	17 ½ lb	1.75 kg	8.75 kg
Ingredients					
Pork and pork fat		3 lb	15 lb	1.5 kg	7.5 kg
Pork rind		½ lb	2 ½ lb	250 g	1.25 kg
Salt		1 tbsp	2 ½ oz	15 g	75 g
Black pepper		¾ tsp	4 tsp	1.5 g	4 g
Garlic, crushed		1 tsp	5 tsp	4 g	20 g
Sage, ground		¼ tsp	1 ¼ tsp	0.25 g	1.25 g
Marjoram		¼ tsp	1 ¼ tsp	0.25 g	1.25 g
Thyme		¼ tsp	1 ¼ tsp	0.25 g	1.25 g
Dry white wine		2 oz	10 oz	60 ml	3 dl

Procedure:

1. Cut the meat into cubes small enough to fit into the grinder. Chill the meat thoroughly.

2. Simmer the pork rind at least 2 hours in salted water, until very tender. Drain and chill.

3. Grind the meat once with the ¼-inch or ⅜-inch plate and then once with the ⅛-inch plate.

4. Repeat this grinding procedure with the pork rind. Mix the ground pork rind with the ground meat.

5. Mix the salt and spices with the wine. Add to the ground meat and mix thoroughly by hand.

6. Stuff into hog casings.

PORK SAUSAGE

		U.S.		Metric	
YIELD:		**3 lb**	**15 lb**	*1.5 g*	*7.5 g*
Ingredients					
Pork and pork fat		3 lb	15 lb	*1.5 kg*	*7.5 kg*
Salt		1 tbsp	2½ oz	*15 g*	*75 g*
Quatre épices		1 tsp	5 tsp	*2 g*	*10 g*
Cold water		3 oz	1 pt	*1 dl*	*5 dl*

Procedure:

1. Cut the meat into cubes small enough to fit into the grinder. Chill the meat thoroughly.

2. Grind once with the ¼-inch or ⅜-inch plate, then once with the ⅛-inch plate.

3. Mix the salt and spices with the cold water. Add to the ground meat and mix thoroughly by hand.

4. Stuff into hog casings or sheep casings.

Variations

Toulouse Sausages

Use the ingredients specified, but do not grind the meat. Chop the meat coarsely with a knife to achieve the characteristic texture of this sausage. Stuff into hog casings.

Toulouse sausages should have a fat content of at least 33 percent, that is, one part fat to two parts lean.

Crépinettes

Weigh out 3½-oz (100-g) portions of sausage meat. Shape it into somewhat elongated patties. Cut squares of caul fat (see page 415) and wrap the sausage portions in the squares. Cook by panfrying, glazing (see page 437), or grilling.

Other ingredients are often mixed with the sausage meat. Some classic additions include blanched, peeled pistachios (2 to 3 oz per lb of sausage meat, or 125 to 175 g per kg); chopped, cooked chestnuts (4 oz per lb, or 250 g per kg); or fresh, diced truffle (whatever quantity the budget allows).

Other sausage mixtures, such as those in the other recipes in this section, may be used to make crépinettes.

VEAL OR BEEF SAUSAGE

		U.S.		Metric	
YIELD:		**3 lb**	**15 lb**	*1.5 kg*	*7.5 kg*
Ingredients					
Pork and pork fat		2 lb	10 lb	*1 kg*	*5 kg*
Veal or beef, lean		1 lb	5 lb	*500 g*	*2.5 kg*
Salt		1 tbsp	2½ oz	*15 g*	*75 g*
Quatre épices		1 tsp	5 tsp	*2 g*	*10 g*
Cold water		3 oz	1 pt	*1 dl*	*5 dl*

Procedure:

1. Cut the meat into cubes small enough to fit into the grinder. Chill the meat thoroughly.

2. Grind once with the ¼-inch or ⅜-inch plate for coarse sausage. For a finer texture, grind once more with the ⅛-inch plate.

3. Mix the salt and spices with the cold water. Add to the ground meat and mix thoroughly by hand.

4. Stuff into hog casings.

Variations

Instead of the meat ratios given in the main recipe, use equal parts pork (including fat) and veal or beef. These proportions make a somewhat leaner sausage with more of the flavor of the veal or beef.

Venison Sausage

Prepare as in the basic recipe or the first variation above, substituting venison for the veal or beef. Add 2 juniper berries, crushed to a powder, for each 3 lb (1.5 kg) of meat mixture. Substitute red wine for the cold water.

HOT ITALIAN SAUSAGE

		U.S.		Metric	
	YIELD:	**3 lb**	**15 lb**	*1.5 kg*	*7.5 kg*
Ingredients					
Pork and pork fat		3 lb	15 lb	*1.5 kg*	*7.5 kg*
Salt		1 tbsp	2½ oz	*15 g*	*75 g*
Black pepper		1 tsp	5 tsp	*2 g*	*10 g*
Fennel seeds		1 tsp	5 tsp	*3 g*	*15 g*
Paprika		2 tsp	10 tsp	*4 g*	*20 g*
Crushed red pepper		1 tsp	5 tsp	*2 g*	*10 g*
Ground coriander		½ tsp	2½ tsp	*1 g*	*3 g*
Sugar		1 tsp	5 tsp	*5 g*	*25 g*
Cold water		3 oz	1 pt	*1 dl*	*5 dl*

Procedure:

1. Cut the meat into cubes small enough to fit into the grinder. Chill the meat thoroughly.

2. Grind once with the ¼-inch or ⅜-inch plate.

3. Mix the salt and spices with the cold water. Add to the ground meat and mix thoroughly by hand.

4. Stuff into hog casings.

Variations

Mild Italian Sausage

Omit the paprika, crushed red pepper, and coriander.

Spicy Garlic Sausage

Omit the fennel and coriander. Add the following:

Oregano		1 tsp	5 tsp	*1 g*	*5 g*
Chopped garlic		1–2 tsp	5–10 tsp	*3–5 g*	*15–25 g*

FRESH BRATWURST

		U.S.		Metric	
YIELD:		**3 lb**	**15 lb**	*1.5 kg*	*7.5 kg*
Ingredients					
Pork and pork fat		3 lb	15 lb	*1.5 kg*	*7.5 kg*
Salt		1 tbsp	2 ½ oz	*15 g*	*75 g*
White pepper		1 ½ tsp	7 ½ tsp	*3 g*	*15 g*
Mace		⅛ tsp	¾ tsp	*0.25 g*	*1.25 g*
Ground coriander		½ tsp	2 ½ tsp	*1 g*	*5 g*
Ginger		¼ tsp	1 ¼ tsp	*0.5 g*	*2.5 g*
Cold water		3 oz	1 pt	*1 dl*	*5 dl*

Procedure:

1. Cut the meat into cubes small enough to fit into the grinder. Chill the meat thoroughly.

2. Grind once with the ¼-inch or ⅜-inch plate, then once with the ⅛-inch plate.

3. Mix the salt and spices with the cold water. Add to the ground meat and mix thoroughly by hand.

4. Stuff into hog casings.

Variation

Double the quantity of cold water. After mixing in the water and seasonings, chill the mixture thoroughly. Then process in a food processor until smooth. Stuff into hog casings. Poach in water until cooked through, about 20 minutes. Drain and chill for storage.

LAMB SAUSAGES

		U.S.		Metric	
	YIELD:	3 lb	15 lb	*1.5 kg*	*7.5 kg*
Ingredients					
Lamb shoulder (see note)		3 lb	15 lb	*1.5 kg*	*7.5 kg*
Salt		1 tbsp	2½ oz	*15 g*	*75 g*
Garlic, chopped		2 tsp	10 tsp	*10 g*	*50 g*
Paprika		1 tbsp	5 tbsp	*6 g*	*30 g*
Cayenne		½ tsp	2½ tsp	*1 g*	*5 g*
Black pepper		½ tsp	2½ tsp	*1 g*	*5 g*
Ground cumin		1 tbsp	5 tbsp	*6 g*	*30 g*
Oregano		1 tsp	5 tsp	*1 g*	*5 g*
Cinnamon		½ tsp	2½ tsp	*1 g*	*5 g*
Cilantro, chopped		2 tbsp	10 tbsp	*6 g*	*30 g*
Cold water		3 oz	1 pt	*1 dl*	*5 dl*

Note: Include some fat with the lean or, if desired, include some pork fat. If pork fat is used, the finished sausage must be cooked to the well-done stage. If all lamb is used, the sausage may be served slightly rare.

Procedure:

1. Cut the meat into cubes small enough to fit into the grinder. Chill the meat thoroughly.

2. Grind once with the ¼-inch or ⅜-inch plate.

3. Mix the salt and spices with the cold water. Add to the ground meat and mix thoroughly by hand.

4. Stuff into hog casings.

Variations

For a simpler, somewhat more straightforward flavor, omit the oregano, cinnamon, and cilantro.

Herbed Lamb Sausage

The flavor of the sausages made by the main recipe is characteristic of the Middle East or parts of North Africa. For a lamb sausage of a more European or American character, omit the paprika, cumin, oregano, cinnamon, and cilantro. Add the following ingredients:

Thyme		1 tsp	5 tsp	*1 g*	*5 g*
Rosemary		1 tsp	5 tsp	*1 g*	*5 g*
Shallot, chopped		½ oz	2½ oz	*15 g*	*75 g*

DUCK SAUSAGES

		U.S.	U.S.	Metric	Metric
	YIELD:	**3 lb**	**15 lb**	*1.5 kg*	*7.5 kg*
Ingredients					
Boneless duck meat and fat		3 lb	15 lb	*1.5 kg*	*7.5 kg*
Salt		1 tbsp	2 ½ oz	*15 g*	*75 g*
Quatre épices		1 tsp	5 tsp	*2 g*	*10 g*
Pine nuts, toasted, or pistachios, blanched and peeled		3 oz	1 lb	*90 g*	*450 g*
Marinated sundried tomatoes, drained and chopped		3 oz	1 lb	*90 g*	*450 g*
Thyme		¼ tsp	1 ¼ tsp	*0.25 g*	*1.25 g*

Procedure:

1. Cut the duck meat and fat into pieces small enough to fit into the grinder. Chill the meat thoroughly.

2. Grind once with the ¼-inch or ⅜-inch plate.

3. Mix the salt, spices, nuts, and sundried tomatoes. Add to the ground meat and mix thoroughly by hand.

4. Stuff into small hog casings.

BOUDIN BLANC (WHITE SAUSAGE)

		U.S.		Metric	
YIELD:		3 lb 8 oz	14 lb	1.75 kg	7 kg
Ingredients					
Chicken breast, boned and skinned		12 oz	3 lb	375 g	1.5 kg
Lean, white pork		1 lb	4 lb	500 g	2 kg
Pork fat		12 oz	3 lb	375 g	1.5 kg
Onion, chopped		6 oz	1 lb 8 oz	185 g	750 g
Milk		8 oz	1 qt	2.5 dl	1 l
Fresh bread crumbs		4 oz	1 lb	125 g	500 g
Eggs		2	8	2	8
Salt		1 ½ tbsp	3 oz	22 g	90 g
White pepper		1 tsp	4 tsp	2 g	8 g
Mace		¼ tsp	1 tsp	0.5 g	2 g
Chopped parsley (optional)		4 tbsp	½ pt	15 g	60 g

Procedure:

1. Cut the chicken, pork, and fat into cubes small enough to fit into the grinder. Chill the meat thoroughly.

2. Grind once with the ¼-inch or ⅜-inch plate, then once with the ⅛-inch plate.

3. Simmer the onions in the milk until they are tender. Pour this mixture over the bread crumbs in a bowl. Let cool.

4. Combine the milk mixture with the ground meat mixture. Purée in a food processor until smooth.

5. Beat the eggs with the salt, white pepper, and mace. Mix into the meat mixture.

6. If desired, mix in the chopped parsley at the same time.

7. Stuff into hog casings.

8. Poach the sausages by simmering them slowly in water until cooked through, about 20 minutes. Drain, cool, and refrigerate.

Variations

Other white meats, such as veal or rabbit, can be used instead of chicken.

Truffled White Sausage

Mix in ¼ to ½ oz of minced black truffle per pound of sausage mixture (15 to 30 g per kg).

Sweetbread and Spinach Sausages

Assemble the following ingredients in addition to those in the main recipe:

Sweetbreads	1 ½ lb	6 lb	*750 g*	*3 kg*
Spinach, AP	1 lb	4 lb	*500 g*	*2 kg*
Cayenne	⅛ tsp	½ tsp	*0.25 g*	*1 g*
Ground coriander	¼ tsp	1 tsp	*0.5 g*	*2 g*

Process, blanch, and press the sweetbreads as directed on page 412. Cut into small dice. Trim and wash the spinach, discarding stems. Blanch in boiling water, drain, and rinse in cold water. Squeeze the spinach dry, and chop it coarsely. Include the cayenne and coriander with the spices in the main recipe. Mix the sweetbreads and spinach into the sausage mixture.

CASSOULET

		U.S.		Metric	
PORTIONS:		**8**	**32**	*8*	*32*
Ingredients					
White beans (such as great northern, white haricot, white kidney)		1 lb	4 lb	*500 g*	*2 kg*
Fresh pork hock		1	4	*1*	*4*
Carrot, pared		1	4	*1*	*4*
Garlic cloves, peeled		2	8	*2*	*8*
Onion, medium, peeled		1	4	*1*	*4*
Whole cloves		4	16	*4*	*16*
Rendered pork fat, duck fat, or salt pork		2 oz	8 oz	*60 g*	*250 g*
Onion, chopped		1 lb	4 lb	*500 g*	*2 kg*
Garlic cloves, chopped		4	16	*4*	*16*
Pork shoulder, boneless and trimmed		1 lb	4 lb	*500 g*	*2 kg*
Slab bacon		8 oz	2 lb	*250 g*	*1 kg*
Peeled tomato, fresh or canned, with juice		1 lb	4 lb	*500 g*	*2 kg*
Tomato paste		1 oz	4 oz	*30 g*	*125 g*
Pork stock or other white stock		8 oz	1 qt	*2.5 dl*	*1 l*
Duck or goose confit (p. 321)		1 lb 8 oz	6 lb	*750 g*	*3 kg*
Toulouse sausages (p. 440)		1 lb	4 lb	*500 g*	*2 kg*
Garlic sausages, fresh (p. 439) or cured		1 lb	4 lb	*500 g*	*2 kg*
Fat from the confit, or other fat, as needed					
Fresh bread crumbs tossed with a little melted butter or other fat		4 oz	1 lb	*125 g*	*500 g*

Procedure for Preparing the Beans:

1. Soak the beans for several hours or overnight.
2. Drain the soaked beans. Combine the beans, pork hock, carrot (cut into several pieces), and garlic cloves in a heavy pot. Pierce the onion(s) with the cloves (4 cloves per onion) and add to the pot. Add enough water to cover by 2 inches (5 cm).
3. Simmer slowly until the beans are cooked but still firm enough to hold their shape. Check on the level of liquid from time to time during cooking to make sure that the beans do not dry out. Add additional water if necessary.
4. When the beans are done, remove and discard the carrot and onion. Taste the beans and adjust the seasoning.
5. Remove the pork hock and bone out. Discard the bones and fat, and reserve the skin (if desired) and meat. Cut the skin, if used, into medium or small dice.

Procedure for Preparing the Meat Stew:

1. Cut the salt pork into small dice. Render it in a heavy pot, then remove and discard the solids.

2. Add the onion and garlic to the rendered fat and brown lightly.

3. Cut the pork shoulder meat into chunks of 2 oz (60 g) each. Cut the slab bacon into 1-oz (30-g) chunks. Add the pork and bacon to the onions in the pot and brown very lightly.

4. Crush or chop the tomatoes and add them to the pot with their juice. Add the tomato paste as well. Simmer a few minutes.

5. Add the stock and bring to a simmer. Simmer slowly until the pork is tender.

6. Add the confit of duck or goose and simmer 10 to 15 minutes. Taste the stew and adjust the seasonings.

Procedure for Preparing the Casseroles:

1. Select baking dishes according to desired presentation. Small dishes can be used to serve one or two portions each, or large ones to serve larger numbers. Use baking dishes that can be presented at the table. Also, the dishes should be large enough to hold 1 to 1 ½ pints (5 to 7 dl) per portion; cassoulet is a hearty dish that is traditionally served in large portions. (Of course, the portion size can be reduced, in which case the number of portions will be greater than indicated in the recipe.)

2. Drain the beans and reserve the liquid. Divide the beans into two equal quantities, then divide half the beans equally among the baking dishes.

3. Stiffen the sausages by cooking them slowly in a little fat for about 10 minutes. Divide the sausages equally among the baking dishes.

4. Remove the confit, the pork shoulder, and the bacon from the onions, tomatoes, and liquid of the stew. Divide these meats, plus the meat (and skin, if used) from the pork hocks, among the baking dishes. Similarly, divide the rest of the stew equally among the dishes.

5. Divide the remaining beans equally among the dishes. Add a little bean liquid as necessary to moisten the casseroles. They should be quite moist but not soupy.

6. Top with a generous layer of buttered bread crumbs.

7. Bake at 325°F (160°C) for 1 to 2 hours, depending on the size of the casseroles. If the beans appear to be getting dry during cooking, add additional bean liquid, stock, or water. The dishes are done when they are very hot and bubbling all the way through to the center. Remember that they must cook long enough to finish cooking the sausages. Also, the top should be browned and crusty.

8. A traditional way to cook cassoulet is to push the crumb crust down into the bean mixture after it has become brown. A new layer of additional fresh crumbs is added, and this procedure is repeated several times. This method thickens the cassoulet (so more liquid should be used at the beginning of cooking) and also enhances flavor by permeating the mixture with the flavor of the toasted crust.

Presentation:

Present the casseroles to the diners at the table. Then spoon some of the meats and beans onto dinner plates. Leave the casseroles at the table, along with serving spoons and forks, so that diners can serve themselves with additional beans and meats.

Variations

À la carte or advance preparation

The procedures for preparing the beans and the meat stew may be done in advance. In addition, in Procedure for Preparing the Casseroles, step 3, cook the sausages until they are completely cooked. To guard against food-borne disease, chill all the cooked components of the cassoulet before assembling. Assemble the casseroles as indicated in the procedure. Cover and refrigerate. Bake to order. Because the casseroles are chilled, baking will take a little longer. Make sure they are heated through before serving.

The selection of meats may be varied. Different versions of cassoulet may contain other sausages, pieces of lamb, or various ham products or other types of cured pork.

A simplified cassoulet may be made with fewer types of meat and without the crumb crust.

ITALIAN SAUSAGES WITH TOMATO CONFIT AND POLENTA

	U.S.		Metric	
PORTIONS:	**4**	**16**	*4*	*16*
Ingredients				
Garlic, sliced	2–3 cloves	8–12 cloves	*2–3 cloves*	*8–12 cloves*
Olive oil	1 oz	4 oz	*30 ml*	*125 ml*
Tomatoes, fresh or canned, peeled, seeded, and chopped	12 oz	3 lb	*375 g*	*1.5 kg*
Capers, rinsed and drained	1 tbsp	4 tbsp	*15 g*	*50 g*
Black olives, European style such as calamata, pitted and coarsely chopped	½ oz	2 oz	*15 g*	*60 g*
Salt				
Pepper				
Italian sausage links (p. 442), about 5 oz (140 g) each	4	16	*4*	*16*
Hot polenta (p. 503), soft and freshly cooked	16–24 oz	4–6 lb	*500–700 g*	*2–2.8 kg*
Italian (flat-leaf) parsley sprigs				

Mise en Place:

1. Sweat the garlic over moderate heat until lightly cooked; do not brown.
2. Add the tomato. Stir and cook until the liquid evaporates.
3. Add the capers and olives. Cook another minute.
4. Season to taste. Cool the mixture and refrigerate if it will not be served for an hour or more.

Cooking:

1. Grill or panfry the sausages.
2. Pour the freshly cooked polenta onto dinner plates. Spread it to cover most of the center of the plates.
3. Slice the sausages. Arrange the slices overlapping on the center of the polenta.
4. Place a spoonful of the tomato mixture on each side of the sausage.
5. Garnish with several sprigs of parsley.

Variations

Grilled polenta squares or triangles (page 504) can be substituted for the soft polenta. This is especially appropriate if the sausages are grilled. In this case, place the polenta alongside, not underneath, the sausage.

Other sausages, such as duck sausages (page 445) or spicy sausages (page 442) may be used instead of Italian sausages.

Tomato Ragout with Garlic and Olives (page 525) may be substituted for the tomato mixture in this recipe.

SALAD OF GRILLED LAMB SAUSAGE WITH NEW POTATOES AND WATERCRESS

		U.S.		Metric	
PORTIONS:		4	16	4	16
Ingredients					
New potatoes, preferably yellow variety, or red-skinned		1 lb 8 oz	6 lb	700 g	2.8 kg
Garlic, minced		¼ tsp	1 tsp	½ g	2 g
Chives, chopped		1 tbsp	4 tbsp	5 g	20 g
Red bell pepper, raw or roasted and peeled, cut brunoise		1 oz	4 oz	30 g	125 g
Mustard Vinaigrette (p. 72) made with olive oil and balsamic vinegar		6 oz	1 pt 8 oz	2 dl	7.5 dl
Lamb Sausage (p. 444)		1 lb 4 oz	5 lb	600 g	2.4 kg
Watercress		1–2 bunches	4–8 bunches	1–2 bunches	4–8 bunches

Mise en Place:

1. Boil the potatoes until tender. Leave the skins on the cooked potatoes or peel them, as desired. Cut into thick slices.

2. Mix together the warm potatoes, the garlic, the bell pepper, and one-half the vinaigrette.

3. Trim the coarse stems from the watercress. Wash, drain, and refrigerate.

Finishing:

1. Grill the sausages.

2. If the sausages are small links (lamb casings), leave them whole. Otherwise, cut them into thick slices on the diagonal. Arrange the sausage along the front edge of the dinner plates.

3. Plate the potato salad just above the sausage, at the center of the plate.

4. Toss the watercress with the rest of the vinaigrette. Place the watercress at the top of the plate.

SAUSAGES WITH RED CABBAGE

	U.S.		Metric	
PORTIONS:	**4**	**16**	*4*	*16*
Ingredients				
Red cabbage	1 lb	4 lb	*500 g*	*2 kg*
Bacon, diced	2 oz	8 oz	*60 g*	*250 g*
Onion, sliced	3 oz	12 oz	*90 g*	*375 g*
Apples, peeled, cored, and diced	2 oz	8 oz	*60 g*	*250 g*
Cinnamon	pinch	¼ tsp	*pinch*	*½ g*
Ground cloves	⅛ tsp	½ tsp	*¼ g*	*1 g*
Pepper	⅛ tsp	½ tsp	*¼ g*	*1 g*
White stock, preferably pork stock	4 oz	1 pt	*125 ml*	*5 dl*
Red wine vinegar	1 oz	4 oz	*30 ml*	*125 ml*
Sugar	2 tsp	8 tsp	*10 g*	*40 g*
Fresh pork sausages, such as Toulouse (p. 440) or garlic sausages (p. 439)	16–24 oz	4–6 lb	*500-700 g*	*2–2.8 kg*
Hot mashed potatoes	12–16 oz	3–4 lb	*400–500 g*	*1.6–2 kg*

Mise en Place:

1. Cut the cabbage into quarters, removing and discarding the outer leaves and the core. Shred the cabbage.

2. Render the bacon. Add the onion and cook over moderate heat until very lightly browned.

3. Add the cabbage and stir to coat lightly with bacon fat. Sweat for a few minutes until the cabbage begins to wilt.

4. Add the spices and stock. Cover and braise until the cabbage is tender.

5. Add the vinegar and sugar. Cook for several minutes. Taste and adjust seasonings.

Finishing:

1. Cook the sausages by any desired method (see page 436).

2. Plate the sausages with the cabbage and mashed potatoes.

GAME DISHES

The term *game* is used to refer to a variety of poultry and meat animals normally found in the wild. In the United States, however, various laws place restrictions on the hunting of wild game for commercial purposes, and much of the "wild" game that has become so popular on restaurant menus is actually from farm-raised animals. Venison farms in particular have become numerous and productive, supplying a growing demand.

Farm-raised game birds are discussed in detail along with other poultry in Chapter 7. This section is concerned with furred game.

Although a great variety of game, large and small, can be found on hunters' tables, the supply of game for the restaurant and retail markets is limited primarily to venison, which is the main subject of this section. Other products, such as boar and hare, are occasionally available as well. In addition, domestic rabbit is considered here, although its meat has little in common with true game.

The selection of recipes in this section is intended to give a sample of various techniques, both classic and modern, rather than to provide a complete repertory of game dishes. Most of the main recipes are for venison, although many of them are applicable to other meats as well, as suggested by the variations. The venison recipes in this chapter have been tested with farm-raised meat, while the recipes for hare and boar have been tested with wild game.

The French terms for various game meats are often used on menus and in various cooking manuals and references. To clarify these terms, a list of those most commonly used follows:

Chevreuil: often translated as "venison," but refers specifically to the roe deer, the most prized European variety

Cerf: red deer; often farm raised

Daim: fallow deer; often farm raised

Marcassin: young boar, especially boar under 6 months of age.

Sanglier: boar

Lapin: rabbit

Lapereau: young rabbit

Lièvre: hare

Levraut: young hare

Venaison: usually translated as "venison," the term in fact refers to the meat of any game animal

Venison

Several varieties of deer are raised on farms for use as meat, including the red deer and the smaller fallow deer. At present, most of the venison on the market in this country comes from farms in the United States and New Zealand.

An important advantage of farm-raised venison, besides its year-round availability, is that the cook can be assured that it is from young, tender animals. In the wild, young animals less than two years old are likely to have tender meat, but the meat rapidly becomes tough as the animal matures and ages. The tradition of marinating game for several days in strong wine marinades originates in large part from efforts to tenderize hunted game enough to make it palatable.

Marination, Flavor, and Tenderness. The first thing to be said about farm-raised venison is that it is milder in flavor than venison hunted in the wild. It has little if any of the strong, gamy flavor that is usually associated with wild game. In fact, a farm-raised venison steak tastes rather like an especially flavorful cut of beef. Those who enjoy strong, gamy flavors may even find farmed venison a little bland.

Although it does have some tenderizing effect, marination is not necessary to tenderize commercially raised venison because the meat is already tender. Nevertheless, marinating is widely used as a flavoring technique. Much of the flavor associated with venison, in fact, is due less to its "gaminess" than to the red wine marinades that were invariably used. As we have already discussed in Chapter 8, these same marinades can be used to make beef taste like venison.

Flavor, specifically the traditional flavor of wild venison dishes, is the main object of marinating in a classic red-wine game marinade. Examples of such dishes include the classic roast of venison Grand Veneur (page 461) and various old-fashioned stews (page 467). Ironically, another reason that hunted wild game is marinated, besides tenderizing, is to cover up some of the meat's strong flavors. Thus, in many classic recipes, whether made with wild or domesticated meat, the primary flavors are due more to the marinade than to the meat.

To retain more of the natural flavor of the meat, cook without any marination (see, for example, page 465), or let it marinate for only a short period (30 minutes to 3 or 4 hours) with the desired seasonings and flavoring ingredients (see page 464, for example). Modern quick marinades are often very simple and may contain only a few ingredients.

Fat Content. Venison, like other game, is very low in fat. This makes it especially popular with health-conscious diners. It also makes the meat likely to become dry unless care is taken by the cook.

The loin and leg, being tender, are best if cooked by dry-heat methods and served rare or medium-done. If cooked longer, they will dry out. Roast these cuts whole, either bone-in or boned out, or cut them into steaks, cutlets, and noisettes, and sauté, panfry, or broil them, taking care not to overcook.

Whole leg of venison, completely boned, seamed, and vacuum packed, is available. Weights range from 5 to 10 lb (2 to 4.5 kg). Whole bone-in saddle weighs from 5 to 20 lb (2.3 to 9 kg), while the loin muscle weighs about half that much after boning and trimming.

Tougher cuts, chiefly the shoulder, neck, and breast, are braised, stewed, or made into ground meat or sausage. These cuts are also lean, but because they are higher in connective tissue and gelatin, they take more readily to stewing and braising.

To generalize, farm-raised venison can be treated like very lean beef. Take care not to cook it to the point of dryness.

Boar

Boar is a type of wild pig. Its meat is somewhat similar to pork, except that it is leaner and its flavor is fuller and richer. Boar is now raised commercially on a few farms and is available in limited quantities.

Boar is somewhat more difficult to cook than venison and other game because, like pork, it must be cooked until well done. At the same time, it is leaner and less tender than domestic pork, so that it often tends to be somewhat dry and chewy. So special care must be taken to cook it adequately, but not to overcook it. Because boar is usually tougher than farm-raised venison, its legs or hams are better suited for braising or slow roasting, while the loins can be used for roasts or cut into medaillons and sautéed.

Because of boar's similarities to pork, many pork recipes can be used to cook it. For example, the recipe for Roast Loin of Pork Stuffed with Dates and Gorgonzola in Chapter 8 can be used for loin of boar as well, adjusting cooking times as appropriate. White wine marinades, befitting white meats, are suitable for boar as for pork. For example, the recipe variation for Roast Boar with Chestnuts and Apples (page 463) can be made with white wine instead of red, although of course the results will be quite different.

Traditionally, boar is handled much like venison, and typical recipes call for red wine marinades. Although marinating a white meat in red wine may seem strange at first, this treatment actually works very well with boar. The red wine accentuates the more pronounced flavor of boar (as compared with pork) and makes it taste more like game.

With two exceptions, the boar recipes in this chapter are simply variations of venison recipes. Please note, however, that the boar is not just a substitute for venison. The results will be quite different when the recipe is applied to boar. In addition, the special cooking and handling characteristics of boar, as discussed previously, must be taken into account, and the cooking times, temperatures, and other procedures must be adjusted as necessary.

Other Large Game. Various other meats are sometimes found in food-service kitchens. Elk, caribou, moose, and antelope are all similar to venison and are handled in much the same way. The first three of these, especially moose, are larger than deer, so it may be necessary to allow for longer cooking times when using venison recipes for them.

Buffalo, or American bison, is raised on Western ranches and is handled like beef. Flavor and cooking characteristics are similar to those of beef, but the meat is somewhat richer in flavor and has less fat and cholesterol than beef.

Rabbit

Domestic rabbit is a versatile meat that can be cooked in most of the same ways as chicken. In fact, in some countries it is classified as poultry. A few typical recipes for rabbit are included in this chapter, but nearly any chicken recipe can be used for domestic rabbit as well. In addition, many recipes for veal or pork, such as the recipe for Pork Chops with Prunes (page 398), are adaptable to rabbit.

Rabbit's light, delicate meat is often compared to chicken, but there are some differences. It is somewhat more flavorful than chicken, with a mild but distinctive taste that is not exactly like that of other poultry or meat. Also, it is very lean (more like chicken or turkey breast than legs) and can become dry if overcooked. Rabbit is sometimes larded or barded to supply the deficient fat.

Rabbit takes well to marination, and of course it can also be cooked without prior marination. Either way, it can be cooked by long, slow simmering, braising, or stewing, or it can be quickly cooked by sautéing, grilling, or roasting.

The structure of rabbit, of course, is like that of other land animals rather than like that of poultry. Cutting methods divide the meaty hind legs, the bonier forelegs, and the choice saddle or back section (*râble* in French). The whole carcass, cut up, is used for stews and sautés, while the saddle alone is often roasted. It may be boned or bone-in, stuffed or unstuffed (see Figures 9.6 and 9.7 for cutting methods).

Small rabbits, 3 pounds (1.5 kg) or less, are the best for cooking. Mature rabbits, weighing about 4 to 5 pounds (about 2 kg) tend to be tougher and drier.

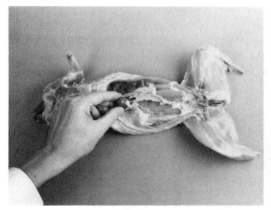

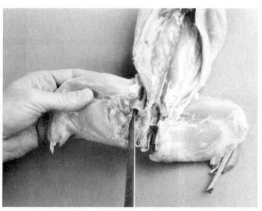

FIGURE 9.6. Cutting rabbit for stews and sautés. (a) The kidneys are located inside the body cavity against the backbone. Pull or cut them out.

(b) Cut off the hind legs, separating them at the hip joint.

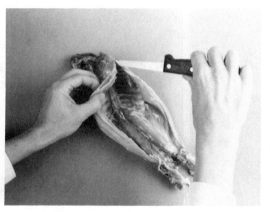

(c) Cut off the forelegs by cutting under the shoulder blade.

(d) Cut through the breast bone to open up the rib cage.

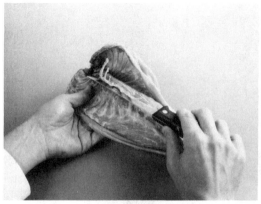

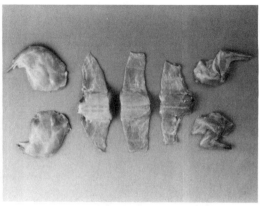

(e) Carefully separate the thin rib bones from the flesh and remove them. The saddle can then be cut crosswise through the backbone into pieces.

(f) This is the cut up rabbit, with the forelegs on the left, three pieces of saddle in the center, and the hind legs on the right.

FIGURE 9.7. Boning and stuffing a loin of rabbit. (a) Remove the tenderloins from the underside of the backbone.

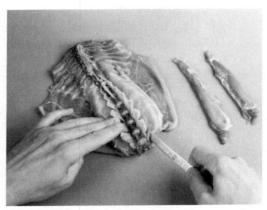

(b) Cut around the backbone to separate it from the loin muscle.

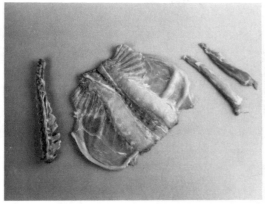

(c) The boned saddle is in the center, with the backbone on the left and tenderloins on the right.

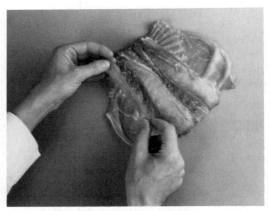

(d) Replace the tenderloins on the underside of the loins, placing the thick part of the tenderloin against the thin part of the loin so that the meat will be of more uniform thickness from end to end.

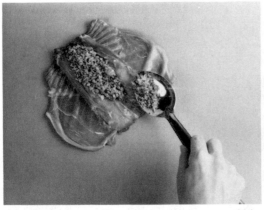

(e) Place the stuffing down the center of the saddle.

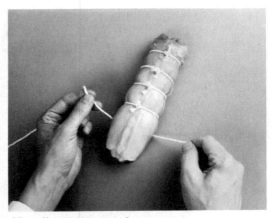

(f) Roll and tie securely.

Hare

Hare is a wild cousin of the rabbit. (Please note that rabbits and hares are different animals; the American jackrabbit, for example, is actually a hare, not a rabbit.) Unlike domestic rabbit, with its light-colored, delicate meat, hare has flesh that is dark reddish-brown and gamy.

Hares 7 to 8 months old, weighing about 6 pounds (2.7 kg) make the best eating. Larger ones, more than 8 pounds (3.6 kg), are likely to be tough and stringy.

Because its structure is the same, hare is cut the same way as rabbit, as shown in Figures 9.6 and 9.7.

Roast Saddle of Hare. Like other game, hare is very lean and therefore becomes dry if overcooked. If roasted, it should be removed from the oven while rare or at least still pink. Rare roast hare has an attractive, deep red color. A typical classic preparation of saddle of hare is as follows. Note that this is also the classic treatment for roast venison.

1. Marinate it in a red wine marinade (such as the venison marinade on page 460).
2. Brown it on top of the stove and roast it rare or medium done (about 15 minutes at 425°F or 220°C).
3. Remove the loin muscles from the bone and cut lengthwise into thin slices. Remove the tenderloins from the underside of the saddle and leave whole or slice as desired.
4. Serve it with a poivrade sauce.

Civet de Lièvre. A civet (pronounced "see-veh" or "see-vay") is a game stew (usually furred game rather than feathered game), traditionally made with red wine. The meat most often associated with civets is hare, and because it is such a classic, a recipe is included in this chapter, even though hare is not often cooked in this country.

Note that the recipe for venison stew (page 467) is similar to the civet recipe. In fact, the venison recipe, which is a typical game stew based on red wine, could also be called a civet.

The most important difference between the two recipes is the blood liaison in the hare recipe. Classical authorities insisted that a stew was not a true civet without a blood liaison. Today, however, infrequent availability, combined with restrictive health regulations, makes the use of this technique fairly uncommon in the United States. As an alternative, thicken the stew with a starch as indicated in the variations following the main recipe.

If blood is available, the classic version can be made. The technique for adding the blood is basically the same as the technique for using an egg-yolk-and-cream liaison. The coagulation of the blood proteins (like the coagulation of the egg proteins) thickens the sauce. Just before serving, the blood should be tempered and added slowly to the hot liquid. Once it has been added, the sauce should never be allowed to boil or the blood will curdle and separate.

MARINADE FOR VENISON

	U.S.		Metric	
YIELD (APPROXIMATE):	**1 pt**	**2 qt**	**5 dl**	**2 l**
Ingredients				
Carrots, chopped fine	1 oz	4 oz	30 g	125 g
Onions, chopped fine	1 oz	4 oz	30 g	125 g
Garlic, crushed	1 clove	4 cloves	1 clove	4 cloves
Parsley stems	6	25	6	25
Thyme	½ tsp	2 tsp	½ g	2 g
Bay leaves	1	4	1	4
Sage, ground	½ tsp	2 tsp	½ g	2 g
Peppercorns, crushed	¼ tsp	1 tsp	½ g	2 g
Cloves	1	4	1	4
Red wine vinegar	2 oz	8 oz	60 ml	2.5 dl
Red wine	1 pt	2 qt	5 dl	2 l

Procedure:

1. Combine all ingredients in a nonreactive container (e.g., stainless steel, glass, plastic; do not use aluminum).

2. Marinate meat as desired or as indicated in recipe. Marinating times may vary from a few hours to several days. After marinating, use the liquid as a cooking medium and as the base for a sauce.

SADDLE OR RACK OF VENISON GRAND VENEUR

		U.S.		Metric	
PORTIONS:		4	16	*4*	*16*
Ingredients					
Saddle(s) or rack(s) of venison, 2½–3 lb (1.1–1.4 kg) each		1	4	*1*	*4*
Marinade for Venison (p. 460); quantity variable, as needed		1 qt	4 qt	*1 l*	*4 l*
Barding fat, as needed (quantity approximate)		6 oz	1 lb 8 oz	*175 g*	*700 g*
Venison Sauce (p. 47)		8 oz	1 qt	*2.5 dl*	*1 l*
Chestnut Purée (p. 513)		8 oz	2 lb	*250 g*	*1 kg*

Mise en Place:

1. Trim the venison, removing all silverskin. Because venison is very lean, there will be very little fat to remove.
2. Marinate the venison for 2 days, using enough marinade to cover the meat completely.
3. Bard the meat by covering the meat with thin sheets of fat and tying them in place.

Cooking:

1. Roast the meat at 450°F (230°C) until rare, about 30 to 45 minutes.
2. Meanwhile, if you have not already made the sauce, use the leftover marinade to do so.
3. When the meat is done, set it aside in a warm place for 15 minutes. Degrease the roasting pan and deglaze it with a little marinade or red wine. Reduce it and strain it into the sauce.

Presentation:

1. Carve the venison like saddle of lamb (see Figure 8.8) or remove the meat from the bone and slice it into medaillons.
2. Arrange the sliced meat on plates or platters and garnish with portions of chestnut purée. Another vegetable or two may be included, depending on availability. Present the sauce in a sauceboat and add it to the plate at serving time, or allow the diners to serve themselves.

Variations

Leg of Venison Grand Veneur

Leg of venison can be prepared and served in the same way. A whole leg of venison weighing 4 to 5 lb (about 2 kg) yields about 8 to 10 portions. This larger cut should be marinated slightly longer, 2 to 3 days. Also, it may be larded instead of or in addition to being barded.

ROAST VENISON WITH APPLES AND CHESTNUTS

		U.S.		*Metric*	
PORTIONS:		**4**	**16**	*4*	*16*
Ingredients					
Boneless venison from loin or leg		1 ½ lb	6 lb	*700 g*	*2.8 kg*
Marinade:					
Red wine		8 oz	1 qt	*2.5 dl*	*1 l*
Shallot, chopped		1 oz	4 oz	*30 g*	*125 g*
Carrot, sliced		2 oz	8 oz	*60 g*	*250 g*
Ground ginger		pinch	¼ tsp	*pinch*	*½ g*
Cinnamon stick		1-inch piece	1 stick	*2-cm piece*	*1 stick*
Salt		¼ tsp	1 tsp	*1 g*	*5 g*
Chestnuts		12	48	*12*	*48*
Brown stock, as needed					
Apples		1	4	*1*	*4*
Butter		½ oz	2 oz	*15 g*	*60 g*
Cinnamon		pinch	¼ tsp	*pinch*	*½ g*
Sugar		2 tsp	3 tbsp	*10 g*	*40 g*
Lemon juice		1 tbsp	2 oz	*15 ml*	*60 ml*
Demiglaze		6 oz	1 ½ pt	*175 ml*	*7 dl*
Butter		1–2 oz	4–8 oz	*30–60 g*	*125–250*
Purée of potato and celery root (p. 544)		6 oz	1 ½ lb	*175 g*	*700 g*
Brussels sprouts		8 oz	2 lb	*225 g*	*900 g*
Butter, as needed					

Mise en Place:

1. Prepare and trim the meat. If the meat is from the leg, it is best, for the sake of uniform cooking and presentation, to separate the individual muscles and cut them lengthwise into the shape and size of boneless loin.

2. Combine the marinade ingredients. Bring to a simmer, then cool thoroughly. Place the meat in the marinade and let marinate for about 4 or 5 hours.

3. Blanch and peel the chestnuts. (Canned, whole chestnuts may be used in place of fresh chestnuts; in this case, the blanching and peeling are not necessary.) Combine the chestnuts in a covered saucepan with enough brown stock to cover by about one-third. Cook slowly until the chestnuts are tender; by the end of cooking, the stock should be well reduced so that there is just enough to glaze and moisten the chestnuts. During cooking, many of the chestnuts will break up. If any remain whole, break them into 3 or 4 pieces.

4. The apple-chestnut mixture is best prepared at the last minute, but it can also be prepared a little in advance. Peel and core the apples, and cut them into ½-inch (1-cm) dice. Sauté slowly in butter for a minute, then add the cinnamon and sugar. Continue to sauté until crisp-tender. Combine with the chestnuts. Add the lemon juice and cook a few minutes to reduce the liquid.

5. Trim the bases and any wilted leaves from the brussels sprouts. Cut them lengthwise into thin slices.

6. Remove the meat from the marinade and set aside. Reduce the marinade by three-fourths. Strain it and add it to the demiglaze. Bring to a simmer and then finish the sauce by stirring in some raw butter. Season to taste.

Cooking:

1. Dry the meat well. In a heavy pan over high heat, brown the meat well on all sides in a little oil or butter.

2. Place the meat in a hot oven (425°F; 220°C) until rare or medium, as desired. Cooking time will vary from about 20 to 45 minutes, depending on thickness of meat and desired doneness.

3. Remove the meat from the oven and set aside to rest in a warm place for about 10 or 15 minutes.

4. While the meat is cooking and resting, cook the brussels sprouts slowly in a little butter until tender but still green and slightly crisp.

Presentation:

1. Place small mounds of the apple-chestnut mixture in the center of dinner plates.

2. Place portions of the brussels sprouts and the potato celery root purée behind the chestnut mixture.

3. Slice the meat. If you are using loins or loin-shaped pieces, you should have three slices per portion.

4. Arrange the slices of meat overlapping each other on the front half of the plate, leaning against the chestnuts and apples.

5. Pour a little sauce around, not over, the meat.

Variation

Roast Boar with Apples and Chestnuts

Substitute boar for venison in the basic recipe. Place the meat in an oven heated to 350°F (175°C); note that this is lower than the roasting temperature for venison. Cook the boar until well-done, but be careful not to overcook it or it will be dry.

NOISETTES OF VENISON WITH RED WINE SAUCE

(Color Plate 15)

		U.S.		Metric	
PORTIONS:		**4**	**16**	*4*	*16*
Ingredients					
Red wine		8 oz	1 qt	*2.5 dl*	*1 l*
Shallots, chopped		1 oz	4 oz	*30 g*	*125 g*
Raspberry purée (see Mise en Place, step 1)		2 oz	8 oz	*60 g*	*250 g*
Lime juice		1 oz	4 oz	*30 ml*	*125 ml*
Juniper berries, crushed		8	32	*8*	*32*
Noisettes of venison, cut from the loin, ¾ inch (2 cm) thick, about 2–3 oz (60–90 g) each		8	32	*8*	*32*
Butter or oil for sautéing					
Butter		2½ oz	10 oz	*75 g*	*300 g*
Chopped parsley (optional)		2 tbsp	1 oz	*7 g*	*30 g*

Mise en Place:

1. To make raspberry purée, force fresh or frozen (thawed) raspberries through a sieve. Measure the resulting purée.

2. Combine the red wine, shallots, raspberry purée, lime juice, and juniper berries.

3. Add the slices of venison to the mixture and marinate for 2 to 4 hours.

Cooking:

1. Remove the meat from the marinade and dry it well.

2. Reduce the marinade by half over moderate heat. Strain.

3. Sauté the venison noisettes in butter or oil over high heat until browned outside and rare inside.

4. Finish the sauce by swirling in the raw butter. Add the chopped parsley.

5. Serve the venison with the sauce.

Variation

Noisettes of Boar with Red Wine Sauce

Substitute boar for venison in the basic recipe. After browning, lower the heat and cook at a lower temperature. Cook until well done but not dry.

NOISETTES OF VENISON POIVRADE WITH CASSIS

		U.S.		Metric	
PORTIONS:		4	16	4	16
Ingredients					
Noisettes of venison, cut from the loin, ¾ inch (2 cm) thick, about 2–3 oz (60–90 g) each		8	32	8	32
Salt					
Pepper					
Butter or oil for cooking					
Chicken stock		2 oz	8 oz	60 ml	2.5 dl
Poivrade Sauce (p. 46) or Pepper Sauce (p. 57)		6 oz	1 ½ pt	2 dl	8 dl
Creme de cassis (black currant liqueur)		½ oz	2 oz	15 ml	60 ml

Cooking and Presentation:

1. Season the noisettes with salt and pepper. Sauté them in butter or oil, keeping them rare.
2. Remove the meat from the sauté pan and set it aside in a warm place.
3. Degrease the sauté pan. Deglaze it with chicken stock and reduce the stock by one-half.
4. Add the sauce and the cassis to the pan and bring to a simmer. Strain the sauce.
5. Serve two noisettes per portion. Spoon the sauce around the meat, using about 1 ½ oz (45 ml) per portion. Garnish the plate with appropriate seasonal vegetables.

Variations

Loin of Venison with White Pepper and a Juniper Red Wine Sauce

Do not cut the loins into noisettes, but leave them in pieces large enough for 2 to 4 portions each. Roll the trimmed loins in lightly crushed white peppercorns; let stand several hours or overnight, if possible, so that the pepper flavor has time to penetrate the meat.

Omit the cassis in the basic recipe. In place of the poivrade sauce, make a red wine sauce as directed on page 58, but flavor the sauce by reducing the red wine with some crushed juniper berries.

Sauté the meat to order, let it rest a few minutes, and slice it. Degrease, deglaze with chicken stock, and add the red wine sauce as in the basic recipe. Finish the sauce by adding heavy cream or crème fraîche, about ½ to 1 oz (15 to 40 ml) per portion; reduce to desired consistency.

Noisettes of Boar Poivrade with Cassis
Loin of Boar with White Pepper and a Juniper Red Wine Sauce

Prepare as in the preceding recipes, substituting loin of boar for the venison. Cook until well done, but be careful not to let the meat become overcooked and dry.

GRILLED VENISON WITH LIME BUTTER

		U.S.		Metric	
PORTIONS:		**4**	**16**	*4*	*16*
Ingredients					
Boneless, trimmed venison (see Mise en Place, step 1)		1 lb	4 lb	*500 g*	*2 kg*
Sichuan peppercorns, toasted		½ tsp	2 tsp	*½ g*	*2 g*
Lime juice		1 tbsp	2 oz	*15 ml*	*60 ml*
Salt					
Butter		1 oz	4 oz	*30 g*	*125 g*
Sichuan peppercorns, toasted and crushed		¼ tsp	1 tsp	*¼ g*	*1 g*
Grated lime zest		1 tsp	4 tsp	*2 g*	*8 g*
Lime juice		¼ tsp	1 tsp	*1 ml*	*5 ml*
Salt, to taste					

Mise en Place:

1. Select a piece or pieces of venison suitable for broiling whole and slicing, in the manner of London broil. Make sure it is well trimmed of all silverskin.

2. Rub the meat with sichuan peppercorns. Sprinkle with lime juice and salt. Let marinate 30 minutes.

3. Make a seasoned butter by softening the butter and mixing in the crushed sichuan peppercorns, zest, lime juice, and salt. Refrigerate until needed.

Cooking and Presentation:

1. Grill or broil the venison until rare or medium rare. Remove from the heat and let rest for a few minutes.

2. Cut on the bias, across the grain, into thin slices, like London broil.

3. Arrange the slices on plates. Top each portion with a small slice of lime butter (about ½ tbsp or 8 g).

RAGOUT OF VENISON

		U.S.		Metric	
PORTIONS:		4	16	4	16
Ingredients					
Venison shoulder, boned		1 lb 12 oz	7 lb	800 g	3.2 kg
Marinade for Venison (p. 460)		1 pt	2 qt	5 dl	2 l
Oil or bacon fat, as needed					
Brown stock or game stock		12 oz	3 pt	3.5 dl	1.4 l
Salt					
Cranberry sauce (optional)		2 oz	8 oz	60 g	250 g
Beurre manié or other starch thickener, as needed					
Crème fraîche or heavy cream		4 oz	1 pt	125 ml	5 dl
Garnish:					
Small onions, cooked and browned		4 oz	1 lb	125 g	500 g
Mushrooms, sautéed (see Cooking and Presentation, step 8)		6 oz	1 lb 8 oz	175 g	700 g

Mise en Place:

1. Trim the meat well and cut it into large cubes, about 1 ½ inches (4 cm) across.
2. Combine the meat and marinade. Marinate for 2 days.

Cooking and Presentation:

1. Remove the meat from the marinade and dry it. In a heavy saucepan or braising pan, heat the oil or fat and brown the meat well on all sides.
2. Meanwhile, in a separate pan, bring the marinade to a boil. Simmer 5 minutes and then strain it.
3. Add the strained marinade and the stock to the meat. Cover and simmer, in a slow oven or on top of the stove, until the meat is tender. This will take 1 to 2 hours, depending on the meat.
4. If the cranberry sauce is used (for flavoring the sauce), add it to the meat during the last half hour of cooking.
5. Remove the meat from the cooking liquid. Reduce the liquid over moderately high heat until there is about 2 to 3 oz (60 to 90 ml) per portion.
6. Thicken the liquid as necessary with beurre manié or other thickener.
7. Add the crème fraîche or heavy cream to the sauce. Simmer a minute. Adjust the seasoning and strain the sauce.
8. Combine the meat, sauce, and garnish of onions and mushrooms. (*Note:* Wild mushrooms, especially chanterelles, are especially good in this dish.)
9. Serve in soup plates or other deep plates, accompanied with noodles or boiled potatoes.

BOAR MEATBALLS WITH ROSEMARY AND ORANGE

		U.S.		Metric	
PORTIONS:		4	16	4	16
Ingredients					
Onion, minced		2 oz	8 oz	60 g	250 g
Garlic, minced		1 clove	4 cloves	1 clove	4 cloves
Butter		1 ½ oz	6 oz	45 g	175 g
Ground boar meat		1 lb	4 lb	500 g	2 kg
Fresh bread crumbs		1 oz	4 oz	30 g	125 g
Rosemary, crumbled		¼ tsp	1 tsp	¼ g	1 g
Salt		½ tsp	2 tsp	3 g	10 g
Pepper		¼ tsp	1 tsp	½ g	2 g
Grated orange zest		½ tsp	2 tsp	1 g	4 g
Oil or clarified butter					
Chicken stock		4 oz	1 pt	125 ml	5 dl
Rosemary		¼ tsp	1 tsp	¼ g	1 g
Orange zest, julienne		1 tbsp	4 tbsp	10 g	40 g
Dijon-style mustard		2 tsp	1 ½ oz	10 g	45 g
Crème fraîche or heavy cream		8 oz	1 qt	2.5 dl	1 l
Salt					
Lemon juice					

Mise en Place:

1. Sauté the onion and garlic slowly in butter until tender, but do not brown. Cool.

2. Mix together the cooked onions and garlic, ground boar, bread crumbs, rosemary, salt, pepper, and grated orange zest. Make small meatballs, so that you have 5 balls per portion.

Cooking:

1. Brown the meatballs well in oil or butter.

2. When the meatballs are browned, pour off any excess fat, if necessary, leaving the meatballs in the pan.

3. Add the stock, cover, and simmer 10 minutes.

4. Remove the meatballs with a slotted spoon and keep them warm. Degrease and strain the cooking liquid.

5. Add the rosemary and julienne of orange zest. Reduce the liquid by three-fourths over high heat.

6. Add the mustard and cream. Reduce by one-third, or until the sauce is slightly thickened.

7. Season the sauce to taste with salt and lemon juice.

Presentation:

1. Plate the meatballs and garnish with fresh noodles and an appropriate vegetable in season.

2. Ladle the sauce over the meatballs.

Variations

Venison Meatballs with Rosemary and Orange

Prepare as in the basic recipe, substituting venison for boar.

Rosemary Orange Sauce (for venison or boar cutlets, steaks, and noisettes)

Combine the chicken stock, rosemary, and julienne of orange zest. Reduce by three-fourths. Continue with steps 6 and 7 in the main recipe to finish the sauce. Served with sautéed or grilled venison or boar.

BRAISED BOAR WITH PORCINI

		U.S.		Metric	
PORTIONS:		**4**	**16**	*4*	*16*
Ingredients					
Dried porcini mushrooms		¾ oz	3 oz	*20 g*	*80 g*
Hot water		8 oz	2 pt	*2.5 dl*	*1 l*
Olive oil		1 oz	4 oz	*30 ml*	*125 ml*
Boneless leg of boar		1 lb 8 oz	6 lb	*700 g*	*2.8 kg*
Shallots		1 oz	4 oz	*30 g*	*125 g*
White wine		4 oz	1 pt	*125 ml*	*5 dl*
Red or white wine vinegar		1 oz	4 oz	*30 ml*	*125 ml*
Salt					
Bay leaves		1	4	*1*	*4*
Juniper berries, crushed		1 ½ tsp	2 tbsp	*3 g*	*12 g*
Peppercorns, lightly crushed		¼ tsp	1 tsp	*0.5 g*	*2 g*
Oregano		pinch	½ tsp	*pinch*	*0.5 g*

Mise en Place:

1. Soak the mushrooms in the hot water for 30 minutes, until they are soft. Drain. Strain and reserve the soaking liquid. Rinse the mushrooms and chop them coarsely.

2. Cut the boar into large dice, about 1 ½ inches (4 cm) across.

3. Peel and mince the shallots.

4. Tie the bay leaves, juniper berries, peppercorns, and oregano into a square of cheesecloth.

Cooking:

1. Heat the olive oil in a heavy braising pan. Add the boar and brown lightly on all sides. Remove from the pan with a slotted spoon.

2. Add the shallots to the pan and brown lightly.

3. Add the wine, vinegar, and the soaking liquid from the mushrooms. Return the meat to the pan and add the mushrooms, a good pinch of salt, and the spice bag. Bring to a simmer, cover, and braise slowly over low heat or in a slow oven until the meat is tender.

4. Remove the meat and mushrooms with a slotted spoon. Remove and discard the spice bag.

5. Skim excess fat from the cooking liquid and return the pan to the heat. Reduce over high heat until the liquid is of good consistency and there is about 2 oz (60 ml) per portion. Adjust the seasoning with salt and pepper. Return the meat and mushrooms to the pan.

Presentation:

This stew goes very well over a bed of soft polenta.

Variation

This recipe can also be used to braise hare. Preferably use the legs of the hare and save the saddle for roasting (see page 459).

RABBIT WITH MUSTARD

		U.S.		Metric	
PORTIONS:		4	16	*4*	*16*
Ingredients					
Rabbit		2–2 ½ lb	8–10 lb	*1 kg*	*4 kg*
Oil					
Butter		¼ oz	1 oz	*8 g*	*30 g*
Shallot, chopped		½ oz	2 oz	*15 g*	*60 g*
Mustard, dijon-style or grainy		1 oz	4 oz	*30 g*	*125 g*
Salt					
Pepper					
Thyme		pinch	½ tsp	*pinch*	*½ g*
White wine		4 oz	1 pt	*125 ml*	*5 dl*
Chicken stock		4 oz	1 pt	*125 ml*	*5 dl*
Heavy cream		4 oz	1 pt	*125 ml*	*5 dl*

Mise en Place:

Clean and cut up the rabbit for stewing, as in Figure 9.6.

Cooking:

1. Brown the rabbit in oil in a heavy pan.
2. Remove the rabbit from the pan and keep it warm. Degrease the pan.
3. Add the butter to the pan. Sweat the chopped shallots in the butter but do not brown.
4. Add the remaining ingredients, except for the cream, to the pan and return the browned rabbit to the pan. Cover and braise slowly over low heat or in a low oven until the meat is cooked.
5. Remove the rabbit from the liquid and set aside. Reduce the liquid by about one-third.
6. Add the heavy cream. Simmer and reduce until the sauce is lightly thickened. Adjust the seasonings. Return the rabbit pieces to the sauce.

CIVET DE LIÈVRE

		U.S.		Metric	
PORTIONS:		4	16	4	16
Ingredients					
Hare, cleaned and dressed		2 ½ lb	10 lb	1.1 kg	4.5 kg
Blood from the hare		4–5 oz	16–20 oz	125–150 ml	5–6 dl
Lemon juice or red wine vinegar		1 oz	4 oz	30 ml	125 ml
Marinade:					
Onion, sliced		2 oz	8 oz	60 g	250 g
Carrot, sliced		2 oz	8 oz	60 g	250 g
Bay leaves		1	3	1	3
Thyme		¼ tsp	1 tsp	¼ g	1 g
Black peppercorns, crushed		6	25	6	25
Parsley stems		6	25	6	25
Red wine		1 ½ pt	3 qt	7.5 dl	3 l
Salt pork		2 oz	8 oz	60 g	250 g
Small white onions, peeled		16	64	16	64
Garlic, chopped		2 cloves	8 cloves	2 cloves	8 cloves
Water, as needed					
Button mushrooms, trimmed		6 oz	1 lb 8 oz	175 g	700 g
Butter					
Hare livers or chicken livers		1	4	1	4
Cognac or other brandy		1 tbsp	2 oz	15 ml	60 ml
Heavy cream		1 oz	4 oz	30 ml	125 ml
Salt					
Toasted french bread slices		8–12	32–48	8–12	32–48
Chopped parsley					

Mise en Place:

1. If possible, obtain the hare's blood along with the hare and save all blood that collects when cutting up the hare. Mix the blood with a little lemon juice or vinegar to keep it liquid. If blood is not available, see the variation following the main recipe.

2. Carefully trim all silverskin from the hare. Cut it up for stewing, as in Figure 9.6.

3. Combine the marinade ingredients in a nonreactive container (stainless steel, plastic, glass; not aluminum). Add the hare. Marinate 1 day.

4. Cut the salt pork into small dice.

Cooking:

1. Render the salt pork in a heavy sauté pan.

2. Remove the hare pieces from the marinade and dry them. Brown them lightly in the rendered fat over moderate heat. Remove the meat from the pan with a slotted spoon and transfer it to a braising pan or casserole.

3. Add the pearl onions to the fat remaining in the sauté pan and brown them lightly. Remove them with a slotted spoon and add them to the hare.

4. Degrease the sauté pan and deglaze it with some of the marinade. Add the deglazing liquid and the rest of the marinade to the hare. If there is not enough liquid to cover the hare, add a little water.

5. Bring the casserole to a boil, cover it, and place it in an oven heated to 300°F (150°C). Braise for 1 ½ to 2 hours, or until the meat is tender.

6. When the meat is cooked, remove it and the pearl onions from the cooking liquid and keep them warm.

7. Degrease the cooking liquid. Reduce it if necessary until there is about 3 to 4 oz (1 dl) per portion. Strain it. (*Note:* The dish can be prepared in advance up to this point; refrigerate the liquid and meat in separate containers, to be reheated later. To reheat, combine the meat and sauce and reheat slowly; then proceed with the rest of the recipe.)

8. Shortly before serving, sauté the mushrooms in a little butter. Set aside with the hare.

9. In a blender or food processor, purée the liver with the blood. Add the brandy and mix in.

10. Remove the sauce from the heat and let it cool until lukewarm. Carefully beat a little of the sauce into the blood to temper it. Then slowly beat this mixture into the hot sauce. Return it to the heat and heat it slowly, stirring constantly, until the sauce thickens slightly. Add the cream. Do not let the sauce simmer or it will curdle and separate. Add salt to taste.

11. Combine the hare and mushrooms. Strain the sauce over the meat.

12. Plate the hare and spoon the sauce over it. Accompany with 2 or 3 slices of toasted french bread. Sprinkle with chopped parsley.

Variation

If blood is not available to thicken the sauce, thicken it with beurre manié, arrowroot, or other starch thickener, or add some flour to the pan when browning the meat.

ROAST SADDLE OF RABBIT STUFFED WITH VEGETABLES AND HERBS
(Color Plate 16)

		U.S.		Metric	
PORTIONS:		**4**	**16**	*4*	*16*
Ingredients					
Saddles from small rabbits (see note)		4	16	*4*	*16*
Butter		½ oz	2 oz	*15 g*	*60 g*
Shallots, chopped very fine		1 oz	4 oz	*30 g*	*125 g*
Carrots, chopped very fine		1 oz	4 oz	*30 g*	*125 g*
Zucchini, chopped very fine		1 oz	4 oz	*30 g*	*125 g*
Mushrooms, chopped very fine		2 oz	8 oz	*60 g*	*250 g*
Garlic, chopped		½ tsp	2 tsp	*2 g*	*10 g*
Basil leaves, fresh, chopped		2 tbsp	1 oz	*7 g*	*30 g*
Parsley, chopped		1 tbsp	4 tbsp	*4 g*	*15 g*
Rabbit liver or chicken liver		1	4	*1*	*4*
Bread crumbs, fresh		4 tbsp	½ oz	*4 g*	*15 g*
Salt					
Pepper					
Oil, for cooking					
Dry white vermouth or white wine		2 oz	8 oz	*60 ml*	*2.5 dl*
Rabbit stock or chicken stock, rich and concentrated		6 oz	1 ½ pt	*2 dl*	*8 dl*
Vegetable stock (p. 101) or additional rabbit stock or chicken stock		4 oz	1 pt	*125 ml*	*5 dl*
Butter		1 ½ tsp	1 oz	*8 g*	*30 g*
Salt					
Mashed potatoes		8 oz	2 lb	*250 g*	*1 kg*
Butter		½–1 oz	2–4 oz	*15–30 g*	*60–125 g*
Steamed, buttered swiss chard or spinach		8 oz	2 lb	*250 g*	*1 kg*
Carrots, small dice, cooked		1 oz	4 oz	*30 g*	*125 g*
Zucchini, small dice, cooked		1 oz	4 oz	*30 g*	*125 g*

Note: This recipe calls for small rabbits yielding boneless saddles of 6 oz (175 g) or less. If these are not available, use larger ones, allotting 2 portions per saddle.

Mise en Place:

1. Bone out the rabbit saddles (see Figure 9.7). Use the bones to make stock for the sauce (or use chicken stock). Reduce the stock as necessary to concentrate it.

2. Heat the butter over low heat and add the shallots, carrots, zucchini, mushrooms, and garlic. Sweat until tender but not browned. Do not cover, so moisture can evaporate as it cooks out of the vegetables.

3. While the vegetables are cooking, purée the liver and force it through a sieve. Measure 1 tbsp (15 g) for each 4 portions (2 oz or 60 g for 16 portions).

4. Mix the basil, parsley, and puréed liver with the hot vegetables. The heat of the vegetables will cook the liver instantly.

5. Stir in the bread crumbs. Season to taste with salt and pepper. Cool completely.

6. Lay the saddles on the worktable, skin side down. Replace the tenderloins, placing the thick end of the tenderloin against the thin end of the loin, so that the meat is of more uniform thickness, as shown in Figure 9.7.

7. Spoon the vegetable mixture down the center of each saddle. Roll up the saddles into a sausage shape to enclose the stuffing. Tie securely. Refrigerate until ready to cook.

Cooking:

1. Brown the saddles well on all sides in oil. Transfer to an oven heated to 450°F (230°C). Roast for 15 minutes.

2. Remove the saddles from the pan and keep warm. Degrease the pan. Deglaze with vermouth and reduce by half.

3. Add the rabbit or chicken stock and the vegetable stock. Reduce by two-thirds. Finish the jus with butter. Season to taste.

Presentation:

1. Enrich the potatoes with extra butter. They should be quite soft.

2. For each portion, place a tablespoon (15 g) of potatoes on each quadrant of the plate.

3. Cut each saddle into 4 slices. Place each slice on top of each dab of potatoes, with the most attractive side of the slice up. (If using larger saddles yielding 2 portions each, modify the presentation as necessary. For example, cut the saddle into 6 slices, 3 per portion. Six slices from larger saddles will be thinner but broader.)

4. Place a mound of chard (or spinach) in the center of each plate.

5. Place a few pieces of diced carrot and zucchini on the plate between the slices.

6. Spoon the jus onto the plate around the meat.

BRAISED RABBIT WITH CELERY AND OLIVES

		U.S.		Metric	
PORTIONS:		4	16	4	16
Ingredients					
Rabbit		2 lb 8 oz	10 lb	1.1 kg	4.5 kg
Olive oil		2 oz	8 oz	60 ml	2.5 dl
Celery		8 oz	2 lb	250 g	1 kg
Onion		4 oz	1 lb	125 g	500 g
Sugar		2 tsp	3 tbsp	10 g	40 g
Red wine vinegar		1 ½ oz	6 oz	45 g	175 g
Green olives, pitted		2 oz	8 oz	60 g	250 g
Cayenne		pinch	¼ tsp	pinch	½ g
Salt					
Pepper					
Chicken stock		2 oz	8 oz	60 ml	2.5 dl
Red bell pepper		1 oz	4 oz	30 g	125 g
Olive oil					
Chopped parsley		2 tbsp	1 oz	7 g	30 g

Mise en Place:

1. Cut up the rabbit for stewing.

2. Cut the celery and onion into thin slices.

3. Slice the olives.

4. Cut the red pepper into brunoise.

Cooking:

1. In a heavy pan, brown the rabbit in the olive oil. Remove from the pan when brown.

2. Add the celery and onion to the fat remaining in the pan. Brown lightly.

3. Add the sugar and continue to brown until the sugar is slightly caramelized.

4. Deglaze the pan with the vinegar.

5. Return the rabbit to the pan and add the olives, cayenne, salt, pepper, and chicken stock. Braise very slowly, over low heat or in a low oven, until the rabbit is cooked, about 30 minutes. Because there is very little cooking liquid, care must be taken so that the pan does not become completely dry, allowing the meat and vegetables to burn.

6. If there is any liquid left in the pan when the rabbit is cooked, remove the cover and reduce it until syrupy.

7. While the rabbit is cooking, sauté the red pepper briefly in a little olive oil to soften.

Presentation:

Place the vegetables (celery, onions, and olives) on plates or on a platter. Arrange the rabbit pieces on top of the vegetables. Top with the sautéed diced red pepper and a little chopped parsley.

CHAPTER

10

Vegetables

*F*resh vegetables appear to be more important in today's restaurants than they have been in many years. Not long ago, vegetables were often merely afterthoughts, prepared and served indifferently and not carefully planned into the menu.

Today, on the other hand, vegetables are getting as much, and sometimes even more, attention than meats, poultry, and fish. A number of famous restaurants are renowned for their expertise in serving vegetables and have, in fact, developed special relationships with farmers in their areas who supply them with the top-quality produce that the restaurants' customers have come to expect and demand.

Several factors play a role in the recent prominence of vegetables. Among these are greater nutritional awareness on the part of both restaurateurs and customers, greater understanding of freshness and quality factors, availability of more kinds and varieties of produce, and an appreciation of the seasonal nature of fresh vegetables and fruits.

Restaurateurs know that imaginative vegetable preparations help them give variety and interest to their menus and that their efforts are likely to be rewarded with increased customer satisfaction.

This chapter is devoted to helping cooks who have learned the basics of vegetable preparation to expand their repertoire of techniques and recipes.

VEGETABLES AS GARNISH

In order to understand the role of vegetables in modern plating practices, it would be helpful to review briefly the meaning of the word *garnish*.

Many people think of a garnish as a small item, such as a sprig of parsley, that is used for decoration but that is not intended to be eaten. In classical cooking, however, the term *garnish* refers to any item placed on a plate to accompany the main item. Any vegetable dish that accompanies a meat or fish item is considered a garnish. Although many kinds of foods could be used (veal quenelles and lardons of bacon are two examples of garnish made from meat), in actual practice most classical garnishes consist of vegetable preparations. For example, the garnish for Tournedos Niçoise (page 357) includes tomatoes cooked with garlic, small potatoes cooked in butter, and green beans.

Garnish, in other words, is used not only for the sake of appearance but also to complete the dish. The important point here is that the garnish is an integral part of the preparation and presentation, not just something added on. If the Tournedos Niçoise were given a different garnish, for example, it would no longer be Tournedos Niçoise.

Modern cooks once again appreciate the significance of Escoffier's dictum that a vegetable—or any other garnish—should always have some relationship to the meat or fish item it accompanies. While they may insist on buying fresh vegetables daily and selecting only the best and freshest, they also buy them in sufficient variety so that the combinations of main items and vegetables are always appropriate and harmonious.

To emphasize the important role that vegetables play as part of the whole rather than as something added on, many recipes for fish, poultry, and meat in the preceding chapters include recipes for the vegetable components of the dish within the main recipe. In other cases, specific vegetable garnishes are indicated with a reference to recipes in this chapter.

In the remaining main-course recipes, no garnishes are indicated, but this does not mean that any vegetable accompaniment is as good as any other. It is up to cooks to use their judgment to choose appropriate vegetables for each main dish.

UNUSUAL AND UNCOMMON VEGETABLES

Increased interest in fresh vegetables has resulted in a greater variety available in the markets. Some of these are relatively new to us, having been introduced via foreign and ethnic cuisines. Thus, we are enjoying an abundance of Chinese and other Asian vegetables, for example.

Others have always been with us, but only in limited use. Collards, for example, have always been important in parts of the South, while various chile peppers are nothing new to Americans of Mexican heritage, but only recently have these vegetables been widely available nationwide.

What follows is a review of various vegetables that were not often seen a decade or two ago but that are now regularly available in the fresh produce markets. The list is by no means exclusive; in particular, those vegetables that are used almost entirely in foreign cuisines are beyond the scope of this book. In addition, many uncommon varieties of common vegetables, such as white eggplant, are omitted.

Cabbage Family

The cabbage family provides many of our most familiar vegetables, including white or green cabbage, red cabbage, brussels sprouts, cauliflower, and broccoli, as well as several less familiar items.

Savoy or European Green Cabbage. This is a round-headed cabbage with crinkly or curly leaves (see Figure 10.1). It is deeper green in color than our regular white or green cabbage. More flavorful and at the same time more delicate than white cabbage, it is often braised and served as an accompaniment to sophisticated meat, game, poultry, and even fish dishes.

Chinese Cabbage. Chinese cabbage, also called *napa* or *nappa cabbage* or *celery cabbage*, comes in two forms: a long, narrow head and a shorter, thicker head (see Figure 10.1). Both are milder and sweeter in flavor than regular cabbage, with less of a mustardy bite. The leaves and ribs are crisp and juicy but very tender, making this cabbage especially good when eaten raw in salads. It can be quickly sautéed or stir-fried to preserve its crispness, or it can be braised until very tender, soft, and smooth.

FIGURE 10.1. **From left to right: bok choy, savoy cabbage, kale, napa or Chinese cabbage, kohlrabi.**

Bok Choy. Bok choy (*pak choi* or *Chinese white cabbage*) is shaped not like a head cabbage but as a bunch of stalks (see Figure 10.1). The thick tender stems are usually white, although they are pale green in some varieties. It is similar in flavor and usage to Chinese cabbage, although it is usually cooked rather than served raw.

Broccoli Raab. This is a type of nonheading broccoli, also called *broccoli rabe, broccoli di rape,* and *rapini.* It is leafy, with thin stems and sparse, scattered buds, and it is more strongly flavored than heading broccoli, with the bitterness and pungency of mustard. For a milder flavor, blanch for a minute in boiling water and then rinse in cold water and drain. Broccoli raab is often sautéed with garlic and olive oil.

Chinese broccoli (*choy sum*) is similar in appearance but has thicker stems and milder flavor.

Kohlrabi. Kohlrabi is a bulbous vegetable that is actually an enlarged stem (see Figure 10.1), which explains its similarity in flavor and texture to the crisp interior of a broccoli stem. It is handled and prepared like turnips, except that it is sweeter, milder, more tender, and needs less cooking.

Kale, Collards, Mustard Greens, and Turnip Greens. These four vegetables are members of the cabbage family that are grown for their leaves. Coarser and heartier than delicate greens such as spinach, they take well to long, slow cooking and are often braised or used in soups. Kale is shown in Figure 10.1.

Peppers

Until recently, only the sweet bell pepper was used with any frequency in the American kitchen—usually in its unripe green form, but occasionally in its red, ripe form. (*Note:* Although green peppers will turn red when they ripen, those that are cultivated specifically to be sold as red peppers are often distinct varieties).

Yellow, orange, and purple varieties of bell peppers have been developed. There are subtle variations in flavor from one variety to the next. Note that purple peppers turn green when cooked, so they are usually used raw.

Cubanelle peppers are often mistaken for hot chile peppers, but they are sweet, not hot. They are light green to yellowish green, or even reddish if they have begun to ripen, with an elongated, somewhat wrinkled shape and thin flesh. They are used in the same way as other sweet peppers.

Fresh *chile* (or chili) *peppers* have been introduced by other cuisines, especially Mexican, and are in wide distribution. The many varieties vary from mild to slightly hot to extremely hot. They are valued for their distinctive flavors as well as their heat levels. Most chile peppers have thinner, less meaty flesh than bell peppers do. The following are some of the more common varieties of chile peppers. Many of these peppers are also ripened and dried, in which case they may take another name. Most chiles are green or greenish when sold fresh and turn red when ripened.

Anaheim. Similar and related varieties include *New Mex, Big Jim,* and *California Chile.* Anaheim peppers (see Figure 10.2) are light to medium green in color, long and narrow, sometimes up to 8 or 9 inches (20 to 23 cm) in length, and mild to moderately hot. When ripened and dried, they are reddish brown and may be called *chiles colorados.*

FIGURE 10.2. **From left to right: Anaheim, poblano, serrano, and jalapeño chiles.**

Poblano. The poblano is a shiny, dark green pepper about the size of a small bell pepper but with a triangular shape and thin flesh (see Figure 10.2). Its heat level varies from fairly mild to moderately hot, and it has a rich, deep flavor. It is sometimes called *ancho pepper*, but this name is more properly used for the red, ripe, dried form (one of the standard components of chile powder). Poblano is the usual pepper used for the classic *chiles rellenos*, or Mexican-style stuffed peppers.

Jalapeño. This is a small, dark green, hot chile, about 2 inches (5 cm) long, with smooth skin, thick flesh, a narrow, slightly tapered shape and a blunt, rounded tip (see Figure 10.2). It is widely available and widely used as a flavoring ingredient. (When dried and smoked, this pepper is called a *chipotle.*)

Serrano. The serrano looks somewhat like a small, thin jalapeño (see Figure 10.2). It is hotter than a jalapeño.

Hungarian Wax. Long, narrow, and tapered, this pepper has a creamy yellow, waxy appearance. A number of varieties are sold with this name or as *banana peppers;* some are sweet and not at all hot, while others may be mildly to moderately hot.

Mushrooms

Although there are hundreds of varieties of edible mushrooms, until recently only the common cultivated mushroom has been used with any frequency in the American kitchen. Now, however, there are many varieties, both cultivated and wild, available in the markets. Some of these mushrooms, especially the wild ones, are very expensive, but the demand always seems to exceed the supply, and these high prices have been readily paid.

Strictly speaking, the term *wild* should be used only for those mushrooms that are not cultivated but that are hunted and gathered in the wild. In the kitchen and on menus, however, exotic cultivated varieties, such as shiitakes, are often referred to as wild mushrooms because they are seen as rare and unusual, like true wild mushrooms, and they are generally more flavorful than the common cultivated button mushroom.

One important advantage of cultivated exotic mushrooms is that they are available all year, while certain wild mushrooms may be in season for only a few weeks a year.

FIGURE 10.3. **From left to right: shiitake, oyster, and enoki mushrooms.**

Cultivated Exotic Mushrooms

Shiitake. Sometimes known as *Black Forest mushroom* or *golden oak mushroom*, the shiitake is also available in dried form as *Chinese black mushroom*. The fresh mushroom (see Figure 10.3) is golden brown to dark brown. It has a firm, fleshy texture and a broad, dome-shaped cap with creamy white gills. Stems are rather tough, so they are trimmed off and chopped fine or used in stocks.

Oyster Mushroom. Also called *pleurotte*, it is a light tan or cream colored, fan-shaped mushroom with a short stem at the side (see Figure 10.3). Tender, with delicate flavor, it is best prepared simply, so its mild flavor is not overwhelmed by stronger-tasting ingredients. (*Note:* The name *oyster* refers to the shape of the mushroom, not its taste.)

Enoki Mushroom. Also called *enokitake* or *enokidake*, this mushroom has a tiny, white cap on a long, slender stem, in clusters or bunches that are attached at the base (see Figure 10.3). The base is trimmed before use. The enoki mushroom has a crisp texture and a fruity, slightly acidic but sweet flavor. Enokis are often used raw (for example, in salads or as garnish) or in clear soups. When used in cooked dishes, they should be added in the last few minutes, so as not to be overcooked.

Cremini Mushroom. The cremini is a variety of the common cultivated mushroom, but it has a brown or tan skin (see Figure 10.4). It may have a slightly more robust flavor than white cultivated mushrooms.

FIGURE 10.4. **From left to right: porto-bello and cremini mushrooms.**

Portobello Mushroom. This is a mature cremini, in which the cap has opened and spread into a broad, flat disk (see Figure 10.4). It may be 6 inches (15 cm) or more across. Portobello caps are often grilled, brushed with olive oil, and served plain as a first course.

Wild Mushrooms. Of the many varieties of edible wild mushrooms, those described here are among the most prized, as well as the most likely to be found on menus. As a rule, they are expensive and of limited availability.

Wild mushrooms should be carefully examined for spoilage or insect infestation. Cut away any damaged parts.

The three varieties described here are also available dried. Dried mushrooms have a high price per pound, but they are more economical to use than fresh wild mushrooms because they are equivalent to about seven or eight times their weight of fresh mushrooms. In addition, they have a more intense, concentrated flavor, so a little goes a long way. To use dried mushrooms, soak them in warm water, drain, and cut as desired. Strain the soaking liquid and use it in sauces, soups, or stews.

Caution: Never eat any wild mushroom that has not been identified by an expert. Many mushrooms are poisonous and some are deadly. Many species are difficult to identify, and some poisonous varieties resemble edible ones.

Morel. Several varieties exist including black, golden, or nearly white. The morel is shaped somewhat like a nearly conical sponge, with a pitted surface, on a smooth stem; it is completely hollow. The most prized of springtime mushrooms, it is usually sautéed or cooked in a sauce and is especially good with cream.

Bolete. Other names for this mushroom include *cep, cèpe* (French, pronounced "sepp"), *porcino* (Italian, pronounced "por chee no"; the plural is *porcini,* pronounced "por chee nee"), *steinpilz* (German, pronounced "shtine pilts"). It is a brown-capped mushroom with a lighter-colored, bulbous stem; the interior flesh is creamy white. The underside of the cap has no gills but many tiny pores. With a meaty but smooth texture and rich, earthy flavor, it is often sautéed or braised with garlic and olive oil or butter. Boletes are available late summer to fall.

Chanterelle. Also called *girolle,* the chanterelle is yellow to orange in color and shaped like an umbrella that has turned inside out. The underside of the cone-shaped cap has ridges instead of gills. It has a rich, woodsy aroma and flavor and is best cooked simply, such as sautéed in butter, perhaps with garlic. It is available summer and fall.

Closely related is the *black trumpet,* also called *black chanterelle, horn of plenty,* or *trompette de la mort* (French name, meaning "trumpet of death," so called because of its black color). In spite of its French name, it is edible and delicious.

Roots and Tubers

Many of our most common vegetables grow underground: carrots, turnips, beets, radishes, parsnips, and potatoes. Underground vegetables are often seen as humble rather than glamorous, but if they are fresh and well prepared they can be as delicious and satisfying as any vegetable. A number of less common roots and tubers vegetables expand the repertoire and add interest to menus.

Jerusalem Artichoke. Known also as *sunchoke, girasole,* and *topinambour,* this is the tuber of a type of sunflower. Looking something like ginger root, it is small and knobby, with a light brown skin. Inside, it is creamy white with a crisp texture when raw and a sweet, nutty taste when cooked. Jerusalem artichokes discolor when cut; to preserve whiteness when boiling, add lemon juice to the cooking water.

Salsify. This vegetable is also called *oyster plant* or *vegetable oyster,* allegedly because it tastes like oysters, although it takes some imagination to discern a similarity. The name *salsify* applies to two different root vegetables, both of which are long and thin with creamy white flesh—one with a tan skin, the other with a black skin. Black salsify is also called *scorzonera.* Both types discolor when peeled or cut, so rub with lemon juice to keep white or place in water with lemon juice added. Salsify becomes mushy if overcooked; it is steamed, added to stews, or boiled with a little lemon juice in the water.

Parsley Root. This is a relative of the herb parsley that is cultivated for its parsnip-shaped roots (see Figure 10.5), with a flavor that suggests celery root, parsley, or carrot. Handle and cook like parsnips.

Jicama. Also called *yam bean,* the jicama (pronounced "hee ka mah," with the accent on the first syllable) looks somewhat like a large, brown turnip (see Figure 10.5). It has crisp, white flesh with a texture like that of water chestnuts and a mild, sweet taste. It is usually used raw, such as in salads, but can also be cooked. It stays crisp when cooked and is added to sautéed or stir-fried dishes.

Daikon. This is a large, white oriental radish (see Figure 10.5). Several varieties can be found, but it is usually long, cylindrical, and slightly tapered. It may be 1 foot (30 cm) or more in length, and it has a typical radish flavor, ranging from hot to mild. Because of its size and uniform texture, it can be cut or sliced into many shapes, making it useful for garnish. It can be eaten raw, quickly sautéed or stir-fried to preserve its crisp texture, or braised until tender; it can be served by itself or in soups and stews.

Yellow-fleshed Potatoes. Varieties include Yukon gold, yellow Finnish, and ladyfinger. These are very firm and waxy, more so than our more common waxy varieties, with a full, rich flavor. They are excellent for boiling. Yellow varieties were merely novelties not long ago, but they are becoming more widely available as their popularity increases due to their high quality.

FIGURE 10.5. **Back row, left to right: celery root and jicama. Center: daikon. Front: parsley root.**

Celery Root. Also called *celeriac* and *knob celery*, this vegetable is a variety of branch celery that is cultivated for its root. Tan to light brown in color, it is bumpy and knobby, with many small rootlets at its base (see Figure 10.5). Inside, it is creamy white and has the distinct aroma and flavor of celery. Small- to medium-size roots that are heavy for their size are the best choice, because they are firm and crisp. Larger ones are often soft and spongy in the center. They are eaten raw in salads, and they are stewed, braised, and puréed.

Other Fresh Vegetables

Several specialty vegetables that don't fit into any of the preceding categories are listed here:

Cardoons. A member of the thistle family, and related to the globe artichoke (which is similar in flavor), this vegetable resembles a large, grayish-green bunch of celery. In Italy, tender young cardoons are eaten raw, but the cardoons available in the United States are usually too tough and bitter and must be cooked. With a vegetable peeler, remove heavy strings from the backs of the stalks and then boil until tender in water containing some lemon juice. Cut and serve the cooked cardoons cold in a salad; sauté or braise in olive oil, butter, or cream; gratiné with garlic, olive oil, and parmesan cheese; or bread and deep-fry.

Fava Beans. While most beans originated in the western hemisphere and were brought back to Europe by early explorers, fava beans (see Figure 10.6), also called *broad beans*, have been grown in the old world for thousands of years. The pods are large and filled with a spongy padding that protects the beans. The shelled beans are usually boiled until tender; then, unless they are very young and tender, the tough skin is removed from each bean. The skinned bean has a brilliant, light green color and a texture that is smooth and not starchy. It is best to serve fava beans simply so the flavor is not buried by other ingredients.

Fennel. Also called *Florence fennel* and (incorrectly) *anise*, fennel is a bulbous vegetable that looks like it might be a swelling at the base of a bunch of celery (see Figure 10.7); the leaves resemble dill. It is aromatic, with light aniselike flavor. (Fennel seeds used as a spice are from a related variety that is cultivated for its seeds rather than as a vegetable.) Tough stems or stalks should be cut away from the bulbous base. Fennel is eaten raw, sautéed, braised, in soups and stews; it goes well with fish and with Parmesan cheese and other Italian-style ingredients.

FIGURE 10.6. **Left to right: fava beans and cranberry or borlotti beans.**

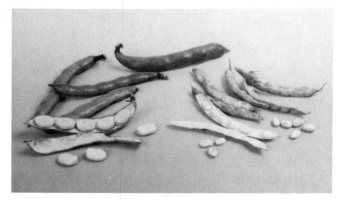

FIGURE 10.7. **Left to right: swiss chard and fennel.**

Fiddlehead Ferns. These are the new shoots of ferns as they emerge from the ground, curled up tightly in the shape of a fiddlehead. *Only the fiddleheads of ostrich ferns should be eaten; other species may be toxic.* Local fiddleheads are available only for a week or two in the spring; earlier or later harvests may be shipped in from areas to the south or north. Fiddleheads are very perishable and keep only a few days; to store an extra day or two, blanch and chill. They are best served simply, boiled and dressed with butter or cream.

Squash Flowers. The large, yellow flowers of various squashes, usually picked just before they open or just after they close, make interesting vegetables. Zucchini blossoms are most often used. Male flowers are more abundant and appear earlier in the season (summer); female flowers with tiny squash attached are especially desirable for elegant presentations (see Figure 10.8). They are very perishable and keep no more than a day. When cleaning, open the flower and look for bees or other insects. Squash blossoms can be sautéed whole or sliced and used as a garnish for plate arrangements or for pasta, rice, and egg dishes. They can also be coated with batter and deep-fried, and they can be stuffed (for example, with cheese, mushroom duxelles, meat or poultry, chiles, nuts, or rice), battered, and fried.

Swiss Chard. Also called *spinach beet, leaf beet,* chard (see Figure 10.7) is the leaf and stalk of a type of beet that develops thick stalks or leaf stems rather than bulbous roots. Varieties with white stalks are most common, but red-stemmed varieties also exist. Chard tastes like beet greens, but often they are milder and sweeter. Leafy parts

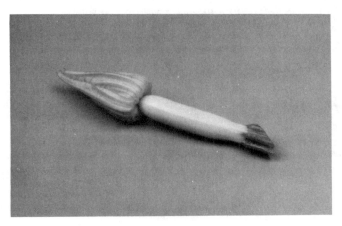

FIGURE 10.8. **Yellow summer squash with attached blossom.**

are trimmed from the stalk and can be cooked like spinach. Stalks are often considered the best part. With a vegetable peeler, pare the backs of stalks to remove the strings, unless the stalks are very small and tender; handle like celery or asparagus. Chard stalks are versatile and combine well with many other foods. They can be sautéed, boiled, steamed, braised, and added to soups.

Legumes

Dried beans, peas, and lentils, which are all seeds that grow in pods, are known as *legumes*. While many of these vegetables can be eaten fresh (such as the cranberry or borlotti beans in Figure 10.6), it is in their dried form that they are one of the world's most important foods (along with grains such as wheat and rice). They are high in protein and other nutrients, and they keep well in storage. Important as they are in more humble diets, they are also becoming more appreciated in upscale restaurants and even in the most elegant dinners. In addition to the familiar favorites (kidney beans of various colors, black beans, white beans such as great northern, lima beans, split peas, black-eyed peas, brown lentils, and chick peas or garbanzos), a number of specialty varieties are becoming more popular as they become more familiar.

Flageolets are the seeds from immature green beans (unlike white beans, which are from mature green beans). Small, pale green, very delicate in flavor, they are especially good with lamb.

Fava beans are the dried form of fresh fava beans (see page 488).

Specialty kidney beans and other colorful beans include many attractively colored beans, such as multicolored, speckled, and mottled varieties. Among them are Swedish brown beans, appaloosa beans, rattlesnake beans, cranberry beans (known in Italian as borlotti), and Christmas limas. As attractive as they are, however, the multicolored types generally lose their colors when cooked. Except for the lima varieties, flavors of most of these are similar to more common kidney beans.

Le Puy lentils are a small, dark green variety of lentil from France. They are valued for their texture and flavor.

Dal is the Indian name for various lentils and beans from the Asian subcontinent. Popular in the United States is *masoor dal* or *red lentil*, a bright red-orange split lentil that turns yellow when cooked. Also available is *mung* or *moong dal*, a yellow dal that is actually the mung bean (source of oriental bean sprouts) that has been hulled and split. These dals are cooked into a soft purée.

VARIOUS FRESH VEGETABLE PREPARATIONS

When fresh vegetables are at their peak of quality and freshness, often the best treatment is simply to steam or boil them and serve them plain, perhaps dressed with a little butter, so their natural flavors can best be appreciated unencumbered by a host of other ingredients and a complex preparation. In such cases, the basic cooking methods— boiling, steaming, sautéing, and so on—are sufficient to prepare delicious vegetable dishes. More complicated techniques are not always necessary.

On the other hand, with vegetables taking a more prominent place on the menu and on the plate, new and interesting vegetable preparations help lend variety and appeal to the menu. An expanded repertoire of vegetable dishes gives the chef more to choose from when matching vegetable accompaniments with main courses.

One must not think, however, that the quality and freshness of the produce is less important when the preparation is more complex. Any dish, simple or elaborate, can be only as good as its ingredients.

Doneness

Before the rise of nouvelle cuisine in the late 1960s and early 1970s, it was common practice to cook, or overcook, most vegetables until they were uniformly soft and textureless. Reawakened interest in fine cuisine, however, led to an appreciation of vegetables cooked *al dente* (Italian for "to the tooth"), that is, lightly cooked vegetables that still retain some texture and crispness. Vegetables that are not overcooked also retain more flavor and nutritional value.

Unfortunately, this situation led to an epidemic of virtually raw, merely warmed-up vegetables. Underdone vegetables can be as unpleasant as overdone ones. Not only are raw carrots, for example, difficult to eat with a knife and fork, but their flavor can be unsatisfying when one is expecting the taste of cooked carrots. Proper cooking changes and generally intensifies the taste of vegetables. It does this in part by breaking down cell walls, thus releasing various flavor components that were previously trapped in the plant cells.

In practice, proper doneness is a relative matter, depending not only on the particular vegetable but also on the type of preparation. Fennel, for example, may be quickly sautéed so that it remains slightly crisp, or it may be braised until soft and meltingly tender.

Cooking vegetables to proper doneness, then, requires judgment and attention to the nature of the dish and the quality of the vegetables. There are no hard-and-fast rules because there are too many variables. The texture of the vegetable and the length of cooking should be appropriate to the specific preparation.

Grilled and Roasted Vegetables

The popularity of grilled meats and fish has been accompanied by more frequent appearance of grilled vegetables on modern menus. The slightly charred, smoky flavor of grilled vegetables makes them seem like more substantial, more satisfying foods than the same vegetables cooked by boiling or steaming.

In general, soft or quick-cooking vegetables or those that can be eaten only lightly cooked are the best candidates for grilling. Popular vegetables for grilling include eggplant (especially small Italian or Japanese varieties), sweet peppers, onions, zucchini and other summer squash, and mushrooms, especially large caps.

The following guidelines are helpful when preparing grilled vegetables:

1. Cut the vegetables for uniform cooking. For example, small, elongated vegetables, such as zucchini or tiny Italian or Japanese eggplants, are cut in half lengthwise. Larger vegetables, such as large eggplants, are generally cut into slices of even thickness. If they are cut in half, they should be scored deeply on the cut side to speed cooking.

2. Baste with oil to help prevent sticking and to reduce drying. Using a flavorful oil, such as olive oil, or a seasoned oil, such as olive oil with garlic and herbs, also adds flavor to the vegetable. Baste several times during cooking for longer-cooking vegetables.

3. Cook to appropriate doneness. Some vegetables, such as eggplant, should be quite soft, while others, such as zucchini, are best served somewhat crisp.

4. Season the vegetables after grilling. Adding salt before cooking draws moisture to the surface; this inhibits browning and results in the loss of some juices.

5. Dressing with a light vinaigrette, perhaps using the same kind of oil that was used for basting, enhances many grilled vegetables. The robust, slightly sweet flavor of balsamic vinegar is especially good with the smoky flavor of grilled vegetables.

Roasting in an oven is, of course, a longer cooking procedure than grilling. Sometimes roasted vegetables are served as is as a garnish (see, for example, the recipe for Roasted Shallots on page 522). More often, perhaps, the roasted vegetable is used as an ingredient in a more complex preparation (see, for example, the Eggplant Purée recipe on page 529, or the Onion Purée on page 532).

Vegetable Mixtures

Another way to increase the variety of vegetable offerings on the menu is to combine two or more vegetables in one preparation. Vegetable mixtures are not a new idea; combinations such as peas and carrots have long been standbys in the simplest lunchrooms. But today's chefs are exploring additional possibilities in vegetable mixtures.

Cooking Vegetables Separately. Most cooking primers advise you to cook vegetables separately and to combine them after they are cooked. The reason for this advice is clear: different vegetables are likely to have different cooking times, and only by cooking them separately does the cook have complete control over the precise degree of doneness of each component. This is true not only for simple mixtures of boiled, steamed, or sautéed vegetables, but also for more elaborate preparations, such as some vegetable ragouts.

Traditionally, a *ragout* is a stew of meat, poultry, or fish, with or without vegetables. Even in classical cuisine, however, the term is also applied to various vegetable preparations, usually of braised vegetables served in a sauce.

For ragouts of mixed vegetables, especially those incorporating the more delicate or quick-cooking vegetables, the best way to control cooking is to prepare the individual vegetables separately, combine them just before serving, and then add the sauce. In most cases, it is best to simmer the completed mixture together for a minute or two before serving. Not only does this assure that the mixture is hot, but it also gives the flavors a chance to blend slightly. Strictly speaking, this kind of preparation is not really a ragout, because the vegetable mixture isn't stewed, but the term *ragout* is often used on menus for this style of dish or garnish. A recipe of this type is given on page 526.

Cooking Vegetables Together. When vegetables are to be cooked until well-done and tender, as in braised vegetable dishes, cooking times do not have to be controlled as precisely as when they are lightly cooked and kept crisp. Consequently, when all the vegetables in a braised mixture require long cooking, they can often be cooked together. Among the vegetables that take well to long cooking are cabbage, celery, fennel, artichokes, eggplant, peppers, tomatoes, onions, leeks, and most root vegetables.

The choice of vegetables in the mixture, the blending of flavors during the long cooking, the type of stock or other braising medium, and the choice of additional flavoring ingredients (such as garlic, herbs, and bacon) all contribute to the character of the dish.

The oriental technique of stir-frying exemplifies another method of cooking vegetables together. The vegetables are added one at a time to the wok or cooking pan, starting with the one that requires the longest cooking. When the additions are timed properly, all the vegetables finish cooking at the same time.

Sautéed, Sweat, and Braised Vegetables

Vegetables are sautéed by cooking them quickly in a small amount of fat, usually over high heat. On the most basic level, the technique of sautéing is used for two main purposes:

- To cook tender, quick-cooking vegetables from the raw to the finished state
- To reheat or to finish vegetables that have already been partially or completely cooked

This basic technique is what might be called a *dry sauté*—that is, no liquid is added, and the pan is left uncovered so that the vegetable's own moisture evaporates rather than being trapped in the pan. Some vegetables, such as mushrooms and zucchini, taste watery when boiled or steamed, so sautéing from the raw state is especially useful for them.

If the heat is kept very low and the pan is covered to trap moisture, the vegetables cook slowly in their own juices without browning. This technique is called *sweating*. It is often used to prepare vegetables that are to be used as ingredients in other dishes, such as soups, stews, and stuffings. The flavor of the fat is an important element in the preparation; butter is usually used, but other fats, such as olive oil or bacon, may be used for specialty items. As the juices cook out of the vegetables, the vegetables become partially saturated with the fat, and their flavor mellows and richens.

A variation on these techniques is useful for cooking those vegetables that require more tenderizing than a quick sauté can provide. First sauté the vegetable over high heat, as in regular dry sautéing, then lower the heat, cover the pan, and cook slowly until the vegetables are tender, as in sweating. Check the vegetables occasionally; if too much of the vegetable's moisture escapes, it may be necessary to add a little water, stock, or other liquid to prevent scorching, unless the heat is very low.

Many vegetables can be cooked this way, including those that must otherwise be blanched or parboiled before being sautéed. Examples include broccoli, cauliflower, cabbage, asparagus, sugar snap peas, and green beans. Cutting the vegetables into small pieces shortens the cooking time. Grating them, cutting them very small, or shaving them into paper-thin slices hastens cooking even more. Even hard root vegetables such as beets, celery root, and turnips can be cooked by this combination sautéing-braising method.

Compared with parboiling and then sautéing, this technique often produces more richly flavored vegetables, because all the juices are retained rather than being lost in the boiling water. The vegetables take on the more robust characteristics of braised vegetables. If stocks or other liquids are added, along with other flavoring ingredients such as herbs, garlic, and mirepoix, the flavor can be further enriched.

Because this method requires first cooking in fat and then trapping moisture with a lid, it is in fact a type of braising, even though some of the vegetable preparations made this way may not resemble classic long-cooked braised vegetables, such as braised celery, braised cabbage, and braised artichokes. Braising is often thought of as a technique with only limited applications. But as the preceding discussion shows, it can be applied to many vegetables. While classic braised vegetables are often cooked for 30 minutes or more, many quick-cooking vegetables or vegetable mixtures may cook sufficiently in 10 minutes or so and still have time for the flavors to blend and develop.

If braised vegetables are billed as a stew or ragout, they are served with the braising liquid, with a sauce made from the braising liquid, or with a sauce made separately and added before serving time. One ounce or so (30 ml) of liquid or sauce per portion is usually sufficient. Do not turn the dish into a soup.

By contrast, the liquid can be reduced to a glaze, which concentrates the flavors and provides just enough liquid to coat and moisten the vegetables.

Gratins

The basic meaning of *gratin* is the brown crust that forms on the surface of various food preparations, primarily those baked in shallow casseroles or dishes. Some dishes naturally form brown top crusts as they bake, such as potato gratin, or gratin dauphinois (page 546). Other vegetables that can be baked in a casserole from the raw state, such as many root vegetables, can be prepared using similar methods.

In most cases, however, the vegetables are partially or completely cooked in advance. They are then baked with a topping that will brown easily and form the desired crust. These gratins are assembled by three primary methods:

Method 1. Arrange the vegetables in an appropriate dish and top with grated cheese, bread crumbs, or both. This is the simplest method and can be applied to many vegetables and vegetable mixtures, including sautéed, stir-fried, braised, and steamed or boiled vegetables tossed with a little butter or oil. Parmesan is the most versatile cheese for gratins, followed by gruyère. Cheddar, American munster, jack, and other cheeses are used for certain preparations. Bread crumbs, if used, may be buttered lightly to improve the flavor and enhance browning.

Method 2. Top or mix the vegetables with a sauce that will enhance browning. White sauces such as béchamel are usually used, especially if they are enriched with butter, cream, or egg yolks. These additions help the sauce brown more readily, as does cheese mixed with the sauce. Thus, sauces enriched with an egg-yolk-and-cream liaison, cheese sauces such as mornay, and egg-based sauces such as hollandaise and sabayon are most useful for gratins. It is best to test a spoonful of sauce under the broiler to make sure it will brown before combining it with the vegetables. Also, sauces that are to be used only as a topping should be thick enough to stay on top and not run to the bottom of the dish.

Method 3. Top or mix the vegetables with a sauce, as in method 2, then top with grated cheese, crumbs, or both, as in method 1. This method is, obviously, the richest and most complex of the three. Take care not to overwhelm the vegetables with sauce and topping. The flavor of the vegetables should predominate.

Shallow baking dishes, called gratin dishes, are usually the best to use, because they allow a large amount of brown crust for a given quantity of vegetable. Also, because they are shallow, the preparation can be heated through quickly.

Following assembly, brown the gratin in the oven (if the dish requires long heating) or under the broiler or salamander (if the dish needs only quick browning).

Transforming a simple vegetable dish to a gratin adds variety and appeal to the menu. For example, instead of serving plain buttered asparagus, arrange the spears in individual gratin dishes, top with parmesan cheese, and brown lightly.

Purées

Vegetable purées have become increasingly popular, in part because they can be used in many ways and fit a great variety of menus, and in part because modern tools have removed some of the drudgery of making them.

Among the uses of vegetable purées are the following:

- An assortment of vegetable purées makes an attractive, multicolored garnish for many entrées.
- A vegetable purée can be used as a bed for a meat, poultry, or fish item. The purée serves to lend its flavor to the main-course item, and it also catches and holds juices that escape from the foods resting on it. For example, see the recipe for Chicken Breast with Onion Purée and Leeks on page 310.
- Vegetable purées can be used as fillings for such items as stuffed vegetables, rolled or stuffed meat items, and savory tarts and other pastries.
- Vegetable purées are used as ingredients for timbales, discussed in the next section, and for mousses and other items.
- When thinned out, a vegetable purée can be used as a sauce. Such a preparation is often called a *coulis* (pronounced "koo-lee"). The most familiar purée-based sauce is a simple tomato sauce, or coulis de tomates, but many other vegetables can be used as well. The subject of vegetable purées used as sauces is also discussed in Chapter 3.

Guidelines for Preparing Vegetable Purées. Techniques for preparing vegetable purées vary depending on the vegetable, the intended use, and the available equipment. The following guidelines, however, are applicable to most preparations.

1. Vegetables to be puréed must be cooked until they are quite tender, so that the purée will be smooth. The usual cooking methods are boiling, steaming, and baking. Boiling and steaming are most often used, but baking is best for many vegetables that have a high water content or that become too watery when boiled or steamed.

2. Vegetables that discolor easily, such as Jerusalem artichokes and globe artichokes, may be cooked with a little lemon juice to preserve their color. Do not use too much lemon juice, however, because acids toughen vegetable fiber and prolong cooking.

3. Purée with the appropriate equipment. Except for the potato masher, which is appropriate for only a few vegetables and is not very efficient for volume production, there are three main tools for this purpose, when making small to medium quantities:

   a. The *food processor* is easy to use and usually produces excellent results, but it has a few drawbacks. First, it makes potatoes and some other starchy vegetables gluey. Second, it will not completely purée stringy or fibrous vegetables, vegetable skins, and hard vegetables that may form lumps.

b. A hand-cranked *food mill* is more time-consuming to use than a food processor, but it produces a uniform purée. It removes strings, skins, and lumps that a food processor would leave intact, and it is excellent for potatoes and other starchy vegetables and root vegetables. Hard vegetables and vegetables that are undercooked may make a rather grainy purée, depending on the fineness of the grid used.

c. A *drum sieve* also called a *tamis* (pronounced "tah mee"), which consists of a fine-mesh screen stretched over a metal or wooden hoop (see Figure 10.9), produces the finest results but is the most difficult and time-consuming to use. It removes all fibers, skins, and lumps and yields a smooth-textured purée. The sieve is used by forcing the vegetables through the screen with a large wooden pestle. To make the job a little easier, purée the vegetables with a food processor or food mill first and then force the rough purée through the sieve.

4. The texture of most vegetable purées should be like that of moist mashed potatoes for most hard or starchy vegetables, somewhat looser for softer, moister vegetables. Moister, more liquid purées can be used as sauces (refer to the section on purée-based sauces beginning on page 49).

5. Vegetables low in starch may be combined with cooked potatoes or rice before puréeing to provide binding or thickening.

6. Season carefully. Purées may require slightly more salt than whole vegetables. Pepper, cayenne, and other spices and herbs may also be used as appropriate.

7. Butter or cream may also be added to purées to provide flavor and richness, but using too much butter or cream can detract from the flavor of the vegetable and make the purée too rich.

8. To transform a vegetable purée into a *mousse,* fold in whipped egg whites, whipped cream, or both. Add egg whites to the purée while it is hot, so that the whites will be cooked and set by the heat of the purée. *Exception:* If the mousse is to be cooked further (for example, tomato mousse used to stuff sole fillets before cooking), fold in the egg whites just before cooking.

Fold in whipped cream only at the very last minute, because the mixture will not hold.

FIGURE 10.9. **A drum sieve and pestle being used to purée cooked carrots.**

Timbales

The basic meaning of the French word *timbale* is kettledrum. Eventually the word came to be used for small, drum-shaped molds or containers for food and, consequently, for the foods prepared in such molds. In classical cuisine, the term is also used for pastry shells baked in these molds, filled with various foods, and used as garnish; this usage is not often encountered today.

The term *timbale* can be used for any kind of food preparation shaped in a timbale mold. A simple rice pilaf, for example, can be packed into a mold and then carefully unmolded onto a plate, rather than just spooned onto the plate. For a similar example, see the Cabbage Timbale variation on page 511.

In most cases today, however, a vegetable timbale is a type of custard—that is, a vegetable purée or other vegetable preparation bound with eggs, cooked in a water bath, and unmolded.

Traditional metal timbale molds of various sizes are shown in Figure 10.10. More widely used today, however, are ceramic ramekins of 2- to 4-oz (60- to-120-ml) capacity; these look like miniature soufflé dishes.

There are many possible variations of vegetable timbales, but the basic principles of preparing custards apply. The basic mixture consists of a liquid or semiliquid mixture (puréed or finely chopped cooked vegetables, usually with the addition of cream or béchamel sauce or both) plus enough eggs to set the mixture when cooked. Overcooking and curdling of the custard is avoided by baking in a water bath and by removing it from the oven as soon as it is set.

Guidelines for Preparing Vegetable Timbales. The following guidelines are suggestions for helping you use timbale recipes, for changing or varying recipes, and for devising new recipes. The basic recipe for vegetable timbales on page 534 is more of a general procedure than a specific recipe. The skeleton of a recipe, so to speak, is provided later in this chapter, with suggestions for specific vegetables provided in the variations.

1. Puréed vegetables usually serve as the base for timbales. Chopped vegetables can also be used, but the timbale may be less firm and less stable; more eggs may be required to make the timbales firmer.

2. Solid vegetable ingredients can be used to give textural or visual interest to the timbale; however, use them with care because the timbale will be more likely

FIGURE 10.10. **Traditional metal molds for timbales, large and small.**

to break apart. Again, more eggs may be needed for extra firmness. Any solid ingredients should be precooked so that they won't exude liquid that would spoil the timbale.

3. Heavy cream, a white sauce such as béchamel, or both are usually added to the puréed vegetable, although they can be omitted for a leaner timbale with a stronger vegetable flavor. Béchamel, because of its starch binder, makes a firmer, more stable timbale. Cream is used instead of white sauce when a more delicate texture is desired.

4. Do not add too much liquid or the timbale may set in layers, with the solids separated from the liquid, unless of course you want the timbale to set in layers for decorative effect. As a rule of thumb, use at least 3 or 4 parts vegetable purée for each part, by volume, of cream or white sauce. Exceptions to this rule include timbales that are basically egg-and-cream custards to which only a small amount of vegetable or other ingredient is added for flavoring, such as mashed roasted garlic.

5. In general, 3 to 4 eggs are added to each pint of mix, although more or less may be used depending on the following factors:
   a. The firmness desired.
   b. The size of the timbales. Larger ones must be firmer to hold up when unmolded. Very small ones, no more than 1 or 2 ounces, are sometimes made with only egg yolks, which give a more delicate texture.
   c. The texture of the vegetables and other ingredients (see guidelines 1 and 2).
   d. The thickness of the mix and the presence or absence of starch binders. Other ingredients, such as cheese, may also help to thicken and bind the mixture.

6. Butter the timbale molds before filling them so that the cooked timbale can be unmolded.

7. Blanched leaves, such as spinach, cabbage, and chard, can be used to line the buttered molds for a decorative effect. Let the leaves hang over the rim of the molds and then fold them over the top after filling to completely enclose the timbale mixture. This technique may not work well if the timbale mixture is too liquid, because the mix may leak between the leaves and the mold, spoiling the appearance of the finished, unmolded timbales.

8. To convert a timbale to a soufflé, separate the eggs. Add the yolks to the mix. Whip the whites and fold them into the mix just before cooking.

9. If the mixture is cooked in a shallow dish or mold rather than a timbale mold, it is like a quiche without a crust and may be called a *flan* or *gateau de legumes* (vegetable cake). If the flan becomes browned on top, it can be called a *gratin* (see page 494). Because it doesn't have to support much height if unmolded, it can be made with a lower proportion of egg. An unmolded *gateau de legumes*, perhaps with a purée of a contrasting vegetable as a sauce, can make a light, elegant first course or luncheon dish.

Compotes, Confits, Chutneys, Relishes, and Other Condiments

A number of specialized vegetable and fruit preparations are served not as side dishes but as condiments to complement the flavors of the main dishes. Many of these items are tart or sweet or both. Classic examples of these kinds of condiments are the cranberry relish served with roast turkey, applesauce served with pork, and mint jelly served with roast lamb.

Modern chefs have devised a great variety of such preparations to give additional interest and variety to their menus. These preparations are of so many types that it is impossible to give any general procedures or even to give any precise definition to the terms in the heading of this section. Usually, however, they have one or more of the following characteristics: sweetness, often from the addition of fresh or dried fruit; tartness, from vinegar, citrus juices, or acidic vegetables such as tomatoes; and spiciness, from hot peppers or other flavorful spices. They are usually very flavorful and hence served in fairly small quantities.

Some examples of these kinds of preparations include the following recipes:

Onion Compote (page 520)
Confit of Shallots (page 522)
Tomato Raisin Chutney (page 537)
Pear Ginger Chutney (page 538)
Lentil Relish with Corn (page 536)

Special Fried Vegetable Preparations

Thin slices and shavings of vegetables, deep-fried until light and crisp, make attractive and interesting garnish for many dishes. Even something as ordinary as potato chips, when freshly made on the premises, seem special, but many other vegetables can be cooked the same way. They are quick and easy—as long as the deep-fryer is on—and require no recipe. Simply cut the vegetables into paper-thin slices or julienne and fry until crisp. Cooking time is usually about 10 to 15 seconds.

The following are some suggestions. Experiment with these as well as other vegetables and cuts.

Chips. Slice thin, preferably with a mandoline, dry on towels if necessary, and fry.
  Red beets
  Celery root
  Carrots (sliced lengthwise)
  Parsnips (sliced lengthwise)
  Lotus root
  Mushrooms
Shreds and julienne. Cut, dust lightly with flour and shake off excess, and fry.
  Leeks
  Carrots
  Celery
  Asparagus peelings
Leaves. Separate from stems, dry well, and fry.
  Celery
  Parsley
  Cilantro
  Sage

Special Potato Preparations

Potatoes are perhaps the most important fresh vegetables in American cuisine; consequently, they get a great deal of attention in cooking texts and general-purpose cookbooks. With the many changes that have transformed culinary practices in the last few decades, potatoes have gotten even more attention as cooks have looked beyond the basic baked, mashed, and french-fried standbys to find more variety. A typical cook of today may be familiar with dozens of potato dishes.

Cooks may look to foreign and ethnic cuisines to find ideas for new potato dishes or may combine potatoes with other vegetables in new ways. A number of the potato recipes in this chapter are examples of this approach to recipe development.

In addition, the following topics discuss some techniques that cooks have found particularly useful. Potato gratins, related to traditional American scalloped potatoes, are not at all new, but they have become especially popular. The surge in popularity of plain, old-fashioned mashed potatoes has led cooks to experiment with potato purées. Variations of potato galettes, related to various classics such as hashed browns and Anna potatoes, have found many uses as garnish.

Potato Gratins. The classic potato gratin is the *gratin dauphinois*, a rich, creamy dish that has been a staple of French bistros for many years and has more recently become an international favorite. This dish, in its basic form, consists of sliced potatoes baked in a shallow dish with milk and cream until the potatoes are tender and creamy and the top is nicely browned.

As with most classic recipes, the subject of gratin dauphinois stimulates strong opinions. Many cooks feel that there is only one correct way to prepare this dish, but there are many different opinions on what the correct way is. Some of the points of disagreement are the following:

- Some cooks insist that it is essential to rinse the sliced potatoes to wash off starch. Others say that they should never be rinsed.
- Some prefer firm, waxy potatoes for this dish; others prefer starchy ones.
- Some use milk and cream; others use only cream.
- Some simmer the potatoes in milk to start the cooking; others put the raw ingredients in the gratin dish and bake them without precooking.
- Some add cheese to the dish (gruyère or Emmenthal); others insist that the classic gratin is made without cheese.
- Some add not only cheese but also egg to the gratin; others feel that nothing should be added to the potatoes except milk, cream, and butter.

Each of these variations has its adherents, so one could say that there are many "correct" versions of the dish. The recipe on page 546 outlines one method. You may want to experiment with the recipe by introducing some of the variables in the above list, in order to find a version that you like best.

Potato Purées. Potato purées appear in many forms on modern menus. Chefs have experimented with many variations on this old-fashioned classic, taking advantage of the many varieties of potatoes available and of the fact that potatoes combine well with many ingredients. Some of the techniques used to create variations on the basic recipe follow. For additional guidelines, refer to the section on vegetable purées (page 495). In particular, remember that potatoes should not be whipped too long or puréed in a food processor, or they will become pasty.

- Traditional mashed-potato recipes call for starchy or all-purpose potatoes, but waxy or new potatoes can also be used. The purée will not be as fluffy or starchy, and the flavor will be somewhat sweeter. It may be necessary to reduce the quantity of milk or cream in the recipe when waxy potatoes are used. They have less starch and will absorb less liquid.

- Increasing the amount of butter and cream in the recipe results in a rich, soft purée with almost the texture of a cream pudding, unlike the lighter, fluffy texture of traditional mashed potatoes. One well-known chef has earned a reputation for a popular potato purée that contains nearly 1 pound of butter for every 2 pounds of potatoes, although many chefs make delicious, rich-tasting purées with much less fat. In spite of the concerns of dieters, these rich dishes have proved extremely popular.

- Olive oil can be substituted for all or part of the butter to make a purée that goes especially well with dishes from southern France and the Mediterranean area. Other fats, such as bacon fat, can also be substituted for butter for different results.

- A great variety of flavoring ingredients can be added to potato purée, including herbs, bacon, mushrooms, cheese, and purées of other vegetables. Garlic-flavored mashed potatoes are especially popular. (See the recipe and variations on pages 544–545.)

Potato Galettes. Galettes are thin, round cakes. Small potato galettes, nicely browned and crisp, are useful garnishes for a variety of main-course dishes and are simple to make, consisting of nothing more than potatoes, butter, and seasoning. There are three basic types, as described below. Recipes for the first two are included in this chapter.

1. *Galettes made of sliced potatoes.* Cut the peeled potatoes (trimmed into even, cylindrical shapes for uniform slices) into paper-thin slices, preferably on a mandoline. Arrange the slices, overlapping one another, to form small, round disks on a well-buttered sheet pan, as shown in Figure 10.11. Top with melted butter and bake until browned and crisp. The potato disks should hold together when done, but handle them gently because they are fragile.

FIGURE 10.11. **Potato slices arranged to form a galette, ready for baking.**

These can be made in a sauté pan on top of the stove, but they must then be turned over to cook both sides. Care is necessary to avoid breaking the galettes.

To form perfect rounds of uniform size. Place a tart ring or flan ring on the baking sheet and arrange the potato slices inside it. Remove the ring and repeat for the next galette.

2. *Galettes made of julienne potatoes.* The basic method is the same as for the first type, but use long, thin julienne of raw potatoes instead of slices. Place a portion of the julienne on the buttered sheet pan, flatten into a thin round, and cook as in the first method.

   As explained in Method 1, these can also be made on top of the stove. Also, a tart ring can be used to shape the rounds.

3. *Galettes made of cold boiled potatoes.* Grate the cooked potatoes and panfry like hashed browns, except make the cakes smaller and much thinner. Use a generous amount of butter or oil and fry until well browned and crisp on the outside.

SPECIAL GRAIN PREPARATIONS: RISOTTO, POLENTA, COUSCOUS, AND BULGUR

Primary techniques for the preparation of grains such as rice form an essential part of a cook's education. A cook with only the minimum of experience or training is able to make boiled or steamed rice and basic rice pilaf.

On the other hand, four grain preparations—risotto, polenta, couscous, and bulgur—may not always be included in a cook's basic training because they may have been considered too specialized or exotic. In recent years, however, these imported dishes (the first two are Italian, the third North African) have become so popular that any cook would do well to become familiar with them.

Risotto

The classic Italian dish, risotto, is made with special varieties of short-grain rice, the most common of which is called Arborio. The basic steps in making risotto are listed here. A distinguishing feature of this dish is that starch is released from the rice as it is stirred and cooked, giving it a creamy texture. *Note:* This risotto is not the same as the preparation that is called risotto in France; French risotto is actually a pilaf, in which the liquid is added all at once and then cooked, covered, without stirring.

1. Sauté the rice in a little butter or other fat, usually with some chopped onion or shallot.

2. Add a small amount of hot stock or other liquid. Stir over moderately low heat until the rice has absorbed nearly all of the liquid.

3. Add a little more stock and repeat the procedure. Continue until the rice is tender but still firm in the center. The texture should be moist and creamy.

4. Raw butter and grated parmesan cheese are usually, but not always, added at the end of cooking, after the pan is removed from the heat.

5. The finished risotto must be served immediately. It does not hold well.

Perhaps the most important classical versions of this dish are *risotto alla parmigiana*, flavored with a generous quantity of parmesan cheese, and *risotto Milanese*, flavored with saffron. Today's cooks, however, add a great variety of ingredients, including vegetables, seafood, and meat, to create dishes substantial enough to serve not just as side dishes or appetizers but also as main courses.

These ingredients may be added to the risotto at any point. Some ingredients that need long cooking or that need time to release their flavor are sautéed with the onion in the first step or added to the rice with the first ladleful of stock. Others, such as blanched or precooked vegetables, quick-cooking vegetables, or cooked meats and seafood, are added near the end of the cooking time, giving them just enough time to heat up and blend with the rice.

A number of suggestions for additions to basic risotto follow the recipe on page 551.

Polenta

Polenta is, to put it inelegantly, Italian cornmeal mush, but this description doesn't do it justice. Polenta is an especially delicious and versatile dish that has found its way from the Italian family table to many restaurants in the United States and elsewhere, including the most elegant and exclusive establishments.

Preparation of polenta is relatively simple and, once the general proportions of cornmeal and water are known, doesn't require a recipe. The following procedure gives the details:

Procedure for Cooking Polenta

1. Measure the cornmeal, water, and salt. The following quantities will produce the approximate yields indicated:

	YIELD:	1 lb 6 oz	5 lb 8 oz	600 g	2.5 kg
Water		20 oz	5 pt	6 dl	2.5 l
Salt		¾ tsp	1 tbsp	4 g	15 g
Polenta (Italian coarse-grained yellow cornmeal)		4 oz	1 lb	125 g	500 g

2. Bring the water and salt to a boil in a heavy sauce pot.

3. Slowly sprinkle the cornmeal into the boiling water, while stirring constantly. Take care to add the meal slowly enough so that lumps are avoided.

4. Cook over low heat, stirring almost constantly, for about 15 to 20 minutes. Stirring not only helps the polenta cook evenly without lumping, but it also causes some starch to be released from the cornmeal into the water. This creates the proper texture.

5. If the polenta is to be served freshly cooked and hot, it should be fairly soft. Stop the cooking when the polenta reaches the desired consistency. If desired, stir in a little butter to enrich the polenta and make it softer. Plate and serve at once.

6. Polenta to be cooled and sliced should be slightly stiffer. When it is done, pour it out onto a lightly buttered sheet pan (or, if you want to avoid the butter, onto a sheet pan lined with plastic film). With a spatula, spread it into an even layer of desired thickness. Cool. Cut into desired shapes. Grill or panfry.

There are two basic ways of serving polenta, as the preceding procedure indicates:

1. Hot, freshly cooked polenta is an excellent accompaniment for many stews and other braised dishes that provide plenty of flavorful juices or sauce for the polenta to soak up. Soft, freshly cooked polenta, often enriched with an addition of raw butter, is also traditionally served as a bed for roasted and grilled meats and poultry.

2. Cooled, firm polenta can be cut into slices and grilled or panfried. A great advantage of this method is that the polenta can be cooked ahead of time, cooled, and then finished to order. Slices of polenta prepared in this fashion are a versatile and popular accompaniment or garnish for many kinds of main-course dishes. For an example of how this preparation is applied, see the recipe variation on page 451.

   Slices of cold polenta can also be baked in a casserole, layered or topped with sauces, meats, cheese, and other ingredients, somewhat like baked pasta dishes such as lasagne.

Couscous

Couscous is made from semolina or hard-wheat flour (although, in its homeland of North Africa one may occasionally find couscous made from other grains). It is not a grain itself, as many believe, but is actually a type of pasta formed into a kind of coarse meal.

The traditional method of preparing couscous is to steam it over a stew and then serve the couscous and the stew together. This dish, the grain and stew combined, is also referred to as couscous. The couscous pot, or *couscousière* (see Figure 10.12) consists of a large bottom section, which holds the stew, and a top section to hold the couscous. This part has a perforated bottom. It is lined with cheesecloth, to keep the grain from falling through the holes, and fitted on top of the stew pot so that steam rising from the stew passes through the couscous, cooking it.

While couscous is an excellent accompaniment to spicy North African stews, American and European cooks have also discovered that it is a good accompaniment to many western dishes when used in place of rice or other starches.

FIGURE 10.12. **A couscousière.**

There are several brands of packaged "instant" couscous available, which are prepared by adding hot liquid to the couscous, letting it stand to absorb the liquid, and then fluffing it with a fork. Instant couscous is useful, but it does not have the texture and flavor of the regular couscous steamed in the traditional way. Although the longer procedure is somewhat time-consuming, it is beneficial to be familiar with it because of its superior results.

Procedure for Steaming Couscous

1. Assemble equipment. The following items will be needed.
   a. A couscousière or other steamer. A convection steamer with a perforated pan, or a pot with a perforated bottom or even a colander that can be set snugly over a pot of boiling water will do nicely.
   b. A length of cheesecloth, double thickness, sufficient to line the bottom and sides of the perforated steamer.
   c. A large bowl or pan for the initial soaking of the couscous, plus a sieve or strainer for draining it.
   d. A large shallow pan such as a roasting pan or hotel pan.
2. Put the couscous in the large bowl. Pour water over it, using about 3 parts water for each part, by volume, of couscous. Stir for a few seconds. Using the sieve, drain off all excess water. Return the couscous to the bowl and let it stand about 15 minutes to absorb the moisture.
3. With wet hands, very gently stir the couscous to begin breaking up lumps. Pick up handfuls of it, gently roll it between the hands, and let it fall back into the bowl. Work it lightly and do not pack it together. Continue until all lumps are broken up. The couscous should begin to feel light and fluffy.
4. Line the steamer pan with dampened cheesecloth. Put the couscous into the pan. Let it fall lightly into the pan; do not pack it.
5. Steam, uncovered, about 20 minutes.
6. Pour the couscous into the large, shallow pan. Add a little salt, and moisten the couscous by sprinkling it with a little cold water and tossing gently. It should be damp but not wet.
7. Oil your hands, and stir and work the couscous as in step 3 to fluff up the grains and break up lumps. The oil on your hands will lightly oil the couscous, which helps keep the grains from forming lumps. If you are making a large quantity, you may need to oil your hands several times.
8. The couscous is now ready for its final steaming, or it can be held, covered with a damp towel, for several hours. If it is held, check to make sure it is not dried out before final steaming. If necessary, moisten it again as in step 6, immediately before steaming, and work it with the hands to break up lumps.
9. Steam a second time, as in steps 4 and 5. Serve at once.

Bulgur

Bulgur is a type of cracked wheat that has been partially cooked or parched. It is usually available in coarse, medium, and fine granulations.

Because it has already been partially cooked, its preparation time is shorter than for regular cracked wheat. In fact, fine and medium granulations need no actual cooking; they can be prepared simply by soaking them in boiling water or stock. A classic preparation of this type is tabbouleh, a salad made by mixing the cooled, soaked bulgur with lemon juice, olive oil, seasonings, and herbs (see the recipe on page 143).

Coarse-grained bulgur is too coarse to be prepared effectively by this soaking method and is usually cooked. Normally, it is cooked by the same method used to make basic rice pilaf (see page 549 for a recipe).

RECIPES FOR VEGETABLE AND STARCH DISHES

The recipes that conclude this chapter are intended to supplement the basic repertoire of vegetable garnishes and side dishes, as well as to illustrate some of the special techniques and procedures discussed in this chapter.

In addition to these recipes, many other recipes for vegetable side preparations are included elsewhere in the book as parts of meat, poultry, and fish recipes. For convenient reference, the following is an alphabetized list of those preparations.

ARTICHOKES EN MIREPOIX

		U.S.		Metric	
PORTIONS:		4	16	*4*	*16*
Ingredients					
Artichokes, large		4	16	*4*	*16*
Lemon juice		½ oz	2 oz	*15 ml*	*60 ml*
Onion, brunoise		1 oz	4 oz	*30 g*	*125 g*
Carrot, brunoise		1 oz	4 oz	*30 g*	*125 g*
Olive oil		1 oz	4 oz	*30 ml*	*125 ml*
Salt					
Pepper					
Chopped parsley					

Mise en Place:

1. Trim and pare the artichokes to the hearts, discarding the leaves, choke, and green outer skin, but leave the stems (peeled) attached. Cut the hearts in half and then cut them into thin slices or thin wedges.
2. Put the slices in a bowl with enough water to cover and add the lemon juice to keep them from discoloring.

Cooking:

1. Over moderate heat, sauté the onion and carrot in the olive oil for about 1 minute.
2. Drain the artichoke slices well and add to the pan with the onion and carrot. Toss to coat lightly with oil. Cover and braise over low heat until tender, about 10 to 15 minutes. Check the moisture level as necessary. There should be enough to provide some steam and to keep the vegetables from burning, but it should be completely reduced at the end of cooking.
3. Season to taste with salt and pepper. Add a little chopped parsley before serving.

Variations

Cut the artichoke hearts into brunoise instead of slices. Use the cooked vegetable brunoise mixture as a garnish or a bed for roast or sautéed meats or seafood.

Gratin of Artichokes and Potatoes

Potatoes, waxy, peeled		12 oz	3 lb	*375 g*	*1.5 kg*
Parmesan cheese, grated		1½ oz	6 oz	*45 g*	*175 g*

Double the quantity of onions in the recipe and slice them instead of cutting them into brunoise. Omit the carrot. Prepare the quantity of potatoes indicated by slicing them very thin, as for potato chips. When the artichokes are tender, mix them with the raw potatoes and place in a gratin dish. Bake at 400°F (200°C) for 15 minutes. Remove from the oven, stir slightly, then top with the cheese. Return the gratin to the oven and bake until the potatoes are tender.

ASPARAGUS STIR-FRY

		U.S.		Metric	
	PORTIONS:	**4**	**16**	*4*	*16*
Ingredients					
Asparagus		1 ¼ lb	5 lb	*575 g*	*2.3 kg*
Butter		½ oz	2 oz	*15 g*	*60 g*
Soy sauce		1 ½ tsp	2 tbsp	*7 ml*	*30 ml*

Toasted sesame seeds, as needed

Mise en Place:

1. Snap the woody bottoms off the asparagus spears. Peel the bottom portions of the trimmed spears.
2. Cut the spears diagonally into 1-inch (2 ½-cm) lengths.
3. Blanch the asparagus in boiling salted water until about half cooked.

Cooking:

1. Heat the butter in a sauté pan. Add the asparagus and stir-fry for 2 minutes.
2. Lower the heat, add the soy sauce, and cook for another minute or two, until the asparagus is cooked but still firm.

Presentation:

Plate the asparagus or mound it in a serving dish. Top with a generous sprinkling of toasted sesame seeds.

BEET GREENS WITH BROWNED SHALLOTS

		U.S.		Metric	
PORTIONS:		*4*	*16*	*4*	*16*
Ingredients					
Beet greens		1 lb	4 lb	*500 g*	*2 kg*
Shallots		2 oz	8 oz	*60 g*	*250 g*
Olive oil		1 oz	4 oz	*30 ml*	*125 ml*
Salt					
Pepper					

Mise en Place:

1. Clean and trim the beet greens, discarding the stems. Wash well and drain.

2. Blanch the greens in boiling salted water. Drain. Cool under cold water and drain again, squeezing out excess water.

3. Chop the greens coarsely—that is, do not mince, but cut the lump of squeezed-out greens into chunks.

4. Peel, trim, and mince the shallots.

Cooking:

1. Heat the olive oil in a pan. Add the shallots and sauté until tender and brown.

2. Add the greens. Toss and sauté until the greens are hot.

3. Season to taste with salt and pepper.

Variations

Prepare other greens, such as kale, collard greens, swiss chard, and spinach. Robust greens such as collards and kale can be flavored with garlic and hot pepper flakes added to the pan at the same time as the shallots.

Roast Beets with Beet Greens

Roast whole, unpeeled beets in an oven at 375°F (190°C) until tender. Peel. Cut into small dice. Prepare the greens according to the procedure in Mise en Place, steps 1 through 3. Before serving, heat the beets and greens by sautéing together in butter. This combination, with its complementary red and green colors, makes an especially attractive garnish for many dishes.

As an alternative method, sauté diced, cooked beets and add a few raw shredded beet greens, sautéing until they are wilted.

Roast Beets with Beet Greens in Walnut or Hazelnut Vinaigrette

Prepare the beets and greens as in the preceding recipe but do not sauté in butter. Toss with a little vinaigrette made with walnut or hazelnut oil and flavored with a little garlic.

BELGIAN ENDIVE DORÉ

		U.S.		Metric	
PORTIONS:		**4**	**16**	*4*	*16*
Ingredients					
Belgian endive		8 oz	2 lb	*250 g*	*1 kg*
Butter					
Water					
Salt					
Butter		½ oz	2 oz	*15 g*	*60 g*
Salt					
White pepper					
Sugar					

Mise en Place:

1. Wash the endive. Cut out the root ends so that the leaves separate.
2. Butter a saucepan or casserole and put the endive in the pan. Add enough water to cover and salt lightly.
3. Cover and bring to a boil. Simmer until tender, about 20 minutes.
4. Drain. Taste a leaf to see if it is bitter (see Cooking, step 1).

Cooking:

1. Heat the butter in a saucepan or braising pan. Add the endive and season with salt and pepper. If the endive is bitter (see Mise en Place, step 4), add a little sugar.
2. Cook slowly until browned on all sides.

Note: This is a somewhat intensely flavored dish that makes it a good accompaniment, in moderate quantities (about 2 oz or 60 g), for various meat and fish dishes, but it may be a bit strong to be served as a large vegetable side dish.

BRAISED SAVOY CABBAGE

		U.S.		Metric	
PORTIONS:		4	16	*4*	*16*
Ingredients					
Savoy cabbage		1 lb	4 lb	*500 g*	*2 kg*
Butter		½ oz	2 oz	*15 g*	*60 g*
Salt pork or bacon, julienne		1 oz	4 oz	*30 g*	*125 g*
Onion, small dice		1 oz	4 oz	*30 g*	*125 g*
Water or white stock, as needed					
Salt					
Pepper					

Mise en Place:

1. Trim the cabbage, removing the core. Remove the coarse ribs from the large outer leaves, if desired. If the outer leaves are tough, separate and blanch them in boiling water for 1 minute.
2. Cut the cabbage into ½-inch (1-cm) dice or shred it.

Cooking:

1. Heat the butter in a braising pan and add the salt pork or bacon. Sauté it over low heat until it begins to brown.
2. Add the onion and sauté 1 minute.
3. Add the cabbage and toss to coat lightly with fat. Cover and cook over low heat. If the cabbage is tender and still wet from washing, it may not be necessary to add any water or stock to the pan to braise the cabbage. As the cabbage cooks, check it occasionally to see if the pan has become completely dry. Add liquid as needed. Cook until tender but still with some texture and a fresh green color.
4. Season to taste with salt and pepper.

Variations

Alternative method for last-minute preparation: In advance, cook the cabbage in simmering salted water until done, then drain and cool under cold water. Drain and reserve. At service time, add to some sautéed bacon and onion in a pan and toss until hot.

Cabbage Timbales

Line small, greased timbale molds with tender, blanched cabbage leaves. Pack them tightly full with braised cabbage. Let them stand a few minutes so that they will retain their shape when unmolded. To serve, unmold and plate. *Note:* The molds must be fairly small so that the timbales will be stable and not fall apart when plated.

CELERY ROOT SAUTÉ WITH FENNEL

		U.S.		*Metric*	
PORTIONS:		**4**	**16**	*4*	*16*
Ingredients					
Celery root, peeled		12 oz	3 lb	*350 g*	*1.4 kg*
Olive oil		1 ½ tsp	1 oz	*8 ml*	*30 ml*
Fennel seeds		½ tsp	2 tsp	*1 g*	*5 g*
Lemon juice		1 ½ tsp	1 oz	*8 ml*	*30 ml*
Salt					
White pepper					
Chopped parsley (optional)					

Mise en Place:

1. Cut the celery root into small dice.
2. If the mise en place is being done in advance, drop the diced celery root into cold water containing some lemon juice to keep it white.
3. Lightly crush the fennel seeds.

Cooking:

1. Heat the olive oil over moderate heat in a saucepan or sauté pan. Add the fennel seed.
2. Add the celery root and sauté slowly for about 5 minutes.
3. Add the lemon juice. Add salt and pepper to taste. Cover and braise slowly until tender, about 5 to 10 minutes.
4. If desired, add chopped parsley at serving time.

Variations

Cut the vegetable into other shapes, such as large dice, batonnet, julienne, slices, and so on. Adjust the cooking time as necessary, depending on the size of the cuts.

Celery Root and Carrot Sauté with Fennel

Prepare as in the basic recipe, using half celery root and half carrot.

BRAISED CHESTNUTS

		U.S.		Metric	
PORTIONS:		4	16	*4*	*16*
Ingredients					
Chestnuts		1 lb	4 lb	*500 g*	*2 kg*
Celery		2 oz	8 oz	*60 g*	*250 g*
Brown stock or white veal stock, as needed					
Sugar		1 oz	4 oz	*30 g*	*125 g*
Salt					

Mise en Place:

1. With the point of a paring knife, cut a cross in the shell of each chestnut. Blanch the chestnuts for 3 to 4 minutes in boiling water or for a few seconds in a deepfryer.
2. Peel the chestnuts, removing both the shell and the inner skin.
3. Trim and wash the celery. Leave it in large pieces to make it easy to remove after cooking; it is for flavoring purposes and is not to be served.

Cooking:

1. Place the chestnuts and celery in a saucepan. Add enough stock to cover. Add the sugar and a pinch of salt.
2. Cover and simmer until the chestnuts are tender. This can be done on the range or in a moderate oven. Cooking in the oven agitates the chestnuts less and helps to avoid breakage.
3. Remove and discard the celery.
4. Drain the chestnuts. Reserve the liquid for later batches or for another use. (See also the variation for glazed chestnuts, which follows.)

Variations

Glazed Chestnuts

Do not drain the stock. Instead, uncover the pan and let the liquid reduce until it is syrupy and coats the chestnuts with a glaze.

Chestnut Purée

	U.S.		Metric	
Butter	1 oz	4 oz	*30 g*	*125 g*
Heavy cream	1 oz	4 oz	*30 ml*	*125 ml*

Omit the sugar in the basic recipe. Drain the braised chestnuts, reserving the stock. Purée the chestnuts and add the butter and cream. Add enough of the reserved stock to bring the purée to the consistency of mashed potatoes.

CORN WITH CHILES AND CHEESE

		U.S.		Metric	
PORTIONS:		**4**	**16**	*4*	*16*
Ingredients					
Butter, corn oil, or olive oil		1 oz	4 oz	*30 g*	*125 g*
Anaheim chiles or substitute (see note 1)		3–4	12–16	*3–4*	*12–16*
Corn, fresh (see note 2)		12 oz	3 lb	*375 g*	*1.5 kg*
Salt					
Mild cheddar, monterey jack, or American munster		4 oz	1 lb	*125 g*	*500 g*

Note 1: Other green chiles or other peppers can be substituted, depending on availability (see discussion of chiles beginning on page 483). For each Anaheim, substitute one poblano, or for every two Anaheims, substitute one green bell pepper plus one jalapeño.

Note 2: If fresh corn is not available, use frozen corn and add a little heavy cream or sour cream to the corn during cooking (see Cooking, step 2).

Mise en Place:

1. Char the skins of the peppers over a gas flame or under the broiler. Wrap and let the peppers steam for 15 minutes to loosen the skins. Peel them and remove cores and stems.

2. Cut the peeled, roasted peppers into small dice.

3. Grate the cheese.

Cooking:

1. Heat the butter or oil in a sauté pan. Add the chiles and sauté briefly.

2. Add the corn (and cream, if used; see note 2). Sauté for 1 or 2 minutes, until the corn is just barely cooked.

3. Season to taste with salt.

4. Put the vegetable mixture into a large gratin dish or individual gratin dishes.

5. Top with the grated cheese. Bake at 400°F (200°C) until the cheese is melted or lightly browned, as desired.

Variation

Add sautéed chopped onion or diced zucchini or both to the corn mixture.

GREEN BEANS WITH SUNDRIED TOMATOES

		U.S.		Metric	
PORTIONS:		**4**	**16**	**4**	**16**
Ingredients					
Green beans, preferably small, slender, young beans		1 lb	4 lb	*500 g*	*2 kg*
Sundried tomatoes, with their oil		3 oz	12 oz	*90 g*	*375 g*
Shallots, minced		½ oz	2 oz	*15 g*	*60 g*
Garlic (optional), minced		½ tsp	2 tsp	*2 g*	*8 g*
Fresh basil, chopped		1 tsp	4 tsp	*1 g*	*4 g*
Chopped parsley		1 tbsp	4 tbsp	*4 g*	*15 g*
Salt					
Pepper					

Mise en Place:

1. Trim the ends of the green beans.
2. Blanch the green beans until about three-fourths cooked. They should remain crisp and green. Cool.
3. Drain the oil from the tomatoes and reserve it. Cut the tomatoes into julienne.

Cooking:

1. Heat the reserved oil in a sauté pan (add additional olive oil if necessary). Add the shallots and garlic and sauté gently over low heat until soft, but do not brown.
2. Add the beans. Sauté until cooked.
3. Add the tomatoes and chopped herbs. Toss the mixture briefly over heat until the mixture is hot.
4. Season to taste.

STEWED LEEKS

		U.S.		Metric	
PORTIONS:		4	16	4	16
Ingredients					
Leeks, white part and a little of the green		1 lb	4 lb	500 g	2 kg
Butter		1 oz	4 oz	30 g	125 g
Water (see variations)		4 oz	1 pt	125 ml	5 dl
Butter		1 oz	4 oz	30 g	125 g
Salt					
Pepper					

Mise en Place:

Clean the leeks well. Cut them into small dice.

Cooking:

1. Sauté the leeks lightly in the first quantity of butter until wilted.
2. Add the water (or other liquid), cover, and simmer about 5 minutes.
3. Remove the cover and continue to cook until all the liquid has evaporated.
4. Just before serving, swirl in the second quantity of butter. Season to taste.

Variations

White veal stock or chicken stock can be used instead of water, if the fuller flavor is desired and if it is appropriate to the dish the leeks are to accompany. For a garnish for fish dishes, use fish stock instead of water, or use half stock and half white wine. Use water if the pure taste of the leeks is desired.

Heavy cream or crème fraîche can be added at the end in place of or in addition to the butter.

Cut the leeks into other shapes and sizes (julienne, large dice, etc.) to change the texture of the dish. Cutting them into brunoise makes the dish almost a coarse purée or sauce.

LEEK PANCAKES

		U.S.	*Metric*
YIELD:		24 small pancakes	*24 small pancakes*

Ingredients

	U.S.	Metric
Leeks, white part only	8 oz	*250 g*
Butter	1 oz	*30 g*
Salt		
Egg	1	*1*
Flour	3 ½ oz	*100 g*
Milk	⅔ cup	*160 ml*

Mise en Place:

1. Cut the leeks in half lengthwise and wash well. Slice crosswise into very fine slices.

2. Sweat the leeks in the butter until the leeks are tender and all moisture has evaporated. Season with salt.

3. Cool completely.

4. Beat the egg in a bowl.

5. Sift the flour. Beat the flour, egg, and milk together to make a thin batter. Stir in the leeks.

Cooking:

1. Heat a nonstick pan over moderately high heat. Spoon 1 tbsp (15 ml) of leek batter onto the pan to make a small pancake. Cook until set and lightly browned on the bottom. Turn over and cook a few seconds on the other side.

2. Repeat with the remaining batter.

Variation

Jerusalem Artichoke Pancakes

	U.S.	Metric
Jerusalem artichokes, pared and grated	1 lb	*500 g*
Lemon juice	1 tsp	*5 ml*
Eggs	2	*2*
Flour	2 tbsp	*15 g*
Salt		

Make a batter with these ingredients and quantities (see preceding Mise en Place, steps 4 and 5). Do not precook the Jerusalem artichokes. Note that there is no milk in this recipe. Cook in a little butter or oil over moderately low heat.

MUSHROOM BLANQUETTE

		U.S.		Metric	
PORTIONS:		4–6	16–24	4–6	16–24
Ingredients					
Assorted fresh, wild mushrooms, or a mixture of wild and cultivated (see Mise en Place)		1 lb	4 lb	500 g	2 kg
Butter		1 oz	4 oz	30 g	125 g
White veal stock or chicken stock		3 oz	12 oz	1 dl	4 dl
Thyme		pinch	½ tsp	pinch	0.5 g
Heavy cream		2 oz	8 oz	60 ml	2.5 dl
Liaison:					
Heavy cream		1 oz	4 oz	30 ml	125 ml
Egg yolks		1	4	1	4
Salt					
White pepper					
Lemon juice					

Mise en Place:

Clean and trim the mushrooms. The mixture should include at least 50 percent wild or exotic mushrooms, such as morels, boletes, chanterelles, shiitake, or oyster mushrooms. Leave small mushrooms whole. Cut up larger ones into halves, quarters, or as desired.

Cooking:

1. Sauté the mushrooms quickly in the butter for 1 or 2 minutes.

2. Add the stock and thyme. Simmer 5 to 10 minutes, until the mushrooms are cooked (some varieties are tougher than others).

3. Add the cream and simmer another 2 minutes.

4. Beat together the cream and egg yolks for the liaison. Stir a little of the hot cooking liquid into it to temper it and then carefully stir this mixture back into the mushrooms. Heat gently until lightly thickened. Do not let it simmer or it will curdle.

5. Season with salt, white pepper, and lemon juice.

Variation

Gratin of Mushrooms

Place the finished blanquette in gratin dishes. Top with grated swiss or gruyère cheese. Brown under a salamander or broiler.

BROILED SHIITAKE WITH GARLIC BUTTER

		U.S.		Metric	
PORTIONS:		4	16	*4*	*16*
Ingredients					
Large shiitake mushrooms		8 oz	2 lb	*250 g*	*1 kg*
Garlic butter		2 oz	8 oz	*50 g*	*250 g*

Mise en Place:

Cut the stems off the mushrooms. Discard the stems or use them for stock. Clean the mushroom caps.

Cooking:

1. Brush the mushroom caps generously with garlic butter. Let them stand 15 minutes to allow them to absorb it.
2. Broil the mushroom caps until cooked, basting them with additional garlic butter.
3. Season with salt and pepper if necessary (depending on the seasoning in the garlic butter).

Variations

Large white cultivated mushroom caps or portobello mushrooms can be prepared in the same way.

ONION COMPOTE

		U.S.		Metric	
PORTIONS:		**6 oz**	**1 lb 8 oz**	*200 g*	*800 g*
Ingredients					
Onions		1 lb	4 lb	*500 g*	*2 kg*
Water		2 oz	8 oz	*60 ml*	*2.5 dl*
Red wine		12 oz	3 pt	*4 dl*	*1.5 l*
Water		8 oz	2 pt	*2.5 dl*	*1 l*
Red wine vinegar		2 oz	8 oz	*60 ml*	*2.5 dl*
Butter		1 oz	4 oz	*30 g*	*125 g*
Sugar		½ oz	2 oz	*15 g*	*60 g*
Salt					
Pepper					

Mise en Place:

Peel the onions. Cut them into small or medium dice or ¼-inch thick (5-mm) slices, as desired.

Cooking:

1. In a nonreactive saucepan (such as stainless steel), combine the onions and the first quantity of water. Cover and simmer 5 minutes.

2. Add the red wine and the second quantity of water. Simmer, uncovered, very slowly until the onions are tender and most of the liquid has evaporated.

3. Add the vinegar. Mix well and continue to simmer.

4. By the time the vinegar has reduced, the onions should be very tender. If not, add a little more water, cover, and steam gently until they are soft. Remove the cover and reduce again if necessary.

5. Stir in the butter and sugar. Stir and heat gently, if necessary, to dissolve the sugar.

6. Season with salt and pepper.

Presentation:

Serve as a condiment with meat, poultry, or fish dishes (see, for example, the recipe on page 236).

ROASTED PEPPERS IN VINAIGRETTE

	U.S.		Metric	
PORTIONS:	4–6	16–24	4–6	16–24
Ingredients				
Green, yellow, or red bell peppers	1 lb 8 oz	6 lb	750 g	3 kg
Olive oil	1 oz	4 oz	30 ml	125 ml
Garlic, minced	½ tsp	2 tsp	1 g	4 g
Shallot, minced	1 tbsp	4 tbsp	5 g	20 g
Lemon juice or red wine vinegar	1 tbsp	2 oz	15 ml	60 ml
Salt				
Pepper				

Mise en Place:

1. Wash the peppers. Leave them whole.
2. Make a vinaigrette by combining the remaining ingredients.

Cooking:

1. Char the peppers on a grill, over an open burner, or under a broiler. Continue until the skins are blackened all over but don't char them so much that the flesh is burned.
2. Wrap them in plastic wrap or in towels. This holds in steam, which helps to loosen the skins. Leave them wrapped for 15 minutes or longer.
3. Rub off the skins. Rinse briefly to remove all the blackened skin.
4. Cut the peppers in half lengthwise and remove the core, seeds, and membranes.
5. Leave the peppers in halves or cut them into quarters or smaller strips, as desired.
6. Combine with the vinaigrette. Let stand a few minutes before serving to allow the flavors to blend slightly.

Variations

A small amount of minced jalapeño or other hot pepper can be added to the vinaigrette.

For a slightly different flavor, sauté the garlic, shallot, and jalapeño in the olive oil. Cool completely and then complete the vinaigrette by adding the lemon juice or vinegar, salt, and pepper.

Charring peppers to peel them is a basic technique for preparing all kinds of peppers. The procedure not only removes the skins but also gives the peppers a pleasant smoky taste. Roasted, peeled peppers, without the vinaigrette, are used in many ways.

ROASTED SHALLOTS

Ingredients

Large shallots, as needed (3 to 5 per portion)
Oil
Salt
Pepper

Procedure:

1. Remove the outermost peel from the shallots but try to leave on a little stem. Carefully cut off the root ends without cutting into the shallot.

2. Place the shallots on a sheet pan or other flat pan. Pour a little oil over them. Roll them around so that they are well coated with the oil.

3. Roast at 350°F (175°C) about 1 hour, until very soft. Serve as a garnish for meat or poultry items.

Variations

Confit of Shallots

Peel and trim the shallots as in the basic recipe. Put them in a heavy sauté pan. For each pound of shallots, add about 2 oz butter and 2 oz sugar (60 g butter and 60 g sugar per 500 g shallots). Add enough water to cover about one-third of the shallots. Simmer very slowly, stirring occasionally, until the water has evaporated and the shallots are soft and caramelized.

Roasted Garlic

Use whole heads of garlic. Do not separate or peel, but slice off the tops (stem ends) of the heads to expose the cloves. Place cut side up on sheet pans, coat with oil as in the basic recipe, and add about ½ inch (1 to 2 cm) of water to the pan. Roast as above. Use as a condiment or flavoring ingredient.

SPINACH WITH WALNUT SAUCE

		U.S.		Metric	
PORTIONS:		4	16	*4*	*16*
Ingredients					
Spinach (approximate quantity; see note)		1 lb	4 lb	*500 g*	*2 kg*
Walnuts		1½ oz	6 oz	*45 g*	*175 g*
Sugar		¼–½ tsp	1½ tsp	*1–2 g*	*6 g*
Soy sauce		4–5 tsp	3 oz	*20 ml*	*90 ml*
Water, as needed					

Note: Quantity of spinach may vary, depending on the trimming yield. You will need enough to yield about 3 oz (90 g) of trimmed spinach per portion, before cooking. Because this dish has a somewhat rich, intense flavor due to the walnut sauce, small portions, no more than about 2 oz (60 g) are best.

Mise en Place:

1. Trim the stems from the spinach and discard any damaged leaves. Wash the spinach well in several changes of water to remove all sand.
2. Grind the walnuts in a food processor. Mix with the sugar and soy sauce. Stir in enough water, a few drops at a time, to bring the mixture to the consistency of a sauce.

Cooking:

1. Bring a pot of salted water to a boil. Drop in the spinach and cook for about a minute.
2. Drain the spinach. Cool thoroughly under cold water. Drain. Squeeze lightly to remove excess moisture.
3. Toss the spinach with the walnut sauce.
4. Serve cold or warm. If it is to be served warm, heat it lightly just before serving.

Variation

Spinach with Sesame Sauce

Substitute sesame seeds for the walnuts. Toast the seeds lightly in a dry pan, and then grind them in a spice mill. Garnish each portion with a sprinkling of additional toasted sesame seeds.

SPAGHETTI SQUASH WITH PEPPERS

		U.S.		Metric	
PORTIONS:		4	16	*4*	*16*
Ingredients					
Spaghetti squash		1 lb	4 lb	*500 kg*	*2 kg*
Red bell peppers, cored and seeded		3 oz	12 oz	*90 g*	*350 g*
Green bell peppers, cored and seeded		3 oz	12 oz	*90 g*	*350 g*
Olive oil, as needed					
Fresh basil, chopped		1 tbsp	¼ cup	*3 g*	*15 g*
Salt					
White pepper					
Optional garnish:					
Toasted pignoli nuts					

Cooking:

1. If the squash or squashes are whole, steam, bake, or boil until done. For smaller quantities, cut the squash in half, place cut side down in a pan, and bake or steam until done. Cut in half (if whole), remove the seeds, and scrape the spaghettilike flesh out of the squash.

2. Cut the peppers into julienne. Sauté them in olive oil until slightly tender but still a little crisp.

3. Add the squash to the peppers and toss to mix and to heat the squash. Add the basil. Season to taste with salt and pepper. Add additional oil if necessary to lubricate the squash, but do not make it too oily.

4. If desired, sprinkle the top of each serving with a few toasted pignoli nuts.

TOMATO RAGOUT WITH GARLIC AND OLIVES

		U.S.		*Metric*	
PORTIONS:		4	16	*4*	*16*
Ingredients					
Olive oil		1 oz	4 oz	*30 ml*	*125 ml*
Garlic		½ oz	2 oz	*15 g*	*60 g*
Onion		2 oz	8 oz	*60 g*	*250 g*
Tomatoes		1 ½ lb	6 lb	*750 g*	*3 kg*
Black olives, pitted (see note)		2 oz	8 oz	*60 g*	*250 g*
Glace de viande		1 ½ oz	6 oz	*50 ml*	*2 dl*
Salt					
Pepper					

Note: Use imported, Mediterranean-type or similar olives, such as niçoise or kalamata. California black olives have little flavor and do not work well in this dish.

Mise en Place:

1. Cut the garlic and onion into thin slices.

2. Peel and seed the tomatoes. Cut into large dice.

3. Slice the olives or, if they are small, leave whole or cut in half.

Cooking:

1. Heat the olive oil in a sauté pan. Add the garlic and onion. Sauté until they start to become soft.

2. Add the tomatoes, olives, and glace de viande. Simmer until most of the liquid has evaporated, about 4 to 5 minutes. Do not cook until completely dry; juice continues to exude from the tomatoes during cooking and attempting to reduce it completely may result in a thick paste.

3. Season to taste with salt and pepper.

RAGOUT OF VEGETABLES

		U.S.		Metric	
PORTIONS:		4	16	*4*	*16*
Ingredients					
A selection of 4 to 6 fresh, young vegetables, such as the following (trimmed weight):		1 lb	4 lb	*500 g*	*2 kg*
Carrots					
Peas or snow peas					
Asparagus					
Tiny onions or scallions					
Zucchini or yellow summer squash					
Small green beans					
Lima beans					
Fava beans					
Baby turnips					
Vegetable stock, chicken stock, or vegetable cooking liquid		1 ½ oz	6 oz	*60 ml*	*2 dl*
Butter		1 oz	4 oz	*30 g*	*125 g*
Salt					
White pepper					

Mise en Place:

1. Trim and cut the vegetables as desired. Note that the weights given are for the vegetables after trimming and cutting.

2. Cook each vegetable separately with any appropriate method, such as simmering, steaming, or stewing in a little butter.

Finishing:

1. Reheat the vegetables as necessary and mix them together as necessary.

2. Bring the stock or other liquid to a boil in a small saucepan. Reduce slightly.

3. Remove from the heat. Whip in the butter (monter au beurre).

4. Season to taste with salt and white pepper.

5. Pour the butter sauce over the vegetables and toss gently. Serve at once.

Variations

Gratin of Vegetables I

Prepare the Ragout of Vegetables as in the basic recipe. Place the vegetables in gratin dishes. Top with grated parmesan and/or gruyère cheese. Brown under a broiler or salamander.

Gratin of Vegetables II

In place of the butter sauce in the Ragout of Vegetables basic recipe, use a light cream sauce mixed with a little gruyère cheese. Place the vegetable mixture in gratin dishes, top with buttered bread crumbs, and brown under a broiler or salamander.

SAUTÉED WATERCRESS

		U.S.		Metric	
PORTIONS:		4	16	4	16
Ingredients					
Watercress		10–12 oz	2½–3 lb	300–350 g	1.2–1.4 g
Butter		½ oz	2 oz	15 g	60 g
Salt					

Mise en Place:

Cut the coarse bottoms of the stems off the watercress. Wash. Drain well. Cleaning is best done in advance, as this gives the watercress time to dry somewhat. Excess water clinging to the leaves will make the finished dish very watery.

Cooking:

Heat the butter in a sauté pan. Add the watercress and sauté until wilted. Add salt to taste. Serve as a garnish in small portions, about 1½ to 2 oz (50 g) each.

Variation

Use olive oil instead of butter. Sauté a little garlic in the oil before adding the watercress.

GRATIN OF ASPARAGUS, SNAP PEAS, AND ARTICHOKES

		U.S.		Metric	
PORTIONS:		4	16	4	16
Ingredients					
Asparagus		1 lb	4 lb	500 g	2 kg
Snap peas (see note)		4 oz	1 lb	125 g	500 g
Artichokes		2	8	2	8
Garlic		1 clove	2–4 cloves	1 clove	2–4 cloves
Shallots		1	4	1	4
Carrot, grated		1 ½ oz	6 oz	50 g	200 g
Olive oil		1 oz	4 oz	30 ml	125 ml
Slivered almonds		1 oz	4 oz	30 g	125 g
Butter					
Olive oil, as needed					
Salt					
Parmesan cheese		1 ½–2 oz	6–8 oz	50 g	200 g

Note: If snap peas are not available, substitute snow peas or a combination of green beans (cut into short pieces) and shelled regular peas.

Mise en Place:

1. Trim the bases from the asparagus. Peel the lower portions of the stalks. Cut on the diagonal into 1-inch (2.5-cm) lengths. Blanch until crisp-tender.

2. Trim and blanch the snap peas.

3. Trim and pare the artichokes down to the hearts, discarding the leaves, choke, and green outer portions. Cut into slices ¼ inch (5 mm) thick. Mince the garlic and shallots. Braise the artichokes, garlic, shallots, and carrot in the olive oil until tender. Add a little water to the pan as necessary to prevent scorching.

4. Brown the almonds lightly in a little butter.

Finishing:

1. Mix together all the vegetables and the almonds. If necessary, add a little more olive oil so that the vegetables are all lightly coated. Salt to taste.

2. Arrange the vegetables in gratin dishes. Top with the cheese.

3. Place in a hot oven until the vegetables are hot and the top is lightly browned. If the vegetables are hot before the top is browned, place under a broiler or salamander for a few seconds.

EGGPLANT PURÉE WITH CREAM

		U.S.		Metric	
PORTIONS:		**4**	**16**	**4**	**16**
Ingredients					
Large eggplants		1 lb	4 lb	*500 g*	*2 kg*
Garlic		1 clove	2–4 cloves	*1 clove*	*2–4 cloves*
Lemon juice		½ oz	2 oz	*15 ml*	*60 ml*
Olive oil		2 tsp	1 ½ oz	*10 ml*	*40 ml*
Heavy cream		2 oz	8 oz	*60 ml*	*2.5 dl*
Salt		½ tsp	2 tsp	*3 g*	*10 g*
White pepper		pinch	¼ tsp	*pinch*	*¼ tsp*

Procedure:

1. Cut the eggplants in half lengthwise. Cut the garlic cloves in half and rub the cut surfaces of the eggplants with the cut sides of the garlic. Reserve the garlic.
2. Score the cut sides of the eggplants deeply with a knife. Brush first with lemon juice and then with olive oil.
3. Place the eggplants cut side up in a baking pan. Cover lightly with foil. Bake at 350°F (175°C) until soft, about 45 minutes.
4. While the eggplant is baking, combine the cream, the reserved garlic, and the salt and pepper in a saucepan. Bring to a simmer, remove from the heat, and let stand 15 minutes.
5. When the cooked eggplants are cool enough to handle, scrape out the flesh and purée it.
6. Remove the garlic from the cream and discard it. Add the cream to the eggplant; mix well. Heat over a low burner. Season if necessary with additional salt, pepper, and lemon juice.

Variations

Eggplant Purée with Sesame Paste

Sesame paste (tahini)		1 ½ oz	6 oz	*45 g*	*175 g*
Olive oil		2 oz	8 oz	*60 ml*	*2.5 dl*
Mashed garlic, to taste					

Omit the cream from the basic recipe and add these ingredients.

Smoky Eggplant Purée

Instead of baking the eggplants, toast them under a broiler, over a gas burner, or directly on a flattop range until the skin is charred black and the eggplant is soft. Peel off the charred skin under running water and cut off the tops. Let the pulp stand in a sieve or china cap to drain excess moisture. Purée and proceed as directed in the basic recipe or the Eggplant Purée with Sesame Paste variation.

PURÉE OF ROOT VEGETABLES

		U.S.		Metric	
PORTIONS:		**4**	**16**	*4*	*16*
Ingredients					
Root vegetables, peeled and diced (see variations)		1 lb 4 oz	5 lb	*600 g*	*2.5 g*
Butter		1–2 oz	4–8 oz	*30–60 g*	*125–250 g*
Heavy cream (optional)		1–2 oz	4–8 oz	*30–60 ml*	*125–250 ml*
Salt					
Other seasonings and flavorings as desired					

Procedure:

1. Review the discussion of vegetable purées on page 495. Steam the vegetables or boil in salted water or stock until tender. Drain well.

2. If the vegetables seem to be watery, dry them briefly by setting them in a pan over low heat or in an oven, uncovered.

3. Purée the vegetables in a food mill or other equipment (page 496).

4. Stir in the butter and, if used, the cream.

5. Season to taste.

Variations

Any of the basic root vegetables, alone or in combination, can be prepared in this way. In addition, winter squash and pumpkin, which have a solid texture like that of root vegetables, can be prepared in this way.

Potatoes are often combined with other vegetables because their starch acts as a binder. Starchy root vegetables, such as potatoes and sweet potatoes, can be made into a stiffer purée than can nonstarchy ones, such as beets and carrots.

Vegetables other than root vegetables can be prepared in the same way, except that quantities may need adjustment, depending on the water content of the vegetables (see the discussion of purées in the text).

The following list of root vegetables can be used. In addition, a few specific recipe suggestions follow the list.

Beets	Potatoes
Carrots	Rutabagas
Celery root	Salsify
Jerusalem artichokes	Sweet potatoes
Parsnips	Turnips

Purée of Sweet Potatoes and Carrots

Sweet potatoes, peeled	14 oz	3 lb 8 oz	*425 g*	*1.75 kg*
Carrots	6 oz	1 lb 8 oz	*175 g*	*750 g*

Cook the sweet potatoes and carrots in chicken broth, drain, and proceed as in the basic recipe. Season with a little nutmeg.

Parsnip Purée with Madeira

Purée parsnips using the basic recipe. Flavor with a little Madeira wine and a generous pinch of sugar.

Dilled Carrot Purée

Follow the basic recipe using carrots, but purée some sautéed shallots with the carrots. Flavor the purée with fresh dill.

Vegetable Cakes

Prepare a purée of root vegetables without cream, keeping it as stiff as possible. Chill it and form it into small, round, flat cakes. Dredge in flour and brown in butter.

Vegetable Coulis

Purées of fresh vegetables, including vegetables other than roots and tubers, can be used as a sauce when thinned out with stock, vegetable broth, vegetable cooking liquid, or water. Prepare as in the basic recipe, and then thin to the consistency of a sauce with the desired liquid. Butter or cream can be added as well.

ONION PURÉE

	YIELD:	U.S.		Metric	
		8 oz	**2 lb**	*250 g*	*1 kg*
Ingredients					
Onions		12 oz	3 lb	*375 g*	*1.5 kg*
Heavy cream		4 oz	1 pt	*125 ml*	*5 dl*
Salt					
White pepper					
Nutmeg (optional)					

Procedure:

1. Leave the onions whole and do not peel them. Place them on a sheet pan or baking pan and bake at 350°F (175°C) until soft, about 45 to 60 minutes.

2. Peel the onions. Purée the pulp.

3. Mix in the cream. Season to taste. Reheat as needed.

Variation

Onion Purée with Leeks

Mix the purée with half its weight of stewed leeks (page 516).

PARSLEY PURÉE

		U.S.		Metric	
YIELD:		**6 oz**	**1 lb 8 oz**	*190 g*	*750 g*
Ingredients					
Parsley bunches		8 oz	2 lb	*250 g*	*1 kg*
Shallot, minced		¼ oz	1 oz	*7 g*	*30 g*
Butter		½ oz	2 oz	*15 g*	*60 g*
Heavy cream		1 oz	4 oz	*30 ml*	*125 ml*
Salt					

Cooking:

1. Remove the stems from the parsley. Wash and drain the parsley leaves.

2. Blanch the parsley for 5 minutes in boiling salted water. Drain, cool under cold water, and drain again. Squeeze out excess moisture.

3. Purée the parsley coarsely or chop it fine by hand. It should not be a smooth purée but should have some texture.

4. Sweat the shallot gently in the butter.

5. Add the parsley to the shallot and butter. Mix well and heat. Or, if the purée is being prepared in advance, cool the shallot and butter and mix with the parsley.

6. Mix in the cream. Season to taste.

BASIC VEGETABLE TIMBALES

		U.S.		Metric	
PORTIONS:		4–8	16–32	4–8	16–32
Ingredients					
Seasoned vegetable purée, (see variations)		14 oz	3 lb 8 oz	400 g	1.6 kg
Heavy cream		2 oz	8 oz	60 ml	2.5 dl
Eggs, beaten		3–4	12–16	3–4	12–16

Cooking:

1. Mix the ingredients together well.

2. Butter small timbale molds of 2- to 5-oz (60- to 150-ml) capacity.

3. Transfer the timbale mixture to the molds. Do not fill them all the way to the rim because the mixture may expand somewhat as it cooks.

4. Set the molds in a hot water bath and bake at 375°F (190°C) until set. This may take from 20 to 45 minutes, depending on the size of the molds, their spacing in the water bath, and other factors.

5. When set, remove them from the oven. Let them stand 10 minutes to allow them to settle.

6. The timbales can be kept warm for a short time in the water bath. At service time, unmold and serve at once.

Variations

Review the discussion of timbales on pages 497–498, regarding the techniques for making timbales and for varying the recipes and procedures. Appropriate vegetables for this recipe include the following:

Asparagus	Fennel bulb
Broccoli	Red bell pepper
Carrot	Spinach
Cauliflower	Turnip
Celery root	Zucchini
Eggplant (with garlic)	

For a more stable but less delicate timbale, substitute béchamel sauce for all or part of the heavy cream.

For those vegetables that combine well with cheese, mix into the timbale mixture a small amount of grated swiss or gruyère cheese or a combination of swiss and parmesan.

Vegetable Mousse or Soufflé

Reduce the amount of cream in the mixture to keep it rather stiff. Separate the eggs. Omit the yolks or add them to the purée, as desired. Whip the whites and fold them into the mixture just before baking.

Gratin of Puréed Vegetables

Add some grated gruyère or swiss cheese to the timbale mixture, using about 2 to 3 oz of cheese per pound of mixture (150 g per kg). Put the mixture into small, buttered gratin dishes. Top with a little more cheese or buttered crumbs. Bake at 375°F (190°C) until the mixture is set and the top is browned. If necessary, brown under a broiler or salamander for a few seconds.

GARLIC TIMBALES

		U.S.		Metric	
	PORTIONS:	4	16	4	16
Ingredients					
Garlic cloves		4	16	4	16
Heavy cream		6 oz	1 pt 8 oz	2 dl	8 dl
Milk		2 oz	8 oz	50 ml	2 dl
Salt					
Egg yolks		2	8	2	8

Cooking:

1. Peel the garlic cloves but leave them whole and uncrushed.
2. Combine the garlic, cream, and milk in a saucepan. Simmer slowly until the garlic is very soft and the cream mixture is reduced by about one-half.
3. Purée the garlic and cream in a blender.
4. Salt to taste.
5. Beat the egg yolks. Cool the cream somewhat if it is hot (to avoid curdling the yolks) and add it to the yolks. Mix well.
6. Butter small timbale molds (1½- to 2-oz capacity, or about 50-ml capacity).
7. Pour the timbale mixture into the molds. Bake in a hot water bath at 300°F (150°C) until set, about 30 minutes.
8. Remove from the oven and let stand about 10 minutes. Unmold and serve at once.

Variation

For a firmer texture, substitute whole eggs for *half* of the egg yolks.

LENTIL RELISH WITH CORN

		U.S.		Metric	
YIELD:		**1 lb**	**4 lb**	**500 g**	**2 kg**
Ingredients					
Green (Le Puy) lentils		4 oz	1 lb	125 g	500 g
Chicken stock, as needed					
Butter or olive oil		½ oz	2 oz	15 g	60 g
Shallot, chopped		½ oz	2 oz	15 g	60 g
Jalapeño, minced		1 tsp	4 tsp	3 g	12 g
Red bell pepper, small dice		1 oz	4 oz	30 g	125 g
Jicama or water chestnut, small dice		½ oz	2 oz	15 g	60 g
Fresh corn kernels		2 oz	8 oz	60 g	250 g
Cilantro, chopped		2 tbsp	8 tbsp	6 g	25 g
Hot red pepper sauce					
Salt					
Pepper					
Lime juice					

Procedure:

1. Soak the lentils in cold water for several hours or overnight. Drain and rinse.

2. Place the lentils in a pot with enough stock to cover. Simmer just until tender but still whole. Do not cook until soft and broken up. Drain and spread out on a sheet pan to cool quickly.

3. Heat the butter or oil in a sauté pan. Add the shallot, jalapeño, and bell pepper. Sauté for 1 or 2 minutes, keeping the vegetables somewhat crisp.

4. Add the jicama and corn. Cook another 1 or 2 minutes.

5. Add the lentils and heat through. Stir in the cilantro.

6. Season with a generous quantity of red pepper sauce (the dish should be spicy) and salt and pepper.

7. Just before serving, season with a few drops of lime juice. Serve hot or cold.

TOMATO RAISIN CHUTNEY

		U.S.		Metric	
YIELD:		**1 pt**	**2 qt**	**5 dl**	**2 l**
Ingredients					
Vegetable oil		1 oz	4 oz	*30 ml*	*125 ml*
Cumin seeds		½ tsp	2 tsp	*1 g*	*4 g*
Onion, chopped fine		2 oz	8 oz	*60 g*	*250 g*
Garlic cloves, minced		1	4	*1*	*4*
Fresh ginger, grated		1 tbsp	4 tbsp	*6 g*	*25 g*
Tomato, peeled, seeded, and chopped		1 lb	4 lb	*500 g*	*2 kg*
Salt		1 tsp	4 tsp	*5 g*	*20 g*
Black pepper		pinch	½ tsp	*pinch*	*1 g*
Ground coriander		1 tsp	4 tsp	*2 g*	*8 g*
Cayenne		⅛ tsp	½ tsp	*0.25 g*	*1 g*
Golden raisins		3 oz	12 oz	*90 g*	*375 g*
Sugar		2 tsp	8 tsp	*10 g*	*40 g*
Red wine vinegar		½ oz	2 oz	*15 ml*	*60 ml*

Procedure:

1. Heat the oil in a stainless steel or other nonreactive sauce pot. Add the cumin seeds and fry for a few seconds, until they begin to darken.

2. Add the onion, garlic, and ginger. Brown lightly.

3. Add the remaining ingredients. Simmer slowly until somewhat reduced and thickened, about 15 to 30 minutes.

4. Taste and adjust the seasonings with additional salt and vinegar if necessary. The chutney should not be too tart but should have enough acidity to balance the sweetness of the raisins.

5. Serve hot or cold as a condiment.

PEAR GINGER CHUTNEY

		U.S.		Metric	
YIELD:		24 oz	6 pt	7.5 dl	3 l
Ingredients					
Pears, pared and cored		1 lb 8 oz	6 lb	750 g	3 kg
Brown sugar		4 oz	1 lb	125 g	500 g
Fresh ginger, grated		2 tbsp	½ cup	12 g	50 g
Onion, minced		4 oz	1 lb	125 g	500 g
Cayenne		pinch	½ tsp	pinch	1 g
Cinnamon		¼ tsp	1 tsp	0.5 g	2 g
Ground cloves		¼ tsp	1 tsp	0.5 g	2 g
White distilled vinegar		4 oz	1 pt	125 ml	5dl

Procedure:

1. In a food processor, chop the pears until they make a coarse, lumpy purée. Do not purée until smooth.
2. Combine all the ingredients in a stainless steel or other nonreactive sauce pot. Simmer slowly until thick. Adjust the seasonings.
3. Serve warm or cold as a condiment.

SPICED POTATOES WITH ONIONS

		U.S.		Metric	
PORTIONS:		4	16	4	16
Ingredients					
Potatoes, waxy or all-purpose		1 lb	4 lb	500 g	2 kg
Oil		1 oz	4 oz	30 ml	125 ml
Cumin seeds		½ tsp	2 tsp	1 g	4 g
Fennel seeds		½ tsp	2 tsp	1 g	4 g
Mustard seeds, preferably black mustard seeds		½ tsp	2 tsp	1 g	4 g
Black pepper		pinch	¼ tsp	pinch	0.5 g
Ground cardamom		pinch	¼ tsp	pinch	0.5 g
Cayenne, to taste					
Salt		½ tsp	2 tsp	3 g	10 g
Onions, sliced		4 oz	1 lb	125 g	500 g
Lemon juice		2 tsp	1 ½ oz	10 ml	40 ml

Cooking:

1. Boil the potatoes in their skins. Peel them and cut them into large dice or chop them coarsely.

2. Heat the oil in a sauté pan. Add the cumin, fennel, and mustard seeds. Cook them about 15 seconds, just enough to toast them lightly.

3. Add the pepper, cardamom, cayenne, salt, and sliced onions. Sauté until the onions are lightly browned.

4. Add the potatoes. Sauté for 5 to 10 minutes, until the potatoes are lightly browned.

5. Add the lemon juice. Toss to mix and cook 1 or 2 more minutes.

Variations

Spiced Potatoes with Spinach

Spinach, blanched, squeezed dry, and chopped	6 oz	1 lb 8 oz	*200 g*	*800 g*

Add the spinach to the basic recipe, mixing it with the potatoes after they have started to brown. Omit the lemon juice.

Spiced Potatoes with Tomato Sauce

Tomato purée	6 oz	1 pt 8 oz	*2 dl*	*8 dl*

Cut the potatoes into larger pieces than in the basic recipe (for example, into quarters or halves). Omit the mustard seeds, cardamom, and lemon juice. At the same time that the potatoes are added to the sauté pan, add the tomato purée. Cook, partially covered, until the liquid is reduced by one-half and clings to the potatoes.

POTATO GALETTES I

		U.S.		Metric	
	PORTIONS:	4–6	16–24	4–6	16–24
Ingredients					
Potatoes, baking type		1 lb	4 lb	500 g	2 kg
Butter, melted		2 oz	8 oz	60 g	250 g
Salt					
White pepper					

Cooking:

1. Peel the potatoes. Cut into very thin slices, preferably on a mandoline.

2. For each portion, place a 4-inch (10-cm) tart ring (see variations) on a well-seasoned or nonstick baking pan or sheet, generously buttered.

3. Place one slice of potato in the center of the ring, then arrange additional slices, overlapping, in a circle around it and touching the inside edge of the ring. The purpose of the ring is to facilitate making uniform, round galettes.

4. Brush the top of the potato cake generously with additional melted butter. Sprinkle with salt and pepper.

5. Remove the ring and repeat with the remaining potatoes.

6. Bake at 400°F (200°C) until browned and crisp.

Variations

Galettes of various sizes are made by using rings of various sizes (refer to page 501 for a discussion of potato galettes).

Instead of using a baking pan, arrange the potatoes (as detailed in Cooking, step 3) in a well-seasoned or nonstick, buttered skillet or sauté pan. Cook on top of the stove, turning once to brown both sides. Turn them very carefully to avoid breaking the slices apart.

POTATO GALETTES II

		U.S.		Metric	
PORTIONS:		*4–6*	*16–24*	*4–6*	*16–24*
Ingredients					
Potatoes, peeled		1 lb	4 lb	*500 g*	*2 kg*
Butter, melted		1 oz	4 oz	*30 g*	*125 g*
Salt					
Pepper					
Oil or melted butter for cooking					

Cooking:

1. Cut the potatoes into fine julienne, preferably on a mandoline. Do not rinse the julienne or hold them under water, so that the starch does not wash off.

2. Toss the potatoes with the melted butter.

3. Heat a well-seasoned or nonstick skillet or sauté pan over moderately high heat. Add a little cooking oil or melted butter to coat the bottom. For each portion, quickly place a 3- to 5-inch (8- to 12-cm) tart ring in the pan. Place a portion of the potatoes inside the ring and flatten into a thin cake. The purpose of the ring is to facilitate making uniform, round galettes.

4. Remove the ring and cook over moderately high heat, turning once to brown both sides well. Cook until brown and crisp.

5. To reheat or recrisp for later service, arrange in a single layer on a sheet pan and bake at 400°F (200°C).

Variations

Omit the melted butter in the basic recipe. Grate or julienne the potato and mix with beaten egg, using one egg per pound (450 g) of potato.

Galettes of Potato and Sweet Potato

Use half potato and half sweet potato in the basic recipe.

SAUTÉED POTATOES WITH SHALLOTS AND GARLIC

		U.S.		Metric	
PORTIONS:		4	16	*4*	*16*
Ingredients					
Potatoes, waxy		1 lb	4 lb	*500 g*	*2 kg*
Olive oil		1 tbsp	2 oz	*15 ml*	*60 ml*
Salt					
White pepper					
Butter		1 oz	4 oz	*30 g*	*125 g*
Shallot, minced		2 tbsp	1 oz	*15 g*	*60 g*
Garlic, minced		1 tsp	4 tsp	*2 g*	*10 g*
Chopped parsley		1 tbsp	4 tbsp	*4 g*	*15 g*

Cooking:

1. Boil the potatoes. Peel and dice them.

2. Heat the olive oil in a sauté pan. Add the potatoes. Season to taste with salt and white pepper. Sauté until they start to brown.

3. Add the butter. Continue to sauté until the potatoes are golden brown.

4. Add the shallot and garlic. Toss over heat for another minute. Do not cook too long; the essence of this dish is the fresh, lightly cooked flavor of the shallot and garlic.

5. Add the chopped parsley. Toss and serve.

Variation

Sautéed Potatoes with Garlic and Anchovy				
Anchovy fillets, chopped	2	8	*2*	*8*

Add the chopped anchovies to the pan at the same time as the potatoes. Continue as in the basic recipe.

POTATOES AND CHILES

		U.S.		Metric	
PORTIONS:		**4**	**16**	*4*	*16*
Ingredients					
Large green chiles, preferably poblanos (p. 484)		4	16	*4*	*16*
Potatoes, waxy		12 oz	3 lb	*375 g*	*1.5 kg*
Onion		4 oz	1 lb	*125 g*	*500 g*
Oil		2 oz	8 oz	*60 ml*	*2.5 dl*
Salt					

Cooking:

1. Roast and peel the chiles, following the procedure in the recipe on page 521. Discard the seeds and core. Cut the chiles into short strips about ½ inch (1 cm) wide.

2. Boil, peel, and dice the potatoes.

3. Slice the onion.

4. Heat the oil in a sauté pan. Add the onion and sauté over moderate heat until tender.

5. Add the chile strips. Sauté about 2 to 3 minutes.

6. Add the potatoes. Season with salt to taste. Cook over moderate heat until the potatoes begin to brown. Taste and adjust the seasoning.

Variations

Bell peppers, of one or more colors, can be used in place of chiles to make a dish of somewhat different character. Use a smaller quantity of peppers, because bell peppers have thicker flesh than do chiles.

Potatoes with Chiles and Chorizos

Add sliced chorizo (spicy Mexican sausage) to the pan at the same time as the potatoes. Use about 1 oz (30 g) sausage per portion, or as desired.

Potatoes with Kale

Omit the chiles from the basic recipe. Use olive oil for cooking and reduce the quantity of oil as necessary. Add chopped garlic to taste to the potatoes. After the potatoes are lightly browned, add some kale, which has been boiled, drained, squeezed out, and chopped. Use about 1½ oz (50 g) kale per portion. Toss to mix with the potatoes. Cook just until the kale is hot.

HERBED POTATO PURÉE

	PORTIONS:	U.S.		Metric	
		4	**16**	*4*	*16*
Ingredients					
Potatoes		1 lb	4 lb	*500 g*	*2 kg*
Milk		2 oz	8 oz	*60 ml*	*2.5 dl*
Butter		1 oz	4 oz	*30 g*	*125 g*
Chives, chopped		1 tsp	4 tsp	*1 g*	*4 g*
Parsley, chopped		2 tsp	3 tbsp	*2 g*	*10 g*
Tarragon, fresh, chopped (see note)		½ tsp	1 tsp	*0.5 g*	*2 g*
Heavy cream		1–4 oz	4–16 oz	*30–125 ml*	*1–5 dl*
Salt					
White pepper					
Nutmeg (optional)					

Note: If fresh tarragon is not available, substitute one-third its volume of dried tarragon.

Cooking:

1. Pare the potatoes. Boil or steam until tender. Purée with a food mill.

2. Heat together the milk and butter until the butter melts. Mix with the potatoes. At the same time, add the chives, parsley, and tarragon.

3. Add enough cream to bring the potatoes to the desired consistency. The purée should be soft and moist.

4. Season to taste with salt, white pepper, and a dash of nutmeg if desired.

Variations

Substitute waxy new potatoes for regular starchy potatoes. The texture and flavor will be different, and it may be necessary to reduce the quantity of milk or cream.

Purée of Potato and Celery Root

Use half potato and half celery root. Reduce the quantity of milk as necessary. Omit the tarragon; omit the other herbs as well if desired.

Potato Purée with Garlic and Herbs

Boil peeled garlic cloves (2 to 6 per lb, or per 500 g, of potatoes). Purée them with the potatoes.

Potato Purée with Sorrel

Sorrel leaves	2 oz	8 oz		*60 g*	*250 g*
White stock	3 oz	12 oz		*1 dl*	*4 dl*

Omit the milk, cream, and herbs from the basic recipe. Shred the sorrel with a knife. Bring the stock to a boil and add the sorrel to wilt it. Add this mixture with the butter to the potato purée.

Potato Purée with Scallions

Omit the tarragon and chives from the basic recipe. Omit the parsley if desired. Add desired quantity of chopped scallions to the potato purée. Garnish the top of each portion with a sprinkling of additional chopped scallions.

Potato Purée with Browned Onions

Onions	6 oz	1 lb 8 oz		*375 g*	*1.5 kg*
Butter, as needed					

Cook the onions slowly in butter until they are well browned and very soft. Omit the herbs in the basic recipe. Add the onions to the potatoes along with the hot milk and butter mixture. Reduce or omit the quantity of cream as desired.

Potato Purée with Bacon or Pancetta

Omit the tarragon from the basic recipe. Render some bacon in a dry skillet or render some minced pancetta (Italian unsmoked bacon) with a little olive oil. Substitute the rendered fat for the butter in the basic recipe. Mix the crisp rendered pancetta or crumbled bacon with the potatoes.

Potato Purée Gratinée

Using the basic recipe or one of the variations, make a purée and put it in one or more buttered gratin dishes. Smooth the top with a spatula. Pour a little cream or crème fraîche over the top. Heat in a hot oven until the top is lightly browned. If necessary, run it under a broiler or salamander to brown the top.

POTATO GRATIN (GRATIN DAUPHINOIS)

		U.S.		Metric	
PORTIONS:		4	16	*4*	*16*
Ingredients					
Garlic		1 clove	1–2 cloves	*1 clove*	*1–2 cloves*
Butter					
Potatoes, waxy		1 lb	4 lb	*450 g*	*1.8 kg*
Salt					
White pepper					
Nutmeg					
Optional: grated gruyère cheese		2 oz	8 oz	*60 g*	*250 g*
Milk		4 oz	1 pt	*125 ml*	*5 dl*
Heavy cream		4 oz	1 pt	*125 ml*	*5 dl*

Additional milk or cream as needed

Mise en Place:

1. Cut the garlic clove(s) in half. Rub the insides of one or more gratin dishes with the garlic. Butter the insides of the dishes well.
2. Peel the potatoes. Cut them into thin slices, preferably using a mandoline. Put the sliced potatoes in a bowl of cold water, to keep them from discoloring and to rinse off excess starch.

Cooking:

1. Remove the potatoes from the water and dry them between towels.
2. Place a layer of the potatoes in the gratin dish or dishes. Season with a little salt and pepper and a very small amount of nutmeg. Continue until the potatoes are about 2 inches (5 cm) or a little less deep in the dishes. When cooked, they will settle to about half this thickness.
3. Combine the milk and cream in a saucepan. Bring to a simmer. Pour the cream mixture over the potatoes; pour it over the entire surface so that all the potatoes are moistened.
4. Bake at 375°F (190°C) until the potatoes are tender, the top is browned, and there is no excess liquid in the dishes, about 40 minutes. The potatoes should be moist but not juicy. If the potatoes become too dry during cooking, add a little more hot milk or cream, pouring it over the top of the potatoes.
5. Remove from the oven and let stand a few minutes to settle before serving.

Variations

See the discussion on page 500 regarding variations on the potato gratin and disagreements about techniques.

SPLIT PEA PURÉE

		U.S.		Metric	
PORTIONS:		*4–6*	*16–24*	*4–6*	*16–24*
Ingredients					
Split peas		6 oz	1 lb 8 oz	*175 g*	*750 g*
Chicken stock, vegetable broth, or water		1 ½ pt	3 qt	*7.5 dl*	*3 l*
Onion		1 small	1 large	*1 small*	*1 large*
Cloves		1	2	*1*	*2*
Bay leaves		1	2	*1*	*2*
Salt					
Butter		1 oz	4 oz	*1 oz*	*4 oz*

Procedure:

1. Pick over the peas and rinse them in cold water.

2. Place the peas in a sauce pot with the stock or water.

3. Stick the bay leaves to the onion with the cloves. Put the onion in the pot with the peas.

4. Simmer uncovered until the peas are soft, about 45 minutes. Check the pot occasionally to see if the peas are drying out. This is a purée and not a soup, so the liquid should be well reduced by the end of the cooking time, but not so that the peas scorch to the bottom.

5. Discard the onion, cloves, and bay leaves.

6. Purée the peas. The purée should be stiff enough to hold its shape softly and not spread out on a plate. If it is too moist, reduce slightly in a wide pan.

7. Add salt to taste. Stir in the raw butter.

Variations

Purées of dried beans, lentils, and dals (see page 490) can be prepared in the same way and served as a side dish or accompaniment to meats and other main dishes. This basic recipe can be used, but soaking and cooking times for beans are generally longer than for split peas. Many bean purées are excellent when flavored with some chopped garlic that has been sautéed in a little butter or olive oil.

LENTILS WITH TOMATO

		U.S.		Metric	
PORTIONS:		**4**	**16**	*4*	*16*
Ingredients					
Garlic		½ clove	2 cloves	*½ clove*	*2 cloves*
Onion		2 oz	8 oz	*60 g*	*250 g*
Celery		2 oz	8 oz	*60 g*	*250 g*
Oil		½ oz	2 oz	*15 ml*	*60 ml*
Lentils, cleaned and rinsed		6 oz	1 lb 8 oz	*175 g*	*750 g*
Chicken stock		12 oz	3 pt	*4 dl*	*1.5 l*
Tomato, peeled, seeded, and chopped		4 oz	1 lb	*125 g*	*500 g*
Red wine vinegar		2 tsp	1 ½ oz	*10 ml*	*40 ml*
Salt					
Pepper					
Olive oil (optional)		1–2 tbsp	2–4 oz	*15–30 ml*	*60–125 ml*

Cooking:

1. Chop the garlic, onion, and celery very fine.

2. Heat the oil in a heavy pot. Add the chopped vegetables and sweat for several minutes.

3. Add the lentils and stock. Simmer, covered, until the lentils are tender but not disintegrating, about 30 to 45 minutes.

4. When the lentils are cooked, add the tomato and vinegar. Season to taste with salt and pepper. Simmer about 5 minutes longer.

5. If desired, finish with a little fruity, flavorful olive oil.

Variation

Southwestern Lentils

Jalapeño pepper, minced		½–1 oz	2–4 oz	*15–30 g*	*60–125 g*
Cilantro, chopped		2 tbsp	1 oz	*7 g*	*30 g*

Omit the celery from the basic recipe and double the quantity of onion. Add the jalapeño at the same time as the tomato. Just before serving, add the cilantro.

BULGUR PILAF WITH LEMON

		U.S.		Metric	
PORTIONS:		4–6	16–24	4–6	16–24
Ingredients					
Butter		½ oz	2 oz	15 g	60 g
Onion, chopped fine		2 oz	8 oz	60 g	250 g
Bulgur, coarse		1 cup	4 cups	2.5 dl	1 l
Grated lemon zest		2 tsp	8 tsp	4 g	15 g
Chicken stock, hot		12 oz	3 pt	3.75 dl	1.5 l
Salt					
Pepper					
Chives, chopped		2 tbsp	½ cup	30 ml	125 ml

Procedure:

1. Heat the butter in a saucepan. Add the chopped onion and sauté gently without browning, until the onion is soft.

2. Add the bulgur. Stir to coat with butter. Stir over heat for 1 minute to lightly toast the grain.

3. Add the grated lemon zest and stir to mix.

4. Stir in the hot chicken stock. Add salt and pepper to taste. Bring to a simmer.

5. Cover the pot and cook over low heat or in an oven heated to 350°F (175°C) until the bulgur is tender, about 20 minutes.

6. Uncover and fluff the grain with a kitchen fork. Add the chives and toss to mix in.

BARLEY WITH WILD MUSHROOMS AND HAM

		U.S.		Metric	
PORTIONS:		4–6	16–24	4–6	16–24
Ingredients					
Dried porcini mushrooms		½ oz	2 oz	15 g	60 g
Hot water		2 oz	8 oz	60 ml	2.5 dl
Oil		½ oz	2 oz	15 ml	60 ml
Onion, small dice		2 oz	8 oz	60 g	250 g
Celery, small dice		2 oz	8 oz	60 g	250 g
Barley		5 oz	1 lb 4 oz	150 g	600 g
Brown stock, chicken stock, or vegetable broth		10 oz	2½ pt	3 dl	1.25 l
Cooked ham, small dice		2 oz	8 oz	60 g	250 g
Salt					

Mise en Place:

Soak the dried porcini in hot water until they are soft. Drain the mushrooms and squeeze them out, reserving all the soaking liquid. Strain or decant the liquid to remove any sand or grit. Chop the mushrooms.

Cooking:

1. Heat the oil in a heavy pot. Add the onion and celery. Sauté briefly.

2. Add the barley and sauté briefly, as for making rice pilaf.

3. Add the stock and the mushroom liquid. Bring to a boil. Stir in the chopped mushrooms and the ham. Add salt to taste.

4. Cover tightly. Cook on top of the stove over low heat or in the oven at 325°F (160°C), until the barley is tender and the liquid is absorbed, about 45 to 60 minutes.

Variations

Add other vegetables to the barley, such as diced carrots, turnips, fennel, or parsnips. Add them at the same time as the onion and celery or cook them separately and add them at the end of cooking.

BASIC RISOTTO

		U.S.		Metric	
PORTIONS:		**4**	**16**	*4*	*16*
Ingredients					
Butter		½ oz	2 oz	*15 g*	*60 g*
Oil		½ oz	2 oz	*15 ml*	*60 ml*
Onion, chopped fine		½ oz	2 oz	*15 g*	*60 g*
Arborio rice		8 oz	2 lb	*225 g*	*900 g*
Chicken stock, hot (approximate measure)		1 ½ pt	3 qt	*7.5 dl*	*3 l*
Butter		½ oz	2 oz	*15 g*	*60 g*
Grated parmesan cheese		1 ½ oz	6 oz	*45 g*	*175 g*
Salt					

Mise en Place:

1. Heat the butter and oil in a large, straight-sided sauté pan. Add the onion and sauté until soft. Do not brown.

2. Add the rice and sauté until well coated with fat.

3. Using a 4- to 6-oz (1.5- to 2-dl) ladle, add one ladle of stock to the rice. Stir the rice over medium heat until the stock is absorbed and the rice is almost dry.

4. Add another ladle of stock and repeat the procedure. Do not add more than one ladleful of stock at a time.

5. Stop adding stock when the rice is tender but still firm. It should be very moist and creamy, but not runny. The cooking should take about 30 minutes. The quantity of stock indicated is only approximate; you may need more or less. If much more is needed, water may be used for the additional quantity.

6. Remove from the heat and stir in the raw butter and the cheese. Salt to taste. Serve at once.

Variations

Risotto Milanese

Saffron		¼ tsp	1 tsp	*0.16 g*	*0.7 g*

Soak the saffron in a little of the hot stock. Prepare the risotto as in the basic recipe. Add the saffron-infused stock near the end of the cooking time.

Asparagus Risotto with Walnuts

Asparagus	1 lb	4 lb	500 g	2 kg
Walnuts	1 ½ oz	6 oz	45 g	175 g

Trim the bottoms of the asparagus spears and peel the lower portion of the stems. Simmer until done. Cut into 1-inch (2.5-cm) lengths. Use the cooking water for part of the stock. Chop the walnuts coarsely and toast them briefly in a dry sauté pan. Add the asparagus and nuts to the risotto along with the butter and cheese. If desired, substitute walnut oil or hazelnut oil for one-half of the raw butter.

Risotto with Artichokes

Prepare Artichokes en Mirepoix (page 507) but omit the carrot. Combine the artichokes with the risotto when it is about half cooked.

Risotto with Radicchio

Radicchio	1 lb	4 lb	500 g	2 kg
White wine	3 oz	12 oz	1 dl	4 dl

Separate the leaves of the radicchio; wash and drain them well. Cut with a knife into thin strips. Follow the procedure for basic risotto but add the radicchio to the sautéed onion. Before adding the rice, sauté the radicchio until it has completely wilted (add more butter to the pan if necessary). Add the rice and sauté it as usual. Add the wine to the pan before the first ladleful of stock. *Note:* The radicchio will turn very dark, almost black, during cooking.

Risotto with Mussels

Mussels, in shells	2 lb	8 lb	1 kg	4 kg
Shallots, chopped	½ oz	2 oz	15 g	60 g
White wine	3 oz	12 oz	1 dl	4 dl
Chopped parsley	2 tbsp	1 oz	7 g	30 g
Olive oil				

Scrub the mussels well and remove the beards. Place in a heavy, covered pot with the shallots and wine. Set over moderate heat and steam until the mussels are all opened. Strain the broth. Remove the mussels from the shells and reserve. Prepare Risotto Milanese using the mussel broth plus water instead of the chicken stock. Add the shelled mussels when the rice is cooked. *Omit the final butter and cheese.* Instead, finish with the chopped parsley and a little olive oil.

Risotto with Seafood

Prepare like Risotto with Mussels but use a mixture of cooked mussels, cooked shrimp, and sliced, cooked squid instead of just the cooked mussels. Supplement or replace the mussel broth with fish or shellfish stock. Use any seafood broth or stock for up to about one-half the amount of cooking liquid; using too much may make the flavor of the risotto too rich and cloying. Do not use parmesan cheese for seafood risottos.

Seafood Risotto with Squid Ink

Squid ink	1–2 tsp	4–8 tsp		*5–10 g*	*20–40 g*
Tomato, peeled, seeded, and chopped	4 oz	1 lb		*125 g*	*500 g*

Prepare Risotto with Seafood but stir the squid ink into the rice before adding the first ladleful of stock. Add the tomato just before serving. Top with chopped parsley.

CHAPTER

11

Cold Foods

*T*he techniques and procedures presented in this chapter belong to the culinary department known as *garde manger* (pronounced "guard mawn zhay"), a term whose basic meaning is larder or food storage place. Especially in the days before modern refrigeration, the food storage room was separate from the kitchen so that it would remain cooler. Consequently, it was the best area for the preparation of cold foods. Thus, the work carried out in the storage area, or garde manger, became known by the same name.

Today the art of garde manger refers primarily to the preparation, decoration, and presentation of cold foods for buffets. It includes the techniques of cold-food decoration, cold-platter design and presentation, and design and planning of whole buffets. Garde manger is an intricate and complex discipline that is the subject of whole books and of extended courses of study.

This book is primarily concerned with à la carte style cooking; buffet service is beyond its scope. Nevertheless, à la carte restaurants have inherited from classical garde manger a number of special food preparations that can be served in single portions as well as on buffet platters. Pâtés, terrines, galantines, and mousses are not only ideal for buffets, they are also popular in many restaurants. This chapter serves as an introduction to these preparations.

Many of these items are less common now than they were several decades ago. The reason for this is simple: they are costly to produce because they require a great deal of time and labor. Back in the days when large kitchen brigades were the rule, pâtés and galantines were considered good ways of utilizing trim and less expensive cuts of meat. Today, not many restaurants can afford to make them. Nevertheless, they are basic skills, and an educated cook must be familiar with at least the rudimentary techniques.

THE HANDLING AND SERVICE OF COLD DISHES

The fact that the dishes in this chapter are served cold means that various factors relating to the handling and service of these dishes require special consideration. These factors have to do with sanitation and with presentation.

Sanitation and Storage

Hot foods that have been handled in a sanitary manner and that are served at or above a temperature that kills microorganisms can usually be considered safe and sanitary to eat. Cold foods, on the other hand, present special problems because they have been stored and handled after cooking. During this time, they may be exposed to disease-causing organisms. Because these foods will not be subjected to further cooking, the organisms will not be destroyed.

For this reason, it is particularly important to follow all the rules of safe food handling. Make sure tools, containers, and work surfaces are clean and sanitary. Keep ingredients refrigerated when they are not being worked on, and keep the finished product refrigerated until service time.

The length of time terrines and other cold foods can be stored in the refrigerator depends on the ingredients, the type of item, and the method of preparation. Meat terrines that have been sealed with a layer of fat (see page 575) and have not been cut may keep as long as several weeks (although the quality may start to decline after a week or so), while seafood or vegetable terrines may keep no more than two or three days, or even less. Pâtés en croûte (see page 569) will not keep as well as terrines because the pastry loses its freshness. Aspics should be kept covered or wrapped to prevent them from drying out.

Presentation

Attractive plating or presentation of foods is, of course, always important, but it could be argued that it is even more important for cold foods than for hot foods. Foods presented hot and steaming, directly from the sauté pan or carving board, have an immediate appeal to the nose as well as the eye, but cold foods must rely more completely on visual impact to make their first impressions.

Furthermore, because there is not the same urgency in getting the plate from the kitchen to the dining room before the food cools down, the cook has more time to arrange cold foods on the plate. This does not mean, however, that the most elaborate or intricate presentation is the best. "Keep it simple" is a good rule of thumb. Food is not made more appetizing by excessive handling.

Arrangements should be kept neat, but this does not mean that they must always be symmetrical or regular. As in the case of salads, a deliberate casualness in the arrangement can be appetizing when it suggests that the dish has been freshly assembled with minimum handling and rushed to the table.

In the case of pâtés and terrines, careful handling is essential to the presentation. Slice them carefully and plate each slice with the best side up. To make neat slices, use a sharp, thin-bladed slicing knife. Before each slice, wipe off any residue from the previous slice and dip the blade in hot water. Slice the pâté with a gentle sawing motion, using the full length of the blade. Don't force the knife straight down or make little jagged cuts; this will make the cut surface uneven rather than smooth.

If the cut end of the pâté has discolored somewhat from exposure to air, plate the first slice with this side down. In contrast to pâtés for buffet presentation, slices of pâté for à la carte service are often garnished with greens or other colorful items, which enliven the sometimes drab appearance of a plain meat pâté. In addition, greens and other vegetable garnish provide a pleasant flavor contrast to the somewhat rich, processed flavor of the pâté or terrine.

Tart or piquant garnishes and accompaniments, as well as tart sauces such as vinaigrette or mayonnaise variations, help to counter the richness of pâtés, which are often rather fatty. This is why sour pickles and mustard are classic accompaniments for these foods.

Consideration must be given to the serving temperature of cold foods such as aspics, pâtés, and terrines. A common error is to serve these items too cold. At refrigerator temperature, their flavors are masked. Furthermore, their textures are too firm; the fat in pâtés and the gelatin in aspics will both be firmly congealed. A little warmer temperature is necessary to enable them to melt pleasantly in the mouth.

To bring them to suitable serving temperature, remove individual portions from refrigeration and let stand at room temperature for about 5 or 10 minutes, but no longer. Remember the sanitation guidelines discussed earlier. This period is long enough to let them warm up slightly, but not long enough to give any possible microorganisms time to start multiplying. Keep in mind, too, that this short period of tempering applies only to those portions to be served right away. Whole pâtés from which portions were cut, for example, should be returned immediately to refrigeration.

ASPIC AND CHAUD-FROID

Aspic jelly or *gelée* (pronounced "zhuh lay") is clarified stock that contains enough gelatin so that it solidifies when cold. The gelatin may be naturally extracted from bones or added from a package. Any good stock naturally contains a certain amount of gelatin, but in most cases it must be supplemented with additional unflavored, packaged gelatin.

Aspic jelly may be nearly colorless ("white" aspic) or various shades of amber, but in most cases it must be crystal clear. This clarity is achieved by clarifying it like a consommé. White or light-colored aspic is used when the natural colors of the foods and decorations must show through. Amber or golden aspic enhances the brown color of foods such as roasted meats and poultry.

Aspic is used as a coating for foods and as a binding ingredient. When it is used as a coating, it has three main purposes:

1. To protect foods from the air, which would dry them out and discolor them
2. To improve appearance and give shine
3. To add flavor

This last purpose is, of course, best accomplished if the stock is of high quality

As a binding ingredient, aspic is used in various mousses, terrines, and aspic molds, as discussed later in this chapter. It is also the binding agent in chaud-froid sauce (see page 560). *Note:* When aspic is used as a binding agent for such items as mousses, it need not be perfectly clarified.

In addition, when congealed and chopped or cut into various shapes, aspic jelly is used as a garnish for platters or servings of pâtés, terrines, and other cold items.

Preparing Aspic Jelly

The best aspic is a well-made, naturally gelatinous stock. It has a superior texture and flavor, but it is time-consuming to make because it requires making a separate batch of stock in addition to the normal stock production. Consequently, most aspics are made by reinforcing regular stock with extra gelatin. In addition, aspic powders or mixes are available, but the flavor of aspic made from them does not compare with that made from stock. They can be useful in an emergency, however, or for pieces used purely for display or decoration.

Classic Aspic Jelly. Prepare classic aspic jelly as you would white or brown veal stock, but with the addition of products that will release a good deal of gelatin, such as split calves' feet or pigs' feet, pork skin, and veal knuckle bones. If enough of these items are used, the stock will contain enough natural gelatin to be used as an aspic jelly.

Follow basic stock-making procedures, except do not brown the added feet and pork skin when making brown stock. When the stock has been made, use the following steps to convert it to aspic jelly:

1. Test the stock for gelatin content. Ladle a small amount of cooled stock onto a small plate or saucer and refrigerate.
   a. If the stock becomes firm, no additional gelatin is needed.
   b. If it sets but is not firm enough, add about ½ oz or 2 tbsp (15 g) powdered gelatin per quart (liter) of stock, or 2 oz (60 g) per gallon (4 liters).
   c. If it does not set at all (which is unlikely if the stock is properly made) but merely becomes thicker, add about 1 oz or 4 tbsp (30 g) powdered gelatin per quart (liter), or 4 oz (125 g) per gallon (4 liters).

Add the gelatin by first stirring it gradually into a little cold water, avoiding making lumps, and letting it soften. Then add the softened gelatin to the stock.

2. Clarify the stock as for consommé. For white aspic (made with white stock), omit the carrots from the mirepoix.

3. After the stock is clarified, remove all traces of fat. The aspic jelly is now ready to use.

Note in the preceding procedure that when extra gelatin is needed, it is added before the stock is clarified. This is to make sure that the aspic is crystal clear. Slight impurities in the gelatin or carelessness in dissolving it could result in cloudiness or lumps.

Regular Aspic Jelly. This is a normal meat, poultry, or fish stock reinforced with gelatin and clarified. Regular stock rarely has enough natural gelatin to enable it to be used as a jelly, so extra gelatin must be added. To test stock for gelatin content and to convert it to aspic jelly, follow the same procedure as for classic aspic jelly, as described earlier. However, note that if the stock contains very little gelatin and stays watery when chilled, more than 4 oz (125 g) gelatin may be needed per gallon (4 liters).

Aspic Powder. Aspic powder is unflavored gelatin mixed with a powdered stock base. To prepare, follow the instructions on the container. Additional unflavored gelatin may be needed for some purposes.

Procedures for using aspic jelly are discussed following a brief consideration to a related topic, chaud-froid sauce.

Chaud-Froid

Described in simplest terms, *chaud-froid sauce* is a white sauce containing enough gelatin so that it will set like an aspic. The name "chaud-froid" is French for "hot-cold"; the sauce is so called because it is made hot but eaten cold.

Today, chaud-froid sauce is rarely used except for display pieces on buffets. Its main purpose in such cases is to provide a smooth, uniformly white background for colored decorations. Since it is not eaten in these cases, it does not have to have a good flavor, and it may be made out of a simple béchamel sauce thickened with roux made with white shortening.

Nevertheless, chaud-froid sauce finds occasional use in some cold dishes, for example, as a component of some aspic molds and terrines. So a brief discussion is warranted without going into the kind of detail found in books on *garde manger*.

Many different kinds of white sauces may be used as a base for chaud-froid, including cream sauces, white stocks enriched with cream or cream and egg yolks, veloutés, and mayonnaise. There are also colored chaud-froid sauces, but they are not often used. Red sauce can be made with the addition of tomato paste and sometimes paprika. Green sauce is colored with spinach and watercress, puréed with some of the hot sauce and strained. Brown chaud-froid can be made by combining one-third glace de viande, one-third tomato sauce, and one-third aspic jelly.

Preparing Chaud-Froid Sauce. Two basic types of chaud-froid sauce are considered here, one based on white stock and cream, the other based on mayonnaise. Both of these are of good eating quality and can be used for first-class cold foods. Heavier types based on roux-thickened sauces may be more economical to make, but are more appropriate for nonedible display pieces.

Procedure for Preparing Classical Chaud-Froid Sauce

Note that this sauce is essentially an aspic jelly with the addition of cream or of a cream-and-egg-yolk liaison. In fact, it can be made by combining aspic and cream, but it will then have to be reinforced with extra gelatin because of the quantity of cream.

1. To make 2 qt (2 l) of sauce, assemble the following ingredients:
   1 qt (1 l) white stock (veal, chicken, or fish)
   1 qt (1 l) heavy cream
   ½ to 1 oz (15 to 30 g) unflavored gelatin (depending on the gelatin content of the stock)
   optional: 2 to 4 egg yolks, for liaison

2. Soften the gelatin in about one-third of the cream.

3. Bring the stock to a simmer. Add the gelatin mixture to the stock and return to the simmer.

4. a. If the egg yolks are used, beat the yolks with the remaining cream to make a liaison. Stir a little of the stock mixture into the liaison to temper it, then add it back to the hot stock. Heat it carefully to cook the egg yolks, but do not let it simmer or the yolks will curdle.
   b. If the yolks are not used, simply temper the remaining cream with a little of the hot stock and then add it to the stock.

5. Strain through a cheesecloth.

Procedure for Preparing Mayonnaise Chaud-Froid

Mayonnaise chaud-froid, also called mayonnaise collée, which means something like "glued mayonnaise," is simply a mixture of aspic jelly and mayonnaise. It is easy to make and, if the two ingredients are of good quality, is a tasty and useful chaud-froid.

The basic proportion is equal parts aspic jelly and mayonnaise. The proportion can be varied to taste, however, from one-third aspic and two-thirds mayonnaise, to one-third mayonnaise and two-thirds aspic jelly.

If you are using a homemade mayonnaise, it is best to prepare the chaud-froid at the last minute and use it at once. Reheating it to remelt it could cause the mayonnaise to break. Commercial mayonnaise, on the other hand, can generally be remelted without damage, but it is still best to use it as soon as it has been made.

The procedure is as follows:

1. Stir the mayonnaise, if necessary, so that it is smooth. If it has just been removed from the refrigerator, let it warm up to cool room temperature. If it is too cold, the first drops of aspic may congeal as soon as they hit it, causing lumps.

2. Melt the aspic over a hot water bath. Then cool it to thicken slightly (see page 562 for the procedure for cooling aspic). It should be at about the same temperature as the mayonnaise.

3. Using a stirring whip (as opposed to a ballon whip, used for whipping in air), stir the aspic into the mayonnaise. Stir carefully to avoid making bubbles. If the gelatin begins to set before the mixing is complete, carefully remelt over the hot water bath.

4. Set the chaud-froid over ice to thicken (see page 563 for procedure). When ready to use, it should be about the consistency of heavy cream. Use at once.

Using Aspic Jelly and Chaud-Froid Sauce

As discussed earlier, aspic and chaud-froid are used to enhance both the appearance and the flavor of cold foods. For best results, the aspic and chaud-froid, as well as the foods to be coated, should be prepared and handled in specific ways. The following sections detail general procedures for handling these products. Specific applications, such as recipes for aspic-based terrine molds, are included later in this chapter.

Aspic jelly must be cooled to just above congealing temperature before it is used to coat foods. If it is too warm, it will not have enough body to coat and will just run off.

Procedure for Cooling Aspic Jelly

The following procedure is used for chaud-froid as well as aspic jelly.

1. If the jelly is congealed, it must first be melted. Set the pan or container of jelly in a hot water bath. Stir it gently from time to time until it is completely melted.
2. Place the warm aspic jelly in a stainless steel bowl.
3. At all times be careful not to make any bubbles. Bubbles in the jelly may get transferred to the surface of your food item and mar its appearance.
4. Select a ladle that fits the curvature of the bowl. Set the bowl in crushed ice, pushing it in so that it sits in a well of ice. With the edge of the ladle against the inside of the bowl, rotate the bowl so that the ladle continually scrapes the inside of the bowl. This method prevents the formation of lumps that would occur when jelly touching the cold bowl solidifies too quickly.
5. Continue to rotate the bowl until the jelly is thick and syrupy but not yet set. The jelly is now ready for use. Remove from the ice bath and work quickly, because it will set very fast.
6. Remelt and recool the jelly as necessary.

Procedure for Coating Foods with Aspic Jelly

1. Chill the food to be coated. For best results, the surface of the item should be as smooth and as fat-free as possible.
2. Place the item on a wire rack over a tray or sheet pan. Excess aspic that falls onto the tray can be remelted and reused.
3. Cool the aspic jelly according to the preceding procedure.
4. Use the aspic as soon as it is ready. Various methods can be used to coat foods with aspic, depending on the sizes and shapes of the items.
   a. For smooth, regularly shaped items, use a large ladle and nap them with a single smooth stroke, as illustrated in Figure 11.1. Working too slowly may produce an uneven, bumpy coat.
   b. Large items and items with steep sides or irregular shapes are harder to coat. Using a ladle, coat the sides first and then the top for best results.
   c. For small items, it may be more convenient to use a kitchen spoon rather than a ladle.
   d. A pastry brush can be used to coat small items. A brush is often used for small portions, such as canapés, that need only a light glaze rather than a perfectly smooth coating of aspic.
5. Chill the items until the jelly is thoroughly set.
6. Repeat with additional coats, if necessary, until aspic is of desired thickness.

FIGURE 11.1. A smooth, regularly shaped item can be covered with an even layer of aspic using one stroke of the ladle.

7. To decorate, dip pieces of decoration in liquid aspic and place on the product in the desired pattern. Some items appropriate to use for decorating aspic include the following:

Leek leaves

Fresh herbs, especially flat-leaf parsley and tarragon

Black olives

Truffles, real or artificial

Tomato peels

Carrots

Hard-cooked egg whites and yolks

As appropriate, cut the items for decoration into very thin slices and then into desired shapes. For most vegetable decorations, such as carrots and leek leaves, blanch to make them more limber and to intensify the color.

8. If decorations have been used, cover the decorated item with a final layer of aspic jelly to protect the design.

Coating with Chaud-Froid. Apply chaud-froid sauce using the same procedure as for aspic. Because most chaud-froid is thicker than aspic, it is usually kept a little warmer when poured.

If the first layer of chaud froid is too transparent or not thick enough, apply one or two additional layers.

After the chaud-froid has chilled and set, apply decorations if desired. Finish with a layer of aspic, for best appearance.

Procedure for Lining a Mold with Aspic Jelly

Many instructions for lining molds say to chill the mold, then pour in a little liquid aspic jelly and turn and tilt the mold until the bottom and sides are coated. This method works and is suitable for some purposes, but it will not produce a smooth, even layer of aspic.

It is not always necessary to line a mold with aspic. Many aspic molds are made by first pouring a thin layer of aspic into the bottom of the mold, chilling it, then adding layers of ingredients (vegetables, meats, mousses, and so on) and covering each layer with a little aspic. The mold is chilled after each layer is added to allow the aspic to set. As long as the layers of solid ingredients are not allowed to touch the sides of the mold, the liquid aspic will fill in these spaces and, in effect, line the mold.

FIGURE 11.2. **Lining a mold with aspic jelly.**
(a) Bury the mold up to the rim in crushed ice.

(b) Fill the mold with cooled liquid aspic.

(c) After ten seconds, quickly but smoothly pour out the aspic that is still liquid.

(d) An even layer of aspic jelly lines the mold, as can be seen by comparing it with an empty mold.

(e) The mold can be decorated at this point by dipping vegetable cutouts in liquid aspic and carefully setting them in place in the mold.

If a mold must be lined with a perfectly even thickness of jelly, the following method is used (see Figure 11.2):

1. Press the mold into a bed of crushed ice so that the ice comes all the way to the top edge.

2. Fill the mold with cooled liquid aspic jelly. Leave the mold in place for 10 seconds. Immediately remove the mold from the ice and quickly dump out the jelly that is still liquid. If the layer of jelly remaining inside the mold is too thin, repeat. If it is too thick, remove it, clean the mold, and repeat the procedure, leaving the mold on ice for less time.

3. Decorate the inside of the mold as desired, by dipping decorations in liquid aspic and then arranging them in place. Chill. Then fill the mold with the selected food product.

SPECIAL FORCEMEAT DISHES

This section is concerned with classic meat and poultry dishes called pâtés, terrines, and galantines. There are terrines based on vegetables and other items rather than meats, but they are the subject of a later section. The main ingredients of the items discussed here are a *forcemeat* and, usually but not always, a *garnish*.

A forcemeat may be defined as a mixture of seasoned, ground meats used as a stuffing or filling. The name comes from the French word *farce*, which means stuffing.

The garnish in a pâté or terrine is not just a decoration, but a major ingredient that adds body, flavor, and nutritional value as well as appearance.

Garnish usually consists of meats or other foods cut in dice, strips, or other shapes, or left whole if they are small. Classic pâté garnishes include:

Ham
Veal
Chicken, duck, or turkey breast
Chicken, duck, or goose livers
Foie gras
Game
Fresh pork fatback
Tongue
Pistachios
Truffles

Basic Forcemeats

A forcemeat, as defined above, is a mixture of seasoned, ground meats. As such, it is basically a form of sausage meat, except that the grind is generally, but not always, finer. Consequently, many of the guidelines for making and handling sausage meat, discussed in Chapter 9, apply here as well. It may be helpful to read or to review pages 430–432 in conjunction with the following discussion of forcemeats.

Basic forcemeat consists of the following:

50 to 65 percent lean meat
35 to 50 percent fat
Seasonings

There are many variations on this basic formula, depending on the ingredients used and how they are combined.

Meat. Pork is the basic ingredient, but many other meats can be included in addition to or instead of pork, including veal, chicken, turkey, ham, duck, rabbit, and game of all kinds.

Liver. Chicken, goose, duck, or pork liver is often included in forcemeats. They give flavor and also act as a binder.

Fat. Equal parts fat and meat are classic proportions. Many forcemeats, however, contain less than 50 percent fat, especially in recent years as people have become more attentive to nutrition and dietary considerations (see the discussion of the fat content of sausages on page 430). Nevertheless, a certain amount of fat is necessary for both moisture and flavor. A pâté with too little fat tastes dry. Hard fat, such as pork fatback, gives best results. Heavy cream is sometimes used to add fat as well as liquid to a forcemeat.

Note that this discussion of fat content refers only to the solid fat specifically added as a measured ingredient. There is, of course, some fat in the lean meat as well.

Other Ingredients. Eggs or egg whites may be added as binders. Flour or other starches may be added for the same purpose. Extra binders are not absolutely necessary in a forcemeat made up purely of meat and fat because the meat proteins are sufficient to bind the product when cooked. On the other hand, when brandy, cream, and other liquids are added to the forcemeat, extra binders may be needed or may at least be beneficial.

The Grind. Forcemeat may be ground coarse, medium, or fine. Country-style pâté, or *pâté de campagne* (pronounced "cawm pah nyuh"), is characterized by a coarse texture. Galantines, on the other hand, are usually made from finely ground forcemeats.

Preparing Forcemeats. As discussed here, many if not most pâté and terrine forcemeats contain some liver. Chicken livers or other poultry livers, both economical and widely available, are the most often used. For the best results, livers should be soaked in milk and then cleaned according to the following procedures. Pork liver or other larger livers can be cut into pieces and then prepared in the same way.

Procedure for Preparing Poultry Livers for Forcemeats

1. Rinse the livers in cold water, drain, then soak for 24 hours in enough milk to cover.
2. Drain and rinse thoroughly in cold water. Drain again.
3. Remove all fat and connective tissue. At this point, the livers are ready to be used whole as garnish for pâtés and terrines. If they are to be added to forcemeats, continue with steps 4 and 5.

4. Blend in a blender until liquid.

5. Strain through a fine china cap or strainer to remove all traces of connective tissue.

The following recipe can be used with many different garnishes to make a great variety of pâtés, terrines, and galantines. It can also be changed according to any of the variations listed by using different meats. Once the basic technique is understood, any kind of pâté can be produced.

The recipe should be viewed as a basic procedure that can be varied in ways other than those indicated following the recipe, just as sausage meat can be varied. The varieties and quantities of spices can be changed. In addition, the fineness of the grind can be varied to make pâtés of varying textures.

The proportion of fat can be increased or reduced, but remember that making the forcemeat too lean will reduce its eating quality. Although at first glance, the recipe looks as if it calls for 50 percent fat, this is not the case, since the liver should be included as part of the meat; the proportion of fat is 44 percent. Taking the first column of ingredients as an example, using 1 lb lean pork, 12 oz fat, and 4 oz liver lowers the proportion of fat to 38 percent (not counting, of course, the smaller amount of fat within the meats). Using 12 oz lean pork, 1 lb fat, and 4 oz liver raises the fat proportion to 50 percent.

BASIC PORK FORCEMEAT

		U.S.		Metric	
YIELD:		**2 lb**	**8 lb**	*900 g*	*3.6 kg*
Ingredients					
Lean pork		14 oz	3 lb 8 oz	*400 g*	*1.6 kg*
Fresh pork fat		14 oz	3 lb 8 oz	*400 g*	*1.6 kg*
Marinade (see note 1):					
*Shallots, minced		1 ½ oz	45 g	*6 oz*	*175 g*
*Butter		½ oz	2 oz	*15 g*	*60 g*
*White wine		2 oz	8 oz	*60 ml*	*2.5 dl*
*Bay leaves		2	8	*2*	*8*
*Brandy		1 oz	4 oz	*30 ml*	*125 ml*
Salt		2 ½ tsp	12 g	*1 ½ oz*	*50 g*
Pâté spice or quatre épices (see note 2)		½ tsp	2 tsp	*1 g*	*5 g*
White pepper		¼ tsp	1 tsp	*0.5 g*	*2 g*
Chicken livers, soaked, cleaned, and puréed, (see p. 566)		4 oz	1 lb	*100 g*	*400 g*
Eggs (see Procedure, step 6)		2	8	*2*	*8*

Note 1: Marinating the meats before grinding is optional, but beneficial. For a simpler procedure and less complex flavor, omit the ingredients marked with an asterisk (*), omit steps 3 and 4 in the procedure, and add the salt and spices as indicated in step 6.

Note 2: Pâté spice may be purchased in various blends, or you may make your own blend to taste. Pâté spice usually contains black and white pepper, cloves, nutmeg, ginger, cayenne, bay leaf, thyme, and marjoram. Grind very fine and sift through a sieve. For quatre épices, see page 438.

Procedure:

1. Before beginning, make sure that all equipment and all ingredients are well chilled. Forcemeats must be kept cold at all times to prevent the fat from softening or melting.
2. Cut the fat and meat into small dice. If the meat is to be marinated, continue with step 3. If not, skip directly to step 5.
3. Sweat the minced shallots in the butter until soft. Add *one-half* the white wine and reduce by half. Cool completely.
4. Combine the meat and fat with the shallots, the rest of the wine, the brandy, bay leaves, salt, spice, and pepper. Toss to mix well. Cover and refrigerate it overnight.
5. Remove the bay leaves. Grind the meat and fat twice through the fine blade of a meat grinder.
6. Combine the ground meats, liver purée, and—if the meats were not marinated—the salt, spice, and pepper. Beat the eggs lightly and mix in thoroughly. *Note:* The eggs are optional and are omitted in many pâtés.
7. Make a quenelle (a small ball of forcemeat) and poach in simmering water. Cool. Taste and correct the seasonings.
8. Keep the forcemeat chilled until ready to use.

Variations

Omit the *fat, pork, livers, and eggs* in the basic recipe. In place of them, substitute the following ingredients and quantities. Seasonings may be varied to taste.

Veal Forcemeat

Lean pork	9 oz	2 lb 4 oz	*250 g*	*1 kg*
Lean veal	9 oz	2 lb 4 oz	*250 g*	*1 kg*
Fresh pork fat	14 oz	3 lb 8 oz	*400 g*	*1.6 kg*
Eggs	3	12	*3*	*12*

Chicken Forcemeat I

Lean pork	9 oz	2 lb 4 oz	*250 g*	*1 kg*
Chicken meat	9 oz	2 lb 4 oz	*250 g*	*1 kg*
Fresh pork fat	14 oz	3 lb 8 oz	*400 g*	*1.6 kg*
Eggs	3	12	*3*	*12*

Chicken Forcemeat II

Chicken meat	1 lb 2 oz	4 lb 8 oz	*500 g*	*2 kg*
Fresh pork fat	14 oz	3 lb 8 oz	*400 g*	*1.6 kg*
Eggs	3	12	*3*	*12*

Duck, Pheasant, or Game Forcemeat

Lean pork, or mixture of pork and veal	7 oz	1 lb 12 oz	*200 g*	*800 g*
Duck, pheasant, or game meat	7 oz	1 lb 12 oz	*200 g*	*800 g*
Fresh pork fat	14 oz	3 lb 8 oz	*400 g*	*1.6 kg*
Livers, soaked, cleaned, and puréed	4 oz	1 lb	*100 g*	*400 g*
Eggs	1	8	*1*	*8*

Terrines and Pâtés

Terrines and pâtés are baked forcemeats, often but not always containing one or more types of garnish. Strictly speaking, the difference between the two lies in how they are baked. By definition, a *terrine* is baked in an earthenware dish; the dish itself is also called a terrine, a name that is derived from the French word *terre*, meaning "earth." Today other materials besides earthenware, such as glass or metal, may be used for terrines. Terrines may be presented in their baking dish, or they may be unmolded.

A *pâté* is, by definition, baked in a crust. The word *pâté* (with an accent on the *e*) is derived from the word *pâte* (without the accent), meaning "pastry." Today, however, the word *pâté* is often used for various terrines baked without a pastry crust. To avoid confusion, the term *pâté en croûte* is then used to specify a pâté with a crust. In this book, the terms *terrine* and *pâté* are used in their traditional, literal senses.

It should be noted that many different kinds of products are called terrines because they are prepared in terrine molds. The terrines discussed in this section are those based on the forcemeats that we have just considered. Other kinds of terrines are discussed in a later section.

Preparing Pâtés. The essential difference between a pâté and a terrine is the crust. Although a heavy pastry crust may not be suitable for all kinds of terrine mixtures, the typical baked forcemeat-type terrine under consideration here can usually be made with or without a crust.

This section concentrates on the specific procedures for making the pastry and finishing the assembled pâté. Making the meat filling is the same as for terrines and is not repeated here. To make a pâté en croûte, apply the following procedure to the Veal and Ham Terrine or to any of the variations following the basic recipe (see pages 576–577).

Pastries used to enclose pâtés are of various types, but the most commonly used are similar to pie pastries but sturdier. A recipe for this type of *pâte à pâté*, or pâté pastry, is included here. Its advantage over many other types of pâté pastry is that it is relatively good to eat. Some authorities argue about whether the dough around a pâté is intended to be eaten. But since not everyone may be aware of this argument, it is best to use a pastry that will be reasonably pleasing to eat.

Traditional English pâtés, or raised meat pies, use a hot water pastry that can be modelled like clay and that is very sturdy when baked. Pastries used for display, that is, for show platters not intended to be eaten, are also made to be very sturdy and easy to handle. These pastries are not considered here.

The procedure for assembling a pâté follows the pastry recipe and is illustrated in Figure 11.3.

PÂTÉ PASTRY (PÂTE À PÂTÉ)

		U.S.		Metric	
	YIELD:	**1 lb 12 oz**	**7 lb**	*900 g*	*3.6 kg*
Ingredients					
Flour		1 lb	4 lb	*500 g*	*2 kg*
Butter		4 oz	1 lb	*125 g*	*500 g*
Lard		3 ½ oz	14 oz	*100 g*	*400 g*
Eggs		1	4	*1*	*4*
Cold water		3 oz	12 oz	*1 dl*	*4 dl*
Salt		1 ¼ tsp	1 oz	*7 g*	*30 g*

Procedure:

1. Place the flour in a large mixing bowl. Add the butter and lard. Rub them in until no lumps of fat remain.
2. Beat the eggs with the water and salt until the salt is dissolved.
3. Add the liquid to the flour mixture. Mix gently until it is completely absorbed.
4. Gather the dough into a ball. On a work surface, knead the dough for a few minutes until it is smooth.
5. Place the dough in pans and cover with plastic film. Refrigerate until needed, or at least 4 hours.

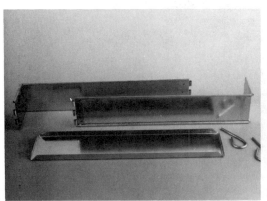

FIGURE 11.3. **Making a pâté en croûte.**
(a) Collapsible molds are used to make pâtés en croûte so that they can be removed from the mold without damage. Assemble the mold and grease the inside well.

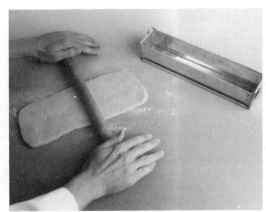

(b) Lightly roll out the pastry into a rectangle, keeping it thick.

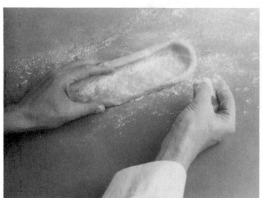

(c) Work the dough into a boat shape. Dust the inside heavily with flour and fold the dough lengthwise to make a pocket.

(d) Roll out the double thickness of dough into a rectangle the size of the mold. Open the pocket.

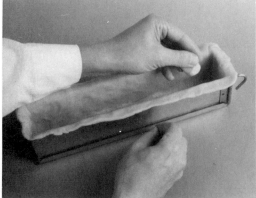

(e) Fit the dough into the mold. Carefully work the dough to fit snugly inside the mold. A ball of dough dipped in flour helps to fit the dough into the corners without tearing it.

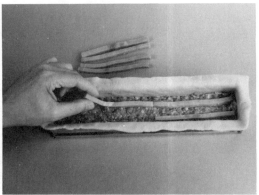

(f) Fill the mold partially with forcemeat and arrange the garnish according to the instructions in the specific recipe.

FIGURE 11.3. (Continued)
(g) Finish filling the mold, mounding the force-meat slightly.

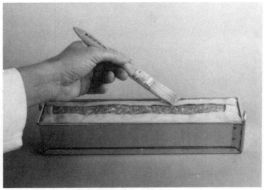

(h) Fold over the rim of dough. Lay the pastry for the top on the mold, cut it to size, and remove it again. Brush the rim of dough with egg wash. (A variation of this procedure is used for show pieces—see the accompanying text.)

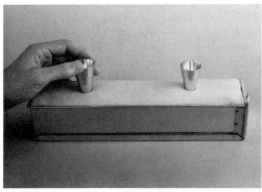

(i) Fit the top pastry in place and make sure it is sealed to the rim of dough below it. Make holes in the top and fit pastry tubes in them to serve as chimneys to allow the escape of steam and to prevent melted fat from bubbling over the top crust as the pâté bakes.

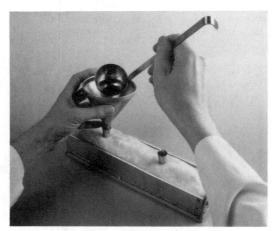

(j) After the pâté has baked and cooled, pour cooled liquid aspic through the chimneys to fill the spaces left when the forcemeat shrank during baking. Chill the pâté.

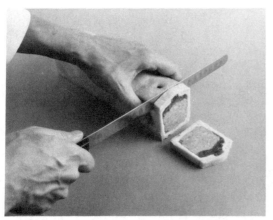

(k) Using a thin-bladed slicing knife, slice the pâté with smooth, steady strokes.

572

Procedure for Lining and Filling Pâté Molds and Finishing Pâtés

1. Prepare the pastry in advance so that it has plenty of time to rest. Remove it from refrigeration long enough ahead of time to allow it to warm up slightly.

2. Prepare the molds by greasing them well on the inside. The directions here pertain to standard rectangular pâté molds. These usually are hinged and collapsible, so that it is easy to remove the pâté without damaging it. If you are using bottomless molds, then also grease the sheet pans on which they are to set. For molds of other shapes, modify the pastry-molding procedure as necessary to fit the shape.

3. For best results, mold the pastry so that it is of even thickness, has no seams, and fits the mold perfectly. First, work the pastry with the hands for a few seconds to make it pliable. Then shape it into a rectangle and roll it slightly with a rolling pin to flatten it, keeping it quite thick.

4. Make an indentation down the center of the dough with the fingers, gradually making a sort of boat shape. Dust the inside of the dough shape well with flour (to keep the two layers of dough from sticking together) and fold the dough along the indentation to make a pocket.

5. Gently roll out the dough to make a rectangle the size of the mold. Be careful not to roll the dough too thin, which would make it fragile. Open up the pocket.

6. Fit the opened pocket into the mold. Carefully mold the pastry to the shape of the mold by pushing the dough with your fingers. Make sure that there are no air bubbles between the dough and mold. A ball of dough dipped in flour is useful to push the dough into the corners of the mold without tearing the dough.

7. If the pâté is to be made without a top crust, trim off the excess dough, leaving a rim of dough about ¼ inch (5 mm) above the top of the mold. Crimp this rim to make a decorative border.

   If there is to be a top crust, leave a rim of about ¾ inch, and let it hang over the sides of the mold. (For display pieces, see the note at the end of step 9. For an alternative method, see step 10.)

8. The mold is now ready to fill. For display pieces, it is common practice to line the inside of the dough with thin sheets of fatback. For pâtés to be eaten, however, it is more appetizing to omit the fat lining. Fill the mold with the desired forcemeat and garnish, as for terrines (see page 574). Mound the filling slightly so that the top crust, if used, will have an attractive domed shape. The dough should hold this shape even as the forcemeat shrinks and settles during baking.

   If the pâté is not to have a top crust, it is now ready for baking; skip to step 12. Baking without a top crust is easier, and allows you to make an attractive aspic glaze with decorations for the top.

9. Fold the rim of the dough from the sides of the mold over the top of the filling. Roll out a sheet of dough for the top crust, if used. Lay the sheet of dough on top of the mold and trim it to size. Remove it, brush the edges of dough from the sides of the mold with egg wash, then return the pastry top to the mold and fit it in place, gently sealing it to the eggwashed dough.

   Note: For display pieces, it is common practice to leave a larger rim of dough (see step 7), which is folded over the forcemeat and trimmed so that the sides meet in the center. The top crust is then fitted in place. This method results in a thicker top crust, but one that is of uniform thickness.

10. As an alternative method for fitting the top crust, leave a ¼-inch (5-mm) rim of dough as in step 7. Brush the inside of this rim with egg wash. Roll out and cut

a top crust slightly larger than the top of the mold. Place on top of the filled mold. Crimp or pinch the two layers of pastry together with the fingers to seal.

11. Decorate the top crust with pastry cutouts, if desired. Seal them to the crust with egg wash. Make one or two vent holes in the top crust to allow the steam to escape. Fit pastry tubes into these holes to form chimneys in order to keep juices from running over the top crust and spoiling its appearance.

12. Preheat an oven to 400°F (200°C). Place the pâté on a sheet pan (if you are using a bottomless mold, it will, of course, already be on a sheet pan). After 10 minutes, reduce the heat to 350°F (175°C); the higher initial temperature helps to brown the pastry. Bake at this lower temperature until the internal temperature reaches 160° to 165°F (72°C). For an average rectangular mold, the baking time will be about 1 to 2 hours. Small molds that make 1 to 4 portions will take 45 minutes or less. For very large molds, use a baking temperature of 325°F (160°C) so that they will cook evenly; extend the baking time accordingly.

13. Remove from the oven and let the pâté cool to room temperature in its mold. For a pâté made without a top crust, first let it cool until it is warm. Then let it finish cooling with a weight on top in order to give the pâté a firmer texture. The weight should be large enough to cover the meat but small enough so that it doesn't touch the pastry rim. This can be accomplished by cutting a board to the proper size, laying it in place on the pâté, and placing the weights on the board. (Obviously, this cannot be done if there is a top crust.)

14. When the pâté is cool, prepare an aspic jelly; melt it and flavor it, if desired, with a little sherry, port, or madeira wine. Cool it according to the procedure on page 562. Fill the pâté with the aspic. If it has a pastry top, pour the aspic through the vent hole or holes, using a funnel, until the pâté is completely full. If it has no top crust, fill it with enough aspic to completely cover the top of the meat. Refrigerate until the aspic is set.

15. Remove the pâté carefully from the mold.

16. Pâtés without a top crust may now be decorated and reglazed with aspic if desired. Decorate as desired (using the materials suggested on page 563) by dipping the decorations in liquid aspic and setting them in place. Chill briefly and then apply a little more aspic to glaze the top.

17. For storage, handling, and presentation, see page 557.

Preparing Forcemeat Terrines. Terrines, like pâtés, may be baked in molds of various shapes and sizes. Traditional oval molds, for example, have long been popular. For ease of portion control, however, rectangular molds are the most appropriate.

A terrine may be lined with thin sheets of fatback, although this is optional. The layer of fat does not contribute significantly, as is widely believed, to keeping the meat moist during baking; after all, the terrine itself is more moisture proof than the layer of fat. Although such a fat lining is traditional, today's diners are more likely to find a rim of fat unappetizing. Of course, this layer of fat can be removed before serving. Alternatively, a sheet of caul fat (see page 415), which is much thinner than a sheet of fatback, can be used to line the mold.

Procedure for Preparing Forcemeat Terrines

1. Prepare the desired forcemeat (see pages 565–569).

2. Prepare the selected garnish. Meat garnishes are usually cut into strips, which will be laid lengthwise in the mold.

3. Marinate the garnish as desired. This step is optional but adds to the flavor.

4. Prepare the mold. Do not use a hinged or collapsible mold, which cannot be placed in a water bath. If desired, line the mold with thin sheets of fatback (sliced on a slicing machine) or with a sheet of caul fat, letting the excess hang over the sides. Make the sheets of fat sufficiently large so that the amount of fat hanging over the sides can be folded over to cover the top completely. If the mold is not lined with fat, grease it well.

5. Place a layer of forcemeat in the bottom of the mold (or, if no garnish is used, simply fill the mold). Spread the forcemeat evenly and rap the mold sharply on the workbench to dislodge any air bubbles.

6. Arrange a layer of garnish on top of the forcemeat.

7. Continue adding forcemeat and garnish until they are all used, ending with a layer of forcemeat on top. Two or three layers of garnish are usually sufficient.

8. If a fat lining has been used, fold the excess fat over the top of the forcemeat to cover it.

9. Cover the top with a sheet of aluminum foil, but cut a few holes in the foil to allow steam to escape.

10. Place the mold in a water bath that is deep enough to allow the hot water to come halfway up the sides of the mold. Bake at 350°F (175°C) until the internal temperature registers 165°F (74°C).

11. Remove the terrine from the water bath and place it on a rack to cool. When it has cooled somewhat but is still warm, finish cooling it with a weight, as explained in the procedure for making pâtés. It should not be weighted when it is still hot, because it is too fragile when hot and may split or fracture, and the weight may force out too much juice. If a looser texture is desired, cool the terrine without weighting it.

12. When the terrine is completely cool, cover and refrigerate it.

13. The terrine may be sealed with a layer of fat or aspic. These protect the terrine from air and help preserve it.

    a. To add a layer of fat, melt lard (or rendered duck fat or other fat appropriate to the terrine), then let stand until cool but still liquid. The terrine should be cool, about 50°F (10°C). Pour in enough fat to cover the meat completely. Let stand until the fat has congealed, then cover and refrigerate. The purpose of this fat is only to extend the keeping qualities of the terrine. It should be removed before serving.

    b. Add aspic to a terrine in the same way as adding a layer of fat; see also the procedure for adding aspic to a pâté, page 574. Unlike melted fat, aspic extends the storage life of a terrine only a few days because the aspic itself will dry out. On the other hand, aspic contributes to both flavor and appearance. If desired, apply decorations to the top of the terrine and add another layer of aspic to glaze.

VEAL AND HAM TERRINE

	U.S.		Metric	
YIELD (APPROXIMATE):	**2 lb**	**8 lb**	*1 kg*	*4 kg*

Ingredients

Veal Forcemeat (p. 569)	2 lb	8 lb	*1 kg*	*4 kg*
Garnish:				
Veal, lean, trimmed	4 oz	1 lb	*125 g*	*500 g*
Smoked ham	4 oz	1 lb	*125 g*	*500 g*
Fresh pork fatback	1 oz	8 oz	*60 g*	*250 g*
Brandy	2 oz	8 oz	*60 ml*	*2.5 dl*

Fresh pork fatback or caul fat for lining
  molds (optional)

Procedure:

1. Prepare the forcemeat according to the recipe on page 568. Refrigerate it until it is very cold.

2. Cut the veal, ham, and fatback for the garnish into strips about ¼ inch (6 mm) thick. Mix with the brandy and marinate in the refrigerator for one hour or longer.

3. For each 2 lb (1 kg) of forcemeat, have ready a 2-qt (1-l) rectangular terrine mold.

4. If using fatback to line the molds, have the fat very cold. Cut it on a slicer into broad, thin slices, less than ⅛ inch (3 mm) thick. Line the mold with the slices, overlapping them by about ¼ inch (5 mm). Let the tops of the slices hang over the edge.
   If using caul fat, line the molds with large sheets of caul, letting the edges of the sheets hang over the edge of the mold.
   If not using caul or fat to line the mold, grease the mold well.

5. Fill the terrine with alternating layers of forcemeat and garnish, beginning and ending with a layer of forcemeat, and laying the strips of garnish lengthwise in the terrine. Press the meat firmly into the terrine so that there are no air bubbles.

6. If using sheets of fat to line the mold, fold the overhanging fat over the top of the forcemeat to cover.

7. Cover with foil.

8. Set the terrine in a hot water bath. Bake at 350°F (175°C) until the internal temperature is 165°F (74°C).

9. Remove from the oven and cool thoroughly. Refrigerate overnight.

10. Remove from the terrine mold and remove all fat. Slice and serve, or return to the terrine, fill the terrine with aspic, and serve from the terrine.

Variations

Veal and Ham Terrine with Foie Gras

Prepare as in the basic recipe, but place a layer of sliced, cooked foie gras down the center of the terrine. Use slices of foie gras terrine (page 600) or canned foie gras pâté. A row of sliced truffles may be placed on top of the foie gras layer.

Veal and Tongue Terrine

Use cooked, cured beef tongue in place of the ham.

Rabbit Terrine

Bone out a rabbit, keeping the loin meat in two long strips. Make a rabbit forcemeat by following the veal forcemeat recipe, but substituting meat from the rabbit legs. Soak, clean, and liquify the rabbit liver according to the procedure on page 566, and add it to the forcemeat. Omit the garnish from the basic recipe, instead using the rabbit loins marinated in the brandy. Fold the thin end of each loin back on itself so that it is of uniform thickness. When filling the terrine, put half the forcemeat in the mold, lay the loins end to end down the center of the terrine, then fill with the remaining forcemeat.

   Optional step: Make a stock with the rabbit bones. Reduce the stock to a glaze, cool, and mix with the forcemeat.

   Optional step: Add a small quantity of nuts, such as skinned pistachios, to the forcemeat.

Game Terrine

Prepare as in the basic recipe, using Game Forcemeat (page 569), and using strips of game meat instead of the veal and ham for garnish. Optional: Add a small quantity of green peppercorns, rinsed and drained, to the forcemeat.

Duck Terrine

Bone out a duck (or several ducks, depending on the quantity being produced). Use the leg meat and any trimmings for making Duck Forcemeat (page 569), and use the duck liver in the forcemeat. Flavor the forcemeat lightly with grated orange zest, using the zest of half an orange for each 2 lb (1 kg) of forcemeat. If desired, flavor the forcemeat with duck stock reduced to a glaze and cooled. Use the breast meat for the garnish, omitting the veal and ham from the basic recipe, but keeping the fatback. Cut the breast meat into strips and marinate in the brandy with the fatback strips.

Country Terrine

Use pork forcemeat, keeping the grind rather coarse. Chop the garnish coarsely and mix with the forcemeat.

Galantines

A *galantine* is a ground meat mixture—that is, a forcemeat, that is wrapped in the skin of the product it is made of, such as chicken or duck. A galantine is almost always poached, although in some occasions it may be roasted.

A galantine is made by rolling up a forcemeat in a large piece of skin, giving the galantine a cylindrical or sausage shape that yields round slices. Consequently, the name galantine is also given to forcemeats or other mixtures (such as mousselines) that are rolled into a sausage shape in a piece of parchment, plastic film, or other material.

A finished galantine is often displayed whole, decorated and glazed with aspic, and with a few slices removed to show a cut cross section. For à la carte service, slices of galantine are served in the same way as slices of pâté and terrine.

The following is a representative recipe for a galantine. The procedure is illustrated in Figure 11.4.

CHICKEN GALANTINE

		U.S.		Metric	
YIELD (APPROXIMATE):		**3 lb**	**12 lb**	*1.25 kg*	*5 kg*
Ingredients					
Roasting chickens, about 5 lb (2.25 kg) each		1	4	*1*	*4*
Brandy		4 oz	1 pt	*125 ml*	*5 dl*
Salt					
White pepper					
Chicken Forcemeat I, p. 569, made with part of the leg meat (see Procedure, step 3)		1 lb	4 lb	*450 g*	*1.8 kg*
Livers from the chickens					
Garnish:					
Leg meat from the chicken		8 oz	2 lb	*225 g*	*900 g*
Smoked ham		2 oz	8 oz	*60 g*	*225 g*
Cured beef tongue, cooked		2 oz	8 oz	*60 g*	*225 g*
Pimientos, rinsed and dried		1 oz	4 oz	*30 g*	*110 g*
Truffles (optional)		1 oz	4 oz	*30 g*	*110 g*
Pistachios, blanched and skinned		2 oz	8 oz	*60 g*	*225 g*

Procedure:

1. One day in advance, prepare the chicken. Cut off the wings at the second joint. Slit the skin of the chicken along the backbone and carefully bone out the chicken, following the procedure on page 283. Be careful not to pierce the skin, and leave the breast meat attached to the skin. Pull the legs and wings out of their skin, leaving the skin intact and attached to the rest of the chicken. Set the legs and wings aside.

2. Trim the skin into a rectangular shape and remove all fat and connective tissue. Spread the skin out on several layers of moistened cheesecloth on a tray, with the skin down and breast meat on top. Pull off the tenderloins in the center of each breast and remove the tendon in each. Butterfly them and lay them over areas of skin that have little or no meat attached. Butterfly the remaining breast meat in thick areas and spread out the meat so that the skin is covered by a relatively uniform thickness of meat. Sprinkle the chicken with salt, white pepper, and *one-half* of the brandy. Cover and marinate in the refrigerator for 24 hours.

3. Remove the meat from the legs, thighs, and wings, and trim away all fat and connective tissue. Set aside enough of the meat to make the forcemeat and garnish. Mix the leg meat for the garnish with the remaining half of the brandy and marinate, refrigerated, for 24 hours. If any leg meat is left, save it for another use.

4. Make stock from the carcass and giblets.

5. Prepare the forcemeat with the ingredients listed in the recipe on page 569. Grind the forcemeat very fine, using a food processor or by passing it three times through the fine blade of a grinder. Keep it cold at all times.

6. Soak, clean, and liquify the livers according to the procedure on page 566. Mix the liver purée with the forcemeat.

7. Cut the chicken leg meat, ham, tongue, pimiento, and truffle into small dice.

8. Mix the diced garnish and the pistachios into the forcemeat until well combined.

9. Drain the brandy from the chicken skin and pat dry with a clean towel.

10. Form the forcemeat into a cylinder about 1 inch (2.5 cm) shorter than the length of the skin. Place the forcemeat on the skin and roll it up with the aid of the cheesecloth.

11. Roll the galantine in the cheesecloth and tie the ends. Then roll the galantine in a sheet of parchment, working to get the roll as smooth as possible. Tie the roll loosely at 2-inch (5-cm) intervals. (This method is used when the galantine must be completely smooth, with no tie marks. For a simpler method, just tie the cheesecloth roll in 3 to 4 places and at the ends.)

12. Poach the galantine slowly in chicken stock until the internal temperature is 160°F (71°C). This will take about 45 to 60 minutes. Retie the galantine, which will have shrunk, and then let it cool completely in the stock.

13. Remove from the stock, unwrap, and decorate as desired.

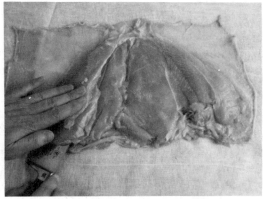

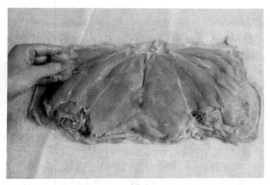

FIGURE 11.4. Making a chicken galantine.
(a) Bone a chicken through the back as in Figure 7.5, removing the legs and wings for use in the forcemeat. Shape the skin into a rectangle and remove the tenderloins from the inner side of the breast. Butterfly the breast meat so that it covers more of the skin with an even thickness of meat.

(b) Butterfly the tenderloins and lay them over uncovered areas of the skin.

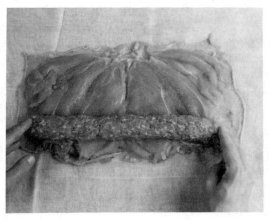

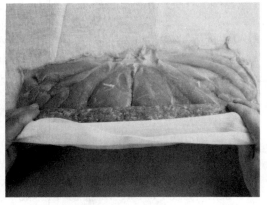

(c) Shape the forcemeat into a cylinder and place it along one edge of the rectangle of chicken as shown.

(d) With the aid of the cheesecloth, roll up the forcemeat in the chicken skin. (Do not roll the cheesecloth into the chicken.)

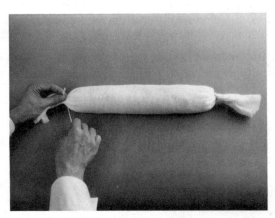

(e) Tie the ends of the cheesecloth securely. Proceed as indicated in the recipe on page 579.

OTHER TERRINES AND MOLDED DISHES

In addition to the baked forcemeat terrines discussed earlier in this chapter, there are several other types of cold dishes made in terrines and other molds. These terrines are generally unmolded and served in slices like traditional forcemeat terrines and pâtés. The ingredients may be arranged in the terrine so as to make an attractive, colorful pattern when the terrine is sliced.

Single-portion molds can also be made using the same techniques and recipes. In this case, the attractive appearance of the dish depends on the shape of the mold, the pattern of ingredients used to line the mold, or the pattern of ingredients suspended in a clear aspic, rather than on the pattern revealed in the slice.

When one first surveys the great variety of terrine recipes created by today's imaginative chefs, it seems that there must be hundreds of types with little relation to each other. In fact, however, the majority of recipes fit into the four basic categories discussed in this section. For the purpose of explaining basic procedures, we will give these four categories the following names:

1. Mousselines
2. Egg mixtures
3. Mousses
4. Aspics

The first two categories are *cooked* terrines. That is, they are cooked after assembly, usually by baking in a water bath. Alternatively, they are sometimes cooked in a steamer. Then they are chilled before serving.

The third and fourth categories are *uncooked* or *chilled* terrines. They are not cooked after assembly, but are chilled until set. Any ingredients that require cooking are cooked before assembly.

The names given here to these groups are not traditional, but they serve to clarify production by emphasizing the primary techniques common to all the recipes in each category. Each of these types is discussed in general terms below. Recipes for terrines that illustrate many of these techniques begin on page 584.

Terrines Based on Mousselines

The body of most fish terrines, as well as some vegetable terrines and other specialty items, consists of a mousseline, also called a mousseline forcemeat. These terrines are made like traditional terrines discussed earlier in this chapter, except that a mousseline takes the place of the traditional ground-meat-and-fat forcemeat.

A mousseline forcemeat, as explained in earlier chapters, consists of raw, puréed fish, poultry, or meat, combined with heavy cream and, usually but not always, eggs or egg whites. Complete procedures and recipes for making seafood and poultry mousselines are included in Chapters 6 and 7 and need not be repeated here (refer to pages 220–222, 259, and 307).

The procedure for assembling and cooking a mousseline terrine is the same as for making a regular forcemeat terrine (see page 574) except that the internal temperature when done is slightly lower, about 158° to 160°F (70°C).

Cooked vegetables, fish fillets, and other appropriate items are used as garnish. Two or more mousselines can be layered in the mold to make multicolored terrines. Alternatively, a mousseline forcemeat can be spread on the bottom and sides of the mold, which is then filled with another mousseline plus garnish, and then topped with a layer of the first mousseline.

Terrines Based on Egg Mixtures

The base mixture for some terrines is made by mixing eggs with puréed or chopped ingredients. Liquids such as stock or cream are often added. These custardlike bases are similar to those used for vegetable timbales, discussed on pages 497–498, except that the mixture must usually be fairly thick in order to support solid garnish and to be firm enough to slice when cooked and cooled. This thicker texture is achieved by eliminating or reducing the amount of cream and other liquids added.

While vegetable purées are most commonly used for this kind of terrine, protein items such as puréed or finely ground cooked meats or soft, smooth cheeses such as ricotta can also be used.

Mousselines, as we have seen, also contain eggs as a binding ingredient. The difference between mousselines and custards is that in mousselines, the egg is used only to help strengthen the binding power of the raw fish or meat proteins. In custard-type bases, on the other hand, egg protein is the only, or at least the primary, binder or coagulating ingredient.

Egg-based terrines are not seen very often, perhaps because they don't seem to be as versatile as the other types. In addition, they can be harder to make because even slight overcooking can break down the egg proteins and ruin the texture of the dish.

Terrines Based on Mousses

A savory cold *mousse*, as used for the base of a terrine, is a preparation of puréed meat, poultry, fish, vegetable, or other food, bound with gelatin and usually lightened with the addition of partially whipped heavy cream. (It is true that the terms *mousse* and *mousseline* are often used more or less interchangeably, but we use them here in two distinct senses in order to avoid confusion.)

The gelatin used to bind or set the mousse may be added in the form of an aspic jelly or as powdered gelatin softened and dissolved in another liquid ingredient.

Because mousses, like aspics, are not cooked after assembly but merely chilled, they are often prepared not only in terrines but in various decorative, irregularly shaped molds. Cooked terrines, on the other hand, are best made in regularly shaped, symmetrical molds so that they will cook uniformly.

The production of mousses is relatively simple. The procedure consists of four main steps:

1. Purée the main ingredient.
2. Add the aspic jelly or dissolved gelatin.
3. Fold in the lightly whipped cream, and season to taste.
4. Pour into the prepared mold.

Molds are usually lined with aspic jelly and decorated, according to the procedures on page 563. As with other kinds of terrines, garnish, if any, is either mixed with the mousse or arranged in the mold as the mousse is added.

Although this method is really little more than mixing together the ingredients in a given order, two precautions must be taken:

1. Carry out the entire procedure, including the pouring of the mixture into the mold, quickly and in one continuous process. If you stop part way through the procedure, the gelatin is likely to set, and you will have a lumpy, poorly mixed product.
2. Do not overwhip the cream. Whip it only until it forms soft mounds. When cream is overwhipped, it breaks and becomes grainy. This same effect can be caused by

the extra beating the cream gets when it is being folded into the mousse mixture. A mousse made with overwhipped cream tastes dry and grainy, not smooth and creamy.

Mousses can also be made without gelatin or other binders. A soft mousse is simply a puréed or ground food with the addition of lightly whipped cream. Although these soft mousses are too soft to be used in terrines, they can be spooned into neat, oval quenelle shapes onto salad plates, garnished attractively, and served as elegant first courses.

Terrines Based on Aspics

Aspic-based terrines are simply glorified gelatin molds. That is, they consist of various solid ingredients held together by gelatin, in the form of aspic jelly.

The proportion of aspic to solids can vary greatly. At one extreme, there may be just enough aspic to hold the solid ingredients together, so that the aspic jelly itself is almost not evident. On the other hand, the aspic may predominate, with various solid ingredients suspended in it at intervals. For this latter type to succeed, the aspic jelly must be of excellent quality, with good flavor, not too firm a texture, and sparkling clarity.

The majority of aspic terrines fall somewhere between these two extremes.

The following general procedure is applicable to the production of most aspic terrines and other aspic molds:

1. *Either* line the mold with aspic, following the procedure on page 563, *or* pour a layer of aspic into the bottom of the mold. Chill until firm.
2. Arrange a layer of garnish in the mold.
3. Add just enough aspic jelly to cover the solid garnish. Chill until firm.
4. Repeat steps 2 and 3 until the mold is full.
5. For best storage, leave the aspic in the mold, covered tightly with plastic film, until service time.

Terrines made by this method depend on a crystal-clear aspic jelly for their appearance and are often very elegant. Another approach is simply to combine the jelly with a mixture of ingredients and fill the terrine with this mixture. A clarified aspic may not be necessary for this method. Terrines made this way range from coarse, peasant-style dishes to more elaborate constructions such as the Lentil and Leek Terrine on page 596.

Headcheese and a number of other commercially made luncheon-meat loaves are examples of this type of terrine. Tripes à la Mode de Caen (page 428), when properly made, can also be chilled until solid and unmolded because it contains enough natural gelatin from the calves foot and other ingredients. Jambon Persillé or Parslied Ham (page 593) is another example of a country-style, aspic-based terrine made with unclarified jelly.

Vegetable Terrines

As awareness of health and nutrition has cut down on the consumption of meat terrines rich in fat, it has also increased the popularity of terrines made with vegetables.

Vegetable terrines do not, however, constitute a separate type of terrine. There are many kinds of vegetable terrines, and most of them are made by the techniques discussed above. For example:

• *Terrines based on mousseline.* A garnish consisting of an assortment of cooked vegetables, bound together with chicken mousseline forcemeat. In addition, chopped vegetables (such as cooked spinach) may also be mixed directly with the mousseline to provide color as well as flavor.

- *Terrines bound with egg.* Vegetable purées or chopped vegetables, bound with egg, layered in a terrine with or without solid vegetable garnish, and baked.
- *Terrines based on mousses.* Vegetable purées forming the base of the mousse, with the possible addition of solid vegetables as garnish.
- *Terrines based on aspic.* An assortment of cooked vegetables bound together with aspic jelly.

Lining Terrine Molds

Uncooked terrines, that is, mousse-based and aspic-based terrines, are usually lined with aspic jelly. In addition, other decorative items can be used to line both cooked and uncooked terrines, both to improve appearance and to add flavor, bulk, and nutritive value. The following are a few suggestions:

Thin slices of vegetables	Crêpes
Leaves of cabbage, spinach, and other leafy vegetables	Slices of smoked salmon (only for uncooked terrines)
Eggplant skin	Thin slices of a different terrine
Sheets of pasta	

For cooked terrines, the mold is greased well before the lining is applied. For uncooked terrines, the preferred method is to coat the mold with a thin layer of aspic before applying the lining.

An alternative method, favored by some chefs, is to line the terrine with plastic film to aid in unmolding. If this method is used for cooked terrines, be sure to use a good, heat-resistant plastic. Plastic lining may not be appropriate for many aspic molds because any small wrinkles in the plastic will show in the surface of the aspic. Besides, aspic molds are easy to unmold without the aid of plastic film by dipping them in hot water and turning the aspic out onto a platter.

TERRINE OF VEGETABLES WITH CHICKEN MOUSSELINE

		U.S.		Metric	
YIELD:		2 lb	8 lb	1 kg	4 kg
Ingredients					
Chicken Mousseline (p. 307)		1 lb 8 oz	6 lb	750 g	3 kg
Chopped parsley		2 tbsp	1 oz	7 g	30 g
Tarragon, fresh, chopped		1 tsp	4 tsp	1 g	4 g
Glace de volaille, melted (optional)		½ oz	2 oz	15 g	60 g
Zucchini, small, trimmed		2 oz	8 oz	60 g	250 g
Red bell pepper, cored and seeded		2 oz	8 oz	60 g	250 g
Carrots, trimmed and pared		2 oz	8 oz	60 g	250 g
Green beans, trimmed		2 oz	8 oz	60 g	250 g
Shiitake mushroom caps		2 oz	8 oz	60 g	250 g

Procedure:

1. Mix the chicken mousseline with the chopped herbs and with the glace de volaille, if used.

2. Trim the zucchini and cut it into strips about ¼ to ½ inch (1 cm) wide. Blanch 2 minutes, drain, and chill.

3. Char and peel the red pepper (see page 521 for procedure). Cut it into strips.

4. Trim and peel the carrots; cut into strips like the zucchini. Blanch 3 minutes, drain, and chill.

5. Trim the green beans; blanch for 1 to 2 minutes, depending on their tenderness.

6. Cut the shiitake caps in half. Blanch for 30 seconds, drain, cool, and pat dry to remove extra moisture.

7. Select appropriate terrine molds. Use a 1½ qt (1.5 l) mold for each 2 lb (1 kg) terrine (smaller or larger molds can be used if the cooking time is adjusted accordingly). Butter the bottom and sides of the molds well.

8. Spread one-third of the mousseline onto the bottom of the mold, being sure to eliminate air bubbles.

9. Arrange the carrots and beans lengthwise in the mold, pushing them partway into the mousseline. Keep the vegetables at least ¼ inch (5 mm) from the sides of the mold (see Figure 11.5).

10. Spread a thin layer of mousseline over the vegetables. Arrange the mushroom caps down the center of the mold, then cover with another thin layer of mousseline. About one-third of the mousseline should be left.

11. Arrange the pepper and zucchini strips lengthwise in the mold, adding a little more mousseline as necessary.

12. Top with the remaining mousseline, again spreading it carefully to avoid air bubbles. Rap the terrine sharply on the work bench to eliminate any remaining air bubbles. Smooth the top of the mousseline with a spatula.

13. Cover tightly with foil and bake in a hot water bath in an oven heated to 325°F (165°C) until set firm, about 1 hour and 15 minutes.

14. Cool thoroughly, then chill well in the refrigerator.

15. Unmold. Slice carefully with a knife dipped in hot water. Serve garnished with a few salad greens and an appropriate cold sauce.

Variations

Instead of the vegetables indicated, select your choice of seasonal vegetables.

For a more luxurious terrine, include some thin slices of truffle with the garnish, or omit the parsley and add some minced truffle to the mousseline.

Fish Terrine with Vegetables

Use a fish mousseline instead of the chicken mousseline. Reduce the number and quantity of vegetables. Add to the garnish some strips of smoked fish, such as smoked salmon, or some fresh fish that has been lightly sautéed until about half cooked.

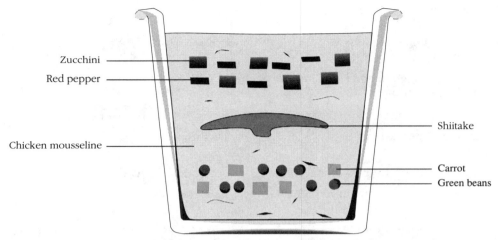

FIGURE 11.5. **Cross-section diagram of Terrine of Vegetables with Chicken Mousseline.**

SALMON TERRINE WITH SWISS CHARD AND POTATO

		U.S.		Metric	
YIELD:		**2 lb**	**8 lb**	*1 kg*	*4 kg*
Ingredients					
Swiss chard leaves, green part only (stems and center ribs reserved for another use)		6 oz	1 lb 8 oz	*175 g*	*700 g*
Potatoes, waxy type		12 oz	3 lb	*375 g*	*1.5 kg*
Heavy cream		6 oz	1 ½ pt	*2 dl*	*8 dl*
Eggs		4	16	*4*	*16*
Salt					
White pepper					
Nutmeg					
Salmon fillets		8 oz	2 lb	*250 g*	*1 kg*
Butter					

Procedure:

1. Blanch the chard leaves until just tender. Drain, rinse under cold water to cool thoroughly, and drain again. Squeeze dry and chop coarsely.

2. Boil or steam the potatoes until tender. Cool. Peel and cut into ¼-inch (6 mm) slices. Reserve the best, most uniform slices, totaling one-third of the potatoes, for garnish and set aside.

3. Put the remaining two-thirds of the potatoes through a food mill to purée. Then combine them in a food processor with the cream and eggs. Process until smooth.

4. Transfer this mixture to a bowl and stir in the chard leaves. Season to taste with salt, white pepper, and nutmeg.

5. Cut the salmon into long, wide strips of uniform thickness.

6. Sauté the salmon lightly in butter until about half cooked. Remove from the sauté pan and pat off excess butter with paper towels.

7. Use a 5-cup (1.25-l) terrine for each 2 lb (1 kg) of mixture. Butter the bottom and sides of the terrine well. (To facilitate unmolding, the terrine may also be lined with a sheet of heat-proof plastic film or a piece of parchment paper cut to fit, after the terrine is buttered.)

8. Pour one-third of the egg mixture into the terrine. Arrange the salmon strips and potato slices in the terrine, alternating layers of potato and salmon with another one-third of the egg mixture. Then fill with the remaining one-third of the egg mixture (see Figure 11.6).

9. Cover with foil. Bake in a hot water bath in an oven heated to 350°F (175°C) until the terrine is set firm, about 1 ½ to 2 hours.

10. Remove from the water bath, cool thoroughly, then chill well. To serve, unmold, slice with a sharp knife dipped in hot water, and plate with an appropriate cold sauce and garnish.

Variations

Line the buttered mold with additional blanched chard leaves. This makes the terrine more attractive if it is to be presented whole.

Spinach may be substituted for the swiss chard.

Lobster Terrine with Swiss Chard and Potato

Omit the salmon. For each 2-lb (1-kg) terrine, steam or boil a 1 ½-lb (700-g) lobster about 4 minutes, until it is about one-half to three-fourths cooked. Cool and remove from shell. Use the tail and claws in place of the salmon for garnish. Purée the rest of the meat with the potatoes, cream, and eggs.

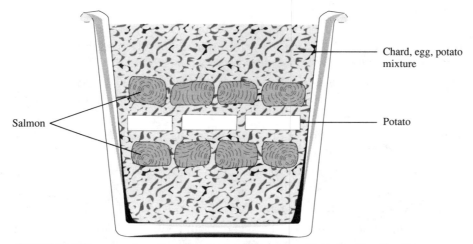

FIGURE 11.6. **Cross-section diagram of Salmon Terrine with Swiss Chard and Potato.**

HAM MOUSSE

		U.S.		Metric	
YIELD:		**2 lb**	**8 lb**	*1 kg*	*4 kg*
Ingredients					
Cooked, lean smoked ham		1 lb	4 lb	*500 g*	*2 kg*
Chicken velouté		5 oz	1 pt 4 oz	*1.5 dl*	*6 dl*
Madeira wine		1 tbsp	2 oz	*15 ml*	*60 ml*
White pepper					
Dry mustard					
Salt					
Gelatin powder		¼ oz	1 oz	*7 g*	*30 g*
Cold chicken stock		4 oz	1 pt	*125 ml*	*5 dl*
Heavy cream		8 oz	2 pt	*2.5 dl*	*1 l*

Procedure:

1. If desired, line a mold or molds with aspic and decorate them according to the procedure on page 563. Keep chilled until needed.

2. Grind the ham until it is very fine.

3. Mix the velouté with the puréed ham. Add the Madeira and season to taste with white pepper, dry mustard, and salt. No salt may be needed if the ham is salty.

4. Soften the gelatin in the cold stock. Heat the stock until the gelatin dissolves, then cool the liquid aspic, but do not let it set.

5. Whip the cream until it forms soft mounds.

6. Add the aspic jelly to the ham mixture and stir until well combined.

7. Quickly and thoroughly fold the cream into the ham mixture. Taste and adjust seasonings if necessary.

8. Fill the prepared molds. Chill several hours or overnight until set firm. Unmold just before serving.

Variations

For a denser but less rich mousse, reduce the quantity of cream as desired.

Substitute prosciutto for one-eighth to one-fourth of the smoked ham.

Instead of velouté, substitute mayonnaise that has been thinned out with cream to the thickness of velouté.

Mousses of other meats, poultry, and fish may be prepared according to the same procedure, substituting an appropriate stock (such as fish stock for fish mousse) and using appropriate seasonings in place of the mustard and Madeira (for example, salmon mousse flavored with dill, cayenne, and white wine).

TRICOLOR VEGETABLE TERRINE

	U.S.		Metric	
APPROXIMATE YIELD:	1 lb 12 oz	7 lb	800 g	3.2 kg
Ingredients				
Spinach	1 lb	4 lb	450 g	1.8 kg
Shallot, minced	¼ oz	1 oz	7 g	30 g
Butter	¼ oz	1 oz	7 g	30 g
Gelatin powder	1 tsp	½ oz	4 g	15 g
Cold chicken stock, vegetable stock, or water	1 oz	4 oz	30 ml	125 ml
Salt				
Heavy cream	2 oz	8 oz	60 ml	2.5 dl
Cauliflower, trimmed	5 oz	1 lb 4 oz	150 g	600 g
White turnips, pared	2 oz	8 oz	60 g	240 g
Gelatin powder	1 tsp	½ oz	4 g	15 g
Cold chicken stock, vegetable stock, or water	1 oz	4 oz	30 ml	125 ml
Salt				
Heavy cream	2 oz	8 oz	60 ml	2.5 dl
Carrots, trimmed and pared	7 oz	1 lb 12 oz	200 g	800 g
Gelatin powder	1 tsp	½ oz	4 g	15 g
Cold chicken stock, vegetable stock, or water	1 oz	4 oz	30 ml	125 ml
Salt				
Heavy cream	2 oz	8 oz	60 ml	2.5 dl

Procedure:

1. Have ready an appropriate mold or molds. Use a 1-qt (1-l) mold for the smaller quantities above. Use either four 1-qt (1-l) or two 2-qt (2-l) molds for the larger quantities. For ease of unmolding, line the molds with plastic film.

2. Trim the stems from the spinach and wash it well in several changes of water. Cook in boiling, salted water until done, about 2 minutes, and drain. Rinse under cold water to cool, and drain. Squeeze dry.

3. Chop the spinach into fine pieces by hand or in a food processor.

4. Sweat the shallots in butter until soft. Add the spinach and cook slowly until quite dry. Cool thoroughly but do not chill.

5. Soften the gelatin in the stock and then heat until it is dissolved. Cool and stir into the spinach. Season with salt.

6. Quickly whip the cream until it forms soft peaks. Immediately fold it into the spinach mixture. Pour it into the mold(s) and smooth with a spatula. Chill until set.

7. Steam the cauliflower and the turnips until they are tender. Purée in a food processor. For the smoothest texture, force the purée through a sieve. Mix the two vegetables together. Heat slowly in a large sauté pan to dry out the purée slightly. Cool thoroughly but do not chill.

8. Repeat steps 5 and 6 to make the white mousse, pour it into the molds on top of the green mousse, and chill.

9. Trim, cook, and purée the carrots in the same way and dry the purée as above. Repeat steps 5 and 6 to make the orange mousse and add it to the terrine (see Figure 11.7).

10. Unmold the terrines and slice to serve. Garnish as desired and serve with an appropriate cold sauce.

Variations

Other vegetable purées may be substituted for those in the basic recipe.

For a low-fat version, omit the gelatin powder, stock, and heavy cream. In place of the stock and cream, use an equal quantity of a strong aspic. Mix the aspic with the vegetable purée.

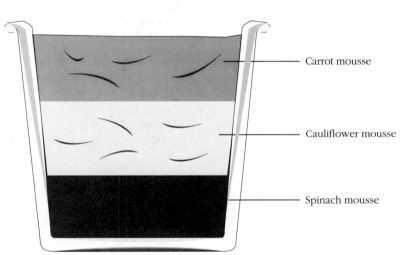

FIGURE 11.7. **Cross-section diagram of Tricolor Vegetable Terrine.**

MOUSSE OF FOIE GRAS

		U.S.		Metric	
YIELD:		**1 lb**	**4 lb**	*500 g*	*2 kg*
Ingredients					
Foie gras (see note)		8 oz	2 lb	*250 g*	*1 kg*
Aspic jelly		4 oz	1 pt	*125 ml*	*5 dl*
Heavy cream		4 oz	1 pt	*125 ml*	*5 dl*
Salt					
White pepper					

Note: See page 598 for a discussion of foie gras. Cooked, not raw, foie gras is called for in this recipe. Terrine of Foie Gras (page 600) may be used. If fresh foie gras products are not available or are too costly, canned foie gras may be used.

Procedure:

1. Force the foie gras through a sieve to purée it.

2. Melt and cool the aspic according to the procedure on page 562. Add it to the foie gras, mixing it in thoroughly.

3. Whip the cream until it forms soft mounds. Quickly and thoroughly fold it into the foie gras.

4. While folding in the cream, taste and adjust the seasonings with salt and white pepper. It is best to do this while folding in the cream so that there is no delay that would allow the gelatin to set too early and so that excess mixing, which may overwhip the cream, is not necessary.

5. Pour at once into a terrine or other mold. Cover tightly and chill at least one day.

6. This dish is very rich and should be served in small quantities, about 2 oz (60 g) per portion. Serve by dipping a spoon into hot water and drawing it across the surface of the terrine, as though scooping ice cream. Place the spoonful in the center of a plate and serve with melba toasts and some raw vegetable garnish or salad greens.

JAMBON PERSILLÉ (PARSLIED HAM IN ASPIC)

	U.S.		Metric	
APPROXIMATE YIELD:	**2 lb**	**8 lb**	*1 kg*	*4 kg*
Ingredients				
Pig feet, split	2	8	*2*	*8*
Onions, each stuck with one clove	1	4	*1*	*4*
Sachet:				
Garlic cloves	1	2	*1*	*2*
Bay leaves	1	2	*1*	*2*
Thyme	½ tsp	2 tsp	*0.5 g*	*2 g*
Tarragon	½ tsp	2 tsp	*0.5 g*	*2 g*
White wine	12 oz	3 pt	*3.5 dl*	*7.5 dl*
White stock, as needed				
Mild-cure ham, in one or more large pieces	1 lb 8 oz	6 lb	*750 g*	*3 kg*
Chopped parsley	½ cup	4 oz	*30 g*	*125 g*
Wine vinegar	½ oz	2 oz	*15 ml*	*60 ml*
Salt and pepper, if needed				

Procedure:

1. Put the pig feet, onions, sachet, and wine in a heavy pot. Add enough white stock to cover. Simmer 2 hours, adding additional stock or water as needed.

2. Add the ham to the pot. Add additional stock as needed. Simmer until the ham is tender. Cooking time will vary greatly, depending on the ham.

3. Remove the ham. Trim off any fat and skin. Dice the ham. Remove any meat from the pig feet, chop it, add it to the ham. Chill the meat.

4. Skim and strain the cooking liquid. The stock may be clarified, if desired, to improve the appearance, but clarification is not necessary if a more rustic look is desired. The feet should have yielded sufficient gelatin, but test it to make sure and add additional gelatin if needed to make a strong aspic; see the procedure on page 559.

5. Melt the aspic (if it has congealed), and add the vinegar and parsley. Taste and add salt and pepper if necessary.

6. Select the desired molds; large salad bowls are traditionally used for this classic dish from Burgundy. Line the bottom of the mold with a thin layer of the parsley aspic. Chill until firm.

7. Combine the ham and aspic and pour into the mold. Chill until set.

8. To serve, unmold and slice. Serve unadorned or plated with some salad greens and vinaigrette.

TERRINE OF VEGETABLES AND CHICKEN IN ASPIC

	U.S.		Metric	
APPROXIMATE YIELD:	2 ½ lb	10 lb	1.1 kg	4.5 kg
Ingredients				
Cooked chicken breast, boneless, skinless	6 oz	1 lb 8 oz	175 g	700 g
Mayonnaise chaud-froid (p. 561)	2–4 oz	8–16 oz	100 g	400 g
Vegetable garnish (as-purchased quantity):				
Carrots	4 oz	1 lb	115 g	450 g
Artichokes, medium	2	8	2	8
Lemons, as needed				
Spinach	8 oz	2 lb	225 g	900 g
Tomatoes, whole, fresh	4 oz	1 lb	115 g	450 g
Green beans	3 oz	12 oz	90 g	350 g
Asparagus	6 oz	1 lb 8 oz	175 g	700 g
Aspic jelly (p. 559) (approximate quantity)	1 pt	4 pt	5 dl	2 l

Procedure:

1. If the chicken pieces are large, cut them in half lengthwise. They should be no more than about 2 or 2 ½ inches (5 to 6 cm) wide. Arrange them on a rack, with the best sides up, and coat them with a thin layer of a well-seasoned chaud-froid sauce (see page 563). Chill until set.

2. Trim and peel the carrots. Cut into long batonnet shapes. Cook the carrots until tender but still firm. Chill.

3. Trim the artichokes down to the bases, rubbing with lemon to keep them from darkening. Cook in water with a little lemon juice until tender. Drain and chill. Cut crosswise into strips about ¼ inch (6 mm) thick.

4. Trim the stems from the spinach and rinse in several changes of water. Blanch, drain, rinse in cold water, and squeeze firmly to remove excess moisture. Chop coarsely.

5. Peel the tomatoes, cut them in half horizontally, and remove seeds and juice. Place them on a cutting board cut side down and slice vertically into slices about ¼ inch (6 mm) thick. Salt the slices lightly and let drain. Dry lightly on clean toweling.

6. Trim the green beans and cook until tender but still firm. Chill.

7. Remove the woody bottoms from the asparagus spears. Peel the lower ends of the spears. Cook until tender but still firm. Chill.

8. Melt and cool the aspic jelly according to the procedure on page 562.

9. Select appropriate terrine molds; for example, use a 1 ½-qt (1.4-l) mold for each 2 ½ lb (1.1 kg) of yield.

10. Either line the mold with aspic according to the procedure on page 563, or else ladle a ¼-inch (6-mm) layer of aspic onto the bottom of the mold. Chill until set.

11. Arrange the carrots and then the spinach in the mold. Add just enough aspic to cover (see Figure 11.8. Note that this diagram shows only the relative positions of the ingredients. The actual proportion of vegetables is greater than shown.). Chill until set.

12. Arrange half of the chicken pieces down the center of the mold, chaud-froid side down. Place the artichokes and beans along side the chicken. Add just enough aspic to cover. Chill until set.

13. Arrange the rest of the chicken, the tomato, and the asparagus in the mold. Add enough aspic to cover. Chill overnight, until set firm.

14. For service, unmold and slice carefully with sharp knife dipped in hot water. Serve with a vinaigrette.

Variations

Substitute other appropriate vegetables in season.

Terrine of Vegetables with Foie Gras in Aspic

Substitute slices of foie gras terrine (page 600) for the chicken. Omit the chaud-froid.

Other items, such as turkey, rabbit, fresh or smoked fish and seafood, can be substituted for the chicken, or omit the protein item entirely and increase the quantity of vegetables.

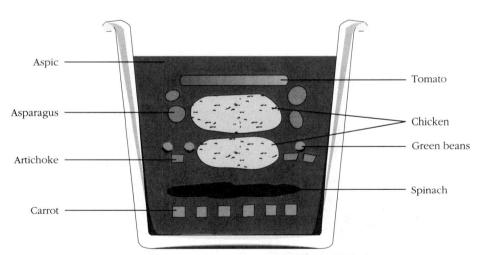

FIGURE 11.8. **Cross-section diagram of Terrine of Vegetables and Chicken in Aspic.**

LENTIL AND LEEK TERRINE WITH SMOKED TURKEY AND PROSCIUTTO

		U.S.		Metric	
APPROXIMATE YIELD:		**2 lb**	**8 lb**	*1 kg*	*4 kg*
Ingredients					
Lentils, preferably green Le Puy variety (see note 1)		5 oz	1 lb 4 oz	*150 g*	*600 g*
Carrots, brunoise		2 oz	8 oz	*60 g*	*250 g*
Medium onion, whole		1	2	*1*	*2*
Cloves		2	4	*2*	*4*
Bay leaves		1	2	*1*	*2*
Leeks, small (approximate quantity; see note 2)		2 lb	8 lb	*1 kg*	*4 kg*
Smoked turkey		6 oz	1 lb 8 oz	*185 g*	*750 g*
Prosciutto, sliced tissue-thin		2 oz	8 oz	*60 g*	*250 g*
Chicken stock		5 oz	1 pt 4 oz	*1.5 dl*	*6 dl*
Gelatin powder		½ oz	2 oz	*15 g*	*60 g*
Salt					

Note 1: Green Le Puy lentils give the best result, as they retain their shape well and have the best appearance.

Note 2: The amount of leeks needed depends on the trimming yield, which can vary greatly. You will need enough trimmed, cooked leeks to cover the top and bottom of the terrine mold. Very small leeks are best, because they cover the top and bottom of the terrine without filling it too much. Larger leeks can be cut in half lengthwise (see Procedure, steps 6 and 8).

Procedure:

1. Soak the lentils several hours or overnight. Drain. Combine with the carrots, the onions stuck with the cloves, and the bay leaves in a heavy pot, and add enough water to cover by several inches. Simmer until tender but still firm and whole. For green lentils, this takes less than 10 minutes. Drain in a fine strainer. Discard the onions, cloves, and bay leaves. Cool the lentils.

2. Trim the root ends and the coarse leaves from the leeks, leaving the lighter green parts attached so that the leeks will be as long as possible. Wash carefully. Steam or simmer until tender. Chill.

3. Cut the turkey into long strips about ½ inch (12 mm) wide. Wrap each strip in a slice of prosciutto.

4. Soften the gelatin in the stock, then heat to dissolve it. Cool the aspic slightly. Because this is a very strong aspic, it should be kept slightly warm or it will solidify too quickly when mixed with the lentils.

5. Mix the aspic with the lentils. Add salt to taste. From this point, the terrine must be assembled quickly so that it is finished before the aspic sets.

6. Select a 1 ¼-qt (1.25-l) terrine for each 2 lb of yield. Line the terrine(s) with plastic film to make unmolding easier. Cover the bottom of the terrine with a layer of leeks arranged lengthwise and end to end. Arrange them tightly against each other so that there are no gaps (see Figure 11.9). If using large leeks, cut them in half lengthwise and arrange in the mold cut side up.

7. Fill the terrine with the lentils, alternating with the turkey strips; arrange the strips lengthwise and at intervals so that they are distributed evenly in the lentils.

8. Top with another layer of leeks, pressing them down firmly and leveling the top. If using large leeks, cut in half lengthwise and place them cut side down on the terrine.

9. Cover and chill overnight, until set firm.

10. Unmold and slice with a sharp knife dipped in hot water. Plate and garnish with a few salad greens. Serve with a vinaigrette, preferably one made with walnut or hazelnut oil.

Variations

Various items can be used instead of the turkey and prosciutto, such as ham, duck breast cooked rare, or loin of rabbit.

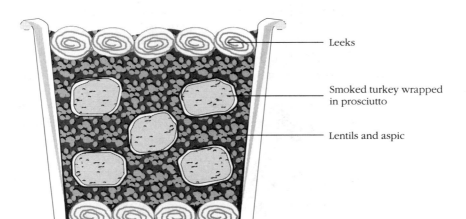

FIGURE 11.9. **Cross-section diagram of Lentil and Leek Terrine with Smoked Turkey and Prosciutto.**

FOIE GRAS, LIVER TERRINES, AND RILLETTES

The chapter concludes with three traditional terrines that require somewhat different techniques from those already discussed. It should be noted that, although these items are especially high in fat and cholesterol, they are as popular as they have ever been, even in these times of diet-consciousness.

Foie Gras Terrines

The most prized and perhaps the most famous ingredient for pâtés and terrines in classical cuisine is *foie gras* (pronounced "fwah grah"). This term in French means "fat liver." Foie gras is the fatted liver of specially fed varieties of ducks and geese. Until recently, only canned or processed foie gras products were available in the United States. Now, however, the breed of duck that is raised to produce foie gras (called the *mullard*, a cross between the muscovy and white pekin ducks) is grown on American farms. Consequently, fresh, raw duck foie gras is now sold in this country. Its availability has created a great deal of enthusiasm among American cooks, in spite of its high price.

The special feeding of the ducks makes the livers very large, more than 1 lb (500 g) as a rule, with a high fat content. A good quality fresh foie gras is a pale yellowish tan color with a smooth, velvety texture, almost the feel of butter. The liver has two lobes, one large and one small. Many chefs like to use the small lobe for slicing and sautéing, and reserve the large lobe for terrines.

It is important to be aware that foie gras consists mostly of fat. Indeed, the rich flavor of the fat is the whole reason that foie gras is so highly prized. Any fat that cooks out during preparation is carefully saved and used for another purpose. Those who must avoid fats, especially animal fats, should probably steer clear of this delicacy. For the rest of us, the high price of foie gras helps to protect our health by making overindulgence unlikely.

There are usually two grades of domestic duck foie gras. The A grade is larger, usually 1 ¼ lb (600 g) or more, with relatively few blemishes and blood spots. The B grade is smaller and has more blood spots and veins.

Preparing Foie Gras for Cooking. No matter how a raw foie gras is to be prepared, it should first be rinsed in cold water and examined closely for green spots. These are caused by bile; they must be cut or scraped away because the bile has a strong, bitter taste. Also, if there are any bits of external fat, remove them.

Next, the liver should be soaked. Place it in lightly salted, ice-cold water or milk to cover, and let stand 2 or 3 hours, no longer. Remove from the salted liquid and rinse in fresh, cold water.

For hot preparations, the liver is now ready for cooking. Usually, the liver is sliced and sautéed quickly in a hot pan. See page 134 for a typical recipe for sautéed foie gras. For cold preparations such as terrines and mousses, the liver should first be deveined. It is possible to skip this procedure, but the veins will detract from both the texture and appearance of the finished product.

To devein the foie gras, first let it come to room temperature. Its fat content makes a cold liver too brittle to devein without excessive breakage, which in turn results in more cooking loss. When the liver is at room temperature, even the heat of the hands melts the fat, so it is important to handle the liver lightly and to work quickly.

Begin by separating the two lobes and laying them, smooth side down, on a clean work surface. Carefully trim off any bloody spots. Grasping a lobe with your thumbs at the sides and fingers underneath in the center, very lightly bend the lobe lengthwise. The top, rough surface should open up slightly, revealing a heavy vein that runs lengthwise through the liver. (If it does not open up, help it along with a shallow incision with the point of a paring knife.) Carefully pull out this vein, along with any other heavy veins that are attached, all the while being careful to keep the liver as intact as possible. Repeat with the other lobe. The foie gras is now ready to be made into a terrine.

No matter how a foie gras is cooked, it is essential to avoid even the slightest overcooking. The liver is very delicate, and the fat cooks out very quickly. Even a few seconds too long in a sauté pan can reduce a slice of foie gras to a few specks of connective tissue floating in a puddle of very expensive grease.

Liver Terrines

Liver terrines, often called liver pâtés, are popular, inexpensive appetizers—except of course for those made with foie gras. The classic liver terrine is a mixture of liquified livers—that is, cleaned, soaked, blended, and strained according to the procedure on page 566—with eggs and seasonings, baked in a terrine until set. An example of this type of recipe can be found on page 602.

This kind of liver terrine generally contains flour as a stabilizer. Because the liver forcemeat is liquid, the flour helps to improve the texture of the cooked product by helping to bind the moisture. Heavy cream is also included in most recipes as a source of fat. Other sources of fat that are sometimes used in addition to or in place of the cream are ground pork fat, ground bacon, marrow, and rendered foie gras fat left over from making terrines.

Another type of liver terrine consists of a basic pork forcemeat with a liver content high enough so that the flavor of the liver predominates. To make this type of terrine, make the forcemeat on page 568, but use six times the quantity of liver. The forcemeat will be quite soft. Follow the basic procedure for making forcemeat terrines (see page 574), using whole, trimmed chicken livers marinated in brandy as the garnish.

A quick and simple substitute for these more elaborate terrines might be considered a type of rillettes (see the next section), since it consists of a seasoned mixture of cooked meat (liver, in this case) and fat. This is the type of "chicken liver pâté" found on delicatessen and coffee-shop menus. To make this type of pâté, sauté some chicken livers, mash or purée them, and mix the purée with about one-eighth its weight in rendered pork fat, soft butter, or other fat, or else with one-fourth its weight in cream cheese. Season as desired, with salt, pepper, herbs, brandy or sherry, and/or sautéed minced onion.

Rillettes

In France's Loire valley, the first thing that customers are likely to be served in a typical neighborhood restaurant, whether they order it or not, is a crock of rillettes and some country bread to spread it on. Variations on this unpretentious dish have become widely popular and are served even in elegant American restaurants.

Rillettes (pronounced "ree yet") is a dish made of pork cooked slowly until it is very tender, shredded, mixed with its own fat, seasoned, and packed into crocks or terrines.

Variations of the classic dish can be made by using other meats in addition to or instead of pork. Items rich in fat, such as duck and goose, are especially appropriate. Rillettes of lean meats, such as chicken, turkey, and rabbit, can be made, but some pork fat or other fat must be added to them when they are cooking.

Some chefs even serve rillettes made from fish such as salmon or cod. The basic procedure is the same, except that the cooking time is, of course, much shorter. The cooked fish is shredded, mixed with just enough butter or other fat to give it a pleasant texture, and seasoned well.

A typical recipe for classic pork rillettes is on page 603. Follow the same basic procedure to make duck rillettes and other variations. A recipe for rillettes made with fish is on page 604.

TERRINE OF FOIE GRAS

		U.S.		Metric	
PORTIONS:		6	24	*6*	*24*
Ingredients					
Fresh, "A" grade duck foie gras, about 1 ½ lb (700 g) each		1	4	*1*	*4*
Salt		1 tsp	4 tsp	*5 g*	*20 g*
White pepper		¼ tsp	1 tsp	*0.5 g*	*2 g*
Choice of wine or liquor: port, Madeira, Sauternes, cognac, or armagnac		½–1 oz	2–4 oz	*15–30 ml*	*60–125 ml*

Procedure:

1. Soak, rinse, and devein the foie gras as described on page 598.

2. Place the liver in a bowl and season with salt and white pepper. Add the selected wine or liquor, using the smaller quantity for cognac or armagnac; if using a sweet wine, use up to but not more than the larger quantity indicated. Turn the livers gently so that all sides are moistened.

3. Cover and refrigerate. Let marinate for 24 hours.

4. Remove the livers from refrigeration about 2 hours before cooking and let them come to room temperature. This is essential to the proper cooking of the terrine.

5. Pack the large lobe or lobes into the selected terrines, smooth side down. Top with the small lobes, smooth side up. Press the livers in firmly to eliminate air spaces. Cover with foil.

6. Place several folded kitchen towels on the bottom of a roasting pan or other pan used as a hot water bath. (This helps to insulate the terrine from strong bottom heat.) Place the terrine or terrines in the pan and add *warm, not hot, water* to come halfway up the sides of the terrine.

7. Place the terrine in an oven preheated to 200° to 215°F (100°C). Bake until the proper doneness, as determined by an instant-read thermometer (see the following paragraph). Depending on the size of the terrine, this will take from 45 minutes to a little over an hour.

    The terrine is done when the thermometer reads from 113°F (45°C) to 130°F (54°C). At the lower end of this range, the cooled terrine will be rather pink in the center, with a soft, creamy texture. At the higher end of the range, the terrine will be firmer and less pink, but more fat will have cooked out, resulting in a lower yield. The right degree of doneness is a matter of personal preference.

8. Remove the terrine from the hot water bath and set on a rack to cool. After it has cooled for about 10 minutes, weight it down with a board that just fits inside the top of the terrine, or with another terrine, and several pounds of weights. When the terrine is almost cool but the fat is still liquid, pour off all melted fat and juices. Separate and discard the juices. Reserve the fat. Put the weights back on the terrine and continue to cool.

9. When the terrine is cold, unmold it and remove and discard any bits of blood or juice on the bottom of the foie gras. Clean out the mold and put the foie gras back in it. Heat the reserved fat just until it is melted and pour it over the terrine. Refrigerate until cold, then cover the terrine tightly and store in the refigerator for 3 to 5 days so that the flavors can develop.

10. To unmold, dip the terrine in warm water for a few seconds, then invert the terrine on a platter or cutting board. Slice with a sharp knife dipped in hot water before each slice. Serve with a little chopped aspic and toasted brioche, or else with some salad greens and a mild vinaigrette made with walnut oil.

CHICKEN LIVER TERRINE

		U.S.		Metric	
YIELD:		**2 lb**	**4 lb**	*1 kg*	*2 kg*
Ingredients					
Chicken livers		1 lb	2 lb	*500 g*	*1 kg*
Heavy cream		8 oz	1 pt	*2.5 dl*	*5 dl*
Eggs, lightly beaten		5	10	*5*	*10*
Flour		2 oz	4 oz	*60 g*	*125 g*
Salt		2 tsp	4 tsp	*10 g*	*20 g*
White pepper		½ tsp	2 tsp	*1 g*	*2 g*
Brandy		1 ½ oz	2 oz	*50 ml*	*1 dl*
Optional: caul fat or thin slices of pork fatback for lining the mold					

Procedure:

1. Soak, rinse, liquify, and strain the livers, following the procedure on page 566.

2. Mix in the remaining ingredients until smooth. If necessary, strain to eliminate lumps.

3. If possible, cover and refrigerate this mixture overnight. This helps eliminate air bubbles that may have gotten mixed in and allows the flour to absorb moisture.

4. Line a terrine mold with caul or fatback, or else grease it very generously with butter or lard.

5. Cover with foil. Bake in a water bath at 300°F (150°C) until set. The water in the water bath should come up to the same level as the forcemeat. Cooking time will depend on the size and shape of the terrine; approximate time will be about 2 hours. Check it periodically after about 1 ½ hours, so that it does not overbake.

6. Remove from the water bath and cool on a rack. Refrigerate overnight or longer. Unmold and slice, or serve directly from the terrine.

Variations

Substitute calf liver or pork liver for the chicken liver.

RILLETTES OF PORK

	U.S.		Metric	
APPROXIMATE YIELD:	**1 lb**	**4 lb**	***500 g***	***2 kg***
Ingredients				
Pork butt or shoulder, with fat but without skin and bones	2 lb	8 lb	*1 kg*	*4 kg*
Bay leaves	2	4	*2*	*4*
Thyme	pinch	½ tsp	*pinch*	*0.5 g*
Onions, small, each studded with 2 cloves	1	2	*1*	*2*
Water	2 oz	8 oz	*60 ml*	*2.5 dl*
Salt	1 ½ tsp	1 oz	*7 g*	*30 g*

Procedure:

1. Cut the meat, with all the fat, into large dice.

2. Cut off an ounce or two of the fat and render it slowly in a large, heavy pot. Add the meat and brown it lightly and gently over moderate heat.

3. Add the remaining ingredients. Cover and cook slowly in a low oven or on the range over very low heat, until the meat is very tender. This will take several hours. Check from time to time to see if the meat has become dry. If it has, add an ounce or two of water.

4. Remove the bay leaves, onions, and cloves. Place the contents of the pot in a colander set over a large bowl. Press firmly on the meat, and collect the fat and drippings in the bowl. Separate the fat from the juices; discard the juices or save for another use, and reserve the fat.

5. Pound the meat with a large pestle or mallet, then shred it with two forks until the meat is a mass of fibers and no lumps. This is time-consuming but necessary.

6. Add as much of the rendered fat as desired and mix it well with the shredded meat. Taste and adjust the seasonings.

7. Pack into crocks or terrines and smooth the top. If the rillettes are to be kept for more than a day or two, seal the surface from the air by covering with a layer of melted fat. Refrigerate overnight or longer. Remove the layer of fat before serving.

8. Serve with crusty bread and sour pickles.

Variations

Rillettes of Duck, Goose, Rabbit, Turkey, or Chicken

Substitute any of the above meats for all or part of the pork. Lean meats should be cooked with additional pork fat to supply enough rendered fat to blend with the shredded meat.

RILLETTES OF SALMON, HADDOCK, OR FINNAN HADDIE

		U.S.		Metric	
YIELD:		**10 oz**	**2 lb 8 oz**	*300 g*	*1.2 kg*
Ingredients					
Salmon, haddock, or finnan haddie, skinless and boneless		8 oz	2 lb	*250 g*	*1 kg*
White wine		4 oz	1 pt	*125 ml*	*5 dl*
Butter, unsalted		2 oz	8 oz	*60 g*	*250 g*
Lemon juice		1 tsp	4 tsp	*5 ml*	*20 ml*
Salt					
White pepper					
Hot pepper sauce					
Caviar, for garnish, as desired					

Procedure:

1. Combine the fish and wine in a saucepan or sauté pan. Poach the fish gently just until it is done. Because there is not enough wine to cover the fish, it will be necessary to turn it over occasionally during cooking so that it will cook evenly.

2. Drain the fish and cool completely.

3. Break the fish into small pieces, then mash with a fork until there are no lumps.

4. Soften the butter and then mix it with the fish until uniformly blended. Season to taste with lemon juice, salt, white pepper, and hot pepper sauce.

5. Pack the mixture into small ramekins or crocks for individual service. Chill.

6. Top each portion with a small spoonful of caviar just before serving. Use salmon caviar for salmon rillettes, or any desired caviar for haddock or finnan haddie rillettes.

7. For service, place the ramekin on a small plate lined with a folded napkin or a doily. Arrange some slices of toast or bread on the underliner around the ramekin, or serve the toast on the side.

APPENDIX

1

Basic Recipes

This appendix contains basic recipes referred to in the text or required as components of other recipes.

BASIC WHITE STOCK

		U.S.		Metric	
YIELD:		**1 gal**	**4 gal**	*4 l*	*16 l*
Ingredients					
Bones: chicken, veal, or beef		5–6 lb	20–24 lb	*2.5–3 kg*	*10–12 kg*
Cold water		5–6 qt	5–6 gal	*5–6 l*	*20–24 l*
Mirepoix:					
Onion, chopped		8 oz	2 lb	*250 g*	*1 kg*
Carrot, chopped		4 oz	1 lb	*125 g*	*500 g*
Celery, chopped		4 oz	1 lb	*125 g*	*500 g*
Sachet:					
Bay leaf		½	2	*½*	*2*
Thyme		pinch	½ tsp	*pinch*	*0.5 g*
Peppercorns		⅛ tsp	½ tsp	*0.25 g*	*1 g*
Parsley stems		4	16	*4*	*16*
Whole cloves		1	4	*1*	*4*

Procedure:

1. Cut large bones into 3- to 4-inch (8–10 cm) pieces. Fish and chicken bones don't need to be cut, but whole carcasses should be chopped up.
2. Rinse the bones in cold water. If desired, chicken, beef, and veal bones may be blanched.
3. Place the bones in a stock pot or steam-jacketed kettle and add cold water to cover.
4. Bring the water to a boil and then reduce to a simmer. Skim the scum that comes to the surface.
5. Add the chopped mirepoix and the herbs and spices.
6. Simmer for the recommended length of time: 6 to 10 hours for beef and veal bones, 3 to 4 hours for chicken bones. Do not let the stock boil. Skim the surface as often as necessary during cooking.

7. Skim the surface and strain off the stock through a china cap lined with several layers of cheesecloth.

8. Cool the stock quickly in a cold-water bath.

9. Cover and refrigerate.

BASIC BROWN STOCK

		U.S.		Metric	
YIELD:		**1 gal**	**4 gal**	*4 l*	*16 l*
Ingredients					
Bones: chicken, veal, or beef		5–6 lb	20–24 lb	*2.5–3 kg*	*10–12 kg*
Cold water		5–6 qt	5–6 gal	*5–6 l*	*20–24 l*
Mirepoix:					
Onion, chopped		8 oz	2 lb	*250 g*	*1 kg*
Carrot, chopped		4 oz	1 lb	*125 g*	*500 g*
Celery, chopped		4 oz	1 lb	*125 g*	*500 g*
Tomatoes or tomato purée		8 oz	2 lb	*250 g*	*1 kg*
Sachet:					
Bay leaf		½	2	*½*	*2*
Thyme		pinch	½ tsp	*pinch*	*0.5 g*
Peppercorns		⅛ tsp	½ tsp	*0.25 g*	*1 g*
Parsley stems		4	16	*4*	*16*
Whole cloves		1	4	*1*	*4*

Procedure:

1. Cut large bones into 3- to 4-inch (8–10 cm) pieces.

2. Do not wash the bones. Place the bones in a roasting pan in one layer. Roast in a hot oven (400° to 450° F or 200° to 225° C) until well browned.

3. Remove the bones from the roasting pan and place them in a stock pot and cover with cold water. Bring to a simmer. Skim and continue to simmer.

4. After draining off most of the fat from the roasting pan, brown the mirepoix in the pan.

5. Add the mirepoix, tomato, and other flavorings to the stock pot. Deglaze the roasting pan with water and add this liquid to the stock pot.

6. Simmer for 6 to 10 hours. Do not let the stock boil. Skim the surface as often as necessary during cooking.

7. Skim the surface and strain off the stock through a china cap lined with several layers of cheesecloth.

8. Cool the stock quickly in a cold-water bath.

9. Cover and refrigerate.

FISH STOCK OR FUMET

		U.S.		Metric	
YIELD:		1 gal	4 gal	*4 l*	*16 l*
Ingredients					
Butter		1 oz	4 oz	*30 g*	*125 g*
Mirepoix:					
Onion, chopped fine		4 oz	1 lb	*125 g*	*500 g*
Carrot, chopped fine (optional)		2 oz	8 oz	*60 g*	*250 g*
Celery, chopped fine		2 oz	8 oz	*60 g*	*250 g*
Mushroom trimmings (optional)		2 oz	8 oz	*60 g*	*250 g*
Bones from lean fish		4–6 lb	16–24 lb	*2–3 kg*	*8–12 kg*
Dry white wine		8 oz	1 qt	*2.5 dl*	*1 l*
Cold water		1 gal	4 gal	*4 l*	*16 l*
Sachet:					
Bay leaf		½	2	*½*	*2*
Peppercorns		¼ tsp	1 tsp	*0.5 g*	*2 g*
Parsley stems		6–8	24–32	*6–8*	*24–32*
Whole cloves		1	4	*1*	*4*

Procedure:

1. Butter the bottom of a heavy stock pot or sauce pot. Place the mirepoix in the bottom of the pot and the bones over the top of it. Cover the bones loosely with a round of parchment.

2. Set the pot over low heat and cook slowly for about 5 minutes, until the bones are opaque and begin to exude some juices.

3. Add the wine and bring to a simmer. Add water to cover and add the sachet.

4. Bring to a simmer again, skim, and let simmer for 30 to 45 minutes.

5. Strain through a china cap lined with several layers of cheesecloth.

6. Cool in a cold-water bath and refrigerate.

ROUX

		U.S.		Metric	
YIELD:		8 oz	2 lb	250 g	1 kg
Ingredients					
Clarified butter		4 oz	1 lb	125 g	500 g
Flour		4 oz	1 lb	125 g	500 g

Procedure:

1. Melt the butter in a heavy saucepan.

2. Add the flour and stir until the fat and flour are thoroughly mixed.

3. Cook, stirring, to the required degree:

   a. White roux is cooked for just a few minutes over moderate heat, just enough to cook out the raw taste. Stop the cooking as soon as the roux has a frothy, chalky, slightly gritty appearance, before it has begun to color. White roux is used for béchamel and other white sauces based on milk.

   b. Blond roux or pale roux is cooked a little longer, just until the roux begins to change to a slightly darker color. Cooking must then be stopped. Blond roux is used for veloutés, sauces based on white stocks. The sauces have a pale ivory color.

   c. Brown roux is cooked until it takes on a light brown color and a nutty aroma. Cook over low heat so that the roux browns evenly without scorching. For a deeper brown roux, the flour may be browned in an oven before adding to the fat. A heavily browned roux has only about one-third the thickening power of white roux but contributes flavor and color to browned sauces.

Variations

Other fats, such as chicken fat or beef drippings, may be used instead of butter when their flavor is appropriate to the sauce.

BÉCHAMEL SAUCE

		U.S.		Metric	
YIELD:		1 qt	1 gal	1 l	4 l
Ingredients					
White roux		4 oz	1 lb	125 g	500 g
Milk		1 qt	1 gal	1 l	4 l
Whole onion, peeled		1 small	1 large	1 small	1 large
Whole cloves		1	2	1	2
Bay leaves		1	2	1	2
Salt					
Nutmeg					
White pepper					

Procedure:

1. Prepare the roux and set it aside.

2. Bring the milk just to a simmer.

3. Beat in the roux. Bring the sauce to a boil, stirring constantly. Reduce the heat to a simmer.

4. Stick the bay leaves to the onion with the cloves and add to the sauce. Simmer for at least 15 minutes or, if possible, for 30 minutes or more. Skim the surface and stir occasionally.

5. Adjust the consistency with additional hot milk as necessary.

6. Season very lightly with salt, nutmeg, and white pepper.

7. Strain through a china cap lined with cheesecloth. Cover or spread melted butter on the surface to prevent skin formation. Keep hot in a hot-water bath or cool it in a cold-water bath for later use.

VELOUTÉ SAUCE

		U.S.		Metric	
	YIELD:	**1 qt**	**1 gal**	*1 l*	*4 l*
Ingredients					
Blond roux		4 oz	1 lb	*125 g*	*500 g*
White stock, hot		1 qt 8 oz	5 qt	*1.25 l*	*5 l*

Procedure:

1. Beat the roux into the hot stock. Bring to a boil and then reduce to a simmer, stirring constantly.

2. Simmer very slowly for an hour. Stir occasionally and skim the surface as necessary. Add more stock if needed to adjust consistency.

3. Do not season the velouté, since it is not used as is but as an ingredient in other preparations.

4. Strain through a china cap lined with cheesecloth. Cover or spread the surface with melted butter to prevent skin formation. Keep hot in a hot-water bath or cool it in a cold-water bath for later use.

BROWN SAUCE OR ESPAGNOLE

		U.S.		Metric	
YIELD:		1 qt	1 gal	1 l	4 l
Ingredients					
Mirepoix:					
Onions, medium dice		4 oz	1 lb	125 g	500 g
Carrots, medium dice		2 oz	8 oz	60 g	250 g
Celery, medium dice		2 oz	8 oz	60 g	250 g
Butter		2 oz	8 oz	60 g	250 g
Flour		2 oz	8 oz	60 g	250 g
Brown stock, hot		3 pt	6 qt	1.5 l	6 l
Tomato purée		2 oz	8 oz	60 g	250 g
Sachet:					
Bay leaf		small piece	½	small piece	½
Thyme		pinch	¼ tsp	pinch	0.25 g
Parsley stems		2	6–8	2	6–8

Procedure:

1. Sauté the mirepoix in butter until well browned.
2. Add the flour and stir to make a roux. Continue to cook until the roux is browned.
3. Gradually stir in the brown stock and tomato purée, stirring constantly until the mixture comes to a boil.
4. Reduce the heat to a simmer and skim the surface. Add the sachet and let simmer for about 2 hours, until the sauce is reduced to the desired quantity. Skim as necessary.
5. Strain through a china cap lined with several layers of cheesecloth. Press on the mirepoix gently to extract juices.
6. Cover or spread melted butter on the surface to prevent skin formation. Keep hot in a hot-water bath or cool it in a cold-water bath for later use.

DEMIGLAZE

		U.S.		Metric	
YIELD:		1 qt	1 gal	1 l	4 l
Ingredients					
Brown sauce		1 qt	1 gal	1 l	4 l
Brown stock		1 qt	1 gal	1 l	4 l

Procedure:

1. Combine the sauce and stock in a saucepan and simmer until reduced by one-half.
2. Strain through a china cap lined with cheesecloth. Cover to prevent a skin from forming. Keep hot in a hot-water bath or cool it in a cold-water bath for later use.

TOMATO SAUCE (WITH ROUX)

		U.S.		Metric	
YIELD:		**1 qt**	**1 gal**	*1 l*	*4 l*
Ingredients					
Salt pork, diced		1 oz	4 oz	*30 g*	*125 g*
Butter		½ oz	2 oz	*15 g*	*60 b*
Onion, medium dice		1 oz	4 oz	*30 g*	*125 g*
Carrot, medium dice		½ oz	2 oz	*15 g*	*60 g*
Celery, medium dice		½ oz	2 oz	*15 g*	*60 g*
Flour		1 oz	4 oz	*30 g*	*125 g*
White stock		12 oz	3 pt	*175 ml*	*7.5 dl*
Tomatoes, canned or fresh		1 lb	4 lb	*500 g*	*2 kg*
Tomato purée		1 pt	2 qt	*5 dl*	*2 l*
Sachet:					
Bay leaf		small piece	1	*small piece*	*1*
Garlic cloves, crushed		1 small	2	*1 small*	*2*
Thyme		pinch	¼ tsp	*pinch*	*0.25 g*
Peppercorns, crushed		4–5	½ tsp	*4–5*	*1 g*
Salt					
Sugar					

Procedure:

1. In a heavy saucepan over medium heat, sauté the salt pork in butter until partially rendered.

2. Add the onion, carrot, and celery and sauté until they are slightly softened.

3. Add the flour, stir to make a roux, and cook until the roux is just slightly browned.

4. Slowly add the stock, while stirring, and bring to a boil. Add the tomatoes and tomato purée and again bring to a boil. Reduce heat to a simmer.

5. Add the sachet. Simmer over very low heat for 1 to 1 ½ hours, until the sauce is reduced to the desired consistency.

6. Remove sachet and strain sauce or pass through a food mill. Season to taste with salt and sugar.

TOMATO SAUCE (WITHOUT ROUX)

		U.S.		Metric	
	YIELD:	1 qt	1 gal	1 l	4 l
Ingredients					
Bacon		1 oz	4 oz	30 g	125 g
Onion, medium dice		2 oz	8 oz	60 g	250 g
Carrots, medium dice		2 oz	8 oz	60 g	125 g
Tomatoes, canned or fresh, coarsely chopped		1 qt	4 qt	1 l	4 l
Tomato purée, canned		1 pt	2 qt	5 dl	2 l
Ham bones or browned pork bones		4 oz	1 lb	125 g	500 g
Sachet:					
Garlic cloves, crushed		1	2	1	2
Bay leaf		small piece	1	small piece	1
Thyme		pinch	¼ tsp	pinch	0.25 g
Rosemary		pinch	¼ tsp	pinch	0.25 g
Peppercorns, crushed		pinch	¼ tsp	pinch	0.5 g
Salt					
Sugar					

Procedure:

1. Render the bacon in a heavy sauce pot but do not brown it.

2. Add the onion and carrot. Sauté until slightly softened but do not brown.

3. Add the tomatoes and their juice, the tomato purée, bones, and sachet. Bring to a boil, reduce heat, and simmer over very low heat until reduced to desired consistency.

4. Remove sachet and bones. Strain sauce or pass it through a food mill.

5. Adjust the seasoning with salt and, if desired, a little sugar.

HOLLANDAISE SAUCE

		U.S.		Metric	
YIELD:		**1 pt**	**2 qt**	**5 dl**	**2 l**
Ingredients					
Butter		1 lb 4 oz	5 lb	*550 g*	*2.2 kg*
Peppercorns, crushed		⅛ tsp	½ tsp	*0.25 g*	*1 g*
Salt		⅛ tsp	½ tsp	*0.5 g*	*2 g*
White vinegar or wine vinegar		3 tbsp	6 oz	*45 ml*	*175 ml*
Cold water		2 tbsp	4 oz	*30 ml*	*125 ml*
Egg yolks		6	24	*6*	*24*
Lemon juice		1–2 tbsp	2–4 oz	*15–30 ml*	*60–125 ml*
Salt					
Cayenne					

Procedure:

1. Clarify the butter. Keep it warm but not hot.

2. Combine the peppercorns, salt, and vinegar in a stainless steel saucepan. Reduce au sec.

3. Remove from the heat and add the cold water. Transfer the diluted reduction to a stainless steel bowl.

4. Add the egg yolks and beat well.

5. Hold the bowl over a hot-water bath and beat the yolks until they are thickened and creamy. Do not overcook them or they will curdle.

6. Remove the bowl from the heat. Using a ladle, slowly and gradually beat in the warm, clarified butter, adding it drop by drop at first. If it becomes too thick to beat before all the butter is added, beat in a little of the lemon juice.

7. When all the butter has been added, beat in lemon juice to taste and adjust the seasonings with salt and cayenne. If necessary, thin the sauce with a few drops of warm water.

8. Strain through a cheesecloth and keep warm, not hot, for service. Hold no longer than 1 ½ hours.

Variations

To avoid having to strain the finished sauce, the diluted reduction may be strained before adding the egg yolks, but some of the flavor will be lost in the cheesecloth.

A simpler hollandaise can be made by omitting the reduction and using a little extra lemon juice for flavoring.

BÉARNAISE SAUCE

		U.S.		Metric	
	YIELD:	1 pt	2 qt	5 dl	2 l
Ingredients					
Butter		1 lb 4 oz	5 lb	550 g	2.2 kg
Shallots, chopped		1 oz	4 oz	30 g	125 g
White wine vinegar		4 oz	1 pt	125 ml	5 dl
Tarragon		1 tsp	4 tsp	1 g	4 g
Peppercorns, crushed		½ tsp	2 tsp	1 g	4 g
Egg yolks		6	24	6	24
Salt					
Cayenne					
Lemon juice					
Chopped parsley		1 tbsp	4 tbsp	3 g	12 g
Tarragon		½ tsp	2 tsp	0.5 g	2 g

Procedure:

1. Clarify the butter. Keep it warm but not hot.

2. Combine the shallots, vinegar, tarragon, and peppercorns in a stainless steel saucepan. Reduce by three-fourths.

3. Remove from heat and cool slightly. Transfer the reduction to a stainless steel bowl.

4. Add the egg yolks and beat well.

5. Hold the bowl over a hot-water bath and beat the yolks until they are thickened and creamy. Do not overcook them or they will curdle.

6. Remove the bowl from the heat. Using a ladle, slowly and gradually beat in the warm, clarified butter, adding it drop by drop at first. If it becomes too thick to beat before all the butter is added, beat in a little lemon juice.

7. Strain through a cheesecloth.

8. Season to taste with salt, cayenne, and a few drops of lemon juice. Mix in the parsley and tarragon.

9. Keep warm, not hot, for service. Hold no longer than 1 ½ hours.

CONSOMMÉ

		U.S.		Metric	
YIELD:		**2 qt**	**1 gal**	*2 l*	*4 l*
Ingredients					
Lean beef, preferably shank, ground		8 oz	1 lb	*250 g*	*500 g*
Mirepoix, chopped into small pieces:					
Onion		4 oz	8 oz	*125 g*	*250 g*
Celery		2 oz	4 oz	*60 g*	*125 g*
Carrot		2 oz	4 oz	*60 g*	*125 g*
Egg whites		4 oz	8 oz	*125 g*	*250 g*
Canned tomatoes, crushed		4 oz	8 oz	*125 g*	*250 g*
Parsley stems, chopped		4	8	*4*	*8*
Thyme		small pinch	pinch	*small pinch*	*pinch*
Bay leaf		½	1	*½*	*1*
Whole cloves		1	2	*1*	*2*
Peppercorns, crushed		¼ tsp	½ tsp	*0.5 g*	*1 g*
Cold beef or veal stock, brown or white, or chicken stock		5 pt	5 qt	*2.5 l*	*5 l*

Procedure:

1. Combine the beef, mirepoix, egg whites, tomatoes, herbs, and spices in a tall, heavy stock pot. Mix the ingredients vigorously with a wooden paddle or a heavy whip.

2. Add a small amount of cold stock and stir well. Gradually stir in the remaining stock, making sure it is well mixed with the other ingredients.

3. Set the pot on moderately low heat and let it come to a simmer very slowly. Stir occasionally. When the simmering point is approaching, stop stirring.

4. Move the pot to lower heat and simmer very slowly for about 1 ½ hours. The solid ingredients will rise to the top and form a "raft." Do not disturb this raft. Do not cover and do not let it boil.

5. After 1 ½ hours, very carefully strain the consommé through a china cap lined with cheesecloth. Avoid stirring or breaking up the raft, as this may cloud the consommé.

6. Degrease thoroughly and season to taste.

TART PASTRY

		U.S.		Metric	
YIELD:		**1 lb 8 oz**	**6 lb**	*750 g*	*3 kg*
Ingredients					
Flour, preferably pastry flour		12 oz	3 lb	*375 g*	*1.5 kg*
Butter		6 oz	1 lb 8 oz	*185 g*	*750 g*
Egg yolks		1 oz	4 oz	*30 g*	*125 g*
Cold water		3 oz	12 oz	*90 ml*	*375 ml*
Salt		¾ tsp	½ oz	*4 g*	*15 g*

Procedure:

1. Sift the flour into a mixing bowl.

2. Add the butter and rub it in until it is well combined and no lumps remain.

3. Beat the egg yolks with the water and salt until the salt is dissolved.

4. Add the liquid to the flour mixture. Mix gently until it is completely absorbed.

5. Place the dough in pans, cover with plastic film, and place in the refrigerator for at least 4 hours. For use, scale portions as needed.

PUFF PASTRY

		U.S.	Metric
YIELD:		**5 lb 10 oz**	*2.8 kg*
Ingredients			
Bread flour		1 lb 8 oz	*750 g*
Cake flour (see note)		8 oz	*250 g*
Butter, soft		4 oz	*125 g*
Salt		1 tbsp	*15 g*
Cold water		18 oz	*560 ml*
Butter		2 lb	*1 kg*
Bread flour		4 oz	*125 g*

Note: All-purpose flour may be substituted for the bread and cake flours.

Mixing Procedure:

1. Place the first quantities of flour and butter in a mixing bowl. With the paddle attachment, mix at low speed until well blended.

2. Dissolve the salt in the cold water.

3. Add the salted water to the flour mixture and mix at low speed until a soft dough is formed. Do not overmix.

4. Remove the dough from the mixer and let it rest in the refrigerator for 20 minutes.

5. Blend the last quantities of butter and flour in the mixer until the mixture is the same consistency as the dough, neither too soft nor too hard.

6. Roll in the butter as directed in the following procedure, giving the dough four four-folds.

Rolling-in Procedure:

1. Dust the bench lightly with flour. Roll out the dough into a rectangle about three times as long as it is wide and about ½ inch (1 to 1.5 cm) thick. Make the corners as square as possible.

2. Spot the butter (from step 5 of Mixing Procedure) evenly over two-thirds the length of the dough, leaving a 1-inch (2.5-cm) margin around the edge.

3. Fold the unbuttered third of the dough over the center third.

4. Fold the remaining third on top. All ends and corners should be folded evenly and squarely. This step, enclosing the butter in the dough, does not count as one of the folds. The folding procedure begins with the next step.

5. Turn the dough 90 degrees on the bench so that the length becomes the width. This step must be taken before each rolling out of the dough so that the gluten is stretched in all directions, not just lengthwise. Failure to do this will result in products that deform or shrink unevenly when baked.

6. Roll the dough out lengthwise into a rectangle. Make sure that the corners are square. Roll smoothly and evenly. Do not press down when rolling or the layers may stick together and the product will not rise properly.

7. Brush excess flour from the top of the dough. Fold the two ends to the center. Make sure the corners are square and even. Again brush off excess flour.

8. Fold the dough in half like closing a book. You now have given the dough one four-fold. Refrigerate the dough for 15 or 20 minutes to relax the gluten. Do not refrigerate it too long or the butter will become too hard. (If it does, let it soften a few minutes at room temperature.) Give the dough another three four-folds, as in steps 5 to 8. After another rest, the dough is ready to be rolled out and made up into the desired products.

A *PPENDIX*

2

Measurement

UNITS OF MEASURE — U.S. SYSTEM

1 pound	= 16 ounces
1 gallon	= 4 quarts
1 quart	= 2 pints
	or
	4 cups
	or
	32 (fluid) ounces
1 pint	= 2 cups
	or
	16 (fluid) ounces
1 cup	= 8 (fluid) ounces
1 (fluid) ounce	= 2 tablespoons
1 tablespoon	= 3 teaspoons
1 foot	= 12 inches

Abbreviations of U.S. Units Used in This Book

pound	lb
ounce	oz
gallon	gal
quart	qt
pint	pt
fluid ounce	fl. oz *or* oz
tablespoon	tbsp
teaspoon	tsp

BASIC METRIC UNITS

Quantity	Unit	Abbreviation
weight	gram	g
volume	liter	l
length	meter	m
temperature	degree Celsius	°C

Divisions and Multiples of Metric Units

Prefix/Example	Meaning	Abbreviation
kilo-	1000	k
kilogram	1000 grams	kg
deci-	1/10	d
deciliter	0.1 liter	dl
centi-	1/100	c
centimeter	0.01 meter	cm
milli-	1/1000	m
milliliter	0.001 liter	ml

Metric Conversion Factors

Weight
1 ounce equals 28.35 grams
1 gram equals 0.035 ounce
1 pound equals 454 grams
1 kilogram equals 2.2 pounds

Volume
1 fluid ounce equals 29.57 milliliters
1 milliliter equals 0.034 ounce
1 cup equals 237 milliliters
1 quart equals 946 milliliters
1 liter equals 33.8 fluid ounces

Length
1 inch equals 25.4 millimeters
1 centimeter equals 0.39 inch
1 meter equals 39.4 inches

Temperature
To convert Fahrenheit to Celsius, subtract 32, then multiply by $\frac{5}{9}$.

Example: Convert 140°F to Celsius.

$$140 - 32 = 108$$

$$108 \times \tfrac{5}{9} = 60°C$$

To convert Celsius to Fahrenheit, multiply by $\frac{9}{5}$, then add 32.

Example: Convert 150° C to Fahrenheit.

$$150 \times \tfrac{9}{5} = 270$$

$$270 + 32 = 302°F$$

Note: The metric quantities in the recipes in this book are not exact equivalents of the U.S. quantities (see page 7 for an explanation.)

APPROXIMATE WEIGHT-VOLUME EQUIVALENTS OF VARIOUS FOODS

Bread flour, sifted
  1 lb = 4 cups
  1 cup = 4 oz

Bread flour, unsifted
  1 lb = 3 ⅓ cups
  1 cup = 4.75 oz

Granulated sugar
  1 lb = 2 ¼ cups
  1 cup = 7 oz

Cornstarch, sifted
  1 lb = 4 cups
  1 cup = 4 oz
  1 oz = 4 tbsp = ¼ cup
  1 tbsp = 0.25 oz

Cornstarch, unsifted
  1 lb = 3 ½ cups
  1 cup = 4.5 oz
  1 oz = 3 ½ tsp
  1 tbsp = 0.29 oz

Gelatin, unflavored
  1 oz = 3 tbsp
  ¼ oz = 2 ¼ tsp
  1 tbsp = 0.33 oz
  1 tsp = 0.11 oz

Salt
  1 oz = 5 tsp
  ¼ oz = 1 ¼ tsp
  1 tsp = 0.2 oz

Cinnamon
  1 oz = 17 tsp
  ¼ oz = 4 ¼ tsp
  1 tsp = 0.06 oz

Ground spices, except cinnamon
  1 oz = 14 tsp
  ¼ oz = 3 ½ tsp
  1 tsp = 0.07 oz

Rice (raw)
  1 cup = 7 oz
  1 lb = 2 ¼ cups

Eggs
  1 large egg, without shell, is about 1 ⅔ oz, minimum weight.
  1 large egg white is about 1 oz.
  1 large egg yolk is about ⅔ oz.

Bibliography

The following list includes basic cooking references and texts as well as a small sampling of recipe collections by noted chefs. New works by prominent cooks appear regularly, and readers in search of new recipes should visit libraries and bookstores for a full selection of recent titles.

Bertolli, Paul, and Alice Waters. *Chez Panisse Cooking.* New York: Random House, 1988.

Bickel, Walter, ed. *Hering's Dictionary of Classical and Modern Cookery.* London: Virtue, 1987.

Bocuse, Paul. *Paul Bocuse's French Cooking.* New York: Pantheon, 1977.

Culinary Institute of America. *The New Professional Chef*, 5th ed. New York: Van Nostrand Reinhold, 1991.

Educational Foundation of the National Restaurant Association. *Applied Foodservice Sanitation*, 4th ed. New York: Wiley, 1992.

Escoffier, A. *The Escoffier Cookbook.* New York: Crown, 1969.

Gisslen, Wayne. *Professional Baking.* New York: Wiley, 1985.

———. *Professional Cooking*, 2nd ed. New York: Wiley, 1989.

Grigson, Jane. *The Art of Making Sausages, Pâtés, and Other Charcuterie.* New York: Knopf, 1976.

Luard, Elizabeth. *The Old World Kitchen.* Toronto: Bantam, 1987.

McClane, A. J. *The Encyclopedia of Fish Cookery.* New York: Holt, Rinehart & Winston, 1977.

McGee, Harold. *On Food and Cooking.* New York; Scribner's, 1984.

———. *The Curious Cook.* San Francisco: North Point Press, 1990.

Madison, Deborah. *The Greens Cook Book.* Toronto: Bantam, 1987.

Maximin, Jacques. *The Cuisine of Jacques Maximin.* New York: Arbor House, 1986.

Montagné, Prosper. *Larousse Gastronomique,* New American Edition. New York: Crown, 1988.

Ogden, Bradley. *Bradley Ogden's Breakfast, Lunch, and Dinner.* New York: Random House, 1991.

Pauli, Eugen. *Classical Cooking the Modern Way,* 2nd ed. New York: Van Nostrand Reinhold, 1989.

Pepin, Jacques. *The Art of Cooking.* New York: Knopf, 1987.

Point, Fernand. *Ma Gastronomie.* Wilton, CT: Lyceum Books, 1974.

Saulnier, L. *La Répertoire de la Cuisine.* Woodbury, NY: Barron's, 1976.

Schneider, Elizabeth. *Uncommon Fruits and Vegetables: A Commonsense Guide.* New York: Harper & Row, 1986.

Sonnenschmidt, Frederic H. *The Professional Chef's Art of Garde Manger,* 4th ed. New York: Van Nostrand Reinhold, 1988.

Tannahill, Reay. *Food in History.* New York: Crown, 1988.

Wells, Patricia. *Simply French: Patricia Wells Presents the Cuisine of Joël Robuchon.* New York: William Morrow, 1991.

White, Jasper. *Jasper White's Cooking from New England.* New York: Harper & Row, 1989.

Willan, Anne. *La Varenne Pratique.* New York: Crown, 1989.

Glossary

Note: This book follows the traditional practice of spelling certain French verbs with an *-é* in place of the *-er* ending (pronounced, approximately, "-ay"). For example, the verbs *sauter* and *poêler* are spelled *sauté* and *poêlé*, respectively, in English usage.

Abats Another word for variety meats.

Aiguillette Long, thin slices of poultry breast or some other meats.

Aioli A type of mayonnaise heavily flavored with garlic.

A la carte (1) Referring to a menu on which each individual item is listed with a separate price. (2) Referring to cooking to order, as opposed to cooking ahead in large batches.

Al dente Firm, not soft or mushy, to the bite. Said of vegetables and pasta.

Allemande (1) German style. (2) A sauce made of velouté (usually veal), a liaison, and lemon juice.

Allumette Cut into matchstick shapes.

Andouillette A sausage made from tripe or intestines.

AP weight As purchased; the weight of an item before trimming.

Arborio rice A variety of Italian short-grain rice.

Aspic jelly A clarified stock that contains enough gelatin so that it solidifies when cold.

AS weight As served; the weight of an item as sold or served, after processing and/or cooking.

Au sec Until dry.

Bain marie A container of hot water used for keeping food hot.

Ballotine A cooked dish made by tying a piece of meat or poultry into a bundle to enclose a stuffing.

Barbecue To cook with dry heat created by the burning of hardwood or by the hot coals of this wood.

Bard To tie thin slices of fat, such as pork fatback, over meats with no natural fat cover to protect them while roasting.

Batonnet Cut into sticks, about ¼ × ¼ × 2½ to 3 inches.

Béarnaise A sauce made of butter and egg yolks and flavored with a reduction of vinegar, shallots, tarragon, and peppercorns.

Béchamel   A sauce made by thickening milk with a roux.

Beluga   The largest type or grade of sturgeon caviar.

Beurre blanc   A warm butter sauce made by swirling a large proportion of butter into a small amount of flavored liquid so that the mixture forms a creamy emulsion.

Beurre fondu   Melted butter.

Beurre manié   Equal parts raw butter and flour mixed together into a smooth paste; used for thickening.

Beurre noir   Butter heated until it is dark brown, flavored with vinegar.

Beurre noisette   Whole butter heated until it is light brown.

Bisque   A cream soup made from shellfish.

Bleak roe   A type of salted roe or caviar from a Baltic fish.

Blanch   To cook an item partially and very briefly in boiling water or in hot fat.

Blanquette   A white stew made of white meat or poultry simmered without preliminary browning and served with a white sauce.

Boeuf à la ficelle   French term meaning "beef on a string." Beef poached in broth, generally with vegetables.

Boeuf à la môde   A large cut of beef braised in red wine.

Bordelaise   A brown sauce flavored with a reduction of red wine, shallots, pepper, and herbs and garnished with marrow.

Boudin blanc   A sausage made of puréed white meat, such as pork or chicken.

Bouquet garni   A combination of fresh herbs tied together, used for flavoring.

Braise   (1) To cook, covered, in a small amount of liquid, usually after preliminary browning. (2) For vegetables, to cook slowly in a small amount of liquid without preliminary browning.

Broil   To cook with radiant heat from above.

Brunoise   (1) Cut into very small (⅛ inch or 3 mm) dice. (2) Garnished with vegetables cut in this manner.

Bulgur   A type of cracked wheat that has been partially cooked.

Butterflied   Cut partially through and spread open to increase the surface area.

Canard   French word for "duck."

Cannelloni   Tubes or rolled squares of pasta, filled and, usually, baked.

Capon   A castrated male chicken.

Cappelletti   Small, filled pastas.

Caramelization   The browning of sugars caused by heat.

Cardoon   A vegetable in the thistle family; resembles a large bunch of celery.

Carpaccio   Thin slices of meat or fish served raw, usually with a cold sauce or dressing.

Carry-over cooking   The rise in temperature in the inside of a roast after it is removed from the oven.

Caul   A thin, lacy membrane of fat surrounding the abdominal cavity of pigs and other animals.

Cassolette   A small heat-proof casserole used for heating and serving single portions of foods.

Cassoulet   A baked mixture of white beans and various meats and sausages.

Caviar   The salted roe of sturgeon and certain other fish.

Celsius scale   The metric system of temperature measurement, with 0°C set at the freezing point of water and 100°C set at the boiling point of water.

Centi-   Prefix in the metric system meaning "one-hundredth."

Cèpe   A bolete mushroom.

Cerf Red deer, a type of venison.

Cervelle French word for "brain."

Chateaubriand A thick beef steak cut from the center of the tenderloin.

Chaud-froid An opaque sauce containing gelatin, used to coat certain cold foods.

Chèvre A cheese made from goat's milk.

Chevreuil French word for "venison"; specifically, the roe deer.

(en) Chevreuil Cooked in the style of venison.

Chile Any of a variety of capsicum peppers, ranging from mildly spicy to very hot, used as vegetables and as flavoring ingredients.

Chitterlings Pork intestines.

Chutney A highly seasoned relish.

Cilantro The leaves of the coriander plant, used as an herb.

Civet A game stew.

Clearmeat A mixture of ground meat, egg whites, and flavoring ingredients used to clarify a consommé.

Coagulation The process by which proteins become firm, usually when heated.

Cocotte A type of casserole dish.

(en) Cocotte Referring to poultry or other foods served in a casserole with various vegetables or other garnish.

Collagen A type of connective tissue in meats that dissolves when cooked with moisture.

Compound butter A mixture of raw butter and various flavoring ingredients.

Concassé Chopped coarsely. In the case of tomatoes, it means peeled, seeded, and chopped coarsely.

Confit French for "preserved." (1) Referring to duck, goose, and some other meats cooked in their own fat and then packed and stored in this fat. (2) Referring to vegetables cr fruits cooked with sugar or with sweet ingredients, in the manner of preserves or marmalade.

Consommé A rich, flavorful, seasoned stock or broth that has been clarified to make it perfectly clear and transparent.

Coral The roe or eggs of certain shellfish.

Coulis (1) A purée of vegetables or, sometimes, of fruit, generally used as a sauce. (2) In classical cooking, a purée soup or cream soup made of poultry, game, or fish.

Court bouillon Water containing seasonings, herbs, and usually an acid; used for cooking fish and certain other foods.

Crecy Garnished with or containing carrots.

Crème fraîche Heavy cream that has been lighly cultured to give it a slightly tangy favor and to thicken it slightly.

Crepinette A small cake of sausage meat wrapped in caul fat.

Crouton Bread that is sliced or cut into various shapes and toasted or fried in butter or oil.

Crustaceans Sea animals with segmented shells and jointed legs, such as lobsters and shrimp.

Cuisse de grenouille Frog leg.

Daim Fallow deer; a type of venison.

Dal East Indian term for various dried beans and lentils.

Deci- Prefix in the metric system meaning "one-tenth."

Deglaze To swirl a liquid in a sauté pan or other pan to dissolve cooked particles or food remaining on the bottom.

Demiglaze; demi-glace   A rich brown sauce or stock that has been reduced by half.

Drawn   With entrails removed.

Dressed   (1) Poultry market form: killed, bled, and plucked. (2) Fish market form: viscera, scales, head, tail, and fins removed.

Drum sieve   A type of sieve consisting of a fine screen stretched over a metal or wood hoop.

Duchesse potatoes   Potato purée mixed with butter and egg yolks.

Duxelles   A coarse paste or hash made of finely chopped mushrooms sautéed with shallots.

Elastin   A type of connective tissue in meats that does not dissolve when cooked.

Emincer   To cut into thin slices.

Emulsion   A mixture of two unmixable liquids.

EP weight   Edible portion; the weight of an item after all trimming is done.

Escargot   French word for "snail."

Espagnole   A sauce made of brown stock and flavoring ingredients and thickened with brown roux.

Estouffade   A French term for "stew."

Etuver, étuvé   To cook or steam an item in its own juices; to sweat.

Fermière   Garnished with carrots, turnips, onions, and celery cut into uniform slices.

Fettuccine   Flat egg noodles.

Feuilleté   (1) A dish made of puff pastry or other flaky pastry, usually topped or layered with other foods. (2) The baked pastry used to make such a dish.

Fiber   A group of indigestible carbohydrates in grains, fruits, and vegetables.

Fillet, filet   (1) Meat: boneless tenderloin. (2) Fish: boneless side of fish.

Flash baking   The process of baking small or thin pieces of food at very high temperatures for very short times.

Florentine   In the style of Florence, Italy. Usually refers to dishes garnished with or containing spinach.

Foie gras   Liver of specially fattened geese and ducks.

Fond lié   A sauce made by thickening brown stock with cornstarch or similar starch.

Forcemeat   A seasoned mixture of ground meats and other foods, used as a filling or stuffing or as a base for terrines and pâtés.

Forestière   Garnished with mushrooms.

Fricassée   A white stew in which the meat is cooked in fat without browning before liquid is added.

Fumet   A flavorful stock, usually fish stock.

Galantine   A forcemeat that is wrapped in the skin of the product it is made of, such as chicken or duck, or rolled into a cylinder without the skin.

Galette   A thin, flat cake.

Garde manger   (1) The cook in charge of cold food production, including salads and buffet items. (2) The department of a kitchen in which these foods are prepared.

Garni   Garnished.

Garnish   Food items added to a serving of another food to complement, embellish, or decorate it.

Gastrique   A mixture of caramel and vinegar, used as a base for various fruit sauces served with duck and some other foods.

Gazpacho   A cold Spanish soup made of puréed raw vegetables.

Gelatinization   The process by which starch granules absorb water and swell in size.

Gelée   Aspic jelly.

Glaçage   A sauce used for glazing.

Glace de poisson   Fish glaze; a reduction of fish stock.

Glace de viande   Meat glaze; a reduction of brown stock.

Glace de volaille   Chicken glaze; a reduction of chicken stock.

Glaze   (1) A stock that is reduced until it coats the back of a spoon. (2) A shiny coating, such as a syrup, applied to a food. (3) To make a food shiny or glossy by coating it with a glaze or by browning it under a broiler or in a hot oven.

Gluten   A substance made up of proteins present in wheat flour that gives structure and strength to baked goods.

Gorgonzola   An Italian blue-veined cheese.

Gram   The basic unit of weight in the metric system; equal to about one-thirtieth of an ounce.

(au) Gratin, gratiné   Having a browned or crusted top, often made by topping with bread crumbs, cheese, and/or a rich sauce and passing under a broiler or salamander.

Gratin dauphinoise   A dish consisting of sliced potatoes baked with milk and cream and, sometimes, cheese.

Gravlax   Cured salmon.

Grenouille   French word for "frog."

Grill   To cook on an open grid over a heat source.

Hollandaise   A sauce made of butter, egg yolks, and flavorings, especially lemon juice.

Hongroise   Hungarian style.

Jambon persillé   Parslied ham in aspic.

Jardinière   Garnished with fresh vegetables, such as carrots, turnips, green beans, peas, and cauliflower.

Julienne   (1) Cut into small, thin strips, about $\frac{1}{8} \times \frac{1}{8} \times 2\frac{1}{2}$ inches (3 mm $\times$ 3 mm $\times$ 6 to 7 cm). (2) Garnished with foods cut in this manner.

Jus   Unthickened juices from a roast or other meat or poultry.

Jus lié   Thickened juices from a roast.

Kasha   Toasted buckwheat groats.

Kilo-   A prefix in the metric system meaning "one thousand."

Lapereau   Young rabbit.

Lapin   Rabbit.

Lard   (1) The rendered fat of hogs. (2) To insert strips of fat in meats with a special needle.

Lasagne   Broad, flat egg noodles, or a baked casserole made with these noodles.

Leading sauce   A basic sauce used in the production of other sauces. The five leading hot sauces are béchamel, velouté, espagnole, tomato, and hollandaise. Mayonnaise and vinaigrette are often considered leading cold sauces.

Levraut   Young hare.

Liaison   A binding agent, usually made of cream and egg yolks, used to thicken and enrich sauces and soups.

Lièvre   Hare.

Liter   The basic unit of volume in the metric system; equal to slightly more than a quart.

Lyonnaise   Containing or garnished with onions.

Magret   The meaty breast of the mullard or moulard duck.

Maître d'hôtel butter   Compound butter containing parsley and lemon juice.

Marcassin   Young boar, especially boar under 6 months of age.

Marinate   To soak a food in a seasoned liquid.

Marsala   A flavorful sweet to semidry wine from Sicily.

Malossol   Russian for "little salt." Refers to a type of caviar containing a relatively small proportion of salt.

Matelote   A type of French fish stew made with wine.

Mayonnaise   A semisolid cold sauce or dressing consisting of oil and vinegar emulsified with egg yolks.

Medaillon   A small, round cut of meat or fish.

Mesclun   A mixture of baby salad greens.

Meter   The basic unit of length in the metric system; slightly longer than 1 yard.

(à la) Meunière   Fish prepared by dredging in flour and sautéing, served with brown butter, lemon juice, and parsley.

Milli-   Prefix in the metric system meaning "one-thousandth."

Mince   To chop into very fine pieces.

Mirepoix   A mixture of rough-cut or diced vegetables, herbs, and spices used for flavoring.

Mise en place   French term meaning "put in place." The setup for production. All the preparations and organization that must be made before actual production can begin.

Mollusk   A soft-bodied sea animal, usually inside a pair of hinged shells, such as clams or oysters. Squid are also mollusks.

Monter au beurre   To finish a sauce or soup by swirling in raw butter until it is melted.

Mornay   A sauce made of béchamel and gruyère cheese.

Mousse   A soft, creamy food, either sweet or savory, that is made light by the addition of whipped cream or whipped egg whites or both.

Mousseline   (1) A sauce made by combining hollandaise and whipped cream. (2) A forcemeat made of puréed fish, poultry, or meat, heavy cream, and usually egg whites.

(à la) Nage   French term meaning "swimming"; referring to poached fish or other foods served with their broth.

Navarin   A brown lamb stew.

Niçoise   (1) Prepared in the style of Nice, France. (2) Garnished with or containing tomato concassé cooked with garlic.

Noisette   (1) French word for "hazelnut." (2) A small, boneless slice of meat cut from the loin or rib section. (See also *beurre noisette*.)

Nouvelle cuisine   A style of cooking that emphasizes lightness of sauces and seasonings, shortened cooking times, and new and sometimes startling combinations of foods.

Offal   Another name for variety meats.

Osetra, ossetra   The second largest type of sturgeon caviar.

Paillard   A thin slice of meat, usually grilled.

Panade   Any of various starch pastes used as a base for a forcemeat.

(en) Papillote   Wrapped in paper or foil for cooking so that the food is steamed in its own moisture.

Parmentier   Garnished with or containing potatoes.

Pasteurized   Heat-treated to kill bacteria that might cause disease or spoilage.

Pâté   A dish made of a baked forcemeat, usually in a crust.

Pâte à choux   A soft dough used for making eclairs and cream puffs; also called eclair paste.

Pâte à pâté   Dough or pastry used to make a crust for pâtés.

Pâté en croûte   A pâté in a pastry crust.

Petite marmite   A dish consisting of various meats, poultry, and vegetables simmered in a broth.

Pilaf   Rice or other grain product that has been first cooked in fat and then simmered in a stock or other liquid, usually with onions, seasonings, or other ingredients.

Piquage   The insertion of small pieces of food beneath the surface of larger pieces of food.

Poach   To cook very gently in water or other liquid that is hot but not actually bubbling, about 160° to 180°F (71° to 82°C).

Poêlé   To cook, or cooked, in an enclosed casserole with butter for basting but with no added liquids, usually on a bed of aromatic vegetables.

Polenta   Italian cornmeal, or a cornmeal mush or porridge made from it.

Pot-au-feu   French for stock pot (literally, "pot on the fire"). A home-style dish in which meat and vegetables are simmered in water.

Pot roast   A large cut of meat cooked by braising or poêléing.

Poussin   A type of small, young chicken.

Profiterole   Tiny round pastry made from eclair paste.

Provençale   In the style of Provence, France. Garnished with or containing tomatoes, garlic, parsley, and sometimes mushrooms and olives.

Puff pastry   A light, flaky pastry made from a rolled-in dough and leavened by steam.

Purée   (1) A food product that has been mashed or strained to a smooth pulp. (2) To make such a pulp by mashing or straining a food.

Quatre Epices   French for "four spices." A mixture of spices used to flavor sausages and forcemeats.

Quenelle   A forcemeat dumpling.

Ragout   A stew or stewlike dish, made of meat, poultry, fish, vegetables, or a combination of any of these.

Raft   The coagulated clearmeat that forms when stock is clarified.

Ravioli   Dumplings consisting of egg noodles filled with any of a variety of fillings.

Reduce   To cook by simmering or boiling until the quantity is decreased; often done to concentrate flavors.

Reduction   (1) A liquid that has been concentrated by cooking it to evaporate part of the water. (2) The process of making such a liquid.

Rillettes   A seasoned mixture of meat, such as pork, and fat, mashed to a paste; served as an appetizer.

Risotto   A moist Italian dish of rice cooked in butter and stock.

Roe   Fish eggs.

Rolled-in dough   Dough in which fat is incorporated into the dough in many layers by using a rolling and folding procedure.

Roquefort   A blue-veined cheese made in Roquefort, France, from sheep's milk.

Rotisserie   An item of cooking equipment that rotates meat or other foods in front of a heating element.

Rouille   A thick, spicy cold sauce flavored with hot peppers.

Roux   A cooked mixture of equal parts flour and fat.

Royale   A type of savory custard used to garnish soups.

Sabayon   A sauce, either savory or sweet, made by whipping egg yolks and liquids together over low heat.

Sachet A mixture of herbs and spices tied in a cheesecloth bag.

Salade tiede Warm salad.

Salamander Small broiler used primarily for browning or glazing the tops of certain items.

Salmis A stew or sauced dish made of roasted game.

Sanglier Boar.

Sauce A flavorful liquid, usually thickened, that is used to season, flavor, and enhance other foods.

Sausage A mixture of ground meat (usually pork) and seasonings stuffed into a casing.

Sauté To cook quickly in a small amount of fat.

Semolina A hard, high-protein flour used to make certain macaroni products.

Sevruga The smallest type of sturgeon caviar.

Shred To cut into thin but irregular strips, either with a knife or with the coarse blade of a grater.

Simmer To cook in water or other liquid that is bubbling gently, about 185° to 200°F (85° to 93°C).

Slurry A mixture of raw starch and cold liquid, used for thickening.

Small sauce A sauce made by adding one or more ingredients to a leading sauce.

Soufflé A light, fluffy dish made by mixing whipped egg whites into a base and baking. May be sweet or savory.

Spaetzle Small dumplings or noodles made from an egg-and-flour batter.

Squab Young pigeon.

Standard breading procedure The procedure for coating a food product with bread crumbs by passing it through flour, then egg wash, then crumbs.

Steam To cook by direct contact with steam.

Stew (1) To simmer a food or foods in a small amount of liquid that is usually served with the food as a sauce. (2) A dish cooked by stewing; usually one in which the main ingredients are cut into small pieces.

Stock A clear, unthickened liquid flavored by soluble substances extracted from meat, poultry, fish, and their bones, and from vegetables and seasonings.

Suprême sauce A sauce made of chicken velouté and heavy cream.

Sweat To cook in a small amount of fat over low heat, sometimes covered.

Sweetbreads The thymus glands of calves and other young animals, used as a food.

Tabbouleh A salad made of bulgur.

Temper To raise the temperature of a cold liquid gradually by slowly stirring in a hot liquid.

Terrine (1) An earthenware casserole dish. (2) A food prepared in such a dish; usually refers to cold forcemeat preparations and similar items.

Timbale (1) A drum-shaped mold or dish. (2) A mixture of eggs, liquids, and purées placed in such a dish and baked in a water bath.

Tobiko A salted roe or caviar from flying fish.

Tomalley The liver of lobsters and some other shellfish.

Tortellini Small, filled pastas.

Tournedos A small beef steak cut from the tenderloin. (Note: Both the singular and plural forms are spelled with a final *s*, which is not pronounced.)

Trichinosis A food-borne disease caused by a parasite sometimes found in undercooked pork.

Tripe The muscular stomach lining of beef or other meat animals.

Truffle A white or black tuberlike fungus or mushroom that grows underground; used primarily for flavoring and decoration.

Truss   To tie poultry into a compact shape for cooking.

Variety meats   Various organs, glands, and other meats that don't form part of the dressed carcass.

Velouté   A sauce made by thickening white stock with a roux.

Viande   French word for "meat."

Vin blanc   White wine.

Vin rouge   Red wine.

Vinaigrette   Dressing or sauce made of oil, vinegar, and flavoring ingredients.

Whitewash   A thin mixture or slurry of flour and cold water.

Zest   The colored part of the peel of citrus fruits.

Index